When the State Trembled
How A.J. Andrews and the Citizens' Committee Broke the Winnipeg General Strike

The Winnipeg General Strike of 1919, which involved approximately 30,000 workers, is Canada's best-known strike. *When the State Trembled* recovers the hitherto untold story of the Citizens' Committee of 1000, formed by Winnipeg's business elite in order to crush the revolt and sustain the status quo.

This account, by the authors of the award-winning *Walk Towards the Gallows*, reveals that the Citizens drew upon and extended a wide repertoire of anti-labour tactics to undermine working-class unity, battle for the hearts and minds of the middle class, and stigmatize the general strike as a criminal action. Newly discovered correspondence between leading Citizen lawyer A.J. Andrews and Acting Minister of Justice Arthur Meighen illuminates the strategizing and cooperation that took place between the state and the Citizens. While the strike's break was a crushing defeat for the labour movement, the later prosecution of its leaders on charges of sedition reveals abiding fears of radicalism and continuing struggles between capital and labour on the terrain of politics and law.

(The Canadian Social History Series)

REINHOLD KRAMER is a professor in the Department of English at Brandon University.

TOM MITCHELL is a university archivist at Brandon University.

When the State Trembled

How A.J. Andrews and the Citizens' Committee Broke the Winnipeg General Strike

Reinhold Kramer and Tom Mitchell

UNIVERSITY OF TORONTO PRESS
Toronto   Buffalo   London

© University of Toronto Press Incorporated 2010
Toronto Buffalo London
www.utppublishing.com
Printed in Canada

ISBN 978-1-4426-4219-5 (cloth)
ISBN 978-1-4426-1116-0 (paper)

Library and Archives Canada Cataloguing in Publication

Kramer, Reinhold, 1959–
When the state trembled : how A.J. Andrews and the Citizens' Committee
broke the Winnipeg General Strike / Reinhold Kramer and Tom Mitchell

(Canadian social history series)
Includes bibliographical references and index.
ISBN 978-1-4426-4219-5 (bound). – ISBN 978-1-4426-1116-0 (pbk.)

1. General Strike, Winnipeg, Man., 1919. 2. Citizens' Committee of One
Thousand (Winnipeg, Man.) – History. 3. Andrews, A.J. (Alfred Joseph),
1865–1950. I. Mitchell, Tom, 1949– II. Title. III. Series: Canadian
social history series

HD5330.W46K73 2010   331.892'50971274309041   C2010-903386-8

This book has been published with the help of a grant from the Canadian
Federation for the Humanities and Social Sciences, through the Aid to
Scholarly Publications Program, using funds provided by the Social Sci-
ences and Humanities Research Council of Canada.

University of Toronto Press acknowledges the financial assistance to its publishing program of the Canada Council for the Arts and the Ontario Arts
Council.

 Canada Council   Conseil des Arts
for the Arts   du Canada  ONTARIO ARTS COUNCIL
CONSEIL DES ARTS DE L'ONTARIO

University of Toronto Press acknowledges the financial support of the
Government of Canada through the Canada Book Fund for its publishing
activities.

To David Williams

For the late Gordon Rothney

Contents

Acknowledgments

Alvin Esau initiated this project by inviting Tom Mitchell to look at some files he had collected for a book on Manitoba legal history. His colleagues Wes Pue, DeLloyd Guth, and Roland Penner provided invaluable legal and historical advice. Trevor Anderson contributed detailed accounts of the lineages of several Winnipeg legal firms. Thanks to Sharon Reilly, Curator of Social History at the Manitoba Museum, for crucial leads on the Employers' Association of Manitoba. Dale Brawn directed us to valuable information contained in the Robert Graham fonds at the Archives of Manitoba and generously provided access to his research on the Manitoba legal community.

For assistance on the Russell jury, we would like to thank Allan Anderson, Barbara Brown, Malcolm Dewar, Lucien Frechette, Frederick Hassett and his wife, Edwin Pritchard, Jane Stevenson, Reg Tolton, and Wallace Tolton. In our research on the non-British Strike leaders, we received important information from Harvey Blumenberg, Dr Eleanor Blumenberg, Val Werier, Joy Rodriguez, Henry Trachtenberg, and Roz Usiskin.

Catherine Bailey, Louise Caron, Mark Levene, Michael MacDonald, David Rajotte, and Bill Russell at Library and Archives Canada responded to inquiries about Justice, the Immigration Department, and Cabinet records. At the Archives of Manitoba, Chris Kotecki was always willing to provide finding aids, and advice; Sharon Foley, Janelle Reynolds, Julianna Trivers, and Paula Warsaba responded to our inquiries about tapes, photographs, and assorted archival records. Louise Ayotte-Zaretski, Monica Ball, Nancy Evenson, Leesa Girouard, and Louise Sloane of the Manitoba Legislative Library provided photographs and biographical material on the Citizens. At the law library of the University of Manitoba, Regena Rumancik led us to 1941 Samuel

Blumenberg trial documents, while John Eaton and Muriel St John helped with Privy Council records and biographical data. Brian Hubner, Shelley Sweeney, Brett Lougheed, and Lewis St George Stubbs at the University of Manitoba Archives fielded a number of our inquiries. At the University of Winnipeg Archives, Gabrielle Prefontaine provided information about the provenance of the Citizens' post-Strike dinner photograph. Thank you as well to Allan Finebilt, QC, for access to the records of the Law Society of Manitoba.

In the Brandon University library, Carol Steele and Randy Paton were always ready to help with inter-library loans; Heather Coulter and Sandi Richards helped us with our inquires about federal and provincial government documents. Jan Mahoney in the Faculty of Arts office transformed several important documents into typed versions. Christy Henry helped with the research for this book and kept the S.J. McKee Archives running while the book was being written. Donna Lowe contributed ideas for our book cover.

At various points in the development of the book, advice, information, encouragement, and insight was offered by many colleagues, including Ian Angus, Peter Campbell, Lyle Dick, Michael Dupuis, Gerald Friesen, Alvin Finkel, Lee Gibson, Philip Girard, Gordon Goldsborough, Hugh Grant, Peter Hanlon, Greg Kealey, David Millar, Bill Morrison, Desmond Morton, Morris Mott, James Naylor, Don Nerbas, Bryan Palmer, Todd J. Pfannestiel, Steve Robinson, Philip Stenning, Jonathan Swainger, Doug Smith, and Meir Serfaty. Duncan Fraser gave us access to the unpublished manuscript of Jack Walker's account of the 1919 sedition trials. Ian McKay offered several suggestions for improvement to the manuscript that he will recognize in the final text. Drew Mitchell provided timely access to legal texts unavailable to the authors. Randy Kostecki, of Manitoba Heritage and Culture, kindly identified the location of the march of the Specials, which appears on our cover. Thank you to Len Husband for his editorial guidance, to the University of Toronto Press readers and John St James for their thoughtful suggestions for revision, and to Wayne Herrington for shepherding the manuscript to final completion.

We would also like to acknowledge the patience, support, insight, and editorial suggestions provided by Bonnie Mitchell and Rita Kramer.

When the State Trembled
How A.J. Andrews and the Citizens' Committee Broke the Winnipeg General Strike

Introduction

It was Natalie Zemon Davis who brought to the forefront one of the great reclamation projects of the late twentieth century, the attempt to resurrect the histories of those forgotten by history: losers, victims, ordinary people.[1] In a small way, our *Walk Towards the Gallows: The Tragedy of Hilda Blake, Hanged 1899* contributed to that ongoing project. But in the historiography of the 1919 Winnipeg General Strike, losers, victims, and ordinary strikers have sometimes nudged aside cabinet ministers. Counter-intuitively, the forgotten subjects of history have been the shadowy *victors*, the members of the Citizens' Committee of 1000. No surprise in one sense: the Citizens shrunk from advertising their individual roles in squelching the prophesied workers' utopia. Historians followed the Citizens' lead by treating the conflict as a struggle between the workers and the Canadian state. The usual stories run thus: around 1919, workers decided to improve their meagre condition by standing up for collective bargaining; or, alternatively, workers sensed for the first time that a general strike could blow up the boss, labour subservience, the whole damn system. With either revolution or decent wages threatening to arrive, Canada played the liberal democratic state's assigned role in crushing the challengers. The state sent mounted police officers swinging clubs into the crowds, then swung laws at radical heads. In these stories, the pressing historical questions revolve around the motives of the Strike leaders. Were they or weren't they revolutionary? Did they intend to overthrow the government or did they only want a living wage? Did the state fear chaos or did it cry sedition so as to hammer down the smallest gain by the workers?[2] Important questions all; but phrased in this dichotomous way they imply that the state was a juggernaut before which strikers must fall.

In existing accounts of the Strike, the Citizens' Committee of 1000 was little more than an outcrop on the state, furnishing it with volunteers for essential services and for a militia. At most, the Citizens' Committee was Canada's evil conscience, grimly reminding the state of its job to repress. But in fact, large tracts of the 'state' were either technically neutral (the provincial government, which held the monopoly on criminal prosecutions) or predisposed towards a negotiated settlement (the City of Winnipeg, represented by Mayor Gray). Even the federal government, represented by the acting Minister of Justice Arthur Meighen and Labour Minister Gideon Robertson, had to be prodded along – now willingly, now with misdirection – so that onlookers would be convinced that the *state* had ordered the prosecutions of the Strike leaders. Who held the prod? The shadowy Citizens' Committee of 1000 and the former boy-mayor of Winnipeg, Alfred J. Andrews.

Historians have mistakenly characterized Meighen, Prime Minister Robert Borden's factotum, as the author of reaction, the antagonist in labour's story.[3] After the strike was over, Bill Pritchard, a Strike leader, insinuated as much, saying that for a 'fine Italian hand,' one need look no further than Meighen.[4] However, during the Strike, Meighen and Andrews communicated regularly, and with the release (under the Access to Information Act) of the Meighen/Andrews correspondence, which previous historians had no access to, we can tell the full story of the Citizens' Committee of 1000.[5] Who authorized the prosecutions of the strikers? The federal government wouldn't say. As early as 1922, E.J. McMurray, defence attorney for the strikers, asked to see ministerial correspondence on the Strike. Again in 1926, J.S. Woodsworth requested the information in Parliament.[6] They got nowhere.

It wasn't until the late 1980s that the crucial papers surfaced. The University of Manitoba's Faculty of Law was preparing to celebrate its seventy-fifth anniversary, and Dean Roland Penner suggested that it publish a book on noteworthy Manitoba legal cases, one chapter per case. Professor Alvin Esau, director of the Legal Research Institute, took on the project. In 1989 and 1990 he was dispatched to Ottawa, where he amassed a mountain of photocopies on a number of trials, among them the sedition trials following the Winnipeg General Strike. Esau invited Tom Mitchell into the office where the photocopies were stacked in separate piles, and said, 'Choose one.' At the time, Mitchell was working on the Hilda Blake murder case, but as he began to dig through the massive file on the Strike he recognized material unknown to historians. It's ironic that Penner unwittingly set the ball rolling: his father, Jacob Penner, had been a Strike organizer, a member of the Defence Committee immediately afterward, and later a Communist alderman for Winnipeg.

Roland, descendant of strikers, served as Manitoba's NDP attorney general from 1981 to 1987.

'We rarely hear,' Adam Smith said, 'of the combinations of masters; though frequently of those of workmen. But whoever imagines, upon this account, that masters rarely combine, is as ignorant of the world as of the subject. Masters are always and every where in a sort of tacit, but constant and uniform combination, not to raise the wages of labour above their actual rate. To violate this combination is every where a most unpopular action, and a sort of reproach to a master among his neighbours and equals. We seldom, indeed, hear of this combination, because it is the usual, and one may say, the natural state of things which nobody ever hears of.'[7] What had been tacit in Manitoba, the Meighen/Andrews correspondence made explicit. A combination of masters actively shaped the federal government's response to the Strike.

The Meighen/Andrews correspondence illuminates Meighen's reluctance to take action against the Strike, his candid thoughts about what actions might be legally defensible, and Andrews's skilful roping in of the state's resources and machinery.[8] Andrews had no *official* role, but Winnipeggers knew that at a certain point he received Meighen's blessing. The correspondence also makes clear that for a long time Meighen had no clue that Andrews would wander far outside of official provincial channels. Since Andrews carried the unofficial imprimatur of the state, he, *in appearance*, became the state, and, by playing upon the various levels of government, he brought the state to the very brink of illegality. Ultimately, the story is much larger than what happened in Winnipeg in 1919: Winnipeg was simply the place where Canada and Canada's liberal order trembled, and therefore the place where reaction proved crucial. In Andrews and the Citizens' Committee of 1000, we see the response of commercial society to a crisis with the potential, so business leaders reasonably feared, to erode the foundation of commercial society, threaten private property, and undermine the decorum by which individuals of all ranks lived together in seeming peace.[9]

Recovering the story of the Citizens is a reclamation project, but not the sort that Zemon Davis had in mind: it is the story of a publicity-shy *winner*. Here, against the grain of the existing historiography, we search for a powerful and triumphant and yet bashful historical subject. In the Winnipeg's Legislative Library you won't find a file on the Citizens' Committee of 1000, and the entries for the Committee in the Provincial Archives of Manitoba are trivial. The Citizens left behind no body of organizational records; membership was secret; with one exception, members hid their affiliation from *Who's Who* entries and obituaries. What's left? A series of attempts to enter the public sphere anonymously:

A photograph purported to be of the Citizens' Committee at a banquet held after the Strike. (Western Canada Pictorial Index, image 38698, contact sheet A1292)

the *Winnipeg Citizen* newspaper, with its anonymously written articles; a brief account of the organization and activities of the Committee; a short submission to the Robson royal commission; ads in the Winnipeg dailies; court records. Except for the court records, these are all studio portraits, the Citizens tailoring themselves in the clothes of The Ordinary Citizen for public consumption, as in the one photograph purported to be of the Citizens at a post-strike banquet.[10] Only now, with the unintended revelations in the Meighen-Andrews correspondence, can we fully assess the meaning of the Citizens' public self-representation. To Winnipeg General Strike historiography's almost exclusive preoccupation with history-from-below, with labour, we add history-from-above, the story of how business leaders in one commercial society stifled a potentially catastrophic threat.

'A "history from above" – of the intricate machinery of class domination – is no less essential than a "history from below"' – so said Perry Anderson.[11] Such a project of historical recovery engages contemporary debates concerning class, industrial relations, the state, the role of law, and the role of discourse and ideology in a divided society. Our aim is to pull the reluctant Citizens, in the persons of Isaac Pitblado, Travers Sweatman, James B. Coyne, Ed Anderson, Ed Parnell, and especially A.J. Andrews, back onto the stage.[12] We will suggest a number of larger and smaller theses in what follows, but the story itself is richer than the argument. The actions of the strikers and the reaction of the Citizens are best seen not in abstract or categorical investigations, but in narrative form ... as day-by-day responses to the situation on the ground. Events, advantages, governments tilting in one direction, then another – these make up the flux of human time, in which a slice of polemic printed on Tuesday can have a very different effect from the same line tossed into a crowd on Saturday. If Benjamin's 'angel of history' reminds us that a storm from Paradise is blowing us ever further from the wreckages of the past, at least we can try to remember that wreckage, not as a single overriding thesis, but as humans acting in time.

Marx's call for revolution was successful in Russia in 1917; why not in Canada in 1919? For an answer, we must look to the Citizens' Committee of 1000 – look backstage to see the manipulation that allowed the Citizens to wield state power; look at the public sphere to see what it was in Winnipeg's political consciousness that gave the Citizens a critical mass of support. Here, the historian is tempted to invoke 'ideology,' so that the victors in the Strike become cynical manipulators of propaganda, while the underclasses become either underdog heroes if they defy the dominant consensus, or stooges if they don't. But ideological repression is not the whole story of the Strike. Certain features of the Citizens' notion of public order had a broader appeal than just to the masters of industry. We don't intend a revisionist history that somehow excuses the state and the Citizens – they manipulated people, churned out propaganda, and hid behind 'ideology' – yet at the same time, we can't ignore the Citizens' *own* sense of what they were doing: their fears of the end of civil society and their intent, therefore, to lay siege to the public sphere. Further, we cannot ignore the fact that many Winnipeggers accepted the Citizens' version of events. 'Strike,' said labour. 'Revolution,' the Citizens called it. According to Philip Corigan and Derek Sayer, one need only press society a bit in order to see its 'seemingly neutral and timeless social forms' in more ruthless shape.[13] The 'knowledge' that wealth was a product of industry and intelligence, the implicit acceptance of one's station in life, and the politeness that allowed people of different classes to greet each other every morning might serve the upper classes well. But we cannot forget the shock to the gut that people felt at the Strike, the fear that order and freedom were under threat. Russia had fallen to the Communists; Germany and Italy were in chaos. One might compare 1919 to the immediate aftermath of 9/11. The burning question was, 'When will it happen here?'

Leninist revolution in Russia, but in the Western world, including Winnipeg, only disappointment for Marxists. Marx gave the Russian revolutionaries and the Winnipeg strikers who read him a far-reaching account of the capitalist mode of production. However, when it came to a *political* theory of the liberal-democratic state, he had little to say.[14] It was left to Antonio Gramsci, meditating on 1919, to try to explain why liberal society had successfully defended itself against an uprising from below. Gramsci couldn't help noticing that the 'advanced' liberal-democratic states had a remarkable fund of resilience, even *in extremis*. In these states, the complex structures that were commonly called 'private' were somehow not overwhelmed by labour's mortar shells dropping round about. Trench-systems, Gramsci called these structures: 'In Russia the State was everything, civil society was primordial and gelatinous; in the West there was a proper relation between State and civil society, and when the State trembled a sturdy structure of civil society was at once revealed. The State was only an outer ditch, behind which there stood a powerful system of fortresses and earthworks.'[15] And the defenders occupying the trenches were far from demoralized. They neither abandoned their positions nor lost faith in their strength and their future.

In 1919, the executive members of the Citizens' Committee were the human faces of Gramsci's defenders. The General Strike had called Winnipeg's commercial society out of its decorum, but the Citizens organized a fierce and unrelenting opposition. They frustrated the Strike Committee's determination to shut the city down. Although only the hesitant provincial government could legally prosecute criminal matters, the Citizens' executive, through a working alliance with the federal government, engineered the suppression of the Strike, prosecuted and convicted the Strike leadership, and, above all, shaped the immediate historical meaning of 1919. If a large number of Winnipeggers hadn't perceived the Strike as a potential revolution, then all the conviction in the world wouldn't have won the battle for the Citizens. The story of the Citizens discloses not only the relationship between the state and 'private' structures in civil society during periods of deep social crisis, but also says something about state formation, the public sphere, the languages of rule, and, most particularly, the post-war idiom of Canadian citizenship.

1

Permitted by Authority of the Strike Committee

Something that appears in certain particulars much like Bolshevism has arisen in Canada. It started in Winnipeg on May 15.

The Outlook, 4 June 1919

Thursday, 15 May

Although they had a good idea of what was coming, at 11:00 in the morning on Thursday, 15 May 1919, the upper classes looking down at Winnipeg streets from above felt a sudden vertigo. Winnipeg's entire street railway grated to a halt. Milk deliveries having been suspended and the pasteurization system shut off, a great stench arose as thousands of gallons of milk began to sour at railway stations and Crescent Creamery. Delivery of bread ceased too. The flour mills shut down and bakeries stopped baking. The city's many single male and female renters could no longer step out, as was habit, to downtown restaurants for their meals – all restaurants were closed. In this, the hottest May for forty years, the thermometer shooting up to 95° Fahrenheit, no one could get ice delivered to keep food cold,[1] except a select few who owned cars and struggled to haul their own ice.[2] Even the water supply was limited, 'rationed' to 30 pounds pressure, enough to do the cooking and washing in the first storey of a house – working-class strikers mostly inhabited little one-storey houses – but no higher. Industry languished, as did the wealthy in their three-storey homes, as did those who lived in the upper floors of the city's fashionable apartments.

To jaded historians and to those schooled in what Bertrand Russell ironically called 'the superior virtue of the oppressed,'[3] such a recitation has lost the power to startle. But it ought to startle. One of the greatest ruptures between the workers and the upper classes in the history of commercial society (second only to the Paris Commune of 1871) had opened.[4] About 30,000 unionized and non-unionized workers put down their tools.[5] Labour leader R.B. Russell, who pegged the number somewhat higher at 35,000, claimed that, with an average three-person family, strikers represented 105,000 people, more than half of Winnipeg's 200,000. Even pro-business alderman Fisher could estimate strikers and their families at no fewer than 70,000.[6] Both inside and outside of Canada, the Winnipeg General Strike gripped newspaper readers, including, half a world away, a leading figure in the Italian Socialist Party (PSI), Antonio Gramsci, who told readers of *L'Ordine Nuovo* that Canadian strikers were trying to install a soviet regime.[7]

Canadian law had barricaded itself against strikes in the Criminal Code and the wartime Industrial Disputes Investigation Act (IDIA): picketing had no legal basis; workers under contract were forbidden to strike; wildcat strikes in public utilities were illegal; intemperate talk could bring the speaker a conviction for sedition or seditious conspiracy; and employers could sue unions in civil prosecutions for damages due to a strike. Winnipeg's upper classes expected that at least some of those barricades would hold. Yet on 15 May, workers threw aside safety, defied the law, and ignored the cooling-off period mandated by the IDIA. Workers, even those with no specific grievance, simply walked off the job.[8]

All over the city, superintendents and managers watched their power drain away. At 11:00 o'clock, 1500 strong left the Winnipeg Electric Railway Company. No matter that the trainmen were, at the time, the focus of an inquiry chaired by Judge Thomas Metcalfe under the IDIA. The men had disregarded the inquiry, and when the call came from the Strike Committee, they walked.[9] F.J. Foster, who operated a cake bakery, tried to take seventy-five cases of eggs 'fresh cracked' to Manitoba Cold Storage, but found the place empty, except for one manager, who wouldn't let Foster in without a special permit from the Strike Committee, in addition to the one already attached to Foster's bread wagon.[10] Theatre and café owners similarly had to petition the Strike Committee, explaining why it was in the strikers' best interest that certain businesses be kept open. In some cases, the Strike Committee granted permission, but only on condition that the businesses prominently display the sign 'Permitted by Authority of the Strike Committee.'[11] Even then, according to A.E. Fulljames of the Kensington Café, strikers intimidated some employees. Discipline became impossible and the café was forced to close again two days later. Angry, Fulljames ripped up the Strike Committee's permit cards. T. Kernaghan of the Venice Café claimed that

when he approached his employees at their homes, he 'had been surrounded by crowds of from 200 to 400 booing and jeering.'[12]
William M. Gordon, superintendent for the Dominion Express Company, watched all 205 of his employees exit the building. They had no dispute with him or his company, and had, in fact, just agreed to a contract two weeks earlier. No matter. The Strike notice received from the Labor Temple trumped the contract.[13] Workers at the Arctic Ice Company had likewise recently negotiated a one-year deal effective May 1st, but they walked too. The next day, managing director Charles H. McNaughton, like baker F.J. Foster, was forced to go to the Labor Temple cap in hand, begging to be allowed to take ice to hospitals. His petition was granted, as long as the driver displayed permission cards on the wagons. Later, the Committee sent additional 'orders' about where ice could and couldn't be delivered.[14]

Yes, ice was permitted for the Winnipeg General Hospital. Dr Herbert O. Collins, general superintendent of the hospital, wrote a letter asking also that employees be allowed to work, and he carried it in person to the Labor Temple, where he presented it to John Queen and the Strike Committee. He was told to expect a reply. None was received, though hospital employees encountered no opposition when they remained on the job.[15] Not everyone got satisfaction. Crescent Creamery employed 300 to 350 men and provided milk and cream to between 125,000 and 150,000 Winnipeggers. Its manager, James M. Carruthers, wrote both to the Trades and Labor Council and to the Strike Committee in hopes of keeping the Creamery open. No reply.[16] Unlike hospital officials, he had no expectation that the Strike Committee would let the Creamery continue business as usual.

Other employers, small and large, were forced to petition the Strike Committee. Some received permission cards; some didn't.[17] In short, authority had fled City Hall, crossing over Main Street to roost on the James Street Labor Temple. If, as E.P. Thompson says, class is an event that occurs when some people begin to articulate their interests against people with other interests,[18] then in Winnipeg on 15 May class was happening.

The Strike's immediate cause was the breakdown in negotiations between management and labour in Winnipeg's building and metal trades. Strikers wanted better wages, better working conditions, and, above all, that appalling thing that raised the hair on the necks of employers everywhere: industrial unionism. With the newly minted weapon of the general strike, industrial unions could shut down a major city. Employers knew that at the recent Calgary Conference of Labour, workers had urged each other to band together in the revolutionary One Big Union (OBU). In any dispute, a massive union could stack the deck in labour's favour, since, in theory, even the smallest demand held the hammer of a general strike behind its back. R.B. Russell, a Machinists' union organizer, spoke bluntly when Canada sent soldiers to fight against the Russian Communists in Siberia: 'Drafts are being shipped to Vancouver so that they can go across to Russia to massacre the proletariat there. Let us have justice and if not, then blood will be spilled in this country. Capitalism has come to that point where it must disappear.'[19] Russell's rhetoric and the way that the Strike quickly spread far beyond the building and metal trades gave the OBU the appearance of fate. No matter that technically the OBU hadn't been created yet – a general strike was an OBU tactic, and Strike leaders such as Russell didn't doubt that the OBU would be the fulcrum to start history rolling down the road to utopia.

Friday, 16 May

The next day, Friday, more bad news for employers. Pressmen deserted the big daily newspapers, the Strike Committee punishing the press for its bias against the Strike. This chilled many Winnipeggers. No more freedom of the press: suddenly the *Western Labor News*, a house organ of the Winnipeg Trades and Labor Council and the Strike Committee, monopolized information. How could one get news that hadn't been doctored by socialists and radicals? Also, how could businessmen convince their employees that yes, somebody *else* may have been treating workers unfairly, but a *general* strike was a ludicrous, scatter-shot affair, and ought to have nothing to do with *our* business? John Dafoe, editor of the *Manitoba Free Press*, hadn't been fully committed to the business owners' side of the dispute, but when he saw his workers abandoning their type, he too cried that Winnipeg was in the throes of revolution.

Forget about communicating with the outside world. Government-employed telephone operators, linemen, and postal workers had joined the striking pressmen on Friday; as did telegraphers on Saturday. You couldn't send a telegram; you couldn't move anything. Even if you wanted to work, it was punishable bad manners to defy your striking co-workers. There were reports of intimidation and of police refusing to intervene.[20] Stranded on the job – by the authority of the Strike Committee – stood a few lonely but essential workers, including a skeleton crew of telegraphers who relayed death notices, news of returned soldiers, and government communications about the Strike. Police officers wanted to leap in with the strikers, but the Strike Committee asked police to hold off. In past strikes, employers had shot back with replacement workers and injunctions against picketing. But with the whole city standing still, such measures would be ineffective at best, or at worst could escalate the Strike into a national affair. Ditto for the IDIA, which (under PC 2525) still threatened a $1000 fine or six months in prison for any striking public utilities worker.[21]

For the most part, the streets remained orderly, but people feared picket-line violence, and rumours about the strikers planning to attack the militia at the Osborne Barracks ran in undercurrents through the city.[22] 'The effects temporarily were complete and staggering. The disorganization of community activity was complete.'[23]

As this wave of labour tumult broke in public, a counter-force had already mobilized itself in private. At the latest by Tuesday, 13 May, two days *before* the Strike, and informally long before that, a group had met and organized itself in anticipation of 'a general tie-up of all industries.'[24] The group was a force that, even as it prepared to influence the public sphere, shunned the spotlight; a force that within days would publish its own anonymous newspaper, but wouldn't reveal its members; a force that would make a loose pact with the federal government: the Citizens' Committee of 1000. Even after the Strike was over, when E.J. McMurray, defence attorney for the Strike leaders, asked for a list of Citizens' Committee members, Magistrate R.M. Noble explained that these were private citizens and that it was his duty to protect them.[25]

Where did the Citizens come from? They didn't spring *sui generis* from the troubled soil of 1919 as a kind of spontaneous response to working-class revolt. There are at least four narratives of the Citizens' origins, none fully satisfying. The Citizens themselves gave a rather spiritual and mythical story: we are an eclectic group, they implied, born out of a sudden, shared wish for freedom of the press, for freedom of movement, for individual liberty – all the great British liberties hitherto shared by every Canadian as a birthright. 'How is it,' the *Winnipeg Citizen* demanded early on, 'that 25,000 [strikers] can dominate and dictate to 150,000 people? Solely because those 25,000 are organized and the 150,000 are not.'[26] Such was the Lockean fiction, making the Citizens a kind of town cousin to working-class unions, a union for the honourable and oppressed 'middle' class. Whereas the strikers autocratically limited freedoms, this middle-class union would defend freedoms; whereas the strikers planned for cliques to rule the nation, this middle-class union would stand up for the individual; whereas the strikers championed Russia, the members of this middle-class union would die for the British Constitution.

Nonsense, said labour, you're a bunch of employers united by greed. You're the dark inverse of unionization. As soon as you saw powerless workers joining each other in a body far stronger than the individual worker, you formed a vigilante group, and, under the cover of anonymity, you conspire to destroy the worker's freedom. There is some truth to this second story, but it's far too simple.

A third story, coming in more measured tones from historians of the Strike – and affirmed by the Citizens themselves[27] – suggests that the 1919 Citizens' Committee of 1000 was born out of the 1918 Committee of 100, a group that had averted a potential civic employees' strike a year earlier. But even this measured story isn't satisfactory, since there were, as we will show, very crucial differences in the composition and tactics of the two committees.

Into the mix comes a fourth, broader story of historical filiation. All over Britain and the United States, well before 1919, groups had sprung up to fight unionization: Anti-Socialist Unions, Economic Leagues, Law and Order Leagues, Citizens' Committees, and Citizens Protective Leagues. Unlike Winnipeg's 1918 Committee of 100, these groups emphasized not conciliation but repression.[28] A number of Winnipeggers had been paying attention to the 'Protective League' phenomenon, particularly, as we will see in chapter 2, to the Minneapolis Citizens' Alliance, and, as early as March (when labour took the first steps towards the OBU in Calgary) the Royal North West Mounted Police was compiling secret reports that Winnipeg's upper classes predicted riots, and that they planned to organize a Citizens Protective Association. No need for divine inspiration in March to prophesy riots – there had already been riots of a sort on 26 and 27 January. Of a sort: the rioters weren't immigrants or labour radicals, but returned soldiers who felt it their patriotic duty to terrorize immigrants. The soldiers had heard reports of a socialist labour meeting at the Majestic Theatre a week before, where speakers proposed a peaceful revolution in Canada, praised the Russian Revolution, and intimated that they'd be ready 'to shed blood if the capitalist wished to use force in keeping the working class from obtaining their rights.'[29] Encouraged by the *Winnipeg Telegram*, by army officers, and by members of the Board of Trade, the soldiers had decided that Winnipeg's immigrants needed schooling in Canadian morality. About 300 men fought each other for three hours, mainly with fists but eventually with planks torn from gates as well.[30] After a German insulted the Union Jack, the police stood aside while a group of soldiers assaulted Germans and other aliens, and wrecked a few places: the Edelweis Brewery; the German Club, where a piano was thrown out of the second floor and smashed to bits; the offices of the

Socialist Party of Canada (SPC), where a large red flag was burned; an automobile dealership owned by Michael Ert, who wasn't a socialist;[31] and the Minneapolis Dye House, a business owned by Sam Blumenberg, who was. Unable to find Blumenberg hidden in the attic, the soldiers dragged his wife out into the street and invited her to kiss the Union Jack.[32] Well might Winnipeg's elite predict riots, when its own Board of Trade members had started one, and its Citizens Protective Association had announced its intent to take direct action against socialist leaders and foreigners.[33]

While this riot can't for certain be called the debut of the Citizens, their connection to the rioters can't be dismissed either. Throughout the period leading up to the Winnipeg General Strike and even during it, the SPC had been trying, not always successfully, to persuade soldiers and police that their lower-class identities ought to trump their ethnic identities. Although we have found no list of members for the Citizens Protective Association, its name and its connections to the Board of Trade suggest that it was a precursor to the Citizens' Committee of 1000. Ideologically (and possibly in some of their members) the two groups of 'Citizens' were congruent, as would become even clearer several weeks into the Strike when the Citizens' Committee began to target aliens with hate literature. Months before the Strike, then, the Citizens Protective Association incited soldiers to riot, even as it proposed to save the city from still-hypothetical alien rioters.

Monday, 19 May

By the time that the Citizens' Committee of 1000 sent its proxies into the public square, the vigilante aspects of the Citizens Protective Association had been laid aside, at least publicly. The Citizens' Committee of 1000 made its first official appearance neither as a group nor as individual men – either of these would have nailed its members uncomfortably to their social roles and their affluence, and might have confirmed the strikers' belief that the Winnipeg General Strike was class war. Instead, the Citizens 'revealed' themselves as a way of speaking, a set of reasons: first in the form of an ad in the 15 May *Free Press*, and then as a new newspaper, the *Winnipeg Citizen*.[34] The pre-emptive ad was written two days before the Strike; later, the Citizens would manage to forget this public birthday and declare that the Committee had been formed within twenty-four hours of the Strike's commencement,[35] as a response to, not a pre-emption of, events. The ad mentioned only that the Citizens were interested in maintaining law, order, and fire service, in protecting the supply of water 'for domestic use' and the supply of gas 'for cooking purposes.'[36] No whisper of industrial uses. With the water pressure during the Strike fixed at 30 lbs, obviously no one was dying of thirst – domestic use was satisfied – so the Citizens' rhetoric about 'necessities' soon transmuted itself into a different rhetoric about freedom.

Only three days after their lives and businesses had been body-checked by the Strike, the Citizens were organized enough to send the first edition of the *Winnipeg Citizen* out into the streets.[37] On Sunday, the four-page newspaper arrived at church doors;[38] on Monday morning, all over the city. Although the *Citizen* did reveal – how else to mobilize volunteers? – that the headquarters of the Citizens' Committee lay in the Board of Trade Building (also known as the Industrial Bureau) at the corner of Main and Water, the newspaper itself had no masthead beyond 'Published in Winnipeg in the Interests of the Citizens.' For a long time there was no way to identify the editors; the authors and contributors are unknown to this day. W.H. Plewman, the correspondent for the *Toronto Star*, couldn't uncover the editors or authors.[39] Even people as closely connected with the executive as Capt. F.G. Thompson, the Great War Veterans Association's delegate to the Citizens, had no idea who was editing the *Winnipeg Citizen* until near the end of the Strike.[40] After the Strike was over, Theodore Kipp, the general superintendent of Ogilvie Mills who assisted the Citizens in the operation of the Fire Department, claimed that he didn't know who the editor was.[41] If one had a quarrel with an article, one couldn't approach the editor directly, but, as with Kafka's castle, the only access for ordinary mortals was to find someone who knew someone who knew someone else.

In contrast, the *Western Labor News* masthead was more revealing – 'Published by the Strike Committee, Labor Temple' – and everybody knew that William Ivens was editor. Within a week, the *Western Labor News* published a list of the Strike's Central Committee members.[42] The *Winnipeg Citizen*, however, seemed to come from nowhere and yet everywhere, from no particular social group and from all 'citizens' at once: 'This publication is not issued on behalf of the workers, nor on behalf of the employers, nor in opposition to either of them as such.' The employers, declared the *Citizen*, already had means of communication and didn't need a newspaper. Rather, the paper's purpose was to keep the '150,000' citizens who weren't involved in the Strike informed.[43]

All the declarations of neutrality were a simple disguise, of course. As befit the growing ideal of objective journalism, articles in the *Winnipeg Citizen* pretended to a certain amount of diversity. One article urged Winnipeggers to curtail their 'joy-riding' (a less pejorative term than it is now), while another reported on the doctors' reaction to the Strike. In fact, however, articles shook hands across the newspaper. That is, a problem raised in one article – that doctors feared for invalid soldiers and the sick during the incommunicado enforced by the Strike Committee – would fortuitously be answered by another article, in which the Citizens' Committee announced that it had been formed especially to help 'little children, invalid soldiers, and the sick generally.' At fire halls no. 9 and no. 12, reported one article, strikers gave firefighters the option of leaving the job or getting their halls smashed up;[44] another article, in the same paper, reported that the Citizens' Committee had arranged to have the fire-halls staffed.[45] Many writers probably contributed articles, but evidently a unified editorial hand bound them all.

If the new *Winnipeg Citizen* wouldn't admit that employers held its leash, in content it broadcast its allegiances, but always phrased as allegiances to moral and patriotic ideals. Everywhere in that first edition, it lashed at the strikers. Telephone operators, clearly lacking a moral sense, refused to stay on the job to allow calls to hospitals.[46] 'Six-sevenths of the people of Winnipeg are trodden just as pitilessly under foot as were the people of Belgium beneath the heel of the Hun. It is for those six-sevenths that *Winnipeg Citizen* is published.'[47] Hyperbolic invocation of 'the Hun' during any sort of argument came as quickly and as instinctively in post–First World War Canada as the word 'Nazi' would come to the lips of late-twentieth-century polemicists. The strikers inevitably gravitated towards the same language as the Citizens, working just as polemically to establish their version of moral reason in the public square: 'Where do the bosses stand? We remember the arrogance of the Hun. We remember their determination to dominate the situation.'[48]

The need to put bread on the table could potentially trump broader questions of rights and liberties, and the *Winnipeg Citizen* understood this. Labour had begun at a fundamental level, demanding '1. THE RIGHT TO COLLECTIVE BARGAINING, and 2. THE RIGHT TO A LIVING WAGE.'[49] Yet this prioritizing of demands ineptly undermined labour's stance. How could the right to life be the *second* issue? If it was, then something other than survival must be at stake. The debate soon moved from matters of survival to matters of moral right, where *reasons* must be given. In the early days of the Strike, the *Winnipeg Citizen*, too, couched its approach at the level of necessity, a level that would trump reasoned argument, by repeatedly insisting that Winnipeggers couldn't get the necessities of life. Initially, the Citizens weren't far off the mark. Workers, expecting overwhelmed employers to cave in within two or three days, announced that they were prepared to starve.[50] The sudden blow to the chains of supply and distribution suggested that the workers might be serious.

The interruption of supply and distribution occurred in part because the *general* strike hadn't been fully theorized. Though 'general' strikes of workers in particular industries were commonplace, the calling of a general strike across a city or country was stunning. The First International refused to endorse such action.[51] Under the Second International, Marxist doctrine spoke of the inevitability of working-class revolution, but only in the fullness of time when the contradictions of capitalism broke society apart. German socialists too – the most prestigious and influential force in the Second International – initially turned up their noses at the general strike. To Wilhelm Liebknecht, a general strike was 'general nonsense.'[52] On the brink of the First World War, it was suggested that a general strike might prevent Armageddon, but when 4 August 1914 arrived, labour quailed at direct action, and salved itself by making toothless assertions that war should be opposed 'by any means deemed suitable.'[53]

A few socialists hoped that general strikes might reform or curb capital. Three times between 1893 and 1913, Belgian labour called week-long general strikes to press – unsuccessfully – for universal suffrage.[54] Italian workers mounted a five-day general strike across the country in September 1904 to protest the government's use of the army in labour disputes. Italy's 'five days of the dictatorship of the proletariat' descended into an orgy of violence and achieved nothing.[55] 'Pure utopia,' the Italian anarchist Errico Malatesta afterwards called the concept of the general strike. 'Either the worker, dying of hunger after three days on strike, will return to the factory hanging his head, and we shall score one more defeat. Or else he will try to gain possession of the fruits of production by open force. Who will he find facing him to stop him? Soldiers, policemen, perhaps the bourgeois themselves, and then the question will have to be resolved by bullets and bombs. It will be insurrection, and victory will go to the strongest.'[56]

In Sweden, 300,000 workers struck in 1909 to protest the repeated use of lockouts by employers in industrial disputes. At first, no trams or steamers ran, gas and electric lights went out, no wood or coal was sold. Vehicles were banned from the streets of Stockholm unless they carried a 'free card' from the strike committee. The press was silenced, allowing the strikers' organ, *Svaret*, to dominate the public sphere. Although the state refused to intervene, volunteers from every social stratum joined a public security brigade termed the 'Frivilliga Skyddskåren' to fight the strike, maintain the food supply, drive cabs, and keep gas, water, and electric services running. After thirty days, the strike collapsed, leaving the general strike discredited among Swedish workers.[57]

Everywhere, the general strike's effects were ambiguous at best ... except in Russia. In Russia, a general strike during the 1905 Revolution paralysed the country, forcing Nicholas II to grant basic constitutional reform. An ad hoc council of workers, the Petrograd Soviet – brainchild of the Union of Unions – set itself up as an alternative to the tsarist authorities, published a newspaper (*Izvestia*), established a militia, distributed food, and promoted the creation of other soviets across the country.[58] When the Romanov dynasty fell in the spring of 1917, the new Kerensky regime faced a rival centre of power in the Petrograd Soviet. Lenin, entering the scene in April, called for the transfer of power to the proletariat, and through the summer of 1917 the Bolsheviks engaged in mass agitation, including general strikes. Then, in October, Lenin audaciously ordered that power be transferred from the Kerensky regime, not to the Petrograd Soviet as expected, but to the Bolsheviks. Gramsci was enchanted – here was an antidote to socialist dithering! 'Why should they wait for the history of England to be repeated in Russia, for the bourgeoisie to arise, for the class struggle to begin, so that class consciousness may be formed and the final catastrophe of the capitalist world eventually hit them?'[59]

In Germany, Rosa Luxemburg, responding to the 1905 Revolution, gave the fullest account of the general strike. Her conclusion: the destruction of the capitalist order required 'the widest and deepest mobilization of the masses.'[60] Luxemburg and Karl Liebknecht – who, unlike his father Wilhelm, embraced the general strike – helped found the Spartacus League on the left fringe of the German Social Democratic movement, and expected that once the Hohenzollerns fell from power, the Spartacus League (renamed the 'Communist Party of Germany') would run a dictatorship of the proletariat via workers' councils.[61] In Spartacist hands, therefore, the general strike was not a tool to achieve limited economic goals, but was theorized as a way to radicalize workers in preparation for all-out revolution.

Karl Liebknecht marched at the forefront of events in January 1919, calling for a general strike and insurrection. At the time, Canadian Prime Minister Borden was in Paris for the Versailles peace conference, and *Manitoba Free Press* editor J.W. Dafoe, also there, sent home reports on the deepening German crisis to Winnipeg readers.[62] The Spartacists and their allies shouted for 'genuine socialists or Communists' to overthrow and replace the Ebert government.[63] Factories stood empty and merchants closed their shops, while the streets seethed with competing parades and placards, some demonstrators shouting 'Down with the Government!' others 'Down with the Spartacus!' Very quickly, rioters and armed combatants replaced the demonstrators. Spartacists managed to occupy public buildings and telegraph offices; and, according to the *Manitoba Free Press*, Russians had snuck into Berlin, 'assisting Dr. Liebknecht and Rosa Luxemburg in fomenting a Bolshevik revolution.' In Düsseldorf, where a Bolshevik republic was declared, hundreds were killed. Revolutionaries jailed the chamber of commerce director, the director of high schools, and a manager of the steel works, while a hundred and fifty prominent citizens fled across the Rhine to Belgian protection.[64]

Liebknecht refused negotiations to end the violence, and on 10 January the Spartacists proclaimed a new government.[65] But the putsch failed catastrophically, and many Spartacists – more than 1000 – were summarily executed on the spot.[66] By 15 January, Liebknecht and Luxemburg had been bludgeoned to death with rifle butts after being arrested and taken to the Eden Hotel, a temporary headquarters for one of the para-military Free Corps supporting the Ebert government.[67] In reporting Luxemburg's death, the *Manitoba Free Press* quoted her own words against her as a fitting epitaph: 'Socialism does not mean the convening of parliaments and the enactment of laws; it means the overthrow of the ruling classes with all the brutality at the disposal of the proletariat.'[68]

Western Canadian labour radicals didn't belong in such company, insists historian David Bercuson. They were pragmatists who meant to win industrial disputes and extract concessions from government, 'but not to topple the government.' They never spoke of 'building the new society within the shell of the old.'[69] In short, one ought to ignore the hyperbolic rhetoric of the Calgary Conference, because the OBUers were not the revolutionaries that the Citizens' Committee portrayed them to be. Probably a sound conclusion, but, given the circumstances of 1919, not a completely satisfying one. Deliberate discussion about general strikes began in Winnipeg in 1918, when Calgary freight handlers struck over the issue of union recognition and the federal government replied by banning all strikes and lockouts for the duration of the war in industries covered by the Industrial Disputes Investigation Act. William Ivens responded: 'The trades congress should call a general strike over all Canada until the order-in-council ... is rescinded.'[70] Senator Gideon Robertson steered his way to a compromise solution, but it was seen as a victory for labour and only made the idea of a general strike more appealing to workers.[71] The Winnipeg Trades and Labor Council (TLC) suggested that general strikes could be called after a simple majority vote of the city's total union members, 'instead of on a majority or two thirds vote of each individual organization.'[72] The *Western Labor News* called this union of unions the 'movement of the near future,' a way of maximizing the power of all workers. Here the general strike appears in a state of transformation from a defensive weapon of last resort to a first-strike weapon, which (via the One Big Union) could shut the country down at a moment's notice. Unions that voted against a general strike would place themselves 'outside the pale of unionism,' and 'be treated accordingly.' Coercion it was – intended to bolster weak unions, but still coercion.[73]

More importantly, Young Turks such as R.B. Russell and R.J. Johns in the Socialist Party of Canada were slowly gaining influence in labour circles, and many clues suggested just what Russell and other radicals hoped to accomplish once they gained control of the TLC. In December 1918 at the Walker Theatre – with Russell among the leaders on stage – 1700 members of Winnipeg's working-class movement proclaimed their solidarity with both the Russian Revolution and Karl Liebknecht.[74] Marx now stood in the shadow of Lenin and Liebknecht: the words *general strike* had acquired a talismanic power.

The 26 and 27 January riots which destroyed German and Jewish businesses in Winnipeg's North End occurred in part because socialists at the Majestic Theatre on the 19th had called for a meeting in Winnipeg's Market Square on the 26th to commemorate Liebknecht and Luxemburg. Returned soldiers were prodded to take offence at this Canadian sequel to the failed German revolution. What is less well known is the battle within the TLC that preceded the riots. It was alleged that TLC secretary Ernie Robinson had cancelled a follow-up to the hugely successful December mass meeting at the Walker Theatre. Was it the Walker Theatre management that had scuttled the follow-up meeting or had TLC officials themselves sabotaged it because the SPC would not collaborate with other socialist parties? George Armstrong thought he knew the answer, blaming Robinson (who rejected the allegation) and secretary of the Dominion Labour Party George Barlow. The SPC decided to sponsor its own meeting at the Majestic Theatre, and when Sam Blumenberg suggested that TLC representatives be invited, he was shouted down with 'We'll have nobody but Socialists.' Armstrong dismissed the leadership of the Dominion Labour Party as 'a bunch of labor fakirs who are using the workers to keep themselves in political jobs.'[75] At the Majestic, Russell paid homage to the fallen Luxemburg and Liebknecht, while Blumenberg called on workers to overthrow the capitalist system.[76]

SPCer Johns brought the dispute to the TLC, and, alluding to the split between Spartacists and supporters of the Ebert government, complained that European socialist infighting was spreading to Winnipeg, but then he went on the attack himself, declaring that some TLC members were frightened of the word 'revolution,' and predicting that socialist ideals would soon triumph in the TLC: 'We are fighting for ideals, and, believe me, we will be fighting with guns before we are through.' Urged by TLC president James Winning to 'get back on course,' Johns responded, 'We are a minority now, but believe me, we are getting a footing on the boards.'[77]

Did this mean that Winnipeg tottered on the cusp of a Spartacus-like uprising, or that the Winnipeg General Strike was, as the Citizens claimed, a prelude to Bolshevik revolution? No. A few hyperbolic statements from Johns didn't amount to a call to the barricades. But these churnings of labour were important. In Winnipeg, socialist and OBU calls for a new order based on soviets and proletarian dictatorship rang discordantly alongside Defoe's reports that terror had chased Düsseldorf's leading citizens to Belgium. All of this, combined with a revulsion against the brutalities of the Russia Revolution, provided a powerful reason for the Citizens to attack the Strike. Knowing who will win and who will lose, the historian sometimes forgets the raw contingency of events. Is there not something unclean about the winner, especially if he does not think like us? Does not a warm halo surround the loser? But in 1919, Winnipeg's upper classes didn't know what might happen; they didn't know they'd win. In Russia and Germany, general strikes led to general insurrection. Well might the upper classes fear Communist-inspired revolution; well might they respond with propaganda and even force.

The voluntary response to the call for a general strike in Winnipeg fit Rosa Luxemburg's prediction of 'independent mass action' by the working class,[78] yet no one among the Winnipeg Strike leaders had thought fully about how to run an entire city. Although Russell was committed to the idea of the OBU with its concomitant general-strike weapon, he 'never worked out exactly how this organization would operate.'[79] The *Winnipeg Citizen* seized on this organizational naivety: 'Lack of ice and lack of milk is causing privation and hardship even for babies – who did not start the strike.'[80] It was true; babies *hadn't* started the Strike! And yet, despite the heavy-handed rhetoric, the situation was fairly dire; the city really was suffering, and the lack of a full theory about how to manage a general strike in a democratic, non-revolutionary context meant that even the strikers themselves were cut off from the food supply for a day or two. Polemical advantage: Citizens.

Nevertheless, what inflamed the upper-class Citizens about the Strike wasn't always what inflamed Winnipeggers in general, and the Citizens, like labour, sometimes stumbled ineptly when it came to prioritizing concerns. Later in the Strike, when lawyer and Citizen spokesperson Isaac Pitblado told a delegation from Moose Jaw about the hardships created by the Strike, the first outrage he reported was that the elevator wouldn't take him to his ninth-floor office. Only after that did he get round to the suffering babies.[81] The cry for bread and milk had quickly become a propaganda device, and Pitblado understood that suffering babies made for great press. But (knowing quite well that milk delivery had been restored) he couldn't help voicing his immediate and more honest concern that he, a high-status lawyer, should be forced to run up nine flights of stairs.

Even by the time that the *Winnipeg Citizen* complained about suffering babies on Monday, milk and bread delivery had already been restored ... provided that drivers carried permission cards. Not only restored, but reported as restored in Monday's *Winnipeg Citizen*, the *very same* paper which carried the complaint. This by no means signified that the strong editorial hand was slipping; it simply meant that no weapon in the propaganda arsenal would be left to rust, especially not one as powerful as suffering babies. Yet with babies drinking milk again, the Citizens realized that they must graduate to a new complaint. They had expected pocket-sized permission cards, not placards, and immediately began to clamour that Winnipeggers couldn't get bread and milk without the strikers' permission.[82] Again, it was the truth, but a truth that one could shape. Demand the necessities of life – everyone must sympathize. After those necessities are met, demand that they be delivered in the freest possible way. The mass of Winnipeggers might not care *how* bread was delivered; but Ed Parnell – owner of Winnipeg's largest bakery (employing 120 men)[83] and member of the Citizens' Committee of 1000 executive – did care. How to convince Winnipeggers that the new bread delivery system was an assault on their liberties?

The beginnings of a discourse of rights and liberties appeared in the *Winnipeg Citizen* as political melodrama: 'This is not a Strike at all ... it is Revolution. It is a serious attempt to overturn British institutions in this Western country and to supplant them with the Russian Bolshevik system of Soviet rule.'[84] It hadn't been the *Citizen* but union members who first cozied up to this melodrama, either in vaunting or in real hope, and they soon found their own words hurled back at them. Earlier that March, the radical Calgary Conference, taking the first steps towards the creation of the OBU, had declared itself in 'full accord' with the Russian Bolshevik and German Spartacist revolutions, and had declared 'full acceptance of the principle of "Proletariat Dictatorship."'[85] At about the same time that Lenin was forming the Communist International in

Moscow to encourage proletarian revolution all over the world,[86] Resolution no. 1 at the Calgary Conference had called for 'the abolition of the present system of production for profit.'[87]

Although 'there was much calculated deceit' in the Citizens' cry of Revolution,[88] the conduct of federal postal employees and provincial telephone workers gave the Citizens reason to fear that the Winnipeg General Strike was 'THE general strike which was plotted out last March at Calgary' by OBU enthusiasts.[89] The *Winnipeg Citizen* was feeling its way towards a narrative in which the Calgary Conference would loom large: 'It was at this meeting that Lenine [*sic*], Trotsky and the German Spartacans [*sic*] were acclaimed as the idols and heroes of the Red movement.'[90] By the spring of 1919, North American newspapers and mass-market publications had already been carrying detailed and negative assessments of the new regime in Russia. Under the heading 'How "Proletarian Dictatorship" Works Out in Russia,' the *Citizen* quoted at length from a *Chicago Tribune* report that described the people of 'Bolshevik Russia' as 'wallowing in despair, disillusion and terror.'[91] The *Canadian Magazine* in February had described Bolshevik rule as a system that 'menaces the welfare of every man who, by individual initiative and ability, has created his own business or established his little shop.'[92] Through the Red Army, Lenin and Trotsky ran 'a clumsy autocracy ... more immediately cruel, more openly unscrupulous, than any that the Ministers of the old regime could have conceived or exercised.' The new Russian state was highly illiberal: the press was 'completely gagged,' individual liberty of action was 'a matter of purchase or evasion,' and corruption was endemic. 'Justice [is] ... a legend, ... human life ... valueless as the rouble in an epidemic of murder and massacre – these are the cold facts of the Bolshevik rule.'[93] And what was the prelude to the Bolshevik seizure of power? A general strike.

At one level, the Strike was fought over wages and other sticking points between employers and employees. At another level, given the Calgary Conference's Resolution #1 against production for profit, the Citizens correctly intuited the battle as one between capital's freedom and the OBU's wish to abolish capitalism. The Winnipeg General Strike would determine how large a union could be, and whether general strikes would now become a regular weapon in the arms race between labour and capital. The Citizens, therefore, called on Winnipeggers to meet the threat with courage and honour, and, though it wasn't said directly, with force if necessary.

The Citizens' most effective hymn was thus the very one that the more intemperate union officials had been singing at the Walker Theatre and in Calgary. By May, Strike leaders in Winnipeg had curbed their intem-

Victoria Park overflows with striking workers. (N2745, Foote
Collection 1679, Archives of Manitoba)

perance and avoided talk of revolution, but the Citizens were quick to
jump on any slips. The *Winnipeg Citizen* reported that on Friday at a
mass gathering in Victoria Park (which once lay between the present
Manitoba Museum and the Red River), *Western Labor News* editor Ivens
had proclaimed 'that Winnipeg was controlled by a Soviet.'[94] One could
also buy Lenin's 'Lessons of the Russian Revolution' there.[95] Even *The
Israelite Press*, sympathetic to labour, belatedly noted that Strike leaders
had altered their discourse depending upon the audience: 'When they
spoke with the bosses, "collective bargaining" was advanced as the
dominant issue, however, [*sic*] these very same leaders spoke differently
at meetings and at parks. Here their talk was revolutionary, instilling the
workers with the highest expectations, ready for big happenings.'[96]

By interpreting Strike leaders' slips, the *Citizen* also strove to *create*
the news of revolutionary intention before reporting it. This wasn't just
a matter of propaganda, as the Calgary Conference Resolution #1 indicates, though propaganda was by no means excluded. It was an attempt
to find a language and a story that would resonate with people either

uninvolved in the Strike or striking reluctantly. During a food committee meeting at which Mayor Gray several times trumpeted that he would ensure that constituted authority would be maintained, Labour councillor John Queen, his craw full, exclaimed, 'Shut up ... I've heard all I want to about constituted authority.'[97] When Rev. Charles Gordon got around to writing his autobiography, it was probably this incident he mythologized:

> The city authorities are powerless. The mayor asks for a conference. Sure! The Strike Committee file [sic] into the Council Chamber and sit with their hats on, smoking cigarettes. The Mayor rises to open the meeting.
>
> 'Shut up and sit down,' orders the chairman of the Strike Committee. 'Who told you to speak?'
>
> The mayor shuts up and sits down. He'd better and he knows it.[98]

In actuality, Gray hadn't been browbeaten by the Strike leaders. Rather he had a full and healthy regard for his own sufficiency during these events, and loved to proclaim to whoever would listen that it was mainly he who bore the responsibility for upholding the Constitution in the face of the strikers. 'If any radical element attempts to interfere with enforcement of law and order,' he boasted, 'we are prepared to smash it immediately.'[99] Although Queen's intemperate response probably had more to do with Gray's grandstanding than with anti-constitutionalism, any dismissal of 'constituted authority' put a sharp point on the Citizens' propaganda.

While the Citizens considered the strikers' incursions on traditional authority as a trademark of Bolshevik revolution, events on the streets bore no similarity to revolution. Travellers coming from Winnipeg reported a calm city. Even though Winnipeggers predicted lean times ahead, the streets thronged with people, and food could still be bought.[100] Toronto reporter W.H. Plewman arrived, expecting to see willing workers held off the job by union threats, and a populace driven into the arms of the Citizens by Bolshevik horrors. But, he said, 'The whole thing is a delusion and a figment of the imagination. There is no Soviet. There was little or no terrorism. The city thus far in the strike had been more orderly than for a similar period in years.'[101] Nevertheless, in their response to the permission signs and to the matter of 'soviets,' the Citizens edged towards a re-articulation of the ideals and beliefs that flowed from the heart of the British political and judicial systems. The Citizens' Committee was the tool of businessmen; it would exaggerate and be cynically deceptive about any number of issues; but if it was right that the Strike threatened the British Constitution, the Citizens could hope for the approval of many Winnipeggers. As we will see, even later, when the Citizens privately acted upon a much more instrumental view of the state, they continued to profess, in their interventions into the public sphere, an allegiance to the higher reasons of British freedom.

If the Citizens' first blast of the trumpet against the Strike lacked nuance, their self-presentation would demand a more careful set of calculations. First of all, the Citizens didn't want to be viewed as strike-breakers but as good Samaritans. While fallacious appeals *ad misericordiam* – to pity – might lack the power to convince, they did constitute an effective way in which the Citizens could deflect attention from their own economic interest. They made much of the telephone operators' work stoppage, accusing the strikers of placing their demands on the backs of sick people and women in childbirth, who, without phone service, would no longer get prompt medical aid. A 'Soviet' was infringing on basic British freedoms and waging war on babies: 'If the city turned on water in a sick person's house in the scarlet fever area, if your starving baby got milk it was "By Authority of the Strike Committee." Here was the equivalent of Soviet government as they have got it in Russia. Here was the beginning of the revolutionary organization of society – the foundation of the intended revolutionary structure.'[102] Yet water had never been turned off, and, by the grace of the food committee (on which strikers and Citizens cooperated) bread and milk delivery had been restored early on.[103] The *Winnipeg Citizen* wouldn't abandon melodrama, making no mention that simple negotiation had brought back services, that the resumption had involved neither the romance of swordplay nor any sort of physical labour by the Citizen-knights.

Yet, from the very beginning, the Citizens tied themselves to 'right.' On the day before the Strike began, Rev. John MacLean had been forced to stop asking the big firms for money to support the Gimli Fresh Air Camp, because Winnipeg businessmen were hunkering down for war.[104] Indebtedness to the charity of Winnipeg's businessmen made it unlikely that the church would criticize the Citizens; MacLean certainly didn't. A subtle gesture slipped the city's churches into anti-Strike ranks. In the absence of the major newspapers, the pulpit suddenly became a useful way of communicating with a large number of Winnipeggers. Mayor Gray asked that his address to the city be read from the city's pulpits. In the address, he warned that if the food supply weren't maintained or if property were threatened, he would spring into action. As for 'Permitted by Authority of the Strike Committee,' sprouting around the city wherever food was being sold, Gray implicitly took aim at alternative author-

ity and invoked God's order as his foundation: 'Support the constituted
authorities with your trust, your confidence, and if necessary your all,
and pray that the Great Master may direct them in honour and wisdom.'
'The future destiny of not only Winnipeg but the whole of Canada,' he
said, depended upon 'the wisdom of our citizens and government in this
crisis.'[105]

Although the Citizens wouldn't tie themselves to Gray – he was more
open to negotiation than they and had refused to join their organization[106] – they piggybacked on his address, so to speak, making their first
major statement on the Lord's Day too, with the first edition of the *Winnipeg Citizen*, dated Monday, apparently distributed to church-goers
already on Sunday.[107] Among the paper's declared objects was 'the
maintenance of law and order'[108] and support for constituted authority,
an approach that would play well in front of church-going readers. The
editors also knew that God, a British patriot, had looked with favour
upon every son sacrificed during the Great War. The *Citizen* noted that
Western Labor News editor William Ivens had been a pacifist during the
Great War, and was an 'ex-preacher.'[109] The first statement was true, the
second deceptive. Ivens, despite being ordained as a Methodist minister,
had left the Methodist pulpit to serve in the Labour Church, as strikers,
too, grasped that the pulpit was an obvious way to communicate with
Winnipeggers. But with Ivens becoming a sort of Protestant anti-Pope,
the Methodist church began disciplinary proceedings to decide whether
his actions constituted insubordination. No decision had been made yet.
If it wasn't the soberest logic to chastise Strike leaders for both pacifism
and revolution, the common thread was clear: anyone was a danger who
undermined the present social order and beliefs. Look, the Citizens'
rhetorical gestures implied, we fear God, and we know that our best
defence against the Strike will come from God-fearing people. At the
same time, the Citizens were careful not to plead virtue or to call upon
God too directly, since strikers might discover that some crucial members of the Citizens – its leading figure, A.J. Andrews, for one – weren't
models of church attendance and moral spotlessness. Enough that the
city should catch a glimpse of the mystical roots of the state, of the
divine order behind Winnipeg's human social order. The Citizens' discourse could therefore seem to come not only from the grassroots 'citizens' below, but also from on high, from 'the fount of all authority.'

In order to pry loose the 'misled' strikers from their pacifist revolutionary leaders, the Citizens outlined a number of right-thinking personality 'types' that they hoped strikers would recognize in themselves,
types rooted in a nineteenth-century idiom of honour: the honourable
employee who thinks the Strike 'childish,' but joins his fellows because

as a federation member it would look 'rotten' for him to abstain; the man who has been coerced into a union because his workplace is a closed shop; the striker, found particularly among female telegraph operators, who has been roused by the ideal of self-sacrifice for a greater cause. Instead of providing reasons for its stance, the *Citizen* provided images, potential faces of the self. Honour *now* consisted of turning against the Strike, and the strikers were honourable people. But the *Citizen* couldn't forbear scolding them, just a bit, for their earlier hasty actions.[110]

The effort to capture the high moral ground and pre-empt the strikers' identities with identities provided by the Citizens emphasizes how the Strike polarized the city's classes. In his account of Vancouver prior to the Great War, Robert McDonald uses a three-class model to describe the social order. He called 'upper class' those 'who owned the means of production (such as land and capital),' top managers, some professionals, and those 'whose interests, aspirations, and skills ... led them to identify with the owners and serve as their agents.' Below this leading stratum sat a middle class, composed of 'small businessmen, lower-level managers, and professionals not closely tied to the upper class.' Also identified with the middle class were 'real estate agents, contractors, commercial travellers, shopkeepers, school teachers, and clergymen.' At the bottom of the social pyramid stood the working class, 'people who worked for wages, whether white-collar office employees and store clerks or blue-collar machinists and street labourers.' Within each stratum an internal hierarchy of status existed, rooted in such markers as skill, job authority, education, disposable income, ethnicity, and religion.[111] Understandably, past approaches to class in the Winnipeg General Strike have tended to use a two-class model, since the Strike polarized people into yeas and nays. But a two-class model fails to capture the complexity of the city's middle class.[112] McDonald's tripartite structure is a better model for Winnipeg too, though even a tripartite structure has descriptive limits when, for example, one tries to assess the class status of municipal workers and policemen, or of working-class leaders whose British ethnicity, wages, and job authority gave them higher status than many middle-class people.

Winnipeg and its class structure were products of the expansion of industrial capital and commercial agriculture into the Canadian West, particularly in the wake of the CPR's construction. As rail lines advanced across the plains, the city emerged as the metropolis for an expanding agricultural hinterland that extended to the Pacific coast, at least until the opening of the Panama Canal in August 1914. The city's most dramatic period of expansion between 1901 and 1914 was a product of the West's increasing settlement and bullish wheat markets. In 1901 there were 42,000 Winnipeggers; in 1919, 200,000. Hopes were high. Who could doubt that the West would soon have a population of 100 million; that it would be the breadbasket of the world; that it would become the centre of gravity for all of Canada? If Canada must soon lead the Empire, and if the West must soon lead Canada, then the West must in short order lead the world. Imperialism, prairie greatness: it was difficult to say where the one left off and the other began.[113] The business and social elite consisted mostly of Eastern Canadian migrants – among them A.J. Andrews and Isaac Pitblado. It was a relatively homogeneous group that in the 1880s had created the 'new Manitoba,' modelled, no surprise, on Anglo-Protestant Ontario.[114] Through a mixture of initiative, ruthlessness, and philanthropy, combined with the prestige and authority derived from their positions in the world of production, members of the elite governed the city's affairs in the pre-war years. Many of them felt a special kinship with 'the man who rose from nothing.'[115] During the General Strike, the upper classes liked to assure strikers that a little spell of hard labour would catapult any worker to the top, that it was only *time* which differentiated between classes in the West – 'We do not believe in the class idea, but that one man is as good as another. **The Canadian laborer does not hate millionaires. He may be a millionaire himself some day … The Man Promoted is the Coming Business Man**' (bold in original).[116] Thomas Deacon, one of the wealthy ironmasters whose intransigence led to the Strike, claimed that he didn't know of a single employer who hadn't started out as a workman or a farmer's son. So forget all this Bolshevik nonsense, and pick up your tools. Of course, Deacon – from his ostentatious Fort Rouge home, which still stands, built of brick and limestone, with eight pillars and a balcony wrapped from the side of the house around to the front – also said that 'manufacturers are not wealthy.'[117] Yet the 'self-made man' mythology wasn't completely inaccurate. In the fluid class boundaries of the Canadian West, class wasn't a destiny tattooed onto a person at birth, but a thing that could be moulded depending upon one's initiative. One cannot speak of an upper class that defined itself across generations or held an ideology distinct from that of the middle class. Indeed, when the men on the Committee of 1000 spoke of themselves as 'representative citizens,'[118] they really believed that they were. Bourgeois mythology, and sometimes experience, had it that the Citizens were only in the vanguard of a large and daily-growing middle class. Paul Nanton, whose father Augustus employed a chauffeur, maids, and servants, professed that 'an 'upper class' was practically nonexistent in Winnipeg.'[119]

But the self-made man mythology was highly exaggerated, and the city was no egalitarian frontier. In practice, it was mostly the Ontario-born who held the needed capital and education to exploit Canada's new investment frontier. A recent assessment of the city's early elite has concluded that *it was* 'tied through familial and business relationships to central Canadian capital – in a very real sense, Winnipeg's elite simply represented an extension of the central Canadian elite.'[120] Eastern European immigrants, by contrast, struggled merely to learn the language. Winnipeg's social and cultural fault line ran along a visible scar – the CPR tracks – splitting the city into north and south. Far south of the tracks, the wealthy inhabited spacious Victorian and Edwardian mansions on the periphery of the city's core at Armstrong's Point (Westgate, Middlegate, and Eastgate) on the Assiniboine in the 1870s, then along Broadway, and later south of the Assiniboine River along Roslyn Road and the Crescent (now Wellington Crescent) in the upscale Crescentwood development. Zoning strictures – all houses directly on the Crescent must cost at least $6000; all houses in the area at least $3500 – kept out the commoners.[121] The city's core, which was least homogeneous in terms of class, was nevertheless 81 per cent British. Among the wealthy south of the Assiniboine, that number rose almost to 87 per cent.[122]

On the wrong side of the tracks stretched the 'North End,' which, as early as 1895, was described as a scene of 'mean and dirty clutter.'[123] Settled in among the grime of railway tracks and manufacturing plants were impoverished working-class immigrants – 50 per cent Slavs and Jews – transplanted from the small towns and steppes of eastern Europe, and shoe-horned into tiny homes, tenements, and boarding houses.[124]

North of the Assiniboine, but south of the tracks, lay residential districts occupied by the British middle and working classes. Their bungalows and two-storey homes radiated from the city centre to the east, south, and especially into the 'West End' and St James as Winnipeg grew.[125] According to the 1921 census, the labour force was divided into just over 6000 managers; 49,000 blue-collar workers; and 19,000 people in what was called 'Service,' a category including everything from char-workers and bicycle repairers to engineers, doctors, and lawyers such as Pitblado and Andrews.[126] The 1916 census indicates 60,600 residents in the North End, 67,000 in the Core, and 48,600 in the South End. Estimating one person in the labour force for every three Winnipeggers, we can see that a good number of 'Service' workers, even beyond Andrews and other professionals, must have been able to afford houses south of the Assiniboine if the South End in 1919 possessed a labour force of over 16,000. The impoverished North End held only about half (over 20,000) of Winnipeg's blue-collar workers. If 30,000 Winnipeggers (including most of the 20,000 north-enders and only few south-enders) joined the Strike, then it seems evident that in Winnipeg's class-mixed core, there was no unanimity: of the over 22,000 workers in the core, close to half joined the Strike. Quality of housing and census numbers indicate that the city's mostly Anglo core held a large and varied middle class, a class that wasn't impoverished and that could potentially be swayed for or against the Strike, given the right approach.

Middle-class values – respectability, morality, self-reliance – held sway in the city, and despite the closing of ranks on both sides, Winnipeg's skilled tradesmen had in many ways embraced those values and their moral grounding. A short novella, 'The Great Tribulation,' serialized in 1902 in the labour periodical *The Voice*, shows this. It places great emphasis on the respectability of Philip Murray, the fictional leader of a Winnipeg general strike that occurs far in the future – in 1960. He drinks tea, treats his mother well, behaves modestly towards women, and if he blames the church for the present state of society, his best friend David Paynter nevertheless happens to be a clergyman who asks him to 'distinguish closely between followers of Christ and followers of the church.' In most ways, the novella is highly conventional. 'All happiness,' the narrator insists, 'proceeds from Love,' making a woman more graceful and queenly, a man more dignified and noble. Although the narrator makes a case for socialism, at the same time he follows the capitalist line that 'self-interest is the mainspring life motive, without which it seems impossible to conceive that anything could live an instant. It gives a tremendous force of character to the individual.' For 'Libertas Brammel,' the anonymous writer (who, A. Ross McCormack suggests, must have been a skilled labourer, an autodidact, and an Anglican recently emigrated from Britain),[127] the problem isn't with the values that the upper class holds, but with the concentration of power in too few hands. Despite Brammel's radicalism, 'The Great Tribulation' has little time for the masses; it wastes little effort on the depiction of social struggle or even of the strike. Instead, the story's interest lies in how Philip rises from a 'small cottage on Arlington avenue' to marry the daughter of Carveth Anstruther, the leader of the employers' syndicate.

Brammel's intent is clearly to dignify socialism. But to do that, he relies on a kind of story beloved of the middle classes – what Michael McKeon calls the 'progressive' narrative. This narrative details how and why a moral hero moves up in station.[128] As a working-class writer, Brammel understandably relies on a popular form more ideologically attuned to the mythology of the rising classes – it must be our *own* work and morality that changed our status, a Lockean faith – than to the classes who worked just as hard without seeing a change in status.[129]

Understandably: who wouldn't want to move up, and who wouldn't want to receive dignity and value as a moral *individual*? Voices as widely divergent as Thomas Hobbes and Max Weber have articulated this human desire for personal value. Hobbes spoke elegantly of 'a vain conceipt of ones owne wisdome, which almost all men think they have in greater degree than the vulgar; that is, than all men but themselves, and a few others.'[130] Weber accepted the importance of class identities in modern societies, but stressed how much people longed for status and identity outside of the economic order. If individual merit, in the form of morality and hard work, allowed a person to rise in class, then deference to authority (in other words, to those who had 'risen') and acceptance of subordination made sense. With these fundamental assumptions of the middle class transplanted from Ontario, one can see why before 1919 the working class didn't seriously challenge the elite. It's tempting to dismiss Rev. Charles Gordon's ventriloquism, since his allegiances lay so clearly with capital, but, even after one accounts for patriotic exaggeration, the speech that in *To Him That Hath* Gordon places in the mouth of a socialist character seems a canny assessment of the Canadianized middle class: 'Gin we were in Rooshie, or in Germany whaur the people have lived in black slavery or even in the auld land whaur the fowk are haudden doon wi' generations o' class bondage, there might be a chance for a revolutionary ... Ye canna make Canadians revolutionaries. They are a' on the road to be maisters.'[131]

In comparison with the middle class, the working class was more divided along lines of ethnicity and skill. Skilled tradesmen of Anglo-Canadian and British lineage viewed themselves as of a higher social standing than unskilled workers, particularly than the non-British who, often unskilled and frequently unorganized, had been driven to Canada by inhospitable homelands and drawn by employment in transportation or construction.[132] Yet under the influence of wartime inflation, a radicalized labour unionism, and the powerful example of the Russian revolution, all earlier bets were off. While the Citizens would soon indiscriminately tar all Strike leaders with the all-purpose stigma of Bolshevism, there were indeed Bolsheviks, especially in the North End ethnic communities, where young socialists, inspired more by the Russian Revolution than by individualism, grew in power. Surprising alliances formed across ethnic boundaries, and young SPCers such as Russell and Johns advocated the One Big Union, while laying siege to labour's old guard. The *Western Labor News* insisted upon class as a primary interpreter of experience. Although it would be misleading to reduce Winnipeggers, even during the Strike, to ciphers in a Marxian class war, nevertheless class identities now took centre stage.[133]

Only one group insisted that class meant nothing: the Citizens' Committee of 1000. McDonald convincingly argues that 'class identities were most keenly felt at the summit of the social structure' than elsewhere.[134] The Citizens, who felt class keenly, deceptively argued that the Strike was the work of a few Machiavells and that the majority of Winnipeg's 'citizens' were a homogeneous family. Yet the Citizens did more than just argue: with the electric streetcars idle, the Citizens 'proved' that class meant nothing by lending out their private vehicles. If 'The Great Tribulation' reveals something about working-class values, it may explain why in 1919, a decade and a half after its publication, even when the high price of living had helped to radicalize the working class, many Winnipeggers were still predisposed to agree in principle with the individualist, 'progressive,' and anti-class arguments of the Citizens.[135] And to agree in practice, when, after several tiring days of tramping through a city bereft of streetcars,[136] they received Free Ride Cards from the Transportation Committee of the Citizens.[137]

2

Who? Who? Who-oo?

In the days before the Strike, as Winnipeg's leading businessmen cast about for an organizational name, they recognized that if they professed to be a grass-roots movement, representing *all* citizens, they must avoid the appearance of elitism. The name they hit upon – the Citizens' Committee of One Thousand – had little to do with the reality. Their later congratulatory telegram, punctuating the arrests of the Strike leaders, would contain thirty-four names; and the possibly apocryphal photograph fewer than fifty people: never near one thousand.[1] Casting back to 1918, the former 'Citizens' Committee of 100' members initially favoured the name 'Committee of 200'[2] for the 1919 committee, nodding to the old committee yet outscoring it, as if twice the number meant twice the legitimacy. In for a penny, in for a pound: why not 'Committee of 300,' *triple* the legitimacy? Bidding finally stopped at '1000,' a name selected on the political principle that the less inclusive the group, the more inclusive the name. At the same time, there were enough uninvolved but sympathetic middle-level managers and enough employees seconded by Winnipeg businesses to do Citizens' Committee drudge work[3] that 1000 names could be trotted out in a pinch. Another, more sinister, provenance for the number 1000 will appear in chapter 8, but the biggest coup of all, really, was for the Citizens to call themselves 'Citizens' and for the strikers to be called 'strikers.'

Committee members spoke of the Kiwanis and Rotary clubs as sister organizations,[4] and these organizations did provide volunteers to drive fire trucks and to deliver milk and food,[5] but it immediately became clear that the Citizens had a kind of cabinet, an executive that didn't require political input from lesser members. A man as significant as James Carruthers, manager of Crescent Creamery and member of the earlier 1918 Committee of 100, *felt* that he was part of the Citizens' Committee, but his language makes it clear that he had no formal role or standing, though he did have the ear of A.J. Andrews: 'I identified myself with the citizens [*sic*] committee ... I would say I was a member, yes.'[6] Drawn from the city's elite, it was the executive, not some representational group of 1000, which directed opposition to the Strike. Deeper into the Strike, the Committee could accurately be called the Citizens' Committee of 10,000 as the Citizens liked to claim.[7] But only thirty-four people had a voice,[8] and an even smaller number were positioned well enough to have any real say.

From among the shadowy Citizens, four faces would emerge early on: an investment manager and three lawyers – respectively A.L. Crossin, Isaac Pitblado, Travers Sweatman, and A.J. Andrews. The Citizens operated out of the Board of Trade Building, and Crossin, who managed investments for Oldfield, Kirby and Gardner,[9] was a former president of the Board of Trade, so his new role was no great stretch. Not that the public knew the exact position of Crossin among the Citizens – people merely knew that he represented their views. Later in life, he would be one of the few to publicize his role in the Committee. In fact, he was an excellent choice for the Committee's public face, since he still carried the aura of wartime patriotism, having been vice chairman of the Victory Loan Campaign.[10]

The three lawyers weren't precisely *captains* of industry. Pitblado would soon protest strongly, 'I never was a capitalist, nor the son of a capitalist.'[11] Despite this, or perhaps *because* of this, the lawyers on the Citizens' Committee would become its fulcrum. They had worked their way up – some, such as Ed Anderson, from poor circumstances[12] – so it was easy for them to believe that effort was always rewarded. Containers of discontent and maintainers of order, Wesley Pue calls lawyers; in Western Canada, most of them were allied with capital, and stood as the most vigilant guardians of bourgeois order.[13] They weren't simply spokespersons for the employers; due to their expertise they held much power themselves. They provided the Citizens with an articulate, measured, and yet uncompromising public voice.

The lawyers had been born and received their degrees variously in Manitoba, Ontario, and the Maritimes. Pitblado and Andrews, in their fifties, were principals of their firms. The Scottish Pitblado had come west at age fifteen in 1882 when St Andrew's Presbyterian Church called his father to the pulpit. Almost forty years later, at the time of the Strike, Pitblado was the head of a large legal firm, chairman of the board of governors at the University of Manitoba, and president of the Manitoba Law Society. 'Mr Freight Rate' he would be called because of his expert-

Isaac Pitblado, ca 1913. (Western Canada Pictorial Index,
Miscellaneous Collection, image 10145)

Travers Sweatman, ca 1925. (Authors' Collection)

ise in that area. Sweatman, ten years younger, with an honours degree in Classics and a Master of Arts, was an up-and-comer, already a substantial member of the elite. He had come from Pembroke, Ontario, in 1879, when his father took a position with Massey-Harris.[14] Like his father, Sweatman served as a lay officer in the Anglican Church.

Some of the lawyers had attended school together and some had worked for each other: Sweatman for Pitblado, and Pitblado for Andrews, Pitblado calling his apprenticeship an eight-year postgraduate course in law.[15] It wouldn't matter crucially during the Strike that Pitblado was a Liberal, or that Sweatman and Andrews were Conservatives. In Andrews's view, they weren't so far apart: he had once offered a $100 reward for anyone who could convincingly explain the difference between a Liberal and a Conservative.[16] Faced with the common enemy, smaller differences among the lawyers melted, just as in Robert Borden's Unionist cabinet of the First World War. In fact, Minister of the Interior Arthur Meighen, who was friendly with Pitblado and Andrews, tried to get them appointed to the Union cabinet (as a way of keeping his own influence ascendant).[17] Meighen tempted Pitblado with the possibility of rendering to Canada a service 'of great and enduring character.'[18] However, when Pitblado saw that other prominent western Liberals were prepared to join the cabinet, he felt able to bow out.[19] Near the end of his life, in his nineties, an alert Pitblado still headed his firm. Although nearly half a century had elapsed in the 1960s and he kept a scrapbook on the 1919 strike, he refused to speak about his role in the Strike or the trials that followed. 'Nothing could be gained,' he said, 'except to stir up old animosities.' He'd much rather talk about stamp collecting.[20]

Like Pitblado, A.J. Andrews was a minister's son; additionally, a veteran of the Northwest Rebellion; additionally, a former mayor – a man to be reckoned with. If there was one person who held the web of Citizens together, it was Andrews. He had already been planning, with Crescent Creamery manager James Carruthers, what to do about the milk situation.[21] Before the dust had settled on the Strike, the *Toronto Daily Star* accurately summed up Andrews's central role, saying that he 'had been here there and everywhere directing the operations of the Citizens' Committee of 1000, finding and assembling evidence against the strike leaders ... drawing up charges, directing raids, supervising arrests and holding innumerable conferences with the authorities, business and labour leaders.'[22]

He was a small man, and, like some small men, compensated for his lack of size with a forceful personality. Although he was clean-shaven, he wasn't finicky about his clothes or general appearance, and his hair, iron-grey and thinning, was long in front and often tousled.[23] He could

A.J. Andrews, ca 1920. (Authors' Collection)

often be seen with a pipe in the mouth. Born in 1865 into a Methodist minister's household at Franklin, Quebec, he had grown up in 'in a bookish atmosphere made austere' by his father's salary of $700 a year – half in cash and half in donations – for a family of six.[24] His father believed 'good conversation to be as important as food on his table,'[25] and 'offered his children a cent from his meager store for every time they caught him in a mispronunciation.'[26] A.J. left the manse at sixteen, heading west to join his older brother in Manitoba. Unlike Eastern European immigrants who came to a foreign land, Andrews came to a brother who practised law in partnership with D.M. Walker, Manitoba's attorney general. A.J. was admitted as a law student to Walker's firm, but interrupted his studies to help defeat Louis Riel during the Northwest Rebellion, though he never came under fire. Military service (and athletic prowess) nevertheless placed him inside a circle of masculine camaraderie, silenced all questions about his patriotism, and made for easy debating points whenever he needed to rebuke those Strike leaders who were pacifists (Ivens and Woodsworth most notably) or who hadn't served in the Great War. Another benefit: service took a year off his articling time. He thus qualified for the Manitoba bar at age twenty, though he had to wait another year for his majority in order to be called to the bar. In 1889 he married Maud Galbraith Watson, the daughter of an implement manufacturer.[27] Andrews became a land speculator and a high flyer, managing to get $25,000 up into the black before falling into the red for $50,000 a year later, and finally back to zero after five more years of sweating blood.[28] As did many of Winnipeg's elite,[29] he found time to race horses. He was never 'overly virtuous' in his behaviour, as one observer delicately put it, and had a reputation as a *bon vivant*. Still, by 1893, he was elected alderman in Winnipeg, and by 1898 was mayor of the city. The 'boy-mayor' they called him, for he was only thirty-two at the time and looked even younger.[30]

He wanted more. Three times – in 1899, 1910, and 1914 – he ran as a Conservative for the Manitoba legislature; three times he was defeated, once by only forty votes.[31] After his first defeat, a reporter asked how he was feeling. 'Brawley, mon,' he replied with affected gaiety, 'I never felt better in my life.'[32] Defeats notwithstanding, Andrews kept his reputation as an astute Conservative strategist. When in 1915 Conservative premier Rodmond Roblin and three of his ministers were accused of receiving bribes in the construction of the new Legislative Buildings, Labour MLA Fred Dixon whaled at Roblin in the Legislature, and Roblin had to call on Andrews to keep him out of jail. Andrews fought the case to a hung jury, though he claimed that the stress turned his hair white.[33]

Andrews wasn't above defending socialists if hired to do so. When Sarah Jane Knight was accused of making seditious utterances, Andrews defended her in front of Justice Sir Hugh John Macdonald, a notoriously harsh judge and a fellow Conservative.[34] Knight's words might be permissible during peacetime, Macdonald said, but they 'could be construed as seditious,' and were therefore dangerous in wartime. Nevertheless, he acquitted her. Andrews was a tactically sharp trial lawyer, respected and feared, not so much because of his legal knowledge – which, as we will see, was sometimes faulty – but because he understood people. Winnipeg's leading businessmen would buttonhole him, looking for advice.[35] When the General Strike dropped on Winnipeg, it wasn't surprising that the acting minister of justice, Arthur Meighen – a lawyer, a Manitoba Conservative, and friendly with Andrews and Pitblado – would soon buy Andrews's analysis of what sort of hell had broken out. And if Andrews had failed to get elected to the provincial legislature, the Citizens' Committee of 1000 provided a cause through which he could exercise his considerable political and legal expertise, and even shape the nation's direction. It would become clear that he wasn't Meighen's lapdog. Very much an individualist, Andrews saw himself as the one who knew best, and while he clearly shared the goals of the Citizens, he was prepared to go against their advice if necessary. During the Strike, he was often seen 'hatless, with a wilted collar dashing about the city.'[36]

Tuesday, 20 May

Since the '1000' imaginary/real Citizens wanted to explain to Winnipeg City Council what exactly they stood for, they couldn't evade the spotlight entirely, and the executive designated Crossin, Pitblado, Sweatman, and Andrews to speak at a special council meeting on Tuesday evening, 20 May, at City Hall. It was Andrews who spoke first. On his death, benchers of the Law Society would say that Andrews 'fought his battles à l'outrance' – excessively – while always remaining 'a happy warrior.'[37] His opening gambit was to throw himself in front of the bullets aimed by the strikers at babies – 'I would go down on my knees to the Trades Council and make my obeisance before them, anything to secure milk for the babies.'[38] Yet he also brandished a more reasoned discourse of civil liberties: 'Under the British flag, all citizens [have] a right to carry on any lawful business,' he said. 'If we are going to exercise our liberties we must have constituted authority in charge of public utilities.'[39] In Andrews's idiom, individual liberties above all meant property rights, which, like other common-law liberties, had been affirmed by the victors of the Glorious Revolution of 1688, and were expressed in the Union Jack, the symbol that the Citizens would soon pin to their breasts.[40] It was no surprise that the Citizens put their trust in him. The freedom to gain a livelihood he characteristically interpreted, with good reason, as the freedom to carry on business. If this were a fundamental freedom, then by keeping the water at 30 pounds pressure the strikers were not harming innocent babies, but infringing on the right of Thomas Deacon of Manitoba Bridge and Ironworks (the metal industries required much water) to make a profit. After the event, the Citizens would worry that the water at 30 pounds pressure had 'threatened the public health with epidemic,'[41] but the best that Andrews could offer in the way of epidemics was dentist N.H. Garvin's testimony that the lack of water to sterilize instruments in his fifth-floor office *could have* resulted in deaths. Had Garvin heard of anyone in Winnipeg dying? He hadn't.[42]

Water was a touchy subject for Andrews because, as mayor, he had pioneered a new British-owned pumping system with a price tag of $1,000,000 so that Winnipeggers could get clean water from artesian wells rather than from the muddy Assiniboine.[43] Later, Thomas Deacon had been elected as mayor in 1913 on the platform of bringing in an even better supply of water from Shoal Lake.[44] That pipeline had finally been completed in the spring of 1919 ... just in time for the Strike.[45] But at Tuesday's City Council meeting, Andrews didn't declaim much about the right to carry on business. Too close a focus on precisely who would gain from the restoration of 'constituted authority' might sabotage the Citizens' cause, so Andrews kept his demand for liberty at a general level. Innocent bystanders, Andrews worried, couldn't get the necessities of life 'untrammeled by orders of any strike committee.' In other words, the bystanders *could* get the necessities of life, but by authority of the Strike Committee. The Trades and Labor Council, in his opinion, was trying to prove that it ruled Winnipeg, and Andrews wouldn't deny that it had so proved: 'He deplored the truth of the statements that policemen remained at their posts "by permission of the strike committee"; that water pressure was kept at 30 lbs pressure "by permission of the Strike Committee"; that public utilities were run in only such a manner as pleased the strike committee. The newspapers were stopped, he continued, and all the citizens could get was what the strike committee chose to give them.'[46] Andrews's style made a strong impression. When Rev. Charles Gordon recalled the Strike in later years, he exaggerated greatly (claiming that water had been cut off, for example), but what he remembered correctly was Andrews's periodic style, piling clause upon clause: 'Not a streetcar moves, not a telephone rings, not a telegram is sent, except by order of the Strike Committee. Not a light bulb shines. No bread, no milk, no water, for 260,000 Winnipeg citizens, except by order of the committee. The picture houses, the dance halls, are run by order of committee.'[47]

Crossin, chair of the Citizens' general committee, naturally spoke at the City Council meeting too. He spoke in a language of authority, and yet, at the same time, of individual rights and resistance to tyranny. Authority: the Citizens, he said, had been created to 'assist in keeping law and order.' Rights: the Committee would 'take what steps were necessary for the securing of the necessities of life,' and 'would not be placed in intolerable subjection by the withdrawal of firemen and the fear of the withdrawal of police protection.'[48] By such statements he attempted to undermine labour's democratic assurances. Labour officials had promised not to take the police off the streets; indeed, they had no desire to do so, since that would invite martial law. Much better to keep order with police officers sympathetic to the Strike. Yet the *Western Labor News* had made it clear that bread and water now available was being supplied by sufferance of the Strike Committee, and could be withdrawn at any time.[49]

For the Citizens, the larger issues of 'freedom' trumped even a possible resolution of the Strike. Initially eager to appear conciliatory, the Cit-

izens had gestured towards negotiation, speaking in their original advertisement of 'the probable justness of some of the [strikers'] demands'
and merely asking, in Monday's paper (reflecting *Saturday*'s consensus)
for a 'just and reasonable settlement.'[50] That offer was quickly withdrawn. Crossin told City Council that, yes, the Citizens would dearly
love to help settle the Strike, but matters of freedom and security must
be settled first. Where Crossin was measured, Andrews was apocalyptic:
'For all time the question must be settled whether the whole city [can]
be thrown into suffering and danger by any one section of the community.'[51] It's not clear who among the Citizens came up with the policy of
non-negotiation. What is clear is that Andrews spoke early on for this
crucial shift in the Citizens' thinking, a shift that would have serious
ramifications. He spoke for hard-line elements among the Citizens just
at the moment that the hard line was becoming policy. The same day that
Andrews was speaking his uncompromising yet vague words before
City Council, the Citizens conveyed their no-negotiation policy privately and much more explicitly in a telegram to George Allan, MP for
Winnipeg South: 'Prevent any government interference with us in
enforcing through lawful means the rights of the Citizens. Do not under
any circumstances allow pressure from well meaning but inadequately
formed persons persuade [*sic*] the government to make any offers of
intervention with a view to settlement. This would be fatal.'[52] A copy of
this demand was forwarded to Gideon Robertson, minister of labour.[53]

If the Strike really was a battle between two opposed systems of
order, and one could pre-empt the future to, in Andrews's telling phrase,
'settle the question for all time,' then it was easy to envision a battle to
the death. The Citizens were already raising the stakes. At the city water-
works, employees had agreed to stay on as long as the pressure remained
at 30 pounds. But the same evening that Andrews spoke at City Council,
A.E. Findlay had been ordered to increase the water pressure. When
employees discovered the change the next morning, they walked off the
job. The Citizens, however, already had a committee assigned to the
waterworks, and citizen volunteers immediately arrived from Vulcan
Iron Works and from Bullman Brothers, companies which, by the
strangest coincidence, needed water the most. Yet Findlay wouldn't
admit that the 'volunteers' had been supplied by the Citizens.[54]

In a battle to the death, any concessions would, Andrews correctly surmised, award a semblance of victory to the strikers. The story of a revolutionary assault on constituted authority held a powerful charge, even
as the Citizens demanded that constituted authority remain passive. A
public that didn't begrudge the workers a few more dollars and better

working conditions might be less friendly if the entire culture were in peril. The Citizens had already intimated that even if the Strike were settled, the unions wouldn't immediately settle down to work. The unions had more up their sleeves, namely a six-hour workday. In 1919, this seemed like a ludicrous proposition to many non-labour people, but the OBU had indeed asked its potential member unions whether they'd support a 1 July nation-wide strike on this issue.[55]

Compared to the British, Canadian workers stood in a profoundly disadvantaged state, and it's no wonder that the OBU had a receptive audience coast to coast. The descent began when the 1892 Criminal Code dealt workers a losing hand for future labour struggles. Previous legal protection of picketing had disappeared from the new code. In 1876, Canada had criminalized intimidation and 'watching and besetting' (the harassment of non-strikers or replacement workers), but stipulated that strikers could nevertheless remain near residences or businesses in order to get or to give information.[56] The result: before the 1892 code, Canadian workers could picket peacefully, but afterwards no such right existed, and employers threw injunctions at strikers gathering outside plant gates. The clampdown tightened in 1901, after the famous Taff Vale Railway case. A British Law Lords court ruled that firms losing money in a strike could sue unions for damages arising out of breach of contract.[57] The British Trades Disputes Act of 1906 soon rescued British unions from this court decision,[58] but the legislation didn't extend to Canada. When strikes broke out, therefore, Canadian employers were free to sue unions, and the frequency of such suits earned Winnipeg the title 'Injunction City.'[59]

In 'Injunction City,' workers faced a business community that through the Board of Trade and the Canadian Manufacturers' Association saw labour as a commodity to be bought at the lowest possible price.[60] Capital defended its interests vigorously. In 1906, when strikers intimidated replacement workers hired by the Winnipeg Electric Railway Company, troops armed with machine guns very quickly appeared. After a strike broke out among machinists, boiler-makers, and blacksmiths at the Vulcan Iron Works that same year, the company's lawyers asked for $25,000 as damages – thanks to Taff Vale – and for a perpetual injunction to keep the unions from interfering with employees – thanks to the 1892 Criminal Code. Justice Mathers concluded that Parliament intentionally omitted the peaceful picketing clause from the code; that the unions' picketing amounted to a common-law nuisance; and that the ninety-two defendants were liable for damages.[61] The injunction was made perpetual and a judgment was entered for $500 against three of the unions involved. An appeal sustained the judgment.[62]

During a meat cutters' strike in January 1917 over the right to collective bargaining, three Winnipeg firms entered damage suits for $25,000 each and applied for perpetual injunctions against picketing.[63] With the $25,000 suits hanging over their heads, the meat cutters retreated, agreeing not to picket if the employers dropped the suits. Replacement workers took over, and, months later, the strike collapsed.[64] In May 1917, machinists at Vulcan Iron Works, Manitoba Bridge and Iron Works, and two other companies struck for higher wages. Vulcan and Manitoba Bridge went to the courts, claiming damages and securing an injunction against picketing. Even the powerful machinist unions surrendered to avoid suits for damages.[65] When young female clerks at Woolworth's struck to increase their pay of $6 a week (at a time when room and board alone cost that), Woolworth's slapped a $25,000 suit against them. Although the judge sympathized with the women and criticized the company, he upheld the injunction against picketing. The company replaced the clerks, refused to recognize the union, and the strike failed.[66] A few months later, Woolworth's proclaimed its generosity towards employees by advertising a 'Clerks' Profit Sharing Sale.'[67]

As long as power could legally be applied in this direct manner, Citizens' committees were unnecessary. However, as the war progressed and labour recognized that only large unions such as the OBU could compete against a stacked law, Winnipeg employers began to view even these powerful anti-labour tools as inadequate.[68] In July 1917, employers moved to a new level of preparedness. The Winnipeg Builders' Exchange hosted a dinner, inviting the Minneapolis Citizens' Alliance and Winnipeg's businessmen to the Hotel Alexander in order to consider the formation of a Winnipeg Citizens' Alliance.[69] Along with its organ, the *Citizens' Alliance Bulletin*, the Minneapolis Citizens' Alliance upheld the 'principle of the Open Shop,' and professed to counter 'the spirit of lawlessness and intimidation which universally governs the efforts of the unions.' The Alliance attacked unions in many dubious ways. Attempts by the International Machinists Association to organize at Minneapolis Steel and Machinery were defeated by means of private detectives, firings, and a city-wide blacklist of union men. When a drive by the National Brotherhood of Teamsters to organize transportation workers culminated in a call for a general strike, the Alliance called together two hundred Minneapolis businessmen. Told that the strike was 'the opening wedge to tie up the city and force in union rule,' the businessmen coughed up $20,000 for lawyers and for special police to guard replacement workers. Mass arrests of picketers broke the strike.[70] Otis

P. Briggs, a metal shops proprietor and the Citizens' Alliance leader in 1919, had only a simple formula to fight labour – 'cut off all negotiations and accept nothing but unconditional surrender'[71] – but a wide variety of methods. As an organizer of the National Founders' Association, Briggs had campaigned to 'have picketing outlawed, to halt anti-injunction bills, workers' compensation and minimum wage legislation and to establish state constabularies.' The Alliance supported its 'Citizens' with strike-breakers, guards, labour spies, blacklists, money, and lawyers to fight strikers. From 1903 to 1917, every Minneapolis Citizens' Alliance president was a member of the exclusive Minneapolis Club.[72]

The Winnipeg chapter of the Canadian Manufacturers' Association endorsed the Minneapolis Citizens' method of correcting 'abuses brought about by organized labour,' and within a week of the Hotel Alexander meeting, three hundred businessmen had signed applications to join the Winnipeg Citizens' Alliance.[73] Here again, we have elements of the fourth story of the Citizens' historical filiation noted in chapter 1, elements more important than the publicized connections to the 1918 Citizens' Committee of 100. On 15 September 1917, twenty members of the Winnipeg Citizens' Alliance met for dinner at the Hotel Fort Garry. Ed Parnell, soon to become a prominent member of the Citizens' Committee of 1000, played host. The Citizens' Alliance declared itself in favour of peace, love, and understanding; it intended to 'promote on a fair and equitable basis industrial peace and prosperity in the community … to discourage strikes, lockouts and all unfair demands by either employer or employees; and uphold the vital principle of the open shop in the city of Winnipeg.'[74] *The Voice*, which had reported regularly on the exploits of Citizens' Alliances in the United States, was blunter: 'With the courts sticking injunctions down our throats why not the able assistance of a citizens' alliance?'[75] In chapter 8 we will note the anti-labour activities of citizens' alliances across the United States, but for now, suffice it to say that when Winnipeg's business community entered the public sphere to fight labour it could not do so as the Winnipeg Citizens' Alliance – a target too well known in its American brand and too easy to hit.

Only a few months after the formation of the Winnipeg Citizens' Alliance in 1918, sympathy strikes broke out when City Council narrowly passed an amendment, proposed by Alderman Frank Fowler, denying civic workers the right to strike.[76] The city's commercial elite couldn't find anything to object to in such an amendment – cheers from the Rotary Club, cheers from the Board of Trade, cheers from the Winnipeg Real Estate Board. But the amendment outraged firefighters, and they walked off the job on 14 May. They were in negotiations that might have proved successful, but the Fowler Amendment rubbed them the wrong way. Ten other unions, including railway workers and city telephone operators, walked out in sympathy. How to meet the threat to municipal services? The City supported the idea of a 'Public Service League.' On the first day of the firefighters' strike, the Citizens' Alliance met to discuss how to respond to the crisis,[77] and Board of Trade members passed a series of resolutions, placing their hands over their hearts and calling for a moratorium on all strikes until the war was over. A day and a half later, 17 May 1918, at the Royal Alexandra Hotel, a Citizens' Committee of 100 was formed, and it quickly endorsed these resolutions. At the time, the Committee was called 'the greatest assembly of those prominent in business and industrial life in the history of Winnipeg.'[78] Yet it was more eclectic than such praise implied. Jack Bumsted points out that only a few Committee members lived on the Crescent and Armstrong's Point.[79] The membership list was public, with the names of those assigned to water, light and power, telephones, police, fire department, cartage, legislation, and transportation subcommittees appearing in the newspapers.[80] Winnipeggers could see that the Committee was indeed community-based, since it included not only male businessmen and the professional elite, but also several clergymen, at least eight women, social service administrators, and, for good measure, even a representative from the Boy Scouts. If one were inclined to count names, they'd add up to exactly 100.[81] A year later, the Citizens' Committee of 1000 would take a less literal, more imaginative line on numbers and inclusiveness.

As might be expected, however, the eclectic 1918 committee wasn't the only means whereby the city's elite tried to solve the sympathy strike. Behind the scenes between 15 and 17 May, a number of wealthy Winnipeggers lobbied George Allan (MP for Winnipeg South), Thomas Crerar (minister of agriculture), and Prime Minister Borden, asking them to employ the War Measures Act to make the strike a criminal offence. Those who wrote included A.E. Boyle (Secretary, Winnipeg Board of Trade), financier Augustus Nanton, and several future members of the 1919 Citizens' Committee of 1000 such as W.H. McWilliams, A.K. Godfrey, Ed Anderson, and Ed Parnell.[82] According to Boyle, all the problems had been caused by the 'unpatriotic action of professional troublemakers,' and Nanton recommended that any striker 'no matter what class he is in' should be immediately conscripted and packed off to war, while anyone advocating a strike should be sent to jail.[83] Since the wealthy weren't in the habit of striking, Nanton's 'no matter what class he's in' rang rather hollow, but the approach of Godfrey and Parnell was more interesting: with the right hand they negotiated at the table as members of the Citizens' Committee of 100, while with the left hand they privately urged the federal government to smash their opponents. Parnell, the bakery owner, wrote not as a private citizen to Prime Minister Borden, but as the president of the Citizens' Alliance, asking for a legislated end to the strike.[84] He sent the identical letter to Crerar. A handwritten response, almost certainly by Crerar, appeared on the reverse of the letter: 'Sorry to hear of your trouble. Why not try paying the people decent wages?'[85]

Borden fobbed Parnell off by saying that municipal employees were ultimately the province's and Premier Norris's problem.[86] Nevertheless, as the federal cabinet would again do in 1919, Borden dispatched Sen. Gideon Robertson (at that time minister without portfolio) to Winnipeg to deal with the crisis. The Citizens' Committee of 100 set about manning civic facilities (such as fire halls) abandoned by strikers, and established a subcommittee to negotiate a settlement. Although Premier Norris headed to Ottawa to urge drastic legislative action, Robertson counselled patience to Borden.[87] By Friday, 24 May 1918, 'more than 6,800 [strikers] from thirteen trades, including such crucial municipal services as fire, water, light and power, and public transportation' were on the street,[88] and things began to look more and more like a general strike. But that same day, Robertson was able to report to Borden, 'Labor troubles satisfactorily adjusted here tonight.'[89] Even before Robertson arrived, the strikers and the Committee had been on the road to an agreement on 'all points except the right of fire department *officers* to belong to a union' [emphasis added].[90] City Council agreed to kill the Fowler Amendment, and civic employees pledged to give the City sixty days' notice prior to any work stoppage. Robertson's task was therefore elementary: get the firefighters to agree that they could unionize but that their officers should be excluded. He succeeded. With celebrations all round, it was reported that (famous last words) 'a recurrence of the trouble will not likely take place again in Winnipeg for many years.'[91]

Within a year, that optimism looked punishingly naive. A negotiated settlement had allowed both sides to retire from battle gracefully, but it was perceived that labour had won the 1918 confrontation. Parnell, for one, disparaged the settlement terms, though he didn't reveal the specific nature of his criticism.[92] Workers believed, correctly, that only working-class solidarity and the threat of a general strike had tilted the field in their favour to nix the Fowler Amendment. R.J. Johns termed this attitude a new 'proletarian morality,' a key to the creation of a just industrial citizenship in post-war Canada.[93] Some members of the Citizens' Committee of 100, on the contrary, felt that they hadn't surrendered to the threat of a general strike, but that many hours of negotiation had saved the day, producing agreement on contracts that bound civic employees legally and morally to their duty. In 1919, those who interpreted the 1918 crisis in this way cried (and rightly so) that the Winnipeg General Strike was a betrayal, because civic employees hadn't bothered to give the promised sixty days' notice before throwing down their tools. The City had bargained in good faith; civic workers couldn't just wave off the 1918 agreement.

In 1918, there had been rumblings, too, that workers wanted not only better wages, but also political control. Then-mayor Davidson had placed a full-page ad in the three newspapers: 'Citizens! *We can run our city*, but we need your assistance'[94] [emphasis added]. A few days later, Sam Blumenberg appropriated Davidson's phrase, speaking to a mass rally of socialists at the Columbia Theatre: 'As to the scabs who took the places of our working men while they are on strike, we will see that they are all fired out cold before we will go back to work … *We are going to run this city* and we will not consent to having any scab working beside us'[95] [emphasis added]. Later Blumenberg increased his geographical reach: 'I meant to go further than this … I was going to say, "We are going to run the Dominion of Canada." It is our aim to change the trades union into a Socialist industrial union. If the capitalist class were not afraid that the strike in Winnipeg would spread throughout the country and grow into a social revolution they would not have settled the strike as easily as they did. They knew that the workers were determined. This was the reason they gave in so easily and thus avoided the overthrow of the capitalist class.'[96] When the 1919 General Strike rolled out so quickly, mowing down all the 1918 promises, little imagination was required for one to agree with the Citizens that the Strike was a second salvo, and that labour would be appeased with nothing less than total victory.

The 1919 Citizens' Committee of 1000 studiously avoided any reference to the Winnipeg Citizens' Alliance, but traced its genealogy back instead to the 1918 Citizens' Committee of 100, and, implicitly, back even further to 1914, when ironmaster and mayor Thomas Deacon, along with Augustus Nanton, got together a committee to create the Winnipeg Patriotic Fund to aid needy families of soldiers. The 1914 committee at first called itself the 'Committee of Forty Citizens.' After a number of prominent Winnipeggers – including A.J. Andrews – rushed to join the patriots, the name was changed to the 'Committee of One Hundred.'[97] The same name was adopted by the 1918 Citizens' Committee. The *Winnipeg Citizen*, mythologizing its origins, explained that the 1918 Committee of 100 'never entirely died, and this year it formed a rallying-point, a nucleus for the organization of a great force – the middle-class citizens who were the innocent victims of revolution.'[98] Bakery owner and president of both the Citizens' Alliance and the 1918 Citizens' Committee of 100, Ed Parnell gave the same story: the Citizens' Committee of 1000 'was simply a continuation, the only difference was that instead of one hundred it was nearly ten thousand at this time.'[99] He, too, kept quiet about the Citizens' Alliance. But the genealogical ties to 1914 and 1918 were deceptive. This story of origins dressed them in the sheep's clothing of 1918's eclectic committee, open to negotiation. There were indeed several holdovers from the Committee of 100 – notably its president Parnell, Pitblado, Sweatman, James Coyne, Crossin, Godfrey, and eleven others.[100] Despite the holdovers, the '1000' Citizens were far more exclusive than the '100.' The new Citizens wisely kept their names out of the newspaper, conscious perhaps that, seeing the leap from 100 to 1000, Winnipeggers might expect a corresponding increase in the eclecticism of the Committee's composition, when in fact the Citizens Committee of 1000 was far narrower. But as long as Winnipeggers forgot about the Citizens' Alliance and confused the Citizens' Committee of 1000 with its predecessor of 100, the Citizens benefited from the accumulated goodwill and benign face of the 1918 Committee.

Even as the 1919 Citizens reaped the 1918 Citizens' goodwill, the 1919 Citizens also made hay out of the previous Committee's inability to produce a lasting peace with labour, damning the Committee with faint praise: 'the "Citizens' Committee of One Hundred" … dealt with the situation to the best of their ability.'[101] The Citizens' Committee of 1000 said that it was prepared to respect the principle of collective bargaining, a right 'conceded,' the Citizens said, 'by all governments for years past,'[102] yet the mood around the table in 1919 was far grimmer than in 1918. If the settlement of 1918 couldn't prevent public employees from shrugging off their contracts whenever some private workplaces encountered labour friction, of what worth was a negotiated settlement? Of what worth was *negotiation*? Conversely, from the strikers' point of view, one short year ago the City, via the Fowler Amendment, had attempted to emasculate civic employees' bargaining powers by denying the right to strike. The 1919 Citizens' Committee of 1000, like its predecessor, helped the City to restore services, but in other ways the 1919 Citizens soon launched into new territory: jettisoning the policy of negotiation, demanding labour's unconditional surrender. If Pitblado, Sweatman, Coyne, Crossin, and Parnell remained from the old Committee, reminding everyone that the 1919 General Strike had betrayed the 1918 contracts, most of the 1919 Citizens were new, especially one important face: A.J. Andrews. The refusal of Andrews & Co. to negotiate showed what a difference a year had made. Labour, by ignoring the 1918 contracts, had ensured that employers would perceive the 1918 settlement as a failure.

Vulcan Ironworks: even by today's standards, it is a massive building, stretching for several city blocks alongside the railway. This was industry on a grand scale, and the opulent houses of metalworks owners such as Thomas Deacon testified about profitability. But it was neither the mulish Deacon nor Vulcan's L.R. Barrett who ran the Citizens. The metal shops needed many men to be productive, and the withdrawal of labour would no doubt have eventually forced Deacon and the others to capitulate, had not subtler minds such as Andrews intervened.

At some point during the first week of the 1919 Winnipeg General Strike, the ironmasters (whose refusal to allow collective bargaining had precipitated the Strike) reconsidered their bluff and sought to reopen negotiations. But after private meetings with the new Citizens' Committee of 1000, the bosses mysteriously resumed their original position, a return which for them had the virtue of justifying their earlier intransigence. After the Strike, Ed Parnell would insist that the Citizens' Committee had been formed only to operate public utilities.[103] But on the evening of 19 May, L.R. Barrett disclosed to the press that 'the whole situation is in the hands of the citizens' committee and we must await action by that committee. In the meantime we are going to sit tight and make no concessions.'[104] Not surprisingly, when Mayor Gray tried to rope the ironmasters into a meeting to negotiate an end to the Strike, they replied that the Citizens' Committee had asked them not to open negotiations. A couple of days later, Gray disclosed this to Council. He had asked for a set of demands from labour. Labour had complied. He had asked for the same from the ironmasters. Silence. A.A. Heaps stated the obvious: 'Then the citizens' committee is standing in the way of a settlement.'[105] The mayor couldn't disagree. Winnipeg had definitively left the tracks of earlier labour disputes.

Wednesday, 21 May

No social order with any moral confidence will hesitate to defend itself. The Citizens were working towards an understanding of their role in history, the burdens, if not always the obligations, of rule. Privately, the Citizens drew employers into military formation, while publicly beginning PR offensives at City Council and in the *Winnipeg Citizen* – but these initiatives weren't enough. Bringing the state to heel was a more delicate operation, requiring political connections. The Citizens lobbied Premier T.C. Norris's provincial Liberal government, demanding that Norris arrest the Strike leaders.[106] On Tuesday evening, Mayor Gray revealed that 'he had a letter from the Premier to the effect that if the Strike Committee placards were removed ... there might be prospects of a settlement.'[107] But apart from ordering provincial civil servants back to work at the risk of losing their jobs, Norris refused to act. Since almost everybody in the Norris cabinet was rural, it's possible that Norris feared the electoral repercussions of mishandling the Strike. He seems to have wished that the Strike were a federal problem.

The federal government, then? The War Measures Act was still technically in force, but Ottawa had been rescinding its more draconian Orders in Council. The OIC allowing for the prosecution of individuals who attended meetings, spoke in support of, or distributed literature for any organization deemed unlawful (PC 2384, approved 25 September 1918) had been repealed by Arthur Meighen, acting minister of justice, on 2 April 1919.[108] Another (approved in July 1918), calling for a voluntary prohibition on strikes or lockouts for the duration of the war, had just been repealed on 1 May 1919. There still remained on the books the 'Consolidated Orders Respecting Censorship,' a potential tool against the strikers.[109] Despite this, the mood in Ottawa was conciliatory. The Borden cabinet had recently (on 4 April) approved the creation of a Royal Commission on Industrial Relations. Chaired by Manitoba's Chief Justice Mathers, the royal commission was expected to give its report shortly, on 1 June 1919.[110]

Mayor Gray begged federal representatives to visit the beleaguered city. Federal involvement seemed to be inevitable, but it would be a mistake to assume that coercion was on Ottawa's agenda or that Ottawa viewed the General Strike as its own problem. Even under the OICs, the onus had been on the *provinces* to prosecute: as a lawyer, Andrews certainly understood the division of powers between Canada and the provinces, and Borden, during the 1918 strike, had made it clear that even OICs must be administered by provincial and civic authorities.[111] Still, the federal government had at its disposal the Royal North West Mounted Police (RNWMP), the militia, the legislative power of Parliament, and the administrative machinery of the state. Winnipeg's business community needed to find a way to move the federal government.

Prime Minister Sir Robert Borden was away in Europe, and not very well besides. The federal Union cabinet, hearing Mayor Gray's appeal and recognizing the seriousness of the crisis, dispatched not one but two cabinet ministers to Winnipeg. Meighen, the senior minister from the West, and Minister of Labour Gideon Robertson were sent to deal with the walkout of Winnipeg's postal workers and to assess the situation generally.[112] On Tuesday, in the comfort of Robertson's private railway car, Meighen and Robertson started west to the besieged city.

The Citizens had advance warning and moved to intercept them. A delegation, including Andrews, Pitblado, Sweatman, and one other – probably either E.K. Williams (a Liberal who later became chief justice of Manitoba) or forty-one-year-old James Bowes Coyne (nicknamed 'Bogus'[113] and also a Liberal) – rushed to Fort William (now Thunder Bay) and caught the ministers there on Wednesday.[114] To the applause of the Citizens, W.T. Cox had told City Council that he was prepared to eat grass rather than capitulate, and that 'the best thing they could tell Robertson and Meighen was "Go back to Ottawa."'[115] There should be no repeat of the negotiations and capitulation of 1918. According to Meighen, the Citizens did most of the talking at Fort William, while he and Robertson listened. The delegation's story was the same one outlined in the *Winnipeg Citizen*: a Bolshevik revolution had gripped Winnipeg; the Citizens feared the worst; please send troops.[116]

Robertson and Meighen, both Conservatives, weren't hard nuts to crack. Later, in July, well-placed Winnipeg lawyer John B. Haig tried to convince Meighen that it had been 'the hot head members of the community who had sent the delegation to ask him to keep his nose out of Winnipeg,[117] but Meighen held the opposite view:

> I knew practically all of [the delegation] personally and knew that they were not citizens who would be easy victims of fear. Their apprehension at this time, nevertheless was very, very great. They were quite certain that what was about to take place in the capital was nothing less than a revolution, and their job was to make us understand that fact.[118]

For different reasons both Meighen and Robertson were susceptible to the story of revolution. Robertson, a former union official of immovable orthodoxy, had only contempt for labour radicalism. He had risen through the ranks of a conservative craft union, the Order of Railroad Telegraphers, which was committed to 'friendly cooperation of workers and employers.'[119] In 1907, the Industrial Disputes Investigation Act imposed a compulsory cooling-off period on public-utilities employees whenever a strike looked inevitable. When the Canadian Trades and Labour Congress in 1913 criticized the IDIA as against the interests of labour, the ORT quit the TLC in protest,[120] Robertson explaining that 'so long as the demands of labour are within the bounds of reason, workmen need have no fear of having their grievances investigated before the bar of public opinion.'[121] Borden, needing a union man to symbolize la-

Arthur Meighen, ca 1920. (Archives of Manitoba)

bour's support for his government, found in Robertson the ideal candidate. Not only was he a strong critic of labour radicals,[122] but he also
gave unqualified support to conscription. Too old for service himself, he
packed two sons off to the Great War.[123] A series of 1918 industrial-
relations crises across Canada, including the near–general strike in Winnipeg, proved Robertson to be an adept conciliator. His was a language
of class collaboration: 'the interests of the employer and the workman
are not diametrically opposed … a view that too many employers and
too many workmen entertain.'[124]

Even closer to the mind of Andrews was Meighen. As a young man,
he had moved to Manitoba and had headed the commercial department
of the Winnipeg Business College in 1898–9, the year of Andrews's stint
as 'boy-mayor.' After his legal studies and his election as MP for Portage
la Prairie, he had proved himself capable of a fierce realpolitik. He knew
the Citizens personally – indeed, Pitblado's law firm handled Meighen's
private business,[125] and Pitblado had given Meighen legal advice on a
business failure involving an 'ill-fated dried-fruit-cleaning machine in

which he had held a half-interest.'[126] Meighen was Andrews's junior in age yet senior in power, and they shared the basic idioms of law, Conservatism, and the story of the state. In a 1921 speech, Meighen showed a keen sense of how the British 'Constitution' lay in the history of past parliamentary acts: 'What are constitutional principles? They are the common law of Parliaments.' And if one were to say that this biased him against radical changes to the polity, he would have agreed. 'Rashness and inconsequence,' he said, 'are alien to the British tradition.' While he spoke of the importance of tradition – 'as lawyers we are traditionists' [*sic*] – he nevertheless left room for the common law to change, quoting Oliver Wendell Holmes that 'the present has the right to govern itself so far as it can.'[127] Certainly Meighen's actions leading up to the Winnipeg General Strike had displayed such attitudes. When the Liberals used procedural loopholes to block a Conservative Naval Aid bill, it fell to Meighen to amend parliamentary process and to justify closure of debate. The Liberals cried that closure was a 'Russianizing' of Canada, that closure was only invoked in European countries where 'they do not know what freedom means' – Edmund Burke and Charles Fox would never have stood for such a thing. But Meighen steered a course that respected common-law precedent – he noted the hundreds of times closure had been invoked in British Parliament, far more often by Liberals than by Conservatives – and yet he stressed that since 1867 Canada constitutionally had the 'sovereign freedom' to do as Parliament thought best. He was quite prepared to honour the great Liberal Fox, and more so Gladstone, who closed debate in an attempt to speed along Irish Home Rule. The crux, Meighen maintained, was 'to see to it that the wheels of Parliament were not clogged, that the arteries of legislation were not stopped, that it was not possible for a small minority to thwart and throttle the whole Parliamentary system.'[128] In order to sway a man such as Meighen, Andrews returned again and again to the narrative of revolution against 'constituted authority.'

The Citizens had been wise to intercept Meighen and Robertson. That the two federal ministers accepted the Citizens' story may be seen in the immediate aftermath of the Fort William meeting. Without hesitation, Meighen wrote to Newton Rowell, minister responsible for the RNWMP, telling him to direct Colonel Cortlandt Starnes, superintendent of the RNWMP in Winnipeg, 'to collect by consent of merchants ... any arms and ammunition in stock ... not now securely safeguarded,' and to report to Meighen any refusals of consent. Meighen declared what the Citizens had primed him to declare, that the 'great purpose [of the Strike] is Soviet control.'[129] Robertson made similar noises to his deputy minister: 'The motive behind this strike undoubtedly was the

overthrow of constitutional government but leaders have already temporarily abandoned hope of success and are frantically endeavouring to
camouflage the issue by pretending to contend for the recognition of the
principle of collective bargaining.'[130] Approvingly, Meighen reported
that the Citizens urged the federal government to 'pursue a strong course
with regard to its own services.'[131] Translated, that meant, 'Force federal employees back to work.' Thus, before he had a chance even to see
strike-locked Winnipeg or to meet with Mayor Gray, Meighen was
already repeating, without qualification, the Citizens' interpretation of
events, saying that 'complete defeat must be achieved.'[132]

Meighen and Robertson would soon meet with provincial authorities
and come away convinced that T.H. Johnson, the attorney general,
wouldn't deal with the crisis. Instead, Meighen leaned on Andrews.
Although it was Andrews who initiated their Strike relationship in Fort
William, Meighen in effect asked Andrews to be his eyes and ears in
Winnipeg. Eventually, on at least two occasions, Andrews would badger
Meighen for arrests, but admit that prosecutions were of course a provincial responsibility. Later, Andrews would surprise Meighen by deploy-
ing criminal law in a way that Meighen had no reason to foresee.

As the Citizens had requested, Meighen recommended a hard line to
Ottawa, and six days later, on the 27th, Borden would respond, 'Law and
order should be maintained ... The Civil Service cannot be permitted
to discard their public duties and to dislocate the public service.'[133] In
other words, postal workers who hadn't returned to work by 26 May
would be fired. Even cabinet members such as Rowell, who viewed
themselves as champions of labour, distinguished between 'men seeking
to overthrow constituted authority, and the sober, serious leaders of the
[labour] movement.'[134] According to his biographer, Rowell, too, agreed
with the Citizens' interpretation of events. It didn't hurt that Citizens'
lawyer James Coyne, who may have been in the Fort William delegation, was Rowell's cousin, or that Rowell knew and respected several
leading Winnipeg Liberals – including Pitblado, Crossin, and E.K.
Williams.[135] Coyne, for one, had already known how to interpret the
Strike six months before it happened, when he commented on the affiliation of the Winnipeg Police union with the Winnipeg Trades and Labor
Council: 'It seems to me that the recognition of the Union means the
inauguration of anarchy by turning over the instruments for the preservation of law and order to the Trades and Labor Council, which is now
largely dominated by labor leaders who are acknowledged Bolsheviki
and whose desire I believe is to substitute a workmen's council with the
Russian motto as the governing force in the municipality instead of the
representative bodies now constituted by law.'[136] Rowell arranged to

send a RNWMP squadron to stand behind Winnipeg's elected officials.[137] If the state wasn't yet *acting* directly against the strikers, it had
always favoured commercial interests. The balance of forces tilted even
more: towards the Citizens and against the strikers.

While the Citizens in Fort William tutored the state on its obligation
to uphold its own power, they cried out against 'tyranny' at home. The
Citizens were astute enough to pitch their story in a variety of registers:
one for Cabinet, a differently inflected one for Winnipeggers. The same
day that Andrews and Co. were briefing Meighen in Fort William, the
Winnipeg Citizen spoke of the strikers' threat against authority, accusing
them of

> an impudent assertion of authority over the police; a claim to control
> the rights of passage on the streets; an assumption of the right to
> license theatres and permit businesses to go ahead; a usurpation of the
> authority of the City Council in the operation of public utilities ...

Thus far, similar to the Fort William delegation. Yet, as the next passage
shows, there were subtle differences between the language addressed to
'the people' and the language addressed to the representatives of 'constituted authority.' To Winnipeggers (who knew that the city was relatively calm), the Citizens didn't warn of potential chaos in the streets. To
'the people,' the *Winnipeg Citizen* depicted the strikers as monarchs
impinging on freedoms. The *Citizen* accused the strikers of 'a tyrannical
interference with the freedom of the Press, which is one of the traditional
bulwarks of British freedom; and as the crowning audacity, a prohibition
of the passage in and out of the city, of His Majesty's mails.'[138] The
focus on union tyranny and British freedom was calculated to appeal to
the common person, who had been hearing altogether too much about
the tyranny of bosses. The *Citizen* did speak to the common person about
a threat to constituted authority, but often within the discourse of *civil
liberties*. For example, interfering with passage on the streets, which
would signal rebellion and chaos to Meighen, was to Winnipeggers presented as a species of tyranny – 'a claim to control.'

With common-law lawyers leading the charge, it's no wonder that
even when those lawyers were off in Fort William common-law principles would resonate throughout the *Winnipeg Citizen*. The *Citizen* called
upon the people to stand up against tyranny, and informed them that in
Russia peasants were rising against the Bolsheviks. The history of
British common law is the story of a defence against the arbitrary
authority of the Crown, a defence against tyranny from *above*, yet one
can understand the Citizens' fears that tyranny could potentially come

from below, from mob rule. But that's not how they articulated the situation to Winnipeggers. To characterize the new situation as mob rule would concede that the Strike was indeed a grassroots movement and that the majority of the strikers supported the actions of the Strike Committee. Instead of voicing their true fears, the Citizens pandered to the strikers' class bias by characterizing the Strike Committee members as royal autocrats and disingenuously insisting that the grassroots was represented by the Citizens' Committee of 1000: 'Do not forget that The Winnipeg Citizen is YOUR PAPER.'

Thursday, 22 May

The Strike was already a week old on Thursday when Meighen and Robertson, well-lobbied, finally arrived in Winnipeg. Meighen would stay until the 27th, Robertson a few days more, consulting with the Citizens and with provincial attorney general T.H. Johnson, but not with the Strike Committee. More surprisingly, Meighen and Robertson didn't bother to speak to Mayor Gray until two days after their arrival. It's conceivable that Meighen and Robertson were too busy to meet with Gray, described by one source as 'an amiable, nervous, and weary politician,'[139] and by another source as demonstrating 'courage and sanity.'[140] It's also conceivable that the Citizens *kept* Meighen and Robertson too busy to meet with Gray, since he seemed to place hope in negotiations. Gray was certainly annoyed at being cut out of the loop:

> I am rather surprised in view of the fact that the burden of maintaining law and order and constitutional government was thrown upon me solely ... that the ministers for whose presence I wired Ottawa did not see fit until two days after their arrival to apprise my officials unofficially that they were here nor what their views were in the matter which was before the whole City of Winnipeg although their subsequent actions will undoubtedly meet with the citizens' approval.[141]

One of the causes for Gray's annoyance was that on Friday he would attempt – blindly, as he realized afterwards – to mediate an end to the Strike. He called together City Council, Strike Committee members R.B. Russell and James Winning, and Citizens' representatives Andrews, Sweatman, and others. But the two powerful federal ministers were touring Winnipeg, being briefed by the Citizens, deciding on the federal government's position, all without hearing a word from the city's mayor. Although Gray didn't realize it, the Citizens had no intention of entering bona fide negotiations, and they instead treated his mediation meeting as a stage from which to play to the crowd, while at the same time issuing a warning to Russell and Winning.

In the Meighen-Andrews correspondence, the nature and function of this theatre becomes apparent, because the Citizens' private lobbying of Meighen in Fort William two days earlier was different from their public self-presentation in Gray's meeting. In keeping with their split discourse for Meighen and for Winnipeggers – the Citizens also split their own identities tactically. To Meighen, they emphasized their economic and political clout. For general consumption, they revealed themselves as innocent lower-case citizens harassed by the Strike.

Meighen could speak sonorously about citizens who wouldn't be easy prey to fear, because, listening to Andrews in Fort William, he knew the Citizens' names, their political affiliations, their net worth in dollars and cents, their reach. After the arrest of the Strike leaders in mid-June, Prime Minister Borden would privately receive a congratulatory telegram with thirty-four signatures. Most Winnipeggers, however, could only make some educated guesses, and, even long after the Strike, speculated about who the Citizens were. Even now, there exists no membership list of the Citizens. Who were these anonymous men who stopped the Strike, the self-declared benefactors of babies and invalids? No one would say. The leaders' names were 'well concealed,' reported Sir Joseph Pope, the first permanent head of the Canadian Department of External Affairs, in response to an inquiry from British intelligence about the utility of citizens as a counter-revolutionary force. 'We are all in this together,' declared one Citizen, 'We don't want anyone to get particular credit, for each man is doing exactly what he can and what seems needed most. Some of us are officers, but we do not feel that we are doing a bit more than the man who is driving a truck. So please don't mention any names.'[142] Of course, it wasn't credit they feared, but reprisals. Yet the *Winnipeg Citizen*, silent about its own staff and funding, wouldn't hesitate, a few days later, to let everyone know which Winnipeg labour leaders had attended the Calgary conference.[143] Important, clearly, for Winnipeg to know the names of those calling for the abolition of the world as they knew it.

All Winnipeggers could gather from the pages of the *Winnipeg Citizen* was that these defenders claimed to be men like themselves – middle-class, patriotic, annoyed by tyranny. 'I never was a capitalist,' Pitblado had said.[144] In the middle of the Strike, faced with the names of radical labour leaders in unforgiving type, the *Western Labor News* would demand, 'Where is the anonymous Citizens' Committee? Who are they? Who is their chairman? Who elected them? ... Who gave them power over the City Council and the Parliaments? ... Who? Who? Who-oo?' In the abstract, the *Labor News* could speculate quite accurately: 'They are rich men, of course ... celebrities of the Manufacturers' Association, the Greater Winnipeg Board of Trade, the Canadian Manufacturers' Association, the Real Estate Men's Association.' These men, said the *Labor News*, believed whole-heartedly in a living wage for themselves, and hadn't hesitated to get *organized*, but when labourers fought to start their own organizations, the manufacturing celebrities suddenly cried foul.[145] Nonsense, replied the *Winnipeg Citizen*, we're not trade and manufacturing associations in disguise – but it immediately qualified that claim: it was certainly possible that *some* members of business organizations might have attached themselves to the committee. Come to think of it, honour belonged to those organizations![146]

Andrews had proclaimed that he spoke for a thousand citizens, 'men drawn from all walks of life, not capitalists.'[147] In fact, however, not a single member of the Citizens' Committee executive came from outside of the upper class – 'he did the deed who gained by it.' Only because the thirty-four-member executive signed the private end-of-strike telegram to Prime Minister Borden, strongly approving of the government's action 'in arresting certain revolutionary leaders in Winnipeg'[148] and letting Borden know the quality of those who approved, do we know for certain who the Citizens were. If it was chancy for the Citizens to name themselves even in private, there would, as we will see, be good tactical reasons after the arrests for the Committee to bowl over Borden and Cabinet with a long list of important Winnipeg names. Only with the release of the Meighen-Andrews correspondence did this telegram become public.

What Louis Silverberg said of citizens' committees in general was true of Winnipeg's Citizens: 'The citizens' committee endeavours to maintain the fiction that it is not merely another expression of employer anti-labor activity, and, therefore, it attempts to show that the personnel of the committee, having no direct interest in a given labor dispute, represents the "public interest" jeopardized by the struggle between employers and workers.'[149] The thirty-four Winnipeggers who revealed themselves to Meighen and Borden, but not to Winnipeg, called themselves 'representative citizens.'[150] In what sense, they didn't say. They claimed to have come from 'all walks of life,' but actually they came only from the top echelons of Winnipeg society and were entirely *un*representative in wealth. Good if Winnipeggers assumed that 'all walks of life' had its usual meaning of 'all jobs,' and if 'representative' had its usual meanings of 'alike in kind' or 'elected.' The Citizens, however, had their fingers crossed, and meant only that they came from a variety of financial, manufacturing, commercial, and legal enterprises, from a variety of service organizations, and from both of the two dominant political parties, the Liberal and the Conservative, as would befit a group petitioning Borden's Unionist government. Judging by the rolls that detail the contributions of men and services to the Citizens' Committee, virtually every *business* in Winnipeg was in some way 'represented.'[151] In effect, the thirty-four executive Citizens used 'representative' in the old feudal sense, referring to a sovereign, who in his divine body 'represents' all the people on his land and in his employ. The 1000, if the number meant anything, referred to the other businesspeople who supported the Citizens, to sons and daughters of the elite, to middle managers, and finally to the low-ranking employees whom the businesses *assigned* to the Citizens – employees who appear as numbers, not names in the contribution rolls.

Celebrities of the Manufacturers' Association and the Board of Trade, the *Labor News* had guessed for the Citizens' identities. Not far off. As a matter of fact, there were no fewer than three recent presidents of the Board of Trade on the Citizens' executive. Besides A.L. Crossin, there was G.N. Jackson, a director of Sovereign Life Assurance and, several years earlier, of the Winnipeg Industrial Bureau. A third, the influential A.K. Godfrey, had been educated as a lawyer, but had made his fortune as a grain and lumber merchant. For a time, he had even presided over the Winnipeg Grain Exchange. Now that the city was in crisis, Godfrey chaired the executive of the Citizens' Committee. Afterwards, he would be one of the very few to reveal his participation to *Who's Who in Canada*.[152]

The Canadian Manufacturers' Association was represented by George Carpenter, who had organized the CMA's prairie division west,[153] and by Melbourne F. Christie. A paint and varnish wholesaler with business interests across the West, Christie had a hand in two of the organizations reviled by the *Labor News*: he not only chaired the CMA's Manitoba branch, but was also vice-president of the Board of Trade.[154] There were other manufacturers too, such as N.J. Breen, a manager in the Lake of the Woods Milling Company;[155] and Frank W. Adams, who ran a harness manufacturing company.[156] The food manufacturer D.J. Dyson, like A.J. Andrews, was a veteran of the Northwest Rebellion – the previous great threat to the Canadian West – and had served as mayor of Winnipeg for three days until a recount deprived him of his position.[157] According to American journalist Samuel Hopkins Adams, who seems to have either observed a Citizens' meeting or received an eye-witness account of one, the Citizens included both 'the extreme Bourbon element of the employers,' which wanted to smash the unions 'so that they will never raise their heads again in this city,' and 'a more progressive and tolerant faction,' which accepted unions in the workplace. An unconfirmed rumour had it that certain Citizens asked Robertson to use the military in combating the Strike.[158] The Bourbons could count among their number a certain 'head of a food company' – either Dyson or William Pitt Riley (Western Grocers) – who made a 'violent' speech against the Strike and asked the Citizens to protect his plant. However, a member of the progressive faction wondered why the speaker had raised food prices 7½ to 10 per cent in the weeks leading up to the Strike.[159]

Many of the Citizens, including Andrews (since 1910), Sweatman, Pitblado, Coyne, Crossin, Godfrey, Ed Anderson, and the Citizens' finance committee chair, W.H. McWilliams (a grain merchant with a variety of other business interests),[160] were members of the exclusive Manitoba Club. So were other elite Winnipeggers who would play important roles in the Strike, almost always on the side of the Citizens: *Free Press* editor John Dafoe, ironmaster Thomas Deacon, Alderman Frank Fowler, Justice Thomas Metcalfe, and Chief Justice T.G. Mathers.[161] It's not surprising, therefore, that when important government officials later met to discuss anti-Strike strategy, Fowler was among them.[162] The Manitoba Club couldn't exactly be called 'representative.' One needed two sponsors, $200, and a favourable vote from more than 80 per cent of the members in order to get in.[163] More accurate to call it the most exclusive club in the province. To enforce a certain amount of class harmony, the club prohibited members from discussing religion or politics, yet, or maybe *because* of this, the Manitoba Club was where the Citizens held their founding meeting.[164] Some Citizens were instead (or sometimes in addition) members at other prestigious clubs: the Carleton Club, the St Charles Country Club, the Winnipeg Canadian Club, the Winnipeg Golf Club, the Lake of the Woods Yacht Club.[165]

Political clout lay alongside the Citizens' economic and social clout. Next to the former mayor, Andrews, on the Citizens' executive sat one soon-to-be mayor – 1918 Citizens' Alliance president Ed Parnell – and two former city councillors: the harness manufacturer Frank Adams and real estate agent A.L. Bond.[166] When the Citizens wanted one of their resolutions to go before City Council – their demand, for example, that council permanently replace striking civic employees, or that firefighters not be allowed to be part of a larger union – the Citizens called on Alderman John Sparling to put forward the motion.[167] A year earlier he had successfully prevented German-born Henry Schlachter from receiving a chauffeur's licence, because Schlachter had said that Americans shouldn't have travelled on the Lusitania after Germany warned them not to do so.[168] Sparling shared the Citizens' goals and met with them throughout the Strike, but wasn't technically on the executive. Under cross-examination after the Strike was over, he could therefore answer with sublime disingenuousness when the defence counsel asked him whether it was the Citizens' Committee of 1000 that had demanded special police. In response, Sparling wondered, 'Was there a committee of one thousand at that time?'[169]

The *Labor News* had also singled out the Real Estate Men's Association as prominent on the Citizens' executive, and indeed real estate interests were represented by A.L. Bond, one of the principals in Berry & Bond,[170] and by Clarence Sheppard, who with a partner had been responsible for developing the exclusive Crescentwood enclave south of the Assiniboine. This neighbourhood for rich families had made Sheppard rich too, and had propelled him into the presidency of the Winnipeg Real Estate Exchange.

Some members of the executive were 'merely' the managers of banks, insurance companies, retail stores, or wholesale enterprises, and thus not technically capitalists: George Munro (Merchants' Bank),[171] J.C. Waugh (Commercial Union Association),[172] Colin Campbell Ferguson (Great West Life),[173] H.M. Tucker (T. Eaton Company),[174] Fred Luke (Canada Cycle and Motor), A.B. Stovel (Stovel Printing), W.P. Riley (Western Grocers), Douglas A. Clark (Clark Brothers building contractors), and C.A. Richardson (Occidental Fire Insurance). Proof that the Citizens weren't just a bunch of capitalists? Easy: the three ironmasters at whose factories the Strike had begun weren't members of the Committee! Nevertheless, one could be forgiven if one mistook the list of the Citizens' executive members for a Who's Who of Winnipeg's commercial elite.[175] Tying all of these businessmen together, mediating between Bourbons and progressives, and representing the 'representative' Citizens, were the powerful lawyers – Andrews, Pitblado, Sweatman, Coyne, and Ed Anderson.

Many of the thirty-four names are only ciphers now, but in 1919 the list told Meighen a very particular class story. It's no surprise that when Rev. Charles W. Gordon, a minister who was one of the Strike's 'neutral' mediators on the Council of Industry,[176] wrote a 1921 novel about the Strike, *To Him That Hath* (under the pseudonym Ralph Connor), he shaped his novel using an aristocratic mythos. In such a mythos, nobility runs deep despite a character's disguises and will always eventually reveal its glory. It's clear that Gordon *wanted* to give his allegiance to democracy. The rich young Rupert Stillwell who says, 'Well, democracy is all right and that sort of thing, but you must drift into your class, you know,' is satirized by Gordon.[177] Yet for all of the novel's expressed disdain for war millionaires, it's clear that some of the upper-middle-class characters are *naturally* better than the weak-willed working class. Such ambivalence between aristocracy and meritocracy is common, especially in North America, because the mythos of 'The Man Who Rose from Nothing' – a progressive, democratic mythos – sits uneasily not only beside the inheritance of English thought (with its aristocratic literary plots), but also beside the paradoxical wish of the *nouveaux riches* to naturalize their status.[178] In Douglas Durkin's *The Magpie*, a 1923 novel more sympathetic to the Strike, the wealthy Mrs Blount is more fully conscious that the aristocratic mythos must be gingerly steered away from bloodlines in order to harmonize with North American notions of a meritocracy. She says, 'Democracy is all right in its place, but – after all – we're not all born equal, or if we are we don't remain equal, do we?'[179]

Despite the Citizens' identities, on Thursday evening at the Board of Trade Building Andrews kept up the charade that they were simple men of the people. In the afternoon, labour got wind of a rumour that Gideon Robertson was supposed to address a larger group of 'Citizens' there, and strikers turned out en masse. Rather than the elected Robertson, they got Citizen appointees Crossin – who took credit on behalf of the Citizens for getting water and bread moving again – and Andrews. The ubiquitous Andrews enjoyed the limelight. If he had failed at politics, he was, after all, a litigating lawyer, not one who toiled away quietly in an office. Now, in this crisis, he could make use of his hail-fellow-well-met style and his gift for argumentation. Tongue-in-cheek, he said that 'he was delighted to see so many desiring to join the Committee of One Thousand.' Even the strikers laughed. Then he spoke of 'the friendly feeling existing between himself and organized labor.' All he wanted, he insisted, was a fair hearing, and if labour's case was valid, they had nothing to fear. Finally, he tried to woo the strikers with historical arguments, suggesting that their kind of experiment had already been tried by the Knights of Labor and the IWW, and had failed. Men in the crowd cried, 'Not the same.'[180] Afterwards, Andrews claimed that he had enjoyed the meeting immensely, what with all the good fellows there. He hadn't enjoyed anything so much in many a month. It was a 'bully time.'[181]

But the names that Andrews had passed on to Meighen on Wednesday had little to do with camaraderie or equality. The names informed Meighen that when Andrews, Pitblado, and Sweatman spoke, Meighen should hear, ventriloquized, the whole of Winnipeg's commercial, legal, and political establishment – Liberals and Conservatives speaking with one voice. No figureheads, the thirty-four. This much the *Winnipeg Citizen* reported accurately: the Citizens had gotten together, they said, and elected a strong executive.[182] At all hours of the day and night, long rows of motor cars lined the street near the Industrial Bureau, because from the outset of the Strike, the executive committee was in 'continuous session,'[183] meeting day and night if necessary, never really adjourning.

Friday, 23 May – Sunday, 25 May

Friday saw a curious spectacle performed at City Council. In the morning's council meeting, Andrews and Sweatman spoke – mostly in conciliatory terms and as if they held little power – yet when Mayor Gray brought together ten representatives of labour and of the Citizens in an attempt at mediation late that evening, Andrews took a much sterner line, and careful observers could see that he was only paying lip service to Gray's hopes. What the Citizens had already decided a couple of days ago slowly became evident: there would be no real negotiations.

In the morning, Andrews pretended to support Mayor Gray, declaring that Winnipeg owed him a debt of gratitude. 'The mayor,' Andrews said, 'worked like a Trojan to bring about industrial peace.' Responding to *Western Labor News* innuendo that far fewer than 1000 people controlled the Citizens' Committee, Andrews boasted that actually more than 2500 people had signed on. But numbers didn't make right, he quickly added, aware that if it came down to headcounts, the strikers might be a few steps ahead. The Citizens, said Andrews, hadn't banded together to oppose the Strike. In fact, they had no business deciding the rights or wrongs of the dispute, and existed merely to keep the public utilities running.[184] He even admitted that possibly workers weren't getting a living wage, though he also restated the Citizens' opposition to sympathetic strikes and to vital public employees affiliating with outside unions. Andrews claimed that the Board of Trade was composed of all classes of the community – a rather curious statement, since it was so patently false and couldn't be kneaded into truth the way that 'representative' could. Was he simply testing how much he could get away with? Labour councillor Queen objected that Andrews's statement was completely untrue, and Andrews retreated, 'Then I am wrong. I understood they were represented. In any case, the board of trade had only been formed to boost the city of Winnipeg.' If such associations weren't fully representative, at least they weren't illegal – correct? If the Manufacturer's Association had been created for an 'illegal' purpose, a law should be made to abolish it!

James Winning queried Andrews about whether the Citizens were in favour of collective bargaining. Andrews replied, 'We have never discussed it.' Felled immediately by guffaws and loud laughter from the gallery, Andrews grew resentful and threatened to leave, but he didn't leave, and instead he nimbly (though unconvincingly) reworded his statement, 'We have never discussed it except with approval.' He claimed that some Citizens might have told the ironmasters not to open negotiations, but the Citizens had never officially undertaken to dictate to any employer what he should do.[185] This was true in the abstract – the Citizens of course had no official power to dictate to the ironmasters – and false in fact: it was Andrews himself who was a prime supporter of the no-negotiation policy.

Sweatman, at that same meeting, adopted a voice that was even more disingenuous than that of Andrews – if such a thing were possible – the voice of the lower-case citizen, unable to speak for any larger group: 'Mr. Sweatman asked what about the rights of the rest of the community, those like himself, who was neither identified with capital or labor.'[186] 'As a private citizen,' he said that he opposed sympathetic strikes, particularly 'when such strikes deprived himself and family from [sic] services which belonged to them in all justice.'[187] It's clear that Andrews and Sweatman were learning to toggle between identities – between 'Citizen' and mere 'citizen'; between, on the one hand, the lawyer who is so closely tied to the concerns of capital that capital entrusts him with its public face and, on the other hand, the average man who only knows that he is the humble inheritor of the great traditions of British liberty.

The upshot of Friday morning's council meeting was that all agreed to let the mayor appoint a representative ten-member committee to work for a settlement. The council meeting was reported in all the major papers – the *Manitoba Free Press*, the *Winnipeg Telegram*, the *Western Labor News* – but not in the *Winnipeg Citizen*. Who was the *Citizen*'s editor? Did he not understand that Winnipeggers might be eager to hear about council's attempt to end the Strike? Did he perhaps not know that Andrews and Sweatman had addressed City Council? The political reasons for the omission aren't difficult to divine. The *Citizen* was less in the business of news than of ideology: much of the paper consisted of polemical articles, which, just as labour kept claiming, hid behind the slogan of 'threats to our institutions.' On page 1, 'Strike Unjustified; Citizens Must Stand Firm'; on page 2 that Saturday, another article, 'Volunteer Brigade Averts Great Tragedy,' about what the *Citizen* called 'one of the worst conflagrations in history.' In plainer terms, a stable adjoining the Hudson's Bay store on south Main Street had caught fire. Instead of news about council meetings and attempts to settle the Strike, readers of the *Citizen* could enjoy self-congratulatory articles of heroic volunteers who, 'tragically handicapped in their efforts by the complete failure of the high pressure service to deliver water,' had saved a stable ... no, the whole city.[188] Unfortunately for the *Citizen*, three days later it had to admit that high pressure had indeed been available and had been used to extinguish the fire.[189]

The other main reason for the *Citizen* ignoring the council meeting can be divined from Andrews's second performance of the day, this time at Gray's evening mediation meeting. The Citizens had no intention of allowing a quick settlement to paper over what they saw as serious problems, and clearly the *Citizen*'s editor saw no advantage in encouraging talk of a settlement. At the mediation meeting Andrews spoke much more as a Citizens' power broker. After condemning the Strike as an act that went well beyond the question of collective bargaining, he contradicted his morning innocence by adding, 'So far as he was concerned there would be no negotiations until the postal employees, firemen, waterworks employees, and telephone operators were back at work. It would be splendid diplomacy for the Strike Committee to yield that point. Afterwards the principle of collective bargaining would be recognized.' But when R.B. Russell pressed him again for assurances on collective bargaining, Andrews toggled quickly back to mere citizen. He said that he couldn't offer assurances because he had no authority to negotiate on behalf of the employers. Instead, he declared that the Strike was wrong and that it went well beyond a dispute between employers and employees: 'We say you've done a wrong. You now have a chance to retire gracefully.' And then, just as quickly as he had become a mere citizen, he toggled forward again to power-broking Citizen: 'If you do not do this, we will line up against you the Dominion, Provincial, and Civic Governments.'[190] Andrews's 'we' was meant to indicate the mass of honest people, middle-class citizens, who, neither labour nor capital, had been harmed by the Strike's effects. *Those* citizens could express their outrage and call upon the government for remedy. Their main power, he implied, wasn't political machination but force of right. Yet, at the same time, he hinted darkly that he had had some assurances that the federal government wouldn't interfere with the Citizens. When Russell brought up the name of Gideon Robertson as a supporter of collective bargaining, Andrews said that the Strike was *not* a Dominion matter.[191] Was it then simply a labour dispute? Not quite that, either. 'This is not a case between employers and employees,' he said. The meeting was finally adjourned at 12:00 with no progress at all made towards mediation.[192]

Addressing a delegation from Moose Jaw in the following week, Sweatman would use the same style of equivocation that Andrews had – speaking for the employers and then protesting that he couldn't speak for the employers. The Citizens were all champions of collective bargaining, Sweatman disclosed. He could not, however, reveal what exactly they might *mean* by 'collective bargaining,' since each member might have a different notion.[193] Andrews's and Sweatman's oratorical sliding between 'Citizen' and 'citizen' was a technique that the *Winnipeg Citizen* had been testing out:

> The fact that the Strike is out of the hands of the both employer and employees, and that it is an issue for the citizens themselves, is demonstrated by an announcement made by Mayor Gray to the City Council today [21 May] ... It is the citizens' fight now, since their right to live as they please has been challenged by the tie-up of food, water and business.[194]

In this ventriloquism, there was still a nominal difference between the *Winnipeg Citizen* and Winnipeg's 'citizens' – the latter treated in the third person – but that difference was meant to disappear in the word 'citizen,' identical with itself. Only the 'Citizens' could best articulate what the 'citizen' wanted.

And only the *Citizen* could suggest the citizen's best course of action. But who was the editor of the *Citizen*? Months later, at the preliminary hearing of the Strike leaders, the answer would come out, making the toggle between identities doubly ironic. Travers Sweatman – so reluctant to put words into the mouths of the employers – and Fletcher Sparling had co-edited the *Winnipeg Citizen*.[195] As mere 'citizens,' Andrews and Sweatman seemed tactically innocent and able to speak only for themselves; they had no promises to make or answers to give for the methods or motives of any Committee. As Executive 'Citizens,' however, they mapped the Citizens' plan of attack, levered the government against the Strike, and shaped the Citizens' public face, including its newspaper. As mere 'citizens' on Friday morning, they went along with Mayor Gray's suggestion that a 10-member mediation board be established. As Executive 'Citizens' that evening, however, they were already torpedoing the mediation.

3

Seven Hundred and Four Years Ago
at Runnymede

What made it possible to slide between the identities of 'Citizen' and 'citizen' was a larger narrative about rights and liberties and about British constitutional history. Standing before the bar of the constitution, in theory everyone was equal; a high-priced lawyer could demand freedoms in the same way that a labourer could. At a practical level, of course, one could not help interpreting the mass movement of the Strike as a revolt of the poor against a collapsing standard of living, against capitalist relations of production, and against the coziness of capital and the state. At an ideological level, however, it's clear that in 1919, 'the peak year of social unrest,'[1] the Citizens also feared a potentially precedent-setting rejection of the British constitution. Labour had constituted itself as a kind of anti-society.[2]

The most explicit expression of the Citizens' reliance upon constitutional narratives didn't come until the middle of June:

> Seven hundred and four years ago tomorrow – on June 15, 1215, at Runnymede the liberties and rights of British citizenship were secured, when the pistol was put to the head of King John and the Magna Charta was placed before him for signature. Many times in the last seven centuries have these rights and liberties been challenged and never once successfully. Those rights have been bought too dearly and too dearly upheld, defended and retained, to be successfully challenged in the Twentieth century in free Canada – in a Canada which is free only by the sacrifices of her sons through four long and bloody years of war.[3]

The timing of this evocation of historical rights and liberties was opportune: someone at the *Winnipeg Citizen* remembered the anniversary, and the *Winnipeg Telegram* fell in line, calling the Citizens' Committee 'the legitimate successor of the barons of Runnymede, the framers of the Bill of Rights, the originators of Habeas Corpus, the true progenitors of British democracy.'[4] But it wasn't a sudden epiphany. Throughout the Strike, the *Winnipeg Citizen* had been moving towards this foundational discourse by repeatedly invoking 'constituted authority' and by pointing at the history of British liberties. Early on, the Citizens spoke of a 'Citizens' Magna Charta.' Its clauses would contain a ban on sympathetic strikes and a prohibition against public service unions affiliating with other unions.[5] Soon the Citizens would also conjure up the Glorious Revolution of 1688 (not by name, of course, since the word 'revolution' might send the wrong message), and they reminded everyone that the coming of William of Orange had completed the British constitution, 'that Constitution which for 200 years has been the wonder of the world and the proudest boast of the Englishman.'[6]

One immediately asks two questions of such material. First, the obvious question: What advantages does this discourse afford the speaker? This is the Gramscian question about politics as propaganda, about ideological manipulation, about a dominant group's self-justification.[7] Pursuing such a question, we would note that in the Citizens' theatre the elected working-class Strike Committee turns out, counter-intuitively, to be the tyrannical King John. Except for 'pistol,' the language is archaic and hieratic, arriving in lofty places where certain words ('rights and liberties,' 'citizenship,' 'British') must not be taken in vain.[8] The question about rhetorical advantage also takes us into the Citizens' attempts to construct an apparently neutral middle class pulled together in opposition to tyranny, 'the great middle class who outnumber either of the other two classes, but who have lacked strength in the past because they have lacked organization.' The Citizens donated both an organization and an identity: 'Who are the middle class ...? In the long run, they are the people who pay the shot when organized labour pushes up the cost of production. Their function in the body politic has been but to pay. These are the people chiefly made to suffer in the revolutionary strike which has taken Winnipeg by the throat.'[9] In such ways, the vocabulary of class could be used to trivialize class distinctions, to discourage the lower classes from acting with class in mind. Homely metaphors were the order of the day: 'Even a goat will get busy if deprived of its food and water supply.' Although water had never been cut off, and bread service had been quickly reinstated by the strikers, the Citizens credited the middle-class goat's butting with the availability of milk and gas, the reopening of Eaton's and Robinson stores, of warehouses and restaurants. Other matters, less dear to 'middle-class' citizens, but of great interest to employers were treated as if they belonged in the same category as milk and bread: the 'dribble of water in the taps' had been returned to normal pressure. And the hated 'Permitted by Authority of the Strike Committee' cards had been removed.[10] Technically, the butting had been done by the executive members of the Citizens, but they graciously conceded thanks to the middle class.

It's tempting to remain at the level of the first question, the level at'' which ideology counts purely as a disciplinary tool, power's deployment of propaganda to put neutral observers off the scent; but there is a second, less easily answered question posed by the Citizens' recourse to the constitution: What, *apart* from propaganda, was compelling about the Citizens' discourse? Of course, what was compelling cannot in performance be separated from the question of ideological manipulation: convincing reasons often arise out of an ideological matrix, and convincing reasons can be expressed in manipulative ways. But that ought not to stop us from isolating the compelling reasons behind a particular social platform. The second question forces us to account for why certain narratives rationally convince us. We must allow that the Citizens (or the middle class or the working class) held certain constitutional commitments in a Rawlsian way – prior to or apart from the their class positions – not just as dressed-up versions of their material interests.[11] It is therefore not enough to ask whether labour had a valid grievance and to assess that grievance from a late-twentieth-century perspective. It is not even enough to ask which story more people consented to. Rather, we enter the territory measured out by Hobbes, Locke, and Adam Smith. On what principles can humans order a society? Where does right (especially right of force) reside? Which story can elicit the widest support – not just in raw numerical terms, but in terms of uniting various enfranchised classes – when it comes to the ordering of society?

An incident, politically insignificant in itself, suggests that Andrews had answered the question of social order to his satisfaction some time before. On 30 July 1904, Andrews was injured at Exhibition Park while participating in a five-furlong (2/3 of a mile) race for 'gentlemen's saddle horses with gentlemen riders.' Rain had made the track greasy. As Andrews was racing, a horse fell in front of him at the turn, he went over top, flew from the saddle, and, with one foot caught in a stirrup, was dragged along the ground some distance before his foot disengaged. His daughters were in the crowd, but at their distance didn't know at first that it was their father who was injured. Having been kicked by the horse on the temple, Andrews lay unconscious for two weeks. Afterwards he claimed that the *Minneapolis Journal* had reported his death, and that he had had the unusual pleasure of reading his own obituary.[12] What is most interesting politically about this event, however, is the name of Andrews's horse: 'King John.' We will pass by the possibility that King John, channelled by a horse, was at this late historical stage avenging himself upon common-law lawyers who always cast him as the enemy of freedom. Rather, we will simply note how near the discourse of the Magna Carta was to Andrews's tongue.

Andrews was a conservative, preoccupied by authority and freedom. He and the other Citizens rooted themselves in classical liberalism, which had been foundational to Canada's public goods of law and order, and security of person and property. The complex ways in which these liberal roots were applied (or not) to 'Permitted by Authority of the Strike Committee' signs, fire alarms, union intimidation, the freedom of the press, sympathy strikes, the breaking of contracts, deference to social 'superiors,' and collective bargaining, helped to determine whether the strikers or the Citizens would win the public debate. In effect, the Citizens said, 'We have a Constitution. Don't tell us where we can and can't go. Don't tell us what we can and can't buy. Don't tell us how we must dispose of our property.'

The strikers could make convincing points about bread prices, profiteering, and the miserable standard of living among workers. Yet when it came to more general assessments of the polity, the *Western Labor News* spoke in Marxist terms about a war between the bosses and the workers, and couched its solutions not in terms of mediation but in terms of class victory. Practically, this meant the wholesale withdrawal of services and labour solidarity; discursively, it meant that what, from the point of view of the strikers below, might sound 'democratic' – the dictatorship of the proletariat or, more euphemistically, 'a parliament of workers'[13] – forecast autocracy to everyone else. The *Western Labor News* spoke of forming local committees (i.e., soviets) to take over the management of businesses, and Strike Committee member Ernest Robinson of controlling the government.[14] On the first day of the Strike, the *Western Labor News* spoke as if labour were asserting its will, not participating in a democracy: 'The profiteers are charging 10c to 20c for an 8c. loaf. The victims bring the bread purchased to the strike committee. This **MUST STOP** and stop **NOW**. Dealers will not be allowed to bleed the workers in this callous fashion. High prices caused the strike. Let a hint suffice' (bold in original).[15] The *Western Labor News* spoke of being prepared to shut down Winnipeg's water supply and everything else – dairies, bakeries, and hospitals – if necessary.[16] On the final page of the paper (and reprinted in the *Manitoba Free Press*) the editors asked, 'How does the idea of using the new parliament buildings for a labour temple strike you?'[17] There was no point in reasoning with capital; power must be seized. In such a context, the invocation of the 'ancient constitution' and natural law theory emanating from Aquinas to Hobbes, Locke, and (*mutatis mutandis*) Adam Smith, made it easy for the Citizens to portray the Strike as tyrannous. One very important and fairly neutral commentator, H.A. Robson, felt that the very strength and thoroughness of the Strike worked against labour, convincing many Winnipeggers that Soviet autocracy lay behind the Strike.[18]

To invoke the Magna Carta and the Glorious Revolution, as the Citizens did, was to situate themselves in a powerful common-law antidote to the pretensions of revolutionary Marxism. The notion of an 'ancient constitution' – rooted not on first principles or an original contract, but on history, experience, and the authority of custom – had provided a justification for Britons to throw off the 'Norman yoke' and to assert their rights against King John. In this story, 1688 was not a revolution, but a reassertion of immemorial rights. Most Whigs and Tories denied that they had carried out a revolution. No claims that sovereignty rested with the people. No insistence upon a negotiable social contract between the ruler and the ruled.[19]

Yet despite the Citizens' invocation of 1688, their homely metaphor of the goat getting busy once his water supply had been cut off translated the conflict into Hobbesian terms, whether the Citizens were conscious of it or not: 'Self-preservation is the first law of nature, and that law has been invoked "by authority of the Strike Committee."'[20] In Hobbes's story, the final cause for humans acceding to the restraints a sovereign power imposes is 'the foresight of their own preservation.'[21] The Citizens invoked constitutional protections by claiming that average citizens 'are treated as having no rights,' but emphasized Hobbesian first principles: 'The right to live is a whole lot more vital than the right of any section to organize or to bargain collectively.'[22] If it had been a stretch for the striking metalworkers to speak of a 'living wage,' it was a correspondingly greater stretch to cast the middle class as a starving goat. But to speak in Hobbesian metaphors in either case – with the capitalists or the Strike Committee as the tyrannical sovereign – one had to speak melodramatically, since only in the most extreme case – when the sovereign didn't allow the initial self-preservation of his or her subjects – could Hobbes's citizens opt out of the Commonwealth. The Citizens' description of the state of Winnipeg – food at a premium, no milk or bread, no ice for hospitals, a dribble of water, no fire protection, no delivery of commodities, a tight gasoline supply, hardly any street transportation, in short, the temporary destruction of 'the whole fabric of our commercial structure'[23] – echoed Hobbes's description of men living without a political umbrella – 'In such condition, there is no place for

Industry; ... no Culture of the Earth; no Navigation, nor use of the commodities that may be imported by Sea; no commodious Building; no Instruments of moving.'[24] From the general acceptance of the notion that commercial exchange is an inherently peaceful activity,[25] it was no great leap to the inverse notion, that interruption of commerce was a belligerent act.

If, as C.B. Macpherson suggests, in a possessive market society the value of a man is determined by the market,[26] then the success of the Citizens' varied enterprises gave them a corresponding sense of their own worth, whereas collective bargaining could be seen as an attempt to do an end run around one's real worth, and, even more sinisterly, as an attempt to extort from worthy individuals a value that one did not have. Many, including *Manitoba Free Press* editor John Dafoe, could give passionate accounts of how Canada and the market combined to produce a naturally superior (and less class-ridden) citizen who, in the idiom of the day, had 'made good.' Dafoe claimed that British aristocrats lost their stiffness and phlegm 'in the atmosphere of go-as-you-please,' the dominant mode of 'Canadian social organization.'[27] Ideas about 'making good' were premised on a bipolar model of society that pretended to be inclusive. Socialism, alternatively, offered a more explicit bipolar model.

In the Citizens' imagined nation there was no class struggle; there were only responsible citizens threatened by a small group of cynical conspirators. The *Citizen* asked Winnipeggers 'to pause and think; Who are the workers? ... By what right do these people who caused the strike regard themselves as "The workers"? Who does not work?' Conceding neither an aristocratic inbred honour nor the Marxist bipolar model of warring classes, the Citizens thought along the lines of atomistic individualism, pushing aside class by claiming that all Winnipeggers, not just the strikers, were workers. In fact, those *not* striking were 'the real workers,' because they respected the rights of others, as expressed in commercial interdependence. To call those who had dropped their tools the 'working' class was 'a deliberate and foul insult' to 'the man and the woman in ordinary walks of life, who work at a desk, or canvas for orders, or who pound a typewriter, or fill columns with figures, who keep stores in a small way – who do their best to live and let live ... Unorganized they may be, but they, and not exclusively the "organized worker," are the real workers, the real proletariat.'[28]

If the Citizens acted as an organized group, they nevertheless didn't express themselves in group terms. The *Winnipeg Citizen* conceded that the 'wealthy manufacturer' did indeed exist, but, like the wealthy merchant, he was 'more fiction than fact.' Winnipeg's richest men

'were the workers of yesterday and if they have some money, it is due
to their own energy, foresight, brains and the money they have spent to
educate themselves. But yet they all work.'[29] To speak in this way was
to idealize conditions in Winnipeg, but the Citizens' great strength was
that their rejection of communal economic identities squared very well
with the great historical calls for individual liberties under the British
constitution.

It's perhaps not surprising that as lawyers of the common law, the
most influential Citizens – Andrews, Pitblado, and Sweatman – understood the Strike's constitutional threat. For many of the businessmen, the
most disturbing threat was to private property, but the Citizens' lawyers
fixed on other indicators, beginning with the permission signs. The Citizens called the signs 'an arrogation of sovereignty and a defiance of the
elected and constituted government,'[30] and this was true in important
ways. The need for the signs arose because union members intimidated
workers who wanted to stay on the job. The police couldn't be counted
on to keep the peace in such situations, since in voting to strike and then
deciding to remain on the job at the request of the Strike Committee,
they had made it clear that their present authority flowed not from the
Crown, but from the Strike Committee. The permission signs described
a real state of affairs, in which an alternate sovereignty operated outside
of the municipal, provincial, and federal governments.

Sign or no sign: it wasn't a simple matter, though both sides portrayed
it so. R.B. Russell protested that he had no interest in attacking the
authority of the state.[31] Indeed, it was imperative for the strikers not to
appear to have so much power that the government would call in the
army. Yet for the psychology of the strikers it was equally imperative to
be *seen* to have power. In practice, bread must move, but only with the
signs prominently displayed. Conversely, the business community was-
n't made up of humanitarians who wanted at any cost to get bread to the
starving. It was important for the business community not just that bread
move, but that it be sold in a free market and without the signs. James
Carruthers, manager of Crescent Creamery, felt sorry for people who
came in a pitiable condition, asking for milk. Even for 'sick people and
children who were living entirely on milk,' he could get no milk, he
lamented. But he, along with City Dairy president Max Steinkopf,
refused to allow the permission signs. Carruthers (who had been on the
old Committee of 100) and Steinkopf took the position that the signs
wasted time and caused discrimination. 'Unless,' Carruthers explained,
'we were able to distribute our product in a way that all the citizens of
Winnipeg would be able to get it, those who had the money to buy it,
there would be no delivery.'[32] This was not a question of the right to life

or of individual freedom. In effect, the issue of bread movement allowed businessmen to piggy-back economic freedom upon cries for the right to life.[33]

Businesses could provoke the strikers into showing that the Strike operated outside of the constitution if the strikers blocked the movement of bread that wasn't properly signed. Theodore Kipp, the general super-intendent of Ogilvie Milling, demonstrated this jockeying for position. He refused to let anyone outside of the proper authority dictate his terms of business, and he therefore removed the permission signs from his company trucks. His drivers were free to carry the cards on their persons to prevent attack, he told them, but he barred them from displaying cards on the trucks. Prodded by the Labor Temple, the drivers quickly closed the plant down. Although office staff and company officials continued to make deliveries, the plant was effectively shut for over a week.[34] Clearly, the fact that the signs were necessary meant that workers were being intimidated; and, just as clearly, the pulling of the signs meant that the Citizens wanted to provoke a confrontation. After the Strike, one of the persistent questions was whether the process of obtaining 'permission' from the Strike Committee amounted to an extra-constitutional procedure. The Strike leaders' defence lawyers claimed that the cards were simply a way of protecting the reputation of drivers against their fellow strikers, but Carruthers laconically testified, 'That is not the way it was put to me.'[35]

It is likely (though not certain) that the Strike leaders' defence counsel Marcus Hyman was satirizing the Citizens' warnings about extra-constitutional powers when he examined the City's sanitary inspectors. Why, he wanted to know, did the inspectors ask the Strike Committee to allow some staff to remain in place? Were the inspectors conspiring to subvert the civic government by taking their request to the Strike Committee? Inspector Ernest Hague was bewildered at Hyman's line of questioning:

Hyman: What made you desirous of clothing the strike committee with power?

Hague: There was no disposition to do so. That was long before there was any suggestion of a Soviet government or anything like that.

Hyman: There was no guilty intention in your mind when you moved that resolution?

Hague: Of what?

Hyman: To transfer the power of the city authorities to that of the strike committee.

Hague: No, not at all.[36]

Hyman took the same ironical tack in questioning inspector Douglas Little. Hyman was suggesting the obvious, that the sanitary inspectors were simply being practical and anticipating future problems – so, too, by analogy, was the Strike Committee.[37] No subversion intended. Of course, Hyman's analogy was deceptive, since the inspectors didn't need large permission signs to prevent intimidation by strikers.

Threats to constituted authority could be apparent or real, and come in innocuous or troubling ways. Andrews liked the sonorous sound of 'His Majesty's mails,' and even though at the post-Strike trials, his witness, Winnipeg Postmaster P.C. McIntyre, persisted in using the more pedestrian 'the mails,' Andrews kept returning to the more exalted phrase,[38] as had the *Winnipeg Citizen* when deploring 'a prohibition of the passage in and out of the city, of His Majesty's mails.'[39] Andrews calculated that the language of royal prerogative conferred dignity and seriousness, and wouldn't irritate Winnipeggers so long as the matter had nothing to do with royal prerogative, but concerned the communication technology of the average citizen. With the postal workers under an ultimatum to return to work, it would be satisfying if one could portray their walkout as somehow constitutionally illegitimate. Yet there was no 'prohibition' of, or systematic interference with the mail – it was merely a work stoppage that had no constitutional bearing.

As a misdemeanour, falsely sounding a fire alarm carried no constitutional significance.[40] A *campaign* of false alarms, however, was another matter. False alarms 'were rung in maliciously and continuously throughout the day and particularly in the small hours of the night from all parts of the City,'[41] so that the fire boxes had to be guarded.[42] Fire halls, of course, were no longer just home to neutral public services: they were also the distribution points for the *Winnipeg Citizen*,[43] therefore symbolic of the way that the state was being manoeuvred by private business. Since the Citizens had called themselves 'workers' too, and had manned the fire engines, the strikers were eager to watch and to jeer their managers and the comfortable sons of the rich scurrying about like peons. The younger siblings of the rich sons saw the newly deputized firefighters in a more romantic light: 'They had little sleep, but there was the spice of adventure as they raced through the streets with bells ringing.'[44] Among the new firefighters was Pitblado's son, whom his father described as 'fractured in an aeroplane fall in France (and God bless him for it, I say).'[45] American journalist Samuel Hopkins Adams was less reverent. He said that many of the volunteers were recruited from the 'gilded youth of the town,' and that 'in the first twenty four hours they had considerable of the gilding and much fat sweated off them, for more than 170 false alarms came in.'[46] Unlike postal workers withdrawing their services, a false alarm campaign did amount to conspiracy – the coordinated undermining of an emergency service run by a duly constituted level of government. The *Winnipeg Citizen* rightly asked, 'Would the people that jeer ... look at the joke in the same way if their own property was burning?'[47]

Similarly, incidents of violence and intimidation – people were booed when they entered stores to buy essentials;[48] Augustus Nanton's barn and twenty horses were torched;[49] crowds stoned delivery drivers;[50] speakers at Victoria Park encouraged strikers to 'deal with' people who returned to work;[51] Helen Armstrong and many others incited violence against workers who tried to cross picket lines[52] – could either be simple criminal matters or constitutional threats depending upon the context. At the Canada Bread Company, twenty or thirty women arrived and entered the bakery, interfering with the men working there. Eventually they were persuaded to leave by the manager, A.A. Riley, but they congregated outside and Riley called the police for protection. When the girls began to block the door and pull men across the sidewalk, the police seemed to find the whole show amusing; they didn't interfere. 'In fact, the police seemed well pleased with the operations.' Later, the mob forced its way up into the shop again, put Riley up against the wall, and shut off the machinery. When police arrived again, a union organizer told them, 'Well, we have the last damned scab out now.' 'That's fine,' the officer said. Afterwards, Riley demanded of the officer how he could speak in such a fashion. The officer responded, 'Our people will not stand for your carrying on business in this way.'[53] Strikers pulled William McCullough, a driver for Eaton's, out of his truck, pushed the truck back across the street, and slashed his tires as he watched. When a police officer arrived, McCullough pointed out the man who had stuck the knife into his tires. 'No, he didn't,' the officer responded.[54] As Adam Smith noted, commerce required 'the equal and impartial administration of justice.' Only such justice, 'by securing to every man the fruits of his own industry,' could give 'the greatest and most effectual encouragement to every sort of industry.'[55]

Were such acts criminal matters or constitutional threats? Were they merely signs of individual wrongdoing or did they tear a hole in a free commercial society? The defence lawyers for the Strike leaders would eventually mock the drivers for being afraid of women, and would speculate facetiously that since the drivers weren't sure of the identities of the crowd, that, for all the drivers knew, the crowd could have been made up of members of the Citizens' Committee.[56] Indeed, most of the violence was small potatoes; and as long as the threats and violence were between private individuals and privately constituted groups, there was no constitutional threat. But when the police refused to uphold the law, the Citizens were correct to argue that the constitution was under attack; and when Roger Bray, who was influential in the Great War Veterans Association, boasted that he had 3000 or 4000 men ready to march on Osborne Barracks and seize the arms of the militia, even the constitutional basis of the state was in danger. If Bray's comment was a joke as he later (and perhaps accurately) characterized it, it was an unwise joke.[57] If in some labour disputes business used private police to intimidate strikers, it's also true that given the limits of state policing, businesses sometimes had to provide their own security. Oral memory recounts that Eaton's manager H.M. Tucker feared that an unruly mob of strikers might march into the store. Tucker directed that a hole be made in the second floor above the Portage Avenue entrance, and he assigned fabric/drapery department employee W.H. Thomson the job of pointing the store's fire hose through the hole to repel any unwelcome patrons.[58] Although in earlier centuries it had been the Crown that had threatened common-law liberties, the real possibility was that now a mass of people, with a sympathetic police force, threatened those liberties.

Socialist journals, commenting after the Strike, tended to sidestep constitutional issues. *The Nation* saw a mass movement from below, a spontaneous outburst that the Strike Committee had to deal with on an ad hoc basis: 'the leaders frankly cannot control it.'[59] New York's *The Call* similarly insisted that 'the unexpected and unprecedented solidarity of workers' forced the Strike Committee 'to become a sort of political and industrial government,' as if the assumption of civic powers had been a chance occurrence rather than a calculated tactic. Silent on the threat to constituted authority, *The Call*, taking a page out of the *Winnipeg Citizen*'s hymnbook, sang of the Strike Committee's chivalry in directing bakers, milk drivers, street cleaners, and theatrical workers to return to their jobs so 'that the population did not starve and that health and general welfare of the city was preserved.'[60]

Within the Manitoba provincial government, opinions were divided about whether the Strike posed a constitutional threat. Attorney General T.H. Johnson created a 'Special Crown Prosecutors Department' in order to 'assist' Robert Graham, Crown prosecutor for the Winnipeg Police Court, in dealing with cases of intimidation and violence caused by the Strike. Graham, who sensed that only public opinion prevented Johnson from sacking him,[61] declined the 'assistance' and felt insulted by the insinuation that he wasn't doing his job. Nevertheless, Johnson dispatched Hugh Phillips, who showed up with his brother-in-law (then a law student), his own stenographer (a barrister from his office), an elaborate filing system, and a squad of special detectives.[62] Phillips became

Andrews's conduit to the Province,[63] and clashed frequently with Graham. According to Graham, the situation wasn't serious: most cases weren't complaints, but had been 'dug up' by the special detectives, and amounted to little more than strikers 'shouting abuse and empty threats.' 'These I dropped,' said Graham. In some cases the strikers were guilty, but the incidents trivial enough for Graham to plea-bargain for suspended sentences, and the only serious criminal cases, Graham felt, were those that occurred at the end of the Strike on Bloody Saturday. Initially, the Citizens imagined that they could attack the strikers through the Crown prosecutor's office. Andrews met with Graham and explained to him how the Citizens planned to prosecute the Strike leaders. But Graham proved uncooperative: 'I intimated that I was still Crown prosecutor and would decide how the cases would be handled.' Eventually Phillips and Graham worked out a modus vivendi whereby they split the cases.[64] Where the Citizens saw a threat to the constitution, Graham saw none, either because most of the incidents were trivial or because he didn't know that the police were highly selective in laying charges.

The initial silencing of Winnipeg's presses was perceived by the Citizens to be another major threat to constitutional liberties. By calling out the pressmen who worked for the three Manitoba dailies (*Winnipeg Telegram*, *Winnipeg Tribune*, and *Manitoba Free Press*), the Strike Committee monopolized the news. The Citizens immediately invoked Locke's liberal account of the natural rights of men. The gagging of the press enabled 'threats and intimidation to rule the city,' while for a short time people outside of Winnipeg couldn't get a true account of what was happening.[65] Even though the *Western Labor News* was far less hyperbolic than the *Winnipeg Citizen*, and was often a calming influence on strikers' passions, the Citizens claimed that there was now no press to 'stifle rumors of rioting, martial law, shooting and bombing, and … contradict the innumerable stories that are afloat and causing disturbances of the mind throughout the whole of the city.'[66] The tyranny over the press was a sign of 'Bolshevik' domination,[67] and a 'challenge to one of the bulwarks of our British Constitution, to wit, the freedom of the Press.' The challenge, said the Citizens, 'was at once taken up by the citizens and the Winnipeg Citizen appeared on the streets for free distribution.'[68]

While there are many similarities between royal censorship (the press's historical antagonist) and 'proletarian' censorship (as in Soviet Russia), it was deceptive to make such an equation in Winnipeg. The refusal to work the presses wasn't the same as political censorship, although the strikers' refusal was *intended* to have a censoring effect. Pressmen deserted the *Winnipeg Telegram* to protest the fact that capital controlled the press. The *Telegram* had set headlines such as 'Bolshevism Denounced and Labour Council Called Undemocratic,'[69] and had long been virulently anti-immigrant, urging that the constitution be suspended to deport aliens: 'The returned soldier who knows the psychology of the Hun from personal and costly contact experiences a very fine scorn for the constitution insofar as it protects the Hun within the gate.'[70] But Labour alderman Ernest Robinson, in defence of censorship, accused the press of more than it was guilty of – 'The reason that we have closed the capitalist press is because those papers said that the streets of Winnipeg were running red with blood' – and the *Winnipeg Citizen* immediately pounced: '(Ed. Note) – This statement of Ald. Robinson is absolutely beside the facts.'[71] The *Citizen* was right. Although the newspapers were biased against labour, neither the very conservative *Winnipeg Telegram* nor the *Manitoba Free Press*, Winnipeg's major paper with a circulation of 80,000, had made any rash claims about the Strike's *events*. The *Telegram* had vehemently criticized Bolshevism, but had also editorialized that socialism was not Bolshevism, that socialism meant cooperation,[72] and that the best way to prevent a strike was to keep the cost of living lower.[73] In the week before the Strike, in fact, the *Telegram* had stepped outside of its usual editorial policy to run an article greatly idealized in *favour* of labour, praising Emiliano Zapata's revolution in southern Mexico.[74]

No matter whether the strikers' position vis-à-vis the press was justified or not, they miscalculated. The *Western Labor News* not only failed to dominate the public sphere and monopolize information, but alienated average people, who said that they missed newspapers more than anything during the Strike.[75] While the accounts offered by the *Labor News* had been internally persuasive to workers, its discourse didn't become authoritative. The press walkouts also alienated newspaper publishers and lined up the mainstream press more squarely against the Strike. Although *The Call* followed Robinson's lead in later claiming that the Strike Committee shepherded its pressmen back to work 'on condition that the newspapers cease printing alarmist reports and refrain from inciting violence,'[76] actually the newspapers resumed publication in spite of the Strike Committee's censorship attempt. Aided by reporters from Chicago and New York, the *Manitoba Free Press* came back on the 22 May,[77] the *Telegram* and the *Tribune* on the 24th,[78] all three rabidly anti-labour.[79] This wasn't much of a leap for the *Telegram*; but now the *Winnipeg Citizen* too was being published, thanks, rumour had it, to the *Telegram*'s presses.[80] Soon Winnipeg would see *Telegram* articles in which, for example, Seattle's mayor called Winnipeg city officials 'yellow' for allowing unions to interrupt civic utilities: 'anyone that tried to deprive a city of water and light might as well put poison in the water.

No one but a lot of yellow backed city officials would let the unions get away with that.'[81] The *Telegram* directly reprinted articles from the *Citizen*,[82] and some articles, such as 'The Logical Autocracy,' simply repeated points made in earlier days by the *Citizen* about the suffering middle class.[83]

Labour's miscalculation was infinitely greater with respect to the *Manitoba Free Press*, since its circulation gave it huge clout. Back during the strike of 1918, editor John Dafoe had spoken of the 'incalculable good' that unions had wrought; he called on both labour and business to compromise rather than to exercise their full powers.[84] Leading up the 1919 General Strike, Dafoe continued to hug the middle of the road. Although there were articles and editorials depicting Russian Bolshevism in a bad light – not a difficult thing to do – most of what appeared in the *Free Press* struck a balance between sympathizing with the workers and warning against a *general* strike: 'Men are no longer concerned about the stock palliatives for poverty or industrial hardship. They have dragged the first principles of the system up to the light of day, and are working with live and explosive elements.'[85] Only in a single page-11 editorial on the day of the Strike did the *Free Press* finally come out against it, saying that because of a dispute between the ironmasters and their employees, it had been proposed that the citizens

Shall do without telephones.
Shall do without street railways.
Shall do without light.
Shall do without water.
Shall do without fire protection.
Shall do without police protection.
Shall do without food.
Of course it will only be necessary to carry the process of self-injury to a certain point and WE SHALL DO WITHOUT LIFE ...
For the sins of some of the people a certain number of lives shall be sacrificed.[86]

Up until this editorial, news articles and most editorials had shown no great bias.

But after seeing his pressmen walk off the job at a moment's notice on 16 May, Dafoe, as soon as he could publish again, made the *Free Press* the 'virtual mouthpiece of the Citizens' Committee,' and he published full-page advertisements on its behalf free of charge.[87] Beginning on 22 May, even the news articles were heavily slanted against the Strike. Front page, centre: 'THE ATTEMPTED SUPPRESSION OF

THE PRESS.' The *Free Press*, so Dafoe's revised narrative ran, wasn't an unintended casualty of the General Strike; no, the *Free Press* had been attacked because the revolutionaries 'did not like its views and feared its influence AT THE MOMENT WHEN THEY WERE ATTEMPTING REVOLUTION.' Dafoe wasn't in the habit of running uppercase letters within stories, but he did so now. Strikers were simply following the lead of 'Lenine [*sic*] and Trotsky, the High Priests of the Winnipeg Reds ... SO ONE OF THE FIRST ACHIEVEMENTS OF THE NEW REGIME IS TO SUPPRESS THE FREEDOM OF THE PRESS!'[88]

Less sensational than the issue of press censorship was a third perceived threat to constitutional liberties, the refusal of many strikers to honour contracts that they had signed in 1918. Crescent Creamery employees had even signed a clause in their contract that there would be no cessation of work for the life of the contract.[89] For all of the *Winnipeg Citizen*'s red herrings – babies dying for lack of milk – and its forays into racist propaganda, the paper had a legitimate constitutional complaint against the strikers: contractual obligation. Common law had always emphasized the sanctity of contracts. The *Winnipeg Citizen* reported Gideon Robertson scolding the civic employees for breaking 'a solemn and binding contract.' 'The ink was not dry upon it before the civic workers had broken it and walked out,' and he protested, 'No honorable man would endorse the action of the civic employees for one moment.'[90] To break a contract, added the Citizens, was to act in the manner of Russian Bolsheviks and the German Kaiser.[91] If a labour contract wasn't exactly a piece of the constitution, the two were nevertheless symbolically linked. How could workers who refused to honour a simple agreement be trusted to honour the more abstract and unwritten portions of the British constitution? If, as Chad Reimer argues, the strikers were trying to negotiate a new social contract,[92] reneging on labour contracts was an inauspicious place to begin such a negotiation.

How could employers feel anything but outrage at the notion of a 'sympathy strike,' a strike in which workers who were satisfied with their pay and job conditions walked off simply because other workers in a more poorly managed company weren't happy? Manager James Carruthers could understand the strike at Crescent Creamery the previous fall, since his workers had gone out of their own volition. This time, however, they presented him with demands and then walked out before he could even present the demands to the board of directors. His employees walked out because they were called out on the General Strike, not because of problems within the Creamery.[93] Just a short year before, the City of Winnipeg's Committee of 100 had acquiesced in a number of labour's demands, anything to keep civic employees off picket lines, and what had happened? A year later, still standing under a valid contract, city employees were again on the streets, not because they had any complaint, but because the *metal trades* had voted to strike.

For social contract theorists such as the Citizens, the very notion of a general strike couldn't help but resonate in disturbing ways, and amounted to a fourth, perhaps the most important, constitutional threat. Bertrand Russell had recently expressed philosophical reservations about the morality of a general strike: a *general* strike did an end run around the constitutional processes of democratic elections and parliamentary law-making.

> Put crudely and nakedly the position is this: the organized workers ... can inflict so much hardship upon the community by a strike that the community is willing to yield to their demands things which it would never yield except under the threat of force. This may be represented as the substitution of the private force of a minority in place of law as embodying the will of the majority.[94]

Almost quoting Russell, the *Winnipeg Citizen*, too, asked 'whether or not any section of the community may deliberately throttle the whole community for any purpose or at any time' – what was this but Bolshevistic dictatorship?[95] Conversely, the collective bargaining envisioned by the Citizens was tightly circumscribed. 'Collective' bargaining, yes; allegiance to large unions, no.[96] Gideon Robertson spoke the same language. The metal trades employees were 'utterly unjustified' in demanding the recognition of union umbrella organizations such as the Metal Trades Council. Using the vocabulary of classical liberalism, Robertson in Parliament defended the right to collective bargaining,[97] but only the craft unions already recognized by employers were acceptable.[98] At present, the *Citizen* claimed, the General Strike stood in the way of any concessions to labour. One could not bargain with open, frank, and confessed revolution, 'as they have it in Russia, Germany and Austria.' The *Citizen* would soon apply the word 'revolution' sweepingly to a wide variety of social actions: 'We are told that 35,000 workers in Winnipeg went on strike, starved babies and injured the sick, just because a mere handful of men, each side admitting the principle, were scrapping over a definition of collective bargaining! It is illogical. It is unreasonable. It is revolutionary!'[99]

As economically and socially troubling as the General Strike was, Andrews, Sweatman, and Pitblado saw beyond the threat to business-as-usual or even the threat to valid contracts. Probably it was Pitblado who felt this first. He was reputed to have a much deeper knowledge of the law than Andrews,[100] and during the Strike he proved the more excitable. Trained, as the lawyers were, in the principles of customary right, they sensed the traditional authority of the state being undermined, and therefore they interpreted the General Strike as a constitutional threat.

Many of the Citizens probably weren't aware of the depth of their ideological ancestry, but the lawyers were, and they cited William Blackstone,[101] whose *Commentaries on the Laws of England* identified the common law with principles derived from reason and justice by individual judges. By the nineteenth century, reason and justice had been superseded by precedent and case law,[102] yet Blackstone remained an authoritative legal text. British common law keeps its eye on the past. It looks always to precedent, to the rule of law against arbitrary will, to a 'constitution' made up of many documents and many judicial rulings. The common law is conservative, since it gives more weight to legal tradition than to juridical activism, even as, paradoxically, it is often activist decisions that become enshrined as constitutional principles. What would stop tyranny? Not bands of workers with their arms raised in rebellion, no matter how justly: to obey them would simply be to trade the tyranny of the king for the tyranny of the mob. Instead, it was hoped that against tyranny would stand law, which required everyone – ruler and ruled – to act within its bounds. And unlike the One Big Union, the Citizens allowed for *both* the sovereignty of the people (in Parliament) and allegiance to kings. This dual allegiance might irritate American-influenced republicans, but it captured the cautious popular imagination of English Canadians. In a partisan situation, where two social groups were battling one another, the common law could be seen as an independent arbiter, a neutral court to which both Crown and Parliament, or owners and proletariat, were petitioners. If contemporary Gramscian understandings of ideology can make such neutrality look naive, one cannot ignore the fact that the law, so conceived, was repeatedly used as an instrument to protect the rights of the individual.[103] These rights, said Blackstone, were threefold: personal security, personal liberty, and private property.

John Locke, another of the Citizens' ideological sources (though not cited by them), followed Hobbes in saying that to banish such insecurity and dread was 'the great and chief end therefore, of Mens uniting into Commonwealths.'[104] Echoes of these thoughts occur in Ed Parnell's description of the Citizens as 'a body of men banded together to keep law and order in this city and run the utilities of the city – endeavour to keep them going.'[105] But Locke's liberal state is no Hobbesian

Leviathan: natural law denies any person or authority the 'right to destroy, enslave, or designedly to impoverish the Subjects.' It follows that 'whatever form the common-wealth is under, the ruling power ought to govern by declared and received laws.'[106] In this way, Locke made theoretical room both for the state's power and for the individual's separate integrity.

It has been suggested that middle-class distaste for labour movements (and, at the same time, for rich industrialists) was at least partially rooted in the notion that the mass industrial system was leaving the liberal individual behind.[107] Though sympathetic to the strikers' grievances, Durkin's *The Magpie* (1923) ends with a pastoral denunciation of both labour and capital. By the end of the novel, the protagonist abandons stock-broking and goes to farm the land, leaving behind dictatorial capitalists and Strike leaders who preach 'a Gospel of Hate.'[108] The humane individual, it seems, can only withdraw from the extremist politics of both sides. However, individualist notions, sometimes against their will, fell into line with the Citizens' interpretation that the Strike drowned the individual and his rights in class-based struggle. The 1902 Winnipeg labour novella 'The Great Tribulation' demonstrates that labour spokespersons felt great affinity with Lockean notions of the individual and republican democracy. The clergyman David Paynter, whom A. Ross McCormack judges to be the mouthpiece of the author, 'Libertas Brammel,'[109] says: 'the first design of the architect and builder of this world of ours for its government, was a republic in form, a government in which each individual would have ample opportunity and be amply qualified in every sense to exercise the duties of his office for his own and the general good.' Yet Brammel seems unaware that the syndicate of employers (the organized enemy of the novel's strike) would have argued from a similar ideological position. He unconvincingly imagines the employers speaking only in terms of their own economic benefit. Such a story has obvious propaganda value for labour (the employers symbolizing naked greed), but Brammel therefore couldn't begin to explain why the ideology of Canadian employers was inviting and why it formed a basis for social cohesion.[110] In Brammel's novella, the six-month strike arises entirely out of economic issues – the workers' pay is too poor – while both employee and employer agree that the quarrel is not between communitarian and individualistic systems of value.

Since the Winnipeg strikers often spoke in terms of a group smaller than the state and larger than the individual, they often looked like a merely self-interested *party*, while the Citizens, though highly partisan, astutely confined themselves to a less partisan discourse, speaking for either the *individual* or the *nation*, and dropping, for example, traditional distinctions of Liberal and Conservative. The Citizens understood how to access the public sphere, and they disparaged any identity based purely on class. Even when many strikers were in effect agitating for new advantages for the *individual*, their rhetoric of group solidarity put them at a disadvantage to the Citizens.[111] In 1919, labour had begun, not very successfully, to create its own democratic institutions: union committees were in place and had some measure of democracy, but only for members; plans for 'soviets' even in theoretical stages carried all of the baggage of recent autocracy in Russia; joint committees with City Council (the bread committee, for example) were the scene of highhandedness by labour and of sabotage by the Citizens. But the middle class *already* had institutions – Parliament, the Bill of Rights – institutions of proven and evolving worth, so why call for new committees? Thus, the Citizens, though they functioned as a highly compromised party, tied themselves rhetorically to the great jurisprudential tradition of the common law, and decried the threat to 'British institutions.'[112] The phrase sounds jingoistic and xenophobic to modern ears, and no doubt it was designed to appeal to such sentiments. However, in the early part of the twentieth century, for most educated Canadians (including the labourite 'Libertas Brammel'), 'British institutions' was a synonym for the common law, democracy, and individual freedoms.

Although Locke and Smith criticized maladministration and disproportionate taxes on the poor,[113] the main thrust of what they said about commercial society fit in well with the Citizens' ideology. Both had made property the *sine qua non* of commercial society. The chief purpose for which men gathered together in Commonwealths, Locke insisted, was for the defence of their property. Smith, too, called government 'the defence of the rich against the poor, or of those who have some property against those who have none at all.'[114] For Locke, mens' freedom consisted of the ability 'to order their Actions, and dispose of their Possessions, and Persons as they think fit, within the bounds of the Law of Nature, without asking leave, or depending upon the Will of any other Man.'[115] In other words, property rights extended to human freedom in all its forms.

This sounds potentially friendlier to labour than in practice it was. In one sense, the working class desperately needed Locke's theoretical foundation. Without it, where could one go but backwards into a history where lords and sovereigns could control one's possessions and even one's person, or, if forward, into a future controlled by some alternative tyranny? Yet Locke was not a modern atomistic liberal. He argued that a class-divided society grew naturally from the fact that the more rational 'man' appropriates more of nature's bounty, and, 'by mixing his labour with it, he makes it his property.'[116] Although possession of 'the work of one's hands' could potentially justify a general strike, according to Locke people without property (as most English workers were) lost full proprietorship of their own persons when they sold their labour to someone else. In this way, C.B. Macpherson explains, Locke naturalized class differentials and thereby provided 'a positive moral basis for capitalist society.'[117]

Only fully rational and industrious men – i.e., property owners – could turf out a government that failed to protect them. When the propertied classes sent James II packing in 1688 and played king-maker to William of Orange, Parliament invoked the common law of the Ancient Constitution, saying that 'the pretended power of suspending of laws, or the execution of laws by regall authority, without consent of Parlyament is illegall.'[118] In Winnipeg, the Citizens lauded that ideological inheritance:

> Since 1215 an Englishman has, in theory, been free; but by the voice of autocratic dictatorship, which bore the semblance of properly constituted authority, the freedom of the Englishman was more or less of a farce until 200 years ago; since when such freedom has been established upon a solid foundation. That foundation was a constitution which was laid seven centuries ago, and which was not completed until William, Prince of Orange, came to England.[119]

The Citizens didn't mention that the great British constitutional tradition, with all of the focus on individual rights, hadn't seen fit to extend the franchise to the non-propertied until the mid-nineteenth century, and, in Canadian federal elections, not effectively until 1898.[120] Nor did the Citizens mention that it was a small oligarchy that controlled Parliament in 1688. Modern conceptions of democracy often emphasize the abolition of privilege, but constitutionalism and liberal democracy of course arose, first, to protect aristocrats, and second propertied burgers, against the monarchy.[121]

The legacy of 1688 was appropriated by both reformers and reactionaries. '1688' and the Bill of Rights had often functioned in the courtroom as a way of protecting private property against raids from above. Now, claimed the Citizens, freedom and property were threatened by raids from below. If it was laughable for ironmaster Thomas Deacon to say of his workers, 'I am paying them all that I possibly can,'[122] or for Thomas Roden of the CMA to claim that going down to a forty-four-hour work week would be suicidal for business,[123] such claims were

The Frozen Breath of Bolshevism

If Bolshevism comes to Canada it will do here what it has done in Russia and what it seeks to do in Germany.

LIBERTY will be destroyed, because Bolshevism means that one class shall rule over all other classes.

PROPERTY will be confiscated without payment to its owners. Your house, your household belongings if you do not own a house, your savings in the bank, your Victory Bonds—you will lose all these.

FOOD will be put beyond the reach of all except those who can seize it by brute strength, for Bolshevism takes the farmer's land, eats the food that is in sight and makes no provision for tomorrow.

LAWS will be annulled and the whole social system thrown into chaos. There will be no courts to adjust wrongs; no punishment for wrong-doers.

GOVERNMENT will be transferred from the elected representatives of the people unto the hands of committees, or soviets, without any central authority—without legislatures or parliaments.

WOMEN AND CHILDREN will be the property of the state. One of the soviets which set the fashion in Russia—the soviet of Vladimir—has already decreed that all women over 18 must register at a bureau of free love and there hold themselves subject to the will of any man who may order them to follow him.

RELIGION will vanish when respect for law and for women and children vanishes. Bolshevism worships not the God of our fathers, but license.

Russia, after her months of Bolshevism, is almost a desert, with millions of her people dead and other millions dying of famine; her industries paralyzed; her government in the hands of ruthless assassins; her law-abiding men and women either murdered or living in hiding, stripped of everything they possessed.

The Canadian idea guarantees every man a free and open opportunity to share in prosperity and happiness. The workman of today may be the millionaire of tomorrow. Labor to be efficient and productive must co-ordinate with capital; both must live under the laws which are made by the elected representatives of the people.

Our greatest bulwark against Bolshevism must be the intelligence, thrift and patriotism of the Canadian workman

This Article is One of a Series—Be Sure to Read Them All.

The wolf of Bolshevism threatens a factory.
(*Winnipeg Telegram*, 27 May 1919)

philosophically familiar territory at least, while the claims of William Ivens – that the gold standard had failed and ought to be replaced with a system in which one hour of 'adult human labour' equalled one unit of exchange[124] – seemed an unworkable utopian flight at best, and at worst an irrational recipe for economic chaos. Was it an attack on liberty for workers to be forced to join a union? Most bosses and a few workers certainly thought so.[125] More sinister were the rumours about confiscation of property, that houses on the Crescent had been allocated to the Strike leaders.[126] If this seems far-fetched, editorial comments that emanated from the *Western Labor News* (reprinted in the *Manitoba Free Press* for the edification of non-labour people) did nothing to squelch such rumours: 'Some employers say that they have a year's supplies in their larders. Well, we hope so, because when ours run out we shall need a boarding house.'[127] How could Winnipeg workers dismiss a Lockean approach to property? Didn't they, often unlike their British counterparts, own property? Didn't they have the franchise?

Locke had also spoken of 'noxious Creatures' who opposed civil society and liberty.[128] In 1919, these 'noxious Creatures' were given a modern face: Bolsheviks. The *Telegram* devoted a full page in large type to 'The Frozen Breath of Bolshevism,' complete with an illustration of a monstrously large wolf towering above a tiny and vulnerable factory. The points underneath combined the Lockean themes of individual liberty and Hobbesian themes of stateless chaos, with the threat of sexual violence thrown in for good measure:

If Bolshevism comes to Canada it will do there what it has done in Russia and what it seeks to do in Germany.

Liberty will be destroyed, because Bolshevism means that one class shall rule over all other classes.

Property will be confiscated without payment to its owners. Your house, your household belongings if you do not own a house, your savings in the bank, your Victory Bonds – you will lose all these.

Food will be put beyond the reach of all except those who can seize it by brute strength, for Bolshevism takes the farmer's land, eats the food that is in sight and makes no provision for tomorrow.

Laws will be annulled and the whole social system thrown into chaos. There will be no courts to adjust wrongs; no punishment for wrongdoers.

Government will be transferred from the elected representatives of the people into the hands of committees or soviets, without any central authority – without legislatures or parliaments.

Women and children will be the property of the state. One of the soviets which set the fashion in Russia – the soviet of Vladimir – has already decreed that all women over 18 must register at a bureau of free love, and there hold themselves subject to the will of any man who may order them to follow him.

Religion will vanish when respect for law and for women and children vanishes. Bolshevism worships not the God of our fathers, but license.[129]

If many of these claims were propaganda, Winnipeggers couldn't deny that some of the functions of government had been taken over by the Strike Committee, and the *Western Labor News* had reprinted speeches of Lenin calling for worldwide revolution.[130]

By mid-June, the Citizens would paint exaggerated images of the Strike leaders to fit in with Locke's 'noxious creatures,' leaders who had no 'understanding of British institutions, of the great foundation fact that this is a land of liberty protected by law.' They were 'born enemies of society ... the kind who should be sent away or put away.'[131] But a more humble and believable anecdote from Ed Parnell suggests something of what the Citizens feared. At a meeting between labour and employers set up by Mayor Gray back in March, Parnell had unsuccessfully advocated a conference of labour and capital to try to create better conditions for all. A 'gentlemanly discussion' ensued, in which 'nothing offensive was said,' but at the end of it, R.B. Russell announced, 'You are all wrong in your economics.' He then gave Parnell a book, *The Soviets at Work,* and added, 'When you get through with it I am satisfied you will know better what you are talking about.' Asked about the book afterwards, Parnell said, 'I consider it revolutionary in its character.'[132] Although Parnell didn't remark directly upon this, it seems apparent in his description of the scene that he was taken aback by the high-handed, yet nonchalant way that Russell dismissed, in its entirety, what might be called 'our way of life,' and wanted to replace it with a system that seemed to be full of tyranny, even if it hadn't actually gotten round to forming a 'bureau of free love.' Parnell wasn't being hypersensitive. Many of the prescriptions in Lenin's *The Soviets at Work* – reducing salaries to the level of the average worker, a six-hour work day, uniting the population in one cooperative, excluding the bourgeoisie from administration of the cooperatives – would have been enough to give the Citizens mild apoplexy, but Lenin went much further, and other of his prescriptions would have alienated not only Winnipeg's British middle class, but also large segments of the working class: peasant tribunals instead of courts, and the requirement in the transition from capitalism to socialism of a dictatorship, an 'iron rule' in which the wills of the thousands must be subjected to the will of one.[133]

The young Strike leaders pose by the Vaughan Street Jail in 1920 (incorrectly identified as Stoney Mountain Jail in previous publications). L–R, back row: Roger Bray, George Armstrong, Ald. John Queen, R.B. Russell, R.J. Johns, Bill Pritchard. L–R, front row: Rev. William Ivens, Ald. Abram A. Heaps. (N12322, Archives of Manitoba)

A brief sentence that appeared in the *Toronto Star* inadvertently put a fine point on Russell's nonchalance: 'Andrews is old enough to be Russell's father.'[134] Indeed, many of the Strike leaders were in their thirties, just coming into a full sense of their manhood and their leadership potential, while the foremost Citizens were in their fifties and at the height of their public and financial achievement.[135] Winnipeg's working class was young, the vast majority under forty years of age, and so were its leaders.[136] Except for Carpenters' Union member and founding member of the Socialist Party of Canada, George Armstrong, who was forty-nine and Canadian-born, the Strike leaders were young or foreign-born or both. Russell, a machinist from the Glasgow shipyards, was a mere thirty. He had listened, at Glasgow Square, to all kinds of radicals, and now he had risen to the national leadership of Canada's Machinists Union.[137] Other Britons among the Strike leaders weren't much older.

Upholsterer and city councillor Abram Albert Heaps was Jewish and thirty-four;[138] John Queen, from Scotland like Russell, was thirty-seven; Fred Dixon, farm labourer, construction worker at the Eaton's store, and MLA – was thirty-eight;[139] William Ivens, the minister who to the dismay of his Methodist superiors had mixed religion and Marxian politics to found Winnipeg's Labour Church, was forty.[140] Charles Gordon's *To Him That Hath* takes this common knowledge that the Strike leaders were young and goes one better. At the end of the novel's strike, seven strikers are jailed: it turns out that six are 'mere boys,' while the seventh was a man embittered by 'a long, hard fight against poverty' in another land, that is, England.[141]

Even more aggravating to the Citizens were the young Eastern European Jews: Sam Blumenberg, Solomon (Moses) Almazoff, and Michael (Max) Charitonoff. Blumenberg had a reputation as one of Winnipeg's most vitriolic radicals, lecturing on socialism, opposing the Great War, and producing his own plays with political themes.[142] Only thirty-three years old, he had been the labour leader who declared, 'We are going to run this city.'[143] In February 1918 at the Columbia Theatre, Socialist Party of Canada speakers had ridiculed the idea that Canadian soldiers were 'fighting for their country – they had no country, the capitalists owned it,' and Blumenberg had appended his defence of the Russian Bolsheviks: 'They had seized the reins of government at the psychological moment to obtain order out of chaos into which the revolution had plunged the country … The Bolsheviki are saving Russia and the workers of Canada cannot do better than emulate them in the Socialist work they have done.' The meeting concluded by omitting to sing the National Anthem.[144] Almazoff, twenty-nine, had told a Jewish audience in January 1918 that the Russian revolution was 'the Greatest Happening of the Twentieth Century.'[145] Charitonoff, the youngest of them at twenty-seven, had edited a Russian-language paper, *Rabochi Narod* (*Working People*) for the Ukrainian Social Democratic Party from mid-1917 until the paper was banned in the fall of 1918. He had applied for permission to publish a new paper. Its seed money came from Bolshevik sources.[146]

In December 1918, at the Walker Theatre, the young radicals had put themselves on public display. An audience of 1700 had listened as Blumenberg, Russell, Armstrong, and Dixon proclaimed solidarity with the Russian Revolution and denounced the Canadian government for its subversion of civil liberties. Charitonoff, only recently relieved of a harsh three-year prison sentence for possession of seditious literature, sat on stage too. The assembly ordered that a 'message of congratulations be cabled to the Bolsheviki,' and John Queen called for 'three cheers for the Russian Revolution.' The meeting ended 'with deafening cries of "Long Live the Russian Soviet Republic! Long live Karl Liebknecht! Long live the working class!"'[147] Soon the Citizens would fashion their own narrative of a Winnipeg conspiracy. When the Great War erupted, so this story went, Reds such as Russell, Queen, Armstrong, Dixon, Blumenberg, had responded with sedition. Afterwards, 'dishonestly masquerading as labor men,' they had hijacked labour to impose the IWW 'under the alias of the OBU,' and in this way planned to import Communist revolution.[148] If the story was inaccurate, a mass of young men cheering for Liebknecht and the Russian Revolution couldn't help but send a chill down middle-class spines.[149]

Should young Eastern European radicals tell Andrews – former mayor, volunteer against Riel – how to run a city? Should the Citizens who had built Winnipeg now sit cross-legged at the feet of the immigrant Russell, young enough to be their son, and be lectured that they were all wrong in their economics? In the minds of older, Ontario-born Citizens such as Andrews, the foreign-born, upstart crows – even the Britons and legislators among them – lacked a full grasp of constitutional government. This was confirmed for the Citizens when reports came of Strike leaders such as Rev. A.E. Smith proclaiming in Victoria Park that 'if the present Constitution stood in the way of progress, the Constitution should be done away with,' and 'if the flag, no matter what color, stood for the obstruction of progress, another flag which stood for the workers should be substituted.'[150]

To invoke the constitutional 'covenant' is, as Peter Brooks suggests, to invoke a master narrative into which each new episode can be fitted.[151] The 35,000 strikers, with their families, might represent half of Winnipeg,[152] but the narrative and emblems of British liberties began to tilt the balance against the Strike. *Toronto Star* reporter W.H. Plewman said:

I was not long in Winnipeg before I found that the flying of the flag on poles and the wearing of a small edition of it on the coat indicated the owners were against Bolshevism or an industrial revolution and against the strike, in so far as the strike represented an attempt to copy Russia's example. The general assumption, but one not entirely correct, is that the wearer of the Union Jack is against the strike. The flag has been adopted as the symbol of the self-styled Citizens' Committee of One Thousand; but while the wearer of it shows that he is against Soviet rule he is not necessarily against the main objects of the strike. For instance, I was given a lift by a business man. He picked up a friend who said: 'A chap back from Siberia had told me about Bolshevism, and as he saw it there, I'm out to fight it to the last.' But as an afterthought he added: 'As to the employers, they should be made to concede the eight-hour day and to recognize the unions.' In so speaking he voiced the feelings of fully 60 per cent of the citizens cooperating with the so-called Citizens' Committee.[153]

The Citizens began to wear the British flag; what could the strikers wear? With some success, the Citizens shoehorned the events of the Strike into the history of British constitutionalism. Methodist minister John MacLean found the rhetoric convincing – 'Some of the Capitalists are to blame for the High Cost of Living, but it looks as if at the bottom of the tactics of the leaders at the Labor Temple there is an attempt at Revolution' – and he worked in committee to force William Ivens to resign from the Methodist ministry.[154] The Citizens' narrative explained some events adequately and distorted others greatly. Above all, their story effectively set the ground rules for what could and couldn't be said, what moves could and couldn't be made. The Citizens' ideological claims against the Strike carried the burden of a long British struggle for rights and liberties. Did the Strike leaders feel the heat of the individual-liberties narrative? Look at it this way: as early as 4 June, they stopped requiring the permission signs.[155]

4

The Anointing of A.J. Andrews

He who wishes to be obeyed must know how to command.

Machiavelli

Monday, 26 May – Wednesday, 28 May

The battle over the meaning of rights and liberties and over the place of the Strike in constitutional history would continue long after the Strike had ended. For the present, the Citizens succeeded in convincing the City of Winnipeg to take a harder line. For the present, even Queen Victoria frowned from beyond the grave at the strikers: City Council decreed that there would be no fireworks for Victoria Day on Saturday if the Strike weren't called off.[1] Until Friday night's mediation meeting, Mayor Gray had maintained at least a modicum of neutrality. Unaware of how thoroughly the Citizens had stage-managed the failure of mediation, he now nailed his colours to the mast and took his frustration out on the strikers, mimicking the Citizens' line about solutions that would last until eternity. In order to move against those civic employees who had joined the Strike, he sought council's approval 'to deal with its employees in a manner befitting their going on strike and to prevent for all time sympathetic strikes in the city's service.' The time for dialogue had passed, and he was determined, again somewhat bombastically, 'to ensure for all time the satisfactory working of our public utilities ... so ably maintained in this time of stress by the citizen volunteers to whom the city owes a debt of lasting gratitude.' Gray asked for authority to fire strikers, and to take back into service only those who would 'be loyal to their signed contracts in the future.'[2] Since every City Council vote taken during the Strike had gone 9–5 against the strikers, there were no worries on Gray's part about the fate of his motion.

City Council's majority also took any surprise out of resolutions that the Citizens prepared concerning the fire department, resolutions that, while piling clause upon clause of self-congratulation and direction, maintained the fiction that the Citizens were only *requesting* change:

> RESOLVED that we as citizens of Winnipeg resent the action of the firemen and other employees of the City of Winnipeg who are engaged in public utility departments in going out on sympathetic strike, whereby the lives, health, and property of our citizens have been greatly jeopardized.
>
> The action of the city firemen is especially to be condemned in view of the arrangements that were made last year by the city council with the representatives of the firemen.
>
> We therefore, while not presuming to dictate to our civic authorities urge upon the mayor and council of the City of Winnipeg that only such striking employees of the City of Winnipeg should be taken back into the service of the city as are thoroughly efficient and are prepared to endorse the principles in the resolution attached.
>
> RESOLVED that this executive committee of one thousand citizens who when the city's firemen abandoned their positions of trust were able to provide for the second time in twelve months a volunteer fire brigade to protect the lives and property of our citizens which volunteer brigade, composed of busy men, have done their duty at great personal sacrifice and have now been on duty a sufficient time to justify the city council in immediately taking steps for the establishment of a permanent, loyal and efficient brigade who may be counted on to stay at their posts no matter what outside influence may try to persuade them to abandon their position of trust, do now request the city council to at once organize such a brigade.[3]

The Citizens, thinking as businessmen, saw the Strike as an opportunity to purge the City not only of disloyal, but also of inefficient workers. Aldermen John Sparling and Frank Fowler brought to Council motions which wouldn't allow firefighters to affiliate with a larger union, and which would require firefighters to sign an agreement banning sympathy strikes, among other things. While these motions weren't identical with the Citizens' resolutions, Sparling and Fowler laid the groundwork for the exclusion of firefighters who resisted the new rules. Even apart from having an inside track with Sparling and Fowler, and the support of seven other councillors, it's clear that the Citizens increasingly carried a kind of *moral* weight because of their constitutional language and also because they had indeed managed to staff the fire halls.

The volunteer fire brigade wore an aura of heroism. Less so the City's sanitation department. Yet the Citizens made a show of equality by volunteering to look after the city's fast-growing mountain of uncollected garbage too. During the meeting at the Board of Trade Building on 22 May, doctors had warned of a potential epidemic due to uncollected garbage, and one witty striker brought the house down by asking 'why in view of the wonderful service rendered the city by the Committee of One Thousand ...: did they not also allay the fears of the medical fraternity by cleaning up the streets and removing the garbage?'[4] No laughing matter, actually: the Citizens wisely took their cue from the joke and organized a garbage detail to clear the piles of refuse. Blustery Alderman Fowler, whose 1918 Amendment to deny civic employees the right to strike had so infuriated unions, declared that he was ready to collect garbage the next day if his services were required, adding, 'I have never been idle in my life and work doesn't scare me in the least.' The *Telegram* (with a large front-page headline) and the *Citizen* reported that the entire executive of the Citizens' Committee had volunteered to collect and destroy this garbage.[5] Of course, it didn't quite come to that. The organizer of the garbage detail, Travers Sweatman, spoke more circumspectly. He simply said that 100 volunteers *supplied* by the Citizens would clean and flush the streets,[6] wording that didn't bind any of the thirty-four executive members to scoop up offal, but allowed the work to be delegated to men supplied and paid for by supportive businesses – men perhaps not quite as full of volunteerism as the public-spirited Citizens, but more willing to pick up garbage for minimal pay.

The *Western Labor News* joked about how the pillars of Winnipeg society would 'demonstrate the dignity of labor by sweeping the streets and removing garbage'[7] – a half-hearted joke now, since even the *appearance* of such labour could only reflect well on the Citizens, and since the *Citizen* could all the more loudly trumpet Lockean ideals: 'The very fact of the Citizens' Committee offering men – offering themselves – to clean the streets and to collect garbage ... is unquestionably the most sensational and pointed evidence of their adherence to their principle – the upholding of constitutional government ... These citizens mean exactly what they say ... They are sincere in word and deed.'[8] In the trials after the Strike, a sanitary inspector, Ernest Hague, said that, yes, he had heard offers from citizens to help with the scavenging. Defence counsel Marcus Hyman wondered aloud if the offer had been made by Mr Sweatman on behalf of the Citizens' Committee, but Hague didn't know.[9] In the end, the supportive businesses didn't even have to waste much manpower on garbage, because when it began to pile up later in the Strike,[10] the health inspector asked Winnipeggers to burn their garbage[11] ... though there *was* a report of two prominent men who helped for several days sorting mail – C.P Wilson, K.C., leader of the Manitoba Bar, and P.A. Macdonald, Utilities Commissioner for the Province.[12] Prominent, but not members of the Citizens' executive. Apparently one banker and several other volunteers wandered down the streets trying to deliver letters, but housewives declined their mail until the Strike was over.[13]

The day before Meighen left Winnipeg, he made the Citizens' status semi-official by anointing Andrews as his bishop. Andrews and the Citizens had been angling for just such a role when they intercepted Meighen in Fort William and when they sabotaged Mayor Gray's mediation attempts. In part, this role was also the result of Meighen's inability to get the provincial attorney general, T.H. Johnson, to bang a few heads together. That Meighen had sidestepped Gray was no great matter constitutionally, but if Meighen wanted to use the courts against the strikers, he had no power to sidestep Johnson – since only the Province could initiate criminal proceedings. After Meighen and Robertson auditioned Johnson, they concluded that the provincial government was too intimidated by the crisis to pursue criminal charges. Meighen later recalled the meeting: 'From the Provincial authorities we could get no assistance whatever. There was no doubt in my mind but that Mr Johnson's state of fear and apprehension was exactly the same as that of the delegation which met us at Fort William.'[14] In all ways but criminal charges, the Province was onside with the Citizens and Meighen: the federal government ordered its employees to return to work or lose their jobs; the Province (and the City too) would soon follow suit. As well, just as the Citizens had urged, the Province declared that there would be no legislation and no compromises until the Strike were stopped. But the reigning provincial Liberals were leery about criminal prosecutions, and the provincial Conservatives, so discredited by the recent legislative building scandal, were in no shape to push anybody. The likeliest goad, the Citizens, were more identified with Conservatives than with Liberals, and couldn't prod the Province into a prosecution either.

If the Province was weak-kneed, Meighen needed someone of his own mind in Winnipeg. Privately, on Monday, Meighen wrote to Andrews, asking this representative citizen now to also 'represent' the federal Justice Department in Winnipeg. What exactly this meant, apart from Andrews now being able to bill the federal government for his time,[15] is not at all clear. Andrews was not, as some have mistakenly suggested, appointed 'acting' minister of justice – that office was already occupied by Meighen.[16] Instead, Meighen gave Andrews a position description that sounded almost like that of a provincial attorney general. Almost: Andrews wasn't empowered to begin any legal proceedings. 'Examine any evidence,' Meighen wrote, 'that may be available touching the conduct of the principle instigators of the present unfortunate industrial disturbance, with a view to ascertaining whether or not the activities of these men is of a seditious or treasonable character and to advise as to what should be done' [sic].[17] Meighen also directed Andrews to confer with the RNWMP should he find it 'in the public interest' to do so. All of these wordings suggest that Meighen was proceeding with great care. Years ago, as a younger lawyer, he had experienced how easily one's words could be misconstrued. He had advised a client to 'plead not guilty with considerable vengeance.' But the client wasn't as linguistically sophisticated as Meighen. Asked by the court what he wanted to plead, the client had replied, 'Not guilty with considerable vengeance.'[18] Meighen gave Andrews much latitude, but no *official* power – he charged Andrews to 'act in co-operation with Attorney-General of Manitoba,'[19] so that any Andrews slip-up wouldn't turn around and bite Meighen.

Andrews interpreted his mandate liberally. Why shouldn't he? He had not only gotten exactly what he had asked for less than a week ago in Fort William, but now he also had Meighen's imprimatur. So, instead of reading 'examine ... advise ... confer ... act in co-operation,' Andrews gave the greatest possible leeway to the word 'represent,' and he interpreted Meighen's words as a *carte blanche* to direct government forces into action. Andrews knew that he'd have to use his permission card discreetly, but he didn't hesitate, the next day, to tell RNWMP superintendent Cortlandt Starnes that he 'had been authorized to deal with General [sic] matters pertaining to the strike, also to take action against agitators if necessary.'[20] In fact, however, Andrews was only a legal adviser. He didn't have authority to take action, but only Meighen knew that. Meighen's reference to 'the public interest' and his invitation to Andrews to collaborate with the RNWMP and the Province allowed the Citizens, through the agency of Andrews, to move beyond supplicant to the state. A short weekend after Sweatman had insisted that he only spoke as a private citizen, Andrews and his closest advisers among the Citizens – Sweatman, Pitblado, and Coyne – had become de facto state security advisers for the Borden government. Andrews was now in a position to directly affect state policy towards the Strike and to direct state resources against labour.

The anointing of Andrews was essentially a private matter, but Meighen had made enough public noises by then to clarify where his blessing lay. The *Winnipeg Citizen* disclosed that Robertson and Meighen had 'let it be known, authoritatively, that they regard the so-called general strike as a cloak for something far deeper – a cloak for an effort to "overturn proper authority."'[21] This invested the *Winnipeg Citizen*'s narrative with legitimacy; more, it verged on the brink of inciting violence, because Meighen added that it was 'up to the citizens of Winnipeg to stand firm and resist the efforts made here to overturn proper authority.'[22] What should loyal citizens do? Could one ignore the common-law notion that each citizen was obliged to defend the state against subversion? Locke had framed the defence of individual freedom as a collective obligation of citizens; and the common law, as Pitblado, Sweatman, and Andrews knew, went even further. It held that citizens were obligated to guard each other's rights,[23] though the defence of freedoms was usually accomplished through the state. Not just the police but the private citizen ought to be prepared to bring offenders to justice and help keep the peace.[24] On this basis, the Citizens' Committee had already broadcast a call to arms at the beginning of the Strike, asking the community to 'guard the rights of the individual member' as well as to 'consolidate and stand solidly behind those public-spirited bands of citizens who are protecting the city.' Winnipeggers should 'be prepared to answer the call at any time when necessary to defend and uphold the free institutions under which we live.'[25] Although this call would eventually have repressive consequences, such a call in and of itself wasn't necessarily repressive, but a fundamental part of the liberal theory of the state. Within a few days, the call had become shriller, less clearly tied to the common law: 'Choose between being a Rebel or a citizen ... There is no middle ground. Revolution and anarchy, bloodshed, famine, death, or the Constitution, Peace, Law and Order! Choose.'[26]

The hieratic word and its common-law corollaries were intended to drive citizens into the arms of the Citizens, to swell out the ranks of the thirty-four businessmen and to get men into the militia under Brigadier-General H.D.B. Ketchen, men who, more than the labour-sympathizing Winnipeg police, would be fully under the control of the state ... and under the control of the Citizens. Like Andrews and many of the Citizens, Ketchen, the General Officer Commanding (G.O.C.) Military District no. 10, was a member of the Manitoba Club[27] and had been present at the organizational meeting of the Citizens' Committee.[28] A former RNWMP officer, he lived in Crescentwood among the rich, and after his retirement would go on to serve two terms as a Conservative MLA.[29] His house, still standing at 111 Nassau, was spacious enough, even if it couldn't quite compare to A.K. Godfrey's beautiful Cape Cod–style mansion at 144 Kingsway (also still standing).[30] The day before the Strike, Ketchen was relatively sanguine. He told Ottawa, 'I do not consider that [the strikers] have the slightest intention of disturbing the peace or causing trouble in the way of disturbances, but unfortunately behind all this trouble there is a well defined element of socialistic and bolshevist tendencies, who may at any moment cause a bad outbreak of rioting and general unruly conduct.'[31] He could commandeer an airplane, the only one in Winnipeg, in case strikers tried to isolate the city, and when he put out a call for a volunteer militia, 'the streets were packed ... The lawyers, doctors, big merchants, city and provincial officials were there, all anxious to be enrolled in what has popularly been termed the citizens' army.'[32] Initially, one thousand men were mobilized, while the others were subject to a call-up by prearranged signal at any time.[33]

Many Winnipeggers joined the militia and the Special Police, but not necessarily because they read the entrails in Meighen's words or acquiesced in the Citizens' story of a threat to the constitution. They joined because the Citizens knew how to organize. In the evidence gathered by the Robson royal commission, it's clear that the Citizens' Committee canvassed Winnipeg businesses for financial support, for the use of business vehicles, and for men. When queried about whether it contributed to any citizens' organization, Wood Valance Ltd Wholesale Hardware responded that it had contributed five men for military and Special Police duty, two three-ton trucks, and three touring cars for one month.[34] Similar responses came from business after business: the owners had sent employees to the militia or for other purposes outlined by the Citizens and had paid the salaries of the men serving. For employees, it wasn't a case of rushing to the Citizens' flag, but often a case of 'join the militia or lose your job.' A few men came from businesses run by members of the Citizens' Committee, but most came from *other* businesses lobbied by the Citizens – one might call this a Chamber of Commerce membership due, the cost of doing business in Winnipeg. What did the men employed by the *Ruthenian* Farmers Elevator Company think when they were dispatched by their employer to the Osborne Barracks to join the militia, and then read in the *Winnipeg Citizen* how aliens from Eastern Europe were to blame for an attempted revolution in Canada?[35]

In the days and weeks to follow there would be long letters from Andrews to Meighen on legal-size paper – Andrews had landed a client with deep pockets. Meighen apparently thought that he was signing on for occasional advice from Andrews. Au contraire, my friend. Only much later, when Andrews sent his bills, would Meighen discover that he had been Andrews's client all day, every day, including most Saturdays and Sundays; and that, a short time later, Meighen had also inadvertently engaged – again all day, every day – the services of Pitblado, Sweatman, and Coyne. From late May to 18 June, Andrews communicated with Meighen nearly every day. Two letters, punctuating important developments in the strike, each extended to over four single-spaced pages. Andrews revealed his anger, his fears, his dismay, his resolution at each new development, though always with a view to shaping Meighen's response. The two Tory lawyers would argue about policy and about the billing, but because they spoke the same idiom, Meighen assumed, not always correctly as we will learn, that Andrews was always under his direction and always spoke for the Citizens' Committee.

Later, when Meighen would part company with the Citizens on the question of criminal prosecutions, Andrews's voice would turn less affable, but through May and June the tone remained professional. In Meighen, Andrews had a sympathetic correspondent, vigilant in defence of the status quo. It wasn't that Meighen simply accepted Andrews's accounts at face value. Nevertheless, he had chosen to place Andrews in a position of influence, and he occasionally circulated copies of Andrews's letters among other federal ministers.[36] Andrews, for his part, knew that Meighen and Cabinet were hearing about Winnipeg from other sources too: Gen. Ketchen reported daily (and on Saturday, 21 June, hourly) to Major-General Mewburn, the minister of militia in Ottawa; Colonel Starnes reported to Commissioner Bowen Perry of the RNWMP, and, through him, to Secretary of State Newton Rowell. In this respect, Andrews's correspondence with Meighen was dialogic, since Andrews, the seasoned criminal lawyer, understood that each of his utterances would supplement or be challenged by the utterances of others. On 26 May, Ketchen told Ottawa: 'Only solution to my mind is have agitator leaders arrested for instigation and intimidation if this was possible consider bottom would fall out of movement to tie up the whole country by sympathetic strikes. Have mentioned this to Ministers here who are giving this consideration but difficulty of procedure and actual proof in support to convict under the existing laws seems to be problem.'[37] Clearly, the Citizens' organizing, lobbying, and publicity campaign was having effect. Although there had been no rioting, Ketchen, for one, was no longer as tolerant as he had been before the Strike, and his messages to Ottawa weren't so different from what one might hear around the Citizens' tables. Still, as we will see, Ketchen's messages weren't quite the same as what Meighen heard from Andrews.

Thursday, 29 May

Andrews's letters to Meighen were confidential, sent via the secure military telegram system. On the supposition that 'enemy' agents were watching, some telegrams were even conveyed in code, Slater's Telegraphic Code, in use thirty-five years earlier when Andrews had volunteered against Riel. Secret agent tactics; and yet at first Andrews predicted a quick end to the Strike. He had good reason for this. General strikes either succeeded or failed – they almost never lasted long – and the Citizens had mounted an effective resistance.[38] If the Strike went two weeks without attaining its object, advantage Citizens. If it lasted four weeks and hadn't been crushed, continuing to block commerce, advantage strikers.

Andrews's early telegrams to Meighen told the acting minister that he ought to consider the situation 'eminently satisfactory' and 'improving daily.'[39] Here at the outset of Andrews's direct association with the state, there was no whisper that the Walker Theatre meeting might have been the first act in a drama of sedition; no extended narrative of conspiracy through the Calgary conference; no call for charges and arrests. Andrews fulfilled his assignment from Meighen, and reported that he had 'sifted' through the evidence, but – in a refrain that he'd repeat several times – he had 'not found sufficient definite ground for justification any arrest [sic].' Meighen had asked for legal advice; Andrews replied with advice and strategy: 'only statements of Ivans [sic] which might justify arrests were made two months ago.'[40] Andrews was itching to arrest Ivens, but since the statements were made at an April meeting of Labour Church,[41] prosecution this late would raise too many eyebrows. The implicit criteria were not legal but pragmatic, political. Evidently, passions weren't inflamed enough for the concern about 'soviets' to be deeply rooted in the public imagination. Andrews claimed that according to Ketchen and Starnes premature arrests would expose the spies among the strikers.[42]

The advice not to arrest, said Andrews, came from Ketchen and Starnes, but Starnes recollected their conversation differently. At fifty-five, Starnes, was close to Andrews's age, and would go on to become commissioner of the RNWMP in 1923. Like Andrews, Starnes had served in the Northwest Rebellion as a young man.[43] A second campaign, no less, for these two loyalists, this time as generals, not soldiers. But Starnes said that it was *Andrews* who felt it unwise to prosecute the Strike leaders for sedition. A conviction was doubtful, and 'the publicity and stir resulting from a trial would do more harm than good.'[44] This is confirmed by the fact that Ketchen lobbied Meighen for arrests.[45] It seems that Andrews was already shaping policy, while pretending to Meighen that he was simply reporting the advice of others. The Citizens – here it's not clear whether on or against the advice of Andrews – asked Gideon Robertson to replace the Winnipeg police with the RNWMP, but Robertson told Starnes that it would damage RNWMP prestige if they were seen as strike-breakers.[46] The Citizens realized that if they wanted to do something about the perceived pro-labour bias and 'extra-consti-tutional' loyalty of the Winnipeg police, they'd have to find a different route. Already by 22 May, Citizens W.H. McWilliams and Ed Anderson had engaged the McDonald Detective Agency,[47] a sign that quite early the Citizens were on the road towards private policing.

In speaking with Andrews, Starnes planted a seed in Andrews's mind about a potential alternative to criminal proceedings. Starnes knew that Ottawa was contemplating changes in the Immigration Act that might make it possible to attack the strikers 'without the cumbersome machin-ery of a jury trial.'[48] Eventually, after the Strike, Andrews would want the public onside in the form of a jury hostile to the strikers, but for the moment, it might be better not to rely on the shifting winds of public opinion, and he took Starnes's hint.

Meighen, having returned to the nation's capital, told the House of Commons that he had no intention of taking the Strike lightly. A general strike, he warned, *always* usurped governmental authority and would challenge the constitutional order: 'It did so result in Winnipeg; it must ever so result.' If every labour dispute in perpetuity would be decided by all unions striking together, 'why then you have the perfection of Bol-shevism.'[49] This was the narrative of Andrews and the Citizens. At the same time, Meighen also mouthed Andrews's soothing line that the Strike 'was not very successful,' even as erstwhile Borden adviser, lawyer C.H. Cahan, tried to ring alarm bells, crying out that a labour leader had predicted that the strikers 'would, within three months, kick the Government off Parliament Hill, without even resorting to arms.' Cabinet, however, as Cahan complained to Borden, treated his warnings with 'contemptuous indifference.'[50] Instead, it took the road that Andrews had advocated, declining to intervene, except with federal employees.[51] Yet while Andrews, with Meighen warily following his lead, predicted a swift good riddance to the Strike, far other things were brewing.

5

The Flag-Flapping Stage

Friday, 30 May – Saturday, 31 May

For the first few days of the Strike, the initiative had been in the hands
of the strikers. By the latter part of May, Andrews reflected a consensus
among the Citizens that the Strike was all but over. The Citizens, acting
in concert with the City of Winnipeg, had arranged to man the firehouse,
the post office, and the water plant. Wives and daughters, such as Grace
Moody (whose sister Maryon would marry Lester B. Pearson), had been
drafted to handle telephone switchboards.[1] Largely because of pressure
from the Citizens, bread and milk were being delivered without discrimination or permission signs, and local men, not imported strike-
breakers, ran the public utilities: the gas works, the streetlights, the
power-house. To move volunteers around the city and to give returning
veterans a ride home, the Citizens commandeered a fleet of 1000 automobiles. Felicitously, this arrangement just happened to permit drivers
to recruit returned soldiers for the militia, in case the Strike turned nasty.
Should the soldiers agree, they didn't have to go home at all, but could
be taken directly from the train to the Minto Barracks for demobilization
and then on to the Osborne Barracks, where the militia waited.[2] A wire-
less plant had been cobbled together atop the Free Press building to re-
establish 'communication' with the outside world, but the first message
wasn't exactly a cry for help: 'Perfect weather conditions have prevailed
since beginning of strike, producing holiday appearance with orderly
throngs on streets. Military not in evidence.'[3]

Nonetheless, for rhetorical purposes the Citizens pretended to be
more on the defensive than they actually were. After the bread problem
had been solved, after the permission cards had been torn up, after the
waterworks employees had been provoked to leave by management

increasing the water pressure, the *Citizen* still cried, 'There is only ONE ISSUE ... THE RIGHT OF THE PEOPLE TO LIVE THEIR OWN LIVES, TO CARRY ON THEIR NORMAL ACTIVITIES, TO HAVE POLICE AND FIRE PROTECTION AND ADEQUATE FOOD AND WATER, without having to ask the permission of a Strike Committee or Soviet.'[4] And yet, the *Citizen* agreed with Andrews: 'So far as Winnipeg is concerned, the strike is broken and the sway of the Bolsheviki threat is diminishing hourly.'[5]

Spoken too soon. Sitting in the upper reaches of society, Andrews and the Citizens operated mostly on second-hand information gleaned from sources closer to the street. If Andrews was more analytical than the Bourbons among the Citizens, he was also frequently wrong or myopic. Ditto Meighen, at third remove. Two developments changed the shape of the Strike and forced the Citizens to change their strategy. First, the rising anger of the war veterans hadn't registered on the Citizens, even though they knew that despite the convenient transportation arrangements returned soldiers weren't flocking to the militia. Instead, businesses were having to assign employees to it. Second, the Police Commission, without consulting the Citizens, decided to tighten the screws on the police by forcing them to sign oaths severing all outside union affiliation.

On the evening of 29 May, after Meighen had repeated Andrews's confident words in Parliament, a number of war veterans sympathetic to the strike held a three-hour meeting in Winnipeg. They were led by Roger Bray, a native of Sheffield, England, who had arrived in Winnipeg in 1903 and had joined the Canadian army in 1916; and by A.E. Moore, president of the Manitoba Command of the Great War Veterans Association (GWVA).[6] The results of Thursday night's meeting became public on Friday morning: two thousand returned soldiers marched on the legislature, shouting for the Province to affirm compulsory collective bargaining and end the Strike. To great cheers, Moore denied any interest in establishing a soviet and proclaimed that returned soldiers would fight against any attempt to do so. They'd call back at the legislature the next day, he vowed, to check on Premier Norris's progress. All that Norris could do was promise to do his best and insist that he greatly *appreciated* the soldiers coming to visit him in the chamber. The protest closed with all singing 'God Save the King.'[7]

It was a bombshell, demolishing part of the Citizens' narrative of a British constitutionalism defending itself against alien ideologies. The Citizens had given rhetorical importance to the war veterans and painted them as defenders of the Canadian order against the Bolsheviks, a narrative easy to accept for Citizens such as Ed Anderson, whose son Joseph had been killed at the Battle of the Somme;[8] or Pitblado, whose wounded son Edward had recently been demobilized.[9] Many on both sides of the Strike were prepared to cheer at each and every hallowing of Great War sacrifices. The Strike had begun sooner rather than later, the Citizens had declared, because the 'rebel leaders' feared 'that it would be dangerous to wait longer ... There were already too many returned soldiers in the country to suit them.'[10] A nice rhetorical flourish ... and reasonably prudent, one would have thought: in the January riots, returned soldiers had beaten up Germans, and just before the Strike – less than three weeks before the pro-Strike veterans marched to Norris – veterans had marched to Norris urging the deportation of 'disloyal' aliens. He had responded that he couldn't step into federal jurisdiction.[11] At the outset of the Strike on 15 May, J.O. Newton, acting president of the GWVA, had traced Bolshevism back to Germany, and had said, 'The returned men are not the men I take them for if they are going to stand for any more of the dirty work of the Hun.' Challenged that he was attacking labour, Newton said that he favoured severe treatment for war profiteers and wouldn't defend capitalists. The GWVA, which one of its executive members estimated was split 50/50 for and against the Strike[12] – he clearly underestimated support for the strikers – eventually adopted a resolution that was neither completely to Newton's taste nor to that of the strikers. Rather, full of ambiguity and threat, the resolution expressed 'full sympathy with the purposes of the present strike,' pledged itself to law and order, and declared that after the Strike was settled returned soldiers and labour would 'get together and discuss the deportation of the enemy alien.'[13] The executive of the GWVA and Winnipeg newspapers, pretending to see only what they wanted to see, took this as a declaration of neutrality.[14] However, of the contending factions among the returned soldiers, those sympathetic to the Strike were the largest, and their repeated appearance in parade formation on Winnipeg streets posed the question of just how long civil order could be maintained. Despite the Citizens' pro-soldier rhetoric, Winnipeg's upper class was afraid. Financier Augustus Nanton set aside his Packard 'with its shining paint and brass,' for 'a rather disreputable Overland car,' and had his chauffeur exchange a smart uniform for an old suit and a cloth cap. On 4 June, 2500 pro-Strike soldiers would parade down affluent Wellington Crescent, and A.L. Crossin would feel that 'these men only needed weapons to become an army.'[15]

When the Citizens had targeted several accurate broadsides at William Ivens, charging him with the shameful sin of pacifism, all the *Western Labor News* could do was to respond lamely that Ivens's *brother* had five war medals for bravery, and that Ivens was born no more than seven miles from *the birthplace of Shakespeare.*[16] Now, however, the returned soldiers were throwing their weight behind the strikers. With the impressive demonstration at the legislature, the Strike Committee could harness the soldiers for its own rhetorical purposes. The soldiers, trumpeted the *Western Labor News*, strongly objected to press descriptions of the Strike leaders as 'English and Scotch anarchists.' The soldiers 'made it absolutely clear that this campaign must be stopped, and stopped at once.' Premier Norris was buttonholed and asked whether he was prepared to call soldiers who sided with the strikers 'Bolsheviks' or 'Aliens.'[17] No, he wasn't. The soldiers demanded that Norris come up with an equitable resolution to the Strike, and they protested the Police Commission's demand for a loyalty oath. Caught up in the wave generated by the soldiers' march, the *Toronto Star* (a progressive though not socialist newspaper) asserted that 'the ex-soldier-citizens have given their full sympathy and support to the strikers in their demands for betterment of their conditions, on the definite understanding that there is to be no disorder or lawlessness.'[18]

Andrews wasn't much moved by the political opinions of the returned 'heroes,' but he had some difficult footwork to do with Meighen. In his 31 May letter, Andrews reported that 'a large and very ugly tempered deputation of returned soldiers' had marched to the legislature to demand compulsory collective bargaining. They were reported as 2000 strong, but he deliberately underestimated their number to Meighen: 'In my judgment 500 would exceed the number, the balance were strikers.' The situation, he continued to insist in face of the evidence, was still 'very favorable.'[19]

The other, simultaneous development that rocked the Citizens was set in motion on 29 May, when the Winnipeg Police Commission sought to crank up the heat on police officers who had voted to join the Strike but who remained on duty at the request of the Strike leadership. The immediate issue was whether the City could get the streetcars running again. The previous evening there had been talk of this at Mayor Gray's office, and Crown Attorney Robert Graham had suggested, 'If you can operate the street cars, the strike will collapse, as that will be the most cogent evidence that you have control of the situation.' But if the strikers interfered with the streetcars, whose side would the police take? Graham added, 'You cannot expect [General Manager of the Winnipeg Electric Railway A.W.] McLimont to try to run the cars unless you can assure him of adequate police protection. You can only call on the military in case of a riot. You cannot give police protection while your police force is under the control of the strikers. It is time to tell the police what they should have been told on May 15th, that they must entirely disassociate themselves from the strikers or turn in their equipment and be dismissed.' Mayor Gray encouraged Graham to advocate this course to the Police Commission.[20] Although Graham declared empathy for police officers – their pay was small and their grievances were ignored – the next day he argued in front of the Commission that the police must either sign anti-union loyalty oaths or lose their jobs. In truth, there was no difficulty at all in convincing the Commission and its chair, Alderman John Sparling. Sparling, who had already done much for the Citizens, probably thought that he was again bearding for them, since the appointment of Special Police had earlier been suggested by members of the Citizens. The Commission gave officers until one o'clock 30 May to sign or be dismissed. The union, conversely, urged its members to ignore the oath, later known as 'The Slave Pact.'[21]

Graham cautioned Sparling against meeting with the police as a group, but if there absolutely had to be a meeting, Graham advised against speeches. Sparling immediately scheduled a group meeting and mounted a platform to make a speech: 'He opened on an almost pathetic note. "When you men signed that strike notice, did you stop to consider the position you were putting ME in? When people speak to me about the police, they don't say THE police, they say YOUR police. As I said to one of MY firemen yesterday –" He got no further. A chorus of "*Your* Police" "*Your* firemen" "When did you buy the police & firemen?" Cat calls & boos' [*sic*]. Graham later offered his assessment of Sparling: 'If his courage and brains had equaled his vanity, he would have been an exceedingly valuable man during the strike.'[22] The upshot of the meeting and a follow-up meeting was that the deadline for the loyalty oath was moved to Tuesday 3 June at 1:30.[23] When leaders of the Citizens heard of the ultimatum, a tactic which Sparling hadn't cleared with them, they would be angry.

On Saturday morning, as promised, the veterans marched a second time down Kennedy Street to the legislature. The *Western Labor News* this time estimated that 10,000 returned soldiers followed the flag: 'The legislative Chamber was packed and thousands stood outside in the drizzling rain.' By encouraging people to wear the Union Jack in their lapels, the Citizens had visually married their cause to patriotism, a clever PR tactic that annoyed the strikers: 'The "Winnipeg Citizen" has come to the flag flapping stage. The strikers are orderly. Their demands are admitted to be reasonable ... So there is but one thing to do. Flap the flag.'[24] Inside the chamber the soldiers saw a man in the press gallery with a flag in his lapel. Believing that the flag signalled affiliation with the Citizens, whom the strikers by now viewed as the principal opponent to a settlement, the soldiers accosted the man. Strikers claimed that they 'respected the flag and they did not want to see it prostituted by the Committee of 1000 … to screen their low down dirty work … Men are wearing the flag these days who spent money with lavish hand to escape military service.'[25] The Citizens found this seizing of flags unpatriotic: 'The men objected to the wearing of the Union Jack by certain of the citizens, calling it prostitution of the flag to use it in this manner. They plucked the little silk square from the breast of several men including the secretary of one of the cabinet ministers.'[26] Reports would come that certain of these men had boys overseas.[27] Outsiders had earlier wondered 'whether the Citizens' Committee served the country well by making the flag a party symbol in an industrial war. It is true that they profess to be standing up for free British institutions, just as though Soviet rule were in force in Winnipeg. But there is no Soviet rule.'[28] In short order, the Citizens would float the idea that it had been enemy aliens, not returned soldiers who had done the flag-plucking: 'Citizens wearing the Union Jack [had] … been publicly insulted by alien enemies who have dared tear the flag from their breast.'[29]

At Saturday's march, Premier Norris again declared his great affection for labour, and pleaded that most of the Strike issues were beyond his jurisdiction.[30] Again Andrews claimed that the *Western Labor News* exaggerated the number of protesters, and he offered Meighen an optimistic assessment of the new threat. According to Andrews, Captain Frederick Thompson, the veterans' representative to the Citizens' Committee, said that the marching soldiers 'had no connection with any of the Returned Soldiers Associations,' and that 'the effect of these demonstrations … will be rather the opposite than the effect desired … It will arouse a feeling of loyalty among the returned men.'[31] Andrews felt sure that the GWVA would fight the 'Bolshevists.' He was wrong. At first, he and the Citizens were taken aback that the returned soldiers supported the Strike. The *Winnipeg Citizen* only gave short page-three reports of the soldiers' marches. Clearly, the growing militancy of the returned soldiers didn't augur well for the Citizens, and they knew only one way of responding, albeit an effective way: exploit the anti-alien feeling among the veterans. Would the veterans be so eager to jump up in support of the Strike if they knew that the Calgary Conference, led by non-Canadians, had advocated revolution?[32] Very quickly, veterans, and therefore aliens, became a central preoccupation of the Citizens.

Sunday, 1 June

On Sunday, Alderman John Sparling arrived at Graham's doorstep upset, saying, 'Graham, you've got us into an awful mess.' He had been at a meeting at Premier Norris's office, where everyone, except for Herbert J. Symington, had said the police loyalty oath ultimatum was a mistake.[33] What did he mean by 'everyone'? Graham wanted to know. Sparling replied, 'Well Isaac Pitblado and several others whose names I cannot recall.' Then the phone rang, and Sparling's wife told him that Citizens' executive chair A.K. Godfrey was at his house and wanted to see him immediately.[34] With Graham beside him, Sparling was forced to listen to the Citizens disparage his actions. He tried to mitigate the criticisms by telling the Citizens that he had pushed back the date of the ultimatum. This impressed Godfrey even less, 'Good God Sparling. That is even worse. Having taken a stand you ought not to have backed up.' But the Citizens hadn't offered help or suggestions, Sparling complained. You neglected to inform us, Godfrey responded.[35] In short order, Sparling was hauled before a group of '75 citizens' at Mayor Gray's house to explain himself. Among those assembled were Premier Norris, Attorney General Johnson, the editors of Winnipeg's three major papers, and, from the Citizens, Godfrey, Pitblado, Coyne, and perhaps others.[36] Sparling defended the loyalty oaths, and after two hours of debate, says Graham, 'the majority were with us.' Graham was perhaps being over-kind to himself, and in the next breath added a more accurate summary of the feeling in the room: 'The rest while still feeling the ultimatum to have been a mistake saw that having been given it must be enforced.'[37]

If Pitblado's and Godfrey's dismay at the ultimatum had been a strategic stance designed to make the civic and provincial authorities heed the Citizens more, they couldn't have come up with a better tactic. But it wasn't a tactic. Andrews, too, despite his hard line, called the loyalty oaths a mistake.[38] No doubt the Bourbons among the employers would have been happy to see repression, and it was true that at the outset of the Strike the Citizens had called for Special Police to leaven the police force, so that it wouldn't be entirely in the hands of the strikers. Some of the Special Police protecting businesses from vandalism were unarmed men,[39] and the Citizens' lawyers understood that at this juncture they were more in the business of public relations than of repression. It wasn't that they sympathized with the police. According to American journalist Samuel Hopkins Adams, it was fear of a wider crisis – 'There won't be a wheel turning between Winnipeg and Vancouver' – that forestalled extreme governmental action, such as martial law.[40] But this was precisely the point. The Citizens understood that too severe a misuse of the state's authority could fundamentally undermine their image. In 1918 there had been talk of invoking martial law,[41] and there is evidence that throughout the 1919 strike, some Citizens demanded martial law,[42] but Andrews knew that what they really wanted was not trouble but business as usual ... on their own terms. They needed a road back to 'normal' circumstances, those glory days when their use of injunctions had effectively hamstrung labour.

The actions of Graham, Sparling, and the Police Commission allowed Andrews to depict himself to Meighen as a mediator between the hardliners who wanted to fire the police and the softies (some of them, he revealed, even among the Citizens!) who wanted Meighen to 'recede' from his 'firm' decision to dismiss postal workers refusing to cross the picket line. Since forty firefighters and several postal workers had already returned to work, Andrews worried that the Police Commission's ultimatum would only provoke the strikers. The police had recently signed a contract and, despite voting to strike, hadn't actually walked out, so 'to insist upon a new term now' would leave the City liable to charges of altering a contract. I'm a pragmatist, Andrews was implying to Meighen, not an ideologue. In Andrews's view, there was no middle course between the regular police force (strengthened, if necessary, with special recruits) and martial law.[43] The commission's action threatened to lead to a wholesale dismissal of police officers, and thence to disorder in the streets because there existed no present alternative to the regular force. If threats brought postal workers and firefighters back on the job, then make good on the threats. If the loyalty oath prevented police from staying on the job, then scrap the oath. Andrews claimed credit for persuading Sparling and the Police Commission to extend the time for the men to sign the oath,[44] though according to the *Western Labor News*, it was the Railway Running Trades Mediation Committee, not Andrews, which did the persuading.[45]

It seemed to Andrews that Mayor Gray and the commission were acting on a false premise: namely, that the RNWMP would step in. But Senator Robertson had already dismissed such a scenario. And in any case, there weren't enough men to undertake the work.[46] Andrews and General Ketchen advised Gray that the RNWMP would not police Winnipeg, so civic authorities ramped up the appointment of special police alongside the regular force. Judging by Andrews's comments, he had been privy to Robertson's decision. Andrews told Meighen, 'It would never do to have the Mounted Police take the place of the striking policemen, it would prejudicially affect our situation throughout Canada, and the Mayor should have realized that he had not a sufficient volunteer force to take the place of the striking policemen.' It was astute of Andrews to echo Robertson without attributing the idea to him. Andrews could seem to be a fount of wisdom: when Meighen discovered that Robertson advised an identical course, it would appear to Meighen that Andrews must be quite dependable, since he and members of Cabinet were on the same tactical page.

As storm clouds gathered, Andrews moved to steel Meighen's commitment to the Citizens' cause. The danger of which Machiavelli warned the 'prince' lay dormant in all of Andrews's dealings with Meighen: 'Each of the counselors will think of his own interests, and the prince will not know how to control them or to see through them.'[47] Downplaying his own substantial role and that of the Citizens, Andrews told the acting minister that the present favourable position was 'directly and solely owing to the stand you took with reference to the postal service.' Andrews congratulated himself for having predicted that 'deputation after deputation, probably even members of the Citizens' Committee themselves' would pressure Meighen to rehire delinquent postal workers. 'All the good you have accomplished,' said Andrews, 'will be undone if you do alter your decision.' In a kind of précis of the moral and pragmatic grounds upon which a just liberal order should base class relations, Andrews explained, 'You treated them with perfect fairness, you gave them every opportunity to come back after they had committed one of the gravest faults possible and any weakness now must result in an entire lack of discipline throughout the whole service.' The assumptions were clear: offences against the sanctity of contract ('one of the gravest faults possible') must be met with a stern face and an awareness of the obligations of rule. Despite the dangerous new developments of the loyalty oath and the veterans' parades, Andrews again concluded with the rosiest possible scenario: unless some serious mistakes were made, the Strike was practically over.[48]

His optimism was for Meighen's consumption. Twenty-four hours later, Andrews concluded that circumstances warranted a daily briefing for Meighen. On Saturday, Andrews had written modestly, 'It will do no harm for me to give my viewpoint.'[49] On Sunday, he told Meighen that 'after discussing the matter with Senator Robertson I thought it wise that I should keep you advised daily by letter.' Andrews wanted his voice alongside Ketchen's and Starnes's at the centre of the state's dialogue on the Strike.

Publicly, Andrews and the other lawyers increasingly took on the role of marshalling the anti-Strike forces. Sunday morning, he and Pitblado addressed delegations from Saskatoon and Moose Jaw. The lawyers were preaching to the choir, and Andrews came away certain that the Saskatoon delegates had been completely convinced that 'there is no justification for a sympathetic strike in their City.'[50] To the Moose Jaw delegates, Pitblado revealed that the husband of one sick woman had to go to the Strike Committee to beg for milk. 'She has since died. I do not know how it affects you, gentlemen, but it makes my blood boil.'[51] The

full story only came out after the Strike, at the preliminary hearing, when
the husband, Leslie Parker, was cross-examined by E.J. McMurray,
defence counsel for the Strike leaders:

McMurray: Your wife was seriously ill and had been for some time,
            I presume.
Parker: Yes.
McMurray: Was she actually on a milk diet?
Parker: No.
McMurray: She was using other food, but expressed a desire that
            she would like to have milk?
Parker: Yes.
McMurray: The doctor did not prescribe milk for her?
Parker: He prescribed everything she wished.
McMurray: Would I be intruding on your feelings by asking what
            was the trouble – pneumonia, or something like that?
Parker: Consumption.
McMurray: It was only a matter of a short time?
Parker: Yes.
McMurray: So that the question of what she ate was not a question
            concerning her death at all?
Parker: No, it had no bearing at all.
McMurray: You don't offer this as a complaint, do you?
Parker: Oh, no. I just said my wife was seriously ill.

Of course, Pitblado never specifically said that the woman had died from
lack of milk – that was left to the Moose Jaw delegates to infer. And he
couldn't be called a liar simply for omitting to mention that the Strike
Committee had readily granted Parker a permission slip for all the milk
his wife wanted.[52] Why should one have to get permission to buy milk?
Pitblado also lamented that the wearing of flags suddenly seemed to
cause offence. The flag wasn't some special Citizens' Committee badge,
but merely a sign that the Citizens stood for constituted authority: 'We
were asked by General Ketchen of this city to … wear our flags to show
we were loyal citizens.'[53] Sunday evening, Andrews addressed eight
hundred of Winnipeg's Citizen volunteers, rallying the troops and giving
the Citizens' version of the events that led to the Strike. The volunteers
'were very pleased at being taken into our confidence and will start out
with new zeal and determination to see this strike through.'[54]

Some objects, Mikhail Bakhtin has said, materialize in the process of
creativity,[55] and this was true in a couple of the Citizens' stories. For
public dissemination, the melodrama of a sick woman dying from want

of milk, and the story of a foreign conspiracy; but for Meighen a more measured story. Andrews had telegraphed Meighen on Thursday – in code, no less – to tell him to disregard suggestions of new evidence against the strikers: 'Find suggestions that different persons had definite evidence not already known by your department are unfounded stop.'[56] This puzzling statement was in all likelihood a pre-emptive heads-up to ensure that Meighen wouldn't be shocked by a news item about to appear in the Sweatman-edited *Winnipeg Citizen*. On Monday's front page, the *Citizen* announced that 'the city solicitor and the minister of justice or his personal representative here have definite information that the revolution was brought to a head by certain men from across the Atlantic, who arrived in Canada seven months ago and who selected Winnipeg as the place wherein to fire the opening gun by a general strike. These men ... have duped the workers into aiding and abetting them.' The organizers were plotting 'to establish a soviet republic in Canada.'[57]

Not to worry, Andrews's coded note told Meighen. Whether the 'minister of justice' was Charles Doherty (currently in Europe), and his 'personal representative' was Meighen (the *acting* minister of justice); or, more likely, whether 'minister of justice' referred to Meighen, and his 'personal representative' to Andrews, it's clear that Andrews had foreknowledge that the front-page shocker would be published, and that it wasn't the work of an overeager maverick. Moreover, Andrews also knew that the material was all spin, long-known facts imaginatively reshaped to inflame Winnipeggers. The story was even known to Meighen ... only it hadn't been decked out in its present finery before. Translated, the mundane facts behind the melodrama of political intrigue only meant that some of the strikers were British-born, that they had emigrated to Canada in the previous year, and that at some point in the past they had mentioned 'soviets' with approbation.[58] The *Winnipeg Citizen* had warned about foreigners and impending revolution before, but now a narrative about dangerous aliens was coalescing around these fragments. For Andrews, this tactic meant that he had to move between two discourses: in private with Meighen, Andrews treated the insurrection story nonchalantly, while publicly he treated it with great seriousness, and he would eventually choose it as the whole story of the Strike. Why use code? Normally, one would rely on code to keep sensitive information or a new tactic from the enemy. In a sense, therefore, the public was the enemy, and code was intended to keep profane eyes from seeing the disconnection between the Citizens' public and private stances.

While Pitblado and the *Citizen* inflamed the public with stories of dying women and conspiracy, Andrews told Meighen in measured tones that nothing had occurred since the beginning of the strike 'to justify any arrests.' His legal partner Frederick Burbidge had examined all the RNWMP evidence, while Andrews had examined General Ketchen's material. Meighen could discount any rumours that Ketchen, Colonel Starnes, or Mayor Gray had material to justify arrests. The Mayor, Andrews said bluntly, 'tells me he has no evidence whatsoever.'

Although there was no evidence, it did not follow that there would never be evidence. If advocacy of alternative economic and political systems wasn't criminal at present, it could be retroactively made criminal, as Andrews hinted: 'The law as it now stands seems to me to be very ineffective in coping with the Bolshevist movement that is taking place.' He reported that Gen. Ketchen had obtained 'a copy of Lenine's [sic] speech on the Russian Soviet Government and a publication issued by the Labor News on the Russian Bolshevik and the Soviet.' 'Lenine's speech' probably referred to *The Soviets at Work*, which young R.B. Russell had before the Strike given to Ed Parnell, assuring the business owner that the pamphlet would clear up his woolly economic thinking. Both pamphlets were 'sold openly' at vendors in Victoria Park. Even more disquieting, agitators were 'addressing large audiences all over the City advocating Bolshevistic and Soviet views.' June 1st had been the date set in March at the Calgary conference for the launching of a general strike in support of the withdrawal of troops from Russia, and if the day was passing relatively quietly in Winnipeg, Andrews was nevertheless apprehensive: 'it would appear to me that the purposes of the Calgary Convention are being accomplished to a limited extent.' In the gap between Andrews's recognition that there was no evidence to justify arrests and his simultaneous request for immediate legislation or an Order-in-Council to deal with the situation, one sees the narrative of a constitutional threat materializing. Andrews closed his Sunday letter to Meighen with word on the street that 'mobs are coming down to wreck the Industrial Bureau [the Board of Trade Building].' Although Andrews dismissed this rumour, he clearly meant it to be ominous.[59]

Monday, 2 June – Tuesday, 3 June

The mob rumoured for Sunday arrived on Monday. Andrews's perspective was narrow, and he concerned himself little with the wellsprings of the Strike's popular support. While he was addressing eight hundred volunteers Sunday evening on the south side of Portage Avenue, north of Portage in Victoria Park church was happening: 'thrilling, pulsating, wonderful.' But the Labour Church never made it into Andrews's letters to Meighen. Denied use of the Board of Trade Building, 'the enormous

Under the Board of Trade Building's cupola and above the left
entrance, a sign reads, 'Headquarters Citizens' Committee of One
Thousand.' (Winnipeg Strike 7/N12298, Archives of Manitoba)

The sign has vanished, courtesy of the angry crowd. (Winnipeg
Strike 8/N12299, Archives of Manitoba)

congregation of 7,000 to 9,000 that surged into the park stood for three hours and listened with rapt attention to address after address packed with information and enthusiasm.'[60] This spilled over into Monday when the returned soldiers, bolstered by many civilians – a much larger crowd than Friday or Saturday – marched on the legislature. Roger Bray again knocked on Premier Norris's door, asking, 'What about the profiteers? What about [pork baron Joseph] Flavelle? – (Boo's) [sic] – What about the 1,000 that raised the rent?' Bray wanted to know why the manager of six telephone girls had been told that the Citizens wouldn't allow the government to reinstate them. Why couldn't the Province solve the problem with pro-labour legislation? Angered when Norris again pleaded impotence, the crowd marched from the legislature towards the St Boniface council chambers, and on the way noticed that the Board of Trade Building at Main and Water had sprouted a bold new sign, 'Headquarters of the Citizens' Committee of One Thousand.' Said the *Western Labor News* euphemistically, the sign 'was soon in [the marchers'] hands.'[61] Andrews was more honest: the soldiers 'being in a very ugly mood wrecked our signs.'[62] 'Most unruly,' was how Ed Parnell characterized the marchers, and he felt that that day 'there was very great danger of serious affairs.'[63] In the end, the marchers also gave a hot time to several Eaton's and Coca Cola drivers, but no violence ensued.[64]

Despite Andrews's earlier sense of calm, and his prophecies of the Strike's collapse, the worm had turned. That same day, anarchists exploded bombs in eight American cities. The homes of Judge Charles C. Nott in New York and of US Attorney General A. Mitchell Palmer in Washington were both damaged, though most Winnipeggers didn't hear of this 'Revenge of Radicals' until Tuesday morning.[65] Some of the Citizens, especially Pitblado, cried for Gen. Ketchen to call in the militia: Pitblado was in a highly nervous and excited condition and was very much afraid of an immediate attack upon the Industrial Bureau where the Citizens' Committee had its headquarters. 'The G.O.C. [Ketchen] refused to be stampeded, and in this he was supported by the mayor.'[66] Andrews, though not quite so inflamed, backtracked from his prophecy of a quick end to the Strike, and said that it was 'the general impression that we may expect violence ... at any time.'[67] There were problems as well with the Citizens' volunteers, who could 'hardly be restrained from resenting the tearing down of our signs and the personal assaults on our members, and the taking from them of their flags.' Rather than re-post the signs, the Citizens chose discretion, as Andrews told Meighen: 'Our Committee has decided not to put up the signs again or do anything that would be a pretext for a riot.'[68]

Premier Norris in action, addressing the Great War Veterans Association on 4 June. (Winnipeg Strike 6/N12297, Archives of Manitoba)

Also under onslaught was Andrews's resolve that the only acceptable outcome would be for the Strike to be defeated unconditionally. He admitted to Meighen that the Railway Running Trades Mediation Committee had complained to the Police Commission that the Citizens were blocking mediation efforts between the ironmasters and metalworkers, that the 'Citizens Committee are not only not helping them to get the metal men to reach a fair settlement, but are trying to prevent this.' Andrews feigned surprise, and said that as soon as he got wind of this, he 'saw members of the Citizens Committee and urged them to rectify this at once.'[69]

It's highly unlikely that Andrews was telling the truth, or that he was only representing the views of his clients. Given the consistent gap between Andrews's public and private comments, it's much more likely that he wasn't yet prepared to let Meighen see a full picture of the Citizens. Better that Meighen should still perceive Andrews as a mediating figure, and that Meighen continue to blame the strikers, not the Citizens, for any impasse. While Andrews sent Meighen down the garden path, the *Winnipeg Citizen* characterized Premier Norris's response to the demonstrators as a vote of confidence in the Citizens' policy – 'Premier Norris took the stand that no negotiations could be instituted until the present sympathetic strike was ended'[70] – and the paper also published an article insisting that the Strike had moved far beyond the original dispute between the ironmasters and their employees. The Citizens formally 'requested' (the word was deceptive, since the ironmasters had agreed to such 'requests' more than a week ago) that the ironmasters and other employers 'leave their disputes in abeyance until the larger questions now involved in the general strike are disposed of.'[71] The next day Andrews cheerfully yarned to Meighen the excellent news wrought by his calming influence: the Mediation Committee was still in session, and the formerly intransigent Citizens were now brokering an agreement between ironmasters and employees.[72]

But there is no evidence of any softening in the Citizens' hard-line stance against a settlement, and in only one area did they retreat slightly. Andrews reported that if the Police Commission couldn't get the police to cut themselves off from all outside organizations, then the Citizens would urge the commission to drop the demands (for now) and accept the far less restrictive declaration of loyalty that the police had already agreed to. On Sunday, Andrews was still hopeful, because Alderman Sparling had hopes for a compromise declaration.[73] Soon it became apparent, however, that the police situation was deadlocked. The police officers rejected the Mediation Committee's loyalty oath; the Police Commission, in response, had decided to fire the whole force, but hadn't yet taken action. By Tuesday, Andrews was concluding, 'It would look as if things were approaching a crisis.'[74]

Even though government buildings were shut down on Tuesday to mark the birthday of King George V, thus giving a brief respite from demonstrations, the quiet was deceptive; meetings were being held at Victoria Park; 'inflammatory speeches' were still, according to Andrews, 'fomenting revolution and the overthrow of all governments.'[75] Yet the *Winnipeg Citizen* spoke as if a rosy-fingered dawn were arriving:

> Hundreds of civic employes [*sic*] are back at their posts; the firemen are back in large numbers; clerical staffs are resuming work; the bookbinders are meeting today to decide upon an urgent demand from a majority of the union that they return to work; railroad employes [*sic*] are hastening to correct their error; retail and wholesale clerks and warehousemen are, in hundreds of cases, returning to work; up to last Monday six thousand strikers had returned to their posts and during the past seven days the number has steadily grown.[76]

Andrews was less sanguine in private. He told Meighen that each day 'a few more' strikers were returning to work, but at the price of an increased danger of riots.[77]

Clearly, Andrews had lost his optimism. Not his resourcefulness, however. One suggestion that he made on Tuesday to Meighen would prove more effective than the others. If the Strike wouldn't collapse on its own, why not apply some legal creativity to snuff it? At present, no law hamstrung the Strike leaders. Andrews urged Meighen, 'If it is at all possible some adequate law should be enacted either by Order in Council or Statute enabling us to reach the leaders in this revolutionary movement. I believe if these leaders could be dealt with firmly it would very soon end the strike.'[78]

To counter the mounting pressure applied by the returned soldiers, the Citizens adopted a two-pronged strategy: they embarked upon a greater rhetorical defence of their 'movement,' and, to divert the soldiers, they increasingly blamed aliens for the labour troubles. Neither strategy was new, but the Citizens, fearing that they might lose the propaganda war, ratcheted up their efforts. They needed to get out from under the repeated charge that their members were drawn from the city's elite. Because they now had volunteers operating in many facets of the public sector, and because more people had chosen sides, they could claim a populist provenance, and could call themselves a Citizens' Committee of Ten Thousand rather than One Thousand.[79] The volunteers could be said to include working men, doctors, lawyers, professionals of every description. 'Thousands of employees' were members, and yes, 'one or two employers' too.[80] The increasing number of volunteers changed nothing in the Citizens' power structure – the executive was still firmly in charge – but now the Citizens' 'middle-class' rhetoric could at least seem less arbitrary. The 'middle class,' said the *Citizen*, consisted of 'the overwhelming majority of our people, the farmers, the greater part of the city dwellers, the prosperous mechanics, the shopkeepers, the clerks, the professional classes and others.'[81] These people were 'the grain between the upper and the nether millstones ... the ham in the industrial sandwich – the Belgium of the industrial world.' In the *Citizen*, the rise in food prices and the spiralling cost of living were magically transmuted into a middle-class grievance against *labour* (rather than against business owners), for the middle classes 'always in the last analysis pay through the nose for an increase in the price of labor or the cost of production of either necessities of life or luxuries.'[82] Now, with the operation of the Citizens' Committee, the 'middle class' was a force to be reckoned with, and only for this reason were the strikers crying foul: 'Because that [middle-class] force insists upon its own rights being permanently safeguarded before any petty quarrels between a group of employers and their employees are considered for adjustment it is accused of bloody intent.' The middle class had no wish to 'bust' the unions. 'It would just as readily 'bust' the employers if the employers trampled upon citizens' rights.'[83] This latter point and its sister point about war profiteers was always made with the clash of cymbals, though in no case was it ever specified *who* was a profiteer or exactly *what* in the repertoire of employers ought to be 'busted.'

The Citizens also ensured that in future demonstrations a contingent of 'loyal' soldiers would neutralize the PR generated by pro-Strike soldiers. Captain Frederick Thompson, GWVA representative on the Citizens' executive, refused to admit that the Citizens had anything to do with organizing the soldiers' Loyalist Association.[84] Andrews's letters to Meighen suggest otherwise: Andrews lobbied Thompson, and afterward told Meighen, 'I am satisfied the executive of the Board of the Great War Veterans will aid us all they can in combating the Bolshevist Revolutionary movement.'[85]

Wednesday, 4 June

June 1919 was one of the hottest Junes in memory; day after day temperatures soaring to new highs.[86] To the heat, to the marches, the strikers added intimidation to stop postal delivery, and a renewed prohibition on milk and bread delivery. Andrews passed on an unsubstantiated rumour that a woman thought her husband, a postal worker, was being murdered when a crowd of two hundred beat and hung an effigy of him on a lamp post.[87] In any case, a principal difficulty facing opponents of the Strike was that strikers and their sympathizers controlled the streets. Andrews thought the situation extremely critical.

The Citizens also sought to increase pressure by attacking aliens. At one level, the Strike was a generational clash, the Socialist Party of Canada and its Young Turks against the older representatives of the established order. But if one wanted to inflame the majority of Winnipeggers, one couldn't hang one's hat on a battle of generations. Better odds exploiting the post-war hatred for Germans and Eastern Europeans. According to C.B. Macpherson, war is a temporary substitute in the nation-state for the old tribal cohesion,[88] and homegrown elites have always known that to cover oneself in the flag is a high-percentage thing to do. This was especially true in 1919, when so many had sacrificed family members for the flag. But even long before the war, the conservative *Winnipeg Telegram* had defined North Enders as barbarians at the gates:

> There are few people who will affirm that Slavonic immigrants are desirable settlers, or that they are welcomed by the white people of

Western Canada ... Those whose ignorance is impenetrable, whose customs are repulsive, whose civilization is primitive, and whose character and morals are justly condemned, are surely not the class of immigrants which the country's paid immigration agents should seek to attract. Better by far to keep our land for the children, and children's children, of Canadians, than to fill up the country with the scum of Europe.[89]

By 1919 Eastern Europe had become nearly synonymous with Bolshevism, and the Citizens asked Winnipeg to choose either 'The Red Flag of class hatred; of autocratic brutality; of utter selfishness; of out-Hunned frightfulness'; or the Union Jack, 'the symbol of pure democracy' that Canadians had followed in the recent war.[90]

During the war, citizenship had centred on the themes of Anglo-conformity, an 'ideology of service' to the state, and subordination to the common good, all derivative from the understanding of the citizen's common-law obligations.[91] In 1919, Anglo-conformity had at least two faces: the much-lauded volunteerism that was now keeping public services operating; and its darker twin, the Citizens' gratuitous attacks on foreign-born workers.[92] Immigration meant the arrival of new and radical ideas; no doubt the Citizens in part feared a rejection of the British constitution and British styles of behaviour. Yet the Citizens also instinctively understood René Girard's notion that to restore harmony a community tends to select a sacrificial victim from its fringes, someone almost, but not quite, human. In the *Free Press*, *Tribune*, and *Telegram* the first of a series of the Citizens' fierce anti-alien ads appeared, calling on the federal government to deport 'the undesirable alien and land him back in the bilge waters of European Civilization from whence he sprung and to which he properly belongs.'[93] There were direct incitements to soldiers to attack foreigners, as the soldiers had done in January: 'During the past four years when aged fathers and mothers, when wives and sisters were bullied and insulted by this element, they consoled each other by saying: "Just wait till the boys come home."'[94] The flag, of course, must shout down all argument: 'CANADIAN HEROES, Will You See the Flag You Fought for Torn Down By Alien Enemies?'[95]

Asked about these ads at the preliminary hearing after the Strike, Ed Parnell said, 'They are my views,' and when pressed as to whether the ads were intended to provoke attacks on Canadian citizens of foreign birth, Parnell retreated into pragmatism: 'When you have danger threatening you, you have to deal with it in a way which will counteract it, and that was the way we thought we would counteract it.' Defence counsel McMurray noted, with some irony, how remarkable it was that those

Great War Veterans Association members counter the Strike by marching against 'enemy aliens' on 4 June. (Winnipeg Strike 4/N12295, Archives of Manitoba)

injured and arrested in the riot of 21 June were nearly all English-speaking – but rumour had already scotched that fact, and Magistrate Noble immediately interrupted, saying that 'the worst rioters,' the ones 'on the roofs' hadn't been caught.[96] Since there was no way to determine the nationalities of those on the rooftops, racism stepped in to insist that they must have been aliens.

Curiously, through the ads the Citizens even addressed *themselves* in a ventriloquized fashion: 'With the formation of the Returned Soldiers Loyalist Association yesterday, began the movement which will speedily clear Canada of the undesirable alien ... MR. EMPLOYER, these men are officially pledging themselves to preserve law and order and to protect your life and property. Do not fail in turn to do your part without stint or limit.'[97] The voice, seemingly that of the 'average' citizen telling employers to fire immigrants and to hire soldiers, was of course the Citizens addressing the Citizens, it being less chancy to do both the talking and the listening. As Charles Taylor notes, 'even where [the public sphere] is in fact suppressed or manipulated it has to be faked.'[98]

In a periodical that Citizen A.B. Stovel published, the Citizens tailored their anti-alien ads to farmers, describing a 'Dastardly' Bolshevik plot by a 'sinister group of secret agents who during the war were the agents of German Sedition in Canada and the United States,' and who were now ramping up the Strike so that they could tie up the movement of wheat after harvest. This news was planned to appear on 5 June, but because of the striking printers, it wasn't published until after the Strike was over.[99]

Already early in the Strike, and playing on post-war Anglo-Canadian nationalism, the Citizens had blamed 'a small junta of avowed Bolshevists' backed by 'an almost solid foreign-born following' for taking control of organized labour in Winnipeg and planning anarchy.[100] In this slightly refocused parody of Marxist doctrine, the Eastern European immigrants were the proletariat, and socialist ideologues the avantgarde. The *Citizen* added: 'There's not a born Canadian in the Red element from *head to tail*. All these trouble makers and strife breeders came here from other lands which probably in most cases they found it convenient to escape from.'[101] That most of the leaders came from 'other lands' was literally true – they came from Britain. But the Citizens didn't name the country because it wasn't politic to criticize the source of Canadian institutions, the flag, and the constitution. In response to a fact threatening to expose the Citizens' rhetoric – the fact that many *Canadians* were striking – the Citizens simply absolved most picketers of responsibility for the Strike: 'Probably not two percent of the English-speaking strikers had the slightest idea of the road which the plotters hoped to lead them.'[102] And who were those 2 per cent? At the level of public support, the Citizens knew that anti-alien *rhetoric* must aim at Germans and Eastern Europeans to maximize propaganda value; yet any *legal* measures must be aimed at the British Strike leadership. One could anticipate, here, another potential clash between the Citizens' public discourse and practical measures. But just as Andrews had hived public melodrama off from the more reasoned discourse used to lobby Meighen, the Citizens now used a virulent anti-alien discourse to agitate the public, while emphasizing legal pragmatism to Meighen.

The Citizens aimed their xenophobia particularly at returned soldiers, reporting, for example, that baker Stephen Brown had had his business shut down when three foreigners, one of whom was Austrian, delivered a letter signed by Ernest Robinson and Helen Armstrong. Brown hoped to bake cakes for returned soldiers, but was prevented.[103] The *Citizen* emphasized that One Big Union supporters at the Calgary conference had approved a resolution calling for 'all organized alien enemies' to be protected by organized labour, and for the federal government to 'deport only such alien enemies as wish to be deported, naturalized or unnaturalized, and that they be given free transportation.'[104] The Citizens construed this to mean that the Strike leaders supported the release of 'those who were actively working for the German government in this country.'[105] To the Moose Jaw delegation Pitblado told an anecdote of a striker confronting a man wearing the flag. The striker said, 'You have no right to wear a flag. You were never in France.' The man replied, 'I have got a right to wear the British Flag if I want to, my three sons have been overseas.' The belligerent striker, Pitblado revealed, was a foreigner.[106] In a full-page, placard-style overture to the returned soldiers on 4 June, the Citizens pointed 'to the prominence in the recent street demonstrations of large numbers of aliens and demanded, since the Alien Enemy Registration Board showed 27,000 alien enemies in Winnipeg, that the alien problem be dealt with immediately.[107] Rumour had it that 'working men' voting not to strike had been outnumbered by aliens 7–1 or maybe 11–1,[108] and that the General Strike 'involving 30,000 workers' had been called 'on the authority of only 8,000 affirmative votes.'[109] Invoking the memory of the war, the Citizens 'unanimously' broadcast the following motion, race hatred decked out in sonorous legal language:

> THEREFORE, be it resolved that the Trades and Labor Council be called upon to immediately submit its records to a Board of Inquiry composed of representatives appointed by the Great War Veterans, the Imperial War veterans and the Army and Navy veterans with authority to report its findings and recommendations so that the public may be informed:
>
> 1 How many aliens and how many registered alien enemies are on the membership rolls of the Unions now on strike.
> 2 The exact number of alien enemies and aliens in each union that voted for the general strike.
> 3 The exact number of votes for and against the general strike cast by each union.
> 4 Why these total votes were pooled and a clear majority decided as sufficient to call a general strike.[110]

On Tuesday the *Winnipeg Citizen* 'learned' – investigative journalism? – 'that all of the large employers of labor in the city have decided that since the aliens in their employ struck work, they will never be taken back.'[111] Perhaps fearing that the point had been lost in the rest of the article, the Citizens added a second motion to Wednesday's placard, under the heading 'JUSTICE TO OUR SOLDIERS.' Aliens had usurped the soldiers' jobs: 'THEREFORE be it unanimously resolved that such aliens ought to be replaced as quickly as possible by our returned soldiers and all employers are hereby urged to take the necessary steps.' And in capitalized bold letters: '**RETURNED SOLDIERS, ARE YOU GOING**

TO PERMIT THESE STRIKING ALIENS TO RETURN TO THE JOBS THAT RIGHTLY BELONG TO YOU?'[112] The Citizens defined themselves as Anglo-conformist, and in faux-parliamentary language – democratic organizations for some reason tend not to phrase their motions 'therefore be it *unanimously* resolved' – they demanded an Anglo-conformist response from Canadians.

It would be interesting to know what Citizens' Committee supporter Max Steinkopf – native of Austria Hungary and owner of City Dairy, which had lost $10,000 in the Strike – thought about this tactic,[113] but the anti-immigrant attitudes of Methodist ministers such as Rev. John MacLean and Rev. Capt. Wellington Bridgman remind us that the Citizens' attitudes were widely shared among British-Canadians. MacLean wrote in his diary on 14 April 1919, 'We are certainly in a sad plight, as there is one alien in Manitoba to every six of loyal British subjects.'[114] Bridgman, after the Strike, was even more vociferous, asking why there were no British people in the criminal dockets, and explaining that credit must go to three hundred years of British character-building and upward moral movement. The most solemn service he ever remembered was during the Great War, when the names of dead sons were read: 'From all that I know of the congregation, if a vote had been asked for the deportation of all Germans, Austrians, Bulgars and Turks the whole of the congregation would have voted for their expulsion.'[115] Immigrants, not capitalists, were the ones whose property was a crime. Bridgman asked, why not allow returned soldiers to adjudicate how much immigrants, upon deportation, should get for their property, say 25 per cent of its value? Since soldiers 'knew the Austro-Hun best,' they could be entirely impartial. And, with the aliens out of the country, it would then be only fair to allow the soldiers to buy the abandoned properties at 5 per cent of their value.[116] A win-win situation for government and soldier. The two Methodist clergymen weren't unique. The citizens' 'protection' society that Anglo south-enders had formed earlier in the year was directed against immigrants,[117] and in January soldiers had rioted against aliens.[118] The Citizens were playing to a sympathetic crowd.

John Dafoe, the editor of the *Manitoba Free Press*, had no trouble blaming 'alien scum,' 'bohunks,' and Laurier-era immigration policies for the impasse at Winnipeg. 'The name of this country is Canada, not Bohunkia,' he declared.[119] The founder of the *Winnipeg Tribune* and MP for Springfield, R.L. Richardson, whose views contrasted sharply with those of the Citizens, was also susceptible to anti-alien propaganda. Richardson urged an inquiry into profiteering, and, even less popular among the upper classes, a federal price board to reduce the cost of living. Yet he also wanted more thorough espionage upon the strikers, especially since a 'foreign element' was mixing with 'a certain band of returned soldiers mostly conscripts.'[120] If even a less biased observer such as Richardson blamed immigrants for the Strike, it's no shock that Andrews would ask for legislation that would attack, or at least seem to attack, aliens.

The powerful effect of the Citizens' anti-alien rhetoric can be measured by the fact that the *Western Labor News* also felt compelled to take it up to avoid being coloured as the enemy. To the amusement of the GWVA executive, labour representatives promised that after the Strike they'd get together with the veterans to sort out the aliens.[121] Later, during the police lockout, Alderman Heaps complained that the City wasn't ensuring that all of the new Specials were British subjects. Enemy aliens, he warned, might be getting the jobs.[122] Labour's official organ tried to mute this concession to racism by inflecting the racial discourse with a labourite emphasis on class: Why doesn't the government deport alien bankers or MPs or railway corporation members? asked the *Labor News* rhetorically, and then answered, 'No, no, the rich alien is all right. It is the poor alien who should be expelled.'[123] So interested was the *Labor News* in keeping the veterans onside, that it allowed the GWVA to censor veterans' news in the paper. The *Winnipeg Citizen*, claiming to speak for veterans, ran a much tighter ship and allowed them no censorship power.

Andrews sent a litany of strife to Meighen during these days, but fed him no populist racism. Instead, Andrews used a more sophisticated anti-foreigner discourse, complaining that an American named James Duncan (secretary of the Seattle District Trades & Labor Council during February's Seattle General Strike) had addressed Winnipeg strikers in the afternoon, and that Immigration authorities had told Andrews that they couldn't legally deport Duncan. Andrews asked, 'Can't enabling legislation be rushed?' Once amendments to the Immigration Act were in place, he explained, Commissioner Perry of the RNWMP was all set to deport 'one hundred dangerous aliens.'[124]

6

To Reach the Leaders in
This Revolutionary Movement

Thursday, 5 June – Friday, 6 June

The decision to amend the Immigration Act was a compromise between the Citizens and federal authorities. 'Citizens clamouring for arrests,' Andrews had telegraphed Meighen on Wednesday. Changing his earlier strategy, Andrews had begun to clamour too. But he was in an awkward position, because he, a Conservative, had to beg his old Liberal nemesis, Tory-hating Attorney General T.H. Johnson, to prosecute the Strike Committee. In the 1910 provincial election, Andrews had run against Johnson (and against the SPC's George Armstrong) in Winnipeg West, losing to Johnson by only forty votes. After the riding boundaries had been redistributed, Andrews took another stab at Johnson in 1914, losing again, this time by 1050 votes. Clearly, there was no love lost between the two, and in 1919 Johnson would only say that he was 'considering' arrests.[1]

There could be no arrests without Johnson's cooperation, Andrews admitted, though later he would find ways of circumventing Johnson. Andrews operated empirically – he assessed and made judgments with a bit of scepticism about his own conclusions. He arranged for Johnson, Mayor Gray, Alderman Fowler, General Ketchen, Colonel Starnes, and Commissioner Perry to meet at Premier Norris's office on Thursday;[2] and when Ketchen, Starnes, and Perry built a convincing case against the immediate arrest of the Strike leadership, arguing that such action would simply fuel sympathetic strikes across the West, Andrews didn't fight the consensus. By reporting the military/police arguments sympathetically to Meighen, Andrews made it clear that he was prepared to side with the majority. This placed Andrews in direct disagreement with Pitblado and the other Citizens. On Thursday, a number of the Citizens including Pitblado, A.K. Godfrey, and Ed Anderson again lobbied Johnson to arrest the Strike Committee, this time for again paralysing bread and milk delivery.[3] The resolution that they brought had been unanimously carried by the Citizens, Andrews not being present. The constitution was being openly defied, the Citizens thundered, and yet the government sat on its haunches. Although claiming that they were doing everything possible to restrain the loyal soldiers, the Citizens also threatened that 'if the Government did not take action the returned soldiers and citizens who are indignant could no longer be held in check and would take the law in their own hands.'[4] Andrews, nevertheless, was canny enough to sail with the prevailing tide, and he prepared to work through other means – deportation – to achieve the results the Citizens sought.[5] Gen. Ketchen was far from sanguine about the situation,[6] but Andrews maintained that the calling out of bread and milk employees was merely a 'last kick,' and all would be well so long as Meighen came through with enabling legislation to deport Bolsheviks.[7]

Meighen did, though not to Andrews's satisfaction. *The Act to Amend the Immigration Act* was adopted on Thursday, and Meighen gave Andrews to understand that it awaited only the Governor General's assent, which would come on Friday at 4:30. The act allowed for the deportation of 'any person unless born or naturalized in Canada who is or becomes of [*sic*] anarchist or undesirable class within the meaning of Section 41.' The revised section 41 specified which acts could lead to deportation, some of which were red herrings, since no new law was needed to outlaw them: advocating the violent overthrow of the Canadian government or of constituted law and authority; advocating the assassination of any government official. A clause that could actually apply to strikers forbade advocating the unlawful destruction of property – and what was the souring milk, now stinking again in warehouses, if not the unlawful destruction of property? Other clauses were vague: inciting riots, belonging to a secret society that extorted money from or in any way attempted to control Canadians by force or threat. Could hot words in Victoria Park constitute the inciting of a riot? Was the One Big Union a secret society? Could the attempt to keep strikers off the job constitute an 'attempt to control' Canadians 'by threat'? One needn't actually belong to a secret society for the act to come into play – one need only belong to it 'by common repute.' The act's vaguest clause forbade affiliation with any organization 'entertaining ot [*sic*] teaching disbelief in or opposition to organized government.' Meighen was astute enough not to name Bolshevism directly and yet the catch-all 'disbelief in organized government' was general enough to snare *any* reform movement, never mind wholesale reappraisals of capitalism. If any immigrant fell prey to such heresy, municipalities could write complaints to the minister of immigration.[8] So that there should be no mistake about the process, Meighen quoted Section 41 verbatim to Andrews, and added that before deporting anyone, Immigration officials must receive notice of precisely how the person offended against section 41.[9]

When Andrews received the changes to the Immigration Act, he was dismayed. He had no quarrel with the vagueness of the offences. That deportations must specify complaints about the person's conduct was acceptable too: when the time came to send foreigners back 'home,' Andrews would simply ignore this requirement. But what disturbed his legal mind was that section 41 applied to 'any person other than a Canadian Citizen.'[10] Not good enough: under the act one could not deport Strike leaders such as R.B. Russell, who, by virtue of British birth and by having been 'domiciled' in Canada for three years, had the rights of Canadian citizenship.[11] Andrews needed a more discriminating strainer. Amid all the public noise about 'enemy aliens,' Meighen hadn't fully twigged to the difference between the Citizens' rhetoric and the actual Strike leaders whom Andrews wanted the law to clobber. No doubt Meighen grasped that 'Huns' weren't at issue, but, given Andrews's complaints, Meighen probably thought that he was aiming at people such as James Duncan, a Seattle General Strike organizer who had come to Winnipeg. Duncan's was the only 'alien' name that Andrews had ever named to Meighen in this regard; he had merely asked euphemistically for legislation 'to reach the leaders in this revolutionary movement.'[12] What Andrews wanted, but hesitated to express in so many words, was legislation to turf the British-born leaders out of Canada.

Thursday night Andrews was too busy to correct Meighen. He had a full plate by now: juggling Police Commission problems, the recruitment of special constables, the issues around the suspension of bread and milk delivery, the Citizens' agitation for arrests, daily meetings with Pitblado, the stalling of the Running Trades Mediation Committee, responses to the veterans' parades. Thursday filled with increasingly aggressive marches and counter-marches, and Andrews wasn't done with his work until 1:00 a.m., his last act the drafting of a proclamation that he had convinced Mayor Gray to issue prohibiting any parades on Friday.[13]

The GWVA executive – less in favour of the Strike than the GWVA membership – had issued a statement reaffirming neutrality and asserting that the soldiers parading to the legislature weren't officially recognized. The *Winnipeg Citizen* proclaimed this as a wholesale defection of soldiers from the Strike.[14] Yet on Tuesday the GWVA membership had passed a vote of support for the Strike by a two-thirds majority. The Citizens dismissed this as the result of a 'packed' meeting, and J.O. Newton, on behalf of the GWVA executive, tried to declare the vote out of order.[15] On Wednesday, the GWVA executive, schooled by the Citizens, declared the vote 'unconstitutional.'[16] This required some logical contortions, since the organization had run on parliamentary lines, but the executive claimed that it could no longer operate in this constitutional manner.[17] The Citizens, meanwhile, tried to emasculate the vote in a more public and effective manner. They organized a fleet of one hundred cars to ferry the 'real' returned soldiers to Broadway and Main for a march,[18] calling it a 'repudiation of the previous parades,' which, according to the Citizens, had included 'draftees, defaulters, enemy aliens and other foreigners.'[19] The real problem for the Citizens was to explain why the same soldiers who hounded anti-conscriptionists such as Ivens and Russell would cheer when those same men led a strike. The Citizens eventually seized on a convenient line that had been floating around for some time: soldiers who supported the Strike were mostly conscripts, while soldiers who sided with the Citizens were mostly volunteers.[20] 'Real' returned soldiers must scorn veterans of the 'battle of London' or the 'French base,' and members of the 'Frosted Trilby clique' or the 'Trench feet brigade'[21] – in other words, men who had dodged the war through minor injuries and postings to headquarters in London or Rouen; and senior officers who in their gold-embroidered Trilbys caps got exemptions based on rank.[22] Unrest from unemployed soldiers was a live fear in Ottawa, and could potentially turn the federal government against the Citizens. Andrews had to make sure that Meighen 'saw' at least as many 'loyalist' soldiers as striking soldiers. For Meighen's benefit, Andrews overestimated the 'loyalists' at 2000.[23]

These 'real' soldiers protested the halt to milk and bread delivery, and marched under banners proclaiming the Citizens' law-and-constituted-order catchphrases. The *Free Press*, doing its bit, asserted that the parade consisted mostly of rank-and-file soldiers, not officers, and that 'there were none of the capitalistic class, one hears so much derided in Victoria park and at the Labor temple.'[24] This wasn't strictly true, since a number of the Citizens hovered at the edge of the masses, but were insulated from them, clapping from behind the windows of their cars. The *Western Labor News* mocked: 'The employers were too dignified to shout, so they tooted the horns of their automobiles while the boys walked to their bidding.'[25] Ed Parnell did evidently step out of his car and march with the anti-Strike soldiers, either because he owned a bakery or because, like the *Winnipeg Citizen*, he wanted to ensure that 'Child Murder Will Be Punished.' His ire had been rekindled by the sus-

pension of bread and milk delivery. 'The citizens must have bread and I
am going to see they get it,' he declared.[26] Nominally, Parnell represented the master bakers on the City's bread and milk committee, but
everybody knew that really he represented the Citizens, and he helped
make a case for Special Police by insisting that bakers couldn't go ahead
without 'ample' police protection.[27] The *Western Labor News* found his
presence at the march ironic: the banners called for a reduction in the
cost of living, yet it was Parnell who, a short time earlier, had increased
the price of bread.[28]

On Thursday morning, both sides were out in full force. About 5000
'returned soldiers loyal to Constitution,' filled the auditorium rink to
capacity,[29] Andrews reported to Meighen. What he didn't tell Meighen
was that this heady total referred to all the volunteers, not simply to
returned soldiers.[30] In the morning's *Winnipeg Citizen*, these 5000 could
read that the previous day some of their number had threatened to go to
the Labor Temple 'and tear it brick from brick.'[31] Taking the hint, Captain Charles Wheeler, president of the Imperial War Veterans, 'called
upon the crowd to clean up the Labor Temple.'[32] Wheeler had been
important in the veterans' protests in February, where he had 'declared
that he had met many Germans in his wanderings but he had never
known a good one unless the Hun had been under a tombstone.'[33]
Andrews, inflating the popular support that the Citizens enjoyed, warned
Meighen that only with difficulty had the Mayor and several officers
persuaded these soldiers not to march on the Labor Temple and not to
'wreck' the crowd of strikers.[34] The most important information that
Andrews kept from Meighen was that during the march the 'loyalists'
had been far outnumbered by Strike sympathizers, estimated by the
Western Labor News to stand at 10,000. The *Winnipeg Citizen* gave a
strangely precise count of the strikers: 800 ex-soldiers and 264 other
strikers, 'cheered on and abetted by an equal number of the foreign element.'[35] Assuming that by 'equal number' the *Citizen* meant another
1064 aliens, from this already underestimated total of 2128 strikers,
Andrews reported only the '800' soldiers to Meighen.[36] The strikers
tried to wrest the constitutional and anti-alien rhetoric from the Citizens
by copying the Loyalist signs of the previous day – 'Fall in Canadian
Corps,' 'Deport All Undesirables,' 'We Stand for Law and Order,' 'We
Stand for Democratic Government.'[37] This unintentionally again
stressed the effectiveness of the Citizens' discourse, and also the limited
ability of the strikers, despite their numbers, to counteract it. The Citizens and their allies didn't need to argue against the message on the
strikers' signs. They only needed to insinuate that many of those carrying the banners 'were speaking in foreign languages.'[38] When the

rumour spread among the strikers that the loyalists were going to march on the Labor Temple,[39] the two demonstrations very nearly confronted one another – which could easily have produced a riot. As it was, there were several fights, and police made arrests.[40]

Andrews and the Citizens decried these arrests and, opportunistically, began to make a more pointed case for reshaping the executive branch of government. Although Andrews worried about the consequences of such a reshaping, the plan had long been on the minds of some Citizens – ever since the police had revealed their sympathies by voting to strike. When General Ketchen, the day before the Strike, had begun to organize a militia in case of civil unrest, he had called together 'senior Militia Officers,' 'returned officers,' and 'influential citizens.'[41] Since Ketchen attended meetings of the Citizens' Committee of 1000, it's a good bet that the 'influential citizens' were mostly Citizens. Drilled and armed, the militia was thus subordinate to capitalist interests, but remained sequestered in the Osborne Barracks. Unfortunately for morale, this 'citizens' army' of several thousands[42] was hemorrhaging daily (it being difficult to keep the men in the barracks)[43] while waiting for an armed rebellion that never came.

Early on in the Strike, the Citizens had briefly but without permission taken over police functions. On 23 May, when the stable fire had threatened the Hudson's Bay store, men with 'S.P.' (Special Police) on their armbands had directed traffic and possibly done other policing tasks, as was revealed in the testimony of Police Commission chair Alderman John Sparling. Sparling was a witness friendly to the Citizens, yet when Andrews tried to get him to admit that since it was no crime for volunteers to fight fires, it was likewise no crime for volunteers to do police work, Sparling had to baulk. At issue was the state's monopoly on the legitimate use of force within its territory.[44] Andrews, and even Magistrate R.M. Noble, tried to deflect the constitutional issue by focusing on whether there were any complaints against the volunteers. Sparling would have none of it:

Andrews: Assuming that you had evidence that there was no one else there to do it, and the police were not there for 45 minutes after the fire started, would you think there was anything greatly wrong about it?

Sparling: As police commissioner I would not have allowed it for 45 seconds.

Andrews: Assuming that I myself, on the way to dinner, find a jam and take it upon myself to try and direct the traffic and straighten it out?

Sparling: I would have no objection to you as a citizen, but if you belonged to some organization, I would have ordered you run in pretty soon.[45]

What Sparling understood was that in a democracy the policing function cannot be delegated by the state to private hands, in which the potential for vigilantism increases dramatically. Captain Frederick Thompson, one of the leaders of the Specials when they did appear, suggested that the rule of law wasn't necessarily a primary consideration. At the Strike leaders' preliminary hearing, he told defence counsel that he proposed to take some men and 'clean up the Bosheviki stuff':

McMurray: You were going to move by constitutional methods?
Thompson: Sure.
McMurray: You were going down and going to wipe that thing out?
Thompson: We would get some of that literature and produce it to the authorities.
McMurray: Irrespective of what might happen?
Thompson: I would take my chance.
McMurray: You didn't ever hear of anything like search warrants and things like that?
Thompson: Sometimes they are slow ...
McMurray: And you would not bother with the Law Courts?
Thompson: I would get my evidence first.[46]

The Citizens' public-spiritedness notwithstanding, elected officials answerable to the people must at all times have oversight on executive functions to ensure the rule of law, and Andrews, as a lawyer and former mayor, certainly knew this. However, he approached the law not idealistically but Talmudically, with a pragmatic approach even to constitutional law. The best story would win, and the story that Andrews had been test-driving for the Citizens was the common-law story in which upon the breakdown of central authority the private citizen steps into the gap. In one sense, the first 'S.P.' armbands were a misadventure, the first draft of a story that wouldn't yet fly, but this misadventure allowed the Citizens' lawyers to hone their story, to learn to do by legal means what they had at first attempted extra-legally. The 'Specials' didn't disappear: the Citizens ensured that armed volunteers patrolled Winnipeg's residential districts at night, not as Special Police or Citizens but as 'citizens,' merely keeping an eye on things for the police.

Early on, since the RNWMP had advised that it wouldn't take sides in the Strike, and fearing a police walkout, civic authorities had slowly begun to appoint special constables alongside the regular force.[47] If the

Citizens couldn't command their own special police, they could get civic officials to create Special Police, and then stack the Specials with returned men loyal to the Citizens' cause. Under cross-examination by counsel for the Strike leaders, Sparling had to be prodded, but was ultimately forthright:

McMurray: Who were the persons who made the demand for special
             police to be put on?
Sparling: Do you mean with regard to this strike?
McMurray: Yes, who were they?
Sparling: There was no definite demand, but it was discussed and
             the gentlemen present were Mr Godfrey and Mr Ingram
             and Mr Sweatman.
McMurray: Were they speaking as individuals or as members and
             representatives of the Committee of One Thousand?
Sparling: Was there a committee of one thousand at that time?
McMurray: I don't think there ever was, but I think this committee
             was formed about that time?
Sparling: I would think they represented the committee of one
             thousand.
McMurray: What do your minutes show on that point?
Sparling: The meeting was called to meet Mr Godfrey, Mr Ingram
             and Mr Sweatman, who stated that they represented the
             citizens' committee of one thousand.[48]

At first, the City refused the demand to replace the police with Specials, but under mounting pressure in early June it acquiesced. Captain Thompson, not only the GWVA representative among the Citizens but also a lawyer, helped Sweatman make the case by hinting at the possibility of riots by returned men. Said Thompson, 'I telephoned Travis [sic] Sweatman who was an older lawyer ... we put it to the Police Commission hot and heavy ... This damn police force is [favourable] to the strike, is not doing a fair job and we want it out or there is going to be real trouble. We had kept it pretty well down. The result is they did fire [Police Chief] MacPherson, and [Deputy Chief Chris] Newton came in.'[49] Captain Wheeler, who commanded one part of the Special Police, was either unaware of this or less truthful; he claimed that the Citizens' Committee had nothing to do with the organization of the Specials.[50]

At the auditorium rink on Thursday, the 5000 'loyalists' were canvassed as to whether they would join the Special Police under Major Hilliard Lyle, Mayor Gray's choice.[51] Gray made the appeal, using the language of the Citizens: 'You men I see in front of me today are going to be the salvation of Canadian democracy! ... This special constable duty is not strike-breaking. It is merely for the purpose of maintaining law and order.' He also promised practical benefits, saying that the streetcars would run as soon as the Specials could protect them.[52] Thompson, meanwhile, kept discipline: 'I remember one chap making a helluva lot of noise and wantin' to cry blue bloody murder ... I knew personally that he'd got, he'd got into a soldier's uniform and never left Winnipeg ... I said, "Look here, you shut up immediately or I'll have some of the boys just force you out of the hall."'[53]

From the meeting, the City hoped to get 2000 Specials at $6 a day, a fairly good salary. This immediately prompted the strikers to crow that capital was unconsciously admitting the need for a 'living wage.'[54] The *Winnipeg Citizen* reported the recruitment drive as if reality had met intentions: 'Before 6 o'clock [Thursday] night the 2,000 special constables were sworn in, and equipped with batons and with arm-bands signifying their badge of authority.' If asked, the newly formed 'Returned Soldiers' Loyalist Association' would supply another 2000 on Friday, and the Specials would serve until 'the revolution' was over.[55] Andrews and Ketchen, not trying to score propaganda victories, reported lower numbers to Ottawa. On Thursday, Andrews told Meighen that four hundred Specials had been sworn in and that he had helped organize them on military organization.[56] On Friday, Ketchen said that the number had risen to 900,[57] while Andrews placed the total at 1500.[58] But even these smaller numbers were bloated. When Crown Attorney Robert Graham told Major Lyle about the possibility that 'loyalist' marchers might cross paths with marching strikers, Lyle was horrified, saying, 'My God, I hope they don't try to parade.' Graham, only slightly facetious, responded, 'Why not. It will be a good chance to try out your men.' Lyle, however, insisted that he couldn't put any men on the street the next day.' Leading 1000 men in theory, he admitted that he didn't have them in fact: 'I have a nominal roll but I haven't seen the men.'[59] The great rush of returned men to the Citizens proved illusory, and a week later Andrews would have to admit to Meighen that the special force on paper never quite materialized as bodies: on paper, the new acting chief of police Newton commanded 1438 Specials; in the flesh, he only had 250.[60]

Were the Citizens justified in asking for Special Constables? Yes, despite the machinations to undermine the regular police. True, the new loyalty oath, dreamed up by the police commission, was engineered as a blow against the Strike, not as a public safety measure. As well, the contract that the City signed with the police contained an article prohibiting both strikes *and* lockouts. When in the coming days the police commission replaced its 210 police officers with Specials, it thus had to pretend that what was occurring was not a lockout, but, in Sparling's words, a series of 'dismissals';[61] or, in the more fanciful language of another Police Commission member, Hugh John Macdonald, the force would be 'purged of all unruly and incompetent members.'[62] He ought to have announced, 'a purging of 9/10s of the police force,' since only about twenty officers signed the loyalty oath and stayed on.[63]

Despite all this propaganda, the perception that the police were biased in favour of the strikers was valid. The police allowed strikers to intimidate workers who didn't wish to strike. The Canadian Oil Companies had cause for complaint, as mobs came down to the filling stations and threatened to wreck them if they weren't closed.[64] Other complaints came from Sunset Manufacturing, from hardware merchant James Henry Ashdown, and from the *Telegram* and the *Tribune*, newspapers hated by the strikers. City Hall had been overrun with strikers, and the Weston fire hall was a particularly hazardous place. Every time that volunteer firefighters attempted to occupy the hall, mobs would arrive to kick them out.[65] There were also reports of threatening letters delivered to the Citizens, though none of the letters was ever produced as evidence in court.[66] During the week leading up to the appointment of the Specials, a number of prominent businessmen complained that the police weren't protecting their private property,[67] and when fights broke out at the Thursday June 5th demonstrations, the *Citizen* complained that police arrested mostly loyalists, treating one man brutally.[68]

The case that day that most incensed the Citizens involved Mayor Gray. Winnipeg police arrested Major Howard, a Dominion secret service officer, for carrying a revolver, even though he had the police chief's permission to carry it. In the first week of the Strike, over strikers' objections that he was 'dishing them out as fast as he could,' the police chief had handed out 126 permits for revolvers, mostly to men hired to guard buildings,[69] but also to men such as Dr Moody, who were fearful of their safety.[70]

When Mayor Gray heard of Howard's arrest, he raced to the police station. He caught the arresting officer outside and ordered him to release Howard. The officer continued to propel Howard forward, while the crowd grabbed the mayor. According to the *Citizen*, 'Two more policemen calmly looked on another twenty feet away, making no move to interfere. Three rioters had the mayor firmly gripped, though they suffered somewhat from his worship's vigorous use of his fists.' S.A. Blair, with a baton, stopped the 'assault' on the mayor. Police made no move to arrest the rioters, but said, 'Stand back, boys, please.' Soon afterwards, Major H.M. Moorhouse, 'a member of the mayor's staff,' helped start a street cleaning truck. Strikers saw a revolver on his person, pulled it from him, and aimed it at him. Police arrested not the striker but Moorhouse. The mayor's secretary, F. Furgeson, went to Moorhouse's aid, but a striker punched him in the throat. Furgeson demanded that the striker be arrested, but police asked Furgeson to produce a warrant. Finally, the mayor re-emerged and forced an officer to arrest the guilty striker.[71]

The *Winnipeg Citizen* was highly untrustworthy, but this story was probably reliable because the *Western Labor News* didn't discredit it. The *Labor News* merely added its own colour to the pursuit of Howard and the officer – 'Mayor Gray rushed after bareheaded like a maniac' – and a different interpretation: thugs had struck a police officer, and Gray should have known that only the police station could revoke the arrest. Why, asked the *Western Labor News*, did we need Special Police when there was no disorder? No strikers had been arrested for creating disorder. It was the Citizens who were trying to create disorder.[72]

A bit of unrest, particularly if directed at foreigners, didn't displease the Citizens, though they knew that for propaganda purposes the violence should originate in the strikers. From the day the Strike began, some Citizens had unsuccessfully 'pressed and jammed' Gen. Ketchen and Mayor Gray for martial law.[73] The emergence of returned soldiers as a force in the Strike, the crisis over policing, and the withdrawal of bread and milk delivery now put martial law on the table again. Although the *Labor News* didn't realize it, the very claim that no strikers had been arrested had an eerie ring. In all the crowds ordering businesses to shut down, in all the shoving matches and fights, was it possible that only non-striking workers and loyalist volunteers were to blame? The *Free Press* claimed that since the beginning of the week, there had been 'at least a hundred serious offences against person and property – assault and battery, open intimidation, destruction of property, indecent and disgusting language, illegal interferences with business operations.'[74] The most likely interpretation of the Strike's 'peacefulness' is partly that intimidators stopped short of direct violence, but also that police were biased in their pattern of arrests. One can readily see why Andrews, and especially Pitblado, shouted revolution: the executive branch of government wasn't under the direction of elected officials, but at the beck of the Labor Temple. The purpose of the Specials was to declare that the authorities had control of the streets, a doubtful proposition.

Not every report of intimidation was equally valid, of course. One may be forgiven for suspecting that the written complaints early on from the law firm Richards, Sweatman and Co. to the Police Commission about lack of protection had more to do with propaganda than crime.[75]

Andrews's report to Meighen on Friday the 6th was exaggerated. He said strike sympathizers had performed numerous assaults 'upon citizens and even upon girls and newsboys, and though the police were present, they refused to interfere ... The police ... arrested a number of our prominent citizens but did not arrest any of the strikers.'[76] In reality, this was a Citizen-coloured interpretation of the Moorhouse/Gray altercation, and of another incident in which two women selling the *Tribune* were accosted by two young female strikers, who, urged on by Helen Armstrong, tore up several copies of the paper.[77] Armstrong was arrested.

Rather than assault, a common treatment was likely that received by the Citizen A.L. Crossin. He complained that on Wednesday night he had been ordered off the sidewalk, and he had noticed others treated with the same lack of deference.[78] The fear was that the young radicals, in razing the foundations of contracts and property, might also lay waste to propriety. The intimation that the strikers had lost their manners – no doubt partly a rhetorical device – showed up in the many references to gentlemanly conduct. In reporting the loyalist soldiers' parade, the *Manitoba Free Press* distinguished between two types of aggression: 'The faces as they passed, showed merry and intelligent with a cheerful aggressiveness, but not of the futile, bitter antagonism of the agitator.' The loyalist leader, Capt. Thompson, not above clubbing a few heads, said, 'We intend to show the premier by our attitude that this is a delegation of gentlemen.'[79] The Citizens couldn't have been happy to remember R.J. Johns in 1918 announcing a new 'proletarian morality,'[80] and Andrews, despite his own insults against the strikers, would later be very quick to cry manners when E.J. McMurray suggested behind-the-scenes manipulation by Gideon Robertson: 'Defendants' counsel should at least be a gentleman, there can be nothing more ungentlemanly or more cowardly than to make a suggestion that would reflect on a Minister of the Crown when he is not here.'[81] The discourse was strongly class-based. In Charles Gordon's fictionalization of the Strike, *To Him That Hath*, when the Strike begins, the workers can't look their friend and manager – who is also their employer's son – in the eye. It is implied that the problem with the unions is that they've lost both the British spirit of fair play and what ought to be synonymous with fair play: the appropriate devotion to one's paternalistic employer. Grant Maitland hired Perrotte, a Frenchman, on the basis of skill, despite Perrotte's race. It would therefore be exceedingly rude, given such magnanimity, for Perrotte ever to challenge his working conditions.[82]

This discourse was partly moral, but moral in a way that revealed its class bias. *To Him That Hath* explains that 'an active interest in clean

and vigorous outdoor sports tended to produce contentment of mind ...
unfertile soil for radical and socialistic doctrines.'[83] *Winnipeg Citizen*
co-editor Fletcher Sparling would declare that 'clean manhood and
womanhood is the first essential to all success,'[84] a statement ideologically similar to quotations attributed to others in his newspaper: returned
soldier William Bathie said that 'clean Trades Unionism and the returned
soldier movement' ought to stifle the strikers, and that 'if we had a man
big enough to draw both returned soldiers and clean labor without its
tinge of "red" the strike could be ended in 12 hours.'[85] Either the editor
Sparling learned something from Bathie, or Sparling 'helped' Bathie to
articulate what it was that Bathie thought.

Still, Andrews's larger point about police sympathies was accurate
and troubling. The partisanship of the police was a growing problem.
And his veiled threat of riots was sure to find a sympathetic ear in
Meighen.[86]

Despite all the turbulence on Thursday, the first thing Friday morning
Andrews sent Meighen an angry, though restrained, wire about the new
section 41 of the Immigration Act:

> section very disappointing does not cover dangerous class not born in
> Canada stop The British Bolshevist and naturalized aliens stop only
> appears to cover non-naturalized aliens stop. Commissioner Perry had
> believed and assumed that could deport any undesirables save Cana-
> dian born stop anything less than this absolutely useless and will not
> meet situation or satisfy citizens who if I inform them of real facts will
> be greatly disheartened and disgusted stop.[87]

By the promptness with which Andrews rejected the legislation as
'absolutely useless,' we know that he must have already had in mind a
list of whose heads he wanted: R.B. Russell, William Ivens, R.J. Johns,
John Queen, George Armstrong, A.A. Heaps, Roger Bray, and Bill
Pritchard – all, except the Canadian Armstrong, British citizens who, by
virtue of domicile in Canada, had all the rights of native-born Canadians. What Andrews needed was a legal situation in which British citizenship and 'domicile' would no longer protect them.

Andrews also related a conversation he had had with James Winning,
the Scottish bricklayer who had became a Winnipeg alderman, president
of the Winnipeg Trades and Labor Council, and a member of the central
Strike Committee. Winning, Andrews claimed, had told him that the
Strike was step one of a broader plan. If the Strike didn't accomplish
labour's goals, a general strike involving every city in Canada would be

triggered. And if that were inadequate, the trains would be stopped.[88] Winning would later testify to the Robson commission that the strikers had no revolutionary intent,[89] but, according to Andrews, 'The idea of the one big union and what it was intended to accomplish by way of revolution, was not to call out the general strike until the 1st of October when the necessity of moving the grain, coal, etc. would paralyze the whole country.'[90] Earlier Andrews had credited Meighen with defeating this design; now he attributed the success to the citizens of Winnipeg for keeping the city running. Most importantly, this was done 'without the aid of force or the intervention of the law in any form.'[91]

Andrews was trying to walk a fine line: wanting to actively combat the strikers, but not to provoke them too much. Clearly, he had refined his earlier, more aggressive position, and didn't necessarily intend to use the Immigration Act amendments immediately. There would be opportunities after the defeat of the Strike to deal with its leaders, especially since Attorney General Johnson, despite his present unwillingness to act, had been intensely lobbied by a 'body' of Citizens on Thursday, and had promised that 'at the proper time' the Province would 'punish' the leaders. How, he didn't reveal. Andrews was collecting evidence for this purpose. Best, however, to let the Strike fail first: 'I believe it will fail, of itself, and because public opinion is against it, it will be exceedingly difficult at any future time to get the large body of labor to strike ... The natural impulse will be to blame the strike leaders.' Use of coercion to break the Strike would simply allow labour to 'claim that they would have won but for the intervention of the Government controlled by the master class.' Andrews didn't want to issue a challenge to labour, and didn't want to risk the Running Trades joining the Strike. Both Mr Beatty and Mr Coleman of the CPR believed that arrests would cause the Running Trades to strike, and that the result would be 'alarming.' As long as no new element – that is, arrests – was introduced, Beatty thought that the Strike's back was broken.[92]

Nevertheless, Andrews did want legislation that would allow him to get at the British Strike leaders if necessary. In this demand, he moved far beyond legal advice. It was arguably the first critical moment in Andrews's campaign, a moment that showed how much he could shape events, and it paved the way for his bolder moves later on. Since Meighen allowed himself to be governed, Andrews recognized that he could employ the Citizens (and Ketchen and Perry and a bit of exaggeration) as sticks with which to drive Meighen, while simultaneously using the powers-that-be – Meighen, Ketchen, and Perry – to rein in the Citizens. Andrews complained to Meighen that the toothless immigration amendments disappointed Ketchen and made him feel that he had 'unintentionally deceived' the returned soldiers. Perry, too, had felt deceived: 'He believed that he could deport any undesirables save Canadian born, that is he could deport them whether they came from Great Britain or elsewhere and aliens whether naturalized or not.' In the guise of protecting Meighen, Andrews also held the Citizens over his head. Andrews said that he hadn't let any of the Citizens, except Pitblado and Coyne, know of the legislation, in hopes that Meighen would come back with better amendments. In effect, Andrews hinted that if Meighen corrected his error post-haste, he wouldn't have to deal with a furious Winnipeg business elite. And finally, the carrot: 'If adequate provisions were enacted by Parliament to enable your officers to deport the class of undesirables that should be deported, very much could be done to stem the tide of revolution. This ought to be done *at once*.'[93]

Meighen proved to be a quick study. The same day, he wired back, 'Fully realized inadequacy of section after first perusal by myself last night.' This implies that it was Meighen's subordinates who hadn't known enough to go beneath the anti-alien rhetoric and had therefore drafted inadequate legislation. But in actuality it was Meighen who had quoted the legislation on Thursday as if he had given Andrews all that Andrews needed. After receiving the telegram on Friday morning, probably before he received Andrews's full arguments in the letter, Meighen remedied his naivety by immediately preparing an amendment 'sufficiently wide to cover all except those born or naturalized in Canada,' and he promised that the new amendment would be law within twenty-four hours.[94] Accordingly, Minister of Immigration J.A. Calder that same day introduced a bill to amend the Immigration Act a second time. The government gave Andrews what he wanted, so that if British immigrants belonged to any of the vague 'prohibited' categories, 'domicile' would no longer protect them. And, to widen the net, the legislation was dated retroactively to 1910. This was intended to ensure plenty of evidence against the Strike leaders: no matter how circumspect they were in their present utterances, any of their words from the past decade could be resurrected to doom them. Explaining the bill to the House of Commons, Calder said, 'The law officers of the Crown have advised that the section as it stands does not really cover all that was intended.'[95] He wasn't very explicit about the targets of the amendments. The more cosmetic changes allowed him to mask what was actually being done to British immigrants. MPs asked him to list the changes to the previous day's bill; he trotted out the wording around 'advocates,' blackmail, and (more significantly) an added clause directed at 'any person who assumes any authority without lawful justification,' but he kept mum about the citizenship changes. Neither did he add that 'law officers' referred to a very specific member of the Citizens' Committee of 1000: the former boy-mayor of Winnipeg.[96]

The new bill not only passed, but passed with incredible speed, Meighen boasting that it 'certainly beat all records.'[97] In a matter of minutes on 6 June, the amendment was adopted by the Commons and Senate and given royal assent. The Immigration Act of 1910 and the 5 June amendment had provided for the deportation of any person 'other than a Canadian citizen' engaged in prohibited activities. The 6 June amendment defined what was meant by a Canadian citizen with the addition of the words 'either by reason of birth in Canada, or by reason of naturalization in Canada.' Calder quietly dropped the clause that had allowed British subjects to be 'domiciled' in Canada. Since British subjects remained technically ineligible for 'naturalization' until the adoption of the Canadian Citizenship Act in 1946, the effect of the 6 June amendment was to leave British-born immigrants (coming to Canada after 1910) exposed to deportation.

Historians have always known that the Immigration Act amendments were an important development in the Strike. What has been less obvious is that a crucial change had taken place in Meighen's relationship with Andrews. Noticing how Meighen had used his legal skills to engineer controversial votes – the motion on Closure (1913) and the Wartime Elections Act (1917), in which he managed to disenfranchise thousands of people who had voted previously – historians assumed that it must have been Meighen who pulled the strings against the Strike. Not so. Andrews not only got what he wanted,[98] but he also had Meighen more or less under rein. Meighen wrote, 'Your telegrams are most useful, and depend upon it I am following every phase and move in Winnipeg with the utmost care.'[99] Nominally, Meighen continued to be in charge. Yet, while he never apologized to Andrews in so many words for initially dropping the legislative ball, Meighen's chastened tone told Andrews all Andrews needed to know.

Saturday, 7 June – Monday, 9 June

One of the other balls that Andrews had up in the air was in danger of coming down: there was danger of a settlement to the Strike. By Wednesday, 4 June, the Running Trades Mediation Committee, having consulted with strikers and employers, had recommended that metalworkers be allowed to negotiate with ironmasters through a Metal Trades Council – exactly the sort of collective bargaining that the work-

ers wanted.[100] The Strike Committee agreed, sensing a potential basis
for ending the General Strike. Andrews and the Citizens were aghast.
They needed the façade of negotiation, but any settlement flew in the
face of their policy of absolute victory. If the Strike weren't called off
before any bona fide negotiations, then labour would continue to bran-
dish the general strike whenever any employer rejected union demands.

Labour Minister Gideon Robertson had earlier promised the Citizens
that the Mediation Committee would offer only the limited form of collective bargaining that had already been rejected by the metal trades
workers. However, when the Strike Committee 'laughed' at that offer,
and told the Running Trades to walk off the job, the Running Trades
Mediation Committee, fearful of its own workers defecting to the OBU,
sided with labour and conceded 'practically all the strikers had asked
for,' namely the aforementioned Metal Trades Council. The employers,
Andrews explained, couldn't accept this.

Damned if they did; damned if they didn't: if the Citizens allowed a
negotiated settlement, the strikers could claim victory; if the Citizens
prevented a settlement, the strikers could claim that the Citizens had
obstructed the process. To avoid these two results, Andrews nominated
Robertson as the stalking horse from behind which the Citizens could
kill the Mediation Committee's new proposal without seeming to do so.
Andrews asked Robertson to come to Winnipeg immediately,[101] and
urged Meighen get him moving.[102] Meighen was confused: 'Please
explain Winnipeg situation especially Citizens Committee asking intervention.' He cited the Citizens' message to MP George Allan of 20 May,
in which the Citizens had asked that there be no 'government interference,' and that 'well meaning but inadequately formed persons' [*sic*] be
prevented from negotiating a settlement.[103] Why, all of a sudden, were
the Citizens now asking for Robertson as a government mediator?
Although Meighen couldn't grasp Andrews's subtle tactics in calling for
Robertson, Meighen did know which outcome Andrews desired, and
spoke in a way that was sure to get his approval: 'Seems to me settlement now under pressure from Minister will be generally accepted as triumph for general strike leaders. This is confidential.'[104] Andrews patted
him on the head: 'Your message shows you understand danger situation
stop Running Trades Committee still working stop Believe Robertson
could greatly assist in preventing tactical mistakes stop Feared committee may report against metal employers and difficulties keeping running
trades from joining strike greatly increased.'[105] Translation: Andrews
thought that he could use Robertson to *prevent* a mediated settlement.
Andrews explained to Meighen:

What we want to avoid if possible is a definite finding by this Committee against the Metal Trades and in favor of the strike Committee as this is bound to have an injurious effect. If on the other hand, this Committee can be persuaded to make no finding at all or a finding that the employers have offered what appears to them to be a fair settlement, no bad results will follow their negotiations.[106]

Although George Allan had to be told back on 20 May not to accept mediation until the General Strike had ended, by now the Citizens' lobbying had taken firm root, and, unaware that the mediation 'effort' was simply a PR exercise, Allan, as confused as Meighen, worriedly telegrammed Augustus Nanton: 'Am informed both Companies and men agreed to accept railway brotherhood officers as mediators stop. Do not quite understand why mediation was accepted while sympathetic strike still on stop. Please explain fully.'[107]

Anti-mediator Robertson duly headed west. David Bercuson has suggested that he had no initial desire to rig the proceedings against the strikers. However, on the prime minister's copy of the letter from Andrews, Meighen wrote the following note: 'This letter shows clearly the purpose Andrews had in suggesting the Minister go west – the opposite purpose than that for which he is going.'[108] The proceedings *were* rigged, and Andrews's 'purpose' was likely by now Cabinet's too, since Robertson earlier acceded to Andrews's interpretation of events, and saw the OBU as anathema to the national interest. In Winnipeg, Robertson quickly took the Citizens' line. He met with the Citizens, the Running Trades Mediation Committee, and officials of the provincial government. By the time that he, after a lot of stalling, reported to Borden on 11 June, there would be a riot, a threat by other railway unions to walk off the job, and the expectation of further violence. Robertson may have hoped for a solution and was prepared to demand concessions from the metal masters, but, following the Citizens' advice, he wouldn't move in that direction until the General Strike had ended.[109] With the existing industrial system of conciliation at risk, he saw the defeat of the Strike as a necessary victory against the OBU, and he needed an end-game strategy other than simple repression. Andrews gave him that strategy.

Andrews may well have had other Machiavellian tactics up his sleeve too. In his telegram of 5 June, he had stated the obvious to Meighen about criminal prosecutions: 'I think it is a matter for the Attorney General rather than your department.'[110] This was basic constitutional law, not something to give an *opinion* on, not something to '*think*' about. Criminal prosecutions were and are the jurisdiction of the Province, and even violations of federal Orders-in-Council had to be prosecuted by the Province. What did Meighen make of Andrews's puzzling letter of the next day? This letter repeated the truism, but in such a way as to call it into question: 'This is a matter purely for the Attorney General and not your department *unless you are strongly of the view that the Attorney General has taken the wrong course and that you should interfere* and I strongly recommend that you leave the responsibility of this matter where it is'[111] [emphasis added]. With the appearance of reaffirming the constitutional status quo, Andrews was already tilling Meighen with the possibility that the federal government – not Andrews – might decide to override Attorney General Johnson and usurp provincial power. Andrews would add to Meighen's confusion later in June when he affected to believe that the federal Justice Department was intent on prosecuting the Strike leadership. The Machiavellian counsellor was dropping into the prince's mind a course of action, hoping that later on the prince might think the idea his own.

Andrews kept himself front and centre by continuing to play mediator, keeping Meighen receptive to his guidance by emphasizing the demands of the more hard-nosed Citizens, and using Meighen's fear of a nation-wide general strike to keep (or to be seen to keep) the more hard-nosed Citizens in line: 'You will be very glad to know that the efforts I have made to curb the impatience of the citizens, has [*sic*] been measurably successful I believe.'[112] Andrews had the CPR's Edward Beatty speak to the Citizens and also to the Running Trades Committee in order to back Andrews's cautious position on state coercion. Beatty spoke about 'the grave fear that if the strike leaders were arrested the railroads might be tied up and the strike situation made more acute both here and at other points.' Commissioner Perry addressed a thousand of the Citizens' rank-and-file volunteers,[113] and Gen. Ketchen managed to receive a 'fair hearing' from the 'red returned soldier element.' Despite the effects of the veterans' parades, and the looming loyalty oath, Andrews continued to claim that as long as authorities could prevent 'any radical thing' from happening, the 'sane' elements within labour would 'depose' the Strike leadership, and the Strike would end. It would be 'a splendid lesson if the strike fails without any hatred or rancor being engendered and the sober workers feel that they have made a mistake.'[114]

Yet on 9 June, the Police Commission kept its ultimatum and dismissed the police officers who hadn't signed the loyalty oath. It was a lockout, but Captain James Dunwoody, who helped organize the loyalist returned men, managed to convince himself otherwise: 'About 3 or 4 days after we had been formed I had a call from the Chief of Police,

[Acting] Chief Newton, who said … 'Dunwoody, my men have gone on strike. You will please take over the control of the city so far as the mounted police are concerned.'[115] It was a lockout and a provocation, precisely what Andrews had hoped to avoid.

7

Time to Act

Tuesday, 10 June

A lot can change in twenty-four hours. Three weeks into the strike, on 5 June, the *Citizen* pretended that the city was the kind of chaotic world that Hobbes and Locke had envisioned preceding the arrival of the state: 'Lawlessness and disorder are rampant throughout the city all day and every night. Men and women are wantonly assaulted upon the streets. Men, women and children are attacked and threatened while going about their lawful avocations.' If the strikers had admitted that the first disruption of the bread and milk supply might have endangered sick children, then a second such disruption must constitute, as a *Winnipeg Citizen* headline put it, 'An Attempt at Wilful Murder.'[1] There had been many cases of intimidation and threat, but the picture of lawlessness and disorder was highly exaggerated, for there were almost no assaults. Yet by opposing a settlement, by fanning anti-alien passions, and by working (despite an initial reluctance) with the Police Commission to replace the police with Specials, the Citizens were helping to create the disorder that they at first had merely imagined.

The Specials under Major Lyle stepped onto the streets on the 10th. Later, stretching the truth, Andrews would say, 'These special police are most of them business men who are not working for the pay that is offered but from patriotism.'[2] All morning they were hooted at and jeered, particularly near Portage and Main, where a large crowd of hecklers had gathered. Finally, at 1:00 or 2:00 p.m., the Specials decided to clean up the street and disperse the crowd. There is a strange menace in the photographs of the Specials that day – men dressed in suits and hats as if they were on their way to work, but forming a wall across Portage

Avenue, carrying spokes from wagon wheels, and striding purposefully towards the strikers.[3]

One might call this a re-enactment of the violent founding of the state. Relying on Nietzsche and René Girard, J.M. Coetzee suggests that for the law to flourish, it must veil its violent origins.[4] But at moments such as June 10th, the state's violence, whether resisted or agreed to in a social contract, reveals itself. The truncheons in the hands of the Specials incensed the strikers, and they threw stones, brickbats, and glass bottles at the Specials, trying, where possible, to wrest away the truncheons.[5] Hand-to-hand combat followed. Mounted Specials under James Dunwoody rushed to the scene to extricate their stranded brethren, including a veteran named Fred Coppins, who had to be taken to the hospital. It was a riot, even though American reporter Samuel Hopkins Adams called the Specials 'an amateur force,' and mocked the scale of the events: 'Apparently the Canadian taste in riots is milder than ours. A running fight of fifteen minutes' duration in the heart of a city between the police and a mob, in which not a shot is fired, not a man is killed, and hardly a window is broken, would scarcely be called a very serious riot in the United States. I hardly know what it would be called; a movie rehearsal perhaps.'[6]

Actually, the riot went on for three hours,[7] and everyone, except over-sophisticated reporters from the United States, considered the events highly serious. Although technically the Specials were now operating within the constitution, their lack of popular legitimacy threatened to subvert the rule of law. They formed a strange hybrid of private and public. Clothed in the uniforms of private life, they nevertheless marched in the military formations of state warfare and state policing. They weren't a fully legitimate police force; but neither, though the *Western Labor News* called them 'thugs,'[8] were they a group of vigilantes. Unlike actual thugs used by some American 'Citizens' Alliance' employers to beat strikers into submission, the Specials weren't a private army usurping a state function: being delegated by the Police Commission to enforce order in the streets wasn't the same as assaulting union officials at night. The Specials were meant to take control of Winnipeg's centre, Portage and Main, to recapture the public sphere that the strikers had illegitimately seized. However, as part of the trench system that Gramsci identified in the West, the Specials were also, and more importantly, meant to capture that *metaphorical* public sphere, described by Jürgen Habermas and Charles Taylor, which had been carved out of aristocratic power. Who had the *right* to inhabit the public sphere? It was High Noon, and the Specials were trying, in a semi-legitimate fashion, to take the town square back for the rule of law. The ordinariness of the uniform could signify either that private citizens were 'rescuing' the state, or that private citizens had managed to grasp state power. If 'Permitted by Authority of the Strike Committee' signs had signalled constitutional dangers on labour's side, so did the deployment of the Specials on the Citizens' side.

From General Ketchen's office window above the street, Andrews looked down on the riot as it played itself out:

> The special police of which a number were mounted proved wholly inadequate and the net result is that they have been chased off the streets, a number of them hurt, some badly wounded and the crowd in possession of a number of their clubs. The crowd hurled brick bats, stones and other missiles and it does not appear to me that there was any kind of an organization to arrest any one. [9]

'My blood boiled with indignation,' Andrews added the next day. It boiled so much that he called Mayor Gray and urged that water hoses and 'the high pressure plant' be used to blow the strikers off the street.[10] With respect to Major Lyle's leadership, Andrews was decidedly unimpressed – 'This man strikes me as being of no ability to cope with the situation'[11] – and in the coming days, after Lyle was dismissed, Andrews grew even harsher, calling him 'more or less a four flusher' and then ending with the typical Citizens' character assassination of anyone who doubted their policy: 'Nobody knows even that he is loyal. He certainly is no organizer and is running around like a chicken without a head.' In Lyle's stead, the Citizens supplied their own man, Major Bingham, 'a real soldier.'[12]

The riot was a turning point for Andrews. He called the situation 'much worse today than it has been since commencement.' Although he had been uneasy about the Police Commission's stand on loyalty oaths, and despite the potential dangers associated with martial law, he immediately insinuated that revolution was under way. Staying with the measured tone designed to assure Meighen of his competence, Andrews hinted but did not claim that constitutional breaches had been made: the trouble, he said, 'had every appearance of being fomented by some organized effort. Whether the old police were at the back of it I cannot say.' If the old police were indeed fighting with the newly authorized police as Andrews implied, this would certainly amount to a crisis of legitimacy, and perhaps even to civil war. But whether it was true or not, Andrews 'couldn't say.' He 'couldn't say' because he had no evidence at all that the old police were at the back of it, but, lacking evidence, he could still insinuate. He began to nudge Meighen towards martial law.

The Citizens were 'indignant' that Mayor Gray had not read the riot act, he said.[13] Indeed, within a couple of days, the *Western Labor News* would report that Gray was beset on all sides: 'The citizens committee has thrown me overboard,' Gray lamented. 'The strikers are against me. Even my old friend [*Winnipeg Telegram* editor] Knox McGee, has declared war on me because I refuse to declare martial law.'[14] The next day, Andrews, to emphasize his point to Meighen, would relay a plan by the strikers to wreck the Citizens' headquarters at the Industrial Bureau, a plan averted by the Strike Committee. Andrews was probably speaking for many Citizens when he suggested that it might be time for the RNWMP or the militia under Gen. Ketchen to appear on stage: 'Unless the special police can be better organized tomorrow will probably witness much bloodshed for General Ketchen cannot close his eyes to the lawlessness that is rife everywhere.' As Andrews now grasped, the City did not have the resources to control the streets. Of the 1200 Specials supposedly available, only 150 could be counted on.[15]

Andrews's tone, though not alarmist, was intended to prepare Meighen for sterner measures advocated by the Citizens. Tuesday evening, the streets were crowded and quiet, but Andrews didn't take any comfort in that. The deceptive quiet held, he thought, because the Specials had backed off and the strikers, not democratically constituted authorities, controlled the streets through intimidation – 'there is no foe in sight.' He looked forward to Wednesday 'with great apprehension.'[16]

Wednesday, 11 June

As the sun rose Wednesday morning, Andrews's earlier prophecies of the Strike's imminent end seemed very distant. General Ketchen, however, was still reluctant to bring in the troops and foreclose the issue. Consent and coercion are the two faces of the liberal order, according to Gramsci. Coercion could have ended the Strike immediately, but was much more safely used as a counterpunch, not as an initiative. The fear was that 'if volunteers with machine guns mow down a crowd of unarmed strikers, no matter on what provocation, all Canada would burst into flame.'[17] Under a British constitution, martial law was a no-man's-land, where the army's commanding officer, in this case Ketchen, could be shelled from both sides. Officers must somehow find 'the exact line between excess and failure of duty.'[18] If Ketchen were too quick to order his soldiers to shoot, he could, potentially, be liable for murder (though in practice such cases were rarely prosecuted); if he were too slow to order his soldiers to shoot, he could, potentially, be liable for not controlling the unrest. Ketchen still hoped that the Specials, now under

Deputy Police Chief Newton instead of Major Lyle, could handle the situation, but Andrews had transposed his confidence to the military. One problem: few returned soldiers were joining the militia. This was clearly a slap in the face of the Citizens, but so that Meighen wouldn't ask difficult questions, Andrews put a hopeful construction on it, saying that the soldiers, 'while they will not join the militia, say they will form themselves into a body in support of the general.'[19]

Reflecting on the riot, but with the purpose of converting the public not cultivating a cabinet minister, the editors of the *Winnipeg Citizen*, unlike Andrews, felt no need to proceed subtly. In the days before the riot, the *Citizen* had used *New York World* reports to allege that the Strike was linked to an international conspiracy based in New York. The author of these reports, Sherman Rogers, a right-wing American investigative journalist, claimed that he had pierced 'the inner council of the Bolsheviki of this continent.'[20] The *Citizen* added that the Winnipeg General Strike was part of a plan to establish OBU control over labour, and that 'almost every move in the enterprise has had its initiative in New York City.'[21] Given Andrews's close consultations with Colonel Starnes of the RNWMP and with General Ketchen, it's highly unlikely that Andrews, Pitblado, Coyne, or *Citizen* co-editor Sweatman believed this claim of an international conspiracy, and on 9 June A.A. McLean, comptroller of the RNWMP, wrote to E.L. Newcombe, deputy minister of justice, that some of the strikers held 'Bolsheviki' *sympathies*, but there was 'little' evidence of actual connections between the Strike 'and enemy or Bolshevik organizations abroad.'[22]

Nevertheless, the 10 June riot allowed the *Citizen* to resurrect, more convincingly, the narrative of revolution. In the earlier, quieter days of the Strike, it had been easy to dismiss as cherry-picking the *Citizen*'s quotations from the Calgary conference and the Walker Theatre meeting. It was less easy now. At the Walker, Russell had said that a workers' revolution would soon overthrow capitalism:

> The blood that is spilled in Canada will depend on the working class. We must establish the same form of government as they have it in Russia so that we may have a Russian democracy here. The only way to prevent the coming revolution in Canada is for the government to establish a form of government such as the Bolsheviks have established in Russia and are now establishing in Germany.[23]

Recounting the injuries to Fred Coppins of the Specials, the *Citizen* announced, 'This IS revolution, with a vengeance. This is THE revolution that has been planned for two years.'[24]

The purpose of such claims was to legitimize their intrusion into the 'extrapolitical' public sphere.[25] In Louis Silverberg's assessment of citizens' committees, 'propaganda is not only a weapon used in conflict, it is a means of intensifying the conflict. It thus serves to prepare the ground for the injection – and justification – of violence into the dispute.'[26] One interpretation of the loyalty oath, the dismissal of the police, the riot, and the press's response is that the *Citizen's* articles convinced no one; they served merely to antagonize strikers and to inflame the Citizens' constituency even further, so that the 10,000 'Citizens' might be goaded into joining the Specials and might become convinced that direct action was necessary. If Andrews can be trusted, the riots initially proved a great spur for militia recruitment, though it was Specials that the Citizens really wanted at this point, not a larger militia sitting uselessly in the barracks.[27]

Despite the provocation offered by a wholesale firing of the police, the Citizens, in recounting the riot, laid all initiative at the strikers' feet. The riot had been designed by 'the Reds to commit all strikers to revolution, by violence, in a desperate effort to save the movement they had started from collapse and incidentally to save their own miserable hides.' The *Citizen* invoked the hierarchical and traditionalist idiom of war-time sacrifice and honour. Honour, gallantry, and heroic patriotism belonged to the Specials, particularly to Coppins, who once had been prepared to lay down his life 'in the blood-soaked miasma of Northern France' for 'God, King, and Country,' and for 'the salvation of a true Canadian democracy.' That same hero now lay wounded for labour's transgressions. The *Citizen* reported that 'at the time of writing, Sergeant Fred Coppin [*sic*], Victoria Cross hero of France, is lying in the Military Hospital and is stated to be dying. He was not expected to live until morning.' Irony of post-war ironies: he had survived the Kaiser's armies in Europe, but now three Austrians had torn him off his horse and tried to kick him to death, 'men whose blood relations he and every other returned fighter fought in France … Are Austrians, enemies of Canada, to be allowed to attempt to murder loyal soldiers, heroes, true Britishers, upon the streets of Winnipeg?'[28]

The Citizens' account illustrates how narrative may be put at the service of ideology. To ensure broader circulation of the story, the Citizens took out an ad in the *Winnipeg Telegram*, describing Coppins's heroic wartime bayoneting of German 'GUN CREW AFTER GUN CREW.'[29] His riot injuries allowed the *Citizen* again to link anti-Strike forces with the patriotism of the Great War: 'Coppin [*sic*] was dragged from his horse while he was fighting for democracy and British institutions just as truly as he fought for them overseas.' He was a particular kind of incarnation, 'the embodiment, the personification of the British Constitution itself.' Coppins, living metaphor of the British constitution, didn't mention that he had been born in the United States and was still an American citizen. [30] By attacking Coppins, a 'peace officer,' the brutal Austrians had attacked the constitution as certainly as the Kaiser had.[31] The *Citizen* passed over the tenuousness of Coppins's own 'constitutional' position – only that very morning he had been sworn into a special police force, days after almost all the police had been locked out.[32] If Coppins were to die, intoned the *Citizen*, the Strike leaders would be 'morally as guilty of his murder as are the curs who put the Prussianist boots to the hero yesterday.' And he probably would die: 'By the time that this appears, he may be dead.'[33]

That same Wednesday, however, Coppins revealed that no one pulled him from his horse, and that he received two broken ribs from a stone thrown by 'a bunch of bohunks.'[34] The day that the *Citizen* was giving a false account of Coppins's potentially mortal injuries, the *Telegram* reported that Coppins's injuries amounted to broken ribs, and that he was rallying quickly.[35] Although the *Telegram* editorialized in favour of the Citizens, praised the Specials, and condemned the 'murderous' assault on Coppins, it retained enough journalistic integrity not to alter the facts of the incident. A telling detail: while the *Citizen* on Wednesday predicted Coppins's imminent death, the Citizens' *advertisement* that same day in the *Telegram* didn't mention death. Clearly, the Citizens realized that their page-two ad in the *Telegram* ought not to directly contradict the *Telegram*'s news report appearing on pages one and three. Yet this didn't prevent the Citizens from printing the false report in their own newspaper on the same day. One must attribute a high degree of cynicism to the *Citizen*'s editors Sweatman and Fletcher Sparling.

As to the 'Austrians,' Gen. Ketchen admitted that the disorder was 'not caused by aliens only. Many labour returned men implicated.'[36] Andrews, too, told Meighen, 'For some reason the Press has blamed the aliens for the riot. I saw it all and that was not my opinion. My opinion was that the strikers were directly the aggressors, and most of them returned soldiers.'[37] Again, the gap between the Citizens' public rhetoric and their spokesperson's private comments suggests cynicism. In any case, if Captain Dunwoody was accurate, the strikers suffered more than the Specials: 'We went back to the barracks, having sustained some casualties, and having caused a good many more.'[38] Dunwoody knew that some of his Specials had drilled holes in their truncheons and filled them with lead in order to give them more heft.[39]

When the facts of Coppins's condition became common knowledge, the *Citizen* didn't issue a retraction. Rather than admitting that yesterday's news had been different, the next day the *Citizen* quietly adjusted itself to the new facts about Coppins's ribs, and instead set to work mythologizing the new day's (Wednesday's) incidents, now turning these, too, into atrocities: 'On the first day one special policeman had his ribs kicked in by a bunch of aliens. On the second day, another policeman was set upon by another bunch of aliens and shot. Winnipeg is in a state of anarchy ... It was purely accidental that [the bullet] did not hit a vital spot. It matters not who fired that shot, the responsibility is upon the men who started the violence that caused it to be fired.' The no-negotiation *Citizen* also accused the Strike leaders of avoiding a settlement.[40] Indeed, there had again been trouble on the streets, but it was the shooting, not the aim, that was accidental. Gen. Ketchen's telegraph explained, 'It transpires [the] Special was not fired on by alien but men in passing car fired a shot to disperse [the] crowd hitting Special in leg: ricochet.'[41] The injured Special, whom the *Citizen* dignified with the title 'Constable' Morson, was shot by another Special – a case of friendly fire. The *Citizen*'s wording – 'it matters not who fired that shot' – suggests that the *Citizen*'s editors knew from the outset that a striker hadn't fired the shot. Strike leaders were now to blame even when Specials accidentally shot each other. The ideological claims of the committee were served, and if only a minimal and belated adjustment to the facts had been made in Coppins's case, the careful wording around Morson's case ensured that no correction would be necessary the next day.

Thursday, 12 June – Monday, 16 June

After two days of riots, the RNWMP planted two operatives to identify US agitators coming into Winnipeg and to gather evidence of treason or sedition among the Strike leaders. At Andrews's insistence, the military also recruited returned soldiers to use as spies.[42] Andrews's secret-service intrigue was a bit of fluff thrown into the air to mesmerize Starnes, Ketchen, and Meighen. Andrews knew that it would be difficult to hang his hat on anything new coming out of the mouths of the Strike leaders, or on US agitators, even though immigrant Strike leaders Sam Blumenberg and Max Charitonoff had come from Eastern Europe by way of the United States, and the less important Oscar Schoppelrei was American.

But Andrews was again planning arrests, and the distraction was intended to make arrests more palatable. The railway Running Trades were making Andrews anxious because the 'younger element' was 'strongly infected with Socialistic views.' Senator Robertson and officers of the 'International Organization' were trying to rein them in. Robertson was dismayed by the apparent spread of disorder, by the recent decision of some CPR and CN members to walk out, and by the practical difficulties of negotiating an end to the Strike.[43] If we take Robertson's and Andrews's word for it, these international union officials were 'very much disturbed' that the government had not yet arrested the Reds leading the Strike.

The ratcheting up of rhetoric by the *Winnipeg Citizen* signalled that it was the Citizens, not international union officials, who were depressed about the situation and wanted arrests.[44] Premier Norris and Commissioner Perry were against arrests under the Criminal Code, though not against use of the newly amended Immigration Act.[45] The Citizens realized that further lobbying of the Province would be a waste of time. 'Their only hope,' said Andrews, 'is the Dominion authorities'[46] – which was to say, 'you, Arthur Meighen.'

Andrews announced to Meighen that the Wednesday issue of the *Western Labor News* contained 'enough evidence ... to convict the whole Strike Committee.'[47] For what crime, he didn't say. Assertions in the *Labor News* that 'the tools of production must no longer remain in the hands of the few' and that the OBU would fix this might have provoked the Citizens,[48] but Andrews's actions a few days later suggest that for him the 'crime' lay in an article about the Specials entitled 'POLICE REPLACED BY THUGS.' Although Andrews had himself been uneasy about the timing of the loyalty oath, now that the course had been taken, he'd defend it to the death, at least in public. The subject of Special Police was especially touchy, since the strikers had identified a constitutional flashpoint: were the Specials an instrument of public order or a private army? Andrews hoped that one hundred of the striking police officers might return to work and sign the oath, but the problem of the Specials hadn't been solved, and although he expected the Police Commission to stand firm on its firing of the police, he predicted that the reappearance of the Specials would again cause riots.[49] Indeed, Alderman John Sparling of the Police Commission admitted that the City didn't have control of the street between 10 and 21 June.[50]

But Andrews had a plan in mind, and all the federal players who were party to his work (as well as historians who didn't have access to Andrews's correspondence) may be forgiven for thinking that he'd bring down the newly amended Immigration Act on the Strike leaders' heads: arrests, brief hearings, deportation. 'I need not forecast this action now,'[51] he said, but pretended to tip his hand, just enough to mislead his superiors. He asked Meighen to 'send certified copy amendments Immigration Act, also instruct Immigration officers here to act promptly at my request. Stop. I may need to act at once.'[52] He hoped that Meighen had 'duly appointed Col. Starnes, Immigration Officer and constituted the proper Board of Inquiry.'[53] More as a courtesy than anything else, copies of the amended Immigration Act were also sent to Attorney General Johnson[54] – his reluctance to act had placed him on the sidelines, and it was Andrews who was in charge now. Minister of Immigration J.A. Calder instructed Mounted Police immigration officers to make arrests as soon as Andrews gave the word, though Andrews still had to clear his moves with Robertson first.

One development that may have helped to steer Andrews away from the Immigration Act was Meighen's warning not to rely on the second sub-clause of section 41, the clause retroactively dating the amendments to 1910.[55] With the sub-clause, Andrews could drag the lake for anything that the Strike leaders had said in the previous decade, including their words at the Calgary conference or the Walker Theatre meeting. Without it, Andrews would have a hard time finding statements advocating even the meagre 'disbelief in organized government,' never mind its violent overthrow. The problem was that earlier on Friday, Tom Moore and John Bruce of the Trades and Labor Council had confronted Prime Minister Borden, first because any *retroactive* law was constitutionally suspect; and, second, because Moore had an agreement with Robertson that 'no legislation affecting labour interests would be passed without notice to him during his absence as Member of [the Mathers] Commission.'[56] Robertson – no lawyer himself – didn't know that Andrews, deprived of the sub-clause, was turning towards the Criminal Code. That Robertson had no idea what Andrews was planning is evident in Robertson's message to Borden: 'Our plan will probably be to move a considerable number directly to train destined Internment Camp KAPUSKASING unless you advise us that accommodation is not available it being thought very desirable that they should be removed promptly from here.'[57] The next day, Robertson was still writing Borden as if Andrews planned immigration arrests.[58]

On Saturday, the day that the youthful revolutionary Antonio Gramsci, probably after reading accounts of the 10 and 11 June riots, told readers of *L'Ordine Nuovo* that in Canada 'industrial strikes have taken on the overt character of a bid to install a soviet regime'[59] – that Winnipeg's militants, like their Russian counterparts, had rejected the lumbering gradualism of Second International Marxism and were about to create a workers' state modelled on revolutionary Russia – Gen. Ketchen told his superiors in Ottawa a similar story: 'Red element has organization prepared to foment trouble at short notice. Propaganda has been wide spread of worst type' [*sic*].[60] But there is scant evidence for what Gramsci welcomed and Ketchen feared. On Friday, the *Western Labor News* headline had read, 'SITUATION LOOKS GOOD.' One story, 'Ugly Action Contemplated,' rumoured martial law, while other stories suggested that the Citizens' anti-alien ads were a subterfuge, and that the Strike wasn't revolutionary. Saturday's headline, 'WE SHOULD WORRY,' was followed by articles about the Specials breaking up gatherings.

It was true that everyone expected a showdown. The *Western Labor News* rumbled about possible arrests, expecting about 100 to 150 strike leaders to be apprehended.[61] But the more ominous propaganda came from the law-and-order crowd. The *Citizen* had taken on a threatening tone, quoting the returned soldier William Bathie, who wanted his fellow veterans to 'get busy and curb' the activities of the strikers, and adding its own gloss to Bathie's 'unmistakable' meaning: 'It is a fact that cannot be blinked by any man, that if British institutions are challenged by violence, in this city or elsewhere, the most harsh of repressive measures must be exercised.'[62] Andrews, too, believed that strikers were preparing to confront the Specials, that they 'were bringing their supporters from St James and all outlying districts.' He advised against placing the Specials, now numbering 400 out of a nominal list of 1438, on the street, and got Crown Prosecutor Robert Graham to persuade the Police Commission to heed the advice: 'Had the men been put on point duty this morning there would certainly have been much bloodshed.'[63] Said Andrews, 'the clash is bound to come but I would like to be thoroughly prepared when it does come.'[64] It wasn't that Andrews was so keen on avoiding bloodshed, but for *strategic* reasons he feared what would happen if he placed the Specials on the street – 'It would embarrass us in what we intend to do.' If the Specials were challenged, he wanted them to triumph.

Heavy rains and 135-kilometre-per-hour winds that tore down wires swept through Winnipeg Saturday night as the drum beat of a possible confrontation sounded.[65] Robertson knew that arrests were imminent – he had to authorize Andrews's plans – but the evidence suggests that Robertson didn't know the *basis* on which the arrests would be made. He was still trying to prevent a general walkout by the railway Running Trades without acquiescing in the recognition of the Metal Trades Council. Already some locomotive firefighters and switchmen, together with trainmen and engineers, had walked off the job in support of the Strike. Nevertheless, Robertson and Cabinet had reason to be optimistic about the stick and carrot. The stick – arresting the leaders – was in Andrews's capable hands. The carrot – forcing ironmasters to accept a lesser form of collective bargaining – would remove the major justification for the sympathetic strike. Robertson knew that some ironmasters had long been willing to bend; they had merely been holding out on the advice of the Citizens. One of the employers, L.R. Barrett of Vulcan Iron Works, continued to be 'very obdurate and quite unreasonable,' insisting that the Strike 'could only be settled by force of arm,' and that 'blood would be shed before a settlement was made.'[66] But Robertson planned to impose a scheme of collective bargaining to 'prevent complete dislocation of transportation in Western Canada.'[67] On Sunday the ironmasters and, more surprisingly, the railway unions agreed to Robertson's terms, the formal recognition of collective bargaining being just enough to keep railway workers on the job.[68] The Strike Committee refused to endorse the agreement. To accept these terms would have amounted to capitulation, as the Metal Trades Council still wouldn't be recognized as the bargaining agent.

None of this altered plans to apply the stick of arrests. Robertson, still thinking of Immigration Act arrests, told Borden, 'Our attitude on the sympathetic strike issue will of course remain unchanged and plans outlined ... yesterday are being matured.'[69]

8

Enough Evidence to Convict the Whole Strike Committee

Tuesday, 17 June

The Province wasn't eager for arrests, especially since it was expected that the new definition of collective bargaining might sap the Strike of its momentum, and Meighen was having second thoughts too, wary of hitching himself permanently to Andrews's wagon and thereby to the Citizens. On Monday he had wired Andrews to the effect that Stony Mountain Penitentiary couldn't be used to hold the Strike leaders because it wasn't an immigration station,[1] and early on Tuesday Meighen wired Robertson: 'Judge Robson wires advising delay in arrests and says Provincial Government so advise [sic]. Andrews and Stearns authorization depends wholly on you. This merely for your information.'[2]

Just as well that it was for information; such queasiness could no longer mean anything to Andrews or the Citizens; the arrests had already taken place. The person supposed to have final authority in the laying of charges, Crown Prosecutor Robert Graham, had been summoned to a meeting at RNWMP headquarters on Monday evening, where nearly one hundred 'citizens' assembled to decide whom to arrest. Mayor Gray, apparently, wasn't invited.[3] Afterwards, members of the Citizens' publicity committee declared that the arrests had come as a complete surprise to them, and that they knew nothing except what they read in the newspapers,[4] but that's misinformation, since Graham was astounded at the size of the crowd.[5] Outside, on what he facetiously called 'Whitewall Avenue,' about fifty automobiles awaited driving orders, and in the Fort Osborne barracks there waited a RNWMP detachment – 175 men of all ranks, with an armoured car and four Lewis guns – should the arrests create insurrection.[6] Neither ignored nor consulted, Graham simply took

his place in the meeting alongside Police Chief Newton and the many
Citizens. Instead of Graham, beside Andrews stood 'Assistant' Crown
Prosecutor Hugh Phillips, who had been more cooperative. Graham had
made it clear that he was opposed to charges. He bore no particular love
for the strikers or their methods, but at the same time he thought that the
case for sedition was weak: 'I do not think there was, in the minds of the
real leaders any thought of revolution. They merely wished to establish
the dominance of organized labour. Further I felt that the strike was on
its last legs ... The strikers knew this but they were holding out in the
hope of obtaining terms of surrender.' Graham blamed some of the subsequent trouble on the arrests.[7] Although Phillips wasn't authorizing the
arrests, and so wasn't exactly overriding Graham, Phillips's presence
helped to legitimize Andrews's actions. Later, when the Strike leaders'
defence counsel, E.J. McMurray, asked Graham about what level of government took the step that night, Graham had no idea:

McMurray:	Do you know if it was made by the authority or under the direction of the Dominion Government or the Provincial Government or its officers?
Graham:	I don't know.
McMurray:	You were not consulted in that capacity at all?
Graham:	No.[8]

At the meeting, Andrews held a lot of blank search warrants and arrest
warrants, and near him sat at least ten typists to fill the warrants in. He
placed a list of about fifty names before the Citizens, and they proceeded
to whittle it down. It's possible that Andrews had a shortlist in mind and
that the consultation was pro forma, but judging by Graham's description, Andrews and Robertson hadn't finalized the list, and the consultation was real. Rather than a level of government taking the lead, the Citizens were deciding who was guilty – not of intimidation or violence
(charges which an individual or business owner might reasonably press),
but of seditious conspiracy and seditious libel. By 9:30 p.m., the Citizens
had settled on twelve of the most active leaders.[9]

Yet the arrests almost didn't happen. Despite the informations, twelve
arrest warrants, and thirty search warrants ready to be executed, Premier
Norris phoned Sen. Robertson at the last moment with 'definite information' that the Central Strike Committee was going to meet with the
'General Committee of Three Hundred' in an effort to call off the
Strike.[10] Robertson returned to the meeting, and said, 'Boys I guess it's
all off ... They have told the premier that if he will appoint a commission to investigate the causes of the strike, the strike will be called off ...

The premier does not wish us to do anything to hamper these negotiations.'[11] There was half a minute of silence, a very long silence for a
meeting as crowded as this one. Then Graham, despite personal misgiv-
ings about the weakness of the charges, asked Robertson whether he
intended to prosecute the Strike leaders even if the Strike were called
off. Robertson said yes. In that case, the pragmatic Graham replied, the
arrests ought to happen immediately, because with this many cooks in
the kitchen, the strikers would soon hear of the government's intentions.
After that, according to Graham, 'Robertson seemed in a quandary.'[12] It
was Sweatman who lifted him out. Sweatman revealed that the Citizens
had a spy on the Strike Committee, who could tell them whether there
really were plans to call off the Strike.[13]

At the same time, the problem of security after the arrests dawned on
Andrews. The provincial jail on Vaughn Street or the City lock-up might
provide a focus for a riot,[14] or even invite a storming of the Bastille.
Miles outside of town, on the bald prairie where the federal penitentiary
of Stony Mountain lay, such unrest would be inconceivable. Therefore,
while Sweatman grilled his informant, Andrews and Robertson rode
'over very rough roads' to Stony Mountain – Saturday's storm earlier
had taken the wires down, so other communication was impossible – and
arranged with the warden a reception for the Strike leaders.[15] When
Andrews and Robertson finally got back to RNWMP headquarters at
1:30 a.m. Tuesday morning, they heard that according to Sweatman's
informant Norris had been deceived, and that no call to end the Strike
had even been discussed, let alone approved. Afterwards, Graham wondered about the source of the information that Norris and Robertson had
received, implying that the information must have been false.[16] However, one might as easily wonder about the convenience of *Sweatman*'s
information.

The raid was launched. In the small hours of Tuesday morning, while
Meighen was still abed, RNWMP Col. Starnes and Acting Police Chief
Newton dispatched five hundred men to guard the Labor Temple while
a search was conducted, and smaller posses went after the Strike lead-
ers. The RNWMP burst in on the homes of Russell, Ivens, Armstrong,
Bray, Heaps (at whose place Queen was also staying), Charitonoff,
Schoppelrei, and Almazoff, rousted them out of bed, collected a mass of
their papers, and escorted the men to new lodgings at Stony Mountain
Penitentiary. Andrews got home about 4:30 a.m.[17]

Mistakenly, Rev. S.O. Irven and Mike Verenczuk were also dragged
out at 4 a.m. With the Anglo-Saxon Irven, the mistake was quickly corrected. Rev. Irven, who lived in the McDougall Methodist parsonage
that Rev. Ivens had inhabited a year earlier, convinced the arresting offi-

cer of the mistake, but other, more suspicious officers returned to the parsonage, and only the marriage register – which proved that Ivens had left the parsonage a year earlier – prevented Irven's arrest. Irven wasn't angry, and pointed out that 'while his name looked like Ivens, his ideas were different.'[18] Mike Verenczuk, mistaken for Boris Devyatkin, didn't fare as well. All the propaganda against aliens took its toll, and Verenczuk, a shell-shocked Canadian war veteran, had to spend seventeen days in jail before Andrews let him go.[19]

For the arrests, Andrews waved around the Immigration Act, but he seems to have used only the Criminal Code provisions for seditious conspiracy and seditious libel. On the 16th, Immigration Minister J.A. Calder reminded Robertson that section 42 of the Immigration Act required the minister's authorization, and Calder told Robertson that Andrews must send Calder the names and particulars so that Calder could issue the order.[20] But Andrews didn't wait for authorization. On the 17th, half a day *after* the arrests, Meighen told Andrews the same thing – that Andrews needed Calder's signature. Too late. The federal government *wanted* to aid Andrews – as long as he used the Immigration Act – but he outran the government, and staged the arrests before the government could authorize his actions. Without comment, Meighen noted, 'Calder just received now 3.40 p.m. these names and particulars and is immediately despatching [*sic*] authorization.'[21] There are several possible reasons for Andrews's haste. Incompetence can't be ruled out, since the fine points of the law weren't Andrews's strength. He was one to act first and ask permission afterwards. However, incompetence is unlikely, since Pitblado, well versed on fine points, was also involved. The most likely reason is that the Citizens, including Pitblado, were exceedingly impatient for arrests. The Strike must be taken down, and if the provincial and federal governments were too cowardly to lead, the Citizens would step in to fill the void. Later, during the immigration hearings, defence lawyers would ask Andrews to produce Calder's original warrant to detain the men, but all Andrews could deliver was a 21 June letter from Calder for Blumenberg's detention. Did the orders *never* come? That's possible, but given Calder's eagerness and Meighen's assurances, it seems reasonable to assume that the order did come, that Andrews for some reason didn't want to display it, and that he destroyed it. We will suggest why in chapter 11.

The warrants, dated 16 June and issued in response to the 'information and complaint of Albert Edward Reams' [*sic*], an RNWMP spy, alleged that the Strike leaders had during May and June 'conspired with one another and divers persons to this informant unknown to excite divers liege subjects of the King, to resist laws and resist persons, same being part of the police force in the city of Winnipeg, in the due execution of their duty, and to bring the said force into hatred and contempt, and to procure unlawful meetings, and to cause divers liege subjects of the King to believe that the laws of this Dominion were unduly administered, and intending to disturb the public peace and raise discontent in the minds of subjects of the King, and to raise and excite tumult and disobedience to the laws.' The defendants had also conspired to publish 'false and libelous statements' concerning the Winnipeg police and the administration of justice.[22] As evidence, Andrews cited the 'seditious' 12 June *Western Labor News*:

> The committee of 1000 has achieved a distinct success in dismissing the Winnipeg police and filling the streets with special police, many of whom are thugs. They have spilled blood, caused booze to be sold openly on the Main Street at 50¢ a drink, and allowed fifteen to twenty bunches to carry on games of 'crap' for hours on the said Main Street without interference. These are the magnificent forces of law and order that replaced the police who were said to have refused to obey law and order.
>
> The special police are paneky [*sic*] and uncontrolled. When one man who kept cool drew his baton and quietly urged the people to get back to the sidewalk, he was charged by another special policeman, and went down under a smashing blow from his baton. So excited were these men that they slashed out at everybody promiscuously, and received a shower of missiles in reply. When one became separated from his fellows he was quickly unhorsed, and understood the meaning of rough-house. Several blackjacks were wrenched from the 'specials' by the strikers, and are now on exhibit at the labor temple. They are heavy chains, loaded with a clevice [*sic*] and bolt, and covered with leather. Whoever made them had murder in his brain.
>
> One fellow was seen to take a daily paper, fill it with filth from the street and wipe the dirty mess all over the face of a 'special.' He spat and swore – and got off the street at the double quick.
>
> The rioting lasted for some time, but was ended when the special police and Mounties dispersed in all directions and left the field to the crowd.
>
> It is understood that Canon Scott begged the mayor to dismiss the thugs and enroll a police of returned men. A strong committee of soldiers left Victoria park and offered Mayor Gray their services to maintain real order if the thugs were removed.
>
> Further, they offered that, provided the special police ceased provocation and that these thugs were sent out without guns, and with short

batons which were concealed, and that the Mounties rode in twos instead of fours, sixes, and eights, that they would not be molested. But if these specials were looking for trouble they would be sure to find it.[23]

In many ways, this was simply an editorializing news report, more aggressive than the usual *Western Labor News* stance, but less aggressive than much of what appeared in the *Winnipeg Citizen*. But the Citizens had put their weight behind the Specials, and now Andrews was elected to show that neither the Citizens nor the Specials could be so easily defied.

In moving to support the Specials and to arrest strikers, Citizens stepped into line, but gingerly, with anti-labour groups all over the Western world. The Citizens looked to these groups for ideology and resolve, but among them Andrews's procedural sophistication and subtle political brokering stood out.

The *Winnipeg Citizen* acknowledged that the Citizens' Committee of 1000 was a 'middle class protective league' like those 'in Britain,' where 'Bolshevists' had unwittingly aroused a strong counter-force standing for 'a square deal for all citizens.'[24] The Citizens spoke of themselves as repeating British history: 'Ten years ago England formed her Anti-Socialist Union with the Duke of Devonshire at its head. That organization was a tremendous success from the start. It successfully fought Socialism and arrested the progress towards the socialization of utility plants. That organization has made socialism impossible.'[25]

A less polemical account of these British leagues would note that increasing labour radicalism after the First World War had spawned a variety of anti-labour organizations. In the spring of 1919, Basil Thomson, director of intelligence for the British Home Office, reported that working-class dissent 'touched its high water mark,' unparalleled since the tumult of the 1830s.[26] He told the government that British workers viewed the Soviet as 'the best form of government for a democracy,'[27] and that they held 'the illusion that the employing class is a small minority for which the manual workers are compelled to toil as "wage slaves."'[28] Prime Minister Lloyd George, too, thought that Europe was 'filled with the spirit of revolution ... The whole existing order in its political, social and economic aspects is questioned by the masses of the population from one end of Europe to the other.'[29] Such a sense of crisis had constitutional implications: observers noticed a 'marked and ominous decline of faith in Parliaments.'[30] British workers seemed convinced that they were being robbed by capitalists,[31] and that the nation's industrial and political institutions were the occupying structures of 'a foreign power.'[32] Kingsley Martin recalled, 'the only time in my life when revolution in Britain seemed likely was in 1919.'[33] No wonder that the *Western Labor News* joked about using the new parliament buildings for a labour temple,[34] or that rumours flew of requisitioning the houses of the wealthy on the Crescent,[35] when in Britain alternate realities had recently been imagined with even greater flair: proletarian leaders occupying Buckingham Place; 'the King working in a mine or driving a lorry.'[36]

In Britain, the reshaping of drifting public opinion couldn't be done by the state, and it couldn't *appear* to be done by capital. A number of related anti-labour organizations claiming independent status (but tied to big business) leapt forward to wage a propaganda war against labour in the name of liberty, property, and the 'middle' class. The Liberty and Property Defence League was founded in 1892, but reconstituted after the First World War to uphold the 'principle of liberty,' to 'guard the Rights of Property ... against undue interference by the State,' and to oppose all who advanced 'revolutionary methods for the overthrow of civilized society.'[37] Despite the middle-class rhetoric, the League was the offspring of railway, banking, and insurance interests, with a chairman who ran a mining company and was on the board of six companies. Similarly, despite its name, the Middle Classes Union – founded 6 March 1919 in London to combat Bolshevism and to represent the interests of 'everybody between organized labor on one hand and organized capital on the other'[38] – included directors of the Bank of Scotland and of Vickers Limited, and could boast one member worth £32,856,000. By October 1919, the Union had seventy branches.[39]

The Reconstruction Society, which appeared in 1919 (though it had begun life in 1908 as the Anti-Socialist Union), fought against Bolshevism with public meetings and pamphlets such as 'The Bolshevik Mad Dog' and 'Bolsheviks and the Nationalization of Girls.' Lord Joicey, a coal millionaire, sat on the executive, as did representatives of engineering, banking, and insurance companies. A leading member was R.D. Blumenfeld, editor of London's *Daily Express*, where several of the society's publications first appeared, including one that announced that 'an organized Bolshevik conspiracy' in Britain was trying 'to break down the fabric of society and render "bourgeois" government – that is Government by Parliament, or democratic majority rule – impossible.'[40]

The anti-labour movement in Britain illuminates aspects of the Winnipeg Citizens' Committee. As in Britain, business interests in Winnipeg sought a discourse and a mode of action that would allow them to enter the public sphere as champions dressed in the public interest, not just in the narrow interests of capital. Nomenclature varied, but disguise was an absolute requirement. The Middle Classes Union's announced constituency of 'everybody between organized labor on one hand and organized capital on the other'[41] was almost identical to the Winnipeg Citizens' evocation of 'the great bulk of the citizens of Winnipeg, who are not employers and who are not of Organized Labour's ranks,'[42] citizens who paid through the nose for every gain by labour. From British anti-labour forces, Winnipeg's Citizens borrowed the themes of property, liberty, patriotism, xenophobia, and stereotyped accounts of that catch-all for anti-labour organizations in this era – the spectre of international Bolshevism. Propaganda campaigns served not only to demonize labour, but also to foster an environment of crisis in which any of labour's demands could seem revolutionary.

If the Citizens' 'patriotism' made it respectable to acknowledge their British mother, we have seen (in chapter 2) that their father was American: the Minneapolis Citizens' Alliance. In the North American context, British appeals to reconstruction, national security, the middle class, or even to liberty and property were trumped by the appeal to citizenship. 'Citizens' carried rights; they could enter the public sphere and assert a 'public' interest; they could make demands on the state. Citizens' committees such as the 'Committee of Forty Citizens,' which later became the Winnipeg Patriotic Fund, served popular causes, for example aiding the needy families of soldiers. When powerful private interests wanted state action, or wished to enter the public sphere without the appearance of self-interest, a committee of 'citizens' could get an advance on the credit of such organizations.

Discussion of Citizens' Alliances in North America usually begins with the Dayton Employers' Association, but that group didn't pretend to be anything other than an employers' association. In contrast, committees that either honestly or in masquerade declared themselves to be broadly based middle-class associations had potential moral force far beyond that of employers associations.[43] In his 1904 account of the 'new employers' association movement,' American investigative journalist Ray Stannard Baker spoke of two classes of employer associations: those which negotiated with unions and those prepared to fight unions.[44] Among the former was the original Citizens' Alliance, founded in Sedalia, Missouri, on 19 August 1901 under *Sedalia Bazoo* founder J. West Goodwin.[45] Membership purportedly included 'bankers, merchants, professional men, artisans and even some workingmen.'[46] Goodwin soon became a missionary in the cause of Citizens' Alliances, whose aims were 'peaceful ... directed in a moral way against strikes and lockouts.'[47] By 1904 he had helped to establish the organization in twenty-eight cities, while other alliances had formed without his involvement. According to Baker, writing in the same year, 'nearly every city in the country making any pretense to industrial importance now boasts a full-fledged Employers' association or citizens' alliance, sometimes both.'[48]

Goodwin said that his organization stood for the 'open shop' principle, under which union men and independent workers were treated identically. Alliances shouldn't achieve their ends through force; rather, they should seek 'to bring about much-needed reforms by the crystallization of a healthy public opinion.' As a result, claimed Goodwin, wherever Citizens' Alliances had been established, about 10 per cent of the population belonged to the group, more wherever labour disturbances and rates of violence were high: 'Lawlessness disappears like the dew before the morning sun and good government takes the place of quasi-government.'[49]

Yet Citizens' Alliances were secret organizations, with 'grips, signs and passwords ... prohibiting any member from telling anyone the names of any other member.'[50] This certainly opened them up to dissimulation and abuse, especially since they presumed to guide the hands of government. Citizens' Alliance members pledged to fight unions that resorted to 'boycotting, or any form of coercion or unlawful force,' including strikes.[51] The implication was clear – unions that opposed the open shop were 'tyrants who oppressed the community and victimized the employer.'[52] What happened when labour unions didn't submit? Citizens' Alliances were supposed to back governments, though descriptions of *how* they did so suggested an inclination to bully elected officials: 'The laws are strong enough in every city to deal with lawlessness, they only need enforcing, and when those whose duty it should be to enforce those laws become derelict in their duties, the Citizens' Alliance steps into the breach, and by sheer moral force compels the officers to do their duty by enforcing the law.'[53] By what mechanisms would 'sheer moral force' prick unbudging authorities forward? And what would happen when the authorities clashed with the 'Citizens' about how laws should be enforced?

Answers were soon provided. The answers revealed that many Citizens' Alliances in fact belonged to Baker's second class of employer associations – the ones keen to break unions. In the summer of 1902, when the operators of mines refused to negotiate, thousands of coal miners in Pennsylvania struck for higher wages, shorter hours, and recognition of their union. The United Miners Workers led the strike from Wilkes-Barre, Pennsylvania. Employers brought in replacement workers, and the inevitable conflict flashed hot. A stuffed effigy, with a placard reading 'J.P. Morgan,' appeared, swinging from a telegraph pole. The local police, apparently in sympathy with the strikers, said that they wouldn't remove the effigy until ordered to do so.[54]

A Citizens' Alliance denying any affiliation with the coal operators quickly surfaced. The Wilkes-Barre Citizens' Alliance declared sympathy with organized labour, but added that, 'over and above it, and above all organized capital, we intend to uphold organized society.' The Alliance entered the fray, offering rewards totalling $5000 for 'the arrest, conviction of all persons engaged in boycotting, hanging in effigies and other criminal acts of intimidating prejudicial to the rights of American freedom.'[55] Through 'sheer moral force,' the Alliance began making citizen arrests. William Fitzinger, a member of the United Mine Workers, was charged with libelling merchants, and the Alliance began a 'citizen' prosecution, hauling him before a magistrate who demanded $7000 bail, an amount that Fitzinger couldn't pay. He remained in jail.[56] The president of the United Mine Workers, John Mitchell, noted that the Citizens' Alliance had ostensibly been formed to maintain 'law and order,' yet, curiously, it focused entirely on the striking miners. He found it strange that no citizens' alliance had been formed 'during the twenty five years when the anthracite coal companies were blacklisting, boycotting, and driving from their homes and families all men who dared to assert their rights and join a labor organization.' What was the Wilkes-Barre Citizens' Alliance except a front for the coal companies and an attempt to crush the miners union?[57]

Citizens' Alliances also arose in the troubled mining frontier of Colorado. The Citizens' Alliance of Denver arose in 1903 under James C. Craig, and, within three weeks had 3000 members and a war chest of nearly $20,000.[58] Soon, Citizens' Alliances appeared in surrounding mining communities, including Cripple Creek, Telluride, and Idaho Springs. No dubious claims of sympathy for organized labour here. These Alliances unambiguously declared their wish to eradicate unions in the state. In July 1903, when the Western Federation of Miners launched a strike for the eight-hour day, the Idaho Springs Citizens' Alliance, claiming a membership of '14,000 businessmen representing every branch of trade,'[59] determined to rid the town of organized labour. The Alliance 'directed law enforcement, held secret strategy sessions, ordered the arrest and interrogation of suspects whom they held incommunicado, watched incoming trains, and warned union sympathizers to leave town.'[60] Union officials were ultimately driven from Idaho Springs.

The Telluride Citizens' Alliance, too, used a corporal version of 'sheer moral force' in March 1904. One hundred members of the Alliance 'armed with rifles and revolvers ... scoured the town ... and [took] into custody between seventy and eighty union men and sympathizers.' The men were marched to the local railway depot, loaded aboard two railways cars, and sent off amidst 'volleys of shots into the air.'[61] Three months later, the Cripple Creek Citizens' Alliance, with the help of the Mine Owners' Association, mounted a 'Death to unionism' campaign in the Cripple Creek area. The Alliance solicited written pledges from employers in the district, promising not to employ anyone belonging to a union.[62] Squads of 'citizens, backed by the militia, made arrests and deposed marshals who refused to act against the union. Strikers, deposed marshals and union officials were rounded up and held in the Citizens' Alliance headquarters.' Lynching was 'freely talked of, and every man [was] ... a walking arsenal.' Again, many arrested miners were thrown on trains and shipped to Denver. One of the miners said, 'I don't know why I was deported ... I have violated no law, destroyed no property, injured no man. So far as I know every one of the men driven with me from home are equally innocent with myself.'[63] These anti-union activities show citizens' alliances moving well beyond the ambit of simple employers' associations: alliances ignored the rule of law, dominated state officials, and, often through proxies, violently attacked union members.

In 1903, when the president of the National Association of Manufacturers, David M. Parry, called for a 'crusade against unionism,' the Citizens Industrial Alliance, a national organization to support the various Alliances, arose. Parry's anti-labour rhetoric was apocalyptic in tone: 'Organized labor knows but one law, and that is the law of physical force – the law of the Huns and Vandals, the law of the savage. All its purposes are accomplished either by actual force or by the threat of force.' He equated organized labour with 'mob-power knowing no master except its own will,' and claimed that it was 'continually condemning or defying the constituted authorities.' Unions had a history 'stained with blood and ruin,' and menaced free government.[64] Since the Citizens Industrial Alliance was the offspring of the manufacturers, it was no stretch for Parry to become its president too. Promotional materials described the Alliance's 'open shop' goals in a more veiled language: 'To promote peace and harmony between employers and employees, to have law and order maintained, and to secure protection for all in the exercise of their divine and constitutional right to work when, where, for whom, and at such rate as they may please.'[65]

Anti-labour vigilante organizations in the United States also called themselves citizens' 'committees,' and in character they often weren't distinguishable from citizens' alliances. In San Diego, a 'Citizens' Committee of 1000,' created in 1912, squared off against IWW activists and pressured the City to limit public speeches to particular areas.[66] Harris Weinstock, special commissioner appointed to investigate the subsequent disturbances, said that the Citizens' Committee of 1000 had been formed, 'ostensibly for the purpose of aiding the duly constituted local authorities in the maintenance of law and order, in deporting so-called undesirables and in preventing their return to the city.' Committee members or thugs hired by the more fastidious members arrested IWW activists, held them without charges, and then drove them to a location outside the city where fifteen or sixteen cars were lined up along the road. A flagpole had been erected. 'Between 60 and 75 men ... part of whom were police officers ... and part private citizens' waited with 'revolvers, knives, night sticks, black jacks and black snakes.' These 'citizens' all wore 'a white hand-kerchief, tied at the elbow of the right arm.' What followed was a Girar-dian ritual re-enactment of the founding of the state: in a theatrical scene lit by headlights and lanterns, the IWW men were first compelled to kiss the Stars and Stripes, and then a 'general clubbing' and horsewhipping followed. Afterwards, the vigilantes loaded the IWW men into automo-biles, transported them to San Ondfre near the county line, and placed them in a cattle pen. Again armed guards beat them. In the morning, they were forced to run a gauntlet of clubs and 'black snakes,' and again kiss the flag. Finally, they were packed off on foot to Los Angeles, 'sore, hun-gry, practically penniless and in deplorable physical condition.' Wein-stock concluded that the San Diego Citizens' Committee of 1000 had 'trampled upon the constitutional rights of other men and proven them-selves to be bitterest enemies of law and order.'[67] But nothing was done about Weinstock's report.

In community after community in the United States, the appellation 'Citizen' camouflaged the use of extra-legal weapons against workers. Because citizens' committees justified themselves on the assumption that law and order had broken down, they had a vested interest in creat-ing 'a fiction of violence and disorder,' masking the real and more mun-dane issues at the root of a conflict. More importantly, the fiction of dis-order provided a pretext for vigilante action, the manipulation of state power, the invasion of workers' homes and labour temples, arrests, imprisonment, denial of bail, suspension of habeas corpus, and deporta-tion. Although citizens' committees publicly advocated labour harmony, privately they often encouraged disorder.[68]

No one on Winnipeg's Citizens' Committee of 1000 referred publicly to the fact that it had taken the same name as San Diego's Citizens' Com-mittee of 1000. Given that the names are identical, it seems likely that at least some of the Citizens saw themselves in light of the San Diego events of seven years earlier. The organization that arose most directly out of American citizens' alliances – the Winnipeg Citizens' Alliance – was instrumental in creating the relatively benign Citizens' Committee of 100 during the 1918 general strike. Yet the Winnipeg Citizens' Alliance hadn't exactly sat on the sidelines during the 1918 conflict. As we have seen, Ed Parnell in 1918 privately wired Robert Borden, demanding Orders-in-Council or other legislation to criminalize the strikers.[69] The employers' next incarnation, the Citizens' Committee of 1000, proved more aggressive, though not as aggressive as San Diego's committee. Whether conveyed directly through Citizens' Alliance members such as Parnell and others, or as a result of watching American developments, a number of practices from the American Citizens' groups found their way into the Winnipeg Citizens' Committee. Like San Diego's Citizens, Winnipeg's Citizens married the flag, and took care to distinguish themselves on the street with the Union Jack rather than just with white armbands. Like their counterparts in Minneapolis, Winnipeg's Citizens took up the policy of no negotiation and put out a newspaper. The Citizens' 'extreme Bourbon element'[70] favoured American strong-arm methods, pressuring Mayor Gray and Gen. Ketchen to declare martial law and to turn the military loose on the city. Was it someone among the Bourbons who suggested an organizational name identical to the highly aggressive San Diego Citizens' Committee of 1000? If Winnipeg's Citizens avoided the violence of Colorado or San Diego, it was a case of, to use Georges Sorel's phrase, the old ferocity being replaced by cunning.[71] No black jacks; no beatings. As in many jurisdictions, but with far greater legal subtlety, Winnipeg's Citizens arranged to jail and deport troublesome labour leaders.

What was most different in Winnipeg was, arguably, the lawyers' political finesse – especially the virtuoso performance of A.J. Andrews. Because of his anointing by Meighen, it appeared that the *state* was pressing charges and mounting prosecutions. No so. Later, when the secretary of state rejected Andrews's request to shut down the *Western Labor News*, Andrews would do it himself with a visit to the printer and a threat of prosecution. He asserted the authority of an attorney general and people responded. Meighen would eventually resist the Citizens' clamour for a federal prosecution of the Strike leaders – a prosecution which would have required an extraordinary constitutional intervention in Manitoba's affairs – only to have Charles Doherty, the actual minister of justice, turn the tables on him and creatively finance the Citizens' prosecution.

Meighen could be forgiven for initially thinking that the arrests were being made under the Immigration Act. He had twice amended the act to

Andrews's specifications in order to make room for such arrests; he had informed Andrews on 17 June that belated authorization was coming from Immigration Minister J.A. Calder for arrests under the act; and Andrews *did* eventually prosecute the Eastern European leaders under the act. Once Meighen became aware that Andrews had used the Criminal Code, Meighen could also be forgiven for thinking that since Andrews had several times noted that authority to prosecute lay with the Province,[72] he must be operating with the consent of Attorney General Johnson.

Under the Criminal Code it was also possible for a private citizen to start a prosecution. In fact, until recently, this had been the norm. Private prosecutions had been carefully protected, as Douglas Hay says, and were considered 'an important constitutional guarantee of civil liberty.' According to Sir James Stephen, they were not only an important legal vent for 'feelings every way entitled to respect,' but also had decided many significant constitutional questions.[73] An individual could go a long way with a private prosecution, especially if everybody thought he was acting on behalf of the minister of justice. Section 5(c) of Manitoba's Crown Attorneys Act obligated the Crown to 'watch over' the conduct of such cases 'without unnecessarily interfering,'[74] though at any time the Attorney General had the authority to stay proceedings.[75] According to the *Toronto Star*, Andrews had been engaged by the *Citizens' Committee of 1000* to lay the charge of treason against members of the General Strike Committee and some city aldermen.[76] That's not quite accurate, even though Citizens' Committee money was available. W.H. McWilliams, the chairman of the Citizens' Finance Committee, asked the Citizens for funds to 'compensate for injury or loss to volunteer workers serving at the request of the citizens' committee.' The fund amounted to approximately $800,000 and he wanted to increase it to $1,000,000. Donations not required to fight the strike would be returned 'on its termination.'[77] It is inconceivable, of course, that any more than a small fraction of the money was actually intended for injury or loss. Rather, it was a hallmark of Citizens' leagues that they could raise massive war chests, which they used to pay 'volunteers' and security guards, and to fund legal action against strikers. Yet, Winnipeg's Citizens neither wanted to cast themselves as the enemy of the people nor to underwrite an expensive private prosecution, and Andrews had no intention of mounting one. They and he wanted the full legal and moral weight of the government to press down on the Strike. But the *Star*'s 'mistake' indicates both the public's misunderstanding of Andrews's legal footwork and, simultaneously, the public's astute estimation that the Citizens somehow must have gained control of government machinery.

If Meighen and Robertson hadn't been fully apprised of the legal niceties of Andrews's plans, at least three other people had been – and they weren't members of any government: Pitblado, Sweatman, and Coyne. Andrews revealed that Pitblado was 'wholly in accord with our proposed line of action.'[78] Working with the other lawyers on the details of the arrests, it wouldn't have been possible for Andrews to hide from them that his operation was extra-curricular. Very likely, the lawyers made the decision as a group, with Andrews and Pitblado leading. The *Telegram*, reflecting public belief, said, 'It is understood that [Andrews] heads an organization of five special representatives of the justice department.'[79] That would have been news to Meighen. Immediately after the Strike leaders' arrests on the 17th, Andrews wrote to him, 'Pitblado, Coyne, Sweatman and other leading legislators not only approve my course but are voluntarily aiding me.'[80] It's unclear whom, if anybody, Andrews meant by 'leading legislators,' and 'voluntarily' had a private meaning for the lawyers (as did many words). It didn't mean 'without pay.' Rather, it meant that no one coerced them to work and to be paid richly. In fact, if one follows the money, the 'voluntary aid' began three days before Andrews spoke of it: the bills given to the Government of Canada for legal work on the Strike point to Saturday the 14th as the turning point. On that day, Sweatman, Coyne, and Pitblado began charging the government for a full day's legal work every day for two weeks, including Sundays. For the two younger lawyers – Coyne and Sweatman – the 14th signalled the beginning of their government pay cheques, though Pitblado had charged the government for daily consultations with Andrews since 26 May, the day that Andrews had been deputized by Meighen.[81] The money, too, shows that in their 'voluntary' service the four lawyers acted as a group.

Andrews knew that there was gold in governmental litigation. No doubt the meagre $15 he received for prosecuting a 'Cruelty to Animals' charge in 1911 paled beside inestimable moral rewards – Andrews being the founder of the Winnipeg Humane Society – but such sums weren't likely to pay his mortgage at 749 Crescent. In a rather different financial league (and at a time when a postal worker made $1419 per annum) were Andrews's paydays of $8125 and $5300 for defending former Conservative premier Rodmond Roblin against charges of kickbacks in the construction of the new Manitoba parliament buildings.[82] Early in the Strike, Andrews expected the Province to eventually prosecute, and he knew that it was important to be well placed in order to get in on the ground floor. A man with sufficient foresight to wade around in places where public money floated would find more than simply moral rewards. What Andrews didn't know was that the Province would never, in fact, agree to prosecute. In telling Meighen that Pitblado, Coyne, and Sweatman were 'voluntarily aiding' him, Andrews let Meighen think that there would be no cost to the federal government: that the work was pro bono, or, more likely, that the Province would soon get on board, or even that the Citizens were underwriting costs.[83] Later, all the lawyers would submit hefty bills, not to the Province or the Citizens but to the federal government, for what initially looked like voluntary public service.

When Meighen heard of the arrests (probably through Gen. Ketchen's wire to the Adjutant General) he revealed a slight irritation with Andrews's haste and presumption. He wasn't certain that the arrests were legal: 'Notwithstanding any doubts I have as to technical legality of arrests and detention at Stony Mountain I feel that rapid deportation is best course now that arrests are made and later we can consider ratification.'[84] Clearly, he still thought that Andrews was proceeding under the Immigration Act. Although Andrews's first wire after the arrests continued to pay lip service to immigration procedures, he added other, rather significant, details without explaining them: 'Ivens, Queen, Heaps, Bray, Verenchuk [*sic*], Almazoff, Charetonoff [*sic*], Armstrong, Russel [*sic*], and Schoppeleri [*sic*] now in Stony Mountain charge seditious conspiracy. Will have Justice remand eight days. Holding till Minister Immigration wires order detainer. Rush this order. We will then hold Court Inquiry at penitentiary. Deport without trying on criminal charges unless evidence insufficient for deportation.'[85]

'Without trying on criminal charges'? Where did that come from? Although Andrews raised the possibility only to dismiss it, why even raise it? Everyone from Borden on down had expected arrests and deportations under the Immigration Act. Meighen's irritation rose again, restrained, in his alarmed response, and he made what one might call a 'Lockean slip': 'Government just received information that ten arrests made last night being detained at Stony Mountain. Yesterday morning I wired you that Immigration Act provides for detention only in Immigration Station and early yesterday afternoon Mr. Calder wired Stearns [*sic*] that authorization for taking into custody and detaining for examination under Immigration Act must come from him personally and asked for names and particulars accordingly. He just received now 3.40 p.m. these names and particulars and is immediately despatching authorization. Presume you are satisfied that there is ■ legal authority for arrests and for detention at Stony Mountain but I would be glad to have full information as to this by wire.'[86] Andrews – 'voluntarily aided' by Pitblado, Sweatman, and Coyne – was freelancing, getting far ahead of Meighen. The typed version of the telegraph includes two letters blacked out in front of the words 'legal authority,' letters that seem to form the word 'no.' Either the typist made a slip, or Meighen dictated exactly what the first part of his letter implies – that there was no legal authority under the Immigration Act for holding the men in a penitentiary – before correcting his unconscious slip.

As to Meighen's understanding that the arrested Strike leaders had to be held at an immigration station rather than at Stony Mountain Penitentiary, Andrews preferred to be guided by Com. Perry and Col. Starnes, who had informed him that in some immigration cases 'police barracks and gaol usual place detention' [sic]. There were, after all, practical considerations: the military and the police were agreed that Stony Mountain, a number of miles from Winnipeg, was the 'only safe place available.' But in the other matters, Andrews knew that he was on shaky legal ground, and although he knew that he had the Citizens' support, he had to soothe Meighen: 'For very purpose justifying arrests I had information laid charging seditious conspiracy which in my opinion could be proved.' Andrews either still planned to fly with the Immigration Act or he wanted Meighen to think so: 'My intention was to drop criminal proceedings when detention order made and proceed deport. If any persons not deportable think should continue criminal proceedings against them where evidence justifies.'[87] 'Think should continue criminal proceedings': on his own authority Andrews, in effect, committed the federal government to an extra-constitutional prosecution. Early in June he had recommended the arrest of the Strike leaders, but the Citizens had had little success with Attorney General Johnson or Crown Prosecutor Robert Graham. Andrews wasn't going to let Meighen sneak away from a decisive stance as Johnson and Premier Norris had.

Andrews and the Citizens faced major obstacles to any prosecution. The biggest was, of course, that the administration of the Criminal Code was a provincial matter. In 1915, then Attorney General Albert Hudson had asked the minister of justice whether the Province or Ottawa should take action in sedition cases falling under Orders-in-Council. Ottawa had replied that the provinces should deal with such cases.[88] During the 1918 general strike Prime Minister Borden had been asked whether the Order-in-Council colloquially referred to as the Anti-Loafing law might be used to force strikers back to work. Borden thought so, but the use of the law was 'a matter for the provincial and civic authorities to act upon as they might be advised by their counsel.'[89] Only in 1969 was the law amended to open the possibility of the federal minister of justice prosecuting under the Criminal Code.[90] Andrews was by no means counsel for the Province. Yet some time during the twenty-four hours after the arrests, Andrews decided to prosecute the British-born strike leaders under the Criminal Code. That raids were occurring across the country on 17 June to search for evidence of seditious conspiracy no doubt made things easier for Andrews,[91] giving the illusion that the arrests were a federal undertaking, but no one outside the Citizens' lawyers, it seems, expected arrests under the Criminal Code.

The response of the federal government to Andrews and the Citizens during this time illuminates the real, yet limited, autonomy of the state in relation to civil society. Historians such as Masters and Bercuson present the federal government as the prosecution in the post-Strike trials. That wasn't the case. It's not that the federal government would have defied the regional business elite, but the government wasn't exactly the 'executive committee of capital' either.[92] The general strike of the previous year had demonstrated the federal government's wish for negotiation. What would happen after the strikers in 1919 dismissed existing labour law as irrelevant and defied it? The Province wasn't prepared to do anything, and Ottawa was prepared to go only so far as quick and painless action under the Immigration Act: the deportation of Eastern European leaders, perhaps a few of the more fiery British leaders. Meighen baulked at arresting and prosecuting the leaders under the Criminal Code, despite the business elite's wishes. However, when the state trembled in 1919, the Citizens stepped forward to become the principal 'subject' shaping the response to the Strike. For the Citizens, there could be no repeat of the 1918 negotiation; just the reverse – scorched earth.

Probably after the riot of the 10th, Andrews began to sense that, as the nexus of so many lines of communication, he could write his own rules. His relations with Meighen were not so much friendly and empathetic as instrumental and pragmatic. Throughout these crucial days, Andrews kept insisting that he did nothing without Robertson's authorization, reassuring Meighen that the federal government was still in control: 'Everything I have done has been at suggestion Senator Robertson but because it might weaken his position with labour I have taken full responsibility for Justice Department.'[93] This was partially true in that Robertson didn't resist Andrews's game plan.[94] But how much did Robertson understand of the legal technicalities? He was no lawyer, and his letters, in which he repeatedly refers to the Immigration Act, suggest that unlike Meighen and Borden, he didn't even know enough to be bewildered by Andrews's bold and extra-legal use of the Criminal Code. To Meighen, Andrews spoke with the authority of Robertson and the Citizens; to Robertson and the Citizens, Andrews spoke with the authority of Meighen. When the press asked Robertson who had ordered the arrests, he could quite honestly say that they were outside of his jurisdiction entirely and had all been made on the authority of the Justice Department.[95] And who was the 'Justice Department' at this time? A.J. Andrews, K.C.

For Andrews, the arrests were a gamble. For other Citizens, less aware of how little was *legally* possible given a baulky Province, the arrests were long overdue, a necessary hand on the collar of a street bully. To Meighen's doubts about legality, Andrews replied testily, 'Events change so rapidly here and telegraph communication so slow you must either trust to my judgment or employ more trustworthy representative.'[96] Despite the offer, it's unlikely that Andrews planned to fall on his sword just yet. Rather, he was gambling that as the voice of Winnipeg's elite he had by now become indispensable to Meighen and the state, and that a display of offended honour would convince Meighen to back off. The next day, Meighen did just that, though not without repeating, 'I had grave doubts as to the legality of our position,' and letting Andrews know that Meighen's 'official' wire (expressing those doubts) was a way of protecting the government and the prime minister in this matter.[97] Meighen wouldn't defy the Citizens, but he was hinting that if the federal government came under too much pressure, he wasn't above cutting Andrews loose.

Why wasn't Andrews satisfied to rely solely on the Immigration Act? A number of reasons loom large, some relating to the feeling that the Strike was escaping the Citizens' control, some relating to Winnipeg's labour history, and some to the feeling that a definitive conclusion was called for. The efficient cause, according to Andrews, was the *Western Labor News* article calling the Special Police 'thugs.' Because the *Labor News* 'openly boasted that policemen's batons, revolvers and other articles were on exhibition at the Labor Temple as trophies of Tuesday's fight,' Andrews became 'convinced' that 'strong measures should be taken to punish the wrong doers.'[98] Andrews had long been waiting for Strike leaders to make 'revolutionary' remarks, and when they didn't, he must have decided that the 'thugs' article was about as close to 'revolution' as they would come.

More importantly, Andrews and the other Citizens felt that the Strike was eluding their grasp. The Strike Committee had rejected the potentially mediating position agreed to by the ironmasters, the Specials could not command the streets, and, most crucially, in the week following the riot the Specials threatened to resign en masse because the City wouldn't let them reassert authority. 'The same situation was true,' Andrews admitted, 'of one thousand and more of our workers and with our volunteer militiamen in the barracks. The inaction of the authorities had so disheartened them that they were all ready to resign and had already commenced to fall off in numbers.'[99] Send the Specials into the streets and have them defeated, or keep the Specials at home and have them resign – either way, the strikers won.

Winnipeg's labour history, which had helped shape the Citizens' no-negotiation policy, also recommended a more decisive action than just immigration hearings. Before 1918, Winnipeg's business community had defeated every challenge of labour through the courts. Even the tough Machinists' Union had been laid low with court-ordered injunctions and fines.[100] In 1918, however, expediency had ruled the day, and, with Ottawa leading the rush to retreat, the City had capitulated to the unions. Nineteen eighteen had taught labour that general strikes worked. How could the general strike as a weapon be wrenched from the hands of labour? The answer was obvious: forget federal mediation; use the courts; criminalize the Strike. It's no wonder that Andrews wanted to meet labour before a judge.

In addition, the Immigration Act would have limited the Citizens' scope. Borden's national political considerations prohibited Andrews from using the sub-clause that retroactively dated section 41of the Immigration Act to 1910, a prohibition that would limit the evidence that Andrews could bring in. And Strike leader George Armstrong had been born of United Empire Loyalist stock on a farm near Scarborough, Ontario.[101] As such, he could not be deported. Either Andrews overlooked this fact initially, or the Citizens felt that it was essential to prosecute Armstrong even though he didn't fit the new immigration law. (Or Andrews, having run against Armstrong in the 1910 provincial election, had a personal stake in ensuring that he was among those arrested.) In any case, it would look strange for the Crown to prosecute a single leader under the Criminal Code while dealing with all the others under the Immigration Act.

Perhaps the most compelling reason for Andrews's use of the Criminal Code was his and the Citizens' growing wish to criminalize the Strike. The leaders must be brought to heel, but the issue of general strikes in Winnipeg must also be settled definitively and publicly. Rather than providing a stage for a broad ideological war, immigration hearings might (and eventually did) turn on legal technicalities, which might leave strikers feeling that they'd merely been outmanoeuvred, and that they ought to return to do battle another day. Above all, it wouldn't capture the imagination of 'the great middle class' that the Citizens made so much of.[102] Far better to have a big public trial on criminal charges and settle the issue with a verdict which no doubt would be unfavourable to the strikers. For the Citizens' warnings to be confirmed as ultimately sound, the Strike leaders must be exposed publicly as Bolsheviks and as serious threats to the established order. It wasn't enough to spank the British Strike leaders behind the tool shed. The appearance of fairness was important: justice must seem to be done.[103] If Russell and his associates were shipped to Kapuskasing and put on a boat in Halifax, the opportunity for a final 'solution' to the Winnipeg General Strike might be lost.[104] The Immigration Act might be well enough for 'aliens,' but a more public rebuke was necessary for British men who ought to have known better. Did Andrews want a show trial? Yes, he did.

9

The Road through Bloody Saturday

Wednesday, 18 June – Thursday, 19 June

Much of the success or failure of the arrests would depend on public reaction, so it was with disagreeable surprise that Andrews and Meighen woke up to Wednesday's *Manitoba Free Press*, which declared that the arrests were unwise and would play into the hands of the radicals by creating martyrs. This from John Dafoe, who was virulently anti-Strike. Of course, Dafoe also knew how to sell papers. Meighen complained, 'It is little short of incredible that any journal should plead for "revolutionaries" who had succeeded for their own unlawful and sinister ends, in demoralizing the industrial life of the whole community.'[1] Although Andrews had no other barometer of public opinion, he pretended that Dafoe's editorial was an anomaly: 'Satisfied public opinion with our action ... Great indignation against Free Press editorial.'[2] In Andrews's circle – among the Citizens – this was no lie. Andrews took the line that the editorial had been based on the same false assumption that Norris had been prey to: that arrests came just as the Strike was about to be called off. Afterwards, Dafoe was reluctant to alter his position, Andrews intimated.[3]

One way of shaping public reaction, despite quarrelsome newspaper editors, was to *be* the public. Having started its own newspaper, and having tried to *be* 1000 citizens, the Citizens understood that if they chorused loudly in the public sphere, the federal government would hear the 'public' applauding all action against the Strike, including iffy Criminal Code prosecutions. Pitblado and Coyne sent one-sentence telegrams to Prime Minister Borden, not praising the arrests that they themselves had helped to engineer, but simply observing, with Olympian detachment, that the public approved. The separate telegrams of Pitblado, Coyne, and

MP George Allan clearly reveal a party line that the Citizens were taking. Each of the three approved of '*government*' action [emphasis added], and referred to the strikers as 'Reds.' Pitblado said 'public generally approve,' while Coyne reached for a different way of putting it, and came up with 'approved ... by general public.' Allan went into a flight of stunning originality by comparison, revealing that the action met the 'approval of Winnipeg's great mass of loyal citizens.' At least thirty-eight individuals, mostly business owners, wired Borden separately from Winnipeg, praising the 'government's' action against 'the revolutionary element,' 'the red element,' or 'the Russian Reds,' and repeatedly saying that the action was endorsed by 'all good citizens,' the 'majority of loyal citizens,' 'all right thinking people,' veterans, or, more honestly, 'my friends.'[4] It's possible that one or two Winnipeggers who wired Borden weren't part of this pre-orchestrated campaign, but the repetitions of wording and content – not to mention the unanimity of opinion – suggest that after taking part in the drama, the Citizens had also arranged to cast themselves as the approving audience. For good measure, eight of those correspondents told Borden to never mind the *Free Press* editorial. And then, wearing their other hats as captains of industry, the Citizens sent a group telegram, also congratulating Borden, with thirty-four signatures attached.

Despite all the on-cue cheering, the elephant in the living room – that many of the Citizens didn't even know existed, and that Andrews and Meighen kept tiptoeing around – was the Province's constitutional responsibility for criminal prosecutions. Early on, Andrews had depicted himself to Meighen as a mediator who was trying to keep the Citizens from acting too aggressively. In the days before the arrests, Meighen had shied away from a direct confrontation, but Andrews had hustled him down the road to criminal arrests. Yet, short of invoking the War Measures Act seven months after the end of the war, the federal government had no legal business prosecuting the strikers. If the prosecution were a private one, the Citizens needed to guard against the charge that they were engaged in a vigilante prosecution, since at any point Attorney General Johnson (who was responsible for preventing malicious prosecutions) could enter a *nolle prosequi* to abort the trial. Also, the Citizens' lawyers were not in the habit of doing work for free. A foretaste of the size and complexity of the criminal prosecution came on Wednesday evening, when Pitblado and Sweatman (if their eventual bills are to be believed) stayed up until 4 a.m., slogging away at the case.[5] Thursday – no doubt at their nudging – Andrews ceased to speak of their 'voluntarily aiding' him, but indicated that (subject, of course, to Meighen's approval) he had 'retained' Coyne, Sweatman, and Frederick Burbidge.[6] This, five days after they had been retained. Either the Province, Ottawa, or the Citizens must foot the bill.

It's possible that Andrews expected that the Province, faced with the fait accompli of criminal arrests, would eventually cough up money. He certainly intimated as much to Meighen. Andrews revealed that (against the Citizens' wishes) the Province had let two Liberals – former Attorney General Hudson and Herbert Symington[7] – negotiate with the Strike Committee's James Winning for the appointment of Judge Robson to look into the causes and conduct of the Strike. Nevertheless, Andrews insisted that the premier was cheering for the Citizens from the sidelines: 'I do not know what stand Premier Norris may be taking officially but he has expressed to Senator Robertson and myself his entire approval of what has been done, particularly in taking the men to Stony Mountain rather than placing them in the Provincial Gaol as he feared a lot of trouble.'[8] It's difficult to tell whether Andrews was using Norris's approval of jail choice to deceptively generalize an approval for the arrests, or whether Norris was pleased with the arrests so long as they weren't dumped in his own sandbox. General Ketchen, reporting to his headquarters five days before the arrests, made it clear that both Norris and Commissioner Perry expected the federal government to use the Immigration Act as planned.[9] When the press asked Norris for a comment on the arrests, he reportedly said, 'Just leave us out of this.'[10]

The likeliest scenario is that Andrews had Norris convinced that Meighen was taking responsibility, and (since the Province was *allowing* the arrests) had Meighen convinced that the Province would eventually take responsibility. Who, the Strike leaders inquired, was in charge of this prosecution? Neither Andrews nor Meighen replied. Only later would Andrews and Meighen grasp that provincial money would never be forthcoming, and that if Andrews wanted a prosecution, he'd have to mount it in a legal twilight zone. On 26 June, Andrews would ask Meighen to let him also retain E.K. Williams, another Citizen.[11] Meighen okayed this if it was 'absolutely necessary,' but added a caution: 'We must not permit of fair criticism that we took undue advantage of greater financial resources in trial like this.'[12] That would be the first inkling that federal dollars *might* be available.

Meighen's agreement should not be taken as an indication that he imagined Ottawa shelling out for the prosecution of eight Strike leaders. The federal Department of Justice did occasionally retain lawyers for legal work on provincial prosecutions. Perhaps the most notorious case during the Great War involved twelve men who allegedly conspired to blow up the home of Sir Hugh Graham, owner of the *Montreal Star*, a newspaper that had vigorously supported conscription. The Dominion Police investigated, and Ottawa helped the province with $3000 for legal services. Effective January 1919, the RNWMP had taken charge of national security matters in Western Canada, and the Strike was the first major crisis under the new arrangement.[13] Meighen's willingness to allow Andrews a bit of leeway in retaining legal assistance to develop his case wasn't unusual, but it didn't amount to agreeing that Andrews could operate without provincial blessing and money. Moreover, Meighen, instead of extending the legal reach of the Department of Justice, had been eliminating the oppressive Orders-in-Council fashioned by Charles Doherty.

Despite Meighen's 'grave doubts about the legality of *our* position' [emphasis added], he decided to support Andrews's arrests. Said Meighen, 'Your message seventeenth received and is quite satisfactory ... I was quite with you in the step you have taken.' He had been caught unawares – 'The fact is, that up to the arrival of your wire last night, I had no information that you had laid charges of seditious conspiracy, the course of the telegrams indicating only an intention to proceed under the Immigration Act' – yet he decided to step alongside, now that his 'deputy' had let the cat-o'-nine-tails out of the bag: 'You and your associates can always feel that your extraordinary efforts on behalf of public law and order, are thoroughly appreciated here ... We at least, can confidently abide the fullest vindication of *our* course' [emphasis added].[14] 'Our' position; 'our' course. Meighen hadn't known what course he was taking until Andrews placed him on it, but now Meighen made a virtue of necessity. The day before, Andrews had reminded him that 'local government would not act,'[15] and now it came to Meighen in a flash of inspiration that if he couldn't legally justify circumventing the Province, at least he could justify the extra-constitutional action on the grounds that he and Andrews and the Citizens were tired: 'As for the Provincial Government, I have exhausted every effort to work hand in hand with them, and I know you and the Citizens Committee have done the same.'[16] Prime Minister Borden took his cue from Meighen, who had taken his cue from Andrews. When Sir Frederick Williams Taylor, acting president of the Canadian Bankers' Association, congratulated Borden on the arrests and urged strong action against the Strike leaders, Borden explained: 'You realize of course, that the administration of the law and the preservation or order are entrusted primarily to the provincial Authorities. In case they fail to act when conditions are serious there is doubtless responsibility on the Federal Government.'[17] The explanation repeated almost exactly the buzz that Andrews had put in Meighen's ear twelve days earlier: 'This is a matter purely for the Attorney General and not your department unless you are strongly of the view that the Attorney General has taken the wrong course and that you should interfere.'[18] Either the prince and his counsellor had serendipitously arrived at the identical position, or the counsellor had convinced the prince that the idea was the prince's own.

As a result of Meighen's effective docility, Andrews could retreat from his threat to quit as Meighen's deputy, could encourage him with good reports, and could reassure him that Andrews perfectly understood Meighen's political concerns about legality and appearances. Andrews not only said that the arrests had greatly pleased 'law abiding citizens' and that some workers were already beginning to trickle back to work, but offered an olive branch to make up for his earlier testy comments: 'You may rely upon my never overlooking the fact that you will be blamed for any of the mistakes that I make and I therefore have tried and will continue to try to be as cautious as possible.'[19] Meighen would still turn leery about money and about entangling the federal government in *criminal* prosecutions, but for now he was in Andrews's corner.

Friday, 20 June

In the wake of the Criminal Code arrests, lawyer T.J. McMurray demanded bail for the Strike leaders. At first, Andrews resisted, saying on Wednesday that it would be 'a fatal error and would be interpreted as weakness.'[20] To plug all the holes, he had posted a Mountie at the Penitentiary, and had several warrants lying in ambush – no wonder that Pitblado and Sweatman were up until all hours – so that if any Strike leader managed to wrangle bail from a soft judge and step out of jail, he'd immediately feel the Mountie's hand on his shoulder, and a new arrest warrant would be waved in his face. The other Citizens, not aware of the legal niceties of Andrews's position, knew only that they wanted the harshest line to be taken with the Strike leaders; meaning no bail. Andrews described his plan to Meighen thus: 'The men will be held under the original warrant until the [Immigration] Board of Inquiry has ordered their deportation or the reverse. My plan is to deport all that are deportable and to try the balance on whatever charges we think will warrant their conviction.'[21]

Then on Thursday, astonishingly, Andrews acquiesced to bail. Howls from many quarters of his own constituency. Gen. Ketchen was opposed;[22] the *Winnipeg Telegram* called the federal government 'yellow';[23] and some of those associated with the Citizens protested Andrews's decision to Ottawa. Businessperson Dick Randolph telegraphed MP George Allan that the Citizens considered the release of the Strike leaders a serious mistake: 'The strong stand taken by Government in making these arrests was approved of by us and inspired great feeling of confidence in citizen at large which feeling has been entirely shattered by releasing these men ... Whole outlook has changed to-day the leaders are arrogant and openly boast of waywardness of Government and are making intrigue plans to create further trouble.'[24] Andrews put his own spin on the reaction. He telegraphed, 'Members voluntary militia seemed quite satisfied when I addressed them,' though he admitted, 'My explanation only fairly satisfactory to citizens committee.'[25] That Andrews was bluffing about the militia is suggested by Gen. Ketchen's response. According to him, the five weeks of sacrifices by the Specials and the militia made them especially hostile to bail.[26] More than a week earlier, Ketchen had complained that the militia was bleeding men to the Specials,[27] whose pay was higher. Now he feared losing even more men.

Andrews was again acting independently of both the Citizens and Meighen, administering the pill that he thought best, even over the patient's protests. Like Meighen, the Citizens evidently thought that deportation was the quickest road to a cure. 'I was,' said Andrews, 'very severely criticized for announcing that the strike leaders arrested would be tried on criminal charges, the deportation proceedings being delayed in the meantime.'[28] He may have had the backing of his fellow lawyers, and he claimed that Sen. Robertson was onside, but he was sailing very close to the wind: his status with Meighen presumed that he spoke for Winnipeg's business elite, yet in the matter of bail, he defied that elite. Why? First of all, optics. Although he spoke of the 'fairest course towards English-speaking prisoners,' what he actually meant was that a clear distinction between Briton and alien would continue to play well: 'I believe public opinion generally will approve this manifestation of fairness on part of Crown.'[29] Second, practical considerations: given a charge that was punishable by only two years' imprisonment (as sedition was), from the perspective of a defence lawyer (as Andrews long had been), it would seem very unusual to deny bail.[30] Third, strategy: Andrews was sure that the British leaders would be easier to convict under the Criminal Code than under the narrow limits of immigration legislation.[31] This after all the tinkering with the Immigration Act and the repeated assurances (which Meighen still believed) that Andrews was pursuing deportations.

Lastly, Andrews was able to get bail conditions that emasculated the Strike leaders. The Strike Committee promised that there would be no public jubilation over the release of the British leaders, and the arrested leaders promised that if bailed they would not only refrain from further involvement in the Strike, but also 'refrain from public speaking, interviews with newspapers and other public utterances' until after their trial.[32] This must have put a grin on Andrews. While most of the Citizens called for heads to roll, and would have joyfully martyred the Strike leaders – indeed, labour MP Fred Dixon was already speaking of their 'crown of martyrdom'[33] – Andrews had found a way to appear magnanimous and fair and constitutionally *British*, while at the same time throwing cold water on the hottest of the firebrands. Andrews crowed, 'When these men were arrested they whined and shivered like curs'[34] – he had never seen 'such an exhibition of cowardice and fear.'[35] Now Russell and the others would tread even more delicately, for fear of handing the Crown additional evidence of sedition. It's possible that Andrews may have still planned to deport the non-British leaders, but by working the space between Meighen and the Citizens, now keeping one in the dark, now the other, Andrews steered a very prudent course.

Behind Andrews's decision was also the post-arrest tumult on Tuesday in Victoria Park, when returned soldiers, a volatile group that he was particularly wary of, shouted support for their imprisoned leaders. The meeting was 'electrified by the arrests' and 'vibrant with emotion.'[36] There was also much fight left in the *Western Labor News*. Unaware that Andrews was already a step ahead, the *Labor News*'s aimed its rhetoric at the denial of bail and the planned deportation of British citizens 'without formality of a civil trial.'[37] If after riots in Liverpool and Cardiff, negroes who were British subjects couldn't be deported, a question naturally arose in Winnipeg: 'Have Scotchmen, Englishmen, and Canadians in Canada less rights than negroes in England?'[38] The *Labor News* concluded by tossing the Citizens' constitutional rhetoric back at them: the abuse of procedure in the arrests was more serious than any charge the workers could formulate 'against the employer-capitalist government.' Under a detailing of the sedition charges the editors placed two quotations, a straightforward and radical claim by Robert G. Ingersoll – 'Whoever produces anything by weary labor, does not need a revelation from heaven to teach him that he has a right to the thing produced' – and a more ironic sentence from Anatole France, cynical in its distrust of what law means in a capitalist society: 'The law in its majestic equality forbids the rich as well as the poor to sleep under bridges, to beg in the streets and to steal bread.'[39] The Victoria Park tumult and the *Labor News* rhetoric culminated Friday in the returned soldiers issuing strongly worded resolutions about 'the denial of free speech' and about the 'Russian methods adopted by the present government.'[40] It didn't soothe labour that the Citizens had gained a symbolic victory by successfully pushing the City to get the streetcars running again.

On Friday evening, the soldiers resolved to make a 'Silent Parade' on Saturday, despite Mayor Gray's proclamation that no marches would be tolerated. Even with bail calming the waters, rumours abounded that the parades would turn into riots, but Andrews tried to wave them away, saying 'these may not occur.'[41] Gen. Ketchen, less thrilled about Andrews's course, was also less optimistic about its calming effect when he telegraphed headquarters: 'This element returned soldiers composed worst type amongst men and incite crowd deliberate disturbance tomorrow.'[42]

Bloody Saturday, 21 June

The Comptroller   Winnipeg Man
    RNWM Police, OTTAWA. Ont.   21-6-1919
At two thirty today at request of the Mayor of Winnipeg and with consent of the Attorney General all available men of the Force mounted and dismounted have been instructed to assist the Civil Authorities in maintaining law and order stop A large body of returned soldiers has decided to disobey the Mayor's proclamation against street parades and defy the Civil Authorities. At this hour they are assembled in large numbers along Main Street. It is probable that the Municipal Forces and Mounted Police will not be able to control the situation and that the Mayor will read the Riot Act and will call upon the Military Forces to act. Every possible attempt has been made to persuade these men not to defy the law. I have been in close consultation with Senator Robertson and Mr Andrews.

                        [RNWMP Commissioner] A.B. Perry

Two fifty. Riots have broken out. Riot Act has been read by the Mayor and Military forces called out. Casualties in the Force two constables injured in the head two horses legs broken.

                                                A.B. Perry

Four thirty. Everything is now quiet Civil Police Mounted Police and troops are occupying the main streets. A large number of rioters has been arrested. Mounted Police were subjected to a very heavy fire of bricks bottles stones and other missiles. Quite a number of casualties but not ·exactly known. Mounted Police in self defence were obliged to use their firearms. Reported that five of the rioters were thus injured. I think the situation is now in hand but further trouble may develop tonight. Officially reported that MIKE SCOBLESCIE [actually Mike Sokolowski] 552 Henry Avenue shot through the heart. This is the only death so far.

                                                A.B. Perry

The Specials muster at the corner of Main and Market. (Foote Collection 1702/N2768, Archives of Manitoba)

Gen. Ketchen's militia arrives in convoy, with mounted machine guns, to suppress the rioting. (Foote Collection 1704/N2770, Archives of Manitoba)

Five thirty PM. At this hour city is quiet. Mounted Police and Military Forces have paraded North end and found all quiet. Turbulent element of returned soldiers holding meeting in Victoria Park. Attitude still defiant.

A.B. Perry

Seven forty PM. About eight arrests made up to present mostly charged with unlawful assembly. Between fifteen and twenty arrested on top of buildings for throwing missiles. City quiet at present.

A.B. Perry[43]

The feared disturbance arrived. Some Citizens later argued that leniency about bail was interpreted as weakness, emboldening the strikers to riot, while Andrews, closer to the truth, claimed the Strike leaders, cognizant of their bail conditions, had tried to *mitigate* the riot.[44] Nonetheless, the strikers massed in the streets, and after the RNWMP made several charges into the crowd, trying to clear the streets, mayhem ensued. The strikers hurled all manner of objects at the Mounties; the Mounties responded with truncheons and guns. In the wake of the Mounties, E.K. Williams, one of the Citizens' lawyers, rode with troops down Main Street.[45]

The Citizens had gotten the streetcars running again on Wednesday, and very soon the crowd focused its anger on that symbol of business-as-usual, overturning a streetcar and setting it ablaze. In General Ketchen's abbreviated version, 'After Mayor read Riot Act much rough work. Police fired on and returned fire. Casualties 20, including 4 mounted police slightly injured, two specials not serious. Of remainder, one foreigner died of gun shot wounds, two others gun shot wounds, serious, likely fatal.'[46] Captain Dunwoody, who led a group of Specials, testified that men with revolvers fired at him and his men a number of times.[47] However, that the 'government' forces came back without a single gunshot wound suggests that this was an after-the-fact rationalization for the Mounties' own use of guns. Ralph Connor's novel of the Strike, *To Him That Hath*, follows this rationalization to its logical conclusion: the novel's dénouement consists of a *striker* accidentally shooting someone, reversing the historical events in which the RNWMP killed one striker and wounded about thirty, one of whom would later die.

After the riot, unrest all night. Rumours ran that strikers would mount an organized attack on the city. In anticipation, Specials blocked all the streets leading into the city centre from the North End. Nothing happened. Crown Prosecutors Graham and Phillips spent the night taking

statements from the hospitalized casualties on both sides.[48] Not everyone, however, was upset by the bullets and truncheons. The Citizens had
all along been pushing towards some sort of conclusion, and the riot at
least had the salutary effect of clarifying which side stood for law and
order, and which side was the enemy. From at least three members of the
Citizens' executive – Ed Parnell, W.R. Ingram, and Robert McKay –
Meighen received telegrams congratulating him on the government's
stern response to the riot.[49]

Monday, 23 June – Monday, 30 June

Bloody Saturday did bring about a conclusion. On Wednesday, the 25th,
the Strike collapsed. The government's harsh suppression of the parade
sapped the will of many of the less radical union members. If Andrews
and the Citizens had little direct role in Saturday's events, they had been
– from their divisive language of 'citizenship' and anti-alien hysteria, to
the hiring of Special Police and the arrests of the Strike leaders – the
shapers of the public climate in which such suppression was conceivable. In the days and months after Bloody Saturday, Andrews and the
Citizens (not always unitedly) sought to shape both the public's and the
government's hindsight too. The judgment of what had been done right
and wrong would in part determine who deserved honour ... and who
could be blamed for the dead and wounded. The apportioning of praise
and blame threatened to open a rift between Andrews and Meighen, perhaps conveniently so for Meighen – partly because he no longer needed
to rely quite so much on Andrews, but also because Meighen began to
grasp that Andrews had misled him on a number of issues.

Having silenced the Strike leaders by means of arrest and bail,
Andrews also sought to silence the *Western Labor News*, claiming that
Monday's paper contained sedition and an incitement to further riot. But
Andrews deflected to Sen. Robertson the praise or blame for closing the
Labor News. Robertson appealed to Secretary of State Martin Burrell to
use one of the wartime Orders-in-Council, but Burrell and Cabinet
refused, saying that it was 'inadvisable and possibly illegal' to use these
OICs for matters not pertaining to the war effort.[50] Lacking federal
imprimatur, Andrews went over Burrell's head, appointed himself censor, and brought pressure to bear on the printers – 'personal friends of
mine and good citizens.'[51] Owner Gustavus Pringle agreed to stop publishing the *Labor News* if Andrews put his request in writing. He did,
signing himself in such a way as to invoke the full powers that he had
never actually been endowed with:

Winnipeg, June 23, 1919

Winnipeg Printing and Engraving Co.,

Gentlemen:–

Certain numbers of the Winnipeg Western Labor News Special Strike Edition have contained objectionable matter in that it is seditious, inflammatory and inciting to riot and this publication must be discontinued. No more issues of this publication must be printed or circulated.

Signed, Yours truly,

ALFRED J. ANDREWS,

Agent, Department of Justice.[52]

The 'Strike Editions' of the *Labor News* must cease; the regular editions of the Trades and Labor Council's *Labor News* could still be published, but the *printers* must assume responsibility to ensure that no seditious articles were published. Winnipeg's other newspapers, unanimously arrayed against the censoring effects of the pressmen's walkout earlier on, felt no outrage at this new censorship. The printers turned over 'manuscripts' of articles that had appeared in the *Labor News*, and on that basis, Andrews was able, finally, to convince the Provincial Government to indulge in some arrests. On Andrews's information, 'Phillips and Graham' (Andrews named the special 'Assistant' Crown Prosecutor Phillips ahead of the less malleable Crown Prosecutor Graham) made out warrants for the arrest of the new *Labor News* editor J.S. Woodsworth, and the writer of many of the articles, Fred Dixon.[53] Here, rather late in the day, Andrews thought that he was finally delivering to Meighen the provincial cooperation that Meighen had desired all along: 'My policy is to encourage Provincial Authorities to act and relieve your Department responsibility. Will only act when deemed necessary and they refuse.'[54] Of course, the Province acted in this way only because the federal government had acted first in arresting the Strike leaders, and the Province kept one leg dangling from the bandwagon, in case it needed to jump off. This latest action would in no way absolve the federal government of responsibility for the earlier arrests, and there was no guarantee that the Province would prosecute Woodsworth and Dixon.

What was the *Western Labor News*'s greatest crime? The only one that Andrews saw fit to mention to Meighen was that the *Labor News* had criticized Andrews for the strict bail conditions he had imposed. This criticism enraged Andrews as a 'direct violation' of his gentleman's agreement with the Strike leaders that they refrain from public speaking, interviews with newspapers, and other public utterances until

after their trial. Andrews didn't say how the article violated their promises, but he had no difficulty in sensing a personal affront: 'These men
... are wholly without honor and can only be dealt with by the sternest
methods.'[55]

A much bigger problem for Andrews, and not so easily swept aside by
an intimidating signature, was the rift that began to open between him
and Meighen. The rift had several intertwined causes. The efficient
cause was the riot: if there had been no riot, there would have been no
political damage to the Borden government, and likely no complaint
from Meighen. But there had been a riot, and some of the Citizens were
blaming the riot on Andrews's leniency about bail. As well, there were
small signs that Meighen was having second thoughts about circumventing the Province by making arrests.

Because Andrews and the Citizens had successfully gone over provincial heads to Meighen, they weren't impressed that Premier Norris
appointed Judge Robson to inquire into the causes and conduct of the
Strike. The Citizens, complained Andrews, were 'much exercised' over
the appointment. With the Strike basically over, the Robson commission
was 'a very great mistake,' and would only convince OBUers 'to hold
their organization together and call another strike later on.' Why not
instead appoint a commission of 'Dominion wide powers' to cast a wider
net and investigate the One Big Union? Such a mandate would dovetail
nicely with Andrews's and the RNWMP's plan to make searches
throughout Canada for more evidence of revolution.[56] Meighen's
response was terse, probably reflecting his worries about Andrews's
freelancing, and hinting at the shaky legal ground for the arrests: 'Before
we can consider matter, must await Robertson's return. Cannot interfere
with Provincial Governments [sic] course.'[57]

Since the question of bail had become so vexed by Saturday's events,
Andrews sought to close the possible rift by undergoing a makeover.
Suddenly, he appeared not only as a stickler about bail but also a stickler about following the proper chain of command. After Strike leader
Bill Pritchard was arrested in Calgary and requested bail, Andrews
telegraphed Meighen: 'Have said will not consent without you direct
unless you think refusal may affect outside organized labour would
refuse. Would suggest consult loyal labour representatives and wire your
decision.' And as to bail for the arrested non-British Strike leaders,
Andrews added, 'Think foreigners arrested should not be bailed if you
think otherwise instruct me.'[58] Evidently fearing that Bloody Saturday
had inflicted political damage, Meighen responded, 'Would think
unwise to consent to bail except with approval legal associates' [proba-
bly referring to Pitblado and Sweatman]. The response shows that,

unlike the Citizens, who had opposed bail, and unlike Andrews, who had favoured it, Meighen had little notion of his own as to whether bail was a good or bad idea. No wonder that Andrews made the decision for him. Meighen's reason for hedging became clear in his subsequent clauses: 'Most important to conform every reasonable way with Winnipeg public sentiment. Assume such was case before previous releases.'[59] In effect, Meighen was hinting that as long as the electorate and the Citizens approved of Andrews's actions, Meighen was onside too. But if the public disapproved? Then he'd be – retroactively – against bail. Given this hedging, it's also no wonder that two days later Andrews would simply inform Meighen that he'd allowed Pritchard's bail.[60]

Despite Meighen's hedging, Andrews wasn't going to take the fall for Bloody Saturday. In his first long letter to Meighen in a week, he tenaciously defended his actions, noting that Commissioner Perry, Sen. Robertson, and Thomas J. Murray (lawyer for the Trades & Labor Council), and a large deputation from the Strike Committee, were all present when bail was arranged. According to Andrews, the Strike Committee was satisfied with the offer from the ironmasters and was about to call off the Strike. After six long weeks of head-butting, everyone was miraculously on the same page: 'everyone' at the meeting took the view that 'if these men were let out on bail it would relieve the situation and help the smaller committee to induce the larger committee to call the strike off.' Andrews also, in defending bail, finally revealed his argument for moving away from deportation and for instead using the Criminal Code. First, he repeated his idealized appeal to fairness, and then he gave the real tactical reason (which he expected Meighen to share): 'You will realize that it will be much harder to legally deport under the Immigration Act than to convict of sedition, assuming that the Board of Inquiry acted purely in a judicial capacity.'

If Meighen insisted upon additional reasons that would play well with voters, Andrews had those ready too. Bloody Saturday could have been much worse if he had opposed bail: 'Those who falsely suggest that my leniency was the cause of the riot on Saturday know very little of the situation. Meetings had been called to protest against keeping these men in gaol without bail and all the strikers were demanding bail.' He was probably right. Of course, the protests could easily be hung around Andrews's neck – he had made the questionable arrests, after all. Was Meighen worried about public sentiment? In that case, Andrews had a bit of food for thought: 'People throughout Canada ... would have blamed the Government for their action in furnishing provocation for the riot.'[61] The government. *Their* action. Meighen would do well to remember who would have taken the fall had worse happened.

A. J. ANDREWS

1909 cartoon of Andrews. (Hay Stead, *Manitobans as We See Em*, 1909, Alfred J. Andrews Collection, N16216, Archives of Manitoba)

Meighen couldn't argue against Andrews's points, but troubling Meighen and widening the rift between the two was his discovery that Andrews didn't always speak for the Citizens. As long as the Citizens were united, Meighen could at least feel confident that he had the considerable clout of Winnipeg's elite at his back. It was only several days later, with Sen. Robertson back in Ottawa, that Meighen realized how much rein Andrews had taken, enough rein that even Robertson *in Winnipeg* hadn't realized that Andrews was acting without the blessing of the Citizens:

'I naturally assumed on receipt of your telegram, stating your intention to release on bail, that those with whom you are associated concurred, and Senator Robertson tells me that it was his understanding that they did concur.' Meighen, wanting whatever it was that the public wanted, didn't necessarily disagree with the bail decision, but thought that in the absence of the Citizens' support, Andrews should at least have delayed the move.[62]

Meighen registered this protest on the 30th, when it could no longer have much bearing: five days earlier, the Strike had been called off. The Citizens had their no-negotiation victory, and Meighen had at least something concrete to show, despite his concerns about Andrews's free-lancing. By the 30th, Andrews wasn't even around to receive Meighen's protest, but had left Winnipeg for the city whose Citizens' Alliance had inspired the creation of the Winnipeg Citizens' Alliance. After all the hours he and the other lawyers put in slaying the dragon, they deserved some time off: 'We are taking brief rest until Wednesday morning as all pretty exhausted.'[63] He was in Minneapolis, golfing.[64]

10

The Only Way to Deal
with Bolshevism

Tuesday, 1 July – Monday, 7 July

Meighen had still cavilled, five days after the Strike was called off, because the victory might still prove to be hollow if 'public sentiment' didn't approve. The Citizens, however, set about occupying the public sphere. A nearly full-page ad that they placed in the *Manitoba Free Press* was intended to leave no doubt that Winnipeg's labour revolt had been tamed: '**Put Him On the Job!**' read the headline. A transcendent voice feigned to speak from beyond the Strike's animosities: 'During the Strike the Citizens' Committee of One Thousand took no issue with Labor as such; no side as between employer and employee. It claims no victory over Labor, but stood uncompromisingly against a sympathetic strike born of plotting revolution. It represented only the General Public.' No victory, yet the accompanying drawing shows many workers in rolled-up sleeves traipsing back towards a factory, watched over by a man in a suit. The low-angle perspective makes him four times the workers' size, towering over them. And the 'neutral' Citizens called for everyone to embrace the shibboleths of capitalist production: 'Turn attention to the work at hand. Six long weeks have been lost to our summer's work. We must catch that up – the only way to do it is by "full steam ahead" in every business and industry in this City.' Of course, not everyone was invited back into the fold. 'The I.W.W., Red Revolutionaries or Bolsheviks' must give their jobs to 'our returned men,' and workers were advised to begin policing radicalism: 'If you neglect to give it your counsel and watchfulness you must not be surprised if the agitator and the plotter creep into control.' Business owners were invited to leave aside 'reckless profiteering' and to take greater cognizance of their employees – 'Stand closer to your men. Think from their viewpoint as to wages and working conditions.' But, above all, production: 'Do not wait now for orders. Start the plant; the goods will move ... All together and advance – without foolishness, delay, red tape, or politics. **Full Steam Ahead!**'[1]

No victory and no politics, the Citizens said, but somehow they had emerged in power ... for the moment. The claim that there had been no victory signified that immediately the battle had shifted its theatre to the *meaning* of the Strike and the arrests. As long as the strikers hindered the flow of necessities and commerce, the Citizens could call them autocrats who were flouting the constitution. Back on the job, however, with the federal government apparently denying the Strike leaders bail, baulking at jury trials, and trying to limit freedom of speech and of association, strikers could broadcast their own call for the British constitutional rights that the Citizens had so feverishly insisted upon. Public battles erupted over bail for the Eastern European Strike leaders, while private battles were fought between the Citizens and Ottawa, and between the provincial and federal governments, over a commission into the Strike and over post-Strike prosecutions. Elected by farmers certain to be luke-warm about an expensive prosecution at a time of rural economic dis-tress, the Norris government was largely immune to demands for a pros-ecution.[2] The pressure was now squarely on Andrews and the Citizens. If a commission apportioned blame to both labour and capital, and if nobody prosecuted the Strike leaders, they'd return to battle another day. No level of government wanted another strike, yet no one wanted to be seen as the oppressor either.

The appeal to the constitution, and the demand for bail for the East-ern European Strike leaders detained under the Immigration Act, landed on Andrews's doorstep quickly. At the first meeting of the Winnipeg Trades and Labor Council since the beginning of the Strike, the secre-tary explained that because the police had taken all his records he was obliged to report verbally. The TLC decided to revive the *Western Labor News*, to fight trial-less deportations, and to embark on a nation-wide campaign to get a trial by jury for every accused. Although Andrews had informally suppressed the *Labor News* and arrested its editors, the strik-ers realized that he had no authority to actually censor the paper, so they put it back on the streets.[3] Said the *Labor News*, 'The federal govern-ment fears that it is facing Niagara because of its criminal neglect in the repression of profiteers, so a campaign of night raids is supposed to be the cure-all for popular discontent.' By subsequently publishing a list of the men whose homes were raided by 'the military police in the wee small hours' of 30 June, the *Labor News* made it a badge of honour to have been arrested.[4]

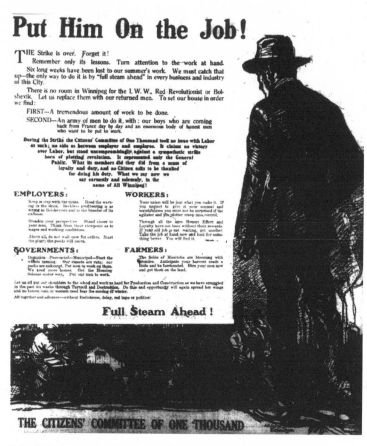

The Strike over, the Citizens urge the resumption of business on their terms. (*Manitoba Free Press*, 28 June 1919)

R.J. Johns, away in Montreal during the arrests, now surrendered and appeared with the other British-born leaders before a reluctant justice, Sir Hugh John Macdonald. There was no 'Crown.' Instead, Andrews 'appeared for the Department of Justice.'[5] Although one might expect that this ought to diminish his authority, it was precisely by stepping into such semi-official roles that he gained a kind of official validation. E.J. McMurray and Marcus Hyman, acting for the accused, insisted that the

Crown, if it had a case, should get on with it. Andrews, tenuously positioned, asked for a remand. Macdonald granted Andrews's request, but 'gave the crown to understand that he would not remand it after the eight days unless the crown produced a pretty strong case for further remand.' That the *Labor News* without qualification used the term 'Crown Prosecutor' for Andrews suggests that the Strike leaders didn't know how tenuous Andrews's position was.[6]

The question of bail conditions was raised as well. Russell, Ivens, Queen, Heaps, Armstrong, and Bray refused to be bound any longer by their bail agreement not to give interviews or speak at public meetings. Judge Macdonald withdrew the limiting conditions, an action that Andrews affected to interpret as a slap in the face, and, since the law was no longer on his side, he resorted to gentleman's language, accusing the Strike leaders of having 'withdrawn undertakings given me'[7] – as if the bail restrictions had been a private promise between them and him, not a legal restriction that he had been briefly able to impose. Andrews asked that bail be doubled to $8000 each, a request Macdonald granted. But no bail for the Eastern European leaders. They had been transferred from Stoney Mountain to the Winnipeg Immigration Hall, pending immigration hearings, and while the British-born leaders enjoyed the constitutional rights of free speech and assembly, at Andrews's insistence the Eastern Europeans (excepting the falsely-arrested Mike Verenczuk) weren't even granted *habeas corpus*.[8] Amid the growing chorus for bail and open trials, Andrews defended his actions to Meighen – 'private reports show men in gaol most dangerous' – even while conceding that the evidence was insufficient to prosecute them criminally. Andrews favoured deportation and no bail, but left the final decision to Meighen: 'You may think differently in view of agitation labor.'[9]

Agitation came from all over Canada. In *To Him That Hath*, a spirit of 'compromise' follows the Strike, and Jack, the son of the factory owner, is acclaimed as the *union's* representative on the post-strike arbitration committee[10] – labour falling gladly in line behind a leading Citizen. Of course, nothing like this happened in actuality. The *Western Labor News* compared the Citizens Committee with the Family Compact,[11] repeated calls for jury trials, and condemned the summary deportations now legislated into the Immigration Act: 'Who conceived the idea? Why did the people who conceived it wish to destroy the British constitutional rights of trial by jury? Why did they stampede it through parliament so drastically that the people had no possible chance to know that the matter was at issue!' In immigration matters, Ottawa could, of course, legally act without provincial consent, but popular outrage against the Star Chamber procedures was mounting. The *Labor News* also condemned the 30 June police raids: 'The government ... came like a thief in the night to do what could much more easily be done in broad daylight.' 'Midnight terrorist tactics' must end at once and the government must adopt methods 'more suitable to British justice.'[12] This raised Andrews's ire, and he wrote Meighen that if Justice Mathers had been 'in the atmosphere of this strike,' his report on industrial relations in Canada wouldn't have been quite so cheery about free speech. Andrews enclosed a copy of the offending newspaper, and although he felt that some action should be taken, he again left it up to Meighen.[13] It was inconceivable that Meighen would suddenly now leap into this fray of his own accord, but Andrews couldn't be entirely displeased, since Meighen assured him that Minister of Immigration J.A. Calder was holding the line on deportation and was searching for a judge to act on the immigration board.[14]

Hard on the heels of the Mathers report, on 4 July the Province added a second commission, appointing Hugh A. Robson as sole commissioner to inquire into the Strike. This fulfilled one of the conditions for labour calling off the sympathetic strike, but angered the Citizens. Even before the announcement, the Citizens were lobbying Ottawa against the commission: on 24 June, using Canadian Manufacturers' Association letterhead, the Citizens had wired Borden, Meighen, and Robertson, urging that 'no Commission should be promised or announced as a condition of calling off the strike.' Robson, a Liberal and a former Court of King's Bench justice,[15] was considered too liberal, and his charge – to investigate the causes of the Winnipeg General Strike – too narrow. How could a provincial commission investigate an international Bolshevik conspiracy? Instead, the Citizens advocated a 'Dominion Commission' with the widest possible powers.[16] Ed Anderson, who was also general counsel to the Winnipeg Electric Railway Company,[17] had kept up a barrage at Meighen on the matter, and Andrews, W.H. McWilliams, and A.K. Godfrey now joined in, aided by MP George Allan.[18] Anderson, citing Pitblado, Coyne, and Sweatman, asked for an investigation of the OBU, 'the Socialistic Party of Canada' [*sic*], the 'Bolshevistic' movement, and especially their 'alterior [*sic*] and revolutionary motives.'[19] The Citizens clearly wanted a royal commission whose conclusion – Bolshevik revolution – would already be anticipated in its terms of reference. Anderson even suggested names, so that the Citizens could be sure of the outcome: 'I think that the Commissioner should be either Judge Duff or Judge Cameron. The latter has some very pronounced views in the right direction.'[20] Like Robson, J.D. Cameron was a Liberal,[21] but with attitudes more in line with the Citizens'. He was the one who had denied the initial bail application of the Strike leaders. If a Dominion-wide commission happened to implicate some of the Strike leaders, then well and good.[22]

At the same time, Andrews was engaged in a more pivotal battle: the constitutional problem of the legal authority to prosecute. Andrews now used the 'sheer moral force' that American Citizens' Alliances had boasted of. The 25 June arrests of J.S. Woodsworth and Fred Dixon, which Andrews had advertised to Meighen as a sign that he had finally got the Province onside, required a decision. Instead of a provincial prosecution, 'Assistant' Crown Prosecutor Hugh Phillips wanted Andrews – that is, the federal government – to prosecute Woodsworth, Dixon, and two other recently arrested men, J.A. Martin and James Grant, for sedition.[23] This could hardly fail to dismay Meighen, but Andrews had primed him by publicizing what a mass of Bolshevik literature had turned up in the raids throughout Canada: 'It will take days to separate and classify it. Whether we are successful in securing convictions or not, we have got written evidence to prove beyond a doubt that Western Canada has been and is seething in revolution, and as a result of these raids we will probably have a number of recommendations as to prosecutions elsewhere.'[24] The public needed to know that he was storing all the revolutionary literature in 'fire-proof vaults' alongside material taken from the Labor Temple and from Winnipeg's radicals.[25] With Meighen, Andrews used the seized literature to make a case for putting more lawyers on the scent: 'I hope you will understand that I am not overlooking the fact that not one dollar of useless expense should be incurred in these proceedings, but at the same time I do not think it is a time when the country can afford on the score of economy to neglect any legitimate means of bringing to light the true situation as it exists in Canada.'[26] A nation 'seething in revolution,' yet Andrews wasn't certain that he could secure convictions. In the end, there would be no charges laid anywhere in Canada except in Winnipeg, by Andrews.

Andrews also primed Meighen by telling him about 'a very largely attended meeting,' in which the Citizens' executive 'expressed very strong appreciation of the action of the Dominion Government and made very complimentary remarks with reference to the counsel you have engaged.' This meant Citizens Pitblado, Sweatman, Coyne, E.K. Williams, and, of course, yours truly, A.J. Andrews. Well might the Citizens sing praise: they were praising themselves. In truth, Meighen hadn't precisely 'engaged' the lawyers – he had engaged Andrews, and Andrews had hauled the others on board, one and two at a time, over Meighen's caution that more lawyers should be engaged only if 'absolutely necessary.' Now Andrews was attributing his own initiative to Meighen and praising Meighen for it.[27]

But despite all of Andrews's petting, Meighen was still leery. In earlier weeks, Andrews had been selectively passing messages between Robertson and Meighen, and although they were still working with material that Andrews had given them, now that Robertson had returned to Ottawa, Andrews could no longer regulate the flow of information between the two. Robertson told Meighen that the Dixon cohort had been arrested 'on instructions of provincial authorities,' just as Andrews himself had claimed. This, if not quite the truth itself – *Andrews* had put Crown Attorneys Phillips and Graham up to the arrests – was at least in the ballpark. But Meighen began to reason in a way counter to Andrews's hopes: the Province had arrested; the Province must prosecute. Why should the federal government conduct the Province's cases?[28] If the Province wouldn't even follow through on its 'own' recent arrests, what hope was there of getting it into the ring against Russell, Ivens, and the others?

Meighen's common-sense approach must have disconcerted Andrews and the Citizens. Treading very carefully, Andrews said, 'My own view would be that it would be just as well for us to take over the prosecution of Woodsworth and Dixon but not [Martin and Grant],' and then quickly added, 'Whatever you have decided will be quite satisfactory as far as I am concerned.' Andrews gave no explanation why only Woodsworth and Dixon should be prosecuted, and the softening of his urgency suggests that he was worried about Ottawa's firmness and was prepared to cut his losses. Yet, even as he left the final decision up to Meighen, Andrews made sure to speak of the prosecution of Russell et al. as a foregone conclusion: 'It is going to be very difficult to be ready to go on at the end of this term but we are going to try if possible to do so as I think it is important to push the matter now by every possible means.'[29]

A few days later, Andrews grew less deferential. If Meighen wasn't going to step up, the Province would simply drop the cases: 'It was at my suggestion that Phillips and Graham took these up and they now wish me to continue to carry them on ... If the legal authorities will not press them I really think you should instruct me to do so.'[30] Then, hardball: 'Prosecution should follow to justify these raids.'[31] In other words, raids and arrests had been made; a decision not to prosecute would mean that the raids had been unjustified, and would harm not the Citizens but the *government*. No matter that it had been the Citizens who had pressed Meighen and Robertson into arrests. As if to underline the point, Ed Anderson also wrote Meighen the same day, and although his focus was on getting the government to appoint a national commission into revolutionary activity, Anderson sent the same warning as Andrews had: 'I think the Government will fall entirely short of justifying its conduct unless it is followed up by energetic action.'[32]

Monday, 7 July – Friday, 18 July

In the second week of July, the entrails didn't look promising for the Citizens. Meighen had ignored Andrews's invitation to take up the prosecutions of Woodsworth and Dixon; the federal cabinet had no plans to impose a Dominion-wide commission over top of the Robson commission; and even the prosecution of the British-born Strike leaders seemed in doubt. Like the Citizens, Winnipeg's labour movement went nationwide in its campaign. Instead of the muzzle that Andrews had fitted them with, Queen, Heaps, and Bray (along with returned soldier R.T. Dunn) now had invitations to speak throughout Ontario, and they roused Ontario audiences by crying out against the Citizens' assault on 'British freedoms,' especially with respect to the non-English-speaking leaders who faced deportation. Queen announced 'a monster petition' on their behalf.[33] At a Winnipeg open-air rally, Dixon shouted that Canadians were having 'their rights and liberties stolen from them by the shabbiest pack of political jackals that ever harassed a civilized country.'[34] Across Canada, individuals, labour councils, women's labour leagues, and informally organized groups of workers petitioned the Department of Justice for 'British justice,'[35] while defence committees raised funds in support of the Strike leaders. J.W. Dafoe continued to suggest in the *Manitoba Free Press* that the arrests amounted to free advertising for the Strike leaders, allowing them to reach an audience in Ontario that they wouldn't normally have reached.[36] Meighen was none too happy at the turn of events, complaining, 'To-day I dispatched letters 2½″ thick of solid paper in answer to petitions from all over the Dominion in behalf of the Winnipeg men.'[37] Senator Robertson worried that the Strike leaders 'being at large' would 'multiply our difficulties in the east,' and he wondered whether the men were breaking their parole by ignoring their undertaking with Andrews.[38] But of course Judge MacDonald had lifted these bail conditions, so Andrews was powerless, except to suggest surveillance on Heaps, Queen, and Bray.

MP George Allan and Citizens A.K. Godfrey, John Botterell, and Andrews continued to lobby Cabinet for a Dominion-wide commission. Like Ed Anderson, Andrews anticipated the commission's conclusion in its terms of reference, and he warned that all the evidence taken in the raids would be lost if a commission weren't appointed. It wasn't seditious to talk about changing the shape of government and the economy, and such talk couldn't convict the Strike leaders in court, but, as Andrews knew, under the right commission chair, all of the material could be knit together into a story of revolution.[39] Botterell, a Conservative grain broker, quite bluntly admitted that a commission would be 'counter-propaganda' against the OBU, and he repeated the other Citizens' suggestion of Judge Cameron as chair.[40] Allan, to avoid wearing the horns, asked Meighen to advise the chair of the Citizens' executive, A.K. Godfrey, personally of the government's decision.[41] Andrews's argument about a connection between a royal commission and the pending criminal prosecutions was devilishly astute: 'We are going to have a good deal of difficulty in establishing our evidence without calling witnesses who are themselves revolutionists which is always dangerous but if this commission were appointed at once we would have no difficulty in disclosing a source of evidence that would make it comparatively easy to proceed with our prosecutions.'[42] How would a royal commission furnish criminal evidence? Unlike in a criminal trial, Andrews could compel informants and accused to testify without legal representation and thus without defence cross-examination. Once the material had entered the public record, he could then use it in a criminal trial to incriminate the Strike leaders. This was not at all far-fetched. Andrews and the other lawyers understood very well what sort of instrument a royal commission could be, since the kickback charges that Andrews had defended former premier Roblin against had arisen out of a royal commission instigated by the Liberals.[43] Almost thirty years later, Citizen E.K. Williams, who had ridden with the Mounties on Bloody Saturday, would use the same technique in the Gouzenko Affair, convincing Mackenzie King to use a royal commission in order to circumvent due process of law.[44] Possibly the Citizens felt that a royal commission was their only hope to bring the Strike leaders to trial. Andrews's suggestion for a judge to lead such a commission? Judge Cameron.

Meighen, for his part, seemed to tire under the Citizens' constant pressure. He told Andrews that the question was 'one primarily for the Labour Department' – that is, Sen. Robertson – almost as if now that the Strike was over, Meighen wanted to pass Andrews on to Robertson. At the same time, he warned that Robertson might not want to hear about a royal commission either: 'Senator Robertson has grave doubts as to the wisdom of such a course.' But, as was the case with so many questions raised by the Citizens, Robertson had not come to a final determination.[45] Coming from Winnipeg, he had carried the Citizens' mail in favour of the commission,[46] but after a few days in Ottawa, he leaned towards Cabinet's views.

In the coming days, it would boil down to the fact that Ottawa did not 'favour' two simultaneous commissions 'for the same purpose,' as Meighen wrote to A.L. Crossin. This set off a small explosion in Winnipeg. Crossin called the Citizens' executive together, gave a public reading of Meighen's letter, and then sent a stern rebuke: the Citizens didn't want two commissions either; they only needed one. Neither a provincial commission nor even a judicial trial could properly expose 'the Bolshevik campaign in Canada.' Growing operatic, he cried that 'a complete exposure of the whole damnable conspiracy ... is imperative if we are to have industrial peace.'[47] Ed Anderson seconded Crossin, though in a gentler tone: 'The Dominion Government has made an excellent start in cleaning up the nasty situation' with arrests and nation-wide search warrants – 'but if you stop there you will utterly fail to accomplish the object that you started out with.'[48] Did Meighen wonder a little about just what object 'he' had started out with? It wouldn't have been surprising if he had yearned for a return to the relative tranquillity of the Strike. Briefly he dangled a compromise offer in front of the Citizens – if the Province didn't object, Robson could be invested with broader powers to look at the situation nationally[49] – but even that offer was soon withdrawn.[50] Cabinet simply wished that the Strike that had gone away would stay away.

Andrews approached Robertson on the questions of the royal commission and prosecutions, making it clear that although the Strike was over, the Citizens weren't going to melt back into the crowd. Perhaps afraid that the federal government might renege on all prosecutions, and yet conscious that the Citizens were loath to spend their own money, Andrews used Robertson's own words as leverage. The Citizens, agreeing with Robertson that 'propaganda must be fought with propaganda,' had decided 'to continue as an organization and to encourage the formation of smaller committees, at different points throughout Canada with a view to forming a Citizens' League throughout Canada to fight the revolution.' The government could help, first by giving the Citizens 'a money grant,' and, second, by distributing 'sound publications,' supplemented by 'a campaign of lectures throughout the country.' The United States was carrying out just such a propaganda campaign to fight labour radicalism; Ottawa should be guided by Washington.[51] Meighen, not quite sure what Andrews was proposing, only heard the request for money, and several days later he gave an impotent, vague response: 'All necessary work must of course be done, but I hope the financial outlay will not be such as to shock the country. It is absolutely impossible to determine from this distance just what is necessary, but your responsibility is to determine that as carefully as possible.'[52] Because Meighen had no notion of what was necessary, he was unwittingly giving Andrews *carte blanche* to hire lawyers ... yet still without authorizing prosecutions.

But Andrews instinctively understood Machiavelli's aphorism, 'He who establishes a dictatorship and does not kill Brutus, or he who founds a republic and does not kill the sons of Brutus, will only reign a short time.'[53] A prosecution would be a good way to kill future strikes: 'There is no time when the public will be in as receptive a mood as at present, particularly when through the medium of this trial, we will be able to disclose the extent to which the revolutionary campaign has been carried on.'[54] Andrews, though he had nothing to base his assessments on, continued to report on the public mood, even labour's mood: 'I hear but one sentiment among the laboring classes, which is that the strike was a tragedy so far as the working men were concerned and they blame the strike leaders and socialists for what has happened. You of course must be prepared for a considerable amount of agitation in support of the men on trial.'[55] In this way, Andrews discounted ahead of time the wave of support for the Strike leaders that was descending on Meighen's office, but the only member of the 'public' whose opinion he quoted was Colonel Starnes. More accurately, Andrews could say, 'I believe there is practically unanimous desire on the part of loyal citizens that these prosecutions should proceed' ... because by 'loyal citizens' he meant the Citizens. Ultimately, the position taken by the Andrews had an instrumental not a popular basis. It was an article of faith for the Citizens that wherever governments took vigorous action (that is, in the United States) revolutionaries fell back in 'fear and confusion,' while in the wake of failed prosecutions they became 'courageous and active.' Again, Andrews begged Meighen for the green light to prosecute. Again, as if he hadn't said the same thing three days earlier, Andrews threatened that the Province was going to drop the prosecutions of Woodsworth and Dixon if Andrews didn't proceed.[56] However, there is no evidence that the Province *ever* intended to prosecute. All that can be said is that Phillips and Graham hadn't set up roadblocks when Andrews had sworn out informations against Woodsworth and Dixon. The two Crown attorneys probably believed that Andrews and the federal government were running the prosecutions.[57] The 'prize' that Andrews had seemingly delivered to Meighen – provincial cooperation – was revealed at this time to be a mirage.

A couple of days later, Andrews – for the third time – told Meighen of the Province's reluctance, and in order to let him taste the urgency,

Andrews sent a wire instead of a letter: 'PHILLIPS FINALLY DECIDED NOT
TO PROCEED WITH WOODSWORTH DIXON AND OTHER SEDITIOUS CASES AS HE
IS NOT SO INSTRUCTED BY LOCAL GOVERNMENT WE ALL AGREE THEY
SHOULD PROCEED PLEASE WIRE ME QUICK IF WE SHALL CARRY THEM ON.'[58]
Still, Andrews managed to get the Province's decision postponed, and,
with respect to the other Strike leaders, he told the press that he hadn't
had enough time to examine the mass of evidence.[59] This may have been
so. But the more important breakdown that stalled Andrews was the federal government's refusal to prosecute. Meanwhile the *Western Labor
News* published polemics such as 'Trial by Jury Destroyed,'[60] and Marcus Hyman, frustrated that his clients were still sitting in the Winnipeg
Immigration Hall, shepherded them into the courtroom to protest against
their continued detention without hearings.[61]

From Andrews's requests, it was clearly the War Measures Act under
which he wanted the federal government to proceed. He complained to
Meighen that he had only received copies of four Orders-in-Council,
although he had asked for *all* the Orders dealing with seditious literature.
The Orders-in-Council under the War Measures Act hadn't yet been
repealed, and could theoretically be used. As the judicial committee of
the Privy Council later noted in the case of *Fort Francis Pulp and Paper
Co. v. Manitoba Free Press Co.* (1923), the federal government had the
authority to decide exactly when the wartime emergency was over. Only
'very clear evidence that the crisis had wholly passed away' could prick
the courts to overrule the government.

But action against the Strike through an Order-in-Council was highly
improbable for a number of reasons. Most obviously, despite the wari-
ness of courts, it was counterintuitive to suggest that the war wasn't
over. As well, wartime prosecutions under the Orders-in-Council had
always been undertaken by provincial governments. Common sense dictated that one couldn't suddenly expect the government to step outside
of its usual sphere of authority in a way that it hadn't done even *during*
the war. By mid-1919, the Canadian state was in transition, no longer
eager to play night watchman and reluctant to intervene as educator of
civic virtue. Government leaders longed for a return to the anti-statist
orthodoxy of pre-1914, when the state merely enforced the ground rules
under which, as Douglas Owram has described it, 'man must be free to
seek his own improvement and be responsible for his own destiny.'[62]
Use of the Orders-in-Council would also have clashed specifically with
Borden's post-war framework, set out in a statement to the Unionist cau-
cus on 26 June 1919. There he outlined a policy of reconstruction which
respected constitutional authority at the federal, provincial, and municipal levels; which abandoned repressive measures necessitated by the

war; and which recognized the 'legitimate and reasonable' aspirations of organized labour.[63] To be sure, Borden weighed in against 'revolutionary or bolshevist propaganda,' but the government had already amended the Immigration Act and the Criminal Code to meet this danger, and was in the process of creating a permanent security force in the reconfigured RCMP.[64] Why revert to wartime legislation?

At a more pragmatic level, use of the War Measures Act might ignite popular opposition. The Great War, the first total war waged under democratic conditions, had triggered a widespread crisis of citizenship. Canada had made unprecedented demands for discipline and sacrifice on its citizens; Canadian progressives had responded with a narrative of solidarity and sacrifice, a citizenship rooted in an 'ideology of service.'[65] After a war waged for democratic values, few were prepared to accept a continuation of government-by-Order-in-Council: calls for British justice landed on Borden's doorstep in heaps. In late 1919, the minister of justice would finally repeal all OICs created under section 6 of the War Measures Act,[66] and the government's repeal of PC 2384 in April had already included the observation that existing laws, rather than the wartime OICs, were quite sufficient to deal with offenders.[67] A 1919 OIC stated that although 'no proclamation has been issued declaring that the war no longer exists, actual war conditions have in fact *long ago* ceased to exist, and consequently existence of war can no longer be urged as a reason in fact for maintaining these extraordinary regulations'[68] [emphasis added].

Andrews mentioned OICs, but his unwillingness to name the War Measures Act out loud to Meighen suggests that Andrews quite understood how politically awkward it would be to use the act. Without provincial cooperation, there were no other options; Meighen, Borden, and the rest of Cabinet decided not to proceed against Woodsworth, Dixon, and the other two recently arrested men. Informing Andrews, Meighen pointedly accepted Andrews's earlier 'delivery' of provincial cooperation at face value, and intimated that the federal government would assume no responsibility for the botch-up: 'Prosecutions referred to your twelfth were undertaken by provincial authorities upon whom is primary responsibility for all criminal prosecutions (stop) consider it undesirable that federal authorities should take on prosecution so launched (stop) you are instructed not to do so.'[69] Meighen didn't rule out future prosecutions,[70] but for the moment, his message couldn't be clearer: 'Council takes ground that Federal government cannot undertake prosecutions as requested your telegram (stop) such prosecutions have everywhere until now been entered and conducted by Provincial authority in usual way and Government feels not justified in now assuming this class of work (stop).'[71] It's possible that Meighen's reference to 'prosecutions' referred not only to prosecutions under Orders-in-Council but included any criminal prosecutions that arose out of the Strike. This could hardly be startling, since Meighen had never expressed a wish to arrest the Strike leaders under the Criminal Code. In early June, Andrews, even as he had tried to cue Meighen for federal prosecutions, had of course admitted that constitutionally there was only one option.[72] Eventually, in January 1920, the Province would put Dixon on trial for seditious libel, but when a jury acquitted him, the Province would drop the Woodsworth prosecution.[73]

In the summer of 1919, while a crowd of five thousand massed at an open-air meeting in Toronto's Queen's Park to hear John Queen preach his interpretation of the Strike – 'What is good for the master classes is bad for you; and what is bad for the master classes is good for you'[74] – Andrews and the Citizens hit a brick wall with the federal government: no royal commission and (so it seemed) no criminal prosecution of the Strike leaders.

All this time, Meighen pondered his worsening relationship with the Citizens. It was not good politics to brush them off – they were, after all, his natural constituency. So he composed a long response to Ed Anderson, acknowledging that the Citizens' letters and telegrams concerned him deeply. The problem was, 'The majority of Council [i.e., Cabinet] could not see their way clear to meet very fully, the wishes of the Committee.' Meighen was a little coy about whether he belonged to the friendly minority or the unfriendly majority. On breaches of censorship regulations, Meighen understood that the Citizens would justifiably 'look to the Government that made the regulations' (the federal government) to prosecute violators. But Ottawa couldn't infringe on the Province's constitutional powers, since all War Measures violations had been provincially prosecuted: 'Every Province in Canada (except perhaps Quebec) and I rather think there have been some prosecutions there, has undertaken and discharged its responsibility in this regard, and why Manitoba should be allowed to succeed in shifting its duty on the Dominion is naturally very hard for a Dominion Cabinet to comprehend.'[75]

Though he knew better, Andrews continued to pay lip service to the notion that the Province would eventually take over the prosecutions. He had to: in the case of Michael Charitonoff's possession of prohibited literature back in January, long before the Strike, the deputy minister of justice, E.L. Newcombe, had made it abundantly clear that the Province was responsible to prosecute, and if it decided not to do so, the federal government would *not* take up the case.[76] Yet Andrews continued to harrow the ground for federal prosecutions. He probably understood that Meighen was now baulking at *all* the Strike leader prosecutions (and only supporting Immigration Act deportations), but Andrews pretended that the baulking was merely at the prosecutions of Woodsworth, Dixon, Martin, and Grant.[77]

Andrews, or perhaps one of the other lawyers, had read the fine print. He reminded Meighen of the fact that the 'Attorney General of Canada' appeared in the censorship Order-in-Council, so that technically the federal government could conduct prosecutions. Yet Andrews also knew that Cabinet could hold out against the Citizens' bullying. He gave Meighen a parting shot: 'It would certainly be a serious thing for the community if from the desire to place the responsibility each upon the other Government, these prosecutions fell through. I fancy that rather than this should happen the Citizens' committee would instruct private counsel to carry on the prosecution of these cases.'[78] This was both a surrender and a threat: a surrender, because Andrews seemed to accept that Ottawa refused to underwrite prosecutions; a threat, because he was informing Meighen that the prosecutions wouldn't evaporate. No federal prosecutions? Then the Citizens would mount private prosecutions.

A private prosecution, acknowledged as such, could have been explosive. It would have involved the Citizens on their own initiative acting as 'the Crown,' and might therefore have emboldened the Strike leaders to counter-sue – to initiate their own private prosecution against the Citizens. In a private prosecution (as in a regular prosecution) the Province would have had to choose sides, throwing either the strikers' case or the Citizens' case or both out of court. *Any* decision could discredit the state and the courts. A decision against the strikers might trigger a national crisis, yet a decision to let the Strike leaders walk free would bring an incalculable political cost. The federal government could either find some way of colluding now or it could pay a heftier price in unrest later. Meighen, who was justly feared for his Machiavellian proclivities, must have admired the Citizens' legal guile.

11

They Are All Dangerous:
Immigration Hearings

14 – 20 July

While Andrews was still wrestling with Meighen and Cabinet over criminal prosecutions, another front in the Citizens' battle opened up: at 2:30 on Monday, 14 July, the board of inquiry into the immigration cases of the 'foreign-born' Strike leaders began. Open to the press, but not the public,[1] the hearings were intended partly as the means to deport several Strike leaders, and partly as an object lesson to immigrants. The Citizens could expect a favourable result: Andrews had personally selected the chair, police magistrate R.M. Noble.[2] Throughout the hearings, Noble would respond impatiently to any defence objections that stood in the way of deportation. Andrews also had a good opinion of a second member of the three-member board, Thomas Gelley, acting commissioner of immigration for Winnipeg. The third member was E.T. Boyce, a Winnipeg employee of the Immigration Department.[3] Who represented the Immigration Department as legal counsel? A.J. Andrews. He could make no claim to knowledge of the Immigration Act,[4] but he could claim to have extensive knowledge of the arrests of the five accused, since he had written out the warrants himself. Much more than Judge Noble or Minister of Immigration J.A. Calder, Andrews directed the proceedings.

Set against him and acting on behalf of the detained men were Marcus Hyman and E.J. McMurray, young lawyers of the Strike leaders' generation. A Jew born in Poland, raised in London (England), and educated at Oxford, Hyman was thirty-six years old. Unlike the detained Jews Blumenberg, Charitonoff, and Almazoff, however, Hyman lived in the right neighbourhood and had been on the right side of conscription: as chairman of the Winnipeg chapter of the British & Canadian Recruiting Mission he had helped to raise several units of men for military service in Egypt and Palestine.[5] He lived at 260 Wellington Crescent, just down the street from Andrews. McMurray, forty-one, had grown up in Ontario, and were it not for his views, he could have easily fit among the Citizens. As an articling law student he had worked for Pitblado, and later for Andrews. Initially, McMurray planned to work as a criminal lawyer, but the real-estate boom of the Laurier era drew him into land speculation. Andrews, recalling his own misadventure in the early 1880s land boom, cautioned McMurray against real-estate bubbles, but McMurray didn't listen, and was saddled with thousands of dollars in debt when the bubble burst in 1913.[6] He returned to a more conventional legal practice to pay off his debts, and rose to become a leading defence counsel.

As one might have predicted, the hearings turned more on questions of procedure rather than on evidence. This was partly because they were the first ever under section 41 of the Immigration Act,[7] but, more importantly, because Andrews wanted a Star Chamber style of prosecution. Early on, when Andrews's plan had still been to use these hearings against even the *British-born* Strike leaders, he had expected that the public wouldn't be admitted, but that the press would. After deciding to pursue deportation only for the Eastern European leaders, and probably to expedite matters, Andrews had persuaded Thomas Gelley to approach Assistant Deputy Minister of Immigration William Scott to see whether the press could be barred from the hearings.[8] Even more problematic would be Andrews's wish for a prosecution in which he could ask whatever questions he wanted of the detainees and float general accusations rather than prove specific illegal acts. Since only Eastern European leaders were now involved, why be so sensitive about British justice? Andrews assured the court that he had good evidence that the men had committed illegal acts, and the court should trust him on this because he didn't want to reveal his informants or evidence. Judge Noble, sharing Andrews's ideological assumptions, went along as far as possible with his procedures, knowing that he couldn't have proceeded without assent from the highest levels: Calder, Meighen, even Borden. At times, Noble would be forced to rein Andrews in, but more often, Noble would compromise his legal principles, conscious always that Cabinet would be happy if Andrews were given much leeway. How much should these quasi-judicial immigration hearings adhere to the constitutional protections offered by a regular court? The answer would prove to be far from self-evident.

In theory, one would have expected the hearings to turn on the question of whether the detained men had become undesirable immigrants, contravening the new section 41 of the Immigration Act. Even if

Andrews couldn't prove that they had advocated violent overthrow of the government, he could presumably prove one of the vaguer provisions: that the men were affiliated with an organization entertaining disbelief in organized government; that according to the new law they had engaged in sedition. One would have then expected something very like a criminal case: long arguments about the definition of sedition and then long arguments about whether the men's words and deeds fit the definition. In practice, however, Andrews's goal with the Eastern Europeans was simply to chase them out of the country as quickly as possible. After all the urgency about section 41, he was prepared to ignore it and to employ technicalities to get the desired result.[9] The board was on the same page. In a letter to board member Thomas Gelley, Deputy Minister Scott delineated the road map of expediency: anyone suspected of entering Canada by 'force or misrepresentation or stealth or otherwise contrary to any provision of the Immigration Act' could be detained and deported.[10] Andrews recognized that he didn't need to address the complex questions raised by section 41 if it could be shown that any of the men had misrepresented themselves when entering Canada. Throughout the hearings, McMurray and Hyman would counter Andrews's expediency with common-law principles and the constitutional rights that obtained in regular court proceedings. To defend their clients against arbitrary treatment, they would canvas the validity of the proceedings under the Immigration Act, the denial of citizenship rights, the denial of bail, and the requirement that the men testify against themselves while criminal charges pended. The cases were interleaved, so that Sam Blumenberg, Oscar Schoppelrei, Max Charitonoff, and Solomon Almazoff were shuttled in and out of the Immigration Hall, often on the same day. Whenever one defendant refused to answer questions, Noble, at Andrews's urging, sent him back to jail, while another defendant was interrogated.

The first case to be heard was Blumenberg's. Jewish and orphaned at a young age, Blumenberg was still technically a Romanian citizen.[11] Although his father had brought the family to the United States, and although Blumenberg had spent his formative years in Minneapolis, he had never become a US citizen. In Winnipeg he ran the Minneapolis Dye House on Portage Avenue.[12] Not only had he spoken often on labour platforms during both the 1918 and 1919 conflicts, but he was also a target for anti-alien fervour because of his opposition to the Great War. Among his radical plays were *The Undesirable Citizen*, *The Modern Shylock*, and *War, What For?* Advertised as 'one of the most radical plays ever produced on any stage,' *War, What For?* opened at the Grand

Theatre in 1915 after the second Battle of Ypres during which nearly six thousand Canadian soldiers died.[13] In 1916, he named his newborn son Karl Marx Blumenberg. Just hours before his arrest, the *Winnipeg Citizen* had said, 'Agitator 'Blumberg,' [*sic*] the man who is keenly interested in turning "wage slaves" into automobile owners and two-hour-a-day-and-half-day-off on Saturday Socialists, is not noted as a worker himself. He is not a wage slave … He never slaves at anything unless it is on a platform with an alien audience where he slaves for an hour in broken English to tell them that they are the salt of the earth and that the earth belongs to them.'[14]

Taking his cue from Scott's catechism, Judge Noble opened the inquiry by announcing that it was concerned with the 'application or right of Samuel Blumenberg to remain in Canada … It seems that the Board of Inquiry opens with the examination of the alien in this case, according to the Act.'[15] If McMurray and Hyman felt a bit at sea in the immigration board procedure, they were not alone. Noble's 'it seems' was an early indication that the chair, too, would often be lost when it came to the Immigration Act and the first-time proceedings under section 41. For his part, McMurray began with objections to Noble's proposed fishing expedition: Blumenberg had been under arrest for some weeks – what exactly was he charged with? Already confused, Noble couldn't say what article Blumenberg had contravened, but only that, 'the charge … is one under the Act for his deportation as an undesirable.'[16] Who had laid charges against Blumenberg? 'Colonel Starnes of the RNWMP,' offered Noble.[17] Andrews came to the rescue, 'It was under Section 41 as amended,' and he quoted the prohibition against anyone who 'by word or act creates or attempts to create riot or public disorder in Canada, who without lawful authority assumes any powers of Government of Canada or any part thereof, or is a member or affiliated with any organization entertaining disbelief in organized government.'[18]

More problematically, Blumenberg had been charged under the Criminal Code, and then, before those charges could be dealt with, he had been summoned to the immigration hearing. McMurray objected that any interrogation of Blumenberg now would short-circuit the criminal trial and his constitutional rights: he would be forced to give evidence against himself. Noble, initially unaware of the other proceedings, seemed oblivious to the complicated legal web that Andrews had created. When Noble realized that a criminal trial might be pending, he still saw no problem with the immigration hearing. In a normal trial such an objection 'might obtain,' he said, but 'here it does not seem to me that it would.'[19] How closely must these novel immigration hearings adhere to the constitutional protections offered in a regular court? Not very closely, at this stage. As in a royal commission, Noble could set his own ground rules.

Instead of sustaining McMurray's objection, Noble scolded him for playing to the press, for attempting to turn the hearing into a political attack on the minister and the Immigration Act.[20] After the scolding, McMurray announced that Blumenberg would 'answer no questions.' Hyman explained the law: Blumenberg, having lived in Canada for several years and having thus acquired Canadian domicile, could claim, under the Immigration Act, rights of citizenship 'over and above those of any person ordinarily applying for leave to enter.' The requirement to answer questions applied only to immigrants applying to enter the country.[21] McMurray put the matter more broadly: unless some particular section of the Immigration Act took away the right, Blumenberg, having established domicile, had 'the common law right of refusing to give evidence against himself.'[22]

Noble equivocated. Maybe defence objections might be valid if 'the questions were not proper.'[23] Gelley took a different tack: Blumenberg was 'not in Canada legally,' so 'domicile' didn't apply. Andrews tried his hand as well. Although the Citizens had loudly proclaimed their common-law defence of the rights of the individual, Andrews argued that Blumenberg, who had domicile but wasn't fully naturalized, couldn't claim all the rights of an individual: 'Blumenberg has not acquired the status of a subject and I think very properly the Legislature has pointed out that he is always subject to investigation.'[24] Noble, with this coaching from Andrews and information from the Immigration Department, now felt himself on firmer ground, and added, 'I understand that the records of the Department show that the accused got into Canada by misrepresentation, so that his standing as a domiciled citizen of the country might not be quite as strong.'[25] Yet Andrews and Noble were wrong. It's unclear whether Andrews intentionally or unintentionally misled Noble and the rest of the board, but section 33, to which Andrews referred, stipulated that a person

seeking to enter or to land in Canada shall answer truly all questions put to him by any officer when examined under the authority of this Act; and any person not truly answering such questions shall be guilty of an offence and liable on conviction to a fine of not more than one hundred dollars or to a term of imprisonment not exceeding two months or to both fine and imprisonment, *and if found not to be a Canadian citizen or not to have Canadian domicile, such offence shall in itself be sufficient cause for deportation* whenever so ordered by a Board of Inquiry or officer in charge ...[26] [emphasis added]

Domicile was domicile – misrepresentations at the border could lead to jail, but deportation was reserved for non-citizens or non-domiciled people.

Another common-law right: the right of the accused person to hear the charges against himself or herself. A complaint had been made against Blumenberg, but, amazingly, as Noble's early confusion underlined, neither Blumenberg nor his counsel had been given any particulars. Hyman demanded that Andrews reveal the charges against Blumenberg and any documentary records. Only then could counsel develop a defence, and only then would questions be put to Blumenberg.[27] Noble grudgingly gave way: 'I suppose if you insist on the actual production of the complaint.' Even Andrews saw no way out: 'We can wire the minister to have the original [complaint] sent here if you wish.'[28] 'I suppose if you insist,' ... 'if you wish' ... the phrases suggest how closely the proceedings verged on a Star Chamber. Unspecified charges had been brought against Blumenberg, and only with reluctance would the magistrate and 'crown' reveal the charges. Yet the response also shows at least a minimal legal conscience, as Noble recognized that although he had the authority to determine the legal process, it must nevertheless adhere in a minimal way to regular Canadian criminal procedure and the constitutional protections established by common law.

Two weeks earlier, Andrews had already laid out his problems before Meighen. It wouldn't be easy to produce evidence under section 41: 'Although Colonel Stearns [sic] has plenty of evidence against these men showing they are all dangerous, it is going to be almost impossible to use his evidence because we cannot uncover his agents whom he is still using.'[29]

Instead, Andrews thought that he could use the improper entries of two or three of the men into Canada to get them deported. The arrests of Blumenberg, Schoppelrei, Charitonoff, and Almazoff had been a product of Andrews's agenda, not Commissioner Perry's or even Colonel Starnes's.[30] Though Perry had apparently told Immigration Minister Calder on 15 June that one hundred aliens had been identified for prosecution under the revised section 41 and that thirty-six of them were in Winnipeg, both Perry and Starnes felt that the prosecution of radicals tended to create martyrs, while also exposing police surveillance.[31]

To Meighen on 14 July, Andrews focused only on the Citizens' continued request for a royal commission,[32] and didn't give even the smallest hint that domicile was an issue: 'The Board of Inquiry has been sitting since Monday and we have I think quite sufficient evidence to deport Blumenberg and Schoppelroi [sic]. We are taking up the other two cases at once. These men are all refusing to answer proper questions which I think alone is sufficient under the Immigration Act to justify their deportation.'[33] When questions about Blumenberg's charges came up in the inquiry, Andrews insisted that he could provide no details. Hyman objected: 'We have in vain asked for particulars, yet we are charged with not answering questions.'[34] Judge Noble was obliged to agree, asking, 'Mr. Andrews, can you give any further particulars?' Andrews responded with a scattershot approach: Blumenberg was a 'professional agitator'; he belonged to 'a revolutionary society'; Andrews had witnesses to testify that Blumenberg had promoted 'disorder.'[35] The last two charges, if accurate, were actionable, but Hyman and McMurray asked for full documentary disclosure. Where were the accuseds' immigration records and their arrest warrants? McMurray hit the nail on the head, saying, 'If the warrant is improper, you have no jurisdiction.'[36] A month earlier, Meighen had acknowledged that the warrant under which Blumenberg and the others had been arrested was seriously flawed, and no doubt Meighen's warning about 'grave doubts as to the legality of our position' were still ringing in Andrews's ears.[37]

On the second day of the hearing, Andrews zeroed in on Blumenberg's conversation with an immigration officer when he had entered Canada. Blumenberg had claimed to be an American citizen, living there for thirteen years and voting in elections, but in fact he had never been naturalized. Andrews was concise: 'I take it from that then you believed you were an American citizen?' 'Yes,' said Blumenberg. 'You know now you were not,' continued Andrews. 'Yes,' Blumenberg was forced to admit.[38]

For the Citizens, the fear, of course, was not of particular misdeeds by individuals either at the border or even during the Strike. What threatened the polity was any broadly socialist orientation. But that wasn't a crime. Although Andrews knew that a scattershot approach of guilt by association could never stand up in court, he also knew that the board shared the Citizens' concerns, and he worked towards generalized critiques of socialism before defence objections pulled him back to the actual charges against Blumenberg. 'What societies of a socialistic character did you belong to?' Andrews started. McMurray advised Blumenberg not to answer, since not only was the question outside the scope of the investigation, but the defence still had not seen the warrant. Noble repeated Andrews's question. Then Andrews repeated the question and, receiving no answer, restated it in a variety of forms: Was Blumenberg a member of the Canadian Socialist Revolutionary Party? Of the Socialist Labor Party of Canada? Of the Socialist Society Local No. 3? Was he perhaps a member of the Russian Progressive Club? The Young Jewish Labor League? The Young Jewish Literary Society? Did he recall a meeting held at the Walker Theatre on 22 December 1918? What part did he play in a meeting at the Majestic Theatre on 19 January 1919? And so on. In Andrews's judgment, every refusal to answer placed Blumenberg in contempt of the hearing, and, as Andrews told Meighen, should be sufficient to justify deportation.[39]

A couple of months later, an appeal of Max Charitonoff's case would confirm what McMurray and Hyman had thought: that domiciled immigrants did have rights. They couldn't maintain a *complete* silence – that would be contempt – but they could refuse to answer certain questions. For the time being, Noble shelved Blumenberg, and asked Andrews to bring forward the other witnesses against him.

Andrews turned to the RNWMP undercover agents, beginning with the legally trained Sergeant Major Francis Edward Langdale. What Andrews could easily prove was a great deal of sympathy among the leaders for the Bolshevik Revolution in Russia; what he couldn't prove was any actual incitements of revolutionary activity in Canada. Although one might have expected the inside story on labour radicalism from the undercover agents, Langdale only offered a rehash of material long available in Winnipeg's newspapers. At the Walker Theatre, amid a crowd that was 50 per cent foreign-born, Blumenberg had appeared wearing 'a flaming red tie' and 'a red handkerchief.' In his speech, he said, 'Bolshevism is the only thing that will emancipate the working class,' and got a laugh when he joked about putting 'on a red flag tie so that there would be no mistake where I stand.' Langdale recounted how Blumenberg led cheers for the Russian Soviet and for Karl Liebknecht. In Langdale's opinion, it was Blumenberg's 22 December speech at the Walker Theatre that provoked returned soldiers to riot against aliens in late January.[40]

McMurray and Hyman found it easy to mock such *post hoc ergo propter hoc* howlers. Andrews and the Citizens, observing what worked and what didn't, were able to use the immigration hearings as a dress rehearsal for their later attacks on the British Strike leaders in the preliminary hearing and trial. Hyman asked Langdale how exactly Blumenberg's comments had led to riots. Langdale responded that 'it was a speech largely in favor of Bolshevik rule.' Asked for specific phrases that might incite people to rush into the streets, the best Langdale could offer was, 'We swear to keep the red flag flying for ever, in spite of the *Free Press*.'[41] Any other phrases that might inflame people? Langdale couldn't remember any.[42] So this was the quality of the evidence that Andrews had been boasting about to Meighen. To make matters worse, Langdale couldn't produce the notes he took at the meeting, only notes made about the original notes.[43]

Cecil Lamont, a reporter for the *Winnipeg Telegram*, took the stand to testify about the Walker meeting, though he, too, no longer had his notes, and he considered it sufficient to read from his published account. Hyman objected. Noble, however, allowed Lamont to continue.[44] Attempting to show that Blumenberg was affiliated with an 'organization entertaining disbelief in organized government,' Lamont testified that R.B. Russell had advocated 'the Russian form of government' for Canada. Asked by Andrews what Russell had to say about revolution, Lamont began, 'Mr. Russell stated ...,' but then Lamont started to read, '[Russell] made an appeal ... for the withdrawal of allied intervention [in Russia], declaring that revolution was about to take place in Canada.' It was all too much for McMurray: 'It is a shameful thing that a newspaper should be put in as evidence, without proof of it at all. It is not evidence.' Andrews tried to keep Lamont rolling: 'Go ahead. What else did he say?' McMurray interrupted again: 'No. That cannot be disposed of so readily.' Noble stopped Andrews from drawing out 'evidence' in this manner, yet Noble did allow Lamont to repeatedly consult his newspaper column while testifying.[45]

Thrown back upon his memory, Lamont could recall only a bit of Blumenberg's speech. With prodding from Andrews, Lamont was able to remember that the accused had worn a red tie, but he couldn't remember what Blumenberg had said about the tie until Andrews gave Lamont leave to peek at his own published article. Then it came to him that Blumenberg had worn the tie in honour of 'the Reds of Russia.'[46] Cross-examination established that in fact Lamont hadn't actually attended the whole meeting, but had derived parts of his article from other newspapermen who had been present. Hearsay, concluded McMurray. But Lamont insisted that what he published about Blumenberg and Russell he had heard himself.[47]

More importantly, McMurray wittily undermined the Citizens' post-hoc narrative in which pro-Communist speeches had caused anti-alien riots:

McMurray: Did you see many of the returned soldiers at that
          [Walker Theatre] meeting?
Lamont: No.
McMurray: So that if the returned soldiers rioted, it would be a
          result of your publication and others similar to it ... You
          think it was your publication [the *Telegram*] that created
          those riots?
Lamont: No ...
McMurray: Did this meeting make you feel like going out to riot?

Lamont: It didn't make me feel like going out to riot ...
McMurray: Did it make [the audience] revolt?
Lamont: I believe it helped.
McMurray: Never mind what you believe. I say, did you see any-
           thing of that kind.
Lamont: It didn't make them go in for·revolution at that time.
McMurray: You saw no drawing of revolvers, or knives?
Lamont: No, not at that time.
McMurray: They went out orderly and quietly ...
Lamont: They went out orderly.[48]

McMurray suggested that Blumenberg's speech hadn't incited anyone to try to establish Soviet government in Canada by force, but that 'he asked the government to establish it.' This was a misleading construction – the Strike leaders expected the workers, not elected Liberals and Conservatives, to compel change – yet so was Lamont's insistence that even if Blumenberg hadn't mentioned force, he had 'suggested' it. McMurray took him to task on that, and on the absurdity of Blumenberg in December 'inciting' the late-January riot that destroyed his own property:

McMurray: He did not suggest that [his Walker Theatre audience]
           should go out red handed and establish that government,
           did he?
Lamont: I don't recollect that he did.
McMurray: He didn't advise them to riot, did he?
Lamont: He didn't advise them to riot.
McMurray: Did he advise the returned soldiers to go down and
           attack his home?
Lamont: No.
McMurray: Or his business.

Andrews's next witness, RNWMP member Albert Edward Reames, had observed the Socialist Party of Canada meeting at Majestic Theatre on 19 January.[49] Reames corroborated Langdale's estimate that 50 per cent of the audience were foreigners, and added that many of them were Jews, 'judging from the appearance.' The speakers all asserted 'that revolution was coming,' hopefully a peaceful revolution, but all were ready 'to shed blood, if the capitalists wished to use force in keeping the working class from obtaining their rights.' Copies of the *Red Flag* were sold,[50] and memorial services were intended for Liebknecht and Luxemburg. Reames said that what he heard was 'very unpatriotic ... and practically hinting at, asking for revolution, and I wondered just how much latitude the government had been giving these people, to let them hold these meetings and say what they said.'

Like Langdale with the Walker Theatre meeting, Reames blamed the January soldiers' riots on the Majestic Theatre meeting the week before, though he couldn't remember Blumenberg himself speaking any revolutionary or inflammatory words. Reames had a lot to say about the riots, and Andrews encouraged him to go on at length, even though the rioters were *anti*-socialists, not socialists. As the Citizens had, Andrews was counting on the anti-foreigner sentiment to carry the day. Scenes of a crowd marching down Elmwood Street, forcing foreigners to show their registration cards, making them kiss the Union Jack, and beating up those who failed to do so, could hardly be flattering to the anti-socialists.[51] But Andrews, knowing the biases of his audience, deemed it sufficient to show that disorder on the streets had followed the Majestic Theatre meeting. Here he was on much safer ground than when he attributed the riots to December's Walker Theatre meeting. He was still operating under the post-hoc fallacy – Blumenberg's opponents, not Blumenberg's audience, had decided to riot – but it was enough for Andrews to show that Blumenberg was tangled up in the events: the crowd had specifically sought him out, attacking his business. Blumenberg's wife had appeared with a gun and threatened to shoot anyone who entered the building, but the returned men seized her, forced her to kiss the Union Jack, and later 'broke everything possible' in the building.

In response to Andrews's methods, Hyman asked Reames if he recalled seeing Blumenberg's address and photograph on the front page of the *Winnipeg Telegram*: 'Do you think that would give the crowd any hint or suggestion as to what they were to do?' Despite this obvious incitement to do harm, Reames stuck to Andrews's party line, answering, 'No … I would say the raid of his place was the result of his speeches in December and January.'[52] McMurray tried a different approach. Reames had been assigned to investigate revolutionaries. Had he investigated returned soldiers who might engage in riots? No, he hadn't. Although he had been present at the Majestic meeting, at the time he had had no inkling of any riots being contemplated until they occurred. Of course, the light dawned on him later, revealing that the Majestic meeting had incited the riots.

Andrews had estimated his audience correctly – how could he not, having convinced the authorities that Noble be named chair. What mattered most, as Andrews understood all along, was the Citizens' control of process. Despite all the setbacks in the Citizens' campaigns against the Strike, despite the lack of provincial cooperation, despite the difficulties in swaying public opinion, the campaign would be successful as long as the Citizens kept their hands on government processes. Although the defence had shown Blumenberg's rights under domicile and had shown the illogic of blaming riots on him, his silence on the vaguer charge under section 41 – of participating in any organization entertaining disbelief in organized government – favoured Andrews. With Andrews at the end of his witnesses, Noble again invited Blumenberg to answer questions about his political beliefs. When Blumenberg didn't cooperate, Noble adjourned the proceedings.[53]

A couple of days later, Andrews finally produced an arrest warrant, though his earlier circumvention of proper legal procedure now came back to haunt him. Andrews was an excellent courtroom performer, but not much of a student of the law, said W.P. Fillmore, president of the Law Society of Manitoba from 1916 to 1918. Andrews not only needed his associates to straighten him out on points of law, but also, in Fillmore's opinion, could not 'pass a third year law exam.'[54] When the defence demanded the original complaint, as required under the act, Andrews couldn't or wouldn't produce it.[55] Andrews produced a 21 July order from J.A. Calder, the minister of immigration, to detain Blumenberg. Yet Blumenberg had been arrested on 17 June, four days earlier. In the arrests Andrews had acted independently, using the Criminal Code, not the Immigration Act. Caught, Andrews backpedalled: 'There must have been a prior telegram.'[56] The Immigration Act had not been adhered to, but Andrews solved the legal problem by lying to the inquiry. He well knew that there was no prior telegram, at least not one he'd admit to. In chapter 8 we saw that Calder and Meighen had begged Andrews to give particulars, and when he finally deigned to do so *after* the arrests, they had said that authorization was on its way. Such a telegram would still have been too late, but only half a day too late, as opposed to four days. If such a telegram once existed, as seems plausible, why did Andrews destroy it? The only convincing answer is that it named the British Strike leaders. However, he now wanted them prosecuted in criminal courts, not in immigration hearings. To reveal the telegrams would be to reveal the questionable legality of Andrews's criminal prosecutions. It would become public knowledge that neither the federal government nor the Province had authorized a *criminal* prosecution. Andrews didn't want the public to realize that, in effect, *he and the Citizens* were prosecuting the Strike leaders,[57] a fact that would chime discordantly with the Citizens' massive *Free Press* ad: 'The Citizens' Committee of One Thousand took no issue with Labor as such; no side as between employer and employee.'[58]

Luckily for the Citizens, they could count on a sympathetic judge. For

Noble's edification, Hyman pointed out that 'this warrant, which pur-
ports to be pursuant to an order from the Minister, is not so.' The
telegram on the 21st was a reply to a complaint dated on the 20th. Nevertheless, Noble was determined to ignore the fatal wound to the hearing's legitimacy: 'I dare say neither you nor I know what information
has gone to Ottawa with reference to these matters, and what the reports
have been.' Noble chose not to delve into the mystery of how Ottawa on
short notice could have communicated with Winnipeg apart from letter
or telegram. He pretended that nothing had changed: 'We have not the
correspondence and I am not interested in it. We have these cases before
us and I propose to proceed with them.'

McMurray protested: 'We have not the warrants we want yet. We
want the warrants instructing them to proceed with this investigation.
We want the warrant from Mr. Calder ... First there comes the complaint; we want a copy of that complaint. That is the information on
which the man is charged with the offence. After that we want the warrant for the trial, the warrant for his arrest, not the warrant to detain him
in jail. We don't care anything about that. What we have are simply warrants of detention.' Noble confessed that he didn't 'know the early history of this matter at all, how [Blumenberg] was arrested, or on what
warrant he was arrested.'[59] Moreover, he didn't want to know. It wasn't
his jurisdiction, he maintained, to decidé whether the men were properly
taken into custody.

In the end, no warrant was needed. Blumenberg gave in and answered
most of the questions. He testified that he had been a member of the
Socialist Party of Canada, and that at the Walker Theatre meeting he had
supported the withdrawal of troops from Russia. But he denied advocating revolution.[60]

Twenty-two-year-old Oscar Schoppelrei couldn't tell the immigration
hearing what country he was a citizen of.[61] He had come from Superior,
Wisconsin, in March 1918 to enlist in the Canadian army, and his six-
teen-year-old Winnipeg wife had died of influenza in April. Remaining
silent about a son given up for adoption, Schoppelrei claimed that he no
longer had any relatives in North America.[62] An unemployed musician,
he had come to the attention of military intelligence through his activities organizing returned soldiers in support of the Strike. He was a very
minor player in the Strike, but Andrews and the Citizens understood that
in terms of publicity, it would certainly help to place an ethnic German
(even if he was a *Canadian* war veteran) alongside the Jewish socialists
on the chopping block. A 14 June report on the formation of a Workmen's and Soldiers' Council played up Schoppelrei's alienness, dismiss-

ing his American birth as irrelevant to his true identity: 'His father was born in German Poland, but is pure German. His mother was born in Russia and is Russian German.'[63] The long arm of the Citizens must have already reached him, because on 25 June, the day that the Strike was called off, he was thrown out of the armed forces for 'Misconduct' – though Schoppelrei claimed that he hadn't heard this news.[64]

As in the case of Blumenberg, the charge and the warrant for Schoppelrei weren't available. Andrews, who still hadn't produced those for Blumenberg, agreed to send for Schoppelrei's. Again, Andrews left aside the charge of sedition, and used the technicalities of entry to try to deport Schoppelrei. Schoppelrei had falsely stated that he had been born in Quebec. Of course, the Canadian army, desperate for recruits of any nationality, had habitually encouraged recruits to lie about their birthplace. The recruitment of Americans into the Canadian army apparently surprised Noble, but Canadian politicians and military officials were well versed in the matter. Sir Sam Hughes, minister of militia and defence, had hoped to lure 60,000 Americans into the Canadian army. This practice was illegal – both the United States Foreign Enlistment Act (1818) and the British Army Act prohibited such recruitment – but Hughes wasn't overly fastidious. While Canadian immigration authorities looked the other way, he lured in recruits from the United States. Some Americans enlisted so as 'to be clothed and fed over winter,'[65] and the unemployed Schoppelrei likely fit into this category. Of his border crossing at Fort Francis, he affected to remember almost nothing: 'I was drunk all the way up.'[66] Hyman implied that the government's encouraging of such irregular entries erased Schoppelrei's culpability. Andrews, however, insisted on the letter of the law. Though he evidently knew the facts of Schoppelrei's entry, he refused to concede anything. Deny, deny, deny: Andrews or someone in the Immigration Department had shrewdly anticipated that defence lawyers might subpoena the recruiting officers – Sergeant Major McLeod (recruiting officer at Duluth) or Lieutenant Bonnar – so that when Hyman demanded to see them, it providentially turned out that Bonnar was somewhere in Siberia, while McLeod had disappeared without a trace.[67]

Canada had not only imported soldiers, but Meighen, certain that soldiers voted in ways that he approved of, had also dexterously arranged The Military Voters Act, 1917 so that soldiers (as long as they were British subjects) could vote. Hyman wrongly interpreted this as a de facto granting of Canadian citizenship to Schoppelrei. Andrews, a step ahead here as well, responded to Hyman's interpretation, 'I am instructed the Department of State has already ruled that service in the Canadian Army does not constitute citizenship.'[68] Andrews didn't seem to know the details of The Military Voters Act, which barred those who weren't British subjects – including Schoppelrei (and the Specials' 'hero,' Fred Coppins) – from voting. If Andrews had known this, he could have clinched the argument.[69] In any case, when Hyman argued that six months of Canadian army service gave Schoppelrei the citizen's right to bail, Gelley refused.[70]

Like Blumenberg's, Schoppelrei's hearing stalled when Andrews began to quiz him about his politics, especially his involvement in the Rank and File Club, a pro-Strike soldiers' group. Hyman objected. With criminal charges of conspiracy, seditious conspiracy, and seditious libel hanging over Schoppelrei's head, he couldn't be expected to give evidence at an *immigration* hearing, evidence that could be used against him later in a criminal trial. Either the Crown should drop the criminal charges (as Andrews had hinted) or close the immigration hearing and proceed with criminal charges. Hyman ·was confused. Sen. Robertson had repeatedly insisted that the 'Eastern European' leaders would be dealt with entirely under the Immigration Act. But now Andrews wouldn't promise to drop criminal charges. To ease Noble's conscience, Andrews insisted that the two judicial actions had no bearing on each other, but the very fact that Andrews refused to promise shows that he was preparing a catch-22 for the Strike leaders.

Andrews ignored Hyman's objections, and turned back to Schoppelrei: 'Do you refuse to answer the question?'[71] Wading into the fray, McMurray declared that this insistence that Schoppelrei incriminate himself before his criminal trial was 'contrary to the past conduct of trials in the courts.' British-born Strike leaders stood free on bail and could look forward to a jury trial. Why not these men?[72] Even Noble agreed. One really oughtn't to prejudice the case of the men if they could still face criminal trials. Yet the remedy that he suggested was utterly inadequate: Schoppelrei and the others should nevertheless answer all of Andrews's questions, and then Noble would offer his own protection 'as far as we can' to everyone who testified. Since Noble had no power to protect the men in future trials, 'as far as we can' in effect meant that the leaders would have a thank-you and hail-fellow-well-met from Noble, but no actual legal protection. McMurray, of course, was unsatisfied: even if evidence from the immigration hearing were excluded from the criminal trial, juries often caught 'some undercurrent of information' though no one could quite say how.[73] But Noble found procedural questions irritating. Although he had seemed to admit the justice of the defence counsel's objections, couldn't they stop their obstinacy and just get on with the hearing? Andrews pushed for a conclusion. Since there was proof of false entry, and since Schoppelrei now refused to answer questions, he should be deported immediately.[74] Noble inclined towards Andrews.[75]

McMurray tried to use this development to Schoppelrei's advantage, wondering whether Andrews had concluded his case.[76] Andrews bethought himself and decided not to conclude so hastily, but, as in the case of Blumenberg, he wanted to bring in evidence from undercover agents, without producing or even naming them. In a letter to Meighen, Andrews explained that 'secret reports' identified Schoppelrei as an organizer of the Rank and File Club, 'perhaps the most dangerous organization of returned soldiers here.' The Winnipeg version of the club, said Andrews, went under the name Returned Soldiers and Sailors Labor Party, and planned 'to bring about a revolution as soon as possible.'[77] In court, Andrews, using portentous language, asked permission from Noble 'to tender under Section 16 of the Act ... certain confidential reports made by Government secret agents, which agents, for State reasons, cannot be named.' Unhappily, the board of inquiry might 'find itself in the position that they will have to act promptly upon evidence that might ordinarily not be received at trials.' Hyman tried to untangle the ambiguous language and put it in plain English: 'Do I understand, Mr Chairman, that the counsel for the Crown proposes to put in hearsay evidence?' 'Yes,' agreed Andrews.[78]

No wonder that papers such as *Dos Yiddishe Vort* would register their outrage: 'People have lived [here] for five or six years and longer. Suddenly they are put under bars [*sic*] ... denied the right of trial before a jury ... Somewhere in a room before three officials, where the public is not allowed, they make a parody of a trial and ... wish to deport them as lawbreakers. There is ... occurring a crime ... against the entire alien population.'[79] Beyond the irony that the Citizens – self-appointed champions of the 1688 constitution and its protections – wished to subvert legal protections, was the simple fact that hearsay evidence was inadmissible in court. Yet Noble, aware of the power of the Citizens, queried Andrews deferentially, as if hearsay evidence didn't have a straightforward legal definition, and that either by some special *form* of presentation or perhaps by thaumaturgy, Andrews might be able to convert hearsay evidence into direct evidence. Noble asked, 'Do the Department think that they can get in evidence of this kind?' 'Do the Department think ...' – Noble spoke as if it was the Department, not he, that had to decide whether to accept hearsay evidence. Since the wavering Noble seemed to want a bit of weighing and measuring, Andrews obliged: 'I have not taken it up with the Legal Head of the department. I have discussed it with those associated with me in the other cases which are pending and that is the view taken by them.' Translation: he had spoken with Pitblado and Sweatman, who were willing to accept hearsay against the Strike leaders. As throughout the Strike, Andrews must seem to be speaking for the federal government, in this case the Immigration Department, when in fact it was the Citizens whom he spoke for ... and now, without Noble's knowledge, Andrews was placing the authority of that informal body above the state as a deciding factor in the state's treatment of the detained men. Hyman, probably unaware of how little consulting Andrews was doing with the Immigration Department, nevertheless put the matter succinctly: 'Surely, the Crown itself cannot say A or X says something or other. We don't propose to produce X. We know who he is; we have him, but we don't propose to produce him, and yet we want this evidence to go in and be binding against the accused. That is an astounding proposition.' Perhaps Noble discovered his legal conscience, or else he got cold feet when Andrews overreached himself by saying that the ruling was important and would influence 'a great number of cases throughout the country.'[80] No, the hearing could not take hearsay evidence from unnamed individuals who wouldn't be subject to cross-examination. Said Noble, 'I do not think that any stretch of the scope in the way of taking evidence, in my opinion, would include that.'[81]

In his closing argument, Andrews pointed to 'a complaint under Section 41 made by Colonel Starnes, who is an immigration officer.' Of course, Starnes wasn't the *minister* of immigration and had no authority to do anything other than complain to the minister. Andrews knew that, so instead of focusing on any actual misdeeds of Schoppelrei's or even on the catch-all of participating in 'an organization entertaining disbelief in organized government,' he urged two grounds for deportation: 'One is that his original entry was obtained by misrepresentation of material facts, and the other is that he has refused to answer proper questions put by the Chairman of the Board.'[82] The defence, in its closing argument, said that although the Crown had claimed to possess certain facts about Schoppelrei, it hadn't brought those facts out.[83] No evidence had been presented that he had attempted to create a riot or that he had assumed the powers of government in the City of Winnipeg. Constitutional protections in the face of a potential criminal trial should allow him to remain silent (though Hyman didn't mention that Schoppelrei's lack of domicile negated this right). Given the lack of original warrants, there were also technical reasons for freeing Schoppelrei.[84] But when Hyman pointed again to Schoppelrei's claim that the military had advised him to lie about his birthplace, Andrews, jealous of Canada's honour, leapt to the defence of his country, saying, 'I resent very much the imputation of my learned friend ... That the Government were a party to any scheme whereby persons were to make misrepresentations.' The Board ordered that Schoppelrei be deported. An appeal would follow.[85]

Solomon (Moses) Almazoff's case, the next one to be heard, went off the rails almost immediately when he demanded bail. Even criminals who had committed serious crimes were granted bail, whereas he – who had to prepare for his university exams or lose an entire year, who had duties to perform for the Kieff Free Loan Association, the Manitoba Free Loan Association, the Nicolaieff Aid Association, and the Western Canadian Jewish War Sufferers Fund – had spent thirty days locked up. Almazoff objected that his detention was a 'torture and punishment,' a violation of his rights 'under the British Flag,' and 'a slap on the face to the Jewish community.'[86] He demanded bail. Then it was Noble's turn to object. He didn't like Almazoff's tone. He didn't like Almazoff's use of the word 'demand.' He didn't like Almazoff dictating to the court. Gelley spoke for the Department of Immigration: 'I refuse to give bail.'[87]

Almazoff revealed that he was a Russian citizen, a Jew from the Ukraine. Resident in Canada for six years, he was studying arts and law at the University of Manitoba while doing bookkeeping and giving language lessons to support himself, his sisters, and his injured father. Almazoff's claim that his arrest was a slap in the face to the Jewish community wasn't an exaggeration. He had been secretary and done publicity for the Jewish war relief, had worked with the sick during the 1918 flu epidemic, and had been elected to the Canadian Jewish Congress.[88] Like Blumenberg, Almazoff initially refused to incriminate himself. As soon as Andrews asked whether Almazoff had been at the Walker Theatre meeting, the hearing ground to a halt.[89]

When it resumed, Almazoff proved more cooperative. Andrews went through his list of suspect organizations as he had done with Blumenberg. Had Almazoff ever been a member of the Russian Progressive Club? No. The Jewish Literary Association? No. The Young Jewish Labor League? No. What about the Socialist Party of Canada? No. Had he attended a meeting on 19 April at the Russian Library in Winnipeg's Liberty Hall? He didn't remember. He revealed that he was a member only of the once-banned Social Democratic Party of Canada and the Dominion Labor Party.

More to the point, Almazoff denied ever having privately or publicly advocated the 'Bolshevist Government in Russia.' But Andrews knew that Almazoff had been in contact with Bolsheviks in New York and that he received the radical publication *Novy Mir*, which counted Leon Trotsky among its former editors. On the way to Montreal as a delegate to the Canadian Jewish Congress in March, Almazoff had stopped in New

York for several days. 'Did you,' Andrews asked, 'go to New York for the purpose of consulting with the leaders of the Bolshevist revolution at New York?' Almazoff denied this. He had gone to New York to see his brother, but had also spoken with a former Winnipegger who edited a Jewish paper. Was that paper *Novy Mir*? No, it was the *Jewish Forward*. Almazoff admitted that he was familiar with *Novy Mir*, but didn't know its editor. [90]

Andrews hoped to connect Almazoff (and eventually Charitonoff) to the rising tide of revolutionary socialism in the United States. In January 1919 the US Senate's Overman Committee – ostensibly formed to investigate the connection between German brewers and German propaganda – began to investigate the threat of Bolshevism and charged that New York was the centre of a Bolshevik conspiracy. The Union League Club's 'Committee on Bolshevism' – aka, the 'Committee of Five' – completed a two-month investigation of working-class radicalism, and concluded that organized labour was falling into the hands of European revolutionary socialists. The Russian émigré community in particular became the focus. At the urging of the Union League, the New York State Senate in March 1919 established the Lusk committee to investigate.[91] Andrews's line of questioning with Almazoff shows that the Citizens were aware of such developments. The mass circulation *Literary Digest* carried detailed reports about testimony before the Overman committee and about Bolshevism generally.[92]

Stymied on the New York tack, Andrews nevertheless established that Almazoff possessed copies of *Novy Mir*, which contravened the Consolidated Censor Orders.[93] He asked whether Almazoff was a Zionist and whether he recognized the manifesto of the Socialist Party of Canada, but Almazoff wouldn't answer.[94] On the subject of attending socialist meetings in Winnipeg, Almazoff answered, but evasively. Whenever Andrews established that Almazoff had been at a meeting, he claimed that he couldn't remember what had been said, sometimes not even the subject. As Andrews knew, Almazoff had praised the Russian Revolution,[95] but he denied having 'spoken' at the meetings, though he may have asked a question. What it was, he could no longer recall. When Andrews asked what other speakers such as William Ivens had said, Almazoff refused to answer.[96]

Almazoff's refusal to answer some questions provided Andrews with leverage. He maintained, and Noble went along with him, that as long as Almazoff didn't answer *every* question, Andrews's case couldn't be concluded. Therefore: no cross-examination by the defence; and repeated adjournments, while the defendant sat in prison. Almazoff pled again for bail. Noble recognized that Almazoff was not before him 'as a criminal or accused person,' but refused to agree that this strengthened the case for bail: 'There are more things to consider than the mere fact of an offense charged, or the likelihood of your appearing, where people are held pending an inquiry for deportation.' He wouldn't elaborate, but Andrews did: Almazoff was guilty of 'a crime,' having been found in possession of two copies of *Novy Mir*, which could merit up to five years in prison. Hyman thought this ridiculous – 'Guilt is conviction not a prima facie case,' he said – while McMurray grew angry. Of all the Eastern European leaders, Almazoff was the best candidate for bail. Yet, while the British-born received bail, the Eastern Europeans languished in prison: 'An outrage is being perpetuated upon these men. In this country there should be no question of race before the law.' Had Ottawa ordered no bail? It hadn't; the matter was in Gelley's hands, and Gelley refused bail.[97]

Like Almazoff, Michael (Max) Charitonoff admitted that he was a Russian citizen and a Jew. Born in Nicolaieff, on the Black Sea,[98] he had landed in New York and spent a few months in Philadelphia before arriving broke at the Manitoba border town of Emerson. Joseph Cherniak provided Charitonoff with the funds required to enter Canada,[99] and although he hadn't become a citizen, he had lived in Canada for five years and five months, long enough to establish 'domicile.' He was married but had no children, and worked for a time in the CPR freight shops.

After the banning of his paper *Rabochi Narod* (*Working People*), he had hoped to publish *Nova Vic* (*The New Age*); the Strike, however, had come along before he could get it off the ground.[100] The defence objected to Andrews's questions about socialist organizations and about Charitonoff's prosecution for possession of prohibited literature. Nevertheless, Charitonoff did answer most questions.[101] He admitted that *Rabochi Narod* had been banned, and that he had been convicted of possessing prohibited literature, but also that the Manitoba Court of Appeal had quashed the conviction.[102]

Andrews tried, unsuccessfully, to link Charitonoff to Moscow money and to A.K. Martens (a Russian representative in New York).[103] However, Andrews knew that after Charitonoff's application to start *Nova Vic* was denied, the Bolshevik seed money had gone into Strike funds. Because of this, the Citizens linked the Strike to agents of Moscow.[104] If this was a slender thread for the Strike, it was not so slender for Charitonoff. Still, he claimed that he had never belonged to 'a secret society or organization that entertained or taught disbelief in or opposition to organized government.' When Andrews pressed him about whether he had ever advocated 'Bolshevist principles,' Hyman asked

Andrews to define 'Bolshevism.' Andrews wouldn't. He found it more convenient to accuse the Strike leaders of revolution without saying what exactly was revolutionary. Charitonoff then declined to answer the question. Andrews did establish that Charitonoff had 'occupied a seat on the platform' during the Walker Theatre meeting.[105] 'Did the meeting send fraternal greetings to the Russian Soviet government?' Did the meeting close with Alderman Queen, the chairman, shouting, 'Long Live the Russian Soviet Government, Karl Liebknecht and the working class!'? Charitonoff pretended not to remember.[106] This no doubt had an effect on the court, as Charitonoff technically 'answered' questions while actually evading them. Because Charitonoff, like Almazoff, refused to answer *every* question put by Andrews, Noble again refused to allow the defence to cross-examine the defendant,[107] and adjourned the sitting.

At the end of the week of immigration hearings, strikers prepared for the first anniversary of William Ivens's Labour Church, coming on Saturday the 19th. Celebrations would include a huge meeting in the Citizens' very home – the Board of Trade Building – where the crowd would fill the large auditorium to capacity and overflow into the streets, where Fred Dixon, speaking of the immigration hearings, would throw back at the Citizens their own shibboleths – 'King John had been forced to sign a pact guaranteeing certain rights to men ... King Charles had lost his life owing to an endeavour on his part to deprive Englishmen of those rights' – where Dixon would wonder aloud 'whether Calder, Meighen and other conspirators were likely to be successful in subverting popular rights,' and where Dixon would conclude by implying that the Citizens were the true Bolsheviks: 'Soon we might hear of a Canadian Siberia being established.'[108] While the Eastern European defendants were lying about their championing of Bolshevism, Andrews went about quietly lobbying Ottawa to take away their constitutional rights. Responding to Andrews, Meighen wired that, just as McMurray and Hyman had argued, the defendants *did* have the legal right to remain silent on some questions: 'Apparently entrants [to Canada] must answer but not so residents.' Domicile *did* confer some rights of citizenship. But Meighen naively thought that new regulations, possibly brought forward as soon as Monday, could put an end to that.[109] Cabinet must have informed Meighen that 'domicile' couldn't be so easily sidestepped, but would require additional (and less popular) amendments to the Immigration Act. No more amendments were made.

Andrews awaited the new regulations, but he was careful not to reveal Meighen's information about domicile to Noble, lest Noble stop insisting that the detainees incriminate themselves. To override Justice Noble's legal qualms about accepting secret reports without allowing the defence to cross-examine the agents, Andrews (through William Scott, deputy minister of immigration) also wanted the Department of Justice to proclaim that such evidence would be acceptable under the Immigration Act. If not, perhaps those regulations too could be jiggled so as to allow secret reports.[110] Andrews had the evidence of a particular man in mind: Harry Daskaluk, 'Secret Service Agent No. 21.'[111] Andrews told Meighen that Daskaluk was 'no longer in the employ of the Mounted Police but ... is very reliable and [his] reports are thoroughly trustworthy.' In the next breath, however, Andrews revealed the price of that trustworthiness: Daskaluk refused to testify unless he were 'protected, given transportation for himself and his wife to Bukowina where he comes from, and $500.00 as well.' Andrews asked Meighen to get Cabinet's opinion on the problem.[112] What Andrews didn't reveal to Meighen was that Daskaluk had also been threatened with deportation if he refused to testify.[113] Eventually, Daskaluk would testify, but the defence would force him to do so under his own name, not as hearsay evidence vouched for by Andrews. Under the harsh light of day, Daskaluk's evidence wouldn't seem quite as compelling as it had been when it was 'certain confidential reports.'

12

They Started the Fire: Preliminary Hearing

21 July – 13 August

Only Schoppelrei's fate had been decided when the immigration hearings were interrupted in mid-flight by a proceeding that held an even greater stake for Andrews and the Citizens: the preliminary hearings for Russell, Ivens, Heaps, Bray, Queen, Armstrong, Johns, and Pritchard. Although Andrews didn't intend to have the immigration hearings interrupted, the recess didn't hurt his game plan. The delay meant that the Eastern European defendants, sleeping every night on prison bunks for more than a month now, would feel increased pressure to answer self-incriminating questions. And even if they escaped deportation, they would have spent time in jail, a cautionary tale to other radicals.

The Eastern European leaders were important to their own constituencies, but, as their unequal treatment suggested, they were only 'aliens.' The British-born leaders (along with the British-descended Armstrong) were of much greater symbolic importance. How could British men have been seduced by radical socialism? To defeat these men would be to defeat British radical masculinity. Andrews and the Citizens must have felt a certain euphoria when through the doors of the Winnipeg Police Court in the new Law Courts building walked the British leaders – most of them relatively young, all eight hand-picked as representative rebels by Andrews and the milling crowd of executive Citizens the night of June 16th. On the streets, capital had been handicapped, but in court Andrews was on home turf, and the referee wasn't public opinion but someone he had chosen. Presiding, again, Justice Noble. This was highly convenient, but not extraordinary – Noble was, after all, one of the two police court magistrates in Winnipeg. Again, Andrews's and the Citizens' control of process translated into control of the outcome. Andrews and Coyne appeared 'for the Crown,' while McMurray, Hyman, T.J. Murray, and Hugh McKenzie appeared for the accused. The defendants, ironically, sat in the jury box, the only place so many could be accommodated.[1]

Historians without access to the Andrews-Meighen letters have generally interpreted the preliminary hearing and trial as the *state* quashing radicalism, and Pitblado later spoke of Andrews as 'chief government counsel.'[2] This might have been true in the immigration hearings, but who exactly was prosecuting the British Strike leaders? Andrews couldn't claim that he was acting for the Attorney General of Manitoba. Had he done so, T.H. Johnson would have felt compelled to correct the public record. Andrews couldn't say that he was acting for Ottawa: a chasm of constitutional propriety might have opened. Yet, he didn't want to say that he was acting on behalf of the Citizens' Committee, and, ultimately, he didn't have to. The question of just *who* occupied the place of the 'Crown' simply wasn't raised. This may have been because private prosecutions were entirely within the law, but, given the nearness of the Citizens to the process, it's more likely that the defence wrongly assumed that the federal government was the Crown. Otherwise, a public outcry would certainly have followed. And why not make the assumption: Meighen had deputized Andrews, and the federal government strongly supported capital.

The law, too, privileged capital, and shaped the stories that could be told by each side.[3] Criminal Code sections on common nuisance (section 221, in particular) made it illegal for workers under contract to go on strike: 'A common nuisance is an unlawful act or omission to discharge a legal duty, which act or omission endangers the lives, safety, health, *property or comfort of the public*, or by which the public are obstructed in the exercise or enjoyment of any right common to all His majesty's subjects' [emphasis added].[4] Firefighters striking despite a legal contract and without grievances, striking merely at the behest of the Strike Committee, could easily be seen as violating section 221. In public utilities – gas, electric works, street railways, telephone, and telegraph – and in industries such as coal mining and railways that were vital to the Canadian economy, workers couldn't strike without mandatory conciliation.[5] The Citizens could bring forward managers from the Winnipeg Electric Railway Company, the Dominion Express Company, and the Artic Ice Company (to name a few) who'd testify that the Strike Committee had counselled their employees to break their contracts and thus the law.[6] Civic workers had been in even greater violation, having in 1918 signed contracts with 'no-strike, no-lockout' clauses.

As well, the Criminal Code contained new sections dealing with sedition. Section 134 promised two years' imprisonment to anyone who 'spoke seditious words, published seditious libel, or was party to any seditious conspiracy.'[7] Because (under section 132) a 'conspiracy' only required that two people join in a seditious intention, union members faced serious legal jeopardy.[8] For sedition cases, the courts tended to give the prosecution wide latitude in submitting evidence, so that the nature and extent of the conspiracy could be addressed. In 1892 Minister of Justice Sir John Thompson had proposed the following definition of seditious intent:

> A seditious intention is an intention to bring into hatred and contempt or to excite dissatisfaction against the person of His Majesty, or the government and constitution of the United Kingdom as by law established, or either the houses of parliament, or the administration of justice ... [or] to excite His Majesty's subjects to attempt otherwise than by lawful means or to raise discontent and disaffection amongst His Majesty's subjects in order to promote feelings of ill will and hostility between different classes of such subjects.[9]

Prophetically, William Mulock argued that such a definition would intrude unhelpfully into 'controversies between labour and capital,' and would gut freedom of speech:

> In a little time you will be clothing your officers with power to prevent public meetings ... The whole history of the institutions of the mother land warrants us in concluding that the greatest safety lies in freedom of discussion. A British mob allows its ill will to pass off by using strong language, while in other countries, where freedom of discussion is prohibited, this ill-will takes the form of deeds of violence and causes the formation of secret societies.[10]

Thompson's definition was left out of the 1892 Criminal Code. However, the thinking behind it remained, since Thompson had taken his definition from Stephen's *English Draft Code of 1880*.[11] *Archbold's Criminal Pleading Evidence & Practice*, which would have been on the desk of every lawyer and judge, also relied upon Stephen. So it's no surprise that Thompson's definition resurfaced as the vague 'teaching disbelief in or opposition to organized government' in section 41 of the Immigration Act, revised to the Citizens' specifications. It also reappeared, back-handedly, in the Criminal Code. Under section 133, one was *not* guilty of sedition if one pointed out, '*in order to their removal* [*sic*], matters which are producing or have a tendency to produce feelings of hatred and ill-will between different classes of His Majesty's subjects' [emphasis added].[12] Although the wording only describes what was *not* seditious, one could reasonably deduce that if one intended to *cause* rather than *remove* feelings of hatred and ill-will between the classes, one might be guilty of sedition. Lack of a clear definition left the bench with a quasi-legislative authority to define sedition, while prosecutors were also free to test-drive their own definitions before a jury.[13] According to Andrews's eventual indictment, the Strike leaders in 1917, 1918, and 1919 'did unlawfully conspire, confederate, and agree with one another ... to excite disaffection against the government, laws and constitution of the Dominion of Canada ... to raise discontent and disaffection amongst His Majesty's subjects in Canada, and ... [to] promot[e] feelings of ill-will and hostility between different classes of such subjects.'[14]

The legal requirement of *mens rea* – the guilty mind – for a conviction was of course important in such a case, but by 1916 in Canada *mens rea* had taken a loose rather than a strict meaning. In Britain (*R. v. Burns*), Justice Cave had ruled strictly, that actual intent to produce a disturbance was needed for a guilty verdict in sedition.[15] In *R. v. Manshrick*, however, the Manitoba Court of Appeal held that in a sedition trial the judge had properly charged a jury when he said, 'It is not what the accused intended, it is not, was it his intention that this should create public disorder,' but would disorder be 'the natural result' of his actions – 'The law presumes that he intended the natural consequences of his acts.'[16]

In Winnipeg, *something* had 'resulted' in a tumultuous six-week-long General Strike and a riot. While Crown prosecutor Robert Graham held to the British notion of *mens rea* – 'I do not think there was, in the minds of the real leaders any thought of revolution'[17] – Bloody Saturday could alternatively be presented to a magistrate as the 'natural consequences' of the Strike leaders' seditious words. The Citizens dusted off the Thompson/Stephen definition of sedition, so near in its wording to the section 41 catch-all, and, armed with legal precedent, drew together evidence to show that the Strike leaders conspired to disaffect Winnipeggers against constituted government.

Noble agreed that *mens rea* didn't require the men to have consciously intended a riot. Since the Strike leaders had been jailed four days before Bloody Saturday, Hyman argued that they couldn't possibly be guilty of inciting a riot, and that RNWMP detective Hugh Campbell's testimony about the riot should be excluded. 'I do not see,' Noble interposed, 'that that has anything to do with it. I will adopt the language of

Mr. Andrews: "They started the fire and it was still burning."'[18] Campbell's testimony was admitted; he testified that Constable Hendrick had been shot, and that Campbell had rescued the semi-conscious Hendrick from a battering by the crowd.[19] It was a significant coup for the Citizens that Noble was operating under a loose notion of *mens rea*, and even more of a coup that Noble had begun quoting Andrews with approval on the subject.

The law thus opened broad avenues for the Citizens to tell a good story, not about how the Strike leaders directly incited violence, but about the myriad strands of historical causation by which seditious words, seeded months earlier, blossomed into burning streetcars, and by which doubts implanted into the minds of the strikers caused their disaffection against the 'duly-constituted' Special Police, the sons and employees of the elite. Judge Noble concurred: 'In a case of conspiracy it is never possible to give evidence that certain people got together in a room and agreed amongst themselves that they would start or put through a conspiracy in the form of an agreement and go on and do a certain thing. You have to take the evidence of what happened and from that deduce that there was a conspiracy to do what happened. That is the only way a conspiracy can be proven.'[20] Noble never made a secret of his bias, and, long before the evidence was in, repeated the Citizens' story: 'The evidence goes to show that away back from the time of the Calgary· convention that a certain number of people put their heads together, and your clients were there – some of them – for the purpose of taking over the whole government.'[21]

At the same time, the law constricted the narratives available to the Strike leaders. The Strike had scoffed at the legal constraints that bound labour to duty: injunctions; criminal sanctions against striking while under contract, against picketing, intimidation, and watching and besetting; the threat of fines arising from civil liability; the requirements of the Industrial Disputes Investigation Act for mediation; and possibly even the sedition clauses of the Criminal Code. This boldness created, in effect, a grand narrative of the empowerment of the working class, but it might easily work against them in court. McMurray and Co. had little choice but to tone down the strikers' very real challenges to property, and instead to tell a story of compliance with law and order. Their defence: workers had criticized the state but within reasonable bounds; workers hadn't used violence (a reasonable claim for much of the Strike); workers had picketed but they hadn't intimidated anyone (a false claim). This was a story of submission to the rights of property and to the prerogatives of the state. A second story that labour and the defence lawyers tried to tell held greater validity: the story of a conspiracy by the

Citizens to prevent a negotiated settlement and to lasso the federal government into questionable prosecutions. However, like their opponents, defence attorneys too lacked direct evidence that certain people had gotten together in a room, and defence attempts to reveal the Citizens' role in heightening the crisis were dismissed as irrelevant by Noble.

In a preliminary hearing, the prosecution must show enough evidence against the accused to warrant a trial. The new information that Andrews filed differed substantially from the information upon which the arrests had been made on 17 June. Originally, the Strike leaders had been charged with 'seditious activity,' but the Citizens' lawyers amended the original information to read 'seditious conspiracy.' In terms of both propaganda and procedure, it was an astute move. Not only did it dovetail with the *Winnipeg Citizen*'s story of an international conspiracy, but it also opened the door for a wide-ranging investigation. As the evidence piled up, a big picture was supposed to form, and the prosecution's story to become self-evident.

In the end, the Citizens couldn't sustain the story of an international revolutionary conspiracy, and had to be satisfied with putting post-war labour radicalism in the dock, charging the Strike leaders with what they could hardly deny: causing trouble between the classes. McMurray considered the charge to be 'a relic of the days of tyranny,' and he offered his own definition of seditious conspiracy: 'It is a very ancient and antiquated machine, very much like the old-fashioned blunderbuss that you filled with scraps of iron, slugs, glass, bolts, and anything you could lay your hands on. The idea was, if you aimed it at someone, you would at least hit him with one slug.'[22] Simple sedition would have been easy to prove: the Strike Committee's taking over of certain government regulatory functions could be understood as disaffection against the constitution; and intemperate statements in Calgary, at the Walker Theatre, and at the Majestic had threatened public order. But simple sedition would have failed to link the Calgary Conference to Bloody Saturday. And why, the defence would have asked, didn't the Crown arrest the leaders when the sedition was uttered rather than much later, when they had toned down their rhetoric considerably? To support the charge of seditious conspiracy, Andrews could only point to words publicly spoken. To support the final charge that the Strike constituted a Common Nuisance under the Criminal Code, he pointed to the vicissitudes of life in Winnipeg during the Strike, with testimony about commercial life being tied up and eggs rotting in warehouses.[23]

With the new conspiracy charges, Andrews left out the Eastern European leaders' names, in effect withdrawing charges against them. This could potentially be to their advantage, though Andrews equivocated. Were the Eastern Europeans successful at the immigration hearings, dropped criminal charges could mean that they wouldn't have to defend themselves twice on the same charges. Were they unsuccessful, they'd of course be denied the right to a proper trial before a jury. McMurray and Hyman tried to get Andrews to say the words – to say that the charges were withdrawn. He wouldn't. All the defence could squeeze out of him was, 'There is only one information now.' Noble observed that Andrews's actions amounted to a withdrawal, but he wouldn't require Andrews to say so. Andrews's unwillingness to take a firm stand makes it clear that he was waiting for the outcomes of the immigration hearings. If the Citizens didn't get satisfaction, he'd turn to the Criminal Code.[24] Effectively, the British leaders were in single jeopardy, the Eastern Europeans in double.

When Andrews began his case, he sketched a broad conspiracy stretching from the Walker Theatre meeting in December, through the Calgary conference in March, to the Strike in May and June. Militants in the Socialist Party of Canada were active agents in the conspiracy, but others were implicated too. Andrews considered every member of the Strike Committee guilty of seditious conspiracy, though only a few were being prosecuted.[25] McMurray responded with a story of apparent openness: that the Strike leaders had made all their speeches in public; so, no conspiracy. When Andrews called to the stand a reporter who had produced a verbatim report of the Calgary conference, F.B. Perry, to identify Russell, Pritchard, Johns, and Armstrong as participants in Calgary, McMurray asked Perry whether one of the conference's purposes in employing him was so that the proceedings could be made public. Perry had to agree.[26]

Because the preliminary hearing, like the Strike, was a media war for the hearts of the middle classes, both the prosecution's and the defence's stories tended to swallow their own tails. Andrews had good procedural reasons for shifting the charge to conspiracy, but his inability to point to secret cabals and hidden plans eviscerated the charge's credibility. He wanted onlookers to put their faith in a mirage. But the defence story, too, was incoherent. To win the middle class, McMurray wanted to tell a story about a group of men who had nothing to hide, of open and brave criticism of big-money profiteering. But to win the court case, he had to plant doubts about whether the leaders had said what they in all likelihood did say. This meant repeatedly questioning the memory and competency of every police observer who testified about socialist meetings. As a result, statements that had been public now looked covert, as the defendants covered their tracks and took back any radical words.

One of the first witnesses at the preliminary hearing, Sergeant Francis Langdale of Military Intelligence, reprised his performance at Blumenberg's immigration hearing. Langdale had produced a report on the Walker Theatre meeting, and he quoted some of the more aggressive speakers: W.H. Hoop had said that capitalists had chained democracy, and that nothing would change until the workers rose up and struck them off. Hoop was also somewhat less than patriotic about the Canadian war effort: 'The blood of our comrades has been spilt on the field of battle and it has been a farce and a shame.' In a similar vein, Ivens had asserted that 'the Germans are our friends' and that German socialists were 'true patriots,' while Blumenberg had shouted that only Bolshevism would emancipate the working class. Any and all references to *revolution* were 'loudly cheered.' In fact, the whole meeting was 'very radical and revolutionary in tone,' with a large contribution from Russell, who stormed, 'Let us have justice, and if not blood will be spilt in this country.' Asked by Andrews about the meeting's effect on the audience, Langdale said, 'It would inculcate revolutionary ideas in their heads.'[27]

McMurray tried to create doubt by getting Langdale to admit that he hadn't taken a verbatim report of the Walker Theatre meeting, that he no longer had his original notes, and that he couldn't even remember on what he'd written them. Perhaps Langdale had written the report after reading the morning newspaper? Langdale thought not, but he wasn't certain.[28] More effective than this attempt to deny what the speakers had said was McMurray's probing of Langdale's definition of 'revolutionary.' 'What revolutionary ideas would they inculcate?' McMurray asked. Langdale didn't want to answer, preferring to speak only generally about the 'tone' of the meeting. But could he cite any revolutionary idea announced at the meeting? Pressed, Langdale answered, 'Yes, possibly that the Russian form of government was vastly superior to the British form of government.' And later, Alderman Queen had mentioned revolution to loud applause.[29]

At the end of the preliminary hearing's first day, history came to the aid of the Citizens. Andrews received a terse wire from Arthur Meighen with some remarkably good news: 'In Justice matters communicate with Mr. Doherty. Am closely following all proceedings.'[30] This simple telegram marked a turning point as fundamental in the efforts of Citizens as Meighen's first deputization of Andrews.

The news was the return to Canada of Borden's minister of justice, Charles Doherty, who had been in Paris since the fall of 1918 helping to negotiate the Treaty of Versailles. Doherty's résumé compared very well with the most accomplished of the Citizens. A native of Montreal, he was educated at St Mary's Jesuit College and then became a gold medal–winning law student at McGill before his call to the bar in 1877. Like Andrews and Colonel Starnes, he helped to put down the Northwest Rebellion, serving as captain in Montreal's 65th Rifle Regiment. His celebrated legal career was capped with an 1891 appointment to the bench, where the Jesuit influence was evident: his judgments were 'terse, closely reasoned, and above all things perfectly lucid.'[31] Elected to the House of Commons in 1908, he was appointed minister of justice in Borden's first government and would remain in that position until his defeat in the 1921 election. In addition to his prominence in law and politics, Doherty was an important figure in the Montreal business community. He served on the boards of the Montreal City and District Savings Bank, the Prudential Trust Company, and the Capital Life Assurance Company, and was president of the Canadian Securities Corporation. As was common for such a man, he also held membership in a number of elite clubs.[32]

Principal legal adviser to the Borden government in August 1914, Doherty faced the crisis of the Great War boldly and comprehensively: he authored the War Measures Act. Ottawa thereby gave itself the authority to set aside the BNA Act and override the provinces whenever it saw fit to do so. Like Andrews, Doherty was prepared to act first and then legalize his actions afterward: 'Some steps,' he admitted, 'had to be taken before this House could be gathered together which were beyond any express legal authorization.' The War Measures Act retroactively ratified those measures.[33] Yet, paradoxically, Doherty thought of himself as a traditionalist when it came to the constitution, and held that the administration of justice was 'absolutely in the hands of provincial governments.'[34] His pessimism about human nature may explain his penchant for coercive state power in times of crisis. He 'once said that if one ever had any doubt as to the existence of a Divine Providence, the operation of democratic institutions was sufficient to dispel that doubt, as nothing short of Divine Power could hold together such elements of chaos.'[35]

As early as the spring of 1918, Borden and Doherty had become increasingly concerned about dissidents in Canada.[36] They had watched the United States, where, in 1917, the federal Department of Justice had helped create a citizens' association – the American Protective League – to monitor German subversives on American soil.[37] Supposed to consist of 'citizens of good moral character,' and financed by 'outside subscriptions or by its members,'[38] the APL became an anti-dissident arm of the War Emergency Division within the US Department of Justice.[39] Ultimately, the APL failed to unearth a single German spy. It did, however, succeed in harassing radicals, dissenters, and Wobblies, and in abusing the civil liberties of Americans.

During the flurry of interest in possible German subversives, Ottawa sent Lt. Col. Vincent Massey, associate secretary of the War Committee of cabinet, 'to study APL methods, with a view to their possible adoption,'[40] and sent Montreal businessman C.H. Cahan to report on anti-war activities in Canada 'by German Agents or with German support.'[41] To nudge Cahan in the right direction, Borden sent along a secret Washington memorandum on the APL.[42] At the same time, Doherty had also asked Sir Percy Sherwood, chief commissioner of the Dominion Police, to report on the IWW and 'kindred organizations.' Canada's state security apparatus was in a primordial state in 1918, and operated under Sherwood's nominal responsibility.

After an exhaustive investigation involving private detectives and police organizations across the country, Sherwood found no trace of IWW activity. Even 'close censorship of the mail' revealed only a single case of the IWW trying to get 'a foot hold in Canada.'[43] Cahan reported back to Doherty in July 1918, saying that German, Austrians, and other aliens hadn't contravened the War Measures Act. In other words, a Canadian version of the APL wasn't needed. According to Cahan, in the United States there had been widespread evidence of German-inspired subversion and the League had played a useful role in 'local man-hunts,' but in Canada manifestations of disloyalty were scattered, isolated, and weak – easily nipped by Dominion and local police. 'Wide-spread unrest and discontent' there certainly was, but it had nothing to do with Germans. What Cahan noticed was 'the growing belief that the Union Government is failing to deal efficiently with the financial, industrial and economic problems growing out of the war.'[44]

Sorry, but the reports didn't meet Doherty's needs. Neither Sherwood's nor Cahan's report would justify beefed-up security or new legislation. Doherty brought in Cahan for a consultation with himself and Deputy Minister of Justice E.L. Newcombe.[45] They must have told Cahan to cast his net more widely – to aliens in general – and by September, Cahan handed in a new report, little resembling the first and much friendlier to Doherty's anxieties. This time, Cahan noted that 'the Russians, Ukrainians and Finns, who are employed in the mines, factories and other industries in Canada, are now being thoroughly saturated with the Socialistic doctrines which have been proclaimed by the Bolshevik faction of Russia.' He discovered that, contra Sherwood, the IWW was spending 'large sums of money' to spread propaganda 'advocating the destruction of all state authority, the subversion of religion, and the obliteration of all property rights.' 'Bolshevik Associations in

The Grasping Hand of the I.W.W.

It is Antagonistic to the Ideals of Honest Labor

Bolshevism offers no possibility of advance for labor. It is an imported theory fomented by foreigners, which is impracticable and incompetent. Men who never knew how to get money will never know how to keep it.

Bolshevism, though doomed to extinction, may not die before several nations of the earth have had a big dose of it. Russian industry is turning somersaults and breaking its neck by turning its factories over to workmen without any directing boss or head. The equable distribution is of little value if little is produced.

In Russia, Bolshevism must be left to burn itself out. In Canada, it must be fought with the ancient weapons of a free people—the applied principles of law and order under a government of the people by the people.

Mr. Samuel Gompers believes that the toilers will see ultimately that there is nothing in the false doctrines of Bolshevism.

The war has revealed that everything depends on the *loyal and continuous support of labor.* Employer and employee came together on one plane of common interest and common effort. The good spirit then developed should never be lost.

Democracy does not always get the best, but it always gets what it wants. It reserves for people the right to make their own mistakes. We do not believe in the class idea, but that one man is as good as another.

The Canadian laborer does not hate millionaires. He may be a millionaire himself some day. Most men of success have labored with their hands and have begun small and raised themselves.

The Man Promoted Is The Coming Business Man

This Article is One of a Series—Be Sure to Read Them All.

Despite the Citizens' propaganda, the IWW had few links to Canada. (*Winnipeg Telegram*, 31 May 1919)

Canada' had formed 'their own Soviets in certain industrial communities' to incite industrial strife and to 'terrorize those of their own nationality who desire to follow their peaceful pursuits.' Upon further reflection, it appeared to Cahan's newly coached eyes that 'Ukrainians and Finns are really under German control, and are undoubtedly being used by Germany to carry on its political propaganda.'

Existing laws were inadequate to meet this conspiracy between Bolsheviks and Germans, and Cahan offered several solutions. 'Unlawful associations,' including the Social Democratic Party and 'any other Society or Organization inculcating the same doctrines or teachings,' must be outlawed. Membership in and attendance at meetings of such organizations must be punishable by jail – no escaping with a fine. Foreign-language publications must be licensed by the federal government.[46] Obviously, Doherty didn't really need Cahan's report itself – only the aura of due process – because within days of the report's submission, on 25 September 1918, the Borden government already had two comprehensive Orders-in-Council (PC 2381 and PC 2384) set to go. In language drawn from American statutes, the OICs outlawed fourteen specific organizations and required that foreign-language publications be federally licensed.[47]

On the other homework assigned by Doherty, Cahan commented, 'Since my interview with you and the Deputy Minister of Justice [Newcombe] last, I have given considerable thought to the matters which were then under discussion,' and the day after PC 2384 was approved, Cahan proposed the creation of a Public Safety Branch and the reorganization of the Dominion Police. Channelling Doherty, Cahan envisioned the Public Safety Branch remaining even after the war until industrial unrest had 'dissipated.' Public Safety would employ lawyers to carry out prosecutions, and would cooperate not only with other branches of the federal government, but also with 'such local private protective associations as it may be deemed advisable to organize on the lines of the American Protective League.'[48] As did the War Measures Act, the Public Safety Branch would have opened the door for federal invasion into any area of provincial jurisdiction. While historians have portrayed Arthur Meighen as the leading exponent of repression in Borden's government – in one account he is described as 'an extremist'[49] – it was, in fact, Doherty who was the more determined apostle of reaction.

Via an Order-in-Council, cabinet approved the Public Safety Branch on 2 October 1918, with Cahan as director. The branch wilted with the departure of Doherty to Europe, and Ottawa never did organize any Canadian counterpart to the APL. But a man of Doherty's views had no difficulty embracing a comparable organization such as the Citizens' Committee of 1000. A seemingly minor point in the OIC's final paragraph would eventually loom very large for Andrews and the Citizens: prosecution of offenders would be chargeable to the War Appropriation.[50]

Perhaps just as important as the War Measures and Public Safety Branch experience was how deeply Doherty had involved himself in the European attempt to create a stable post-war order. As one of five international jurists named by the League of Nations to review proposals for a Permanent Court of International Justice, Doherty believed that the best chance for peace was through international rule of law. At the same time, he was a pragmatist: 'You have to recognize existing conditions, and when you cannot get the whole loaf, it is wisdom to take the half loaf.'[51] Having just returned from Europe, he carried with him an immediate picture of the chaos offered by the Spartakusbund's 'follow-up' to the Russian Revolution. He wasn't likely to shed tears for Liebknecht and Luxemburg. And revolution wasn't planning to stay in Europe. In late July, British Colonial Secretary Milner would cable Borden to inform him that to resuscitate revolution in Canada, the Soviets had put two million rubles at the disposal of Communists in Ottawa, Calgary, Lethbridge, Edmonton, Regina, Victoria, Vancouver, and Montreal.[52]

On 28 June, Doherty signed the Treaty of Versailles below British Prime Minister Lloyd George, and then headed back to Canada to resume his responsibilities as minister of justice and Attorney General of Canada. Prime Minister Borden too returned from Europe, but as a tired, sick man, lacking sufficient energy to breath life into the fading Unionist government. Absent during most of the summer and unable to attend to his responsibilities throughout the fall, he left Ottawa for a warmer climate in January. During Borden's absence, acting prime minister George Foster and Doherty helmed the government.[53] Although Borden would later lament that the two didn't cooperate fully, and 'did not command the confidence of colleagues,'[54] the Citizens would have few complaints.

One of the first things that greeted Doherty on his return was the Winnipeg crisis. At the time of his death, a colleague would remark, 'The intricacy of a legal puzzle, I think, rather attracted him. He would not cut the gordian knot, he would unravel it.'[55] The puzzle that confronted Doherty in July 1919 was how to mount a prosecution of the Strike leaders in the absence of provincial cooperation. Within days of Doherty's return to Ottawa and resumption of the controls in the Department of Justice on 14 July,[56] he solved the puzzle, and Ottawa's unease about the Citizens' methods vanished. If the Citizens would prosecute, the constitutional puzzle was solved; if Doherty stole his own Public Safety Branch idea to finance prosecutions through the War Appropriation (in this case demobilization funds), the Citizens' anger about government inaction would be solved. What Doherty probably didn't anticipate, however, was the size of the Citizens' lawyers' bills.

The first direct sign of a sea change in Ottawa's approach came to Andrews in late July, partway into the preliminary hearing, when Doherty revealed that he was ready to employ article II.7 of the Consolidated Orders in Council on Censorship approved under the War Measures Act.[57] He wasn't prepared to give Andrews *carte blanche*, but said that he'd support a prosecution as long as procedures outlined in the Orders were adhered to.[58] Meighen's views about constitutional propriety fell by the wayside. Like Andrews, Doherty knew that the Consolidated Orders made it possible for the federal attorney general to act unilaterally – he had helped write the orders. Acting unilaterally on the basis of the previous censorship orders would be new, but it wouldn't rise to the more politically difficult level of actually creating *new* OICs under the War Measures Act long after the war. In mid-July letters to Meighen, Andrews had coveted the OICs. Under them, swearing out an information was tantamount to conviction. As Andrews put it, 'The information itself is prima facie proof of all facts alleged therein and would save a great deal of expense and difficulty in securing convictions.'[59] Indeed, it would save expense and difficulty ... there'd be no trial. 'Guilt is conviction not a prima facie case,' Hyman had protested, rooting himself in the constitution during Almazoff's immigration hearing,[60] but under the censorship OICs, guilt *was* defined as a prima facie case. If the government pointed a finger, the accused was guilty. Andrews had fantasized briefly about proceeding in this high-handed manner, asking Meighen to authorize it. This request was a bit surprising, since it wouldn't give Andrews and the Citizens their show trial. Nevertheless, in mid-July Andrews's request for a conviction without a trial made sense: the Province was baulking at prosecutions and he desperately needed some sort of a clear-cut victory over the Strike leaders. Later, Doherty, who would inherit Andrews's request, wouldn't say yes and wouldn't say no. Ideologically, Doherty was completely in Andrews's corner, but politically, Doherty couldn't justify a new OIC. If Andrews had 'special cases' that Doherty should consider (under the old censorship OICs), send him the details. Andrews would, and in early August, Doherty would approve the prosecution of Jacob Miller, co-editor of *Die Volk Stimme* (*The People's Voice*).[61] To maintain rule of law, Doherty wanted to prosecute the Strike leaders. If the Province wouldn't carry the ball, then he'd work with the on-site group that would. On the second day of the preliminary hearing, this was all in the future, and Andrews didn't know for certain what Doherty would do. But given Doherty's ideological orientation, Andrews must have felt buoyant after reading Meighen's terse wire: 'In Justice matters communicate with Mr. Doherty.' The Citizens had their man.

The preliminary hearing's second day got under way in a carnival of disorder. A courtroom full of noisy partisans; Armstrong with his hat on until asked to take it off; Bray puffing on a cigarette until ordered to desist; clashes between counsel that made the Strike leaders guffaw. A woman continually whispered in 'loud, sibilant' tones until a constable waded into the audience to shut her up.[62] Later in the hearing, McMurray would object to the constable's presence, because it left the impression that the defendants were 'a bunch of dangerous criminals.' But Noble, unimpressed by the Strike leaders' lack of decorum, kept the constable on because of 'irregular conduct on the part of the accused,' mainly, it seems, because one of the leaders continually chewed tobacco and spat juice on the floor.[63]

The strongest evidence for the Citizens' story came in testimony about the speeches given by the Strike leaders in the months before the Strike. Andrews, always conscious of what he had learned as a young defence lawyer – 'When you have a point to make, whenever possible, make it through a policeman or official'[64] – put RNWMP Sergeant Albert Reames on the stand again to testify that the speeches at the Majestic Theatre in January were all about 'Capitalist vs. Workers.' Every speaker at the Majestic impressed upon the audience that 'a revolution was coming in the near future,' and that the working classes must educate themselves 'in order that when the revolution takes place they will be in a position to understand what is actually taking place.' The speakers hoped for a peaceful revolution, but declared that they were ready 'to shed blood' if the capitalists forcibly kept workers from their rights. The *Red Flag* and a book entitled *Socialism, Utopian and Scientific* were on sale. Reames concluded: 'These speeches had a very detrimental effect upon returned soldiers.' Despite prodding from Andrews, Reames (probably wanting to avoid the *post hoc* knots of the immigration hearings) wouldn't quite put his finger on the direct cause of the riots of a week later. But he did say, 'They were *indirectly* caused by the speeches I heard in the Majestic Theatre.'[65]

Politically sensitive reading material could certainly be seditious. RNWMP detective W.H. McLaughlin would later testify that at a post-Strike meeting on 3 August, Bill Pritchard, while on bail, had urged his audience to buy *The Communist Manifesto*. McLaughlin had done so. Thus, *The Communist Manifesto* was introduced as evidence against the Strike leaders. When Coyne proposed to read selected passages from the *Manifesto*, McMurray objected and asked that he read all of it or none of it. Noble wasn't about to ask everyone to sit still for the entire *Manifesto*, but since Coyne declared himself willing to let the defence read a few selected passages too, Noble allowed Coyne to begin reading:

In short, the Communists everywhere support every revolutionary movement against the existing social and political order of things.

In all these movements they bring to the front as the leading question in each, the property question, no matter what its degree of development at the time.

Finally they labor everywhere for the union and agreement of the democratic parties of all countries.

The communists disdain to conceal their views and aims. They openly declare that their ends can be attained only by the forcible overthrow of all existing social conditions. Let the ruling classes tremble at a Communistic revolution. The Proletarians have nothing to lose but their chains. They have a world to win.

McMurray was reduced to pointing out that the *Communist Manifesto* was 'on the shelves of the library at Oxford and Cambridge.' 'You might apply that,' Coyne wittily returned, 'to the bacteria in a laboratory.'[66] Although McMurray might have wished that his clients had exhibited a disinterested academic curiosity about Communism, or a respect for Communist goals combined with an aversion to Communist methods, Pritchard's unqualified championing of the *Manifesto* suggests that McMurray was wrong.

Nevertheless, McMurray was able to insert doubt about the value of Reames's testimony and thus the Citizens' narrative, first because Reames's references to bloodshed didn't seem to involve direct quotations from the speakers. McMurray said, 'It struck me that your reports were largely a matter of conclusion you had come to, that you had not given the exact words of the men, but what you concluded.' Reames agreed. McMurray pushed on: did each speaker declare a willingness to shed blood? Reames, initially, would only qualify his testimony slightly, 'Yes, although they might have put it in a different form,' but eventually, under McMurray's questioning, Reames had to admit that the speakers had intimated a willingness to shed blood, but that he could provide no direct incitements. Stressing Reames's admission that the speakers all hoped for peaceful change, McMurray asked, 'Where is there a single place in that address where they said or intimated that they were bringing on a revolution?' Reames was forced to reduce his testimony from facts to exposition and finally to speculation: 'There is nothing in these reports to say they were going to, but what I said was this, that it was very easy to perceive by their speeches and actions that they would like to see one. They were going to do their best with their speeches to bring one along. That is the way I took it.'[67]

Later witnesses for the prosecution would agreed with Reames that remarks by the Strike leaders were intended to raise disaffection towards constituted authority, and a few remarks were even revolutionary. According to the newspapers, RNWMP Detective W.H.

McLaughlin testified that on 10 June, with A.A. Heaps present, Roger Bray claimed to have 'a fully organized army of 3,000 to 4,000 ready to seize arms and take possession of Minto barracks at a given signal.'[68] Bray said that the Strike was bound to end in a fight, and when McLaughlin observed that it was too bad that the strikers had no guns, Bray responded, 'We have got between three and four thousand men ready and instructed to be in certain places when the alarm is sounded, and they will get into the Citizens' cars which are to carry the militia to Minto barracks, pass themselves off as militiamen until they get inside the barracks, get possession of the rifles, turn them on the real soldiers and seize the barracks.'[69] McLaughlin's account appeared in the newspapers, but not in preliminary hearing transcripts. Why? Evidently the statements must have come not from McLaughlin's testimony, but from the reports that were entered as evidence, and to which McMurray unsuccessfully objected.[70] But why didn't Andrews play this evidence up, so damaging to the Strike Committee? Why didn't he elicit the evidence from McLaughlin directly in testimony? The most compelling explanation is that Andrews knew that the statements weren't made seriously, and that his story had too much to lose if that became manifest in court. A consideration of the statements themselves suggests that their facetiousness would indeed become obvious. What revolutionary would reveal to a stranger the method whereby he was about to seize power? One could attribute the claim of a 4000-strong revolutionary army to a moment of bravado in Bray, but to what could one attribute the description of a potential method of infiltration? The most likely explanation is that Bray had unwisely baited McLaughlin.

McLaughlin's evidence also referred to a 2 June mass meeting in Logan Park, where Ivens gave 'thinly veiled hints that the workers must resort to violence.' Ivens alluded to the fact that the government 'had machine guns mounted on trucks,' and advised strikers, 'This means war. We must fight to the finish.'[71] But whether Ivens meant a literal war with guns or a metaphorical labour war wasn't evident.

Incendiary remarks were likewise reported by W.E. Davis, who quoted Ivens as having proclaimed in Victoria Park, 'The parliament of the City is now in the Labor Temple instead of in the City Hall ... The Parliament Buildings on Kennedy Street would make a good Labor Temple, and ... the way things are going we will soon move in.' Ivens bragged about controlling the press, saying that 'there would soon be no dailies published unless the strike committee published one.' In the class war between capital and labour, labour would win: 'This time the lightning will strike upwards instead of downwards.'[72]

In order to discredit Davis, McMurray focused on his business credentials and his chumming with the Citizens. He was an advertising agent from Minneapolis who did business with Winnipeg firms, and he had stayed at the Hotel Fort Garry, seat of luxury. After getting him to admit that he couldn't always hear Ivens and couldn't quote him verbatim, McMurray mocked the fact that Davis seemed only able to recall Ivens's words, not the other speeches:

McMurray: You mentioned the magnificent carrying qualities of the
            voice of Mr. Ivens; you could hear him more easily than
            the others?
Davis: Ivens had a good speaking voice.
McMurray: You were charmed with his voice?
Davis: That is not a fair way to put it.[73]

More damaging to Davis's testimony, however, was the fact that he had made a report to the Citizens. After priming Davis with gentler questions, McMurray went for the neck:

McMurray: Have you been employed to fight labor in any way
            before this?
Davis: No Sir ...
McMurray: Now, after you heard this speech, did you report it to
            any one?
Davis: I won't say 'report it' is the right word; I talked it over
            casually with some friends.
McMurray: Did you report it to the members of the Citizens' Com-
            mittee in the Industrial Building?
Davis: I was asked by someone to make a statement of what I
            had heard that afternoon, because I thought some of my
            friends had said something to the committee about it.
McMurray: And you did make a report?
Davis: I made a statement regarding it; I will not say it was a
            report ...
McMurray: To whom did you make this statement?
Davis: It was in a room [at] the Industrial Bureau; as I under-
            stood it – the organization – I cannot say I knew it was
            the Citizens' Committee, but I presume that it was.[74]

Davis's friendships and affiliations wouldn't worry Judge Noble, but before the court of public opinion, such hints of the Citizens' reach were less benign.

With Sgt. Reames, although Andrews had effectively made his point through a police officer, McMurray was able to strike at a weak chink in the Citizens' story of a seditious conspiracy, and he again performed a *reductio ad absurdum* of the notion that the Majestic Theatre meeting had caused riots a week later. Reames agreed that at the meeting he didn't immediately foresee riots, but that he recognized trouble later in the week after talking with returned soldiers. He wanted to avoid the extravagant claims of *post hoc* reasoning – McMurray might ask him why he hadn't prevented a foreseeable riot – so it wasn't hard for McMurray to show how Reames was hedging his bets:

McMurray:	When you were at the meeting did you think it would produce riots?
Reames:	I was not quite in a position to think anything at that time.
McMurray:	Did you think it would produce riots?
Reames:	If everyone thought the same as I did, who were at that meeting, I would say it should produce riots.
McMurray:	You thought it would produce riots?
Reames:	I am not going so far as to say that.
McMurray:	You can either say 'yes' or 'no.'
Reames:	The answer in this case comes between yes and no. It is neither. It might.
McMurray:	What would it produce then?
Reames:	It would produce discontent amongst the people listening to the speeches, the average person listening …
McMurray:	Is not discontent the father of progress?
Reames:	It may be in lots of cases.[75]

Despite Reames's care, the coup de grace came on the hedging word 'indirectly.' McMurray queried Reames on the causes of the soldiers' unrest, but Reames maintained that this hadn't been part of his investigation. Yet, if Reames was so confident about the 'indirect' cause of the riot, surely he must have a good idea of the direct causes. In fact, no. Asked about the direct cause, Reames responded, 'I am not in a position to say.' McMurray asked again, 'You can find the indirect ones, what were the direct ones?' 'I am not in a position to say,' Reames again replied.[76] Advantage defence.

On the second day of Reames's testimony, McMurray turned to the slipperiness of the sedition charge. The basis for Andrews's arrests on 16–17 June – the criminal information – which prominently featured the word 'seditious,' had been signed by Reames. Reames was able to more or less give *Archbold's* textbook definition of sedition: 'attempting to overthrow constituted authority by unconstitutional means' or 'bringing the government ... into disrepute by utterances which may tend to turn good people against it.' McMurray wondered, did adverse criticism of government amount to sedition? 'It all depends,' Reames fired back, 'upon the character and the intention of the speaker.'[77] McMurray turned to Reames's testimony that statements made at William Ivens's Labour Church were seditious.[78] Could Reames provide an example? Could he identify any meeting in which people were holding secret conversations?

McMurray:	What did you find in [the service on 13 April] that was seditious?
Reames:	Continual hammering at the system, no chance of co-operating with the capitalistic class.
McMurray:	Is that sedition?
Reames:	No, I would not exactly define that as sedition.
McMurray:	In all these addresses you heard no sound or call to arms or advising any rioting or fighting?
Reames:	No, but the seed of discontent was being gradually sown in the minds of the people present at the time, and insidious underhand propaganda was going on at that particular time to have them take over and control all industries.
McMurray:	By political action.
Reames:	By no action, by force ... Ivens in his statements said 'You Capitalist, and there are some of you here listening to me now, you know what I say is true, and you see the writing on the wall. You system [*sic*] is tottering to its fall, and, knowing this, you are frantically trying to get the working man to look favorably upon some scheme of co-operation, but labor with sullen determination refuses to grasp your hand.' Further, 'We do not want co-operation. We intend to take all.'
McMurray:	By force?
Reames:	Take it which way you like. It is for the judge to decide ... I will not swear they were the exact words, but they were the same meaning anyway.[79]

Such cross-examination was double-edged. McMurray could expose the glaring weakness in the Citizens' story of conspiracy and *direct* incitement to violence. Yet, while it might not be seditious to refuse to cooperate with the capitalist classes, statements such as 'We intend to take all' certainly implied an attack on constituted authority. In such matters, the Citizens' story held true.

Towards the end of Reames's testimony, McMurray returned to its weakest point: the Majestic meeting and its 'indirect' role in what McMurray ironically called 'this attempted revolution.' McMurray established that Heaps and Queen didn't speak at the Majestic, making it a puzzle as to why Reames swore out an information against them. When Reames responded that other investigations and reports contributed to the information, McMurray pounced, and declared that the speeches *weren't* the cause of the unrest. Reames fell back on the word 'indirectly' and promised, 'I will not get away from the word "indirectly."' Judge Noble, even if he had to lead the witness, attempted to rescue Reames from the word. Did Reames mean that there were other causes? Reames started to expand on the speeches; Noble gently led him back to what he meant by 'indirectly.' Reames began a long convoluted response, unwilling to let go of the word; Noble interposed, 'I do not think "indirectly" explains what you mean.' Reames still didn't take the cue, and finally Noble had to spell it out, 'What you mean by that is this, – that it was part of the campaign which led up to the riots.' 'Exactly,' Reames agreed.

Noble had meant to rescue Reames from a story of 'direct' (thus real, but in the present case not easily identifiable) causes and 'indirect' (thus hypothetical) causes of the unrest. What Noble wanted to nudge Reames towards was the Citizens' story, in which many strands, each doing 'part' of the work, made up the larger conspiracy. McMurray, however, met this revision of the story head-on. His subsequent questions showed that Noble's rescue had been merely semantic. If the Majestic speeches had been merely 'part' of the causes of revolution, surely Reames could now explain what his secret reports detailed as 'the other causes.'

Reames: No, I will not. I will say they are a very small part.
McMurray: The speeches are the big part?
Reames: They are not.
McMurray: What is the big part?
Reames: Wait until the evidence is introduced by the Crown.
McMurray: The witness can tell me. He was the man who investigated and all the reports came to him. He is unduly modest. Now then, Sergeant, what was the real cause of the strike outside of these speeches.
Reames: Mr. McMurray, if I could answer more clearly on this matter I would gladly do so. The point is this, there

were a large variety of causes, which I am not prepared
personally to give to you.[80]

Both Andrews and Noble leapt in to shield Reames, but clearly there
were only two possible explanations for such hedging. Either Reames
and the Citizens were bluffing – low wages caused the Strike, and the
prosecution's notion of larger 'causes' that could be blamed on the Strike
leaders was a mirage – or Reames had no authorization to speak about
'larger' causes. In other words, larger causes were in the safekeeping of
the Citizens, and even the lead investigator wasn't allowed to explain
knowledge too wonderful for him.

Despite Reames's difficulties, Andrews, in the search for seditious
conspiracy (and not just sedition), continued to usher his witnesses
towards the effects of socialist speeches. A later witness, *Manitoba Free
Press* newspaper cartoonist B.T. Battsford, testified about red neckties at
the Majestic meeting, about the distribution of the *Red Flag*, and, most
damningly, about the leaders' speeches and their effects.[81] George Armstrong spoke against not only war profiteers, but also against 'the system
that permitted such a state of affairs.'[82] Russell 'went severely after the
press and pulpit and censorship, and said the truth had not been told
about Russia ... that there was undoubtedly an organized campaign to
keep the truth back from the people in the rest of the world ... He said
the Russian government had done great things for the workmen.'[83]
Battsford couldn't remember whether Russell had specifically mentioned revolution, but Johns had said that workers must unite, because a
revolution was coming: 'The socialist party could not stop it; no one
could stop it; it was inevitable.' Although Johns 'made a distinct point of
expressing the hope that bloodshed would not be necessary ... if it came
to a showdown and it had to be fought, he would be willing to fight ...
I think he said he was ready to die.'[84] The speeches 'had a very bad
effect on me,' Battsford insisted, 'and I thought it was a thing the authorities should never have permitted; I thought it was pretty close to openly
advocating rebellion in the country.'[85]

McMurray could bring to the fore a bit of Battsford's newspaperman's
sympathy against censorship, and could satirize Battsford's knee-jerk
reaction to the *Red Flag*, but found it hard to argue successfully against
patriotism, in which shallowness of thought wasn't necessarily a
disadvantage:

McMurray: You think the distribution of the Red Flag itself would
            be a serious matter?
Battsford: I thought it was, but, of course, that is not for me to say.

McMurray: Although you don't know what the contents of it was?
Battsford: The reason I thought it was an insidious thing to be
             handed around was because it was called The Red Flag
             ...

McMurray: You would be opposed to 'The Soviets at Work'?
Battsford: On this ground, that it might tend to show that the
             Soviet system was better than the Democratic system
             and a man so impressed might follow the sentiments set
             out there.
McMurray: And the same thing might be said about Tom Paine and
             Rousseau's work?
Battsford: Well, we have to deal with things that are before us and
             not those old works.

Regarding the Strike leaders' speeches, Battsford's testimony was
nearly immune to cross-examination. McMurray turned Armstrong's
speech back to its focus on war profiteers and showed that Battsford
couldn't summarize Armstrong's complex economic analysis. But
McMurray was less successful in blunting the thrust of Russell's words.
While admitting that Russell hadn't laid out a full program for revolution, Battsford nevertheless insisted, 'I tell you that I think they were of
the impression that a revolution was coming ... and they wanted it to
succeed and they wanted to ensure its success.'[86] McMurray was
reduced to implying that Battsford may have mixed up the various
speeches at the Majestic:

McMurray: Supposing it is alleged that Russell at that meeting did
             not speak on the subject that you credit him with at all,
             is it possible that you are mistaken?
Battsford: I am not infallible, but I am honestly giving my impres-
             sions and recollections.
McMurray: Is it possible that you got these speakers mixed up?
Battsford: ... to the best of my recollection that is what transpired.[87]

When Battsford named Russell as the second speaker, McMurray noted
that Russell had been the third speaker and that he didn't speak on Russia but defended the labour party's platform.[88] McMurray hinted that
Battsford had borrowed his testimony from a newspaper account of the
Walker meeting, not at the Majestic. Not possible, replied Battsford,
because he had never read any account of the Walker meeting. 'That is
singular,' returned McMurray, 'because Russell spoke at that meeting on

the Russian government, I understand.'[89] The only early report on the Majestic meeting, appearing in the *Western Labor News* in January, favours McMurray's version against Battsford, though because the account is condensed, it's still possible that Battsford was telling the truth. But no questioning of Battsford's memory or competence could erase his basic and true points: Russell applauded the Russian Revolution and favoured the Soviet system of government.

One of the last witnesses to go into detail about the Strike leaders' speeches was Harry Daskaluk, the former 'Secret Agent #21' for the North West Mounted Police, whose evidence Andrews had tried to introduce without bringing Daskaluk to the stand. As long as Daskaluk was safely off-stage, Andrews could describe his source as 'very reliable,' and his reports as 'thoroughly trustworthy.'[90] Daskaluk testified that at the Liberty Hall on 2 May Ivens had said that 'he found out the truth that preaching was nothing but a lie and an injustice; that he was, as other preachers, spreading untruth and injustice among the poor working class.' Ivens thought that change was possible without bloodshed, but after Almazoff and Saltzmann of the Young Jewish League contradicted him, he grew less insistent upon non-violence. In Daskaluk's account, Saltzmann said that 'if a man in a factory had a six cylinder car and a nice house he would not give that up without a fight and for the workers to get it they had to fight also ... The other side were preparing machine guns and ammunition, while the workers had nothing on hand, so to obtain anything was impossible without revolution or bloodshed.' Then Almazoff 'pointed out there were many thousands of women and children dying in Canada and the United States yearly from the treatment of barbaric and rotten capitalists,' and concluded, 'Why should I be afraid to kill anyone else, and we should kill them as fast as we can get hold of them.' The audience responded enthusiastically, and 'some applauded very loudly saying he was a real socialist, a revolutionist.' Sensing a change in the wind, Ivens agreed with them, and wished them 'good success.'[91] At the same hall at a later date, Tom Cassidy advocated the One Big Union to the Young Jewish Club and insisted that it would take a fight, a revolution, to overthrow the present system.[92]

Under McMurray's questioning, Daskaluk's reliability shone less brilliantly. McMurray established that Daskaluk was an unemployed twenty-five-year-old Ukrainian immigrant who couldn't remember in what month the RNWMP had hired him as a 'detective' to spy on other immigrants. In Russia he had had a liberal education, but in Canada he could only find work as a labourer, moving from job to job.[93]

McMurray: Why did you go and join the police?

Daskaluk: Because I saw this propaganda was going on and if a
job was open why should I not take it ...
McMurray: You had a certain package you wanted to sell and you
went to the police to dispose of it?
Daskaluk: Not exactly ...

McMurray's attack soon revealed that either Daskaluk was withholding
information or he knew almost nothing specific about the ferment in
Winnipeg's North End.

McMurray: I want to know what you knew.
Daskaluk: I knew the propaganda was going on.
McMurray: What did you know?
Daskaluk: The people were attempting to overthrow ...
McMurray: Who were?
Daskaluk: Foreigners and others. I was more acquainted with the
foreigners.
McMurray: Where?
Daskaluk: In the North End of Winnipeg.
McMurray: Tell us any single thing you remember.
Daskaluk: They were not doing anything but they were speaking a
lot.
McMurray: What were they doing? Name your man first.
Daskaluk: They were agitating.
McMurray: Who? Name a person.
Daskaluk: I did not know any person at that time.
McMurray: You were in Winnipeg for four years?
Daskaluk: I did not know anybody. I know them to look at, but did
not know their names.
McMurray: Did you know anybody in Winnipeg?
Daskaluk: The people I know would not be of value here.
McMurray: Who was your school teacher at that night school?
Daskaluk: Mr Furley.
McMurray: Who were any of your associates at that school?
Daskaluk: That school has nothing to do with this.
McMurray: Who were any of your associates there?
Daskaluk: Mr Furley.
McMurray: He was your teacher; anybody else?
Daskaluk: I do not remember.
McMurray: Can you remember the name of a single one?
Daskaluk: No.
McMurray: How long did you go?

Daskaluk: About three months.

McMurray: And you cannot remember the name of a single person
           you met at that school?

Daskaluk: I did not want to find out their names ...

It's difficult to say whether Daskaluk was protecting revolutionary
friends and compatriots – while offering up Jews such as Almazoff and
Saltzmann – or whether, under the pressure of McMurray's cross-examination, he was growing wary.

McMurray: The only man you met in North Winnipeg that you
           knew in the course of six or seven years was Furley?

Daskaluk: Yes sir.

McMurray: It was rather a lonely existence you were having?

Daskaluk: I know more people, but I did not know their names.

McMurray: An educated man, living five or six years in North Win-
           nipeg and didn't know the names of a single person but
           one?

Daskaluk: No.

McMurray: You are just like Robinson Crusoe, he only knew his
           man Friday for a long time?

Daskaluk: Yes.[94]

It's likely that Daskaluk feared the arrest of his friends and also their
reprisals against him and his family, since he requested transportation to
a safe haven in Bukowina.[95]

Daskaluk may well have told the truth about the speeches, but he was
clearly an unreliable witness, and Andrews's instinct to keep him off-
stage had been sound. Daskaluk had testified about meetings, but had
destroyed all his notes. Perhaps fear had caused him to completely
reconsider both his role and his decision to testify, for at times it almost
appeared as if he wanted to assist the *defence*. When McMurray
rephrased Cassidy's statements about revolution and a fight to mean,
'He was simply organizing the labour forces together for the object of
bringing about better conditions of affairs,' Daskaluk quickly agreed.
Andrews got him to repeat Ivens's assent with the revolutionary sentiments of Almazoff and Saltzmann. Noble hoped for something more
meaty, and asked, 'Well, after [Ivens] came back the second time to
speak did he make any reference at all to the shedding of blood?' But
Daskaluk would add nothing: '[Ivens] didn't exactly make reference to
that, but he agreed with what they asked him before.'[96]

Daskaluk's reluctance appeared most debilitating for the prosecution when McMurray asked him about revolutionary sentiments outside of the two Liberty Hall meetings. Daskaluk revealed that he had continued to track Almazoff, but hadn't heard any other revolutionary statements. Daskaluk agreed with McMurray that for three months he had 'worked night and day going to all the meetings [he] could where the foreigners were gathered together,' but he hadn't brought in enough evidence, and the RNWMP laid him off. Asked McMurray, 'During all that time you were working for them the only evidence you could find was these two meetings against these people ... The only time you could smell tracks [of a revolution] was on the 2nd and 9th of May?' Daskaluk didn't deny it.[97]

With Genevieve Lipsett Skinner, an articulate journalist, Andrews should have had no reason to fear the witness box, and indeed the Citizens' story at first seemed to gain ground during her testimony. Her husband, Robert Curtis Skinner, was advertising manager in 1913 at the Hudson's Bay Company, which Fletcher Sparling, one of the editors of the *Winnipeg Citizen*, began to manage in 1915. In 1920 she would surface as a candidate for the Manitoba Conservative Party.[98] Skinner testified that she interviewed John Queen via telephone on 13 January for a *Montreal Star* article on labour radicalism. Later, she offered the piece to the *Winnipeg Telegram*. The *Telegram*'s news editor may have shown her article to Queen and rewritten it somewhat – editing out the damning quotations[99] – but she revealed that during the interview Queen had 'declared himself in favor of Bolshevism,' and had said that 'the workers were going to take over the Industrial plants.' 'Who,' she returned, 'are the workers? We all work.' Either Skinner, long after the event, had borrowed this line from the *Winnipeg Citizen*, or she had heard and repeated capitalist rejoinders to socialism before her January interview. In either case, one of Skinner's questions elicited a seditious answer. What if the owners objected to the workers taking control? Queen answered, 'They would use force if necessary.'[100]

The testimony seemed very damaging to Queen, the more so when Skinner testified that her shock had convinced her to put the collaborator in all of her stories, Mrs Niblett (whose pen name was Mollie Glen), on the phone to verify Queen's answers. Andrews evidently thought he could get extra mileage out of Skinner's testimony, so he put Niblett in the witness box too. She testified, 'I went to the phone and Alderman Queen was on the phone and I repeated her questions.'[101] According to her, Queen gave the same answers, including his vow to use force if necessary.

McMurray, however, was convinced that Skinner and Niblett were perjuring themselves. The neat dovetailing of the 'two' interviews was suspicious, as were the women's exaggerated and unlikely warnings to Queen that he was on the record – Niblett claiming to have heard Skinner say, 'Of course, Mr Queen, this is for publication and you will be careful.' McMurray suggested that the phone connection had been bad and that there had been no interview – that Skinner had talked to someone else and received Queen's views by hearsay. First, McMurray caught Skinner in a claim that she, though she wasn't on the phone, had heard Queen say to Niblett, 'Mrs Skinner heard me correctly.' Skinner had to back down, but Noble tried to extricate her by saying, 'She does not pretend anything more. There is no suggestion that she was hearing it too.'[102] Skinner was a canny witness; Niblett less so. Niblett claimed that Queen said, 'Had you had been at the meeting in the Walker Theatre the other night, you would have known that there was not a dissenting vote when it was decided to send a letter of congratulation to the Soviets in Russia.' But the Walker meeting took place in the afternoon. If her testimony was false, McMurray surmised, she could not invent consistent answers as fast as he could invent questions. He caught her making up the time sequence. First, Niblett said that she had called Skinner who immediately came into the office at 11:00. To try to maintain consistency with other questions, Niblett changed this, to say, 'I phoned her immediately [at 9:30] and she didn't come until 11.' Niblett clearly hoped that the use of the same word – 'immediately' – would obscure the very different time sequences.

Most crucial to McMurray's dissection of the story was the curious procedure of a second reporter getting on the phone to verify the first reporter's story. Niblett could easily repeat, sometimes word for word, what the two women had claimed that Queen had said. But McMurray tried to get Niblett to describe the mechanics of how she had 'repeated' Skinner's questions to Queen.

McMurray: You told my learned friend you repeated her questions.
Niblett: Certainly I repeated the questions that were on the
                    paper. I am not supposed to remember them.
McMurray: There were no questions on the paper?
Niblett: There were notes on the paper.
McMurray: But there were no questions on the paper.
Niblett: Just notes.
McMurray: What do you mean by saying you repeated her questions?
Niblett: I heard her questions.
McMurray: And you repeated them from memory?
Niblett: Yes at the moment …

McMurray: You told my learned friend you were repeating the ques-
            tions to him and you told me a moment ago you read the
            notes and were repeating it from the notes in front of
            you. Now what was on that note, the first thing you
            read?

Niblett: I tell you I cannot remember, I simply interviewed
            Alderman Queen along the lines as I heard Mrs Skinner
            …

McMurray: Well then were you or were you not reading these notes
            as you asked Alderman Queen the questions?
Niblett: I had the notes before me, I suppose.
McMurray: Were you reading them?
Niblett: I suppose they were in front of me, I really cannot tell.
McMurray: You cannot tell whether you were reading it or not?
Niblett: I do not know whether I went off on my own to inter-
            view him, I could not tell you.
McMurray: Did you repeat his answers to Mrs Skinner?
Niblett: I did.
McMurray: She wrote them again.
Niblett: I do not know.
McMurray: Try and recollect.
Niblett: I would not say that …

McMurray established that because Niblett had Skinner's notes, Skinner
couldn't be reading them to verify Queen's answers.

McMurray: And still you were talking for the very purpose of veri-
            fying what she said?
Niblett: Yes.
McMurray: What means of verification had you?
Niblett: I could not tell you if she was taking notes.
McMurray: That is remarkable.[103]

The most likely reconstruction of events seems to point to what any
public figure must face in the media, especially a politician who takes a
controversial stance: two journalists, unable to get the necessary interview for their story on labour radicalism, rely upon hearsay from someone who heard Queen speak at the Walker meeting. The journalists
expect their piece to pay and to vanish, but an enterprising prosecutor
named Andrews gets wind of the story. The last thing that the journalists

can admit is that they got no interview and fudged the quotations. When the actual trials came, Andrews would drop both Skinner and Niblett from his roster of witnesses.

Andrews also steered the hearing towards the Citizens' old story of suffering babies, calling to the stand W.S. Thompson, manager of the Consumers Ice Company. He could testify that ice was not a luxury but 'absolutely essential' to Winnipeggers: 'You would have thought so if you had seen the hundreds of people who came to the plant with their automobiles to get ice and with the calls we had from sick people and people who didn't have any way of getting ice. We had to deliver ice to them in some way.'[104] Under cross-examination by McMurray, Thompson pointed to children living in the upper floors of apartment buildings: 'The milk for the children in these flats could not be kept without you had ice' [*sic*]. Andrews wanted to catch the Strike leaders in the act of usurping the functions of constituted authority or, at the very least, creating a Common Nuisance, but McMurray threw the suffering-baby narrative back at Andrews and implied that it was the Citizens who conspired to prevent a settlement, certainly in ice distribution. He reminded Thompson that the secretary of the Teamsters' Union (representing Thompson's employees) had offered Thompson a contract to sign: 'Why wouldn't you do that? You knew these little children were dying for want of ice – Did you want to let them die?' At first Thompson protested that he wouldn't sign the contract because he hadn't read it over. But it soon came out that he had had no intention of signing it. While he acknowledged that the Strike Committee was prepared to respond positively to requests for ice, he wouldn't sign because the Strike Committee would control distribution.[105] When Thompson's employees returned to work throughout the Strike, no strikers intimidated them. With such cross-examination, McMurray could show that the Strike Committee conspired less, the Citizens more.

Make your point through a policeman or an official. More effective for the Citizens than some of the minor figures that Andrews had corralled was an eager and able witness, Mayor Charles Gray.[106] Even though the Citizens' machinations fleetingly appeared in Gray's testimony, through him Andrews could develop a convincing story of labour's attack on constituted authority. Gray testified that the 1918 contracts satisfied union demands and that civic workers formally promised not to strike 'until grievances were made the subject of an inquiry and a report.' Despite all this, most civic employees flocked to the Strike. Although the police officers hadn't walked out, they had voted to Strike, and when

Gray had asked for clarification, their spokesperson, Sergeant Living-stone, confirmed that if the Strike Committee ordered the police off the job, they'd go.[107] Gray gave evidence of intimidation complaints, and of grocery stores and restaurants forced to close due to fear and lack of sup-plies.[108]

In cross-examination, McMurray got Gray to admit that workers had a right to withdraw their labour. Judge Noble, however, chimed in, 'What would you say about their quitting work where they have a con-tract?' and Gray quite properly added that workers in public utilities had an extra moral obligation. The walkout by the fire brigade put the city in jeopardy, especially during the fire beside the Hudson's Bay Com-pany.[109]

Water, another contentious issue, provided less ammunition for the Citizens' case, since the Strike Committee hadn't cut off that public util-ity, only limited pressure to the first floors of buildings. Nevertheless, babies wailed against the Strike again, as Gray testified that the Strike Committee 'considered 30 lbs was enough pressure for domestic water service, which, of course, was ridiculous and absurd, because the pres-sure was not high enough to reach above the second story and it created great hardship on many citizens of Winnipeg, especially on mothers who had no water for their babies, or for other purposes.'[110] More damning in terms of sedition, if less likely to arouse the emotions, were the roles of city councillors Queen and Heaps. Asked by Andrews whether the two had supported the use of volunteers to man civic utilities, Gray offered a withering denunciation: 'Alderman Heaps and Alderman Queen had several times stated that any men working these utilities were scabs, were strike breakers; in fact, they called the council strike break-ers.'[111] Later, when the City wanted to instruct the engineer to raise the water pressure, Queen and Heaps voted against the measure.[112]

Milk and bread weren't public utilities, but their supply was crucial. Gray began to describe a meeting between council members and repre-sentatives of the Strike Committee on the subject, but Andrews inter-rupted so that he and the Citizens would get proper accolades:

Andrews: Make it quite clear, which was first in point of time. Do
           you recollect certain citizens coming to see you?
Gray: Yes
Andrews: You remember my coming to see you for one?
Gray: Yes ... The first discussion I had upon that was with your-
           self and one or two other gentlemen and shortly after that
           some of the strike committee came over from the Labor
           Temple and discussed this, about half past eleven.[113]

The Strike Committee proposed ration cards, 'but,' added Gray, 'there was strenuous opposition ... I remember you yourself were very much incensed with the idea and also the members of council, and finally it was decided to have the committee go ahead with the delivery of milk and bread, cutting out cream.'[114] Whenever the Strike Committee had to have private consultations during these joint meetings, Queen would leave his fellow councillors to closet himself with the strikers.[115]

Andrews and Coyne pointed at other symptoms of the usurpation of the City's constituted authority, the signs placed on the bread and milk trucks – 'Operating by permission of the strike committee.'[116] Howard Rosling, who rented out rowboats on the Assiniboine, was ordered to close his business. Although he applied at the Labor Temple for permission to remain open, the Strike Committee, functioning as a quasi-governmental organization, denied permission.[117] Sanitary inspectors stayed on the job, but only on authority of the Strike Committee.[118] Ben Blume, manager of the Famous Players film exchange, testified that theatres operated under the Strike Committee's permits, while Andrew Ferguson disclosed that the Exhibitors association, of which he was secretary-treasurer, had submitted to political censorship, pledging not to show films to which labour objected.[119]

The Citizens' story of a struggle for constitutional power was nicely illustrated by Gray's version of the meeting in which Queen had challenged his authority. Gray downplayed his own grandstanding: 'The question came up of constituted authority and Alderman Queen stated that he didn't want to hear of constituted authority; so I said that as Mayor of Winnipeg constituted authority was vested in me and I would see that it was upheld with the dignity due to that position, and alderman Queen told me to sit down, which, of course, I refused to do.'[120] Some 'citizens' demanded special police to augment the police force in dealing with reports of intimidation, but when Gray floated this proposal, quite within the City's constitutional jurisdiction, the strikers threatened the withdrawal of the regular force.[121] Later, after the dismissal of the regular force and the 10 June riot, the Specials were kept off the streets because the City feared the strikers. Clearly, the Strike Committee, and not constituted authority, controlled the streets.[122]

McMurray counterattacked by shifting responsibility for the deepening crisis to the Citizens. Gray conceded that the Strike occurred because employers would not recognize the Metal Trades Council.[123] Yet he qualified his answer, placing it more in line with the Citizens' narrative by describing the Strike as part of a more general malaise: 'like the "flu," it had to come. I am convinced that nothing could have stopped the strike from coming on from what I saw subsequently.'[124] Nevertheless, because the Citizens (especially early on) had skirted around the somewhat bombastic Gray, he was vulnerable in small ways to McMurray's counter-story of a Citizens' conspiracy. Gray explained that initially his attempts to bring the ironmasters back to the table seemed promising. Less than a week into the Strike, they had agreed to talk about a negotiated solution,[125] yet in their 21 May meeting at City Hall, something had changed their attitude. They suddenly told him that 'they had nothing whatever to say at the present time,' that 'they would not negotiate at all and that the matter was in the hands of the Citizens Committee.'[126]

Since Andrews, in the immigration hearings, had made much of the leaders' *secret* ties to Bolshevism, McMurray shone a light at the conspiracy on the other side of the table. Cross-examination showed that the Citizens had led Gray to believe that they were attempting to stay 'neutral' in the negotiations. The Citizens had agreed to meet with the Running Trades union officers, though Gray was unaware if any meeting took place. He seemed surprised to hear McMurray quote a letter in which Mr Lyall of Manitoba Bridge and Iron Works told an MP that Citizens had convinced the ironmasters to avoid all negotiations and settlements until the General Strike had been called off.[127] McMurray also asked Gray about how those 'citizens' had represented themselves early in the Strike:

McMurray: Was my learned friend one of these men?
Gray: Yes.
McMurray: Whom did he say he was representing? Did he say he was representing any association of people?
Gray: No.
McMurray: He came as a citizen?
Gray: He distinctly stated that he was representing no one excepting in so far as a thoughtful citizen would help anyone who was suffering from lack of bread or milk, mentioning particularly the women and children and not the men, because they could take care of themselves.[128]

It came out that on the first or second day of the Strike, the Citizens had asked Gray to join their organization. He had declined, saying that he must represent all citizens.[129]

McMurray tried to get Gray to admit that the Citizens had been the main movers behind the firing of the police and the hiring of the Specials. As far as Gray knew, however, the Citizens hadn't asked for the discharge of the force.[130] Yet when Gray was asked about martial law, his carefully worded reply was revealing.

McMurray: Did the Citizens' Committee of One Thousand urge
            upon you to put military law in force in Winnipeg?
Gray: No, not as a committee.
McMurray: Did many members of the Committee of One Thousand
            urge upon you to put military law in force?
Gray: Not many.[131]

On the issue of violence in the streets, Gray sided strongly with the Citizens. He acknowledged that for a long time during the Strike the city was relatively quiet, but, having been bullied himself, he was in no mood to pat the strikers on the back: 'There was a certain amount of intimidation going on, which is a mild form of terrorism, to my mind.'[132] Gray related his own attempt to intervene in the arrest of Major Howard, saying, 'This mob closed around me and started to go for me to tear my clothes and I had to defend myself. There was a friend with me and he prevented me from going down on the pavement.' The attackers, he testified, 'looked like what we, for the want of a better term, call aliens.'[133]

Other witnesses confirmed Gray's testimony about intimidation, though their experience varied. Managers of companies such as Dominion Arctic and Ice Express testified that their employees feared coming back to work or working outside of the parameters set by the Strike Committee, but the managers could point to very few direct threats and couldn't point to any violence. Under Hyman's cross-examination, William Gordon of Dominion Express revealed that six of his employees had expressed fear, yet he was unable to name any of them.[134] Mike Stodnick, a cook at the Olympia Restaurant, gave evidence of threats, but not of violence. One evening a gang of strikers appeared in the back lane and taunted him, 'You scab, come out.' When he got home, his brother-in-law, a striking CPR mechanic, advised him to stop working and told him that a returned soldier awaited him at the Salter Bridge, intending to kill him. Stodnick moved, but continued to work, and had no trouble during the Strike.[135]

The only report of direct violence came from Robert 'Ginger' Snook, an aged and wealthy eccentric. He was a perennial candidate for City Council, and if John Queen were to run for mayor, Snook said that he'd consider running against Queen. Contracted by the City during the Strike, his garbage and scavenging rigs were assailed by gangs, in one case by up to three hundred men. The strikers forced his drivers to unhitch the horses. Then the strikers chased the horses and drivers home, overturned the wagons, stole the nuts from the wheels, and broke the reach. 'I went into Jerry Robinson's and collared a nice little baseball bat,' bragged the eighty-six-year-old bantam, 'and if I had got there I could have used it as well as any man in this town.' Having trouble hiring drivers after that, he drove himself, and was accosted by returned soldiers. The event proved less satisfactory than the boast. He defended himself with a walking stick, but four soldiers pinned him onto the ground, and were ready to put the boots to 'the old son of a bitch,' when his employee Jack arrived with a pitchfork to rescue him. McMurray treated Snook facetiously, suggesting, 'You should have been one of the special constables,' and saying that the unidentified thugs who attacked Snook's rigs could, for all anyone knew, have been members of the Citizens' Committee. Snook said he didn't know.[136] On some jobsites, workers could continue working without interference during the Strike, but despite McMurray's mocking tone, in other places – especially when mobs were on the prowl – violence lurked just beneath the surface. And occasionally, as in the case of Snook, the strikers were violent. That the violence rarely occurred was more a result of the drivers giving in to intimidation than of the strikers' self-control. Several operators of filling stations, somewhat more prudent than Snook, were threatened by pickets sent out by the Strike Committee. Alexander Fraser, of Prairie City Oil, said that a crowd of fifty men ordered him to close the station and get off the property in an hour. When he didn't comply, they closed down his pump and said, 'Here, you had better "get."'[137] Mackenzie, for the defence, asked, 'Did you think they were serious or merely endeavoring to persuade you to close down?' Fraser replied, 'It didn't look very promising to me.'[138]

Next to Mayor Gray, the most important figure at City Hall during the crisis had been Alderman John Sparling, chair of the Police Commission, and of the City's Fire, Water and Light Committee, and a close associate of the Citizens. McMurray tried to point to that connection, but Sparling disputed that, since he had kept up the façade of neutrality even as he ferried the Citizens' proposals to Council and to the Police Commission:

McMurray: Do you know if the citizens committee had claimed to themselves that they were handling the situation of distributing the milk?

Sparling: No.

McMurray: Were you a member of the citizens committee?
Sparling: You mean the Committee of One Thousand?
McMurray: Well, they called it that.
Sparling: Well, I had nothing to do with that; I was hardly in the
            building.[139]

Andrews used Sparling effectively to relate the story of Strike Committee's control over the police, showing that even though the police had agreed to a contract with a no-strike-or-lockout clause, Sparling received notice on 14 May that the police would strike at 11:00 the next morning. The Strike Committee asked them to remain on duty and they never did walk out, yet one couldn't fault Sparling's conclusion: 'We might not be able to rely on the regular police force.' When the question of 'special police' came up on the first day of the Strike, representatives of the Strike Committee – Ernest Robinson, James Winning, and 'Beech' (actually Harry Veitch) – had threatened that the regular police would walk out if special constables were hired.[140] Clearly, the extra-constitutional Strike Committee controlled the city's police. And between the riot on 10 June and Bloody Saturday, the Special Police didn't have control of Winnipeg's streets.[141]

The Strike Committee's claim to direct the police was confirmed by a highly credible witness, Crown Prosecutor Robert Graham. In a discussion between City officials and Strike leaders, Graham asked, 'Suppose the oil companies can carry on business with non-union labor?' Russell smiled and said, 'They have a right to do that if they can.' As for any trouble that might result, Russell pointed to the fact that the police were still on duty and 'under orders from the chief.' Graham wasn't so sure, 'Are they?' Russell didn't need much prodding, 'Well probably the word "orders" should not be used there, but they were permitted to continue work, they were not called out.' Taking the hint, Graham remarked, 'You can call them out.' 'Certainly,' replied Russell, 'at a moment's notice.'[142]

Other of Sparling's claims were less trustworthy. He said, 'We felt that we had to have more police protection. We had demands from the Bread people, the Milk people and demands to protect the Fire halls and to protect citizens and we thought we had not enough men.'[143] In fact, of course, it was not police numbers but their ideological orientation that was the problem.

There were fewer Specials than regular police officers, and the Police Commission didn't receive a lot more complaints than usual in the first month of the Strike – six rather than the usual three – but the complaints came from the *Winnipeg Telegram*, from the *Winnipeg Tribune*, and from leading hardware merchants, the Ashdowns. Winnipeg's businesspeople were worried, and from them came the call for Specials. McMurray pressed Sparling on why the Police Commission drew up a new contract that included the contentious loyalty oath. Sparling at first said, 'Something had to be done to reassure the general public that the police intended to carry out their duties,' but he soon admitted that the new contract was intended mainly 'to prevent sympathetic strikes.' McMurray established that the City, not the strikers, had broken the contract:

McMurray: As a matter of fact, the city locked them out?
Sparling: They were dismissed.
McMurray: The men kept their contract, the city did not.
Sparling: I would not think so. I would think the situation arose
            was not governed by the agreement.[144]

In addition to this equivocation, Sparling was forced to admit that there had been very little trouble in the city before the Specials were put on the streets; a lot of trouble after.

Hard upon this testimony, Andrews and McMurray exploded at one another. McMurray suggested that the inept leader of the Specials, Major Lyall, may have been brought to Winnipeg by Senator Robertson. Andrews immediately leapt up, saying, 'My learned friend should not make such a suggestion, because I happen to know there is absolutely no truth in it.' McMurray snapped back that if Andrews had anything to say he could go on the stand and say it. It's difficult to tell whether McMurray was goading Andrews or whether, after McMurray's implication that the Police Commission (and by extension, the Citizens) had behaved dishonourably, Andrews needed to jump on any opening to attack McMurray's honour. Andrews was certainly very touchy about the Specials' legitimacy: in the sedition charge information, he had prominently featured the *Western Labor News* article calling them 'thugs.' Furious, Andrews turned to the traditional language with which throughout the Strike he and the Citizens had tried to put the strikers on the wrong side of a class and cultural divide: 'Defendants' counsel should at least be a gentleman. Nothing could be more ungentlemanly, more cowardly than to make a suggestion that would reflect upon a Minister of the Crown when he is not here.' McMurray, familiar with the code and not willing to be out-insulted, took up his former employer's glove, 'The proper answer to an outbreak like that would be a slap across the mouth. I am really astonished.' 'Don't be too fresh, young man,' retorted Andrews, reminding everyone of the difference in age between the labour leaders and the more established members of the business elite. 'We've had bluffers in this court before.'[145]

When bakery owner Ed Parnell took the stand, and admitted that he was a member of the Citizens, McMurray greeted the revelation with great irony: 'Well, that is good; you are the first we have met.' Parnell considered his work as a Citizen to be a service to Winnipeg, and he was eager, unlike many Citizens, to speak of the Committee's role in the Strike. At McMurray's prodding, Parnell even began to name Citizen names: Mr Botterell and Mr Andrews, A.K. Godfrey, Mr Crossin, Mr Pitblado, Mr Sweatman, Mr Adams, Mr Harry Agnew.[146]

McMurray saw a chance to expand the story of a counter-conspiracy by the Citizens to incite race hatred, to make false claims of revolution, and to prevent a negotiated settlement. Andrews tried to block this while pretending not to: 'I have no objection to this evidence, but it cannot be relevant and it takes up time.' Noble was inclined to agree with Andrews, but McMurray fought to keep the Citizens in the spotlight: 'The dealings of the Citizens Committee are exceedingly important. They asked the Mayor to use violence against the strikers. If they were the fomenters of the trouble that occurred surely that is pertinent to the inquiry. I think it would be absolutely unfair if we are not permitted to investigate at this stage the actions of the Citizens Committee. We say it is a misnomer, that it was never a *citizens committee*: that they did not represent the citizens at all, but that they represented the Capitalistic interests here.' Noble allowed McMurray to proceed but without naming 'private' citizens.[147]

Through Parnell, McMurray tried to make several forays into the inner workings of the Citizens, but each time he was stymied. If Andrews allowed Parnell to take the stand because he wouldn't reveal where any bodies lay and would present the benign side of the Citizens, Andrews had calculated well. McMurray could elicit little more than the public version of the Citizens that had been broadcast in the *Winnipeg Citizen*. In Parnell's account, the Citizens cared very little about who would win the Strike, but busied themselves entirely with keeping City services running: 'Throughout the whole of the Citizens' committee's meetings, and I say, I was practically at almost every one of them, I never heard any discussion as to the merits ... of the labour question, the labour situation. They took no part directly or indirectly in that matter, but simply tried to bring about a condition that would prevent bloodshed and keep the utilities going.' McMurray asked, 'Where did you get the name Citizens Committee? I am a citizen here and was never invited to it.' Parnell countered with the party line, that the Citizens were 'simply a continuation' of the previous year's Committee of One Hundred, only this time they were 10,000 strong. In every issue with the slightest possibility for controversy, Parnell professed a lack of knowledge. He didn't think there was a membership list to verify the number 10,000, didn't know who edited the *Winnipeg Citizen*, and didn't even know that it was published on the *Telegram*'s presses, but he thought that somewhere there might have been 'a list kept of the actual executive.'[148]

Andrews had blamed the Strike Committee members for a riot that happened while they were in jail – they 'started the fire.' For McMurray, it proved much more difficult to discover who bore responsibility for whatever it was that the Citizens had started. Had the Citizens' racist ads been approved by the Committee? Parnell said no. From where, then, had these ads crept into the *Free Press*, the *Tribune*, and the *Telegram*? Permitted by authority of whom? Parnell had no idea. He had attended Citizens' Committee meetings regularly and no one had discussed the ads. Stonewalled, McMurray tried at least to call one Citizen to account, and he asked Parnell, 'Don't you think there was a danger of precipitating injuries to the foreign citizens of the country?' Not really: in Parnell's mind, the graveness of the situation called for a response that would counteract the threat. McMurray suggested that the real intent of the ads was to put returned soldiers and aliens at each other's throats. He pressed Parnell, 'Do you think the object of it was to turn loose a body of men upon the alien and drive him out?' Parnell, however, was on the side of the angels, ergo, the hate-fuelled ads must be angelic too, and he answered, 'No, to try and prevent that kind of thing. The whole aim and object of the Citizens Committee was to prevent trouble.'[149] Parnell left the Citizens in the best of their possible worlds: their racist ads had been defended, but no one was any wiser about where they had come from. When McMurray pointed out that those injured and arrested in the riot were almost all English-speaking, Judge Noble, more Catholic than the pope when it came to the Citizens' propaganda, rushed to Parnell's side and insisted that 'the real rioters, or the worst rioters, were not caught at all; those on the roofs and places like that.'[150] McMurray tried to bait Parnell with the Citizens' effective ability to take over the reins of the federal government on the alien question. Parnell replied first with platitudes; and when those proved double-edged, he fell back on denial:

McMurray: Don't you think that was the duty of the government, to take care of the alien question?

Parnell: Unfortunately, there was too much government and not enough common sense.

McMurray: It was the intention of the citizens committee to take the matter out of the hands of the government and deal with the alien themselves?

Parnell: No, not at all. Cut that out; there is nothing in that at all.[151]

Later in the hearings, to legitimize the Citizens' anti-alien stance, Andrews invited the cartoonist Battsford to carp about aliens. Most of those at the Majestic Theatre meeting, Battsford explained, were aliens: 'That was the surprising feature of the meeting to me, that a man of foreign extraction should be allowed to get up in our city and talk to those of foreign extraction and incite unconstitutional methods of obtaining certain resolutions; I thought it was wrong and that the authorities were lax in not preventing it.'[152]

The political *meaning* of Parnell's responses – signifying the Citizens' strategic retreat into 'privacy'– soon became apparent. McMurray got no closer to the castle when he probed the Citizens' warning to the ironmasters not to negotiate until the sympathetic strike had ended. Parnell testified that the ironmasters weren't part of the Citizens Committee, but when confronted with Mayor Gray's admission that the ironmasters wouldn't settle until the Citizens' go-ahead, Parnell again knew nothing. This was completely implausible: one can only conclude Parnell was perjuring himself. Did 'the graveness of the situation' call for perjury? McMurray tried to corner him into saying that if the ironmasters blamed the Citizens for preventing a settlement, then the ironmasters must be liars. But in his reply, Parnell tiptoed across the razor's edge between public and private that the Citizens as a whole continued to walk, allowing him to convince himself that he wasn't committing perjury. The warning, he said, 'might have been done by private individuals but not by the committee.' It was an ingenious equivocation: given their connections, the Citizens could repeatedly manipulate the public sphere, to the point of sabotaging mediation, effecting legislation, and making arrests, but whenever they were questioned, they scooted back into the shell of 'private' citizenship. It's not clear whether Andrews had coached Parnell or whether Parnell had hit upon this solution to the question of responsibility on his own, but Parnell recognized the effectiveness of the response. When McMurray asked why the Citizens, so intent merely upon preserving City services, had had to closet themselves with the federal minister of labour, Sen. Robertson, and whether the Citizens had asked Robertson to use force, Parnell fell back again upon the public/private distinction. 'No,' he maintained, there wasn't a request for force, but, covering himself, he added, 'If it was done it would be by private individuals.' With respect to such public issues, the distinction was absurd – Andrews would have roared had a Strike leader claimed that he applauded the Russian Revolution only as a private individual. The Citizens had also met with the Manitoba cabinet, said Parnell, but with no objective other than 'to get the thing wound up.'[153]

Late in his testimony, Parnell did forget himself slightly, and fell briefly into the more authoritarian discourse that the Citizens had used to get the ironmasters onside, a discourse that didn't mesh so harmoniously with 'private citizen.' McMurray returned to the question of whether the Citizens had tried to settle the dispute between the ironmasters and the strikers, and Parnell responded, 'No, that could not be done. The thing had gone too far.'[154] Clearly, Parnell lied when he claimed not to know about the no-negotiation policy. If the Citizens hadn't lobbied the ironmasters, had limited themselves to supplying City services, there would have been no need to take any stand on negotiations between the strikers and the ironmasters, much less to pronounce that the dispute was incapable of settlement.

But this wasn't enough of an opening for McMurray, and in the end, faced with all of Parnell's sweetness and light, McMurray had to give up in disgust. In the fall of 1920, Parnell would be rewarded for his role in the Strike when 'a Citizens' Committee' chose him to run for mayor (after several aldermen, including Frank Fowler, declined).[155] But after Parnell's smokescreen testimony at the preliminary hearing, McMurray couldn't let him go without leaving a knife in him, and, by implication, in the Citizens, saying, 'You don't think any good thing can come out of Nazareth, do you?' Parnell had won his courtroom battle against McMurray, and the Citizens had won the Strike, but Parnell shouldn't call himself a Christian. Parnell felt the thrust keenly: 'I have just as big an interest in my fellow men as you have and I am only telling what I believe to be the truth.'[156]

The only other witness at the preliminary hearing who admitted being a Citizen, grain broker and vice-president of the Grain Exchange John Botterell, stayed Parnell's course.[157] The Citizens didn't favour business or labour, but existed merely 'to back up constituted authority' and 'to maintain public utilities.' Yet of specifics, Botterell revealed little. He had no knowledge of the Citizens trying to settle the Strike. He had no knowledge of any communication with the ironmasters. He had never heard any Citizen say that the Strike must be defeated. He had heard that there was a Press Committee, but had only a 'hazy' idea of it, and in any case, he didn't think that the published anti-alien ads could create trouble. The most that McMurray could get out of him was that there had been a Citizens' executive of between forty and sixty members.[158] Of the Citizens meeting with Sen. Robertson in Fort William Botterell was aware, but, unlike Parnell, he wasn't going to name names.[159] And yet, after all the camouflage, when McMurray asked, 'I suppose your affairs were not conducted in secret?' Botterell responded, 'We had nothing to hide.' Rewriting history, he recalled that the Citizens' deliberations had been completely open: 'Any citizen who wanted to come in and sit in

our deliberations was welcome.'[160] In fact, however, since the meetings
weren't announced, any lower-case citizen, lacking a personal invitation, might have found it a challenge to discover their time and location.

Of the Strike Committee, Botterell had more precise knowledge. At a
City Hall meeting about the bread and milk supply, the Strike Committee proposed to supply bread and milk through 'the labor temple,' an
idea that Botterell had strongly opposed for practical reasons. Eventually, the Strike Committee made 'a tentative gentlemen's agreement' to
allow bread and milk delivery for the Strike's duration. When, some
time later, Botterell heard that bread and milk were again to be cut off,
he approached James Winning to ask whether the gentlemen's agreement was going to be broken, and Winning said, 'Yes, we are considering whether we will turn the screws on tighter or not.'[161] This was
enough, in Botterell's mind, to show the level of honour one could
expect from the Strike leaders.

Throughout the preliminary hearing, very little that reflected ill on the
Citizens came to light. Andrews's orchestration – from the arrests to the
choice of witnesses – combined with Noble's piety towards the Citizens, ensured that the focus remained almost entirely on the Strike
Committee. The evidence most damning to the Citizens made only the
briefest appearance. When McMurray asked Crown Prosecutor Robert
Graham whether he had been consulted about the arrests of the Strike
leaders, Graham admitted that he hadn't, and he didn't even know
under whose authorization the arrests had been made.[162] But the lead
wasn't pursued, and given Noble's willingness to continue the immigration hearings despite the missing warrants, a protest wouldn't have
made any difference.

On 12 August, Andrews closed the case for 'the Crown,' and McMurray had no plans to submit evidence on behalf of the defendants. He did
note, however, that the preliminary hearing was 'an unusual proceeding,' because every trial that he had been involved in 'had always been
conducted under the Attorney general's department.'[163] 'I suppose,' he
said to Noble, 'on the evidence that has been given you will find they
will be committed for trial?' 'Yes,' responded Noble. Hinting sardon-
ically at judicial biases (including his own) in favour of the Citizens, he
added, 'They are very anxious for a *jury* trial' [emphasis added].[164] Of
course, a lot would depend upon who controlled the process of jury
selection ...

13

Poor Harry Daskaluk:
The Settling of Accounts

1 – 16 August

Even while the preliminary hearing was still going on, the immigration
hearings resumed, Andrews, Noble, and McMurray all playing simultaneously, like chess champions, at several tables at once. Andrews would
probably have preferred less of a grind, but the schedule – one thing at
least – was beyond his control. First up, again, Sam Blumenberg. He had
tried to remain silent, but under Andrews's and Noble's pressure he had
given in, testifying that he had favoured socialism but not revolution. To
counter this, Andrews brought in more witnesses who heard revolution
in his Majestic speech. Instead of saying that Blumenberg's speech had
incited his followers to violence (which, had it happened, would have
been evidence of sedition), Andrews again floated the notion that it was
Blumenberg's fault that returned soldiers had rioted against aliens and
had ransacked his business. Andrews, with much of the preliminary
hearing and a number of the immigration hearings under his belt, now
had a fuller idea of what sort of story he wanted to tell. Either he coached
the cartoonist Battsford well, or Battsford intuitively understood what
was required of him, because his testimony mythologized the organization of the Citizens:

Andrews: What was the likely result of that speech upon the
           returned soldiers?
Battsford: Well, if I can be accepted as a sample of the effect it
           would have on any loyal man, returned soldier or other-
           wise, it would undoubtedly arouse his feelings; it would
           make him feel like organizing something as a counter-
           move.

Andrews: Can you say what effect it did have, from something that
            occurred after?
Battsford: ... It had the effect with the returned soldiers that it was
            their right, if the authorities did not take this matter in
            hand, to take it in hand themselves; and if there were men
            organizing the alien or unpatriotic element of this country,
            that they had the right to do what they could to destroy
            that organization.[1]

Despite articulating this 'right to destroy,' Battsford was independent
enough to express, under Hyman's cross-examination, unease about how
the returned soldiers had targeted aliens. Battsford, following behind the
rioters on 26 and 27 January, watched as a crowd of five hundred or
more soldiers smashed some places, beat up one man, and marched to
the Swift Canadian plant, where they demanded that aliens be handed
over.[2] When the returned men called a second time at Swift, managers
proposed that the aliens would be fired if returned men would take the
jobs. They declined the offer, saying that the plant was 'not fit for a
white man to work in.' Battsford commented, 'To tell you the truth, I
was not very sympathetic with what the body was doing ... I didn't think
it was the constitutional way to do it. If they wanted the aliens out, I
thought they could do it some other way.'[3] Battsford's qualms of conscience didn't make him the friend of aliens. He understood the soldiers'
actions because, as he said, 'You could hardly expect the alien to throw
up his job. He is not built that way.'[4] Hyman managed to get Battsford
to agree that the Briton and the Canadian might not be built that way
either. Of course, Battsford's qualms didn't seriously conflict with
Andrews's story: one could sympathize with the soldiers' outrage but
proceed against aliens such as Blumenberg 'constitutionally' – for
example, by changing the Immigration Act and holding immigration
hearings.

At Solomon Almazoff's hearing, Harry Daskaluk was trotted out again
as Andrews's main card. In addition to the testimony that Almazoff had
declared his readiness to 'kill anybody ... as fast as we can get hold of
them,'[5] Daskaluk also attributed to him the statement that 'revolution is
impossible without bloodshed, because the workers have no guns or
ammunition and the other side are preparing machine guns and rifles and
all other weapons.'[6] At the preliminary hearing, however, Daskaluk had
attributed the same statement to another speaker, named Saltzmann:
'The other side were [sic] preparing machine guns and ammunition,
while the workers had nothing on hand, so to obtain anything was

impossible without revolution or bloodshed.'[7] Probably because of the sheer volume of testimony, the defence didn't notice this strange discrepancy.

What the defence did notice was Daskaluk's limited, heavily accented English, and Hyman brought to the stand Fred Kaplan, the twenty-year-old secretary of the Young Jewish Labor League, who insisted that the discussion involving Almazoff 'was not a discussion whether we should not shed blood.' Rather, Almazoff and the other young Jews were wondering why Ivens had come to the *workers*, 'telling us not to cause bloodshed.' 'The workers, not having any ammunition or guns, did not cause the bloodshed'; Ivens should instead 'go among the capitalists and preach co-operation' there.[8] In order to show the difficulties that Daskaluk would have had in understanding Almazoff, Hyman went through a list of words that Almazoff had used, and asked Daskaluk to define them:

Hyman: Can you tell me the meaning of the word 'degradation'?
Daskaluk: It means to degrade somebody.
Hyman: What does that mean?
Daskaluk: Well, putting them out of a position. Supposing you were
           lieutenant and you were degraded, you would not be lieu-
           tenant any more, you would be corporal ...
Hyman: What is the meaning of the word 'amicable'?
Daskaluk: I don't know.
Hyman: What is the meaning of 'animosity'?
Daskaluk: Animosity? I don't know.
Hyman: What is the meaning of the word 'pangs'?

At this point Judge Noble interrupted the cross-examination, and gave Daskaluk the benefit of the doubt, suggesting that he sometimes caught the glimmer of a meaning, but had difficulty articulating it. Daskaluk, not wanting to disappoint Noble, was thus encouraged to make an attempt at 'pangs': 'Well, there is a word "pangs" in the Roumanian [*sic*]. It means "uplift."'[9] On Hyman led Daskaluk, through a forest of words, most of which Daskaluk didn't know.

At the end of November, when Russell's trial began, Daskaluk would be nowhere to be seen. Defence counsel, however, was eager to cross-examine such a witness, since he had, after all, been a prime card against the Strike leaders during the preliminary hearing, and his name was on the back of the indictment.[10] Andrews refused to produce him: his evidence wasn't required and 'they could not rely on this man.'[11] Edward Bird, Russell's lawyer, revealed that Daskaluk had been promised $500 for his evidence. Bird supplied correspondence in which George Ireland, a relief officer from Vancouver, wrote to G.B. Clarke of the Social Service Council in Winnipeg, and related that Daskaluk, 'his wife and infant child, three weeks old, Ukrainians, are destitute and a public charge in this city.' Relief officers in Winnipeg contacted Colonel Starnes, who reported that 'this man gave evidence for the Crown, and was promised $500 ... and ... as soon as the case is finished they will give him the balance.' Starnes agreed to advance Daskaluk an additional $100.[12] Bird also produced a 1 November letter, addressed to 'My Dearest friend.' In it, Daskaluk himself complained, 'Today at the Court Room I was told that they will deport me if I will not go to Winnipeg. I said alright. You know they only gave me one cup of tea without sugar in 24 hrs. Rotten system and barbaric treatment they use for me. But my brother, I have promised to myself to stay where I am. Even if they starve me to death, I one done wrong, being forced, but not again' [sic]. He signed off, 'Yours for socialism, and better Rights.'[13] 'I one done wrong': Had Daskaluk lied under oath for money? Or had he told the truth, the 'wrong' being his willingness to testify against a compatriot for money? The answer may never be clear. What is certain is that Andrews's 'very reliable' and 'thoroughly trustworthy'[14] Secret Service Agent #21 proved to be an unreliable and reluctant witness.

Taking the stand himself, Almazoff testified that he had not addressed any Strike meetings, though Andrews was ready to debate whether Almazoff's ten-minute 'question' for Ivens wasn't really a speech. Against Daskaluk's testimony, Almazoff claimed that he had never advocated bloodshed, and that he had said to Ivens, 'The workers never want revolution, because it does not pay them. They are always penalized for it.'[15] He hadn't attended the Walker or Majestic meetings, and, rather bad news for Andrews if he wanted a conviction for seditious *conspiracy*, Almazoff hadn't even spoken to any Strike Committee members during the Strike.[16]

On the other hand, Almazoff now gave a closer accounting of his New York trip and Communist connections: he had not only attended relief and Jewish meetings, but also a National Socialist Organization meeting, where the speakers had included A.K. Martens, the Russian representative whom Almazoff had earlier denied meeting.[17] During the Strike, Almazoff had sent telegrams to the New York Jewish newspaper *Forward*, and Andrews grilled Almazoff on them. Andrews zeroed in particularly on a 5 June telegram, which ended, 'Situation grave. Soldier beaten by scabs, died. Theatres closed.'[18] Almazoff insisted, 'I didn't put any phrase which was not in some of the papers,'[19] but there's no evidence of any paper giving an account of replacement workers killing a soldier. Almazoff's use of the word 'scab,' argued Andrews, disclosed his true attitude towards those engaged 'in protecting the lives and property of the citizens of Winnipeg, carrying on the necessary activities to keep the people alive in Winnipeg.'[20] Sedition, in this Citizens' definition, was only rhetorically against the King. In practical terms (seen also in Andrews justifying arrests by citing the *Western Labor News*'s article that attacked the Specials), sedition amounted to any verbal attack on the Citizens and their proxies. Almazoff's propaganda appeared at the same time as the Citizens' first anti-alien ads appeared, and mimicked the *Winnipeg Citizen*'s apocryphal misinformation – the mother who died because the strikers had denied her milk, and the returned soldier Coppins who, acting as a Special, had been attacked during the riot of 10 June and lay 'near death.' Andrews's demand for truth in reporting was quite reasonable, yet, coming from a Citizen, it was also laughable.

Despite the problems with Daskaluk's testimony, Andrews, summing up, called for Almazoff to be deported mainly as a result of Daskaluk's 'direct and convincing evidence … No language I can conceive would be more likely to cause a riot or bloodshed than that used by Almazoff on that occasion.'[21] One person did find language more likely to cause a riot, though this language, too, came from Almazoff. Judge Noble called the phrase 'Soldier beaten by scabs, died' 'a dangerous statement, a false statement, and I can hardly imagine a statement more calculated to fan any flame there was along the line of revolution.'[22] Summing up for the defence, Hyman said that Almazoff was charged with attempting to create a riot and usurping government powers, but 'when boiled down to its essence we have the essence of one incorroborated [*sic*] person who is suspect from beginning to end.'[23]

To show that Almazoff belonged among honourable men such as themselves, Hyman asked Noble and Andrews to allow a statement from Almazoff. Andrews consented. 'In a nervous and agitated tone, standing at the side of Hyman,'[24] Almazoff said, 'It means a death sentence if I am sent out of this country as European Russia is blockaded and I will be sent to [anti-Bolshevik White Russian Commander Aleksandr] Kolchak.'[25] Still, Almazoff would submit if he deserved it.[26] He had never tried to instigate a riot. During 1905's 'Bloody Sunday' in Russia, his brother had been shot down, and Almazoff implied that he wouldn't desire in Winnipeg what he escaped from in Russia.[27] Moreover, during the wartime influenza epidemic, he had nursed patients, one of them 'a rich man in Arlington Street.' He hadn't disdained the rich. Said Almazoff, 'I had never seen such luxury as where I put on for the first time my mask and I assisted that man for several hours until the doctors procured a nurse.' 'We were told there were millions of germs covering your face every minute you stood by the sick ... They sent me to another man until I fell sick myself.'[28]

Couched in honour, Almazoff's statement made an impression on the board. Andrews immediately tested it by noting that this portrait didn't fit with Almazoff's 'truculence' during his arrest. When Hyman protested that a 2 a.m. wake-up visit from the police might give anyone jitters, never mind the high-strung Almazoff, Noble retorted, 'The ordinary Anglo-Saxon at the sight of a policeman becomes calm. He may feel indignant but he is careful not to show it. Some of these other races, I imagine, begin to flare up.'[29] Nevertheless, despite the quibbles over whether Almazoff was fully one of us, and even if Almazoff didn't quite attain the kind of gentlemanly honour that Andrews pretended to, he did turn into a 'face' (to use the language of Emmanuel Lévinas) rather than remaining fully alien. Noble reserved his judgment.

In the end, Almazoff walked free. Two of the three board members were inclined to deport him, and Judge Noble, 'as a layman,' was also so inclined. But Noble's 'legal and judicial conscience' wouldn't allow him to deport on the basis of a single contradicted witness who was himself 'an alien, not of the very highest type.'[30] Noble seemed to think that his not-guilty verdict on Almazoff wouldn't be the final word, since Andrews kept hinting that in his vest he had more evidence against Almazoff.[31] Hinting, but never tabling. Afterwards, reporting to Justice Minister Doherty, Andrews didn't produce any additional evidence either, and he said that Noble had declared Almazoff 'an undesirable,' but that Almazoff had received the benefit of a 'legal doubt.' To convince Doherty that the Almazoff verdict wasn't a defeat, Andrews added, 'It is thought that the lesson [Almazoff] has received, and others, will do him considerable good.'[32]

Blumenberg, Schoppelrei, and Charitonoff the board ordered deported. The grounds? Not sedition, despite all the testimony of revolutionary statements made at the Walker, the Majestic, and elsewhere. Although the *Free Press* called Blumenberg 'prominent ... in the ranks of the extremists here,' and described his speeches as having 'an extremely revolutionary character,'[33] he was deported for making false statements when entering Canada years earlier.[34] Schoppelrei, similarly, was ordered deported for a false statement: for claiming that he had been born in Quebec, not the United States, so that he could fight for Canada in the Great War. The war hero Coppins, whose ribs the strikers had broken on 10 June, had lied about his country of birth too. However, not being on Strike, he wasn't in jeopardy. The board did its homework: it had the Immigration Department query the Department of Justice to make sure that the technicalities would snare Schoppelrei. Was the false statement enough to deport Schoppelrei? Was his refusal to answer questions enough? Could the board deport even though the technicalities had nothing to do with the original complaint against Schoppelrei?[35]

Schoppelrei's biggest problem was that he hadn't been in Canada long enough to acquire domicile, and the Department of Justice, on that basis, sifted the technicalities even more finely than Andrews and the board had. Because Schoppelrei hadn't acquired domicile, he must answer questions. And yes, Immigration could cherry-pick rule violations even if the violations weren't in the original complaint.[36] Finely sifted: W. Stuart Edwards wrote to Immigration that, by itself, Schoppelrei's refusal to answer questions wasn't culpable, but set alongside his lie at the border, it was.[37] The only hesitation was that if the military had encouraged him to lie, it would be unjust to use the lie against him. But Schoppelrei must prove this: 'It should not be difficult to ascertain whether Canadian military authorities were in the habit of advising immigrants to the effect stated by the counsel for Schoppelrei.'[38] In the event – with one recruiting officer disappeared and the other dispatched to Siberia – it proved not just difficult, but impossible to ascertain that the Canadian army was recruiting Americans. The Citizens bagged their German; Schoppelrei was deported.[39]

Charitonoff's case turned out to be the most controversial, so much so that Hyman's frustration got the better of him. Charitonoff had attended the Walker Theatre meeting, and speakers there had called his arrest for possession of seditious literature an example of how the Canadian government opposed free speech. 'While he did not speak,' Noble explained, 'he obviously participated in and countenanced the proceedings ... He was present on the platform, and was referred to by speakers as an example of government injustice ... Canada [is] not ready for the activities of radicals of Charitonoff's kind.'[40] Still, technical grounds, not seditious conspiracy, were again cited – this time retroactively. Charitonoff had been admitted into Canada by Immigration Commissioner J. Bruce Walker, but the board pounced on an earlier rejection by Inspector Counell at Emerson, who had disqualified Charitonoff for not having enough money (PC 924), and for not coming on a through ticket from his country of birth or naturalization (PC 23). Lyle Dick put it best: 'The Board was issuing a border rejection five and one half years after the entry!'[41] The same, except for the number of years, was true of Blumenberg and Schoppelrei.

When Noble announced the decision, Hyman boiled over. After seven weeks of jail for his client, Hyman had been led to believe there must be some conclusive evidence of seditious conspiracy against Charitonoff.

Now, even though an immigration commissioner had accepted him,[42] he was to be thrown out of Canada because five years earlier he hadn't had enough money?

> I had a sleepless night last night. I lay thinking: Am I insane? Is this a nightmare? Is this a delusion I am laboring under that I have to meet trifling, ridiculous charges of this kind under the British Empire and the British Flag? Are we going to have it stand in that way that the first proceedings we have in this city under this amended Act can show the greatest horrors that can be be [*sic*] conceived under British Law will be perpetrated here?[43]

Stung, Andrews pointed out that Charitonoff's participation in the Walker Theatre meeting hadn't been defended, and that 'many had been killed through the prolongation of the war, due to the treachery of the soviets of Russia.'[44] Hyman announced that Charitonoff would appeal.

What could the Citizens show for their efforts in relation to immigrants? Parliament had adopted legislation that undermined the juridical standing of all those British immigrants who had gained citizenship through domicile since 1910. Andrews had been allowed to turn from adviser into prosecutor, and in the end he had rested unsteadily on technicalities to deport two men, one of them (Blumenberg) a significant Strike leader, the other (Schoppelrei) a very minor figure. Charitonoff eventually slipped out of Andrews's grasp. To Doherty, Andrews wrote, 'An appeal is now pending to the Minister of Immigration and will come before you in due course,'[45] as if Doherty, the Citizens' best friend in Ottawa, might be able to pull the necessary strings to deny the appeal. Doherty had to disabuse Andrews, and tell him that appeals to the Minister of Immigration weren't in Doherty's kingdom: 'I do not see that it will call for any decision on my part.'[46] In the event, Justice did have a voice in the appeal, though not the voice that the Citizens wished. A Department of Justice lawyer recognized that to silently sit on a platform while someone else complained about how the government had treated you, wasn't seditious:

> Charitonoff is probably in fact well within the meaning of undesirable, but leaving out of consideration, as must be done, the suppression of his paper and his conviction for having Bolshevik literature in his possession, the case against him is merely that he voted for resolutions in themselves not seditious but which were supported by persons who made seditious utterances. In a court of law I should think Charitonoff

would stand a very good chance of acquittal upon a charge of seditious conspiracy or of participating in an unlawful assembly.[47]

Charitonoff's appeal was granted and he was freed.[48] In sum, the Citizens' hunt of alien socialists was underwhelming in tangible results. Yet, less tangibly, Andrews was probably right to see the hearings as a kind of object lesson for immigrants that would be applauded by many Winnipeggers: conform or else. Almazoff's impassioned plea not to be sent back to his country of birth had succeeded. Could other immigrants be sure of the same if they spoke too loudly on the wrong side of a labour issue?

Poor Harry Daskaluk, rubbed between the upper grindstone of the Citizen-run state and the lower grindstone of his striking family and friends. He was supposed to receive $500 for his troubles. Others, *doing* the grinding, fared considerably better: Andrews, Pitblado, Sweatman, and Coyne. One cannot reasonably argue that the four Citizen-lawyers were in it only for the money – they were convinced that revolution was around the corner – but it would be equally unreasonable to argue that they were indifferent to the fact that their 'public' service paid handsomely. Meighen couldn't have known (Andrews didn't tell him) that he was hiring more than one Citizen when on 26 May he retained Andrews to represent him in Winnipeg. Only later did Andrews reveal the other Citizens who were 'voluntarily aiding' him.[49] For 'daily consultation with Mr. Andrews with respect to strike and strike leaders and the course being pursued by the Dominion Government' between 26 May and 13 June, Pitblado charged $4500. He had helped with the closing of the *Western Labor News*, and was engaged 'continuously in preparation of warrants and search warrants and advising.' Sweatman's bill totalled $3412;[50] Coyne's $3900.[51] For less than three months' work Andrews charged $7600, with another $2500 going to other members of his firm. Between 26 May (the day he had been retained by Meighen) and 16 August, Andrews charged for 76 days – in other words, for every weekday and for 16 out of the 22 Saturdays and Sundays.[52] At $100 a day, he made almost double the prime minister's $57 a day; more than double if one assumes that the prime minister might occasionally work weekends too. On this matter of utmost importance – his fees – Andrews travelled to Ottawa himself.[53] The size of the bill underlines how independently Andrews had acted. Meighen had retained Andrews, but had expected a few quick deportations, not a whole series of criminal prosecutions. All the masquerade of the Citizens taking over the prosecution now dissipated, as Andrews unveiled the bill.

The bureaucratic struggle began over who would pay. Commissioner Perry told the RNWMP's comptroller, Angus McLean, that the force had been 'called upon to pay accounts for services rendered by different parties acting under instructions from Mr. Andrews.' Should Perry pay the accounts on behalf of the Department of Justice? McLean, sure that the force bore no responsibility for such accounts, wrote (secretly and confidentially) to Deputy Minister of Justice Newcombe, asking whether Andrews was authorized by Justice to incur the expenditure, and whether Newcombe wanted the RNWMP to 'defray them on your behalf.'[54] The operative phrase: 'on your behalf.'

Newcombe didn't answer. Instead, on 8 September, the assistant deputy minister of justice, Stuart Edwards, sent McLean a few bills to pay: the legal fees for the prosecution of the Strike leaders; new accounts of $5500 for two other lawyers, E.K. Williams and W.W. Richardson. The grand total amounted to $27,458.50.[55] Edwards had 'the honour to state that Mr. A.J. Andrews, K.C. of Winnipeg has been given charge of the legal services in connection with this matter, and any disbursements which may reasonably be incurred under his direction in connection with the apprehension and prosecution of the several offenders may properly be paid out of your appropriation subject, of course, to certification and audit in the usual way.'[56] Not acceptable – McLean refused to pay. The RNWMP had never engaged Andrews and wouldn't accept 'pecuniary responsibility for his services or actions.' Nor had Andrews ever consulted the RNWMP before incurring expenses. Although the force had been asked to cooperate with him, he had been appointed by the acting minister of justice.[57]

When Andrews heard about the scuffle, he wrote Edwards, saying that there were a large number of accounts that needed to be paid *at once*.[58] Edwards replied that he had no appropriation out of which to pay the lawyers, but promised to alert Doherty.[59] Meighen's hesitancy about the prosecutions might have limited Ottawa's liability. All Andrews had needed to arrest the Strike leaders was a detention order under the Immigration Act from Minister J.A. Calder, but Andrews hadn't provided the necessary information until after the fact, when he had already made *criminal* arrests. Nevertheless, Doherty had fully gone along with Andrews's wish to prosecute, and at some point, Doherty had authorized $150 a day in court for Andrews, Pitblado, and Coyne.[60] Now the problem of where to squeeze out money had to be solved by Justice bureaucrats, preferably not by going to Parliament for 'new' money that might call attention to the questionable nature of the prosecution. The large amount of money involved made it a cabinet-level problem.[61] September came and went without any cheques being sent. Early in October, an

exasperated Andrews wired Doherty about unpaid accounts with witnesses, reporters, and service providers. Careful not to place himself and
the other expensive lawyers at the head of the begging line, Andrews
protested, 'This is very embarrassing and … prejudicial to [the] prosecution.' He called for Doherty to rush the miscellaneous funds and,
almost as an afterthought, 'cheques for lawyers engaged as well.'[62] All
of this was the fallout from the Province's decision not to prosecute.

At that point, Doherty hit upon a solution. Remembering his pet project, the short-lived Public Safety Branch, he also remembered that the
money for the project had come out of the War Appropriation. He could
avoid wandering blindly in the political minefield of new federal powers under the War Measures Act, and he could stay safely within the
BNA Act. The funds had been earmarked for demobilization of Canadian soldiers. Defending the bill in May 1919, the minister of militia,
Major-General Mewburn, had told Parliament that 'every dollar of this
expenditure is simply to pay the allowances of soldiers on active service today, including war service gratuity, deferred pay, which amounted
to some $36,000,000, and separation allowances to dependents of
troops.'[63] But already a year earlier, while most soldiers were still in
Europe, and long before Mewburn promised the soldiers every dollar,
Doherty had already come up with creative ways of spending their
money. Soldiers shouldn't have to come back to labour unrest, should
they? 'An Act for Granting His Majesty Aid for Demobilization and
Other Purposes' (6 June 1919) did, after all, refer to 'measures deemed
necessary or advisable by the Governor in Council in consequence of
the war.'[64] Laurier Liberals sitting in opposition weren't quite so certain that the government's practice would match its rhetoric. Rodolphe
Lemieux wondered, 'What are those measures that are deemed necessary? What are those vague measures that are deemed advisable?'[65]
Another Quebec MP, Lucien Cannon, sharpened the question: Were
these 'necessary' measures simply a revival or extension of the War
Measures Act? No, replied Sir Thomas White, minister of finance and
acting prime minister.[66] Nevertheless, and even though the majority of
Winnipeg's returned soldiers had joined the Strike, on 10 October 1919
cabinet approved an Order-in-Council whereby $35,000 of the soldiers'
settlement money was appropriated to pay for the prosecution of their
labour leaders.[67] The trials of the Strike leaders, what were these
expenses but ways of ensuring order in Canada after the war? All for
the comfort of the returned soldiers.

For the Union government, paying Andrews and the other Citizen-
lawyers with funds already approved had the advantage of masking its
involvement in an extraordinary legal manoeuvre. Still, questions were

raised about whether such expenditures were lawful. The federal auditor general, E.D. Sutherland, objected. He told the Department of Justice that he could not see how *any* Strike expenses fell under the Demobilization Act. The suppression of strikes didn't fit, and the legal expenses arising out of a strike certainly didn't fit under (as 2.a of the Demobilization Act put it) 'the defence and security of Canada.' The auditor general suggested, instead, a separate appropriation and a special vote of Parliament.[68]

Political dynamite, such a step. Federal cabinet ministers must have kicked themselves for repealing the Order-in-Council for the Public Safety Branch.[69] Had they kept the branch alive, the prosecutions could have easily and legally been funded and pursued. As it was, short of using the War Measures Act the federal government had no authority to prosecute or to fund a prosecution. The most that Justice could do was to let the Citizens prosecute, and, for funding, to fall back on the vagueness that Lemieux and Cannon had prophesied as trouble. Newcombe argued that the Demobilization Act allowed for 'many expenditures not foreseen which in one way or another find their origin in the war.' 'Revolutionary activities in Winnipeg and elsewhere' originated in 'war conditions.'[70] It was an easy argument to make: was there anything in 1919 that couldn't in some way be blamed on conditions in 1918?

Ultimately, Sutherland had no power to deny the appropriation. At that time, the auditor general was limited to examining operations and approving or refusing government cheques,[71] while on questions of legality, the minister of justice had the final say.[72] And so, on 16 October, cheques finally winged their way to Andrews,[73] with an additional $4000 advance for the continuing prosecution of the Strike leaders.[74] More money, much, much more, would be required before the Strike leaders were behind bars. In the absence of a budget approved through Parliament, funds had to be provided repeatedly through Orders-in-Council from demobilization monies. Further OICs on 6 November 1919[75] and 31 January 1920[76] were approved for the amounts of $30,000 and $50,000 respectively. Another in April and one in June 1920 furnished an additional $80,000.[77]

The heroic services that the Citizens made to Canada ended not with a bang, but with a holler for money. The cheques that Edwards forwarded on 18 May 1920 to cover the balance on the lawyers' accounts included significant deductions.[78] All claims of extra time spent in court over and above a normal day's trial were rejected. To Andrews, Edwards pointed out that the department only authorized $150 per day in court, and $100 per day out of court. Andrews wanted $26,375; Edwards was prepared to pay only $10,201.

Andrews, particularly irritated that the Liberals Coyne and Pitblado had got more money than he did even though they had spent less time, immediately went over Edwards's head to Doherty, saying that the bills were 'exceptionally reasonable' considering 'the arduous task.' For the 1916 trial of members of Manitoba's former Conservative government ('very much less work and less important work'), chief prosecutor R.A. Bonnar had been paid $30,000, with only slightly less going to his associates.[79] During the Strike leaders' preliminary hearings, the court had gone into extended sessions, and Andrews had worked many Sundays and late into the evening most days. With some validity, Andrews claimed to have slain the beast: 'The position here is exceptionally tranquil, and I think it will be many years before there will be trouble of this kind again in Winnipeg.' Andrews wanted Ottawa to acknowledge him as the Citizen of Citizens – Ottawa still didn't understand what a holocaust the West had gone through, what a dragon he had confronted. Rather than Justice curtailing payments, Andrews considered that he should have received a bonus, 'some special fee.'[80] He more or less got his way. Half of the amounts claimed for the lengthy court sittings were allowed – $9475. Andrews had billed for $26,375; he received $19,676. By the end of 1921, the federal government would send an astounding $227,000 to the Citizens' lawyers to deal with the Strike prosecutions, of which money over $47,000 went to Andrews alone.[81] Harry Daskaluk got $500. For thirteen months' work in 1919–1920, Andrews pulled in $42,000; the prime minister's 1920 salary, by comparison, was $15,000.[82] Apart from any ideological considerations, it had made good business sense for Andrews to insist that the Strike leaders be pursued by all legal means. Yet, what the money *represented* was far more important than any pleasure the lawyers might get out of it. These substantial paydays represented a kind of imprimatur far outreaching Meighen's early anointing of Andrews. The money meant that what had begun as a group of private businessmen reacting against labour's demands had become official state policy. The depth of the state's investment in these lawyers helped to justify their actions and gave a high gloss to their opinions. One might even reverse Andrews's reason for requesting a bonus: if the lawyers received a great reward, the dragon they slew must have been fearsome indeed.

But even $42,000 wasn't the end. Late in 1920, the Department of Justice would retain Andrews for a set fee of $2500 to prepare documents for a British legal firm to oppose R.B. Russell's appeal to the Judicial Committee of the Privy Council. Nevertheless, his charges, landing in Ottawa, had managed to drag in fees for Pitblado, Coyne, and Sweatman totalling about $9500.[83] Edwards was stunned. No arrangements had been made to retain other lawyers, but Andrews had gotten used to bringing in 'voluntary' legal help. Edwards noted that if the bills were paid in total 'the Government will pay $300 for every six pages of instructions issued to English counsel.'[84] The bills were paid in total.

Wednesday, 20 August

If the money from Ottawa made the Citizens' lawyers and their deeds bright with honour, this shine could be seen only among the Citizens and by the Union government. Were the extent of the payments to become public knowledge, not everyone would cheer. How then to memorialize the Citizens' deeds in public and to cement the terms of their ideological victory?

Long before the squabble over the lawyers' fees was settled, the *Manitoba Free Press* headlines cried, 'Citizens of Winnipeg to Form Association: Give Permanence to the Work of Committee of One Thousand – Meeting Tonight.' Here, again, John Botterell's claim that the Citizens' deliberations were completely open was insincere. The new organization planned to 'represent the community as a whole.' However, to pass through the door one needed 'a card of admission.'[85] Tickets for the event at the Board of Trade Building had been sent to the 7800 men and women who had maintained public utilities, manned fire halls, and otherwise helped the City fight the Strike. It's not likely that Harry Daskaluk, witness for the Citizens, was invited to tea, but surely 7800 tickets must signify that the meeting hadn't been restricted to a particular class.[86] The next day, the *Manitoba Free Press* indeed celebrated the notion that 3000 people 'of all classes and creeds, occupations and professions' had come together. If Andrews had reason to complain of the *Free Press*'s lack of enthusiasm after the Strike leaders' arrests, he couldn't complain now. The front page read, 'Citizens Unite in Organizing Strong League ... Deep Sense of Loyalty to Canadian Laws, Protection of Life and Property Paramount Feature.' At the meeting, the old Citizens' Committee had been given a facelift and a new name: the Citizens' League of Winnipeg. The Chair of the Citizens' executive, A.K. Godfrey, also presided over the League. Other stalwarts – Citizens' chair A.L. Crossin and *Winnipeg Citizen* co-editor Fletcher Sparling – took minutes for the League.

In a speech, Godfrey stressed that the old Citizens had no quarrel with 'the better element of the labor party,' and he hoped that this element would join the League. The Citizens' Committee hadn't emphasized the interests of any one class, and neither would the League. Cooperation with labour was the new gospel – 'Their interests are our interests' – but one shouldn't forget the recent troubles that had triggered the Citizens'

Committee, 'because labor had not met its responsibilities.' While Andrews reminded the federal government in private of the dragon the Citizens had slain, Godfrey reminded the public:

> The labor man who remains at home and works in his garden while the agitator is working his organization is not doing his duty, and we as citizens, notwithstanding our regard for labor, cannot forget that element was responsible for the trials and tribulations visited upon us during a period of six weeks. We cannot forget there was a movement started at Calgary last March, endorsed or assisted by American organizations, which was responsible for the launching of a revolution in Winnipeg on May 15 of this year.[87]

Crossin, too, preached on revolution. In Canada, the United States, and Europe had arisen a 'well organized and well financed' campaign that instead of using constitutions to redress grievances, had used 'direct action, which is force.' These radicals wanted to destroy 'the whole of our organized civilization,' but the new Citizens' League would carry on the work of the Citizens' Committee in preventing this.[88] The League, which would hopefully go nation-wide, would devote itself to the best Canadian ideals: constitutional government, respect for Canadian law, the combating of all forms of propaganda against Canadian institutions, the study of industrial questions, 'the dissemination [of] reliable information on this subject,' and the cultivation of a 'closer relationship between employer and employee.' Thus would the work of the Citizens be engraved on the hearts of Canadians.[89]

A few people even in this select crowd thought that for a 'new' start it might be best to keep the connection with the Citizens down to a whisper. If animosity created by the Citizens' Committee hampered the efforts of the Citizens' League, why not delete the clause in the League's constitution referring to the Citizens' Committee? But whatever the future advantage of such a move, those most closely identified with the Citizens understood that such a deletion might imply that the Citizens had been something other than selfless defenders of the constitution. Captain Charles Wheeler, president of the Imperial War Veterans, who had never known a good German 'unless the Hun had been under a tombstone,'[90] lectured the assembly. 'Some of us who are in the know have positive proof that this movement against democracy is being financed by German money,' he thundered. If this harangue wasn't quite on topic, nevertheless it had the desired effect. Only 'about fifty' of the three thousand voted to delete the reference to the Citizens' Committee, and the motion was defeated.[91]

Who, then, should lead this 'new' Citizens' League? A nominating committee composed of members of the old Citizens' executive proposed a list of executive members.[92] Again, objections: not everyone saw in this the wonderful working of democracy. At least twenty executive members of the Citizens' League had served on the executive of the Citizens' Committee, and the four weightiest of the 'new' positions belonged to the old Citizens: president, Isaac Pitblado; first vice-president, A.K. Godfrey; honorary-secretary, Fletcher Sparling; and honorary-treasurer, W.H. McWilliams. Someone pointed out that the executive could perhaps be perceived as 'a clique.' It was decided that the executive members would act as 'temporary' officers, pending an election. After elections, Dr J. Halpenny replaced Pitblado as president, but the rest of the Citizens' League executive looked remarkably unchanged: A.K. Godfrey as vice-president; Sparling as secretary; and Citizens Sweatman, Botterell, Parnell, Crossin, McWilliams, Markle, Bond, Stovel, Ferguson, Munro, Christie, and Tucker on the executive. Reverend Dr Pigeon, of Augustine Presbyterian Church, declared: 'This organization stands for the assistance to every class in the community and for the rebuke and defeat of any aggression on the part of any class when that aggression is against the cherished rights of democratic citizens.' Two very moderate labour-identified men – T.J. Murray and A.W. Puttee – were also nominated for the executive, but other delegates cried foul, and the two were removed.

The reason for inclusive rhetoric but practical exclusions soon became clear: in short order, the Citizens' League put up its own slate in the civic election. The Citizens' advertisements called the election 'THE SECOND ROUND OF THE STRIKE,' and clarified the choice for voters: 'THERE IS JUST ONE ISSUE RED OR WHITE.'[93] Mayor Gray, also up for re-election, agreed.[94] R.A.C. Manning explained that the 'new' Citizens 'would be fighting against those who had laid their plans at the Calgary Red convention with design of getting control of the civic government of the city.'[95] The civic elections in November 1919 indicated a deeply divided city, with the Citizens mobilizing just enough support to maintain the status quo. Labour and the Citizens won an equal number of seats, so the deciding vote went to the chair, Mayor Gray, who retained his post over S.J. Farmer by 15,630 votes to 12,514.

On the level of civic politics, the Citizens' League continued the work of the Citizens. On the level of culture, in October 1919 several Winnipeggers, including Citizen A.B. Stovel and W.R. Bulman (who wasn't listed on the Citizens' telegram to Borden, but who was a prominent businessman and served as president of the Canadian Manufacturers' Association),[96] organized a citizenship conference, and embraced citizenship education as a means of creating class harmony. Ed Parnell was among the attendees.[97] The organizers, slightly less exclusive than the Citizens' League, invited Marcus Hyman to speak. As a lawyer and a graduate of Oxford, he had the appropriate accent to speak as a class insider, while as a Jew and a defender of the Strike leaders he could give the perspective of the outsider – though possibly he might be too soft on socialism. Hyman wasn't impressed by the Citizens' efforts to bring aliens to obedience school. He dismissed references to the 'dignity of labour, and the cooperation ... between the citizens and labour, and the education of labour,' calling all of it 'humbug and cant.' The citizenship of the workers, he insisted, was not in question. It was not the workers who required education in citizenship, but the Anglo-Canadian middle-class conference attendees. From Hyman's comments and from the elections after the Strike, one may gather that although the Citizens had pushed enough levers in government and had (through a mixture of serious constitutional concerns, propaganda, and anti-alien sentiment) marshalled enough of the middle to defeat the Strike, the Citizens had also widened the chasm between the classes. Now that they had inflicted injury, the Citizens were ready for the healing to begin, and they professed eternal devotion to 'good' labour. But the nation was polarized. 'Labour,' said Hyman, 'has no use for us.'[98]

14

Duty to God, Country, and Family:
The Russell Trial

4 November – 24 December

The polarization of classes meant that when the actual trials of the British-born Strike leaders began, everything would depend on who sat in the jury box. Russell's was the first criminal trial, though initially all the leaders were supposed to be tried together. The immigration hearings hadn't taken down all five 'Eastern European' targets, but had nevertheless put the fear of God into the alien, and the preliminary hearing had shown that in front of the right audience, the Citizens' evidence and story would hold fast. All that was necessary at Russell's trial was to confirm what the preliminary hearing had already 'established.' Again, Andrews took a highly polemical tack – sometimes verging on absurdity in his claims – but he combined that polemic with a scientific attention to judge and jury selection, so that his hyperbole would fall on fertile ground.

R.B. Graham, Winnipeg's actual Crown prosecutor, explained the distinction between a Crown prosecutor and a 'paid advocate' who worked merely for his client: 'A Crown prosecutor must be absolutely fair. He must bring out everything that tells in favor of the accused as strongly as what tells against him.'[1] The quasi-Crown Andrews chimed in to the same effect near the end of the Russell trial: 'I am not here, leader of the forces of the Crown, to hound him to justice … I am here to assist you gentlemen in sifting this evidence, and aiding you in determining the innocence or guilt of the accused, and it is my purpose to present that evidence before you in as impartial a light as my capacity enables me to do'[2] – and then he impartially explained that Russell and his fellow conspirators had planned to

King's Bench of Manitoba, 15 November 1909. L–R, Justice W.E.
Perdue, Justice Thomas Metcalfe, Justice T.G. Mathers, Chief Justice
Joseph Dubuc, Justice D.A. Macdonald, Justice A.E. Richards, Justice
J.D. Cameron. (University of Winnipeg Archives, Western Canada
Pictorial Index, image 10813)

wipe out all sentiments of faith in God, respect for fellow men, sanctity of marriage and the family, love of country, regard for life and
property, in a word all principles of religion and nationality and to
overturn and subvert the present system of constitutional government
of the Dominion of Canada, by force, in order to bring about a condition of chaos and tyranny such as exists in Russia and to give control
of the Dominion of Canada or a part thereof to the ambitious conspirators under the guise of a so-called government by the workers, or the
dictatorship of the proletariat.[3]

This movement from polity into barbarism brought Locke's allegori-
cal account of the origins of the state and constitution into line with the
old story of the British empire civilizing a dark and disordered West.
Would a jury of Winnipeggers find such a black-and-white story believ-

able? Andrews was taking no chances. In the summer, the Citizens had favoured trials held outside Winnipeg before a 'whiter' audience, perhaps presided over by Chief Justice Mathers in Portage la Prairie. Andrews, having earlier been stung by the *Western Labor News*'s criticism of him even though he thought that bail conditions had effectively muzzled the Strike leaders, now opposed bail. Even though he pretended to have no opinion on the matter of bail, he told the presiding judges that he knew it for a fact that the men planned to tie up all of Canada on October 1st.[4] Winnipeg judges denied the men bail, but the issue came to Mathers, and his decision to give the Strike leaders bail ended Andrews's affair with country judges.[5] He immediately told Deputy Minister of Justice Newcombe that the Citizens would have 'difficulty in getting in our evidence with [Mathers], much greater in any event than before either Justice Metcalfe or Justice Galt who are taking the Winnipeg assizes.'[6] Result: in late November the Strike leaders were arraigned for trial before Thomas Metcalfe, a man well known to Andrews, though not always in the best of circumstances.[7]

Briefly, it seemed that Andrews might have to sell his story to a jaundiced urban jury after all. But Andrews was nothing if not resourceful. The Crown possessed a virtually unlimited power to reject jurors through its ability to 'stand by' a juror until all other potential jurors were considered.[8] When the assizes opened on 4 November, Andrews received the list of possible jurors. He turned the list over to the RNWMP and the McDonald Detective Agency and a 100-yard dash was on. Armed with copies of a little questionnaire that Andrews had devised, the RNWMP and the McDonald detectives raced to find the jurors, asking,

> Is he a returned man: if so was he a volunteer or a conscript? ...
> What are his views as to the Union Government War Policy?
> Was he ever a member of a Union?
> What are his views on Bolshevism? ...
> What does he think of Trades Unionist Leaders and their methods
>   during the last twelve months?
> What does he think of the Winnipeg Strike?
> Does he think it was justified?
> What does he think of the Citizens' Committee of 1000 and their
>   work? ...
> Is he in your opinion liable to be sentimental in his judgment?[9]

To prevent prejudgment, it was legal for police to ask such questions of people who *knew* the jurors, but it was criminal for someone linked with the prosecutor to ask the questions directly of jury members. That would constitute jury tampering, and the Criminal Code threatened a harsh penalty.[10]

It's possible, but highly unlikely, that the RNWMP and the McDonald Detective Agency used Andrews's questions only on acquaintances of the jurors. Significantly, fifty years after the Strike, the president of the Exchequer Court of Canada, Judge Joseph Thorson, revealed that, as a young, relatively inexperienced Crown attorney for the Province in 1919, he had felt 'an abiding sense of shock' that it was possible to pack a jury in such a way that there was no possibility of acquittal.[11] As well, during the next trial in January, the defence tried to prove that Andrews had tampered with the jury, but Judge Metcalfe barred most of the evidence from court. Joseph Wright, a blacksmith, signed an affidavit saying that the day after he had received a jury summons, a man approached him about how best to sell several lots in West Kildonan. But 'his interest in real estate,' Wright realized, 'was not very great, for he shortly turned the conversation on to the subject of the trial of Robert B. Russell ... and he asked me what was my candid opinion of the matter.' Wright revealed that he considered the Strike to be an ordinary strike, 'the natural result of conditions.' When Wright applied to be excused from jury duty on account of illness, he was excused.[12] It was alleged that Deputy Sheriff Pyniger had given out jury lists, and Pyniger admitted, that, yes, he had turned the list over to the 'Crown' counsel (Andrews), but only at the order of Justice Galt. Pyniger claimed that he had also offered a copy of the list to McMurray, but McMurray denied receiving such an offer.[13] McMurray called a juror, J.W. Hansen, to the stand, and asked him whether anyone had approached him after he was summoned to be on the jury panel. But Andrews objected to the question, and Metcalfe upheld the objection. When McMurray tried to ask RNWMP officers whether members of the force had interrogated potential jurors, Andrews again objected, and Metcalfe ruled that defence questions could only address the possible misconduct of the deputy sheriff, not of the RNWMP.[14]

Andrews's determination to limit the opportunity of the defence to challenge potential jurors fundamentally altered all the trials. In defending the constitution, he criminally violated it. His questions for the jurors reached even into support for Canada's war policy, which had no bearing on Russell's guilt or innocence, but which, Andrews knew, would predispose jurors against Russell, who had opposed the Great War. After the RNWMP and McDonald detectives brought the answers to Andrews in mid-November, he knew all he needed to know, and he jealously guarded that information. Later, when McMurray tried to ask potential juror William Scott whether he was opposed to the cause of labour, Andrews cried foul. It was improper for the defence to get the answers to such questions. Metcalfe, despite the bad blood between him and Andrews, agreed, and sustained the objection.[15] Andrews further skewed the process on 27 November, when, shortly after the trial of all the Strike leaders had begun, he chose to try Russell separately and hold over the trial of the others until January. Andrews was concerned that, with eight defendants, if the defence exercised all the peremptory challenges at its disposal, the available jury panel might be exhausted before a jury was selected.[16] After Metcalfe ruled that the defence could make only four peremptory challenges, it sought to extend the challenges by altering the charges, asking to have Russell tried under the amended Criminal Code.[17] A conviction under the amended Code could potentially increase Russell's sentence from two years to twenty years, but the defence was willing to take the risk, because the threat of a longer sentence entitled the defence to greater peremptory challenges to the jury.[18] But Metcalfe ruled against the defence.

In the end, the only rejected jurors were those 'stood aside' by the Crown, and, even though the trial was in Winnipeg, Andrews got himself a 'white,' country jury that didn't at all reflect the city's ethnic mix. No labour person or immigrant or even Winnipegger would sit in judgment of Russell. The jurors were farmers and rural businessmen: community leaders, Orange Lodge associates, men with relatives who had served and died in the Great War.[19] This is not to say that jurors were all closed-minded or easily managed. Nevertheless, they were the ideal audience for the Citizens, since in sedition cases guilt or innocence isn't decided by facts alone, but by the most compelling story. Like all sedition trials, this one posed basic constitutional questions: How far did Russell's freedom of speech and assembly extend? Should disorder in Europe limit traditional freedoms in Canada? Where did Russell's valid criticisms of the state end and conspiracy begin? Sedition trials turn on political judgment, and the McDonald Detective Agency had ensured that politically these farmers and businessmen belonged to the rural equivalent of the Citizens' constituency.

Once in court, Andrews misled the jury members on the nature of the proceedings, telling them that this trial was a rare 'state trial,' and that he represented 'the Crown,' that is, 'the people of Canada.'[20] On purely technical grounds, he was correct, since a private prosecution is carried forward in the name of the Crown. On moral grounds, he was wrong, unless executive members of the Citizens, so insistent about their 'representative' role, now represented the people of Canada.[21] At the end of the trial Andrews would worry that he hadn't quite covered his tracks, so before the jury deliberations, he ridiculed the defence claim that the trial was a vigilante prosecution led by the Citizens: '[The defence] tried in a weak way to suggest that this prosecution is perhaps tried by somebody else than the local government,' explained Andrews. He pointed to the indictment, 'preferred by the Attorney-General of this province.' He added, 'There is only one crown represented in this case, by the Attorney-General of this province, and I am here as his representative ... Did [the defence] question that when he was in the box?'[22]

Actually, the defence had. But Andrews, with Judge Metcalfe's cooperation, had cut the questions off. McMurray had called Attorney General T.H. Johnson to the stand, asking if Johnson's department had discussed whether the Strike had broken any laws. Andrews leapt up to object because such a disclosure would be 'against public policy.'[23] Making no headway on that front, McMurray, and then lead counsel Robert Cassidy, asked Johnson whether the Province was paying for the prosecution. Once again, Andrews quickly objected, and Judge Metcalfe backed him up – 'in the absence of authority the question could not be answered.' Johnson escaped.[24]

A couple of months later in the Legislature, on 16 February 1920, Johnson couldn't avoid answering. Fred Dixon, just that day acquitted on the charge of seditious libel, asked, '[Are] ... Messrs. Alfred J. Andrews, K.C., Isaac Pitblado, K.C., J.B. Coyne, K.C., and W.A.T. Sweatman, purporting to be Crown Counsel in the case of The King vs. William Ivens, et al., representing His Majesty by virtue of being retained or instructed by the Attorney-General of Manitoba?' 'No,' Johnson answered. Dixon then asked under whose authority they were acting. The Province confessed that Johnson had permitted Andrews to act as Crown, but that Andrews and company were retained by Canada's Minister of Justice.[25] In other words, it was a private prosecution, permitted under the Criminal Code, but curiously (and here silence reigned) paid for by Ottawa out of demobilization funds.

In his address to the jury, Andrews suggested that it forget complex legal questions, and confine itself to the questions that he had set: 'Gentlemen, do you care whether the Dominion as a whole, who might regard this as having a far greater than local import, as something that may settle in this crisis the destiny of this country ... Do you care whether the Dominion or the local government is behind this prosecution? All you ought to care for is that you honestly do your duty and decide the one thing you have before you, the simple problem, the guilt or innocence of the accused.'[26] Andrews didn't say so, but, always pragmatic, he made sure on behalf of the Citizens that the Constitution, that 'proudest boast of the Englishman,' was locked in a safety deposit box offstage. The farmers should decide guilt or innocence; the constitution was best left in the keeping of the Citizens.

Even assessments of the witnesses' reliability were, Andrews judged, too thorny for a mere jury to comprehend. With Judge Metcalfe's complicity, Andrews was able to insist that the defence not address witness reliability, but confine itself to the guilt or innocence of the accused. Defence lawyer Robert Cassidy called to the stand Harry Daskaluk – the divided RNWMP 'secret agent.' His hair in pompadour style, throwing 'into relief a high brow and intelligent forehead,' Daskaluk had answered only a few questions when Andrews objected. Conscious that the defence's focus on Daskaluk's money-bought testimony would taint *all* RNWMP witnesses, Andrews began a systematic series of objections. We are not trying the RNWMP, he roared, and Metcalfe concurred. If Daskaluk was going to give evidence that would influence the jury to discount the other witnesses, Metcalfe simply wouldn't allow it. Cassidy kept asking questions, and Metcalfe kept ruling them out of order. Finally, Cassidy laughed scornfully and gave up: '[Daskaluk] is concealed behind such a defence of protection that I can do nothing.'[27]

The indictment for the Strike leaders boiled down mostly to the proposition that they had sought 'to bring into hatred and contempt and to excite disaffection against the government, laws and constitution,' 'to bring the administration of justice into contempt,' 'to cause discontent,' and 'to promote feelings of hostility and ill will between different classes in the community.' The Strike had 'challenged constituted authority, and set class against class,' and 'was intended to be a step in a revolution.'[28] This sounded as if there had been a call to the ramparts, but Andrews took pains to lower the bar for a conviction. The prosecution, he cautioned the jury, did not assert that Russell and his associates had 'attempted to overthrow the government.' No, all that was charged was that they had seditiously conspired to 'bring about discontent and dissatisfaction and what would be the logical result some day – revolution – some day attempted revolution – some day overturning the government.'[29] In 'discontent' and 'disaffection' Andrews again dusted off the old Thompson/Stephen definition of sedition that never made it into the new Criminal Code but still sat in everyone's law books. To this definition he added that a general strike by its very nature was illegal. It could be nothing other. It was the means by which a 'Soviet' government would be established in Canada. Coyne, too, suggested that if a strike 'causes hostility and disturbs the tranquility of the public,' it must be seditious, and 'it cannot be legalized by hanging a card on it saying that it is a trade combination for the protection of the workman.'[30] Finally, the Strike leaders were also guilty of criminal nuisance, and here, as well, Andrews set a low standard for guilt: every general strike was unlawful since it created a public nuisance.[31] The Citizens couldn't forget that life in Winnipeg during the Strike *hadn't been easy*, and who but the Strike leaders were responsible for that? They had endangered 'the lives, safety, health, property, or comfort of the public' by failing to discharge a duty or had obstructed the public 'in the exercise or enjoyment of any right common to all His Majesty's subjects.'[32] Set alongside the towering charge of sedition, this might seem to be an afterthought, but it wasn't. 'Criminal nuisance' allowed the Citizens to bring into court all the irritations that had pricked them during the Strike, including stories of babies dying from want of milk. Sedition, standing alone, would have narrowed the trial's scope considerably.

If the Criminal Code didn't actually define sedition as the sowing of 'discontent' and 'disaffection,' the Citizens could rest secure knowing that Canadian *case* law (especially during wartime) was friendly to the older catch-all definition, a definition that presented an emotional face to the public while stifling political opposition.[33] Andrews referred the jury to the case of 'Menchoruk' [*sic*], who was convicted of sedition in 1916. When a canvasser for Victory Loans knocked on his door and said that a lot of boys at the front would never return, Morden-area farmer Albert Manshrick – born in Canada but of German extraction – not only refused to donate, but shot back, 'I hope too none of them will come back.' To another canvasser, who warned Manshrick that if the Germans conquered France, they would soon be landing on Canadian beachheads, Manshrick had said, 'Let them come. That's all right. What about it?' Manshrick was convicted of sedition, and spent a short time in jail until he paid his substantial $700 fine.[34]

Andrews pointed out to his jury that the judge (supported on appeal) had deemed Manshrick's words seditious 'because they would provoke a breach of the peace.' The law presumed, said the judge, that Manshrick '*intended the natural consequences of his act* – in this case, of his words. Whether the words did create public disorder, and there is no evidence that they did create public disorder, that has nothing to do with the defense. Were they calculated to create public disorder?' (emphasis added). Yes, ruled the courts, they were so calculated.[35] 'Natural consequences' were of course a screen for '*no* consequences at all.' 'Breach of the peace' meant 'words that shouldn't be said.' It would have taken a subtle dialectician to trace a logical progression from intended consequences to an actual 'breach of the peace' in Manshrick's case, but it was an emotional story, not logic, that dictated the interpretation of sedition law. In a Canada at war with Germans, the canvassers had a good patriotic story, Manshrick a poor story.

The Manshrick judgment suited Andrews perfectly. Russell wasn't on trial for what he said or intended, or even for what other people did as a result of what he said, but rather, Andrews emphasized, for what 'would ... be the natural result of such words.' The law presumed that Russell and the other Strike leaders had intended the natural consequences of their actions or words. Out of Russell's mouth had come the inflammatory expectation of 'blood in the streets.' The meaning was clear to Andrews: 'The burglar comes into your house in the silent watches of the night, and he presents a revolver to your face, and you give up all you have – this is a peaceful robbery – he doesn't shoot you. That is what the accused Russell meant when he said "a threat of a general strike was enough in 1918," and he thought it would be enough in 1919.' For the Citizens, this was the meaning of sedition. Some of them agreed in theory that workers had the right to withdraw their labour, but, in practice, when a strike arrived, it was equivalent to a pistol pointed at your head.[36] Russell's words hadn't created disorder, and Andrews acknowledged this, but it was irrelevant.[37]

The notion of a broad-based conspiracy ensured that the trial of Russell was the trial of all, even though it had been Andrews who had procedurally hived off Russell's trial from those of the other leaders. In the Citizens' story, all socialist-influenced workers belonged to a unified conspiracy. For much of the trial, Andrews turned away from Russell and wandered about in the statements of Russell's colleagues, attributing to labour a solidarity that labourites could only dream about. Since Andrews had found no seditious actions and few seditious words, *faute de mieux* he had to weave together a series of isolated statements from a wide variety of socialist speakers to patch together (in front of the right audience) a conspiracy. He began by digging into Scotland, where Russell had belonged to a 'Socialist Party': 'You will remember Snowden, one of the members of that party, when he attempted to attend a Bolshevist meeting in Russia, could not get the sailors to let him on the boat because they were loyal. These men who had braved the perils of the deep, the treacherous submarine, they would not carry Snowden. Why? Because they felt they would be traitors to their country.'[38] In fact, however, Philip Henry Snowden, a member of the pacifist minority of the Independent Labour Party (the ILP, to which Russell had also belonged), wasn't anything near a traitor. Initiatives to convene an assembly of socialist parties of 'allied' nations culminated in the fall of 1917 in a call to a conference in Petrograd 'with a view to securing a united working-class peace.' The British Labour Party decided to send a deputation, including Snowden, to obtain information about the plans of the Russian Council, but at Aberdeen an official of the Seamen's Union prevented Snowden and two others from sailing.[39] In 1924, Snowden would become Britain's Chancellor of the Exchequer.

Returning to Canadian issues, Andrews pointed at the Strike leaders. What did the Walker meeting participants say? Paraphrasing very loosely, Andrews supplied the answer, 'Oh, they say blood is running in Russia; blood will run in this country from the Atlantic to the Pacific. We are willing to wade in blood to get our rights.' Someone had joked that 'houses in Fort Rouge would make good houses for the Soviet leaders.'[40] Sam Blumenberg had said, 'I put on a red flag tie so that there can be no mistake about where I stand. This Russian question is a world question. It affects the workers of every country.'[41] Tellingly, though perhaps not as seditiously, Blumenberg had been introduced to the audience as 'a building laborer to represent the building laborers in this bona fide labor movement.' Yet the president of the Winnipeg Trades and Labor Council, James Winning, had admitted that Blumenberg 'presses clothes, or something like that.' He probably, Andrews scoffed, never did a day's work as a building laborer in his life.'[42]

Given the jury that they had assembled, Pitblado (who prepared the case)[43] and Andrews calculated that this audience would be prepared to come down hard on Bolshevik sympathizers, and on such things as phoniness, blasphemy, 'prostitution,' and lack of patriotism. Andrews, waxing biblical, preached to the jury, 'By their acts and by their deeds you shall judge them.'[44] He feigned reluctance to repeat blasphemy, but nevertheless managed to spit it out, and to finger Russell's friend, Bill Pritchard: 'the man ... and – I don't know whether I should refer to it – Pritchard the man who blasphemously refers to the late lamented Mr Christ.'[45] If this wasn't precisely seditious, it fit tidily into the category of 'words that shouldn't be said.' Coming from Pitblado, this kind of self-righteous attack might have been unremarkable. Coming from Andrews, it was risible. His father had been a Wesleyan Methodist minister, a devout man for whom 'religion was not a thing to be worn lightly, like a coat in summer weather. He [had] sacrificed himself and his family to his work, feeling it no less than his sacred duty to make the sacrifice.'[46] But Andrews, unlike his father, knew what made 'the world go round,' and, as his friends and colleagues tantalizingly reported, was 'not overly virtuous' in his moral behaviour.[47] It wasn't that Andrews was a malicious person. His colleagues would recall that 'there was never anybody quite like A.J. Andrews,' and that 'he was liked by everyone who knew him.' In his personal life, he was 'the opposite of a stuffed shirt – there was nothing false about him.' However, it was also true that 'the fates wove black as well as white threads into the web they spun for him. He has been human – more human than most men. The saint's thorny crown would sit uncomfortably upon his head.'[48] During the Strike leaders' trials, nevertheless, he knew how to clothe himself in morality and pious outrage. Though he himself might not bear too much scrutiny, he called down divine judgment upon the strikers for the benefit of jurors Roy Tolton, who (after church union) would become known as a United Church man and would vote for conservative premier John Bracken year in and year out;[49] Joseph Fréchette, a devoted Roman Catholic, who would become a big fan of Bible Bill Aberhart during the Depression;[50] William Heale, an Anglican serving on the Rockwood Municipal Council, school, and church boards;[51] and Theo Nugent, at whose house student ministers who led church services stayed.[52]

As indicated by one of Andrews's accusations – that the Strike leaders wanted to 'wipe out all ... sanctity of marriage and the family' – his pious outrage against Russell's colleagues extended into the private sphere. From the Methodist point of view, the family was not only the foundation for worship, but gave civil and political life its character.[53] Facing Russell in the courtroom, Andrews became a model of bourgeois respectability, decrying the Socialist Party of Canada's assault on the family: 'They abolish family, and they take woman that we have put on a pedestal from that pedestal ... There is no place in society where the home is more sacred, where the family is more hallowed, than in the family of the good, honest working man. His home, it may be humble, but it is his home ... I say to you, that the home of the poor man is as sacred and even happier than the home of the rich.' Immigrants and francophones probably wouldn't fully grasp this sacredness: 'We Anglo-Saxons have a word we do not find in the French or other languages, that word home.' Socialists, wanting to dissolve nations, 'would take away that home.'[54] Andrews, voice of rectitude. The imaginary poor-but-happy worker, guarantor of Andrews's sermon.

Judge Metcalfe must have smiled at Andrews running for election on the family values ticket. Metcalfe, a bachelor and 'a rather heavy drinker,' was romantically involved with Maud Andrews, A.J.'s estranged wife,[55] and, once, Andrews 'found his wife in bed with Judge Metcalfe who knocked Andrews downstairs.' After Metcalfe died, Mrs Andrews would take up with a property man named Enderton.[56] Still, Andrews 'trod' the road of life 'cheerfully and happily.'[57] Cheer was possible despite his wife's infidelity because he had his own lady friends, and by agreement with Maud, 'they lived in the same house but led separate lives.'[58] Andrews could get away with his cry for family values and with many things that others couldn't because he had a very colourful court manner, and because of his reputation.[59] In this trial, it didn't hurt that all the jury members came from out of town.

William Ivens, introduced to the jury as a 'co-conspirator' (though the trial was now supposed to be only of Russell), didn't perhaps blaspheme or destroy the family. However, given the conservative Christian separation between the economy and salvation, his troubling and colloquial jeremiads could be branded as false religion, even if the offence wasn't in the Criminal Code. Andrews satirized the Labour Church, 'this camouflage of a church service that these men hold on a Sabbath night, inviting such men as Pritchard, who refers to the late lamented Mr. Christ' – Andrews found himself able to say it again – 'To join these meetings does not impress me with the good citizenship of the accused clergyman, the Rev. William Ivens.' It wouldn't have lessened Andrews's wish to depict Ivens as a 'failed' minister that Andrews's own father had served as pastor of Ivens's former church, McDougall Methodist, for three years in the early 1900s.[60] Ivens wasn't a lapsed clergyman, but Andrews made the most of the fact that Ivens had been removed from the pulpit of McDougall for his pacifism and socialism, and Andrews invited the jurors to dredge up their own knowledge of lapsed clergymen: 'Perhaps your experience would lead you to this belief, that when a clergyman goes from the Church – I mean his own church – he often goes a long way before he stops.' Then – 'Gentlemen, listen to this very carefully' – Andrews turned to statements culled from Ivens's sermons:

> The capitalists owned the forests and all the natural resources, and the land which grew the wheat; they owned the railways that moved the wheat to the elevators; they owned the elevators in which it is stored; they own the mills which grind the wheat into flour; they owned the distributing houses into which the flour went. And the audience must not overlook that they owned the houses in which you poor suckers live.

Andrews asked, 'Did you ever listen to ranker sedition than that?'[61] Observers might be forgiven for scratching their heads, puzzling over what in Ivens's words constituted sedition, but of course if one resurrected the old and elastic Thompson/Stephen definition, sowing disaffection between classes was seditious.

Ivens's sermon had been intended for urban Winnipeggers, but its hyperbole carried enough about those who owned 'the land upon which grew the wheat' to make it grate on the sensibilities of farmers and rural businessmen – who owned their own land. To Andrews's delight, Ivens could be interpreted as implying that rural people belonged to the hated capitalist class. Andrews certainly knew how to play to an audience: 'This reverend gentlemen speaking on Sunday night to a well dressed audience, I fancy, calls them "suckers."'[62] Either the juror-farmers would be struck, Andrews hoped, by the audacity of 'well-dressed' city folk demanding an ever-increasing share of the pie, or the jurors would be appalled by the lack of decorum that this 'lapsed clergyman' observed in the pulpit, calling people 'suckers.' One wouldn't expect juror William Hassett, an Anglo-Irish Protestant farmer who voted Conservative whenever he had the opportunity,[63] to be charmed by Ivens's diatribe. At the very least, the jurors ought to feel that Ivens had replaced salvation with economic panaceas.

In other sermons, Ivens had implicated the justice system in the master class. When necessary, Andrews skirted around the constitution, packed juries, and used his influence to have his cases heard by the right judge – just the sort of influence that Ivens inveighed against – but Andrews could also heatedly champion the law's honour: 'Gentlemen, you know it is a lie; a foul lie that this man is telling – when he told you that the capitalists own the judiciary in Canada.' It was a subtle and effective point, despite Andrews's over-the-top delivery: if the courts were tainted, then this very jury must be tainted too. But the jurors knew that they weren't tainted, so ... The son of a minister could not resist a parting shot against Ivens, especially with Christmas only a few days off: 'This reverend gentleman coming out with language of that kind on the Sabbath, when he should be preaching the gospel of that Christ, whose Birth we will remember in two or three days ... "Peace on earth and good will to men" – and they breathing hatred.'[64]

Phony Blumenberg; blasphemer Pritchard; irreligious Ivens. Also the prostitute Heaps: 'voting every time, prostituting his oath, elected to represent all the citizens, cuts off the city water, encourages the firemen to leave the city prey to the flames.' Likewise John Queen: 'Queen making seditious speeches. Queen in the city council, prostituting his oath of office just as the others.'[65] This time Andrews's vitriolic denunciation came from the heart and didn't require as much posturing. In earlier, more idealistic days between 1893 and 1897, he had been a Winnipeg alderman, and then the city's 'Boy Mayor' in 1898–9: 'A fierce civic pride existed in those days – I have a vivid impression of perfect teamwork among the citizens – everyone worked for the good of Winnipeg.' Allowing for the repainting of nostalgia, Andrews's comment nevertheless shows an unqualified (if self-serving) belief in service and an immense civic boosterism. He drew lessons from the early days of Winnipeg's development: 'You have to have civic spirit to make a city a success and believe me we had it in those days.' In recognition of his civic spirit, on 1 June 1898 Winnipeg's new fire engine had been named 'the A.J. Andrews,'[66] so it was doubly galling for him when the new generation of firefighters leaned towards highly partisan labour councillors such as Heaps and Queen, technically the firefighters' employers. Heaps and Queen, in essence, had advised their own employees to walk out on a contract. Of course, this, again, wasn't sedition in any sense of the word, and it hadn't much to do with Russell.

Finally, Andrews lamented, there was lack of patriotism, epitomized in R.J. Johns, like Russell a machinist, a Socialist Party of Canada member, and an advocate of the One Big Union. Lack of patriotism was, in the Citizens' idiom of Canadianism, tantamount to sedition. Manshrick's crime hadn't only been the voicing of pro-German attitudes – he could and did apologize for those – but also the failure to contribute to the patriotic fund. Nothing to be done about that at his trial, except weakly to lament the state of his finances. With their anti-alien ads, their attempt to characterize the Strike as Hun-inspired, and their singling out of the insignificant Schoppelrei, the Citizens had waved the flag. They certainly grasped the specialized 'ideology of service' in which duty to the state stood far ahead of loyalty to class, ethnicity, or region,[67] or even to humankind. Andrews asked Russell whether the SPC sang God Save the King at its meetings. Russell deftly parried. No, he replied, not at the beginning or the end, 'nor do the Methodists either.' Andrews officially bristled at this joke at the expense of his former Methodist conscience, and he cried for Metcalfe to 'demand order in the courtroom.' Even Metcalfe was puzzled, saying, 'I haven't seen any disorder.'[68]

Johns, then. At the Calgary conference, observed Andrews, it is Johns, 'who says – and it seemed a little thing gentlemen, – Johns the man who reporting at the meeting says "We had to sing *God Save the King* to get the building, but we sat down and got away with it."' Time for Andrews to place one hand on his heart and the other on the flag: 'A poor thing, you may say. Gentlemen, the flag, the Union Jack that waves above us is the emblem of our loyalty; dear to every one of us. We sing "God save the King," not for what the words mean, but because from the depths of our heart it is an outpouring of our loyalty.'[69] Andrews wasn't gunning for reason, but for the biases of the pre-selected jurors such as Harold (Harl) Woodhead, a general merchant in Morris who would serve as the Noble Grand – branch chairman – of the Morris Oddfellows in 1920;[70] and William McClymont, a 'staunch Orangeman' who owned the Hazelridge Mercantile Store and held Orange meetings upstairs there.[71]

Another way at Russell was to attack the platform of his party, the SPC, and, at the same time, to tell the story of the Citizens. Andrews's address

was a post-war manifesto of conservatism, with patriotism at its core –
and if patriotism was the measure, the SPC was woefully lacking.[72] For
many in the Winnipeg legal community these ideas were powerfully felt.
Pitblado's son Edward had fought as a lieutenant in the Canadian Field
Artillery, and twenty-two men from the Pitblado & Hoskin firm had
enlisted as well – five were killed in action.[73] In place of loyalty to
Canada, the SPC substituted 'the abolition of national sentiment' and
'allegiance only to class.' Andrews led the jury in a close reading of the
SPC manifesto: 'The working men have no country,' he read. 'We cannot take from them what they have not got.'[74] Andrews's gloss: this ideology was 'the moral equivalent of that embraced by deserters and opponents of conscription.' As for the associated notion that Canada was a
class-ridden society, he protested, 'I would like to point out to you that
these are horrid lies; there are no classes in this country. There is no master class; there is no slave class in this country.' Indeed, there weren't for
the Ontario-born Andrews, and it's unlikely that independent-minded
farmers and country merchants would notice them either. Since he himself had risen, Andrews saw only the individual and opportunity: 'Thank
God, under the free conditions we have in Canada, my son and my
grandson can be anything that he wishes. Free opportunity for every man
to rise and I trust the time will never come when under the dictatorship
of the proletariat we will all be reduced to one common level.'[75] Rather
than slaves, Andrews saw 'a number of workmen happily engaged in
their labor,'[76] into which paradise Russell and the SPC had planted discontent and had ominously prophesied 'the day,' a final showdown
between workers and capitalists.[77]

Andrews understood his audience and shaped his story accordingly.
All this concentration on class instead of the nation could only have
come from … German subversion! 'Perhaps for ten years before the
Great War,' he explained, 'the German was sowing the harvest among
the people. Hatred of England. They were sending people over to England, spies. They were preparing for the Day … In Berlin we found them
drinking to "Der tag," preparing for the day, and when the day came
Great Britain was not prepared. May God in his great goodness prepare
us for the days of revolution that these men are preparing for us.'[78] Russell's fondness for 'reds' opened a door for Andrews, but that door must
eventually lead to Germany: 'Our soldiers have been fighting the "Reds"
in Russia … It was the Russian Bolshevist, who in conspiracy with the
German in that treaty made with Germany in withdrawing the Russian
soldiers from the eastern front, sent many of our young men to their
death on the fields of Flanders.'[79] While young Canadians had served,
Russell and his associates had demeaned their holy memory: the SPC

manifesto alluded to 'a master class capable of sending millions to slaughter in the field for the extension of its profits.'[80] Suddenly Andrews turned personal with the jury: 'Some of your boys went to war. Did you know that they were offering their lives to extend the profits to capitalists? Don't you think that they went into this war for a principle? And haven't you given of your money, and have not some of our friends given their lives for that principle?'[81] The McDonald Detective Agency's questioning of the jurors had ensured that Andrews could safely display such telepathy. Juror Theo Nugent's son Ethelbert had fought for Canada and caught the Spanish flu overseas, dying shortly after his return to Winnipeg.[82] Frank Heale, younger brother of juror William Heale, had volunteered in the war and paid the 'supreme sacrifice.'[83]

Andrews offered a kind of nationalist catechism of manhood to the jury, a syllabus of virtue to measure the character deficits of Russell and his co-conspirators. 'What is a man's first duty?' For his answer, Andrews gave brief lip service to God, and then turned, more extensively, to the ideology of patriotic service:

We live under the British flag, our first allegiance is to whom? Our first allegiance is to the Great God who made us. That is man's first duty. What is his second? A man's second duty is to his country, such as exemplified by the splendid heroism of our young men who sprang to the aid of their country, willing to sacrifice their lives for their country's honour. They left homes, they left their wives and their little ones and went to France to fight for their country. Why? Because they felt, first, their duty to their God, and second, their duty to their country; third, their duty to their families and to those they loved; and lastly their duty to themselves. It is only by following that creed that we have reached our destiny as a nation.[84]

Russell, conversely, had asserted that 'his first duty was to himself.' In May, the Citizens had made similar statements while encouraging Winnipeggers to mobilize against the Strike: 'Self-preservation is the first law of nature ... Even a goat will get busy if deprived of its food and water supply.'[85] But now Andrews, with a country jury that hadn't read those words, felt no pressure to be consistent, and declared self-preservation a despicable thing: 'Self preservation is ... the law of the animal; it is not the law of the God-Man. Our first duty is not to ourselves.' If Russell thought so, he was ignorant of his duty to God, country, and family. Worse, he had set 'himself up as an educator – an educator to educate the workmen, to make them feel that they are slaves, and to sow among the workmen of this country the doctrine of hate.'[86] The claims wouldn't have been wasted on juror Albert Anderson, a school trustee whose family remembered him as a man devoted to his community. He gave his neighbours a helping hand whenever they needed it. After the Spanish influenza epidemic hit East Selkirk, he risked his life and his family's welfare to take care of ill neighbours. His grandson recalled that one thing that people always said about Albert was that he put others ahead of himself, and sometimes even ahead of his family.[87]

In contrast to the self-serving antagonist Russell were the story's community-minded white knights. Before a rural jury, Andrews could allow himself greater imaginative licence to continue the *Winnipeg Citizen*'s story of heroic and selfless public service: 'Where would [the Strike] have ended had it not been for the splendid heroism of that class which is neither employer or employee, that class of citizens which came between this class that Mr. Russell and his friends are trying to get at each other's throats; if it had not been for their-sacrifice, and their splendid heroism, – God alone knows what would have happened.'[88] If such 'classless' people – neither employer nor employee – were harder to find in Winnipeg than Andrews intimated, they were easy to find in the country and on this jury, so to call them 'selfless' wasn't bad policy. Unless the jurors had relatives with access to the *Western Labor News*, it's unlikely that the jurors would have known that the citizen-heroes were mostly either those upper-class people who benefited from the low wages of workers – the wealthy and their dependents – or those who couldn't afford to defy the wealthy – their non-unionized employees. Russell's lawyers had sought to place blame for the Strike, as Andrews put it, 'upon some Citizens' Committee.'[89] Well, yes, Andrews had been a member of the Citizens Committee of One Thousand. Were jurors surprised, he asked, 'that there were men like myself, who when we saw the children without any fault of ours and without any fault of these children, deprived of the means of life – when we saw the people faced with the impossibility of getting bread, are you surprised that we should at that time, have been willing to submit to the dictation temporarily of this strike committee?' The jurors didn't know that Andrews's compensation for his splendid heroism was nearly triple the prime minister's salary. What the jurors received instead of this information was a challenge to their masculinity: 'Would you ... be willing to crawl on your hands and knees to the labor temple, to bow your head three times for the floor, to get the children of this city milk?'[90]

On the public-spirited shoulders of the Citizens rested democracy, while the SPC suggested that the working class shouldn't let itself be constrained by parliamentary rules.[91] 'It is not a crime,' admitted

Andrews, 'for Mr. Russell to get up and say that he thinks the Russian government is a fine government, but he must not carry it to the limit of getting people to hate our form of government; he must not excite revolt; he must not excite discontent.' But Russell had advocated 'the establishment here of the Russian soviet government system by the same means as it was established there.'[92] The evidence for this was thin, yet the machinations by Russell and the SPC to gain control of the labour movement showed that Andrews wasn't entirely off-base. If Russell hadn't conspired to overthrow the nation, SPC-related correspondence indicated that he *had* planned to overthrow the forces of moderate labour. Andrews reserved most of his commentary for substantive letters to and from Russell. To Joe Knight, the leading Edmonton SPCer and eventual publisher of *The Soviet*, Russell had written on 29 November 1918, 'Well, Joe, I expect we will now be confronted with the horrors of peace, and it is to be hoped that the Reds will wake up now and get in all the propaganda that can be expounded twenty-four hours per day.'[93] What really interested Andrews about the letter was Russell's reference to the Western Labour Conference: 'We will pack it with reds, and no doubt start something.' To confirm the Citizens' story, vague references had to be reworked into specific meanings. Andrews helped the jury make the leap: 'Yes they started something which ended in two men in Winnipeg losing their lives, and the whole population of Winnipeg being put to inconvenience and distress.'[94] All the chance results of the Strike, including the shooting of strikers by the RNWMP, were the natural consequences of the 'something' that the Strike leaders had 'started.'

Andrews relished the famous 3 January 1919 letter from Russell to Chris Stephenson containing Russell's account of the Walker Theatre meeting: 'We held a mass meeting at the Walker Theatre … wakening the latent members to life again.' Andrews fastened on Russell's use of 'we' to make the point that although the meeting had been sponsored by the Winnipeg Trades and Labor Council and the SPC, Russell, writing to Stephenson as 'socialist to socialist,' conflated the two organizations, disclosing that the Reds – Russell, Johns, and their followers – had captured the TLC.[95] Russell's language certainly had a conspiratorial ring. Telling Stephenson about a prospective editor of a new Toronto-based *Machinists' Bulletin*, Russell confided, 'The Comrade who edited the *Marxian Socialist* up until it was banned, has been appointed Editor and the intentions are to get the same line of stuff off, so you can figure the rest yourself.'[96] 'Why,' Andrews mused, 'should he be figuring the rest himself?' Russell, editor of the national *Machinists' Bulletin*, related the dramatic growth in its circulation to 'somewhat around 20,000 … proof that they are swallowing it … Some of the recent issues and although they are not the real thing, you will realize the necessity of me leading them gently' [sic].[97] Andrews fastened on Russell's reference to the 'real thing,' to 'swallowing,' and to 'leading them gently.' While this was far from showing the Strike to be a Bolshevik plot, it did suggest that Andrews was right in attributing ulterior motives to Russell. The real thing, Andrews correctly suggested, was the *Communist Manifesto*. In this, Andrews detected a sinister Russell instilling poison, corrupting workers by slow degree.[98] Russell's letters were enough for Andrews, no stranger to propaganda himself, to uncover a fundamental deceit in Russell's character. For Russell, propaganda involved slowly acclimatizing resistant workers to militancy. The Citizens came at propaganda from a different angle, using the technique of red herrings. As to the question of possible revolution, whereas socialists sometimes denied their own statements, the Citizens could appeal to the detective capacities of Winnipeggers to find more conspiracy than actually existed – so much so that Andrews had had to warn Meighen not to take the *Citizen*'s conspiracy headlines too literally.[99]

In the preliminary hearing, standing before Judge Noble, Andrews had emphasized the constitutional transgression involved in the Strike Committee taking authority in Winnipeg. Now, before a jury, Andrews didn't waste much time on constitutional legalities. Instead, for his farmers, Andrews translated the law into the popular idiom of the *Winnipeg Citizen*'s hyperbole: 'Men dared not go out and deliver milk or bread without protection from the Strike Committee ... There was terror throughout parts of the city. People proposed sending their families out. You can imagine the situation pictured to you ... There were reports of babies that were dying for want of milk.' The country jurors hadn't been there; how could they argue? And the champion of man's first duty to God phrased his words so that he wasn't technically lying: there *had* been reports – false reports, yes, but they were reports – of babies dying. Rather than split hairs with legal definitions, Andrews made sedition a matter of personal opinion: 'Some of us have formed the opinion that policemen and firemen, who are guarding the lives and the property of the city, should not go out on strike ... [The strikers] undertook to punish me, and to punish my children, and to punish the men, women and children of the city for wrongs they had not committed, by holding a gun to them, and not to the Metal works, but to them, to compel compliance to their demands. Open rebellion – open insurrection – open sedition.'[100]

To increase the emotional impact of the story, Andrews made a confession: at one time, much younger, he had thought himself a socialist! He had understood socialism as reform then, 'the doctrine of the God-man, the brotherhood of humanity.' Andrews's revelation was a tactical ploy, but it wasn't pure bluff. Twenty years earlier, a Conservative candidate in the 1899 provincial election, he had in fact been denounced as revolutionary. He had advocated referenda and proportional representation to improve the democratic process in Manitoba. From a surprising quarter – the local Fabian Society – he had received support. The Liberal *Manitoba Free Press*, however, thundered at him for suggesting 'dangerous innovations … in the heart of an election campaign.' In an editorial titled 'Mr. Andrews a Revolutionist,' the *Free Press* had warned voters against a candidate intent on 'over turning … our system of government who will at one stroke topple over the constitution under which we live, and forfeit all the advantages in government for which patriots in the Mother Country have fought and suffered and handed down to us as perhaps the most priceless heirloom that can ever be bequeathed to posterity.'[101] Despite the *Free Press* rhetoric, Andrews's approach had been democratic and constitutional, not revolutionary. By 1919, Andrews was less ready to champion innovations, and the *Free Press* had taught him a pragmatic, even cynical lesson on how to use patriotism to silence one's opponents.

During the Russell trial, Andrews insisted that he had no desire to attack socialism 'as perhaps you and I understand it.' His target was something quite different – 'revolutionary socialism'[102] – and his best evidence came from Russell's OBU work. Russell, Andrews noticed, was an action-oriented man, always going on about wanting to 'start something.' Andrews read from Russell's letter to Stephenson: 'Comrade Johns and myself are elected to represent the Trades and Labor Council at the Calgary meeting, and we are getting a number of the Reds elected by the locals – so let's hope we will be able to start something.' 'Start what?' Andrews asked, and then answered with a series of quotations from Russell: '"When we boys start something" – "start scrap" – "start revolution."' Andrews didn't reveal the context of the last two words, but he disclosed that Russell's final letter had ended, 'Yours for the scrap.'[103] When Russell and his 'boys' arrived at the Calgary conference in March 1919, they had as their goal, Andrews said, 'the dictatorship of the proletariat. The taking over of all property from persons to whom it rightfully belongs by the proletarians – the worker.'[104] If Andrews's wording was more direct than the resolutions at Calgary (which called for the present system of production to be abolished, and for workers to give up on Parliament as means to achieve their ends), he wasn't far off. The 1 May 1919 pre-issue of the *One Big Union Bulletin* announced, 'The Proletarian Dictatorship has been proclaimed in Canada,' and carried the following publishing information: 'Vol. 1, No. 1, Winnipeg, May 1, 1919 – Prov. Sec'y.

Room 14, Labor Temple.' Who occupied Room 14 in the Winnipeg Labor Temple? R.B. Russell.[105]

After the trial's war of words ended, Judge Metcalfe gave a four-hour charge to the jury. It accorded well with the Citizens' views: 'Sedition ... is an offence against the constitution, which we have been in the habit of considering the best birthright which our ancestors left us, and which, with some constitutional improvements as may from time to time occur, is the most valuable inheritance which we can transmit to posterity. When we consider the benefits daily conferred upon our people by the British Constitution, the crowning effort of centuries of bloodshed and sacrifice, it should fill the hearts of all British subjects with gratitude that God has seen fit to place them within the jurisdiction of that constitution; and they should righteously guard and prevent its destruction by unlawful means.' In ideal circumstances he favoured free speech, but the war had altered the ratio: 'In time of stress,' words 'may be likely to cause such discontent, hostility and disturbance as to be seditious. If the words spoken or published are seditious, it is no defence that they are true, and evidence to prove their truth is inadmissible.'[106] And he had no patience for pacifism, which, though it might not be legally seditious, he clearly considered to be so: 'If a man won't fight for his country, as our forefathers fought at Quebec and Queenston Heights, will he fight for his fireside? If such sentiments are to be brought about by illegal strikes, by force exercised thereby, by terror, by combinations of soldiers and workmen, by speeches at soldiers and workmen's councils, or by unlawful means, it is a crime and it is seditious.'[107]

Metcalfe dealt head-on with suggestions that the federal government was mixed up in the prosecution and was paying 'a part' of the cost. He interpreted the issue in the way that the Citizens had: if the Province had declined to prosecute, and if it was unusual to have a private prosecution paid for by Ottawa, it was worse to 'see these offences committed' and be forced to 'marvel at the audacity of the offenders and the inactivity of the Governments.' In this way, he castigated the Province, and even managed obliquely to justify the Citizens' role – 'It is the duty of every individual, or combination of individuals, to observe the law; and to give information of its infraction by others.' He admitted that the administration of justice was a provincial matter – 'as a rule this duty devolves upon the government of the province' – but if an agitation 'too great for the province to deal with' occurred, or if there was danger of the constitution being overthrown, the federal government could supply military force, 'quell the disturbance,' arrest the guilty, and 'aid' the Province in bringing them to trial – 'Otherwise, how could we exist?'[108] There was some force to this argument, but Metcalfe had cut off the defence's ability to question the government's role, and, in effect, he was now admitting that Andrews had misled the jury when he had claimed, 'There is only one crown represented in this case, by the Attorney-General of this province, and I am here as his representative.'[109]

Whatever personal or political friction existed between Metcalfe and Andrews, they belonged to the same class, and Judge closed ranks with Crown. His instructions to the jury members included telling them what decision to make: 'Gentlemen, speaking to you as the Judge, if I were on a jury, there is much in that matter that I would find no difficulty in concluding was seditious.'[110] Andrews had chosen his jurors well, and despite the reservations of Roy Tolton and D.H. Pritchard, by the next morning the jury had finished deliberations. Guilty.

Epilogue: Echo

After Russell was taken out to the woodshed, only the mopping up was left to do. More police were put on the streets, since authorities worried that the city might go up in flames after Bill Pritchard addressed the workers, but the feared riot never took place. Andrews travelled about the city cautiously, with RNWMP bodyguards at his side. In the coming months, Heaps would be acquitted, but Ivens, Pritchard, Johns, Queen, and Armstrong would each be sentenced to one year in jail for several counts of seditious conspiracy. R.E. Bray would be found guilty of being a Common Nuisance, and would be rewarded with six months of hard labour. The sentences, Metcalfe would note, were so short only because he was following the jury's recommendation for mercy.[1] Victoria Park, where the strikers had massed, would be sold by the City to Winnipeg Hydro, so that a steam heating plant could be built.

The Citizens' Committee of 1000 disbanded … at least in name. The Citizens had already planned for their own succession in civic politics with the Citizens' League, and culturally with the October Citizenship conference, but employers still needed an organization that was dedicated to propagating their views more directly. 'Masters are always and every where in a sort of tacit, but constant and uniform combination,' Adam Smith had said.[2] After a couple of months of respect to the dear departed Citizens' Committee, in January 1920 the Employers' Association of Manitoba held its inaugural meeting at the Hotel Fort Garry. As befit a young organization unencumbered by the sins of its predecessor, it called for 'industrial peace and commercial prosperity.' But it had no difficulty remembering who had won in 1919, and it agitated for 'freedom of contract' (i.e., an open shop), and against lockouts and strikes. To ensure that tragedies such as 1919 never happened again, it planned 'to disseminate a knowledge of the fundamental economic laws and conditions upon which successful production depends.' Within three months, the association had enrolled 243 firms, employing 15,317 people.[3] On the 51-member board of directors sat eight former Citizens, and a number of their close associates.[4] Charles Roland – newspaperman, commissioner of the Winnipeg Development and Industrial Bureau, and all-round propagandist for the business community – became the group's principal spokesperson.[5]

For public consumption, the Employers' Association began in 1922 to publish *The Payroll and Labor Legislation Review*, opposing 'radical closed shop practices, intimidation or coercion, violence, destructive agitation, class wars, boycotts, blacklists and all unwarranted and illegal interferences tending to cripple industry and commerce in Canada.'[6] Privately, the association sent members a confidential *Special News Bulletin*. In 1919, the Citizens' Committee of 1000 had demonstrated what feats a combination of masters could accomplish, and if Winnipeg businessmen were inclined to forget this, *Bulletin* #321 was there to remind them: 'If you are not a member of the Employers' Association, why "go it alone" when there is an organization of over 300 other representative concerns ready to help fight your battles for you.'[7] The *Bulletin* also alerted its members, for example, that eight Canadian delegates had attended a 'Red Convention in Moscow,' where 'Nikoli Lenine' had led discussions about the 'prospects of World Revolution.' The *Bulletin* reported that Moscow directed the forces of 'World Communism,' that it maintained close ties with Canadian and Winnipeg Communists,[8] and that 'Under the guise of Labor parties, groups of Socialists representing many types of radicalism and syndicalism are continually seeking representation on City Councils the World over, aiming to change the entire social system and establish the Russian Soviet System.'[9]

When striking miners in Herrin, Illinois, killed eighteen guards and replacement workers, the *Bulletin* announced 'the most frightful crime in America's history,' but detailed nothing of the labour troubles leading up to the murders.[10] When Benito Mussolini's Fascists violently assaulted trade unionists and socialists in Italy, the Employers' Association cheered. Unions, the *Bulletin* declared, had too much power in Italy, and so must be met by a diametrically opposed force. If a strike broke out, the Fascists promptly sent however many men were deemed necessary to break it. 'The members of the order have driven the Communists out of factories and restored the plants to the owners ... Any one having difficulty with their labor should apply to the Fiscisti [*sic*], who will be pleased to furnish them with men.' The strike breakers would announce their arrival to the government authorities – 'the fiscisti movement in every respect is cooperating with the government' – and then would 'proceed peacefully about their work ... If interfered with, however, the retaliation is extreme' [*sic*].[11] 'Peacefully,' in other words, was code for 'violently if necessary.' Like many of Winnipeg's Specials, Mussolini's blackshirts were in part recruited from among the young men of the upper classes: the Fascists were 'the sons of the finest people of Italy.' Although A.J. Andrews had skilfully managed the government, ending the Winnipeg General Strike with little violence, and although the Specials had proved to be duds in Winnipeg, the Employers' Association cast a longing eye towards Italy, where solutions to labour unrest seemed so much simpler and so much more emphatic. Fascism, Italian style, was 'the quickest way to bring around a normal condition in any country and avert a turmoil of the governments of respective countries.'[12]

Praise of fascism; and severe cautions about Manitoba's over-liberal education system: Roland disclosed to Premier John Bracken that the 'Research and Investigation Bureau of the Employers' Association' had discovered that a number of schools were teaching 'revolutionary doctrines that threaten the foundations of citizenship of this province.' 'Under the guise of schools and colleges,' revolutionaries were teaching 'class hatred,' 'Sovietism,' and 'Communism.' Roland urged Bracken to enact laws swiftly to 'stamp out for all time the "Moscow hope" for the overthrow of Canadian government.'[13]

At every moment, and particularly when the Winnipeg General Strike was first declared, employers were tempted to see labour as wholly Other, an alien eruption from the backwaters of Eastern Europe and the slums of England. What the Citizens were able to do, even after the Strike – through newsletters, the Employers' Association, educational initiatives, and political lobbying – was to recast the conflict over wages and power into the idiom of citizenship. The worker no longer belonged simply to the alien mass, but must appear in the freighted role of 'citizen,' either meeting or not meeting the requirements of the Citizens' definition. The citizen was, so to speak, a company with a limited liability. This meant that upper-case Citizens needn't think of themselves in a broadly human relation to their employees – responsibility was strictly limited. As long as the employer upheld his duties to the nation, what happened between employer and employee was private, happening in the inalienable sphere of private property. The paradigm did have some advantages for workers – employers needn't peer too closely into the private affairs of the 'citizen' – but many disadvantages, mainly that employers controlled the criteria of citizenship. Some criteria were unsurprising and uncontested: citizens must not advocate the overturning of the present system of government. Some criteria were more technical and arbitrary: a citizen's border papers must be fully in order if his name were Schoppelrei; more leeway would be given if his name were Coppins. Some criteria were contested: in the slowly accreting right of free speech, could a citizen speak against his country's involvement in a war, as Ivens had done? No, the Citizens answered, and they had little difficulty carrying the argument. Some criteria were still being forged in the furnace, though the Citizens had a strong idea of what the finished product should look like: a closed shop was incompatible with free citizenship; sympathy strikes were certainly incompatible; possibly all strikes were incompatible.

Of course, not all Canadians applauded the Citizens' ideological victory. In the Manitoba provincial election of June 1920, labour elected eleven candidates. Four were elected in Winnipeg, 'three of them political convicts' (William Ivens, John Queen, and George Armstrong), while William J. Tupper, a scion of the Conservative Tuppers, narrowly kept R.B. Russell, 'an inmate of the provincial penitentiary,'[14] out of the legislature. But resistance to the Citizens also came from less ideologically polarized sources. O.D. Skelton – political economist, dean of arts at Queen's University, and later Mackenzie King's undersecretary for external affairs – had in 1911 published *Socialism: A Critical Analysis*, based on his PhD thesis 'The Case against Socialism.' But in 1920, he insisted that Canada had little to fear from revolutionaries, and that few Canadians were likely to fall in behind those who, 'hypnotized by formulas ... shriek for the overthrow of all organized society and the dictatorship of the proletariat.' The war, Skelton warned, had accustomed Canadians to 'the coercion of minorities and the worship of the state,' and the most serious threat to liberty came from hysteria among the wealthy. He said, 'It is hypocrisy to talk of the sacredness of democracy and the constitution if constitutional methods of influencing one's fellow-citizens are forbidden.' In a veiled reference to the Winnipeg sedition trials and Blumenberg's immigration hearing, he denounced 'trials which assume that socialism is sedition and the preaching of doctrines with which you may differ punishable because possibly leading you to commit a breach of the peace against the preacher.'[15]

Despite moderate voices such as Skelton's, the ideological power of the Citizens and the Employers' Association may be measured in the fact that it took ten years for striking postal workers to be fully reinstated. In April 1929, the federal Postmaster General proposed to reinstate postal employees who had struck in 1919 – with reimbursement of lost pay and restoration of seniority. The Winnipeg Board of Trade, the Employers' Association, and the prairie division of the Canadian Manufacturers' Association rose up in anger and sent 'an emphatic denunciation of the proposal' to

Prime Minister Mackenzie King, cabinet ministers, and senators. The Board of Trade telegram stated that 'Winnipeg business men are unalterably opposed to government giving back pay to postal workers who violated their oath of allegiance and refused to go back within the time allotted by the government in 1919.' Any 'surrender' by Ottawa would disastrously affect postal morale right across the country. The Board of Trade was sure that 'the Communist revolutionary element' would immediately advertise its power throughout Canada.[16] Nevertheless, defying the heirs of the Citizens, Ottawa finally passed the Postal and Railway Mail Service Employees Bill. Higher-salaried employees, who had been rehired as postal helpers of the lowest grade after the Strike, finally received backpay ... ten years after having been summarily demoted.[17]

Unlike the postal workers, the Citizens who had major roles in defeating labour flourished after the Strike. Parnell, such an effective public façade for the Citizens at the preliminary hearing, became the city's mayor after Gray, serving two terms. When he died in office, Citizens-affiliated councillor Frank Fowler replaced him. Pitblado took a seat on the boards of a number of companies, received an honorary degree from Dalhousie University, and became president of the Canadian Bar Association. Sweatman, shortly after the Strike, became president of the Board of Trade. Much later, in 1938, he ran for mayor against John Queen, only to lose to the man he had helped put behind bars two decades earlier. But both Pitblado's and Sweatman's firms did very well, the one as Pitblado LLP (now with 60 lawyers) and the other eventually turning into Fillmore Riley LLP (now with 54 lawyers).

And Andrews? He did well too. He served as president of the Law Society of Manitoba from 1922 to 1925, and was lionized as 'the nestor of the Manitoba bar.' In 1936 lawyers and judges held a banquet celebrating his golden anniversary.[18] Today, in the Commodity Exchange tower at 360 Main Street, one can find the offices of Pitblado LLP and Fillmore Riley LLP on the 25th and 17th floors respectively, as well as the 92 lawyers of Aikins, MacAulay & Thorvaldson LLP, which inherited Andrews's firm. From the offices of Aikins, MacAulay & Thorvaldson on the 28th to 30th floors, one can look down on the place where the riots occurred from a far greater height than Andrews, his blood boiling, did in 1919.[19] Near the end of his eighty-four years, Andrews said that life and people had been good to him. 'More than the average allotment of good things of this world has been given to him.' Did he have regrets that ate away at his last days? Not according to his biographer: 'He has lived too strenuously to be beset by the doubts that harass the contemplative mind.'[20]

Notes

INTRODUCTION

1 Natalie Zemon Davis and Randolph Starn, 'Introduction,' *Representations* 26 (Spring 1989), 1. It was Lucien Febvre who first used the phrase 'history from below' when in 1932 he observed that Albert Mathiez, a founding member of the Annales tradition, had sought 'histoire des masses et non de vedettes; histoire vue d'en bas en non d'en haut' ('a history of the masses and not of celebrities; history seen from below and not from the top'). In 1966 the phrase entered English historiography as the title for E.P Thompson's discussion of the New History. Thompson's 1963 *History of the English Working Class*, with his call to rescue ordinary people from the 'enormous condescension of posterity,' inspired a generation of social and labour historians. Zemon Davis's *The Return of Martin Guerre* entered the canon of *history from below*, first as a film adaptation, and later as her fine history of the case. Lucien Febvre, 'Albert Mathiez: Un tempérament, une éducation,' *Annales HES* 4 (1932) 18, reprinted in Lucien Febvre, *Combats pour l'histoire* (Paris, 1992), 347. E.P. Thompson, 'History from Below,' *Times Literary Supplement*, 7 April 1961. E.P. Thompson, *The Making of the English Working Class* (New York, 1963), 12. Natalie Zemon Davis, *The Return of Martin Guerre* (Cambridge, 1983). The translation and reference to Febvre's article on Mathiez, is courtesy of Lex Heerma van Voss, IISH, e-mail to *H-Labor*, Editor's Subject 'History from Below,' 19 May 2006.
2 The standard accounts of the strike include Norman Penner, ed., *Winnipeg 1919 – The Strikers' Own History of the Winnipeg General Strike* (Toronto, 1973); D.C. Masters, *The Winnipeg General Strike*

(1950; Toronto, 1973); Kenneth McNaught and David J. Bercuson, *The Winnipeg General Strike: 1919* (Don Mills, 1974); David Jay Bercuson, *Confrontation in Winnipeg: Labour, Industrial Relations, and the General Strike* (Montreal, 1974); J.M. Bumsted, *The Winnipeg General Strike of 1919: An Illustrated History* (Winnipeg, 1994); and Craig Heron, ed., *The Workers' Revolt in Canada 1917–1925* (Toronto, 1998).

3 For example: 'At the time of the arrests, there is little doubt that Andrews was a restraining influence both upon Robertson and upon the extremists, like Meighen, in the cabinet.' McNaught and Bercuson, *The Winnipeg General Strike: 1919*, 81. 'A programme of drastic action was taken, largely through the influence of the minister of justice, Hon. Arthur Meighen, that able and very determined man, of Ulster descent, who was resolved that the strike must be broken.' Masters, *The Winnipeg General Strike*, 102–3.

4 Bill Pritchard, *Address to the Jury in The Crown vs. Armstrong, Heaps, et al.* (Winnipeg: Defense Committee, 1920), 30–1. Pritchard referred to Meighen's construction of the Wartime Elections Act, and the Immigration Act amendments of 5 June 1919.

5 The correspondence is found in the Department of Justice file on the Winnipeg General Strike. See Library and Archives Canada, Record Group (RG) 13 (Department of Justice), Accession 1987–88/103: box 36, file 9-A-1688, 'William Ivens and Robert Russell the King Vs. the A/M Regarding the Winnipeg Strike' (hereafter LAC, RG 13, Access 87–88/103: box 36, file 9-A-1688). This collection of documents is more varied and extensive in content than what Peter Heenan, Liberal member of Parliament and minister of labour in the King government, disclosed in May 1926. In debate on the Liberal government's budget proposals, Heenan asserted that in 1919 – without the Province's request – the federal government had sent troops to Winnipeg, troops that had shot and killed (*Debates House of Commons*, 11 May 1926, 3286). Meighen denied this (*Debates House of Commons*, 2 June 1926, 3979), and Heenan responded with lengthy quotations from Department of Labour records: the correspondence of Labour Minister Gideon Robertson, Prime Minister Borden, Brigadier-General H.D.B. Ketchen, Minister of Immigration James Calder, and Meighen himself (*Debates House of Commons*, 2 June 1926, 4004–26). However, Heenan did not have access to the Department of Justice files that contained the most revealing account of the relationship between Ottawa and the Citizens' Committee. See also 'The Heenan-Robertson Dispute,' *Toronto Daily Star*, 1 June 1926. Tom Mitchell and James Naylor, 'The Prairies: In the Eye of the Storm,' in Heron ed., *The Workers'*

Revolt in Canada, benefited from access to the files contained in LAC, RG 13, Access 87–88/103: box 36, file 9-A-1688.

6 For E.J. McMurray's request, see *Sessional Papers*, 1922, vol. 5 (Ottawa, 1922), 16. On 9 January 1923, Thomas Mackay, undersecretary of state, wrote to the deputy minister of justice to remind him of the request for documents made in April 1922. Mackay acknowledged that Justice might not be able to provide the documents requested. Still, he wanted a response of some kind from the department. See LAC, RG 13, Access 87–88/103: box 36, file 9-A-1688, pocket #1, Under Secretary of State to Mr Newcombe, Deputy Minister of Justice, 23 January 1923. Nothing was produced. For Woodsworth's attempt and a response from Meighen, see Canada, House of Commons, *Debates*, 25 January 1926, 423–4.

7 Adam Smith, *An Inquiry into the Nature and Causes of the Wealth of Nations*, vol.1, ed. R.H. Campbell and A.S. Skinner (Indianapolis, 1981), I.viii.13, 84.

8 An introduction and index to these papers is available. See Ken Kehler and Alvin Esau, *Famous Manitoba Trials: The Winnipeg General Strike Trials – Research Source* (Winnipeg, 1990).

9 Smith believed that commercial society freed the ordinary person from the subservience and dependency of earlier societies: 'Commerce and manufactures gradually introduced order and good government, and with them, the liberty and security of individuals, among the inhabitants of the country, who had before lived almost in a continual state of war with their neighbours, and of servile dependency upon their superiors.' Smith, *Wealth of Nations*, III.iv.4, 412.

10 Western Canada Pictorial Index, University of Winnipeg, Winnipeg Free Press Collection, 'Members of Citizens' Committee at a banquet held after the Winnipeg General Strike,' image 38698, contact sheet A1292. The provenance of this photograph is not certain. Given the Citizens' secrecy about their identities, it's difficult to believe that they would allow a photograph to be taken of the executive. There is limited information about the photo's provenance, but, as in the case of Billy the Kid, so strong is the wish to *see* the historical subject that, where there is only one photo or portrait, the apocryphal very quickly becomes the canonical.

11 Perry Anderson, *Lineages of the Absolutist State* (London, 1979), 11.

12 Canadian historians have generally limited themselves to accounts of employer associations such as the Canadian Manufacturers' Association and the Canadian Industrial Reconstruction Association. For previous accounts of Citizens' committees, see Desmond Morton with Terry Copp, *Working People: An Illustrated History of the Canadian Labour*

Movement (Ottawa, 1980), 83; Craig Heron, *The Workers' Revolt in Canada 1917–1925* (Toronto, 1998); Tom Traves, *The State and Enterprise: Canadian Manufacturers and the Federal Government 1917–1931* (Toronto, 1979), 15–29; Judy Fudge and Eric Tucker, *Labour Before the Law: The Regulation of Workers' Collective Action in Canada, 1900–1948* (Don Mills, 2001), 19, 21; James Naylor, *The New Democracy: Challenging the Social Order in Industrial Ontario 1914–25* (Toronto, 1991), 189–214; Andrew Yarmie, 'The State and Employers' Associations in British Columbia: 1900–1932,' *Labour/Le Travail* 45 (Spring, 2000): 53–101.

13 Philip Corrigan and Derek Sayer, *The Great Arch: English State Formation as Cultural Revolution* (Oxford, 1985), 3.

14 Perry Anderson, *Considerations on Western Marxism* (London, 1976), 4.

15 Antonio Gramsci, *Selections from the Prison Notebooks*, ed. and trans. Quentin Hoare and Geoffrey Nowell Smith (New York, 1971), 235, 238. Gramsci's various assessments of relations between the state and civil society are not always consistent. While we are indebted to his insights about the durability of the liberal order, we attempt no resolution of what Perry Anderson has referred to as the 'antinomies of Antonio Gramsci.' See Perry Anderson, 'The Antinomies of Antonio Gramsci,' *New Left Review* 100 (November–December 1976), 5–78.

1 PERMITTED BY AUTHORITY OF THE STRIKE COMMITTEE

1 Weather data courtesy Dr Rod McGinn, Geography Department, Brandon University.

2 Provincial Archives of Manitoba, MG 14, C109, M 329, Robert Blackwood Whidden Graham fonds (hereafter PAM, Robert Graham fonds), 81.

3 See Bertrand Russell, *Unpopular Essays* (London, 1950), 80–7.

4 Seattle's general strike in February 1919 lasted a week; Britain's general strike in 1926 would last only 48 hours. The comparison with the Commune is in the duration of proletarian ascendancy in Paris and Winnipeg: Paris for two months; Winnipeg six weeks. Bloody Saturday was nowhere near as violent as the suppression of the Commune. Nevertheless, assertions that the Commune was the creation of the First International, 'whose hidden hand guided, with a mysterious and dreaded power, the whole machine of Revolution,' sound much like the *Winnipeg Citizen*'s charges of Soviet machinations in Winnipeg. For the quotation, see E.B.M., 'The Commune of 1871,' *Fraser's Magazine* 3, n.s. (June 1871), 802, quoted in Kirk Willis, 'The Introduction

and Critical Reception of Marxist Thought in Britain, 1850–1900,' *The Historical Journal* 20, no. 2 (1977), 425 n. 39.

5 The estimate of 30,000 strikers appears in at least two sources unlikely to overestimate: Citizens' Committee of One Thousand, *The Activities and Organization of The Citizens' Committee of One Thousand in connection with The Winnipeg Strike* (Winnipeg, 1919) (hereafter *The Activities and Organization of The Citizens' Committee*), 12. J. Castell Hopkins, ed., *The Canadian Annual Review of Public Affairs, 1919* (Toronto, 1920), 464.

6 *Manitoba Free Press*, 24 May 1919.

7 'The Week in Politics,' Unsigned, *L'Ordine Nuovo* 1, no. 6 (14 June 1919), in Antonio Gramsci, *Selections from Political Writings 1910–1920*, selected and edited by Quentin Hoare (London, 1977), 61.

8 Bryan Palmer has observed that the Strike was indeed 'an act of civil disobedience that threatened treason.' Bryan D. Palmer, 'What's Law Got to Do with It? Historical Considerations on Class Struggle, Boundaries of Constraint, and Capitalist Authority,' *Osgoode Hall Law Journal* 41, nos. 2&3 (Summer/Fall 2003), 479.

9 Provincial Archives of Manitoba, M268–9, Preliminary Hearing, The King vs. Wm. Ivens, R.B. Russell (hereafter PAM, Preliminary Hearing), R.J. Johns et al., J.R. Ong, 1448–51.

10 PAM, Preliminary Hearing, F.J. Foster, 824–6.

11 PAM, Preliminary Hearing, George A. Graham, 863–5; Mr. Davis, Manager Dominion Theatre, 999–1000.

12 *Manitoba Free Press*, Friday 25 July 1919. See PAM, Preliminary Hearing, 196–259.

13 PAM, Preliminary Hearing, William M. Gordon, 609–11.

14 PAM, Preliminary Hearing, Charles H. McNaughton, 616–18.

15 PAM, Preliminary Hearing, Herbert O. Collins, 798–800.

16 A 'Trades Council special meeting' was reported in the *Western Labor News* as follows: 'A communication from the Crescent Creamery was received requesting the Council to consider the claims of the hospitals and children if a strike is called. It was pointed out that this company was shipping butter to Chicago and selling it cheaper than in Winnipeg. This was to maintain Winnipeg prices.' Carruthers denied these charges under oath. PAM, Preliminary Hearing, James M. Carruthers, 243–53.

17 See, for example, PAM, Preliminary Hearing, Howard Rosling, Boat Rental Agency; OL. Marrin, Jobin-Marrin Company, Wholesale Grocers, William McKenzie, bread manufacturer, 669–71, 1249–52, 1443–7.

18 E.P. Thompson, *The Making of the English Working Class* (Markham, 1968), 9–10.

19 Library and Archives Canada, RG 18, Royal Canadian Mounted
    Police, vol. 3314, H.V. – 1 (vol. 4), Winnipeg General Strike and Riot
    1919, Winnipeg, Manitoba, Immigration Board Hearing (hereafter
    LAC, Immigration Board Hearing, vol. 4, Samuel Blumenberg), 15
    July 1919, 34.
20 *Manitoba Free Press*, 7 August 1919.
21 *Statutes of Canada*, 9–10 George V, xcviii–xcix, 1919.
22 PAM, Preliminary Hearing, Ed Parnell, 1035.
23 *Winnipeg Citizen*, 9 June 1919. See Library and Archives Canada,
    Robert Borden Papers, (hereafter LAC, Robert Borden Papers), reel C-
    4341, The Citizens' Committee of One Thousand, 9 June 1919: 61860.
24 Advertisement, *Manitoba Free Press*, 15 May 1919, 7.
25 'City Police Showed Where Sympathy Lay,' *Manitoba Free Press*, 7
    August 1919, 10.
26 'The Strike Situation in Winnipeg,' *Winnipeg Citizen*, 19 May 1919.
27 The Activities and Organization of The Citizens' Committee, 5.
28 K.D. Brown, 'The Anti-Socialist Union, 1908–49,' in K.D. Brown, ed.,
    Essays in Anti-Labour History (Hamden, CT, 1974), 234–61; Stephen
    White, 'Ideological Hegemony and Political Control: The Sociology of
    Anti-Bolshevism in Britain 1918–1920,' *Scottish Labour History Soci-
    ety Journal* 9 (June 1975), 3–20; Arthur McIvor, '"A Crusade for Capi-
    talism": The Economic League, 1919–1939,' *Journal of Contemporary
    History* 23 (4 October 1988), 631–55; *A Report To His Excellency
    Hiram W. Johnson, Governor Of California, As Commissioner
    Appointed On April 15, 1912, To Investigate Charges of Cruelty And
    All Matters Pertaining To The Recent Disturbances In The City of San
    Diego And the County Of San Diego, Including The Causes Thereof
    And The Causes Contributing Thereto* (Sacramento, 1912); Selig
    Perelman and Philip Taft, *History of Labor in the United States,
    1896–1932* (New York, 1935); Elizabeth Jameson, *All That Glitters:
    Class, Conflict, and Community in Cripple Creek* (Chicago, 1998);
    American Protective League – Organized with the Approval and Oper-
    ating Under the Direction of the United States Department of Justice,
    Bureau of Investigation (confidential) (Washington, 1918); William
    Millikan, 'Maintaining "Law and Order": The Minneapolis Citizens'
    Alliance in the 1920s,' *Minnesota History* (Summer 1989), 219–33;
    Louis G. Silverberg, 'Citizens' Committees: Their Role in Industrial
    Conflict,' *Public Opinion Quarterly* 5, no. 1 (March 1941), 17–37.
29 PAM, Preliminary Hearing, Sergeant Reames, 103.
30 'Men on both sides fell … About eight soldiers and 12 foreigners were
    left … unconscious before the foreign element beat a retreat.' *Win-
    nipeg Tribune*, 27, 28 January 1919, quoted in Henry Trachtenberg,

"'The Old Clo' Move'": Anti-Semitism, Politics, and the Jews of Winnipeg, 1882–1921,' PhD diss., York University (Toronto), 1984, 2: 649. Six soldiers and civilians were arrested and sentenced to either fines or two weeks in jail. Ibid., 869 n. 88.

31 PAM, Preliminary Hearing, Frederick William Law, 405.

32 LAC, Board of Inquiry, Samuel Blumenberg, vol. 4, 15 July 1919, 36–9.

33 Donald Avery, *'Dangerous Foreigners': European Immigrant Workers and Labour Radicalism in Canada, 1896–1932* (Toronto, 1979), 82.

34 Henry Trachtenberg reports that the Citizens' Committee may have circulated a leaflet in Yiddish through North End during the Strike. Trachtenberg, "'The Old Clo' Move,'" 2: 656.

35 *Winnipeg Citizen*, 9 June 1919.

36 Advertisement, *Manitoba Free Press*, 15 May 1919, 7.

37 The *Winnipeg Citizen* was set in town and printed in the country. *Montreal Gazette*, 21 May 1919.

38 Norman Penner, ed., *Winnipeg 1919 – The Strikers' Own History of the Winnipeg General Strike* (Toronto, 1973), 211.

39 *Toronto Daily Star*, 23 May 1919.

40 PAM, Preliminary Hearing, F.G. Thompson, 975.

41 PAM, Preliminary Hearing, Theodore Kipp, 1309–10.

42 *Western Labor News*, 22 May 1919.

43 *Winnipeg Citizen*, 19 May 1919.

44 *Winnipeg Citizen*, 19 May 1919, 1.

45 *Winnipeg Citizen*, 19 May 1919, 3.

46 *Winnipeg Citizen*, 19 May 1919.

47 *Winnipeg Citizen*, 19 May 1919, 4.

48 *Western Labor News*, 19 May 1919, 4.

49 'Our Cause is Just,' *Western Labor News*, 21 May 1919, 1.

50 'If workers must starve, it may as well be now as later. This is the reason behind the General Strike.' See 'Why the General Strike,' *Western Labor News*, 17 May 1919, 3.

51 Phil H. Goodstein, *The Theory of the General Strike* (Boulder, 1984), 32–3.

52 James Joll, *The Second International 1889–1914* (New York, 1966), 53.

53 Marc Ferro, *The Great War 1914–1918* (London, 1973), 34.

54 Janet L. Polasky, 'A Revolution for Socialists Reforms: The Belgian General Strike for Universal Suffrage,' *Journal of Contemporary History* 27, no. 3 (July 1992), 449–66.

55 Shepard B. Clough, *The Economic History of Modern Italy* (New York, 1964), 155.

56 James Joll, 'Anarchism and Syndicalism,' in Mary Lynn McDougall, *The Working Class in Modern Europe* (London, 1975), 108. Malatesta made the statement in 1907.

57 T.H. Penson, 'The Swedish General Strike,' *The Economic Journal* 19, no. 76 (December 1909), 602–9.

58 Orlando Figes, *A People's Tragedy: The Russian Revolution 1891–1924* (New York, 1997), 189–90.

59 Antonio Gramsci, 'The Revolution Against "Capital,"' *Avanti!*, 24 December 1917, as reprinted in Gramsci, *Selections from Political Writings 1910–1920*, 36.

60 Perry Anderson, *Considerations on Western Marxism* (London, 1976), 11–14. Norman Geras, *The Legacy of Rosa Luxemburg* (London, 1976), 124. Gramsci noted that Luxemburg disregarded important voluntary and organizational elements in the events of 1905. Gramsci, *Selections from Political Writings 1910–1920*, 233.

61 S. William Halperin, *Germany Tried Democracy: A Political History of the Reich from 1918–1933* (New York, 1965), 120.

62 Henry Borden, ed., *Robert Laird Borden: His Memoirs* (New York, 1938), 861.

63 *Manitoba Free Press*, 8 January 1919.

64 *Manitoba Free Press*, 8, 10, 13 January 1919.

65 'State of Siege Proclaimed in Berlin,' *Manitoba Free Press*, 10 January 1919.

66 Halperin, *Germany Tried Democracy*, 120–2.

67 *Manitoba Free Press*, 18 January 1919. J.P. Nettl, *Rosa Luxemburg*, vol. 2 (London 1978), 772–6.

68 'Liebknecht's Death May Cause Uprising,' *Manitoba Free Press*, 18 January 1919.

69 David J. Bercuson, *Fools and Wise Men: The Rise and Fall of the One Big Union* (Toronto, 1978), 83.

70 'What Ivens Says,' *Manitoba Free Press*, 17 October 1918. Earlier, in the summer of 1918, Ottawa had approved an Order-in-Council advocating a no-strike or lockout policy until the end of the war and urged its adoption 'upon both employers and workmen for the period of the war.' See PC 1743, 11 July 1918, *Statutes of Canada*, 1919, xcvi.

71 See Judy Fudge and Eric Tucker, *Labour Before the Law: The Regulation of Workers' Collective Action in Canada, 1900–1948* (Don Mills, 2001), 102.

72 *Western Labor News*, 13 December 1918.

73 The decision to ask for this vote was approved with two dissenting votes. *Western Labor News*, 13 December 1918. For a detailed account

of how this process worked in May 1919, see Provincial Archives of Manitoba, A0063/GR 6202 (G7529), *The Royal Commission to Investigate the Cause, Effects, Methods of Calling and of Carrying on the General Sympathetic Strike* (hereafter PAM, Robson Commission), 14–16.

74 'Red Letter Day in History of the Labor Movement,' *Western Labor News*, 27 December 1919. In Edmonton, the Socialist Party of Canada published the *Red Flag* – the same name as Karl Liebknecht's magazine; it was available in Winnipeg too.

75 'Socialist Split with Labor Party,' *Manitoba Free Press*, 16 January 1919. *Manitoba Free Press*, 22 January 1919.

76 'Socialist Party Hold Mass Meeting in Majestic Theatre,' *Western Labor News*, 24 January 1919.

77 *Manitoba Free Press*, 22 January 1919. The report in the *Western Labor News* was slightly less melodramatic, but substantially the same. 'Trades Council Report,' 24 January 1919, 4.

78 Geras, *The Legacy of Rosa Luxemburg*, 117.

79 Peter Campbell, *Canadian Marxists and the Search for a Third Way* (Montreal and Kingston, 1999), 180.

80 *Winnipeg Citizen*, 19 May 1919.

81 Provincial Archives of Manitoba,' ME10.B25, 'A Member of the Citizens' Committee of One Thousand' [Isaac Pitblado], 'An Address on the Subject of the Winnipeg Strike Delivered by a Member of the Citizens' Committee of One Thousand to a Deputation of Citizens from Moose Jaw, Sask.' (hereafter, Isaac Pitblado, 'An Address on the Subject of the Winnipeg Strike'), 3.

82 Penner, ed., *Winnipeg 1919*, 51. 'City Police Showed Where Sympathy Lay,' *Manitoba Free Press*, 7 August 1919, 10.

83 'City Police Showed Where Sympathy Lay,' 10.

84 'The Strike Situation in Winnipeg,' *Winnipeg Citizen*, 19 May 1919.

85 Penner, ed., *Winnipeg 1919*, 28–9.

86 Anderson, *Considerations on Western Marxism*, 17–18.

87 *Western Labor News*, 4 April 1919, Supplement.

88 H. Clare Pentland, 'Fifty Years After,' *Canadian Dimension* 6, no. 2 (July 1969), 14.

89 'The Naked Fact of Revolution,' *Winnipeg Citizen*, 27 May 1919. For an astute analysis contradicting this claim, and explaining why the timing of the Strike was not to the liking of those organizing the OBU, see Gerald Friesen, '"Yours in Revolt": Regionalism, Socialism, and the Western Canadian Labour Movement,' *Labour/Le Travailler* 1 (1976), 139–57.

90 'Revolution or Law and Order,' *Winnipeg Citizen*, 22 May 1919.

91 'How "Proletarian Dictatorship" Works Out in Russia,' *Winnipeg Citizen*, 26 May 1919, 3. See also 'The Horrible Example,' *Winnipeg Citizen*, 11 June 1919 and Frank J. Taylor, 'Rule as Tyrants in Liberty's Name,' *Winnipeg Citizen*, 12 June 1919.

92 W.A. Willison, 'Bolshevism,' *The Canadian Magazine* 52, no. 4 (February 1919), 884.

93 Right Hon. Sir George Buchanan, G.C.B., G.C.M.G., 'The Russian Revolution: Its Genesis and Aftermath,' *The Fortnightly Review*, December 1918, quoted in Willison, 'Bolshevism,' 883–4.

94 *Winnipeg Citizen*, 19 May 1919, 1. American journalist Samuel Hopkins Adams, after interviewing several 'men of good character' present at Victoria Park, implies that the statement may have been an invention of the Citizens' propaganda. Provincial Archives of Manitoba, MG 14/B 18, Samuel Hopkins Adams, 'The One Big Union – What the Strike at Winnipeg Really Shows,' *Collier's*, 19 July 1919, 31. As a journalist, Hopkins specialized in investigative reporting and exposés. He became famous in 1905 for a series of articles exposing quack patent medicines. His articles contributed to the passage of the American Food and Drug Act in 1906. *The New Encyclopaedia Britannica*, 15th ed., vol. 1 (Chicago, n.d.), 88.

95 Isaac Pitblado, 'An Address on the Subject of the Winnipeg Strike Delivered,' 7.

96 *The Israelite Press*, 8 July 1919, quoted in Roz Usiskin, '"The Alien and the Bolshevik in Our Midst": The 1919 Winnipeg General Strike,' *Jewish Life and Times* 5 (1988), 44.

97 'City Police Showed Where Sympathy Lay,' 10. 'Strikers Controlled Winnipeg Ten Days,' *Manitoba Free Press*, 29 July 1919, 10. 'We Are Running the City,' *Winnipeg Citizen*, 20 May 1919. PAM, Preliminary Hearing, Charles Gray, 454; Ed Parnell, 1029.

98 Charles Gordon, *Postscript to Adventure: The Autobiography of Ralph Connor* (Toronto, 1938), 360.

99 'Winnipeg Unions State Demands,' *Racine Journal*, 20 May 1919, 2.

100 *Toronto Daily Star*, 21 May 1919.

101 *Toronto Daily Star*, 23 May 1919.

102 'The Shoals of Pernicious Leadership,' *Winnipeg Citizen*, 22 May 1919.

103 *Winnipeg Citizen*, 19 May 1919.

104 Library and Archives Canada, MG29, D65, John MacLean, General Diary 1917–19 (hereafter LAC, John MacLean, General Diary), 14 May 1919.

105 Legislative Library of Manitoba, Mm4, 'Manitoba Strike Papers,' *Winnipeg Citizen*, 19 May 1919, 4; Charles F. Gray to Citizens, 18 May 1919.

106 PAM, Preliminary Hearing, Charles Gray, 556–7.

107 Penner, ed., *Winnipeg 1919*, 211.

108 *Winnipeg Citizen*, 19 May 1919.

109 *Winnipeg Citizen*, 19 May 1919, 1.

110 *Winnipeg Citizen*, 19 May 1919, 3.

111 Robert A.J. McDonald, *Making Vancouver: Class, Status, and Social Boundaries, 1863–1913* (Vancouver, 1996), xvi.

112 Alan Artibise uses the two-class model. See the brief critique of Artibise's Winnipeg in Robert A.J. McDonald, 'The Business Elite and Municipal Politics in Vancouver 1886–1914,' *Urban History Review* 11, no. 3 (February 1983), 12.

113 Gerald Friesen, *The Canadian Prairies: A History* (Toronto, 1984), 342–3.

114 On this theme, see 'The Triumph of Ontario Democracy, 1881–1888,' in W.L. Morton, *Manitoba: A History* (Toronto, 1957), 199–234, and Alan Artibise, *Winnipeg: An Illustrated History* (Toronto, 1977), 28.

115 The phrase is taken from Alexander McLachlan's famous 1874 poem 'The Man Who Rose from Nothing,' in *Canadian Poetry: From the Beginnings through the First World War*, ed. Carole Gerson and Gwendolyn Davies (Toronto, 1994), 96–7.

116 'The Grasping Hand of the I.W.W.,' *Winnipeg Telegram*, 31 May 1919, 15.

117 'Unemployment Insurance and Old Age Pensions are Two Points Agreed Upon,' *Manitoba Free Press*, 13 May 1919, 5.

118 'Citizens' Committee Issues Statement,' *Winnipeg Citizen*, 19 May 1919, 3.

119 Paul Nanton, *Prairie Explosion: Setting the Pace for Canada* (typescript, 1991), 155. Copy courtesy of Peter Hanlon.

120 *Don Nerbas,* 'Wealth and Privilege: An Analysis of Winnipeg's Early Business Elite,' *Manitoba History* 47 (Spring/Summer 2004), 63–4. Nerbas draws conclusions similar to those of Robert A.J. McDonald on Vancouver's business elite, challenging J.M.S. Careless and Alan Artibise, who portrayed Winnipeg's early business elite as a group of self-made men. See J.M.S. Careless, 'The Development of the Winnipeg Business Community, 1870–1890,' *Transactions of the Royal Society of Canada*, series 4, no. 8 (1970); Alan F.J. Artibise, *Winnipeg: A Social History of Urban Growth, 1874–1914* (Montreal, 1975); Alan Artibise, 'An Urban Economy: Patterns of Economic Change in Winnipeg, 1873–1971,' *Prairie Forum* 47 (1973), 189–217; Alan Artibise, 'Continuity and Change: Elites and Prairie Urban Development, 1914–1950,' in *The Usable Urban Past: Plan-*

ning and Politics in the Modern Canadian City, ed. Alan Artibise and Gilbert A. Stelter (Ottawa, 1979) 130–54; and Alan Artibise, 'Boosterism and the Development of Prairie Cities, 1873–1913,' in *Town and City: Aspects of Western Development*, ed. Alan Artibise (Regina, 1981), 209–35.

121 Alan Artibise, 'An Urban Environment: The Process of Growth in Winnipeg 1874–1914,' *Canadian Historical Association Historical Papers 1972*, ed. Jay Atherton (Montreal), 126. Nerbas, 'Wealth and Privilege,' 63–4, 52.

122 Artibise, *Winnipeg: A Social History*, 157, 169.

123 Artibise, 'An Urban Environment,' 11.

124 Artibise, *Winnipeg: A Social History*, 163.

125 Artibise, *Winnipeg: An Illustrated History*, 74.

126 *Sixth Census of Canada*, 1921, vol. 4 – Occupations, table 5 (Ottawa, 1929), 610–31.

127 A. Ross McCormack, 'Introduction,' *Labour/Le Travail* 4 (1979), 188.

128 See Michael McKeon, *The Origins of the English Novel 1600–1740* (Baltimore, 1987).

129 'Libertas Brammel,' 'The Great Tribulation: Winnipeg's First General Strike' (1902), *Labour/Le Travail* 4 (1979), 197, 196, 193.

130 Thomas Hobbes, *Leviathan* (1651; Harmondsworth, Middlesex, 1968), ch. 13: 95.

131 Ralph Connor [Rev. Charles Gordon], *To Him That Hath: A Novel of the West of Today* (New York, 1921)140.

132 Waves of Laurier era immigrants transformed the British and Protestant character of Winnipeg. In 1901, 73.9%, or 31,289 of 42,340, Winnipeggers were British; in 1911, this had declined to 62.1%, or 84,477 of 136,035 people. Meanwhile, the percentage of people of Central and Eastern European origin grew from 12.3%, or 5207, in 1901 to 22.9%, or 31,152, in 1911. In 1921, citizens of Jewish, Slavic, and German origin would constitute 23.3%, or 41,727, of Winnipeg's 179,087 people. See A.J. Artibise, 'Divided City: The Immigrant in Winnipeg Society, 1874–1921,' in Gilbert A. Settler and Alan A.J. Artibise, eds, *The Canadian City: Essays in Urban History* (Toronto, 1977), tables I and IV, 304–5.

133 For an account of the evolution of Winnipeg's working-class movement in the last years of the Great War, see Tom Mitchell and James Naylor, 'The Prairies: In the Eye of the Storm,' 178–180, in Craig Heron, ed., *The Workers' Revolt in Canada 1917–1925* (Toronto, 1998).

134 McDonald, *Making Vancouver*, xix, 240 n. 11.

135 Hopkins Adams, 'The One Big Union,' 14, 22.

136 LAC, John MacLean, General Diary, 20 May 1919.

137 'The Shoals of Pernicious Leadership,' *Winnipeg Citizen*, 22 May 1919, 1.

2 WHO? WHO? WHO-OO?

1 Western Canada Pictorial Index, University of Winnipeg, Winnipeg Free Press Collection, 'Members of Citizens' Committee at a banquet held after the Winnipeg General Strike,' image 38698, contact sheet A1292 (see p. 6 above). On the problems in the provenance of this photograph, see our 'Introduction,' note 10.

2 J.M. Bumsted, *The Winnipeg General Strike of 1919: An Illustrated History* (Winnipeg, 1994), 86. David Jay Bercuson, *Confrontation in Winnipeg: Labour, Industrial Relations, and the General Strike* (Montreal, 1974), 121.

3 PAM, Robson Commission, box 1.

4 'Citizens' Committee Issues Statement,' *Winnipeg Citizen*, Monday, 19 May 1919, 3.

5 'Rotary Global History Fellowship,' 6 June 2006, 3, at http://www .rotaryfirst100.org/clubs/cities/clubs/35winnipeg.htm.

6 PAM, Preliminary Hearing, James Carruthers, 300.

7 'The Citizens' Committee of "One" Thousand,' *Winnipeg Citizen*, 2 June 1919.

8 The telegram of congratulations to Sir Robert Borden after the arrest of the Strike leaders was signed by the crucial 34, while the photograph purported to be the Citizens celebrating after the Strike contains 64 people. Only 50 of the 64 are seated, and it's not clear whether the people standing, some female, some partially obscured, are to be regarded as on the same level as the 50.

9 On Crossin, see the *Winnipeg Tribune*, 22 October 1956; and Bumsted, *The Winnipeg General Strike*, 88.

10 Paul Nanton, 'A.M. Nanton's Years in Winnipeg, 1883–1926,' *Manitoba History* 6 (Fall 1983), 19.

11 Isaac Pitblado, 'An Address on the Subject of the Winnipeg Strike,' 3.

12 University of Manitoba Archives and Special Collections, Gerald Friesen fonds, MSS 154, PC 171 (a.97-20, a.02-26), Ed Anderson, Biographical Questionnaire, 'Edward Anderson,' file 4, box 16. See also Gerald Friesen fonds, file 4, box 16, Edward Anderson, 'Memoirs,' unpublished ms, pp. 1, 3.

13 W. Wesley Pue, 'A Profession in Defence of Capital?' *Canadian Journal of Law and Society* 7, no. 2 (Fall 1992), 267–84.

14 B.M. Greene, ed., *Who's Who in Canada, 1928–29: An Illustrated Bio-*

graphical Record of Men and Women of the Time (Toronto, 1929), 2010.

15 University of Manitoba Archives and Special Collections, MSS 48, PC 58, Pitblado Family Fonds, Series 3, Isaac Pitblado, box 6, folder 32, Isaac Pitblado, '60 Years at the Bar – the Pitblado Story,' 31 January 1950.

16 Dale Gibson and Lee Gibson, *Substantial Justice: Law and Lawyers in Manitoba 1670–1970* (Winnipeg, 1972), 190.

17 Robert Craig Brown, *Robert Laird Borden – A Biography, Vol. II* (Toronto, 1980), 108.

18 John English, *The Decline of Politics: The Conservatives and the Party System 1901–20* (Toronto, 1977), 155–6, 172–3.

19 Ibid., 109.

20 James (Jack) S. Walker, *The Great Canadian Sedition Trials: The Courts and the Winnipeg General Strike, 1919–1920*, ed. Duncan Fraser (Winnipeg, 2004), 6.

21 PAM, Preliminary Hearing, James Carruthers, 293.

22 *Toronto Daily Star*, 27 June 1919.

23 Ibid.

24 *Winnipeg Tribune*, 7 July 1948.

25 Ibid.

26 Roy St George Stubbs, *Prairie Portraits* (Toronto, 1954), 4.

27 Roy St George Stubbs, 'Life Story of A.J. Andrews,' *Winnipeg Free Press Magazine*, 15 June 1940, 5.

28 Sam Street, 'Ex-Mayor Recalls Fierce Civic Pride,' *Winnipeg Free Press*, 9 April 1949.

29 Don Nerbas, 'Wealth and Privilege: An Analysis of Winnipeg's Early Business Elite,' *Manitoba History* 47 (Spring/Summer 2004), 53.

30 St George Stubbs, *Prairie Portraits*, 9. 'Life Story of A.J. Andrews,' PAM, Western Canadian Legal History, Biographical file, 'A.J. Andrews.' Cameron Harvey, ed., *The Law Society of Manitoba* (Winnipeg, 1977), 238–40.

31 Harvey, ed., The Law Society of Manitoba, 238–40.

32 *Manitoba Free Press*, 8 December 1899.

33 Harvey, ed., The Law Society of Manitoba, 231–3.

34 See 'Remarks Result in Arrest of Woman,' *Manitoba Free Press*, 3 October 1918; *Manitoba Free Press*, 7 October 1918; and 'City and District,' *Manitoba Free Press*, 14 October 1918, 5.

35 *Winnipeg Free Press*, 1 February 1950. Gibson and Gibson, *Substantial Justice*, 190.

36 *Toronto Daily Star*, 27 June 1919.

37 PAM, Western Legal Archives, Biography file, 'A.J. Andrews.' Law
Society Minutes, 1950 [n.d.].

38 'City to Replace Striking Water-works Employees,' *Winnipeg Citizen*,
Wednesday, 21 May, 2.

39 *Western Labor News*, 22 May 1919.

40 The Citizens could draw on a venerable body of natural law theory.
Thomas Aquinas observed that though the world was God's property,
and men only its trustees, 'each person takes more trouble to care for
something that is his sole responsibility than what is held in common
by many.' Adam Smith transferred the jurisprudential vindication of
private property into the language of political economy, so that it was
commercial society which gave freedom and security to the meanest
member of society. For the evolution of the natural law of property, see
Istvan Hont and Michael Ignatieff, *Wealth and Virtue: The Shaping of
Political Economy in the Scottish Enlightenment* (Cambridge, 1985),
26–44.

41 The Activities and Organization of The Citizens' Committee of One
Thousand, 7.

42 PAM, Preliminary Hearing, N.N. Garvin, 1143.

43 Street, 'Ex-Mayor Recalls Fierce Civic Pride.'

44 Nerbas, 'Wealth and Privilege,' 50.

45 Sales and Advertising Club of Winnipeg, MB. 'Winnipeg's 75th birthday party, 5–11 June 1949: Official program and a brief history of
Winnipeg,' 15, *Peel's Prairie Provinces* 7139, at http://peel.library
.ualberta.ca.

46 'City Council Asserts Authority,' *Manitoba Free Press*, 21 May 1919,
1 [delivered in 22 May paper].

47 Charles Gordon, *Postscript to Adventure: The Autobiography of Ralph
Connor* (Toronto, 1938), 361.

48 *Western Labor News*, 22 May 1919.

49 *Western Labor News*, 17 May 1919, 2.

50 Advertisement, *Manitoba Free Press*, 15 May 1919. *Winnipeg Citizen*,
19 May 1919, 3.

51 *Manitoba Free Press*, 22 May 1919. See the report of the meeting in
the *Western Labor News*, 22 May 1919.

52 Allan was the trusted conduit for messages from the Citizens to
Ottawa. He mixed the practice of law with various business interests,
and served one term in the House of Commons before returning full-
time to his legal and business interests. He had close connections with,
among others, Augustus Nanton and Thomas Deacon, and at the time
of his death was president of the Great West Life Insurance Company,

chairman of the Canadian Committee of the Hudson's Bay Company, and on the boards of many corporations. See *Winnipeg Free Press*, 6 December 1940.

53 LAC, RG 13, Access 87–88/103: A-1688, pocket #2, A.K. Mclean to Hon G.D. Robertson, reporting a telegram from 'Executive Committee of One Thousand Citizens,' 20 May 1919.

54 PAM, A.E. Findlay, Preliminary Hearing, 1149–52.

55 *Winnipeg Citizen*, 19 May 1919, 1.

56 *Statutes of Canada* 1876, 124–5. Canada's 'An Act to Amend the Criminal Law relating to Violence, Threats and Molestation' enacted the subsection of the English 'Conspiracy and Protection of Property Act' of 1875.

57 Before 1901, unions couldn't be sued, because they weren't legally considered to be corporate entities. On the impact of this decision in Canada, see Judy Fudge and Eric Tucker, *Labour Before the Law: The Regulation of Workers' Collective Action in Canada, 1900–1948* (Don Mills, 2001), 23–4, and Bryce M. Stewart, *Canadian Labor Laws and the Treaty* (New York, 1968), 137.

58 Stewart, *Canadian Labor Laws*, 143.

59 On the use of injunctions to control labour in Canada, see Fudge and Tucker, *Labour Before the Law*, 18–26.

60 For an account of industrial relations in Winnipeg before 1919, see Bercuson, *Confrontation in Winnipeg*, 9–18.

61 Stewart, *Canadian Labor Laws*, 144–5.

62 Ibid., 145.

63 Ibid., 5. *The Voice*, 16 March 1917, 8.

64 *The Voice*, 23 March 1917, 8.

65 *The Voice*, 22 June 1917.

66 *The Voice*, 22 June 1917, 5. In July 1917, the Winnipeg Trades and Labor Council wrote a long detailed letter to the president of the Trades and Labour Congress about the increasing use by Winnipeg employers of injunctions to fight organized labour. The correspondence was published in *The Voice*, 6 July 1917, 4. In 1921, the Congress asked Ottawa to amend the sedition clauses of the Criminal Code, to insert peaceful picketing clauses, and to bring sympathetic strikes within the bounds of legality, as was the case in Great Britain. The request went nowhere. See Bryce Stewart, *Canadian Labor Laws*, 153–60.

67 *Manitoba Free Press*, 18 October 1917, 3.

68 On the spread and radicalization of labour as the war progressed, see Craig Heron and Myer Siemiatycki, 'The Great War, the State, and Working-Class Canada,' in Craig Heron, ed., *The Workers' Revolt in Canada 1917–1925* (Toronto, 1998), 11–43; and Ian McKay, *Reason-*

ing Otherwise: Leftists and the People's Enlightenment in Canada, 1890–1920 (Toronto, 2008), 430–6.

69 'May Form Citizens' Alliance,' *Manitoba Free Press*, 26 July 1917.

70 William Millikan, *A Union Against Unions: The Minneapolis Citizens' Alliance and Its Fight Against Organized Labour, 1903–1947* (St Paul, 2001), 30–9, 75, 92, 95.

71 William Millikan, 'Maintaining "Law and Order": The Minneapolis Citizens' Alliance in the 1920s,' *Minnesota History* (Summer 1989), 220.

72 Millikan, *A Union Against Unions*, 7, 35.

73 'To Make Winnipeg Open Shop City,' *Manitoba Free Press*, 3 August 1917.

74 'Citizens' Alliance Busy,' *Manitoba Free Press,* 15 September 1917.

75 'Jottings from Billboard,' *The Voice*, 3 August 1917.

76 Alderman F.O. Fowler, was the manager of the Winnipeg Grain & Produce Clearing House. A native of Ontario, he arrived in Winnipeg in 1901 after farming in the Brandon area from 1880. He represented South Brandon in the provincial legislature from 1897–1903. Fowler was a member of the Manitoba Club, and the St Charles Country Club. C.W. Parker, ed., *Who's Who and Why – A Biographical Dictionary of Men and Women of Western Canada* (Vancouver, 1913), 255.

77 Bercuson, *Confrontation in Winnipeg*, 61. For a fuller discussion of the Citizens' Alliance, see chapter 8.

78 A. Ernest Johnson, 'The Strikes in Winnipeg in May 1918 – The Prelude to 1919?' MA thesis, University of Manitoba, 1978, 128.The quotation is from the *Winnipeg Telegram*, 16 May 1918, cited in Johnson, 'The Strikes in Winnipeg,' 38.

79 Bumsted, *The Winnipeg General Strike*, 13, 85.

80 *Winnipeg Telegram*, 17 May 1918. *Manitoba Free Press*, 17 & 18 May 1918.

81 The full list of 100 names appears in 'Local Committee of 100 is Chosen by Business Men,' *Winnipeg Telegram*, 17 May 1918, 2, 4.

82 LAC, Borden Papers, reel C-4332, A.N. Nanton to G.W. Allan, 16 May 1918: 54222–4; A.E. Boyle, Secretary, Winnipeg Board of Trade to Sir Robert Borden, 15 May 1918: 54216–17; E. Anderson to G.W. Allan, 15 May 1918: 54218–19; W.H. McWilliams to Geo. W. Allan, 18 May 1918: 54262; and A.K. Godfrey to Hon. G.W. Allan, 18 May 1918: 54263. Many of the letters came to Borden through Allan, who would act as a similar conduit for the Citizens in 1919.

83 Ibid., A.N. Nanton to G.W. Allan, 16 May 1918: 54222–4; A.E. Boyle, Secretary, Winnipeg Board of Trade to Sir Robert Borden, 15 May 1918: 54225–8.

84   Ibid., E. Parnell President The Citizen Alliance [*sic*] to Sir R.L. Borden, 17 May 1918: 54247–8, 54252–3. Bercuson, *Confrontation at Winnipeg*, 62–3.

85   Ibid., Reverse side in handwriting, E. Parnell President The Citizen Alliance [*sic*] to Hon. T.A. Crerar, 17 May 1918: 54252–3.

86   Ibid., Robert Borden to E. Parnell and Citizens' Alliance, 18 May 1918: 54258.

87   Ibid., G.D. Robertson to Rt. Hon. Sir Robert Borden, 21 May 1918: 54274.

88   Bercuson, *Confrontation in Winnipeg*, 62.

89   LAC, Borden Papers, reel C-4332, G.D. Robertson to Sir Robert Borden, 24 May 1918: 54279.

90   On the Committee of One Hundred, see Johnson, 'The Strikes in Winnipeg,' 160–6. See also LAC, RG 13, Access 87–88/103: A-1688, pocket #2, Minutes of a General Meeting of the Citizens' Committee of One Hundred containing the report of its Conciliation Committee.

91   'Big Strike is now Matter of History,' *Manitoba Free Press*, 27 May 1918.

92   PAM, Preliminary Hearing, Ed Parnell, 1066.

93   Bercuson, *Confrontation in Winnipeg*, 67.

94   *Manitoba Free Press*, 15 May 1918, 2, quoted in Johnson, 'The Strikes in Winnipeg,' 129.

95   *Manitoba Free Press*, 20 May 1918, 3, quoted in Johnson, 'The Strikes in Winnipeg,' 156.

96   *Manitoba Free Press*, 27 May 1918, 13, quoted in Johnson, 'The Strikes in Winnipeg,' 172–3.

97   'Committee of Forty Citizens to Appeal for Funds,' *Manitoba Free Press*, 27 August 1914. 'Canvass to Start Today for Fund,' *Manitoba Free Press*, 1 September 1914. 'Subscriptions to Fund Come Freely,' *Manitoba Free Press*, 3 September 1914. Nanton, 'A.M. Nanton's Years in Winnipeg,' 17.

98   'The Winnipeg Revolutionary Strike,' *Winnipeg Citizen*, 9 June 1919.

99   PAM, Preliminary Hearing, Ed Parnell, 1058.

100 Other holdovers were A.B. Stovel, F.W. Adams, C.A. Richardson, George N. Jackson, J.C. Waugh, N.J. Breen, C.D. Sheppard, W.R. Ingram, H.M. Agnew, D.J. Dyson, and F. Luke.

101 The Activities and Organization of The Citizens' Committee of One Thousand, 5.

102 'More facts on the Strike Situation,' *Winnipeg Citizen,* 20 May 1919.

103 'City Police Showed Where Sympathy Lay,' *Manitoba Free Press*, 7 August 1919, 10.

104 *Montreal Gazette*, 20 May 1919.

105 *Western Labor News*, 23 May 1919.
106 LAC, RG 13, Access 87–88/103: box 36, file 9-A-1688, Andrews to Arthur Meighen. 'I have requested Attorney-General to arrest Committee under *code*. They are considering.' LAC, RG 13, Access 87–88/103: box 36, file 9-A-1688, Andrews to Meighen, 4 June 1919.
107 'City to Replace Striking Water-works Employees,' *Winnipeg Citizen*, Wednesday, 21 May, 3.
108 *Statutes of Canada*, 1919, Vols I–II, PC 702, 2 April 1919, lxxx.
109 *Statutes of Canada*, 1919, Vols I–II, PC 1241, 22 May 1918, lxvi.
110 The Mathers Commission actually reported on 28 June 1919, conceding the principle of collective bargaining at the heart of the Winnipeg General Strike. *Report of Commission to enquire into Industrial Relations in Canada*. Printed as a supplement to the *Labour Gazette*, July 1919, 12.
111 'House Discusses Winnipeg Strike,' *Manitoba Free Press*, 21 May 1918, 4.
112 Roger Graham, *Arthur Meighen: The Door of Opportunity* (Toronto, 1960), 236–7.
113 J.E. Rea, *T.A. Crerar: A Political Life* (Montreal and Kingston, 1997), 32.
114 Just who was among this delegation is a bit of a mystery. Penner, *Winnipeg 1919*, 60–1, says that four Citizens came, including Andrews, Pitblado, and Sweatman. Meighen later recollected that either half or most of the Citizens' delegates were Liberals, so it's likely that the other prominent Liberal lawyers on the committee – Coyne and Williams – were there. Meighen named Pitblado as the head of the delegation. 'The Winnipeg Strike,' NAC, Meighen Papers, Series 6 (MG 26, I, vol. 226 A), 149087. David Bercuson claims that Andrews led the delegation. See Bercuson, *Confrontation in Winnipeg*, 132. Bercuson also claims that Robertson and Meighen arrived the evening of the 21st. Meighen's summary asserts that they arrived the morning of the 22nd.
115 Penner, ed., *Winnipeg 1919*, 60.
116 Graham, *Arthur Meighen*, 236.
117 LAC, Accession 87–88/103, box 36, file a-1688, pocket #2, John B. Haig to Arthur Meighen, 8 July 1919.
118 LAC, Arthur Meighen Papers, Series 6 (MG 26, I, vol. 226 A): 'The Winnipeg Strike.'
119 James Foy, 'Gideon D. Robertson, A Conservative Minister of Labour, 1917–1921,' MA thesis, University of Ottawa, 1972, 17–18.
120 Ibid., 31.
121 Ibid., 33.

122 See Gideon Robertson to Robert Borden, 23 August 1917, quoted in Foy, 'Gideon D. Robertson,' 54.
123 Foy, 'Gideon D. Robertson,' 38.
124 Gideon Robertson, Canada, Senate, *Debates*, 2 April 1919, 195.
125 Bercuson, *Confrontation at Winnipeg*, 120.
126 Graham, *Arthur Meighen*, 161.
127 Arthur Meighen, *Unrevised and Unrepented: Debating Speeches and Others* (Toronto, 1949), 106–8.
128 Ibid., 43–55.
129 LAC, RG13, Access 87–88/103: box 36, file 9-A-1688, pocket #2, Meighen to N.W. Rowell, 21 May 1919.
130 LAC, Borden Papers, reel C-4341, Gideon Robertson to Mr F.A. Acland, Deputy Minister of Labour, Ottawa, 27 May 1919: 61587.
131 LAC, RG 13, Access 87–88/103: box 36, file 9-A-1688, pocket #2, Meighen to N.W. Rowell, 21 May 1919.
132 Ibid. In a telegram to E.L. Newcombe, Deputy Minister of Justice, on 22 May 1919, Meighen told Newcombe to prepare a memorandum 'setting out recent history and present state of law in United States Britain and British Dominions relating to restraints on strike or inclusion in labor or other unions of members government service particularly postal unions.' LAC, RG 13, Access 87–88/103: box 36, file 9-A-1688, pocket #2, Arthur Meighen to E.L. Newcombe (telegram), 22 May 1919.
133 This is what Borden wrote to G.V. Andrews, an MP from Winnipeg. Henry Borden, ed., *Robert Laird Borden: His Memoirs*, vol. 2 (Toronto, 1969), 215.
134 Canada, House of Commons, *Debates*, 12 June 1919, 3409–10. N.W. Rowell was a friend of orthodox labourites but an enemy of post-war labour radicalism. For his views, see Margaret Prang, *N.W. Rowell: Ontario Nationalist* (Toronto, 1975), 266–9.
135 Prang, *N.W. Rowell*, 299.
136 J.B. Coyne to W.H. Carter, 31 October, 1918, Winnipeg Board of Trade Council and Executive Minutes, vol. 4, 1918–1925, Provincial Archives of Manitoba, quoted in Johnson, 'The Strikes in Winnipeg,' 178. When the Strike erupted, Coyne was representing the Winnipeg Electric Railway Company in proceedings before Judge T.L. Metcalfe under the Industrial Disputes Investigation Act. After 15 May the street railway workers ignored the proceedings. 'Street Railway Trouble Was under Consideration,' *Winnipeg Evening Telegram*, 13 December 1919.
137 This in addition to the 90th, the 79th, the 100th, and the '106th regiments, the Fort Garry Horse, the 13th Battery, and Winnipeg's regular

detachment of NWMP.' Hon. Sir James Loughheed, on Canada, Sen-
ate, *Debates*, 21 May 1919, 451; Canada, House of Commons,
Debates, 23 June 1919, 3843–5; and Canada, House of Commons,
Debates, 2 June 1926, 4004–5.

138 'Revolution, or Law and Order?' *Winnipeg Citizen*, 22 May 1919.
139 Samuel Hopkins Adams, 'The One Big Union – What the Strike at
Winnipeg Really Shows,' *Collier's*, 19 July 1919, 30.
140 LAC, Borden Papers, reel C-4332, Oliver Mowatt Biggar to Robert
Borden, 5 June 1919: 61803–5.
141 'To Discipline Civic Strikers,' *Winnipeg Citizen*, 26 May 1919.
142 Sir Joseph Pope to the British Colonial Office, 16 August 1919. See
Public Records Office, CO 42/1014, Secretary of State Colonies to
Governor General, 26/7/19; and CO 42/1011/192544, 250–7,455–61.
The existence of this correspondence was reported in Gregory S.
Kealey, 'The RCMP, the Special Branch, and the Early Days of the
Communist Party of Canada: A Documentary Article,' *Labour/Le Travail*, 30 (Fall 1992), 170 n. 6.
143 *Winnipeg Citizen*, 26 May 1919.
144 Isaac Pitblado, 'An Address on the Subject of the Winnipeg Strike,' 3.
145 'The Nameless Ones,' *Western Labor News*, 5 June 1919, quoted in
Penner, ed., *Winnipeg 1919*, 112, 114.
146 'The Citizens' Committee of One Thousand,' *Winnipeg Citizen*, 2
June 1919.
147 'City to Replace Striking Water-works Employees,' *Winnipeg Citizen*,
Wednesday, 21 May, 2.
148 Winnipeg, 18 June 1919. Telegrams to the prime minister received
from Winnipeg Citizens respecting the government's action. See
LAC, RG 13, Access 87–88/103: box 36, file 9-A-1688, pocket #2,
Executive Citizens Committee of One Thousand to Robert Borden, 18
June 1919. The members of the executive were A.K. Godfrey, H.M.
Agnew, A.L. Crossin, Fletcher Sparling, D.A. Clark, I. Pitblado, W.R.
Ingram, C.D. Sheppard, Ed Parnell, A.L. Bond, C.A. Richardson,
Robert McKay, W.P. Riley, A.B. Stovel, F.W. Adams, D.J. Dyson,
George Carpenter, H.M. Tucker, W. McWilliams, T. Sweatman, J.B.
Coyne, J.C. Waugh, E. Anderson, C.C. Ferguson, C.O. Markle, G.N.
Jackson, 'Sr. Blanchard,' M.F. Christie, George Guy, George Munro,
W.A. Mackay, F. Luke, N.J. Breen, and W.M. Governlock. 'Sr. Blan-
chard' was likely Major Cyril F. Blanchard of the 90th Rifles and a
principal in Blanchard and Wood, Financial Agents. Parker, W*ho's
Who and Why*, 57. At the Preliminary Hearing, Ed Parnell admitted
that he was a member of the committee and got around to naming
Godfrey, Crossin, Pitblado, Sweatman, Coyne, Andrews, Adams, and

Agnew before objections shut down this line of questioning. Preliminary Hearing, 1054. Some men who had significant roles on the Citizens' Committee did not sign the telegram. For example, John E. Botterell – a Conservative grain broker – represented the Citizens on the city bread and milk committee, lobbied Meighen, and identified himself as a Citizen at the Preliminary Hearing. PAM, Preliminary Hearing, 1042, 1081. Jack Bumsted also names Winnipeg's leading financier Augustus Nanton as a member of the Citizens (*Winnipeg General Strike 1919*, 107), and he was certainly seen by the strikers as one of their principal opponents (Nanton, *Prairie Explosion*, 154). Most likely, as his telegrams to MP George Allan suggest, Nanton was an *éminence grise*, in close contact with the Citizens, but not taking part in their day-to-day meetings.

Henry Trachtenberg also reports that 'a handful of Jews in business and the professions belonged to the Citizens' Committee of 1000.' He cites an RNWMP report that named Charles Tadman, hardware store proprietor, Hiram and Mordecai Weidman, and Dr Abraham Bercovitch. Charles Tadman 'was given a pistol and ammunition, but disassembled the gun and placed it and the ammunition in different parts of his daughter's safe, the combination of which he did not know.' Trachtenberg also suggests that Max Steinkopf and Harry Wilder were 'probably' members. Sidney Goldstein, later part of the prosecution team in the trials of the Strike leaders 'also may have belonged.' Yet there is no evidence that places any of these members of the Jewish elite on the Citizens' executive. Harry Wilder asserted in *Dos Yiddishe Vort* that it was perhaps a good thing that the Jewish community was represented 'in the camps of both sides.' However, after the Citizens' Committee began its hate campaign against 'aliens,' Wilder denounced those Jews who stayed associated with the Citizens. *Dos Yiddishe Vort*, 20 June and 22 August 1919, quoted in Trachtenberg, '"The Old Clo' Move": Anti-Semitism, Politics, and the Jews of Winnipeg, 1882–1921,' PhD diss., York University (Toronto), 1984, 2: 654–5, 870–1 n. 101. On Goldstein, see D.A. Hart, ed., *The Jew in Canada* (Montreal, Toronto, 1926), 407.

149 Louis G. Silverberg, 'Citizens' Committees: Their Role in Industrial Conflict,' *Public Opinion Quarterly* 5, no. 1 (March 1941), 24. At the time that he wrote the article, Louis Silverberg was assistant to the director of information of the National Labor Relations Board, created to enforce the provisions of the National Labour Relations Act – also known as the Wagner Act – of 1935. The Wagner Act, the product of a tenacious US senator, Robert Wagner, was intended to grant American workers basic rights of industrial citizenship, including the

right to collective bargaining. Harold Selig Roberts, *Roberts' Dictionary of Industrial Relations*, 4th ed. (Manoa, HI, 1994), 515.

150 'Citizens' Committee Issues Statement,' *Winnipeg Citizen*, 19 May 1919, 3.

151 PAM, Robson Commission, box 1.

152 Greene, ed., *Who's Who in Canada, 1928–29*, 380.

153 'G. Carpenter Ends 33 Years with CMA,' *Winnipeg Tribune*, 21 March 1949.

154 *Winnipeg Free Press*, 11 July 1944. Parker, *Who's Who and Why*, 139.

155 Greene, ed., *Who's Who in Canada, 1928–29*, 1319.

156 Parker, *Who's Who and Why*, 4.

157 *Winnipeg Free Press*, 14 March 1949.

158 E.J. McMurray during Ed Parnell testimony, PAM, Preliminary Hearing, 1067.

159 Hopkins Adams, 'The One Big Union – What the Strike at Winnipeg Really Shows,' 30. On W.P. Riley, see Greene, ed., *Who's Who in Canada, 1928–29*, 1492.

160 Parker, *Who's Who and Why*, 571.

161 Other Manitoba Club members among the Citizens were William McWilliams, D.A. Clark, W.P. Riley, H.M. Tucker, C.C. Ferguson, Melbourne Christie, N.J. Breen, Clarence Sheppard, C.A. Richardson, and E.K. Williams.

162 LAC, RG 13, Access 87–88/103: box 36, file 9-A-1688, pocket #2, Andrews to Meighen (telegram), 4 June 1919.

163 Nerbas, 'Wealth and Privilege,' 53. 'The Act of Incorporation, Constitution, Rules and Regulations and List of Members of the Manitoba Club,' Winnipeg: 1913, 10; *Peel's Prairie Provinces*, 2344, at http://peel.library.ualberta.ca.

164 John English, *Robert Borden: His Life and World* (Toronto, 1977), 180.

165 University of Manitoba Archives and Special Collections, Gerald Friesen fonds, Biographical Files, Isaac Pitblado, Travers Sweatman, J.C. Coyne. 'Clarence Shepard, City Realtor, Dies,' *Winnipeg Tribune*, 8 July 1949. Parker, *Who's Who and Why*, 738. *Winnipeg Free Press*, 11 July 1944. Parker, *Who's Who and Why*, 139.

166 Parker, *Who's Who and Why*, 4, 72.

167 'Council Discharges Striking City Employees,' *Winnipeg Citizen*, 27 May 1919, 2.

168 'Strike Not Yet Finally Settled,' *Manitoba Free Press*, 28 May 1918, 9.

169 PAM, Preliminary Hearing, John Sparling, 735.

170 Parker, *Who's Who and Why*, 72.
171 *Winnipeg Tribune*, 28 September 1911
172 Parker, *Who's Who and Why*, 843.
173 Greene, ed., *Who's Who in Canada, 1928–29*, 1267.
174 Ibid., 1903.
175 On employers' associations, see Clark, *The Canadian Manufacturers' Association*, and Andrew Yarmie, 'The Right to Manage: Vancouver Employers' Associations, 1900–1923,' *BC Studies* 90 (1991), 40–74; Andrew Yarmie, 'The State and Employers' Associations in British Columbia: 1900–1932,' *Labour/Le Travail* 45 (2000), 53–101; and Andrew Yarmie, 'Employers and Exceptionalism: A Cross-Border Comparison of Washington State and British Columbia, 1890–1935,' *Pacific Historical Review* 72, no. 4 (2003), 561–615.
176 Mary Vipond, 'Blessed Are the Peacemakers: The Labour Question in Canadian Social Gospel Fiction,' *Journal of Canadian Studies* 10, no. 3 (August 1975), 39.
177 Ralph Connor [Rev. Charles Gordon], *To Him That Hath: A Novel of the West of Today* (New York, 1921), 71.
178 'The Man Who Rose from Nothing' is the title of Alexander McLachlan's famous 1874 poem. For aristocratic and progressive narratives, see Michael McKeon, *The Origins of the English Novel 1600–1740* (Baltimore, 1987).
179 Douglas Durkin, *The Magpie* (1923) (Toronto, 1974), 131.
180 'Meeting of 1000 (?) Proves Fake,' *Western Labor News*, 24 May 1919, 3.
181 'Committee of 10 to Make Attempt toward Settlement,' *Winnipeg Telegram*, 24 May 1919, 3.
182 *Winnipeg Citizen*, 19 May 1919.
183 *Toronto Daily Star*, 21 May 1919. *Winnipeg Citizen*, 19 May 1919.
184 'Committee of 10 to Make Attempt toward Settlement.'
185 'Mayor to Appoint Committee,' *Western Labor News*, 24 May 1919, 4. 'Committee of 10 to Make Attempt toward Settlement.'
186 *Manitoba Free Press*, Saturday, 24 May 1919, 1.
187 'Committee of 10 To Make Attempt Toward Settlement.'
188 'Volunteer Brigade Averts Great Tragedy,' *Winnipeg Citizen*, 24 May 1919, 2.
189 'Correcting an Error,' *Winnipeg Citizen*, 27 May 1919, 3.
190 'Midnight Session Abortive,' *Western Labor News*, 26 May 1919, 3.
191 As John Haig and W.T. Cox said, in passages quoted earlier, the purpose of the Citizens' trip to Fort William had been to convince the federal ministers that they should keep out of the Strike. LAC, RG

13, Access 87–88/103: box 36, file 9-A-1688, pocket #2, John B.
Haig to Arthur Meighen, 8 July 1919. Penner, ed., *Winnipeg 1919*, 60.
192 'Midnight Session Abortive,' *Western Labor News*, 26 May 1919, 3.
193 Isaac Pitblado, 'An Address on the Subject of the Winnipeg Strike,'
12.
194 'Ironmasters Leave Issue in Hands of Citizens,' *Winnipeg Citizen*, 22
May 1919, 2.
195 PAM, Preliminary Hearing, Capt. F.G. Thompson, 375. For the day-
to-day business of publication, 'a competent editor' had been hired
to put the *Citizen* together. See 'The Activities and Organization of
the Citizens' Committee of One Thousand,' 26. This editor has
never been identified, but a strong possibility is Charles F. Roland,
who in 1907 was appointed commissioner of the Winnipeg Development and Industrial Bureau, a collaboration of the City of Winnipeg, the Board of Trade, and over four hundred businesses. See
Manitoba Free Press, 21 March 1912, 13 and 30 March 1913, 9.
During the Great War, Roland worked closely with Augustus Nanton as the secretary of the Winnipeg Patriotic Fund and as organizer
of the Victory Loan Campaign. Roland was appointed Winnipeg
Commissioner under the Soldier Resettlement Act in 1918 and, a
year later, secretary for the Western Canadian branch of the Canadian Reconstruction Association. *Henderson's Winnipeg Directory*
(Winnipeg, 1919). The CRA branch office in Winnipeg was located
in the Electric Railway Chambers on Notre Dame Avenue and
Albert Street, just north off Portage Avenue – in the same building
as the offices of the Winnipeg Electric Railway Company and one
of the leading Citizens, lawyer Ed Anderson. After the Strike, in the
spring of 1920, Roland surfaced as the first managing secretary of
the Employers' Association of Manitoba and the publisher of its
newsletter, the *Special News Bulletin*, which propagandized the
business community. For the Canadian Reconstruction Association,
see Tom Traves, *The State and Enterprise: Canadian Manufacturers
and the Federal Government 1917–1931* (Toronto, 1979), 16–17.
For the address of the Winnipeg office, see *Manitoba Free Press*, 2
April 1919, 2. On Roland, see Parker, *Who's Who and Why*, 704;
Henry James Morgan, *The Canadian Men and Women of the Time*,
2nd ed. (Toronto, 1912), 965; *The Canadian Who's Who* (Toronto,
1910), 196. On Roland's activities during the Great War, see Manitoba *Free Press*, 14 November 1914, 9; 17 July 1917, 5. For his
death notice and a review of his Winnipeg career, see *Winnipeg
Free Press*, 24 August 1936.

3 SEVEN HUNDRED AND FOUR YEARS AGO AT RUNNYMEDE

1   Eric Hobsbawm, *Age of Extremes: The Short Twentieth Century 1914–1991* (London, 1994), 69, 55–71.
2   The reference to an *anti-society* appears in Milorad Drachkovitch, *The Revolutionary Internationals 1864–1943* (Stanford, 1966), 102.
3   'The Truth from the Inside,' *Winnipeg Citizen*, 14 June 1919, 3.
4   'Runnymede, June 15, 1215 – Winnipeg, June 15 1919,' *Winnipeg Telegram*, 16 June 1919.
5   'The Lie as a Weapon,' *Winnipeg Citizen*, 24 May 1919.
6   The Activities and Organization of the Citizens' Committee of One Thousand, 37.
7   See Jeffrey Stout, *Democracy and Tradition* (Princeton, 2004), 230.
8   The terms are borrowed from Mikhail Bakhtin's account of authoritative discourse. M.M. Bakhtin, *Speech Genre and Other Essays*, ed. Michael Holquist and Carl Emerson (Austin, 1986), 242.
9   'The Shoals of Pernicious Leadership,' *Winnipeg Citizen*, 22 May 1919.
10 Ibid.
11 According to Rawls, constitutional rules are best made (i.e., with least prejudice) under a 'Veil of Ignorance,' in which one must argue abstractly and rationally, as if not knowing one's place in the social order. John Rawls, *A Theory of Justice* (rev. ed.) (Cambridge, MA, 1999), 112–23. Stout, *Democracy and Tradition*, 230.
12 *Manitoba Free Press*, 30 July 1904. *Winnipeg Tribune*, 17 July 1948.
13 The phrase comes from William Ivens's address to the Royal Commission on Industrial Relations. 'Labour Declines to Give Any Official Recognition to Industrial Commission,' *Manitoba Free Press*, 12 May 1919, 1.
14 *Western Labor News*, 7 February 1919. For Robinson's comment, see 'Robinson Declares Labour Plans Industrial Control,' *Manitoba Free Press*, 20 May 1919, 1 [Delivered with 22 May 1919].
15 'Bread – Bread – Bread – Up – Up!' *Western Labor News*, 17 May 1919, 1.
16 'A United Front,' *Western Labor News*, 17 May 1919, 2.
17 'Strikelets,' *Western Labor News*, 17 May 1919, 4. Reprinted in the *Manitoba Free Press*, 19 May 1919, 1 [delivered with 22 May paper].
18 Robson, heading the royal commission investigating the Strike, said, 'A limited strike would probably have attained the end for Labour without antagonizing the community.' PAM, Robson Commission, 21. Robson's neutrality may be measured by the fact that although the strikers and the Province agreed to appoint him head of the royal com-

mission, the Citizens opposed his appointment. LAC, RG 13, Access 87–88/103: box 36, file 9-A-1688, pocket #2, Andrews to Meighen (letter), 25 June 1919.

19 H.T. Dickinson, 'The British Constitution,' in *A Companion to Eighteenth-Century Britain*, ed. H.T. Dickinson (Oxford, 2002), 5–6.

20 'The Shoals of Pernicious Leadership,' *Winnipeg Citizen*, 22 May 1919, 1. The Citizens never mention Hobbes directly, but a direct acquaintance between the Citizens and Hobbes is not required by our argument. The point is that the Citizens made use of Hobbesian arguments and mythology.

21 Thomas Hobbes, *Leviathan* (1651; Harmondsworth, Middlesex, 1968), 223.

22 'The Shoals of Pernicious Leadership,' *Winnipeg Citizen*, 22 May 1919, 1.

23 Ibid.

24 Hobbes, *Leviathan*, 186.

25 Charles Taylor, 'Modern Social Imaginaries,' *Public Culture* 14, no. 1 (2002), 104.

26 C.B. Macpherson, *The Political Theory of Possessive Individualism: Hobbes to Locke* (Oxford, 1961), 80.

27 *Manitoba Free Press*, 29 June 1902, quoted in Kurt Korneski, 'J.W. Dafoe and the Labour Revolt of 1919,' paper delivered at 83rd Annual Meeting, Canadian Historical Association (Winnipeg, 2004), 12–13.

28 'More Facts on the Strike Situation,' *Winnipeg Citizen*, 20 May 1919.

29 Ibid. In an era less circumspect about disclosures of wealth, the *Winnipeg Telegram* published an article entitled 'Winnipeg's Ever Widening Circle of Millionaires,' about the fortunes of Winnipeg land speculators. *Winnipeg Telegram*, 19 January 1910.

30 'Revolution, or Law and Order?' *Winnipeg Citizen*, 22 May 1919.

31 'Strike Committee Warned Against Keeping Out Firemen and Postmen,' *Manitoba Free Press*, 24 May 1919.

32 PAM, Preliminary Hearing, James Carruthers, 253, 257. PAM, Preliminary Hearing, Max Steinkopf, 1431.

33 Carruthers was simply expressing the perspective of commercial Winnipeg. Adam Smith captured this fundamental axiom in his observation that 'it is not from the benevolence of the butcher, the brewer, or the baker, that we expect our dinner, but from their regard to their own interest.' Adam Smith, *An Inquiry into the Nature and Causes of the Wealth of Nations*, vol.1, ed. R.H. Campbell and A.S. Skinner (Indianapolis, 1981), I.ii, 2, 26–7.

34 PAM, Preliminary Hearing, Theodore Kipp, 1307–8.

35 PAM, Preliminary Hearing, Carruthers, 298.

36 PAM, Preliminary Hearing, Ernest Hague, 597–8.

37 PAM, Preliminary Hearing, Douglas Little, 601.

38 PAM, Preliminary Hearing, P.C. McIntyre, examined by A.J. Andrews, 1403.

39 'Revolution, or Law and Order?' *Winnipeg Citizen*, 22 May 1919.

40 'False-alarm fiends,' as the *Citizen* called them, were fined up to $50.00 and costs. 'The Crime-Sheet's Significance,' *Winnipeg Citizen*, 24 May 1919, 3.

41 The Activities and Organization of the Citizens' Committee of One Thousand, 6.

42 LAC, John MacLean, General Diary, 19 May 1919.

43 PAM, Preliminary Hearing, J.K. Sparling 745, 752. 'The Strike Situation in Winnipeg,' *Winnipeg Citizen*, 21 May 1919, 4.

44 Paul Nanton, *Prairie Explosion: Setting the Pace for Canada* (typescript, 1991), 152.

45 Isaac Pitblado, 'An Address on the Subject of the Winnipeg Strike,' 4.

46 Samuel Hopkins Adams, 'The One Big Union – What the Strike at Winnipeg Really Shows,' *Collier's*, 19 July 1919, 29–30. Alderman John Sparling said that on average, 20–25 false alarms came in per night, and that police couldn't guard all the alarm boxes, there being 354 in the city. PAM, Preliminary Hearing, J.K. Sparling, 711.

47 'Things Loyal Citizens Would Like to Know,' *Winnipeg Citizen*, 23 May 1919.

48 'The Gagging of the Press,' *Winnipeg Citizen*, 20 May 1919.

49 Paul Nanton, 'A.M. Nanton's Years in Winnipeg, 1883–1926,' *Manitoba History* 6 (Fall 1983), 19. Paul Nanton says, 'The day the barn was destroyed and the horses died, the strike ceased to be an adventure. I hated those men who had done this thing.' Nanton, *Prairie Explosion*, 146.

50 PAM, Preliminary Hearing, J.H. Johansson, 1372.

51 University of Regina Archives, Lusk Papers, New York State Library, Reports on Winnipeg General Strike: New York State Legislature, Committee to Investigate Revolutionary Radicalism [1919], Lusk Committee Agent, 'Report #1,' 9 June 1919 (facsimile).

52 PAM, Preliminary Hearing, Ed Parnell, 1043, 1048, 1071. 'Mrs Armstrong Is to Face Charge,' *Manitoba Free Press*, 6 June 1919, 9.

53 PAM, Preliminary Hearing, A.A. Riley, 1115–16.

54 PAM, Preliminary Hearing, William McCullough, 1365–6.

55 Smith, *Wealth of Nations*, IV.vii.c, 54, 610.

56 PAM, Preliminary Hearing, William McCullough, 1367.

57 'City Police Showed Where Sympathy Lay,' *Manitoba Free Press*, 7 August 1919, 10. Andrews's reluctance to make anything of Bray's

'boast' in the preliminary hearing suggests that it probably was a joke. For a full discussion, see chapter 12. Ed Parnell's striking employees were apparently told by their union's president and secretary to keep their children off the streets, since the strikers intended to raid the Osborne Barracks and take possession of them. PAM, Preliminary Hearing, Ed Parnell, 1035, 1049, 1051.

58 Fred McGuiness (son-in-law of W.H. Thomson) conversation with Tom Mitchell, 17 June 2004.

59 'The Revolution – 1919,' *The Nation* 109 (4 October 1919), 452.

60 *The Call*, quoted in 'Labor Takes Thought to Itself,' *The Independent*, 21 June 1919, 425-6.

61 PAM, Robert Graham fonds, 111–12.

62 PAM, Robert Graham fonds, 109.

63 PAM, Robert Graham fonds, 120–1.

64 PAM, Robert Graham fonds, 109–11. Phillips showed Graham an Order-in-Council empowering Phillips, but the Manitoba Legislative Library has been unable to find a copy of this.

65 'The Gagging of the Press,' *Winnipeg Citizen*, 20 May 1919.

66 Ibid.

67 'To the Citizens of Winnipeg,' *Winnipeg Citizen*, 19 May 1919.

68 The Activities and Organization of the Citizens' Committee of One Thousand, 7.

69 *Winnipeg Telegram*, 14 May 1919, 1.

70 'The Enemy Alien Problem,' *Winnipeg Telegram*, 14 May 1919, 9.

71 *Winnipeg Citizen*, 19 May 1919.

72 'Socialism verses [*sic*] Bolshevism,' *Winnipeg Telegram*, 13 May 1919, 9.

73 Dr Frank Crane, 'The Cure of Bolshevism,' *Winnipeg Telegram*, 13 May 1919, 9. 'The Industrial Relations Inquiry,' *Winnipeg Telegram*, 13 May 1919, 9.

74 'The Fall of Zapata's Republic: An Experiment in Socialism,' *Winnipeg Telegram Magazine*, 10 May 1919.

75 Michael Dupuis, 'The Response of the Toronto Daily Press to the Winnipeg General Strike,' MA thesis, University of Ottawa, 1973, 10.

76 *The Call*, quoted in 'Labor Takes Thought to Itself,' *The Independent*, 21 June 1919, 425–6.

77 Issues for the 17th, 19th, 20th, and 21st were included in the 22 May *Free Press Evening Bulletin*. The *Free Press* itself reports that it resumed publication on 21 May, while Michael Dupuis suggests that it resumed a limited publication on 20 May. Dupuis, 'Response of the Toronto Daily Press,' 13.

78 Dupuis, 'Response of the Toronto Daily Press,' 14.

79 On the *Tribune*, see Dupuis, 'Response of the Toronto Daily Press,' 21.

80 'City Police Showed Where Sympathy Lay,' *Manitoba Free Press*, 7 August 1919, 10. Ed Parnell, PAM, Preliminary Hearing, 1063.

81 'Says Winnipeg Civic Heads Are Yellow,' *Winnipeg Telegram*, 27 May 1919, 4.

82 'Strike Unjustified; Citizens Must Stand Firm,' *Winnipeg Telegram*, 24 May 1919, 1.

83 'The Logical Autocracy,' *Winnipeg Telegram*, 27 May 1919, 9.

84 'The Essentials of the Situation,' *Manitoba Free Press*, 18 May 1918.

85 'The Industrial Unrest Commission,' *Manitoba Free Press*, 14 May 1919, 11.

86 'For Public Consideration,' *Manitoba Free Press*, 15 May 1919, 11.

87 See Ramsay Cook, *The Politics of John W. Dafoe and the Free Press* (Toronto, 1973), 100; and Murray Donnelly, *Dafoe of the Free Press* (Toronto, 1968), 105, quoted in Korneski, 'J.W. Dafoe and the Labour Revolt of 1919,' 29.

88 'The Attempted Suppression of the Press,' *Manitoba Free Press*, 22 May 1919, 1.

89 PAM, Preliminary Hearing, James Carruthers, 246.

90 'Strike Unjustified; Citizens Must Stand Firm,' *Winnipeg Citizen*, 24 May 1919.

91 'Loyalty to Contracts? "Nothing Doing,"' *Winnipeg Citizen*, 28 May 1919.

92 Chad Reimer, 'War, Nationhood and Working-Class Entitlement: The Counterhegemonic Challenge of the 1919 Winnipeg General Strike,' *Prairie Forum* 18, no. 2 (Fall 1993), 219–37.

93 PAM, Preliminary Hearing, Testimony, James Carruthers, 304–5.

94 Bertrand Russell, 'Direct Action and Democracy,' *The Dial*, 3 May 1919. *The Dial* was an American journal of radical opinion.

95 'More Facts on the Strike Situation,' *Winnipeg Citizen*, 20 May 1919.

96 'The Citizens' Magna Charta,' *Winnipeg Citizen*, 23 May 1919.

97 During debate on the Criminal Code amendment bill in the Senate in July 1919, Robertson would seek clarification of the meaning of the word *force*. He had no difficulty in allowing references to violence or physical injury, but he feared that if 'force' included 'economic force,' then Parliament was infringing 'upon the legitimate rights of labour organizations in using economic force' when arbitration had failed. Canada, Senate, *Debates*, 5 July 1919, 913.

98 'Strike Unjustified; Citizens Must Stand Firm,' *Winnipeg Citizen*, 24 May 1919.

99 'They Are "Known by Their Acts,"' *Winnipeg Citizen*, 2 June 1919, 1.

100 Dale Gibson and Lee Gibson, *Substantial Justice: Law and Lawyers in Manitoba 1670–1970* (Winnipeg, 1972), 190.

101 The Activities and Organization of The Citizens' Committee of One Thousand, 40.

102 R.C.B. Risk, 'A.H.F. Lefroy: Common Law Thought in Late Nineteenth-Century Canada: On Burying One's Grandfather,' *University of Toronto Law Journal* 41, no. 3 (Summer 1991), 311–12.

103 Blackstone, *Commentaries on the Laws of England*, Introduction, section 2.

104 John Locke, *Two Treatises on Civil Government*, ed. Peter Laslett (Cambridge, 1966), Second treatise, sec. 124, 368.

105 PAM, Preliminary Hearing, Edward Parnell, 1054.

106 Locke, *Two Treatises on Civil Government*, Second treatise, sec. 124, 368.

107 Vipond, 'Blessed are the Peacemakers,' 39.

108 Douglas Durkin, *The Magpie* (1923) (Toronto, 1974), 190.

109 A. Ross McCormack, 'Introduction,' *Labour/Le Travail* 4 (1979).

110 'Libertas Brammel,' 'The Great Tribulation: Winnipeg's First General Strike' (1902), *Labour/Le Travail* 4 (1979), 201, 198–9.

111 In the cadences of a contemporary Marxist as sophisticated and important as Fredric Jameson, one can still detect a note of disdain for Lockean individuality: 'The loss of (bourgeois) individuality is certainly one of the great anti-utopian themes.' Fredric Jameson, *Archaeologies of the Future* (New York, 2005), 17. Jameson wants to defend utopian thinking from its critics, but he can't help letting the word 'bourgeois' creep in, not just as a historical designator, but as if to sermonize that a certain kind of individuality is the burger's toy, possibly a chimera.

112 'The Strike Situation in Winnipeg,' *Winnipeg Citizen*, 19 May 1919, 1.

113 John Locke, *Works* (1759), ii, 26, quoted in C.B. Macpherson, *The Political Theory of Possessive Individualism*, 223. Smith, *Wealth of Nations*, V.ii.e.5, 725; 6, 842.

114 Smith, *Wealth of Nations*, V.i.b.12, 715.

115 Locke, *Two Treatises on Civil Government*, Second treatise, sec. 4, 287.

116 Macpherson, *The Political Theory of Possessive Individualism*, 200.

117 Ibid., 220.

118 Theodore Frank Thomas Plucknett, *A Concise History of the Common Law*, 5th ed. (Union, NJ, 2001), 59.

119 The Activities and Organization of the Citizens' Committee of One Thousand, 37.

120 Manhood suffrage was instituted in all provincial jurisdictions, with the exception of Quebec, prior to 1898, but at the federal level only in 1898. For the evolution of the national franchise, see Norman Ward, *The Canadian House of Commons Representation* (Toronto, 1950), 211–24. At the Winnipeg municipal level in 1919, plural voting and property ownership requirements biased the electorate in favour of property. See James Lightbody, 'Electoral Reform in Local Government: The Case of Winnipeg,' *Canadian Journal of Political Association* 2, no. 2 (June 1978), 307–32.

121 Ellen Meiksins Wood, 'Demos versus "We, The People": Freedom and Democracy Ancient and Modern,' in *Demokratia: A Conversation on Democracies, Ancient and Modern*, ed. Josiah Ober and Charles Hedrick (Princeton, 1996).

122 'Unemployment Insurance and Old Age Pensions Are Two Points Agreed Upon,' *Manitoba Free Press*, 13 May 1919, 5.

123 'Says Labor Disregards Basic Economic Laws,' *Manitoba Free Press*, 16 May 1919, 1.

124 'Labour Declines to Give Any Official Recognition to Industrial Commission,' *Manitoba Free Press*, 12 May 1919, 1.

125 PAM, Preliminary Hearing, Ed Parnell, 1026.

126 'An Interview with James Dunwoody,' *Manitoba History* 6 (Fall 1983), 23.

127 'Strikelets,' *Western Labor News*, 19 May 1919, 4. Reprinted in *Manitoba Free Press*, 20 May 1919 [delivered in 22 May 1919 paper, 2]. In the trial of the Strike leaders, Justice Metcalfe's charge to the jury included chapter and verse for where the *Western Labor News* advocated attempts to overcome the 'law of property,' to seize land, and to redistribute it to the workmen. See Provincial Archives of Manitoba, P-5613, f-8, The King vs. William Ivens et al., Justice Metcalfe's Charge to the Jury, 26 May 1920, 40.

128 Locke, Second treatise, sec. 10, 291.

129 'The Frozen Breath of Bolshevism,' *Winnipeg Telegram*, 27 May 1919, 8.

130 Justice Metcalfe refers to the *Western Labor News* of 17 January 1919. See PAM, P-5613, f-8, The King vs. William Ivens et al., Mr. Justice Metcalfe's Charge to the Jury, 26 May 1920, 42.

131 'An Awakening Is Coming,' *Winnipeg Citizen*, 13 June 1919.

132 PAM, Preliminary Hearing, Ed Parnell, 1039–40.

133 John Spargo, in *Bolshevism: The Enemy of Political and Industrial Democracy* (New York, 1919), 288–300. Spargo quotes extended passages from *The Soviets at Work*.

134 W.H. Plewman, *Toronto Daily Star*, 27 June 1919.

135 Andrews was 54, Pitblado 52, A.L. Crossin 51, A.K. Godfrey 48, and Ed Anderson 52. Coyne and Sweatman were relatively youthful, 41 and 40 respectively.
136 Of the city's workforce, 27% was under 24 years of age and fully 90% under 49. Data derived from *Census of Canada*, 1921, 424–5, 440–1.
137 Peter Campbell, *Canadian Marxists and the Search for a Third Way* (Montreal and Kingston, 1999), 171–3.
138 *Pioneers and Early Citizens of Manitoba – A Dictionary of Biography from the Earliest Times to 1920* (Winnipeg: Canadian Publicity Company), 1925, 198.
139 James Naylor, 'Dixon, Frederick John,' *Dictionary of Canadian Biography* (forthcoming).
140 Michael William Butt, 'To each according to his need, and from each according to his ability. Why cannot the world see this?' The politics of William Ivens, 1916–1936,' MA thesis, University of Manitoba, 1993, 69.
141 Connor [Rev. Charles Gordon], *To Him That Hath* (New York, 1921), 276.
142 In October 1915, at the Globe Theatre, Blumenberg gave a lecture on 'The Balkan States from a Socialist Viewpoint,' *The Voice*, 15 October 1915.
143 *Manitoba Free Press*, 20 May 1918, quoted in A. Ernest Johnson, 'The Strikes in Winnipeg in May 1918 – The Prelude to 1919?' MA thesis, University of Manitoba, 1978, 156.
144 *Brandon Daily Sun*, 12 February 1918.
145 Trachtenberg, '"The Old Clo' Move,"' 2: 867–8 n. 81.
146 LAC, Immigration Board Hearing, vol. 4, Michael Charitonoff, 16 July 1919, 5–6. *Western Labor News*, 13 December 1918. Other young ethnic militants included Boris Devyatkin, Matthew Popowich, John Navisivsky, and Jacob Penner. On these, except for Devyatkin, see William Rodney, *Soldiers of the International – A History of the Communist Party of Canada 1919–1929* (Toronto, 1968), 25.
147 'Red Letter Day in History of the Labor Movement,' *Western Labor News*, 27 December 1919.
148 Provincial Archives of Manitoba, M1413, In the Court of King's Bench, The King Against William Ivens, Richard J. Johns, Robert B. Russell, William A. Pritchard, John Queen, A.A. Heaps, George Armstrong, and R.E. Bray – Particulars, 20th day of January, A.D. 1920, Alfred Joseph Andrews, Counsel for the Crown (hereafter PAM, Particulars, 20th day of January, A.D. 1920, Alfred Joseph Andrews, Counsel for the Crown).

149 See 'Revolution or Law and Order,' *Winnipeg Citizen*, 22 May 1919.
150 University of Regina Archives, Lusk Papers, Committee to Investigate Revolutionary Radicalism [1919], Lusk Committee Agent, 'Report #7,' 15 June 1919 (facsimile).
151 See Peter Brooks, 'The Law as Narrative and Rhetoric,' in *Law's Stories: Narrative and Rhetoric in the Law*, ed. Peter Brooks and Paul Gewirtz (New Haven, 1996), 21.
152 W.H. Plewman, *Toronto Daily Star*, 23 May 1919.
153 Ibid.
154 LAC, John MacLean, General Diary, 29 May, 4 and 9 June 1919.
155 'Canada's Labor Troubles,' *The Outlook*, 4 June 1919, 3.

4 THE ANOINTING OF A.J. ANDREWS

1 *Montreal Gazette*, 23 May 1919.
2 'To Discipline Civic Strikers,' *Winnipeg Citizen*, 26 May 1919.
3 'Citizens' Committee Resolutions,' *Winnipeg Citizen*, 27 May 1919.
4 'Meeting of 1000 (?) Proves Fake,' *Western Labor News*, 24 May 1919, 3.
5 'CITIZENS OFFER TO SWEEP STREETS,' *Winnipeg Telegram*, 28 May 1919, 1. 'Would Make "Sympathy" Strikes Illegal,' *Winnipeg Citizen*, 29 May 1919.
6 'Fowler Ready to Handle Garbage,' 'Citizens Will Do Garbage Work,' *Winnipeg Citizen*, 29 May 1919, 3–4.
7 'Garbage Service to Be Resumed,' *Western Labor News*, 29 May 1919, 4.
8 'The Bolsheviks and the Soft Pedal,' *Winnipeg Citizen*, 29 May 1919, 2.
9 PAM, Preliminary Hearing, Ernest Hague, 598.
10 'City Council a Tragic Farce,' *Western Labor News*, 11 June 1919, 2.
11 *Manitoba Free Press*, 30 July 1919.
12 PAM, Preliminary Hearing, P.C. McIntyre, 1413. G.W. Allan, MP Winnipeg South, Canada, House of Commons, *Debates*, 2 June 1919, 3063.
13 E.C. Rodgers, 'First Full Story of Canadian Strike: "One Big Union" Is One Big Issue,' *Decatur Review*, 15 June 1919, 14.
14 Library and Archives Canada, Meighen Papers, Series 6 (MG 26, I, vol. 226 A), 149088.
15 LAC, RG 13, Access 87–88/103: box 36, file 9-A-1688, pocket #2, Department of Justice in account with Andrews, Andrews, and Co., 17 August 1919, 8.
16 The error appears, for example, in Roy St George Stubbs, 'A.J.

Andrews: Nestor of the Manitoba Bar,' *Canadian Bar Review* 24 (1946), 193; and Norman Penner, ed., *Winnipeg 1919 – The Strikers' Own History of the Winnipeg General Strike* (Toronto, 1973), 51; and Jon Wooley, *A Century of Integrity: Manitoba Justice 1870–1970* (Winnipeg, 1999), 35. Meighen had been appointed acting minister of justice during the absence of justice minister Charles Doherty in Paris from late 1918 to July 1919. In 1922, in the House of Commons, Meighen tried to clear this up. See Canada, House of Commons, *Debates*, 24 April 1922, 1068–9.

17 LAC, RG 13, Access 87–88/103: box 36, file 9-A-1688, pocket #2, Meighen to Andrews, 26 May 1919.

18 Dale Gibson and Lee Gibson, *Substantial Justice: Law and Lawyers in Manitoba 1670–1970* (Winnipeg, 1972), 214.

19 LAC, RG 13, Access 87–88/103: box 36, file 9-A-1688, pocket #2, Meighen to Andrews, 26 May 1919.

20 Library and Archives Canada, RG 18, Royal Canadian Mounted Police, vol. 3314, file #H V-l, (hereafter LAC, RG 18, Royal Canadian Mounted Police), Superintendent C. Starnes, Commanding Manitoba District, to Commissioner A.B. Perry, 27 May 1919. LAC, RG 13, Access 87–88/103: box 36, file 9-A-1688, pocket #2, Meighen to N.W. Rowell, 21 May 1919.

21 'Strike Unjustified; Citizens Must Stand Firm,' *Winnipeg Citizen*, 24 May 1919.

22 Ibid.

23 William Blackstone, *Commentaries on the Laws of England, Introduction*, sec. 2, Of the Nature of Laws in General, available at http://www.lonang.com/exlibris/blackstone/index.html.

24 Peter Burns, 'Private Prosecutions in Canada: The Law and a Proposal for Change,' *McGill Law Journal* 21 (1975), 271, quotes Sir Theobald Mathew, *The Office and Duties of the Director of Public Prosecutions* (London, 1950), 4, that at one time 'all men were bound to combine themselves in associations of ten, each of whom was responsible for the good behavior of the rest.'

25 'The Strike Situation in Winnipeg,' *Winnipeg Citizen*, 19 May 1919.

26 'Revolution, or Law and Order?' *Winnipeg Citizen*, 22 May 1919.

27 *The Canadian Who's Who*, vol. 2, 1936–7, ed. Charles G.D. Roberts and Arthur Tunnell (Toronto, 1937), 587.

28 David Jay Bercuson, *Confrontation in Winnipeg: Labour, Industrial Relations, and the General Strike* (Montreal, 1974), 121.

29 'Veteran Military Man, General Ketchen Dies,' *Winnipeg Free Press*, 28 July 1959.

30 See *1919 The Winnipeg General Strike: A Driving and Walking Tour* (Winnipeg, 1985).

31 Brig.-Gen. H.D.B. Ketchen to the Secretary, Militia Council, 14 May 1919, quoted in James Eyars, *In Defence of Canada: From the Great War to the Great Depression* (Toronto, 1964), 63.

32 *Toronto Daily Star*, 19 May 1919.

33 *Toronto Daily Star*, 21 May 1919.

34 PAM, Robson Commission, box 1, file 12.

35 PAM, Robson Commission, box 1, file 7.

36 LAC, RG 13, Access 87–88/103: box 36, file 9-A-1688, pocket #2, Meighen to Andrews, 14 June 1919.

37 LAC, Borden Papers, reel C-4341, G.O.C. Winnipeg, 26 May 1919 to Adjutant General, Ottawa: 61584–5.

38 Only the month-long 1909 national strike in Sweden lasted more than a week. See our brief account in chapter 1.

39 These two telegrams were retyped and provided to Meighen as a one-page summary. LAC, RG 13, Access 87–88/103: box 36, file 9-A-1688, pocket #1, Andrews to Meighen, Acting Minister of Justice [n.d.].

40 LAC, RG 13, Access 87–88/103: box 36, file 9-A-1688, pocket #2, Andrews to Meighen (telegram), 28 May 1919.

41 On Ivens's comments, see PAM, Preliminary Hearing, RNWMP Sergeant Albert Reames, 83–92.

42 LAC, RG 13, Access 87–88/103: box 36, file 9-A-1688, pocket #2, Andrews to Meighen, 1 June 1919.

43 W. Stewart Wallace, *The Macmillan Dictionary of Canadian Biography*, 3rd ed. (Toronto, 1963), 711.

44 LAC, RG 18, Royal Canadian Mounted Police, Cortlandt Starnes, Superintendent Commanding Manitoba District to the Commissioner, RNWMP, 30 May 1919.

45 LAC, Borden Papers, reel C-4341, G.O.C. Winnipeg, 26 May 1919 to Adjutant General, Ottawa: 61584–5.

46 Starnes reported Robertson's words. LAC, RG 18, Royal Canadian Mounted Police, Superintendent Commanding Manitoba District to Commissioner, 30 May 1919.

47 LAC, RG 13, Access 87–88/103: box 36, file 9-A-1688, pocket #1, G.W. Allan to Arthur Meighen, 12 May 1920.

48 LAC, RG 18, Royal Canadian Mounted Police, Superintendent Commanding Manitoba District to Commissioner, 30 May 1919.

49 Canada, House of Commons, *Debates*, 2 June 1919, 3037–41.

50 LAC, Borden Papers, OC 564 (1) – OC 566 (M.G. 26, H 1a), vol. 113, C.H. Cahan to Robert Borden, 28 May 1919: 61546.

51 See references to Sir Robert Borden's diary, cited as Borden Papers Private (BPP), 29 May 1919, in Robert Craig Brown, *Robert Laird Borden*, 166 nn. 9 & 10.

5 THE FLAG-FLAPPING STAGE

1 Paul Nanton, *Prairie Explosion: Setting the Pace for Canada* (typescript, 1991), 153.

2 Robert Cooney, a retired Brandon resident, relates how his father Pte. W.J. Cooney, upon returning to Winnipeg on 9 June 1919, was invited by a representative of the Citizens' Committee to join the local militia housed at Minto Barracks: 'He told the Citizens' Committee guy to "go to hell." He was not interested in fighting his own people.' Pte. Cooney fought in France with the 44th Battalion Canadian Infantry. Personal conversation with Robert Cooney, 17 June 2004. See Nominal Role, 44th Battalion C.E.F., Regimental Number 1000963, Cooney, W.J. Pte, 44th & 226th Bn., demob., 8-6-19, Theatre of Service – France, 255, in *Six Thousand Canadian Men – Being the History of the 44th Battalion Canadian Infantry 1914–1919*, ed. E.S. Russenholt (Winnipeg, 1932). Russenholt gives a more prosaic account of the return of the 44th: 'Sunday, June 8. At 9:30 a.m. the train draws into Winnipeg. Crowds pack the station. Sporadic cheers are smothered in a stark quiet. Volunteer automobiles take the men, and the next-of-kin who await them, to Minto Barracks. One by one, the 44th men complete their papers – and walk across the echoing drill floor, through the clanging gate, out into the open air – "civies"!' *Six Thousand Canadian Men*, 229.

3 *Montreal Gazette*, 23 May 1919.

4 'Don't Be Misled – The Only Issue Is Bolshevism,' *Winnipeg Citizen*, 30 May 1919.

5 'Deeds, Not Words, Made Revolution,' *Winnipeg Citizen*, 30 May 1919, 2.

6 David Jay Bercuson, *Confrontation in Winnipeg: Labour, Industrial Relations, and the General Strike* (Montreal, 1974), 143.

7 'Returned Soldiers Wait on Government,' *Manitoba Free Press*, 31 May 1919, 5.

8 University of Manitoba Archives and Special Collections, Gerald Friesen fonds, Ed Anderson, Biographical questionnaire, St Paul's College, 'Memoir,' 5.

9 University of Manitoba Archives and Special Collections, MSS 48, PC 58, Pitblado Family Fonds, Series 4, Lt. Edward Bruce Pitblado, 'Summary of Army Career,' *War Diary, 1915–1919*.

10 'Revolution or Law and Order,' *Winnipeg Citizen*, 22 May 1919.
11 'Cabinet Must Act or Quit,' *Winnipeg Telegram*, 13 May 1919.
12 PAM, Preliminary Hearing, Frederick William Law, 411.
13 *Manitoba Free Press*, Friday, 16 May 1919.
14 See, for example, PAM, Preliminary Hearing, Frederick William Law, 409, and 'Attitude of Veterans,' *Manitoba Free Press*, 14 May 1919, 1.
15 Nanton, *Prairie Explosion*, 145, 150. 'Striking Soldiers Wear Out Shoes on Long March,' *Winnipeg Telegram*, 4 June 1919, 1.
16 'More Suggestions for "The Citizen" Telegram, et al.,' *Western Labor News*, 29 May 1919, 4.
17 *Western Labor News*, 31 May 1919.
18 *Western Labor News*, 30 May 1919.
19 LAC, RG 13, Access 87–88/103: box 36, file 9-A-1688, pocket #2, Andrews to Meighen, 31 May 1919. The *Free Press* outdid even Andrews in estimating low: it suggested that there were only 700 men in total at the protest. 'Returned Soldiers Wait on Government,' *Manitoba Free Press*, 31 May 1919. John Dafoe allowed no mention of the mass protest on the front page, though he found room for articles on the butter situation, on the Police Commission and mediation for the police, on the Trades Council having no authority to call a strike, and on postal workers returning to work. Instead, he buried the protest on page 5, next to church service announcements.
20 PAM, Robert Graham fonds, 87.
21 PAM, Robert Graham fonds, 77, 87, 89, 98.
22 PAM, Robert Graham fonds, 91.
23 PAM, Robert Graham fonds, 81.
24 'Frantic Patriotism,' *Western Labor News*, 24 May 1919, 1.
25 'Returned Soldier Deprecates Abuse of Flag by Citizen's [*sic*] Committee,' *Western Labor News*, 30 May 1919, 4.
26 'Mass Demonstrations Made,' *Winnipeg Citizen*, 2 June 1919, 3.
27 'Wearer of Union Jack Is Assaulted,' *Manitoba Free Press*, 3 June 1919, 8.
28 W.H. Plewman, *Toronto Daily Star*, 23 May 1919.
29 'The Strike Committee, the Soldier and the Alien,' *Winnipeg Citizen*, 4 June 1919, 4.
30 *Western Labor News*, 2 June 1919.
31 LAC, RG 13, Access 87–88/103: box 36, file 9-A-1688, pocket #1, Andrews to Meighen, 1 June 1919.
32 'A Point for the Returned Soldier,' *Winnipeg Citizen*, 31 May 1919, 3.
33 A member of the Manitoba Club, H.J. Symington K.C., served as counsel for the committee investigating the Legislative Building scandal that brought down the Roblin government in 1915. Along with for-

mer attorney general Albert B. Hudson K.C., Symington advised Attorney General Johnson on the handling of the Strike. LAC, RG 13, Access 87–88/103: box 36, file 9-A-1688, pocket #1, Andrews to Meighen, 18 June 1919. B.M. Greene, ed., *Who's Who in Canada, 1928–29: An Illustrated Biographical Record of Men and Women of the Time* (Toronto, 1929), 72.

34 PAM, Robert Graham fonds, 94.
35 PAM, Robert Graham fonds, 95.
36 PAM, Robert Graham fonds, 97.
37 PAM, Robert Graham fonds, 98.
38 LAC, RG 13, Access 87–88/103: box 36, file 9-A-1688, pocket #2, Andrews to Meighen, 31 May 1919.
39 *Toronto Daily Star*, 21 May 1919.
40 Samuel Hopkins Adams, 'The One Big Union – What the Strike at Winnipeg Really Shows,' *Collier's*, 19 July 1919, 30.
41 *Winnipeg Telegram*, 16 May 1918. A. Ernest Johnson, 'The Strikes in Winnipeg in May 1918 – The Prelude to 1919?' MA thesis, University of Manitoba, 1978, 138.
42 *Western Labor News*, 17 May 1919, 4.
43 LAC, RG 13, Access 87–88/103: box 36, file 9-A-1688, pocket #2, Andrews to Meighen, 31 May l919.
44 LAC, RG 13, Access 87–88/103: box 36, file 9-A-1688, pocket #2, Andrews to Meighen, 31 May 1919.
45 *Western Labor News*, 31 May 1919.
46 LAC, RG 13, Access 87–88/103: box 36, file 9-A-1688, pocket #1, Cortlandt Starnes, Superintendent Commanding Manitoba District to the Commissioner, 30 May 1919.
47 Machiavelli, *The Prince*, trans. George Bull, rev. ed. (Harmondsworth, 1971), 27.
48 LAC, RG 13, Access 87–88/103: box 36, file 9-A-1688, pocket #2, Andrews to Meighen, 31 May 1919.
49 LAC, RG 13, Access 87–88/103: box 36, file 9-A-1688, pocket #2, Andrews to Meighen, 31 May 1919.
50 LAC, RG 13, Access 87–88/103: box 36, file 9-A-1688, pocket #2, Andrews to Meighen, 1 June 1919.
51 Isaac Pitblado, 'An Address on the Subject of the Winnipeg Strike,' 5.
52 PAM, Preliminary Hearing, Leslie Horace Parker, 314, 317, 321.
53 Isaac Pitblado, 'An Address on the Subject of the Winnipeg Strike,' 8.
54 LAC, RG 13, Access 87–88/103: box 36, file 9-A-1688, pocket #2, Andrews to Meighen, 1 June 1919.
55 M.M. Bakhtin, *Speech Genre and Other Essays*, ed. Michael Holquist and Carl Emerson (Austin, 1986), 121.

56 LAC, RG 13, Access 87–88/103: box 36, file 9-A-1688, pocket #2, Andrews to Meighen, 29 May 1919 (coded telegram).

57 'They Are "Known by Their Acts,"' *Winnipeg Citizen*, 2 June 1919.

58 It may be that Andrews had access to RNWMP commissioner Perry's report on the OBU and the Calgary conference. Perry, basing his report on information from 'Secret Agent #10' and on Perry's own conversations with Bill Pritchard and V.R. Midgeley, informed Prime Minister Borden that the labour radicals weren't aiming at revolution in the ordinary (violent) sense of the word, but that they wanted to bring about a social and economic revolution. In doing so, they might unchain forces that could endanger Canada's security. Unlike one of his subordinates who suggested that certain labour leaders be made to disappear, Perry advocated the changing of sedition laws so that the more radical leaders could be netted. LAC, MG 26, Borden Papers, OC519 – OC524, H 1 (a), vol. 104, A. Bowen Perry, Commissioner of the RNWMP, Re: Inter-Provincial Labour Convention Calgary, Alta., 56825–36. Meighen certainly would have been aware of this report.

59 LAC, RG 13, Access 87–88/103: box 36, file 9-A-1688, pocket #2, Andrews to Meighen, 1 June 1919.

60 *Western Labor News*, 2 June 1919.

61 'Soldiers Mean Business,' *Western Labor News*, 3 June 1919, 1–2.

62 LAC, RG 13, Access 87–88/103: box 36, file 9-A-1688, pocket #2, Andrews to Meighen, 2 June 1919.

63 PAM, Preliminary Hearing, Ed Parnell, 1053.

64 'Soldiers Mean Business.'

65 'Attempt Made to Blow Up Home of Attorney General Palmer of U.S.,' *Manitoba Free Press*, 3 June 1919, 1. *The Literary Digest*, 14 June 1919.

66 LAC, Borden Papers, OC564(1) – OC 566, MG 26, H a(1), vol. 113, 61804–5.

67 LAC, RG 13, Access 87–88/103: box 36, file 9-A-1688, pocket #2, Andrews to Meighen, 2 June 1919.

68 LAC, RG 13, Access 87–88/103: box 36, file 9-A-1688, pocket #2, Andrews to Meighen, 3 June 1919.

69 LAC, RG 13, Access 87–88/103: box 36, file 9-A-1688, pocket #2, Andrews to Meighen, 2 June 1919.

70 'Mass Demonstrations Made,' *Winnipeg Citizen*, 2 June 1919, 3.

71 'The Citizens' Committee of "One" Thousand,' *Winnipeg Citizen*, 2 June 1919.

72 LAC, RG 13, Access 87–88/103: box 36, file 9-A-1688, pocket #2, Andrews to Meighen, 3 June 1919.

73 LAC, RG 13, Access 87–88/103: box 36, file 9-A-1688, pocket #2, Andrews to Meighen, 1 June 1919.

74 LAC, RG 13, Access 87–88/103: box 36, file 9-A-1688, pocket #2, Andrews to Meighen, 3 June 1919.

75 Ibid.

76 'They Are "Known by Their Acts."'

77 LAC, RG 13, Access 87–88/103: box 36, file 9-A-1688, pocket #2, Andrews to Meighen, 3 June 1919.

78 Ibid. Andrews indicates that he had asked the provincial attorney general to arrest Strike leaders: LAC, RG 13, Access 87–88/103: box 36, file 9-A-1688, pocket #2, Andrews to Meighen, 4 & 5 June 1919.

79 'The Citizens' Committee of "One" Thousand.'

80 Ibid.

81 'Why Not Organize Ourselves?' *Winnipeg Citizen*, 4 June 1919

82 'The Citizens' Committee of "One" Thousand.'

83 Ibid.

84 Provincial Archives of Manitoba, MG14, C46, Frederick G. Thompson Papers, 6 June 1969.

85 LAC, RG 13, Access 87–88/103: box 36, file 9-A-1688, pocket #2, Andrews to Meighen, 1 June 1919.

86 For 14 days in June, the high exceeded 28° Celsius. From 21 May through 30 May, the daily high had never dipped below 26°, and on 28 May it had reached 35° (95° Fahrenheit). Weather data courtesy Dr Rod McGinn, Geography Department, Brandon University.

87 LAC, RG 13, Access 87–88/103: box 36, file 9-A-1688, pocket #2, Andrews to Meighen (letter), 4 June 1919, evening.

88 C.B. Macpherson, *The Political Theory of Possessive Individualism: Hobbes to Locke* (Oxford, 1961), 274.

89 *Winnipeg Telegram*, 13 May 1901.

90 'Which Flag?' *Winnipeg Citizen*, 4 June 1919.

91 Douglas Owram, *The Government Generation: Canadian Intellectuals and the State 1900–1945* (Toronto, 1986), 80.

92 The Citizens defined patriotism as 'Love of country evidenced by service ... Patriotism today calls for Service in the form of volunteers to do something with a view to keeping law and order in the city, and to insure that the mass of people who are not interested concerning the strike, except as onlookers, are not interfered with, inconvenienced or handicapped in getting the necessities of life.' *Winnipeg Citizen*, 26 May 1919.

93 See, for example, *Winnipeg Telegram*, 6 June 1919.

94 'To the Citizens of Winnipeg,' *Manitoba Free Press*, 3 June 1919, 3.

95 'THE ALIEN IN OUR MIDST,' *Manitoba Free Press*, 3 June 1919, 5.

96 PAM, Preliminary Hearing, Ed Parnell, 1060.

97 'THE ALIEN Is On His Way' *Manitoba Free Press*, 6 June 1919, 3.

98 Charles Taylor, 'Modern Social Imaginaries,' *Public Culture* 14, no. 1 (2002), 112.

99 'What It All Means,' *The Nor'-West Farmer*, 5 June 1919, 881.

100 'Revolution or Law and Order,' *Winnipeg Citizen*, 22 May 1919.

101 Ibid.

102 Ibid.

103 'The Citizens' Magna Charta,' *Winnipeg Citizen*, 23 May 1919, 3.

104 *Winnipeg Citizen*, 26 May 1919. 'The Naked Fact of Revolution,' *Winnipeg Citizen*, 27 May 1919, 1.

105 *Winnipeg Citizen*, 31 May 1919.

106 Pitblado, 'Address on the Subject of the Winnipeg Strike,' 8.

107 'The Strike Committee, the Soldier and the Alien,' *Winnipeg Citizen*, 4 June 1919, 4.

108 Rev. (Capt.) Wellington Bridgman, *Breaking Prairie Sod: The Story of a Pioneer Preacher in the Eighties with a Discussion of the Burning Question of To-day, 'Shall the Alien Go?'* (Toronto, 1920), 191.

109 'The Strike Committee, the Soldier and the Alien,' *Winnipeg Citizen*, 4 June 1919, 4.

110 Ibid.

111 'The Strike, the Solder and the H.C. of L.' *Winnipeg Citizen*, 3 June 1919, 3.

112 'The Strike Committee, the Soldier and the Alien,' *Winnipeg Citizen*, 4 June 1919.

113 'Council Takes Prompt Action to Get Milk and Bread for Citizens,' *Manitoba Free Press*, 5 June 1919, 1. 'Max Steinkopf,' Biographical questionnaire, Dept. of History, St Paul's College.

114 LAC, John MacLean, General diary, 14 April 1919.

115 Bridgman, *Breaking Prairie Sod*, 172, 157.

116 Ibid., 215.

117 Donald Avery, *'Dangerous Foreigners': European Immigrant Workers and Labour Radicalism in Canada 1896–1932* (Toronto, 1979), 82.

118 'Dealing with Problem Placing Soldiers,' *Manitoba Free Press*, 3 February 1919, 10; 'Returned Men Demand Aliens Be Sent Home,' *Manitoba Free Press*, 4 February 1919, 1, 6; 'Board of Twenty Down to Business,' *Manitoba Free Press*, 5 February 1919, 10.

119 *Manitoba Free Press*, 11 June 1919. 'Strike Observations,' *Manitoba Free Press*, 7 June 1919, 3.

120 LAC, RG 13, Access 87–88/103: box 36, file 9-A-1688, pocket #2, R.L. Richardson MP to Sir Thomas White and Hon. Arthur Meighen, 3 June 1919 (telegram).

121 'Returned Soldiers Loyalist Association in Operation,' *Manitoba Free Press*, 6 June 1919, 8. Certainly the reporting here may be slanted, but there are enough indications of similar statements to warrant the accuracy of J.O. Newton's testimony on this point. On the other hand, as David Williams notes, during the war many soldiers had become sceptical about patriotism and racism – 'all that rot.' David Williams, *Media, Memory and the First World War* (Montreal & Kingston: McGill-Queen's University Press 2009), 238, 129.

122 'City Council a Tragic Farce,' *Western Labor News*, 11 June 1919, 2.

123 'MAYOR RESCUES GUNMAN: Mayor Goes Crazy,' *Western Labor News*, 6 June 1919, 1, 4. See also PAM, Preliminary Hearing, Frederick William Law, 425, in which labour counsel E.J. McMurray also tries to distance labour from the alien.

124 LAC, RG 13, Access 87–88/103: box 36, file 9-A-1688, pocket #2, Andrews to Meighen (letter), 4 June 1919, evening.

6 TO REACH THE LEADERS

1 LAC, RG 13, Access 87–88/103: box 36, file 9-A-1688, pocket #2, Andrews to Meighen (telegram #1), 4 June 1919.

2 In his report to the adjutant general on 5 June 1919, Ketchen explained that 'Citizens' Committee waited on Premier urging arrest of strike leaders.' LAC, Borden Papers, reel C-4341, G.O.C. Winnipeg to Adjutant General, Ottawa, 5 June 1919: 61808.

3 LAC, RG 13, Access 87–88/103: box 36, file 9-A-1688, pocket #2, Andrews to Meighen, 5 June 1919 (telegram); 6 June 1919 (letter).

4 LAC, RG 13, Access 87–88/103: box 36, file 9-A-1688, pocket #2, Andrews to Meighen, 6 June 1919 (letter).

5 LAC, RG 13, Access 87–88/103: box 36, file 9-A-1688, pocket #2, Andrews to Meighen (letter), 4 June 1919, evening. Ibid., Andrews to Meighen, 5 June 1919.

6 LAC, RG 13, Access 87–88/103: box 36, file 9-A-1688, pocket #2, G.O.C. to Adjutant General, Ottawa, 5 June 1919 (telegram).

7 LAC, RG 13, Access 87–88/103: box 36, file 9-A-1688, pocket #2, Andrews to Meighen, 5 June 1919 (telegram).

8 Ibid.

9 Ibid.

10 'An Act to amend The Immigration Act,' 9–10 George V, ch. 25, 98.

11 The process of being 'domiciled' in Canada applied only to British cit-
    izens, and constituted a third way, besides birth in Canada and natural-
    ization, whereby one could become a Canadian citizen.

12 LAC, RG 13, Access 87–88/103: box 36, file 9-A-1688, pocket #2,
    Andrews to Meighen, 3 June 1919.

13 LAC, RG 13, Access 87–88/103: box 36, file 9-A-1688, pocket #2,
    Andrews to Meighen, 5 and 6 June 1919.

14 'Veterans Repudiate Parades,' *Winnipeg Citizen*, 3 June 1919, 2.
    Ketchen gave a similarly biased statement to his superiors: 'War Veter-
    ans Association published statement abandoning neutrality regarding
    the present strike and now do not support strike.' LAC, RG 13, Access
    87–88/103: box 36, file 9-A-1688, pocket #2, Gen. Ketchen, G.O.C. to
    Adjutant General, Ottawa, 6 June 1919.

15 'G.W.V.A. Endorses Strikers,' *Western Labor News*, 5 June 1919, 1.
    'Organized for Law, Order and Food,' *Winnipeg Citizen*, 6 June 1919,
    4. PAM, Preliminary Hearing, Frederick William Law, 416–17.

16 'Drastic Action by Veterans Confirmed,' *Manitoba Free Press*, 6 June
    1919, 7.

17 'Great War Veterans Are Determined to Suppress Attempt at Bolshe-
    vism,' *Manitoba Free Press*, 5 June 1919, 1.

18 'Committee of 1000 Organize Opposition Soldiers' Parade,' *Western
    Labor News*, 5 June 1919, 4.

19 'The Canadian Corps Is Heard From!' *Winnipeg Citizen*, 5 June 1919,
    4.

20 Andrews's examination, PAM, Preliminary Hearing, Frederick William
    Law, 432.

21 'That Grand Theatre Meeting,' *Winnipeg Citizen*, 12 June 1919.

22 Thanks to Professor Desmond Morton for his interpretation of this
    quotation. E-mail to Tom Mitchell from Professor Morton, 1 April
    2004.

23 LAC, RG 13, Access 87–88/103: box 36, file 9-A-1688, pocket #2,
    Andrews to Meighen (telegram #1), 4 June 1919. The *Western Labor
    News* underestimated the soldiers at 800, while the *Free Press* put the
    crowd at 5000, neglecting (purposely?) to mention how many soldiers
    were in that number. 'Committee of 1000 Organize Opposition Sol-
    diers' Parade.' 'Mass of Returned Men Give Assurance They Stand
    Solid in Defence of Law and Order,' *Manitoba Free Press*, 5 June
    1919, 2.

24 'Mass of Returned Men Give Assurance.'

25 'Committee of 1000 Organize Opposition Soldiers' Parade.'

26 'Child Murder Will be Punished,' *Winnipeg Citizen*, 6 June 1919, 1.

27 'Council Takes Prompt Action to Get Milk and Bread for Citizens,' *Manitoba Free Press*, 5 June 1919, 1.

28 'Committee of 1000 Organize Opposition Soldiers' Parade.'

29 LAC, RG 13, Access 87–88/103: box 36, file 9-A-1688, pocket #2, Andrews to Meighen, 6 June 1919.

30 The *Free Press* said that the auditorium rink was filled to its capacity of 3000, with as many again outside, but didn't specify that the numbers included soldiers. 'Returned Soldiers Loyalist Association in Operation,' *Manitoba Free Press*, 6 June 1919, 8.

31 'The Canadian Corps Is Heard From!'

32 'Committee of 1000 Organize Opposition Soldiers' Parade.'

33 'Returned Men Demand Aliens Be Sent Home,' *Manitoba Free Press*, 4 February 1919, 6.

34 LAC, RG 13, Access 87–88/103: box 36, file 9-A-1688, pocket #2, Andrews to Meighen, 6 June 1919.

35 'Organized for Law, Order and Food,' *Winnipeg Citizen*, 6 June 1919, 4.

36 LAC, RG 13, Access 87–88/103: box 36, file 9-A-1688, pocket #2, Andrews to Meighen, 6 June 1919. According to the *Free Press*, members of the Citizens' Committee had made a careful count and came up with 1350 strikers. 'Another Strikers Parade Yesterday,' *Manitoba Free Press*, 6 June 1919, 3.

37 'Organized for Law, Order and Food,' *Winnipeg Citizen*, 5 June 1919, 4. 'Another Strikers Parade Yesterday.'

38 'Another Strikers Parade Yesterday.'

39 'Ten Thousand March for Justice,' *Western Labor News*, 6 June 1919, 1.

40 LAC, RG 13, Access 87–88/103: box 36, file 9-A-1688, pocket #2, Andrews to Meighen, 6 June 1919. 'Organized for Law, Order and Food.' 'Special City Police Force Is Now Ready,' *Manitoba Free Press*, 6 June 1919, 1.

41 LAC, RG 13, Access 87–88/103: box 36, file 9-A-1688, pocket #1, Adjutant General to the G.O.C. M.D. #10, Winnipeg, Man., 14 May 1919.

42 Samuel Hopkins Adams, 'The One Big Union – What the "Strike" at Winnipeg Really Shows,' 30.

43 LAC, RG 13, Access 87–88/103: box 36, file 9-A-1688, pocket #2, Andrews to Meighen, 10 June 1919.

44 This is, in fact, Weber's very *definition* of the state. See Max Weber, 'Politics as a Vocation,' 173, at http://www2.pfeiffer.edu/~Iridener/ DSS /Weber/polvoc.html. 'Politik als Beruf,' *Gesammelte Politische Schriften* (München, 1921), 396.

45 PAM, Preliminary Hearing, Alderman J.K. Sparling, 748, 754–5.

46 PAM, Preliminary Hearing, Capt. F.G. Thompson, 977–8.

47 However, when intimidation against postal workers and bread and milk trucks flared up again, the RNWMP's Col. Starnes did promise protection.

48 PAM, Preliminary Hearing, Alderman J.K. Sparling, 735–6.

49 Quoted in Frederick David Millar, 'The Winnipeg General Strike, 1919: A Reinterpretation in the Light of Oral History and Pictorial Evidence,' MA thesis, Carleton University, 1970, 254.

50 PAM, Preliminary Hearing, Capt. Wheeler, 1242–4.

51 Major Hilliard Lyle – the *Manitoba Free Press* misspelled his name as Lyall, probably confusing him with H.B. Lyall of Manitoba Bridge and Iron Works – had been in Winnipeg since 1896, but wasn't well known. He served in the Boer War and spent some time during the Great War in the United States training American soldiers. *Manitoba Free Press*, 10 June 1919.

52 'Returned Soldiers Loyalist Association in Operation,' *Manitoba Free Press*, 6 June 1919, 8.

53 Quoted in Millar, *The Winnipeg General Strike*, 250.

54 'MAYOR RESCUES GUNMAN: Mayor Goes Crazy,' *Western Labor News*, 6 June 1919, 1, 4. PAM, Robert Graham fonds, 100.

55 'Organized for Law, Order and Food,' *Winnipeg Citizen*, 6 June 1919, 4.

56 LAC, RG 13, Access 87–88/103: box 36, file 9-A-1688, pocket #2, Andrews to Meighen, 5 June 1919 (telegram).

57 LAC, RG 13, Access 87–88/103: box 36, file 9-A-1688, pocket #2, Gen. Ketchen, G.O.C. to Adjutant General, Ottawa, 6 June 1919.

58 LAC, RG 13, Access 87–88/103: box 36, file 9-A-1688, pocket #2, Andrews to Meighen, 6 June 1919.

59 PAM, Robert Graham fonds, 104.

60 LAC, RG 13, Access 87–88/103: box 36, file 9-A-1688, pocket #2, Andrews to Meighen, 13 June 1919.

61 PAM, Preliminary Hearing, Alderman J.K. Sparling, 709, 739.

62 Macdonald's recourse to the shibboleth 'loyalty' makes it clear that he went along with the Citizens' interpretation of the Strike: 'The Police Force should be reorganized ... and brought up to a standard of efficiency, loyalty and devotion to duty befitting the occupants of such responsible positions.' Quoted in Henry James Guest, 'Reluctant Politician: A Biography of Sir Hugh John Macdonald,' MA thesis, University of Manitoba, 1973, 376.

63 PAM, Robert Graham fonds, 102.

64 PAM, Preliminary Hearing, J.K. Sparling, 710.

65 PAM, Preliminary Hearing, J.K. Sparling, 712–13. A number of other incidents of intimidation are detailed in chapter 3.

66 PAM, Preliminary Hearing, Ed Parnell, 1055, 1057.

67 Guest, Reluctant Politician, 375.

68 'Organized for Law, Order and Food,' Winnipeg Citizen, 6 June 1919, 4.

69 PAM, Preliminary Hearing, J.K. Sparling, 734.

70 Paul Nanton, Prairie Explosion: Setting the Pace for Canada (typescript, 1991), 150.

71 'Lawlessness in Winnipeg,' Winnipeg Citizen, 6 June 1919, 2.

72 'MAYOR RESCUES GUNMAN: Mayor Goes Crazy,' Western Labor News, 6 June 1919, 1, 4.

73 'Gray Adamant on Question of Street Demonstrations,' Winnipeg Telegram, 7 June 1919, 8. Western Labor News, 7 June 1919, 4; 9 June 1919, 4.

74 'Must Be Protections for Citizens' [editorial], Manitoba Free Press, 5 June 1919, 1.

75 PAM, Preliminary Hearing, Ed Parnell, Testimony 1055, 1057.

76 LAC, RG 13, Access 87–88/103: box 36, file 9-A-1688, pocket #2, Andrews to Meighen, 6 June 1919.

77 'Mrs Armstrong Is to Face Charge,' Manitoba Free Press, 6 June 1919, 9.

78 'Strikers Fail in Attempt to Cut Off Bread-Milk Supply,' Manitoba Free Press, 6 June 1919, 4.

79 'Mass of Returned Men Give Assurance They Stand Solid in Defence of Law and Order,' Manitoba Free Press, 5 June 1919, 2.

80 David Jay Bercuson, Confrontation in Winnipeg: Labour, Industrial Relations, and the General Strike (Montreal, 1974), 67.

81 A.J. Andrews, Preliminary Hearing, 744.

82 Ralph Connor [Rev. Charles Gordon], To Him That Hath: A Novel of the West of Today (New York, 1921), 202, 28.

83 Ibid., 186.

84 E.U. Pugsley, 'Courage and Persistence Won Success for Fletcher Sparling,' The Beaver, October 1920, 12.

85 'The Truth – From the Inside,' Winnipeg Citizen, 14 June 1919, 1, 3.

86 LAC, RG 13, Access 87–88/103: box 36, file 9-A-1688, pocket #2, Andrews to Meighen, 6 June 1919.

87 LAC, RG 13, Access 87–88/103: box 36, file 9-A-1688, pocket #2, Andrews to Meighen, 6 June 1919 (telegram).

88 LAC, RG 13, Access 87–88/103: box 36, file 9-A-1688, pocket #2, Andrews to Meighen, 9 June 1919.

89 J.M. Bumsted, The Winnipeg General Strike of 1919: An Illustrated History (Winnipeg, 1994), 127.

90 LAC, RG 13, Access 87–88/103: box 36, file 9-A-1688, pocket #2, Andrews to Meighen, 6 June 1919.
91 Ibid.
92 Ibid.
93 Ibid.
94 LAC, RG 13, Access 87–88/103: box 36, file 9-A-1688, pocket #2, Meighen to Andrews, 6 June 1919 (telegram).
95 Canada, House of Commons, *Debates*, 6 June 1919, 3211.
96 Ibid., 3213.
97 LAC, RG 13, Access 87–88/103: box 36, file 9-A-1688, pocket #2, Meighen to Andrews, 7 June 1919.
98 See Leslie Katz, 'Some Legal Consequences of the Winnipeg General Strike,' *Manitoba Law Journal* 1 (1970), 47–8, for more detail on these changes. Andrews also coached Meighen to amend the Naturalization Act to take naturalization away from anyone who was perceived as a threat, and to ensure that such legislation was 'simple and summary.' The amendments were introduced on 9 June and approved in September. This was too late for use against the Winnipeg strikers, but the amendments remained available for use by the state against future strikers. LAC, RG 13, Access 87–88/103: box 36, file 9-A-1688, pocket #2, Andrews to Meighen, 8 June 1919.
99 LAC, RG 13, Access 87–88/103: box 36, file 9-A-1688, pocket #2, Meighen to Andrews, 7 June 1919 (letter).
100 For a detailed account of this development, see Bercuson, *Confrontation at Winnipeg*, 157.
101 LAC, RG 13, Access 87–88/103: box 36, file 9-A-1688, pocket #2, Andrews to Gideon Robertson, 6 June 1919.
102 LAC, RG 13, Access 87–88/103: box 36, file 9-A-1688, pocket #2, A.L. [*sic*] Andrews to Hon. Sen. Robertson (telegram), 6 June 1919.
103 LAC, RG 13, Access 87–88/103: box 36, file 9-A-1688, pocket #2, A.K. Mclean to Hon. G.D. Robertson, reporting a telegram from 'Executive Committee of One Thousand Citizens,' 20 May 1919.
104 LAC, RG 13, Access 87–88/103: box 36, file 9-A-1688, pocket #2, Meighen to Andrews, 9 June 1919.
105 LAC, RG 13, Access 87–88/103: box 36, file 9-A-1688, pocket #2, Andrews to Meighen, (telegram) 9 June 1919.
106 LAC, RG 13, Access 87–88/103: box 36, file 9-A-1688, pocket #2, Andrews to Meighen, 9 June 1919.
107 Ibid., George Allan to Augustus Nanton, 9 June 1919.
108 Bercuson, *Winnipeg General Strike: 1919*, 211, fn. 51. For the Andrews letter, see LAC, Borden Papers, reel C-4341, Andrews to Meighen, 9 June 1919: 61857-8.

109 LAC, Borden Papers, reel C-4341, G.D. Robertson to F.A. Acland, Deputy Minister of Labour, Following for Prime Minister, 11 June 1919: 61891.

110 LAC, RG 13, Access 87–88/103: box 36, file 9-A-1688, pocket #2, Andrews to Meighen, 5 June 1919 (telegram).

111 LAC, RG 13, Access 87–88/103: box 36, file 9-A-1688, pocket #2, Andrews to Meighen, 6 June 1919.

112 LAC, RG 13, Access 87–88/103: box 36, file 9-A-1688, pocket #2, Andrews to Meighen, 8 June 1919 (letter).

113 Ibid.

114 LAC, Borden Papers, reel C-4341, Andrews to Meighen, 9 June 1919: 61857–8.

115 'An Interview with James Dunwoody,' *Manitoba History* 6 (Fall 1983), 22.

7 TIME TO ACT

1 'An Attempt at Wilful Murder,' *Winnipeg Citizen*, 5 June 1919.

2 LAC, RG 13, Access 87–88/103: box 36, file 9-A-1688, pocket #2, Andrews to Meighen (letter), 18 June 1919.

3 See cover photograph. After the Strike, Charles Gordon mythicized the Specials in *To Him That Hath* by having the novel's hero, Jack Maitland, help to organize them. They agree that no guns will be used, only axe handles. Connor [Rev. Charles Gordon], *To Him That Hath*, 251.

4 J.M. Coetzee, *Giving Offense: Essays on Censorship* (Chicago, 1996), 142.

5 University of Regina Archives, Lusk Papers, Committee to Investigate Revolutionary Radicalism [1919], Lusk Committee Agent, 'Report #2,' 10 June 1919 (facsimile).

6 Samuel Hopkins Adams, 'The One Big Union – What the Strike at Winnipeg Really Shows,' *Collier's*, 19 July 1919, 30. One other source reported that the riot actually extended over three hours. *Manitoba Free Press*, 11 June 1919.

7 *Manitoba Free Press*, 11 June 1919.

8 *Western Labor News*, 11 June 1919, 1.

9 LAC, RG 13, Access 87–88/103: box 36, file 9-A-1688, pocket #2, Andrews to Meighen, 10 June 1919.

10 LAC, Borden Papers, reel C-4341, Andrews to Meighen, 11 June 1919: 61889–90.

11 LAC, RG 13, Access 87–88/103: box 36, file 9-A-1688, pocket #2, Andrews to Meighen, 10 June 1919.

12 LAC, RG 13, Access 87–88/103: box 36, file 9-A-1688, pocket #2,

Andrews to Meighen, 13 June 1919. Deputy Police Chief Newton quickly got rid of Lyle by sending him to Minneapolis to check out used militia uniforms for the Specials.

13 LAC, RG 13, Access 87–88/103: box 36, file 9-A-1688, pocket #2, Andrews to Meighen, 10 June 1919.

14 'Ugly Action Contemplated,' *Western Labor News*, 13 June 1919, 1.

15 LAC, RG 13, Access 87–88/103: box 36, file 9-A-1688, pocket #2, G.O.C. to Adjutant General, Ottawa, 11 June 1919.

16 LAC, RG 13, Access 87–88/103: box 36, file 9-A-1688, pocket #2, Andrews to Meighen, 10 June 1919.

17 Hopkins Adams, 'The One Big Union.'

18 Charles Townshend, 'Martial Law: Legal and Administrative Problems of Civil Emergency in Britain and the Empire, 1800–1940,' *The Historical Journal* 25, no. 1 (March 1982), 167–95.

19 LAC, Borden Papers, reel C-4341, Andrews to Meighen, 11 June 1919: 61889–90. There doesn't seem to be independent verification that this was true. Possibly Andrews was referring to (and turning a blind eye towards) illegal military 'free-corps' groups.

20 'The Winnipeg Revolutionary Strike,' *Winnipeg Citizen*, 9 June 1919.

21 'This Revolution Is Dictated from New York,' *Winnipeg Citizen*, 7 June 1919.

22 LAC, RG 13, Access 87–88/103: box 36, file 9-A-1688, pocket #2, A.A. McLean, Comptroller of the Royal North West Mounted Police to E.L. Newcombe, Deputy Minister of Justice, 9 June 1919.

23 'A Riot Born of Revolution,' *Winnipeg Citizen*, 11 June 1919.

24 Ibid.

25 The language is borrowed from Charles Taylor, 'Modern Social Imaginaries,' *Public Culture* 14, no. 1 (2002), 114.

26 Louis G. Silverberg, 'Citizens' Committees: Their Role in Industrial Conflict,' *Public Opinion Quarterly* 5, no. 1 (March 1941), 27.

27 LAC, RG 13, Access 87–88/103: box 36, file 9-A-1688, pocket #2, Andrews to Meighen, 13 June 1919.

28 'A Riot Born of Revolution.'

29 'FROM THE SIDEWALK THEY CALLED HIM A SCAB ...' *Winnipeg Telegram*, 11 June 1919, 2.

30 Fred Gaffen, *Cross-Border Warriors* (Dundurn Press, 1995), 32.

31 'A Riot Born of Revolution.'

32 PAM, Preliminary Hearing, F.C. Coppins, 1324.

33 'A Riot Born of Revolution.'

34 PAM, Preliminary Hearing, F.C. Coppins, 1326–7.

35 'Sergeant Coppin [*sic*] Rallies Quickly from His Hurt,' *Winnipeg*

Telegram, 11 June 1919, 1, 3. Gen. Ketchen too, that same day, was informing his superiors that Coppins suffered from 'injured ribs and chest,' but was 'improving nicely.' LAC, RG 13, Access 87–88/103: box 36, file 9-A-1688, pocket #2, G.O.C. to C.E.S., 11 June 1919.

36 LAC, RG 13, Access 87–88/103: box 36, file 9-A-1688, pocket #2, G.O.C. to Adjutant General, Ottawa, 11 June 1919.

37 LAC, RG 13, Access 87–88/103: box 36, file 9-A-1688, pocket #2, Andrews to Meighen, 13 June 1919.

38 PAM, Preliminary Hearing, Capt. James Moore Dunwoody, 1436.

39 'An Interview with James Dunwoody,' *Manitoba History* 6 (Fall 1983), 22.

40 'Democracy Must Be Vindicated,' *Winnipeg Citizen*, 12 June 1919.

41 LAC, RG 13, Access 87–88/103: box 36, file 9-A-1688, pocket #2, G.O.C. Winnipeg to Adjutant General, Ottawa, 12 June 1919.

42 Cortlandt Starnes to the Comptroller, 12 June 1919. LAC, RG 13, Access 87–88/103: box 36, file 9-A-1688, pocket #2, G.O.C. to Adjutant General, 14 June 1919.

43 LAC, RG 13, Access 87–88/103: box 36, file 9-A-1688, pocket #2, Andrews to Meighen, 13 June 1919.

44 LAC, RG 13, Access 87–88/103: box 36, file 9-A-1688, pocket #2, G.O.C. Winnipeg to Adjutant General, Ottawa, 12 June 1919. Ibid., Andrews to Meighen, 13 June 1919.

45 LAC, RG 13, Access 87–88/103: box 36, file 9-A-1688, pocket #2, G.O.C. Winnipeg to Adjutant General, Ottawa, 12 June 1919.

46 LAC, RG 13, Access 87–88/103: box 36, file 9-A-1688, pocket #2, Andrews to Meighen, 13 June (letter).

47 LAC, RG 13, Access 87–88/103: box 36, file 9-A-1688, pocket #2, Andrews to Meighen, 13 June 1919.

48 'Collective Bargaining Inevitable under Present Economic System,' *Western Labor News*, 11 June 1919, 3.

49 LAC, RG 13, Access 87–88/103: box 36, file 9-A-1688, pocket #2, Andrews to Meighen, 13 June 1919.

50 PAM, Preliminary Hearing, J.K. Sparling, 725.

51 LAC, RG 13, Access 87–88/103: box 36, file 9-A-1688, pocket #2, Andrews to Meighen, June 13 (letter).

52 LAC, RG 13, Access 87–88/103: box 36, file 9-A-1688, pocket #2, Andrews to Meighen, 13 June 1919 (telegram). See also LAC, Borden Papers, reel C-4341, Prime Minister to Senator Robertson, 13 June 1919 (telegram): 61915.

53 LAC, RG 13, Access 87–88/103: box 36, file 9-A-1688, pocket #2, Andrews to Meighen, 13 June 1919 (letter).

54 LAC, RG 13, Access 87–88/103: box 36, file 9-A-1688, pocket #2, Meighen to Andrews, 13 June 1919 (telegram). Ibid., Adjutant-General to G.O.C., 13 June 1919.

55 LAC, RG 13, Access 87–88/103: box 36, file 9-A-1688, pocket #2, Meighen to Andrews, 13 June 1919 (telegram). Ibid., Adjutant General to G.O.C., 13 June 1919.

56 I.e., the Royal Commission on Industrial Relations, 1919. Prime Minister to Robertson, 13 June 1919.

57 LAC, Borden Papers, reel C-4341, Robertson to the Prime Minister, 13 June 1919: 61915.

58 LAC, Borden Papers, reel C-4341, Robertson to Prime Minister, 14 June 1919: 61932–5.

59 'The Week in Politics,' unsigned, *L'Ordine Nuovo* 1, no. 6, 14 June 1919; reprinted in Antonio Gramsci, *Selections from the Prison Notebooks*, ed. and trans. Quentin Hoare and Geoffrey Nowell Smith (New York, 1971), 61.

60 LAC, RG 13, Access 87–88/103: box 36, file 9-A-1688, pocket #2, G.O.C. Winnipeg to Adjutant General, Ottawa, 14 June 1919.

61 'Ugly Action Contemplated,' *Western Labor News*, 13 June 1919, 1.

62 'The Truth – From the Inside,' *Winnipeg Citizen*, 14 June 1919, 1, 3.

63 LAC, RG 13, Access 87–88/103: box 36, file 9-A-1688, pocket #2, Andrews to Meighen, 14 June 1919.

64 Ibid.

65 University of Regina Archives, Robert Graham fonds, 117; Lusk Papers, Committee to Investigate Revolutionary Radicalism [1919], Lusk Committee Agent, 'Report #6,' 14 June 1919 (facsimile).

66 LAC, RG 13, Access 87–88/103: box 36, file 9-A-1688, pocket #2, Robertson to Borden, 17 June 1919.

67 NAC, RG 13, Access 87–88/103: A-1688, pocket #2, Robertson to Borden (telegram), 14 June 1919.

68 The declaration signed by the proprietors appears in D.C. Masters, *The Winnipeg General Strike* (1950; Toronto, 1973).

69 LAC, RG 13, Access 87–88/103: box 36, file 9-A-1688, pocket #2, Robertson to Borden (telegram), 14 June 1919.

8 ENOUGH EVIDENCE TO CONVICT THE WHOLE COMMITTEE

1 LAC, RG 13, Access 87–88/103: box 36, file 9-A-1688, pocket #2, Meighen to Andrews, 16 June 1919 (telegram).

2 LAC, RG 13, Access 87–88/103: box 36, file 9-A-1688, pocket #2, Meighen to Robertson, 17 June 1919.

3 'Extremists among Strike Leaders Quietly Placed behind Prison Bars,'
   Manitoba Free Press, 18 June 1919, 4.
4 '21 Strike Arrests Today,' *Winnipeg Telegram*, 17 June 1919, 3.
5 PAM, Robert Graham fonds, 115.
6 Robert Graham fonds, 121. LAC, RG24, National Defence, 'General
   Strike Winnipeg, 1919,' Series C-1, reel C-5052, file: 363-46-1, Gen.
   H.D.B. Ketchen, G.O.C., to the Secretary, Militia Council, Ottawa, 17
   June 1919.
7 PAM, Robert Graham fonds, 121–2.
8 PAM, Preliminary Hearing, R.B. Graham, 1079.
9 PAM, Robert Graham fonds, 115.
10 LAC, RG 13, Access 87–88/103: box 36, file 9-A-1688, pocket #2,
   Andrews to Meighen (letter), 18 June 1919.
11 PAM, Robert Graham fonds, 116.
12 PAM, Robert Graham fonds, 116.
13 PAM, Robert Graham fonds, 117.
14 PAM, Robert Graham fonds, 117.
15 LAC, RG 13, Access 87–88/103: box 36, file 9-A-1688, pocket #2,
   Andrews to Meighen (letter), 18 June 1919.
16 PAM, Robert Graham fonds, 118.
17 LAC, RG 13, Access 87–88/103: box 36, file 9-A-1688, pocket #2,
   Andrews to Meighen (letter), 18 June 1919.
18 *Manitoba Free Press*, 18 June 1919.
19 Mike Verenczuk ('Veremchuk' on his attestation paper), who stayed in
   Devyatkin's house while Devyatkin was gone, was a naturalized British
   subject, and had fought in France. After being wounded twice and
   shell-shocked, he was honourably discharged in 1917. Initially arrested
   without a warrant, he spent more than two weeks in custody, and
   finally, when the Citizens could produce nothing against him, he was
   released. A contemporary account of his treatment wasn't far off the
   mark: 'Here was a man who volunteered to help fight for liberty, freedom, and justice, which he was told were in danger – twice wounded
   in that fight ... **and who had been refused bail in any amount or on
   any condition, had been kept in the penitentiary ... in solitude each
   day for seventeen days ... Mr. Andrews, in the name of Law and
   order and constituted authority appeared willing to railroad a perfectly sane and innocent man to a lunatic asylum**' [bold in original].
   Norman Penner, ed., *Winnipeg 1919 – The Strikers' Own History of
   the Winnipeg General Strike* (Toronto, 1973), 158–9, 164, 219. LAC,
   Soldiers of the First World War, Attestation paper no. 425444,
   Mike Veremchuck [*sic*], Canada Over-Seas Expeditionary Force, at

http://www.collectionacanada.gc.ca. Devyatkin (also 'Deviatken' and 'Daveiatkin'), for whom the police did have a warrant, was a 31-year-old Russian Jew who became a member of the Canadian Communist Party by 1921, but left for the United States two years later. Also known as Dick Murzin, he associated with Moishe Stern, a Soviet Military Intelligence (G.R.U.) spy in the United States in the late 1920s and early 1930s. Henry Trachtenberg, '"The Old Clo' Move": Anti-Semitism, Politics, and the Jews of Winnipeg, 1882–1921,' PhD diss., York University (Toronto), 1984, 660. Peter Campbell, *Canadian Marxists and the Search for a Third Way* (Montreal and Kingston, 1999), 196. John Haynes and Harvey Klehr, *Venona: Decoding Soviet Espionage in America* (New Haven, 1999), 373. Johns couldn't be arrested because he was in Montreal. Blumenberg turned himself in on the afternoon of 17th (*Winnipeg Telegram*, 18 June 1919), and Pritchard was arrested in Calgary (*Western Labor News*, 21 June 1919).

20 See RG 76, vol. 627, file 961162, Agitators pt. 1, Calder to Robertson, 16 June 1919.

21 LAC, RG 13, Access 87–88/103: box 36, file 9-A-1688, pocket #2, Meighen to Andrews, 17 June 1919 (telegram).

22 'The Charge,' *Western Labor News*, 19 June 1919, 2.

23 'Special Police Driven from the Street,' *Western Labor News*, 11 June 1919, 1, 4. 'The Charge,' *Western Labor News*, 19 June 1919, 2.

24 'The Citizens' Committee of "One" Thousand,' *Winnipeg Citizen*, 2 June 1919, 2.

25 'A Menace to Capital and Labor,' *Winnipeg Citizen*, 13 June 1919, 3.

26 Basil Thomson, *Queer People* (London, 1922), 276, quoted in S. White, 'Ideological Hegemony and Political Control: The Sociology of Anti-Bolshevism in Britain 1918–1920,' *Scottish Labour History Society Journal* 9 (June 1975), 17 n. 1.

27 Basil Thomson, 'Fortnightly Report on Revolutionary Organizations,' no. 26, 18 November 1918, Cabinet paper G.T. 6328, Cab 24/70, Public Record Office, London, quoted in S. White, 'Ideological Hegemony and Political Control,' n. 2.

28 Basil Thomson, 'Survey of Revolutionary Feeling during the Year 1919,' 15 January 1920, C.P. 462, Cab 24/96, quoted in S. White, 'Ideological Hegemony and Political Control,' 17, n. 2.

29 Lloyd George, 'Some Considerations for the Peace Conference' (draft), 24 March 1919, Cab 1/28/15, quoted in S. White, 'Ideological Hegemony and Political Control,' 3.

30 *Nineteenth Century and After*, vol. 85, May 1919, 894–6, quoted in S. White, 'Ideological Hegemony and Political Control,' 17 n. 2.

31 *Financial Review of Reviews*, March 1919, 42, quoted in S. White, 'Ideological Hegemony and Political Control,' 17, note 2.

32 W. Crotch, *Industrial Anarchy and the Way Out* (London, 1920), quoted in S. White, 'Ideological Hegemony and Political Control,' 17 n. 2.

33 Kingsley Martin, *Father Figures: The Evolution of an Editor, 1897–1931* (Chicago, 1966), 88, quoted in S. White, 'Ideological Hegemony and Political Control,' 17 n. 1.

34 'Strikelets,' *Western Labor News*, Saturday, 17 May 1919, 4. Reprinted in the *Manitoba Free Press*, 19 May 1919, 1 [delivered with 22 May paper].

35 'An Interview with James Dunwoody,' *Manitoba History* 6 (Fall 1983), 23.

36 *National Review*, March 1919, quoted in S. White, 'Ideological Hegemony and Political Control,' 3.

37 Liberty and Property Defence League, *Thirty-Eighth Annual Report*, 1920, 2, 12, 6, quoted in S. White, 'Ideological Hegemony and Political Control,' 8.

38 'British Middle Classes Union as an Active Force,' *New York Times Magazine*, 25 January 1920, 44.

39 The National Security Union, founded in May to combat Bolshevism, had as its honorary treasurer the Earl of Denbigh, a director of eight companies, including the Midland Bank, Indo-Burma Oilfields, and Rio Tinto. S. White, 'Ideological Hegemony and Political Control,' 12, 9.

40 *Reconstruction: Political and Economic* (London, n.d.), 6, quoted in S. White, 'Ideological Hegemony and Political Control,' 8.

41 'British Middle Classes Union as an Active Force,' *New York Times Magazine*, 25 January 1920, 44.

42 'The Shoals of Pernicious Leadership,' *Winnipeg Citizen*, 22 May 1919.

43 See Richard W. Gable, 'Birth of an Employers' Association,' *The Business History Review* 33, no. 4 (Winter, 1959), 541; Desmond Morton with Terry Copp, *Working People: An Illustrated History of the Canadian Labour Movement* (Ottawa, 1980), 83.

44 Ray Stannard Baker, 'Organized Capital Challenges Organized Labor: The New Employers' Movement,' *McClure's Magazine* 23 (July 1904), 282–3.

45 Rebecca Carr Imhauser, *Sedalia* (Charleston, SC, 2007), 30.

46 'Mission Is Peaceful,' *The Galveston Daily News*, 22 June 1904.

47 Ibid.

48 Baker, 'Organized Capital,' 283.
49 'Mission Is Peaceful.'
50 Ibid.
51 J. West Goodwin, 'Sedalia's Citizens' Alliance and Others,' *American Industries*, 1 August 1903, 14, quoted in Selig Perelman and Philip Taft, *History of Labor in the United States, 1896–1932* (New York, 1935), 132.
52 See George G. Suggs's description of the emergent employers' association movement in *Colorado's War on Militant Unionism: James H. Peabody and the Western Federation of Miners* (Detroit 1972), 65–8. For the quotation, see ibid., 6.
53 'Mission Is Peaceful.'
54 'Hang Morgan in Effigy,' *The Fort Wayne News*, 7 June 1902.
55 *Winnipeg Morning Telegram*, 2 July 1902.
56 *Coshocton Daily Age*, 3 July 1902.
57 'Plot Is Formed to Crush Union,' *The Constitution: Atlanta, Ga.*, 10 July 1902.
58 Suggs, *Colorado's War*, 68.
59 'Labor War in Mountain State,' *The Cedar Rapids Evening Gazette*, 31 July 1903.
60 Suggs, *Colorado's War*, 77.
61 'Send Union Men Packing,' *Winnipeg Morning Telegram*, 16 March 1904.
62 'Death to Unionism Is the Slogan at Cripple Creek,' *Reno Evening Gazette*, 9 June 1904. For a detailed account, see Elizabeth Jameson, *All That Glitters: Class, Conflict, and Community in Cripple Creek* (Urbana and Chicago, 1998).
63 *The Ogden Standard*, 8 June 1904.
64 Proceedings of the 8th Annual Convention of the National Association of Manufacturers of the United States of America, 1903, 15–16, quoted in Richard W. Gable, 'Birth of an Employers' Association,' *The Business History Review* 33, no. 4 (Winter, 1959), 541–2.
65 'Movement to Spread the Open Shop Plan,' *New York Times*, 27 November 1904.
66 For a detailed account, see Rosalie Shanks, 'The I.W.W. Free Speech Movement San Diego, 1912,' *Journal of San Diego History* 19, no. 1 (Winter 1973), 25–33.
67 Harris Weinstock, A Report to His Excellency Hiram W. Johnson, Governor of California, As Commissioner Appointed on April 15, 1912, To Investigate Charges of Cruelty and All Matters Pertaining to the Recent Disturbances in the City of San Diego and the County of San Diego, Including the Causes Thereof and the Causes Contributing

Thereto (Sacramento, 1912), 14–15. 'State May Prosecute San Diego Vigilantes,' *Oakland Tribune*, 18 May 1912.

68 Louis G. Silverberg, 'Citizens' Committees: Their Role in Industrial Conflict,' *Public Opinion Quarterly* 5, no. 1 (March 1941), 30, 18.

69 See chapter 2. LAC, Borden Papers, reel C-4332, E. Parnell to Robert Borden, 17 May 1918: 54247–8.

70 Hopkins Adams, 'The One Big Union.'

71 Georges Sorel, *Reflections on Violence*, trans. T.E. Hulme (New York, 1967), 191, quoted in Zygmunt Bauman, *Postmodern Ethics* (Oxford, 1993), 119.

72 See also *Revised Statutes of Canada, 1906*, vol. 3 (Ottawa 1906), chap. 146, 'An Act Respecting the Criminal Law,' sec. 2(2), 2419.

73 Douglas Hay, 'Controlling the English Prosecutor,' *Osgoode Hall Law Journal* 2, no. 2 (June 1983), 166–7.

74 *Revised Statutes of Manitoba*, vol. 1 (Winnipeg, 1892), sec. 5(g), chapter 38, 'An Act Respecting Crown Attorneys,' 460.

75 *Revised Statutes of Canada, 1927* (Ottawa, 1927), sec. 962, part 19, chapter 146, 'An Act Respecting the Criminal Law,' sec. 2(2), 970.

76 *Toronto Daily Star*, 11 June 1919.

77 Penner, ed., *Winnipeg 1919*, 123–4.

78 LAC, RG 13, Access 87–88/103: box 36, file 9-A-1688, pocket #2, Andrews to Meighen, 14 June 1919.

79 '21 Strike Arrests Today,' *Winnipeg Telegram*, 17 June 1919, 3.

80 LAC, RG 13, Access 87–88/103: box 36, file 9-A-1688, pocket #2, Andrews to Meighen, 17 June 1919 (telegram).

81 LAC, RG 13, Access 87–88/103: box 36, file 9-A-1688, pocket #2, The Government of the Dominion of Canada in account with I. Pitblado, 13 August 1919, 14; J.B. Coyne, 14 August 1919, 13; and Travers Sweatman, 14 August 1919, 12.

82 PAM, G8303, 27.9.15 and 11.11.11, *Sessional Papers no. 116* (73–8).

83 LAC, RG 13, Access 87–88/103: box 36, file 9-A-1688, pocket #2, Andrews to Meighen, 17 June 1919 (telegram), #208.

84 LAC, RG 13, Access 87–88/103: box 36, file 9-A-1688, pocket #2, Meighen to Andrews, 17 June 1919 (telegram), #2400.

85 LAC, RG 13, Access 87–88/103: box 36, file 9-A-1688, pocket #2, Andrews to Meighen, 17 June 1919 (telegram), #206.

86 LAC, RG 13, Access 87–88/103: box 36, file 9-A-1688, pocket #2, Meighen to Andrews, 17 June 1919 (telegram).

87 LAC, RG 13, Access 87–88/103: box 36, file 9-A-1688, pocket #2, Andrews to Meighen, 17 June 1919, #208.

88 *Manitoba Free Press*, 12 June 1915, 5.

89 *Manitoba Free Press*, 21 May 1918, 4.

90 *Canada (Attorney General) v. Canadian National Transportation Ltd.*, [1983] 2 S.C.R. 206, file no: 16998, 13.

91 LAC, RG 18, Royal Canadian Mounted Police, 'Report Re: Wm. Ivens et al. – Seditious Conspiracy,' Royal North West Mounted Police, 4 December 1919, Reg. file 175/1006, 'D' Div. file 18/26.

92 'The executive of the modern State is but a committee for managing the common affairs of the whole bourgeoisie.' Karl Marx, *Manifesto of the Communist Party* (Moscow, 1952), 44.

93 LAC, RG 13, Access 87–88/103: box 36, file 9-A-1688, pocket #2, Andrews to Meighen, 17 June 1919 (telegram), #208.

94 Andrews claimed to Meighen that Robertson authorized every step, a claim that Meighen would have challenged had it been untrue. See, for example, LAC, RG 13, Access 87–88/103: box 36, file 9-A-1688, pocket #2, Meighen to Andrews (telegram), 18 June 1919.

95 'Extremists among Strike Leaders Quietly Placed behind Prison Bars,' *Manitoba Free Press*, 18 June 1919, 4. '21 Strike Arrests Today.'

96 LAC, RG 13, Access 87–88/103: box 36, file 9-A-1688, pocket #2, Andrews to Meighen, 17 June 1919 (telegram), #208.

97 LAC, RG 13, Access 87–88/103: box 36, file 9-A-1688, pocket #2, Meighen to Andrews (telegram), 18 June 1919.

98 LAC, RG 13, Access 87–88/103: box 36, file 9-A-1688, pocket #2, Andrews to Meighen (letter), 18 June 1919.

99 Ibid.

100 In 1906, Vulcan Iron Works had asked for a permanent injunction against picketing the premises of the company, and for $50,000 in damages from striking employees. The company was awarded $5000 and the permanent injunction. Early in 1912, Vulcan Iron Works agreed to accept $3000 as full payment of costs and damages. When the local could not pay the total, it had to beg $1850 from the Machinists' Grand Lodge. Manitoba Cases, 'Two Important Decisions with Regard to Picketing,' *Labour Gazette*, April 1909, 1152–4; Manitoba Cases, 'Machinists' Appeals Dismissed,' *Labour Gazette*, April, 1911, 1171–2; Manitoba Cases, 'Injunction against Employees of Vulcan Iron Works Company,' *Labour Gazette*, May 1913, 1323.

101 See J.M. Bumsted, *The Winnipeg General Strike of 1919: An Illustrated History* (Winnipeg, 1994), 78.

102 'The Shoals of Pernicious Leadership,' *Winnipeg Citizen*, 22 May 1919.

103 In 1920, the government would try to repeal the amendments. Gideon Robertson would argue in Parliament that the amendments had only been brought in under great necessity, and that once the emergency

was over, it shouldn't be possible to deport a British subject 'who may have been resident in Canada nearly all his life.' Gideon Robertson, Canada, Senate, *Debates*, 27 May 1920, 417. The repeal wasn't approved until 1928. See Barbara Roberts, *Whence They Came: Deportation from Canada 1900–1935* (Ottawa, 1988), 24–33.

104 As it turned out, Ottawa would not agree to use an alien detention camp to hold the arrested men, so an alternative had to be found. PAM, Robert Graham fonds, 117.

9 THE ROAD THROUGH BLOODY SATURDAY

1 LAC, RG 13, Access 87–88/103: box 36, file 9-A-1688, pocket #2, Meighen to Andrews, 18 June 1919.

2 LAC, RG 13, Access 87–88/103: box 36, file 9-A-1688, pocket #2, Andrews to Meighen, 17 June 1919, #208.

3 LAC, RG 13, Access 87–88/103: box 36, file 9-A-1688, pocket #2, Andrews to Meighen, 18 June 1919.

4 LAC, RG 13, Access 87–88/103: box 36, file 9-A-1688, pocket #2, Telegrams to Sir Robert Borden, 18 & 19 June 1919.

5 LAC, RG 13, Access 87–88/103: box 36, file 9-A-1688, pocket #2, The Government of the Dominion of Canada in account with I. Pitblado, 13 August 1919, 14; Travers Sweatman, 14 August 1919, 12.

6 LAC, RG 13, Access 87–88/103: box 36, file 9-A-1688, pocket #2, Meighen to Andrews, 19 June 1919.

7 Along with Isaac Pitblado, James Coyne, *Free Press* editor J.W. Dafoe, and Minister of Agriculture Thomas Crerar, Hudson and Symington were members of the powerful behind-the-scenes Liberal 'Sanhedrin' that met at the Manitoba Club, and they therefore had a direct line into the Citizens, but operated independently of them. J.E. Rea, *T.A. Crerar: A Political Life* (Montreal and Kingston, 1997), 32. B.M. Greene, ed., *Who's Who in Canada, 1928–29: An Illustrated Biographical Record of Men and Women of the Time* (Toronto, 1929), 72. Robert Bothwell, 'Symington, Herbert James,' in *The Canadian Encyclopedia*, 2nd ed., ed. James Marsh (Edmonton, 1988), 2106; Anna Tillenius, *Learned Friends: Reminiscences – Pitblado & Hoskin, 1882–1974* (Winnipeg, 1974), 27.

8 LAC, RG 13, Access 87–88/103: box 36, file 9-A-1688, pocket #2, Andrews to Meighen, 18 June 1919.

9 LAC, RG 24, National Defence, Series C-1, reel C-5052, file: 363-46-1, 'General Strike Winnipeg, 1919,' G.O.C. to Adjutant General, Ottawa, 12 June 1919.

10   Norman Penner, ed., *Winnipeg 1919 – The Strikers' Own History of the Winnipeg General Strike* (Toronto, 1973), 165.

11   LAC, RG 13, Access 87–88/103: box 36, file 9-A-1688, pocket #2, Andrews to Meighen (telegram), 26 June 1919.

12   LAC, RG 13, Access 87–88/103: box 36, file 9-A-1688, pocket #2, Meighen to Andrews (telegram), 27 June 1919.

13   On the transformation of the RNWMP into a national police agency in 1919–20, see Steve Hewitt, *Riding to the Rescue: The Transformation of the RCMP in Alberta and Saskatchewan, 1914–1939* (Toronto, 2006), 12–28. On the Montreal bombing and prosecution, see J. Castell Hopkins, ed., *The Canadian Annual Review 1918* (Toronto, 1919), 496–7. For a record of the legal expenditures by Ottawa on this case, see 'Prosecution of Dynamiters,' *Auditor General's Report, 1918–1919* (Ottawa, 1919), ZZ –14.

14   LAC, RG 13, Access 87–88/103: box 36, file 9-A-1688, pocket #2, Meighen to Andrews, 18 June 1919.

15   LAC, RG 13, Access 87–88/103: box 36, file 9-A-1688, pocket #2, Andrews to Meighen, 17 June 1919, #208.

16   LAC, RG 13, Access 87–88/103: box 36, file 9-A-1688, pocket #2, Meighen to Andrews, 18 June 1919.

17   LAC, Borden Papers, reel C-4341, Robert Borden to Sir Frederick Williams Taylor, 18 June 1919: 61972.

18   LAC, RG 13, Access 87–88/103: box 36, file 9-A-1688, pocket #2, Andrews to Meighen, 6 June 1919.

19   LAC, RG 13, Access 87–88/103: box 36, file 9-A-1688, pocket #2, Andrews to Meighen (letter), 18 June 1919.

20   LAC, RG 13, Access 87–88/103: box 36, file 9-A-1688, pocket #2, Andrews to Meighen, 18 June 1919.

21   LAC, RG 13, Access 87–88/103: box 36, file 9-A-1688, pocket #2, Andrews to Meighen (letter), 18 June 1919.

22   G.O.C. Winnipeg to Adjutant General, Ottawa, 19 June 1919 (telegram).

23   'Red, Blue and All Yellow,' *Winnipeg Telegram*, 20 June 1919, last edition,1; at http://manitobia.ca/cocoon/launch/en/newspapers/TWT/1919/06/20/13/Olive.

24   LAC, RG 13, Access 87–88/103: box 36, file 9-A-1688, pocket #2, Dick Randolph to G.W. Allan, MP, House of Commons, Ottawa, 20 June 1919. 'Dick Randolph' was probably Richard Randolph Pattinson, who had served in the militia as a Lieutenant Captain in the 90th Winnipeg Rifles, and who, like his friend F.G. Thompson, helped to head up the militia supporting the Citizens. Pattinson was in the process of launching a new brokerage business representing

Gold Pan Mines Ltd. and Falcon Minerals. In 1910 Pattinson rated high enough to be appear in a collection of caricatures of prominent Winnipeggers that included Andrews, Pitblado, and Coyne. In 1919, as a veteran, a Conservative, and a self-employed businessman of long-standing association with the city's elite, Pattinson embraced the cause of the Citizens, but he was no longer an influential figure, and wasn't among the thirty-four who signed the Citizens' telegram to Robert Borden. Still, Pattinson knew many Citizens on a first-name basis, and Allan credited Pattinson's telegram sufficiently to forward it to cabinet. For Pattinson's obituary, see *Winnipeg Free Press*, 22 October 1964, 41. The cartoons appear in *Manitobans As We See Em*, Newspaper Cartoonists Association of Manitoba, 1910, http://www.mhs.mb.ca/docs/people/manitobansasweseeem.shtml. On Pattinson's enlistment, see Richard Randolph Pattinson, LAC, RG 150, Access 1992–3/166: box 7653-35, Officer's declaration form.

25 LAC, RG 13, Access 87–88/103: box 36, file 9-A-1688, pocket #2, Andrews to Meighen (telegram), 20 June 1919.

26 LAC, Borden Papers, reel C-4341, Brigadier-General H.D.B. Ketchen, General Officer Commanding Military District no.10, to The Secretary, Militia Headquarters, Ottawa, 19, 20 June 1919: 62040.

27 LAC, RG 24, National Defence, Series C-1, reel C-5052, file: 363-46-1. G.O.C. to Adjutant General, Ottawa, 10 June 1919, 'General Strike Winnipeg, 1919.'

28 LAC, RG 13, Access 87–88/103: box 36, file 9-A-1688, pocket #2, Andrews to Meighen (letter), 25 June 1919.

29 LAC, RG 13, Access 87–88/103: box 36, file 9-A-1688, pocket #2, Andrews to Meighen, 19 June 1919.

30 LAC, RG 13, Access 87–88/103: box 36, file 9-A-1688, pocket #2, Andrews to Meighen, 25 June 1919.

31 LAC, RG 13, Access 87–88/103: box 36, file 9-A-1688, pocket #2, Andrews to Meighen, 19 June 1919.

32 LAC, RG 13, Access 87–88/103: box 36, file 9-A-1688, pocket #2, Andrews to Meighen, 25 June 1919.

33 'Soldiers' [*sic*] Cheer Prisoners,' *Western Labor News*, 18 June 1919, 1. University of Regina Archives, Lusk Papers, Committee to Investigate Revolutionary Radicalism [1919], Lusk Committee Agent, 'Report #9,' 17 June 1919 (facsimile).

34 LAC, RG 13, Access 87–88/103: box 36, file 9-A-1688, pocket #2, Andrews to Meighen (letter), 25 June 1919.

35 LAC, RG 13, Access 87–88/103: box 36, file 9-A-1688, pocket #2, Andrews to Meighen (letter), 18 June 1919.

36 'Soldiers' [*sic*] Cheer Prisoners.'

37 'The Charge,' *Western Labor News*, 19 June 1919, 2.
38 'British Subjects Cannot Be Deported,' *Western Labor News*, 19 June 1919, 1.
39 'The Charge,' *Western Labor News*, 19 June 1919, 2.
40 'Soldiers' Resolution,' *Western Labor News*, 20 June 1919, 1.
41 LAC, RG 13, Access 87–88/103: box 36, file 9-A-1688, pocket #2, Andrews to Meighen, June 20, 1919.
42 G.O.C. Winnipeg to Adjutant General, Ottawa (telegram), 20 June 1919.
43 A.B. Perry to the Comptroller, RNWM Police, Ottawa, 21 June 1919.
44 LAC, RG 13, Access 87–88/103: box 36, file 9-A-1688, pocket #2, Andrews to Meighen (telegram), 21 June 1919.
45 Dale Gibson and Lee Gibson, *Substantial Justice: Law and Lawyers in Manitoba 1670–1970* (Winnipeg, 1972), 233.
46 G.O.C. to Adjutant General, Ottawa, 21 June 1919.
47 PAM, Preliminary Hearing, Capt. James Moore Dunwoody, 1437.
48 PAM, Robert Graham fonds, 125.
49 Acting Minister of Justice to Ed Parnell, 21 June 1919. Acting Minister of Justice to W.R. Ingram, 21 June 1919. Acting Minister of Justice to Robert McKay, 21 June 1919.
50 Martin Burrell to Senator Robertson, 22 June 1919, 'General Strike Winnipeg, 1919,' RG 24, National Defence, Series C-1, reel C-5052, file: 363-46-1. See also PC 1241 (22 May 1918), which updated the OIC of 17 January 1917. The relevant section is Order II, #7.
51 LAC, RG 13, Access 87–88/103: box 36, file 9-A-1688, pocket #2, Andrews to Meighen (letter), 25 June 1919.
52 'The Latest Desperate Trick of Tyrants,' *Western Star*, 24 June 1919, 1.
53 LAC, RG 13, Access 87–88/103: box 36, file 9-A-1688, pocket #2, Andrews to Meighen (letter), 25 June 1919. Offences created as indictable offences by the Criminal Code are instituted by an Information before the Justice of the Peace, and the offender is brought to trial either by a warrant issued by the Justice of the Peace or by summons. See William B. Common, 'The Administration of Justice in Canada,' *Journal of Criminal Law, Criminology, and Political Science* 43, no. 1 (May–June 1952), 6.
54 LAC, RG 13, Access 87–88/103: box 36, file 9-A-1688, pocket #2, Andrews to Meighen (telegram), 24 May 1919.
55 LAC, RG 13, Access 87–88/103: box 36, file 9-A-1688, pocket #2, Andrews to Meighen (letter), 25 June 1919.
56 LAC, RG 13, Access 87–88/103: box 36, file 9-A-1688, pocket #2, Andrews to Meighen (telegram), 25 June 1919.
57 LAC, RG 13, Access 87–88/103: box 36, file 9-A-1688, pocket #2,

Meighen to Andrews (telegram), 25 June 1919.

58 LAC, RG 13, Access 87–88/103: box 36, file 9-A-1688, pocket #2, Andrews to Meighen (telegram), 24 June 1919.

59 LAC, RG 13, Access 87–88/103: box 36, file 9-A-1688, pocket #2, Meighen to Andrews (telegram), 25 July 1919.

60 LAC, RG 13, Access 87–88/103: box 36, file 9-A-1688, pocket #2, Andrews to Meighen (telegram), 27 July 1919.

61 LAC, RG 13, Access 87–88/103: box 36, file 9-A-1688, pocket #2, Andrews to Meighen (letter), 25 June 1919.

62 LAC, RG 13, Access 87–88/103: box 36, file 9-A-1688, pocket #2, Meighen to Andrews, 30 June 1919.

63 LAC, RG 13, Access 87–88/103: box 36, file 9-A-1688, pocket #2, Andrews to Meighen (telegram), 27 June 1919.

64 LAC, RG 13, Access 87–88/103: box 36, file 9-A-1688, pocket #2, Andrews to Meighen, 2 July 1919 (letter).

10 THE ONLY WAY TO DEAL WITH BOLSHEVISM

1 *Manitoba Free Press*, 28 June 1919. See also PAM, Robson Commission, box 1, file 39, 'Put Him On The Job!' Submitted with a Statement of the Committee of One Thousand, Showing Co-operation Given By The Committee in the settlement of The Winnipeg Sympathetic Strike, May–June 1919.

2 On the Norris government's role, see W.L. Morton, *Manitoba: A History* (Toronto, 1957), 368–73.

3 Evidently, the *Labor News* initially went underground and used a different printer than Gustavus Pringle (of Winnipeg Printing and Engraving), upon whom Andrews had put pressure. Pringle denied printing *The Western Star* and *The Enlightener*, two of the papers that briefly continued the *Labor News*. PAM, Preliminary Hearing, Gustavus Pringle, 59.

4 *Western Labor News*, 4 July 1919.

5 'Strike Leaders Again Remanded; Bail Higher,' *Manitoba Free Press*, 4 July 1919, 5.

6 'Bail Increased to $8,000 Unconditionally,' *Western Labor News*, 4 July 1919, 1. Those remanded included R.B. Russell, William Ivens, W.A. Pritchard, John Queen, A.A. Heaps, George Armstrong, R.E. Bray, R.J. Johns, Sam Blumenberg, Oscar Schoppelrei, Moses Almazoff, Max Charitonoff, and Mike Verenczuk.

7 LAC, RG 13, Access 87–88/103: box 36, file 9-A-1688, pocket #2, Andrews to Meighen (telegram), 3 July 1919.

8 LAC, RG 13, Access 87–88/103: box 36, file 9-A-1688, pocket #2, Andrews to Meighen (telegram), 4 July 1919. Verenczuk was turned

over to Marcus Hyman, who agreed to assume responsibility for him. *Manitoba Free Press*, 4 July 1919, 5.

9 LAC, RG 13, Access 87–88/103: box 36, file 9-A-1688, pocket #2, Andrews to Meighen (telegram), 3 July 1919.

10 Ralph Connor [Rev. Charles Gordon], *To Him That Hath: A Novel of the West of Today* (New York, 1921), 286.

11 'History Repeats Itself,' *Western Labor News*, 4 July 1919.

12 *Western Labor News*, 4 July 1919.

13 LAC, RG 13, Access 87–88/103: box 36, file 9-A-1688, pocket #2, Andrews to Meighen (letter), 7 July 1919.

14 LAC, RG 13, Access 87–88/103: box 36, file 9-A-1688, pocket #2, Meighen to Andrews (telegram), 4 July 1919.

15 B.M. Greene, ed., *Who's Who in Canada* (Toronto, 1939), 213.

16 LAC, Borden Papers, reel C-4341, Citizens Committee of One Thousand to Prime Minister, Minister of Justice, Minister of Labour (telegram), 24 June 1919: 62089–92.

17 B.M. Greene, ed., *Who's Who in Canada, 1928–29: An Illustrated Biographical Record of Men and Women of the Time* (Toronto, 1929), 1550.

18 LAC, RG 13, Access 87–88/103: box 36, file 9-A-1688, pocket #2, G.W. Allan, House of Commons, Ottawa, Canada, to Hon. Arthur Meighen, 5 July 1919 (letter).

19 LAC, RG 13, Access 87–88/103: box 36, file 9-A-1688, pocket #2, Edward Anderson to Arthur Meighen, 7 July 1919 (letter).

20 Ibid.

21 C.W. Parker, ed., *Who's Who and Why – A Biographical Dictionary of Men and Women of Western Canada* (Vancouver, 1913), 116–17.

22 LAC, RG 13, Access 87–88/103: box 36, file 9-A-1688, pocket #2, Edward Anderson to Meighen (letter), 7 July 1919.

23 LAC, RG 13, Access 87–88/103: box 36, file 9-A-1688, pocket #2, Andrews to Meighen (telegram), 3 July 1919. For Phillips's recollection of his role in the Strike, see *Winnipeg Tribune*, 6 April 1949. On Martin and Grant, see the *Winnipeg Evening Tribune*, 25 November 1919.

24 LAC, RG 13, Access 87–88/103: box 36, file 9-A-1688, pocket #2, Andrews to Meighen (letter), 3 July 1919.

25 'Radical Propaganda Discovered in Raids,' *Manitoba Free Press*, 5 July 1919, 3.

26 LAC, RG 13, Access 87–88/103: box 36, file 9-A-1688, pocket #2, Andrews to Meighen (letter), 2 July 1919.

27 Ibid.

28 LAC, RG 13, Access 87–88/103: box 36, file 9-A-1688, pocket #2,

Andrews to Meighen (telegram), 4 July 1919. Meighen had expressed similar views in the Commons. See Canada, House of Commons, *Debates*, 23 June 1919, 3845–6.

29 LAC, RG 13, Access 87–88/103: box 36, file 9-A-1688, pocket #2, Andrews to Meighen, 4 July 1919.

30 LAC, RG 13, Access 87–88/103: box 36, file 9-A-1688, pocket #2, Andrews to Meighen (letter), 7 July 1919.

31 Ibid.

32 Ibid. Anderson claimed that he hadn't had a chance to see Andrews about the matter. That's possible, since the notion of the government having to 'justify' its actions was a common theme among the Citizens at this time.

33 'Winnipeg Strike Leaders in East,' *Manitoba Free Press*, 8 July 1919.

34 *Manitoba Free Press*, 10 July 1919, 5.

35 For a discussion of the workers' public protest, petitions, and letters against the detentions, see James Muir, 'The Demand for British Justice – Protest and Culture during the Winnipeg General Strike Trials,' unpublished paper, University of Manitoba Canadian Legal History Project. For a list of the letters and petitions both supporting and opposing detention, see Ken Kehler and Alvin Esau, *Famous Manitoba Trials – Research Source* (Winnipeg, 1990), 73–85. The actual petitions and letters are contained in LAC, RG 13, Access 87–88/103: box 36, file 9-A-1688, pocket #1.

36 'Capitalizing the Prosecution,' *Manitoba Free Press*, 10 July 1919

37 LAC, RG 13, Access 87–88/103: box 36, file 9-A-1688, pocket #2, Meighen to Andrews, 8 July 1919.

38 LAC, RG 13, Access 87–88/103: box 36, file 9-A-1688, pocket #2, G.D. Robertson to Meighen, 8 July 1919.

39 LAC, RG 13, Access 87–88/103: box 36, file 9-A-1688, pocket #2, Andrews to Meighen, 8 July 1919.

40 LAC, RG 13, Access 87–88/103: box 36, file 9-A-1688, pocket #2, J.E. Botterell to Hon. Arthur Meighen, Acting Minister of Justice, 10 July 1919 (letter). Parker, *Who's Who and Why*, 74.

41 LAC, RG 13, Access 87–88/103: box 36, file 9-A-1688, pocket #2, G.W. Allan to Arthur Meighen, 9 July 1919.

42 LAC, RG 13, Access 87–88/103: box 36, file 9-A-1688, pocket #2, Andrews to Meighen, 8 July 1919.

43 *Royal Commission Appointed to Inquire into Certain Matters Relating to the New Parliament Buildings* (Winnipeg, 1915).

44 Williams noted, 'The Commission has full control over its own procedure and the way in which it will handle all matters coming before it. It may, and in this case should, sit in camera. It need not be bound by

the ordinary rules of evidence if it considers it desirable to disregard them. It need not permit counsel to appear for those to be interrogated by or before it.' E.K. Williams, 'The Corby Case' [Top secret memorandum to William Lyon Mackenzie King], 7 December 1945, 'Primary Documents: Igor Gouzenko, and the Espionage Commission,' *Canada's Rights Movement: A History*, webmaster Dominique Clément, at http://www.historyofrights.com/PDF/williams_memo.pdf. See also *Royal Commission to Investigate the Facts Relating to and the Circumstances Surrounding the Communication, by Public Officials and other Persons in Positions of Trust of Secret and Confidential Information to Agents of a Foreign Power* (Ottawa, 1946).

45 LAC, RG 13, Access 87–88/103: box 36, file 9-A-1688, pocket #2, Meighen to Andrews, 12 July 1919.

46 LAC, RG 13, Access 87–88/103: box 36, file 9-A-1688, pocket #2, Robertson to Meighen, 8 July 1919.

47 LAC, RG 13, Access 87–88/103: box 36, file 9-A-1688, pocket #2, A.L. Crossin to Meighen, 16 July 1919 (letter).

48 LAC, RG 13, Access 87–88/103: box 36, file 9-A-1688, pocket #2, Edward Anderson to Hon. Arthur Meighen, K.C., 16 July 1919.

49 LAC, RG 13, Access 87–88/103: box 36, file 9-A-1688, pocket #2, Meighen to Andrews (telegraph), 17 July 1919.

50 LAC, RG 13, Access 87–88/103: box 36, file 9-A-1688, pocket #2, Meighen to Andrews, 18 July 1919.

51 LAC, RG 13, Access 87–88/103: box 36, file 9-A-1688, pocket #2, Andrews to G.D. Robertson (letter), 9 July 1919.

52 LAC, RG 13, Access 87–88/103: box 36, file 9-A-1688, pocket #2, Meighen to Andrews, 12 July 1919.

53 Machiavelli, *Discorsi*, book 3, ch. 3, quoted in Arthur Koestler, *Darkness at Noon* (London, 1940), 9.

54 LAC, RG 13, Access 87–88/103: box 36, file 9-A-1688, pocket #2, Andrews to G.D. Robertson (letter), 9 July 1919.

55 LAC, RG 13, Access 87–88/103: box 36, file 9-A-1688, pocket #2, Andrews to Meighen, 5 July 1919.

56 LAC, RG 13, Access 87–88/103: box 36, file 9-A-1688, pocket #2, Andrews to Meighen (letter), 10 July 1919.

57 LAC, RG 13, Access 87–88/103: box 36, file 9-A-1688, pocket #2, Andrews to Meighen (letter), 25 June 1919.

58 LAC, RG 13, Access 87–88/103: box 36, file 9-A-1688, pocket #2, Andrews to Meighen (telegraph), 12 July 1919.

59 'Strike Leaders Are Again Remanded by Magistrate,' *Manitoba Free Press*, 12 July 1919.

60 *Western Labor News*, 11 July 1919.

61 'Strike Leaders Are Again Remanded by Magistrate,' *Manitoba Free Press*, 12 July 1919.

62 Douglas Owram, *The Government Generation: Canadian Intellectuals and the State 1900–1945* (Toronto, 1986), 35.

63 Henry Borden, ed., *Robert Laird Borden: His Memoirs*, vol. 2 (Toronto, 1969), 220. On the theme of labour and the state after the war, see James Naylor, 'Workers and the State: Experiments in Corporatism after World War One,' *Studies in Political Economy* 42 (Autumn 1993), 95–6.

64 The process was completed in 1920. On this theme, see Gregory S. Kealey, 'State Repression of Labour and the Left in Canada, 1914–1920: The Impact of the First World War,' *Canadian Historical Review* 73 (September 1992), 281–314; Gregory S. Kealey, 'The Surveillance State: The Origins of Domestic Intelligence and Counter-Subversion in Canada, 1914–1921,' *Intelligence and National Security* 7, no. 3 (1992), 184–91; Gregory S. Kealey and Andrew Parnaby, 'War on Two Fronts: In the Great War, the Canadian State Found Itself Fighting on Two Fronts,' *Beaver* 81, no. 4 (2001), 8–15; Judy Fudge and Eric Tucker, 'Pluralism or Fragmentation? The Twentieth-Century Employment Law Regime in Canada,' *Labour/Le Travail*, 46 (Fall 2000), 251–306; and Steve Hewitt, *Riding to the Rescue: The Transformation of the RCMP in Alberta and Saskatchewan, 1914–1939* (Toronto, 2006).

65 Owram, *The Government Generation*, 80.

66 The act was repealed on 20 December, effective 1 January 1920.

67 *Statutes of Canada 1919*, PC 702, 2 April 1919, lxxx.

68 Quoted in *Fort Frances Pulp and Paper Co. v. Manitoba Free Press Co.* (1923), [1923] A.C. 695 (P.C.), 6. At http://www.dessus.com/TaxInfo/Cases/fortfrancis.html.

69 LAC, RG 13, Access 87–88/103: box 36, file 9-A-1688, pocket #2, Meighen to Andrews (telegram), 14 July 1919. Robert Borden left Ottawa for the balance of the summer on 17 July. Henry Borden, ed., *Robert Laird Borden: His Memoirs*, 2: 983.

70 LAC, RG 13, Access 87–88/103: box 36, file 9-A-1688, pocket #2, Meighen to Andrews (letter), 14 July 1919.

71 LAC, RG 13, Access 87–88/103: box 36, file 9-A-1688, pocket #2, Meighen to Andrews (telegram), 17 July 1919.

72 LAC, RG 13, Access 87–88/103: box 36, file 9-A-1688, pocket #2, Andrews to Meighen (letter), 6 June 1919.

73 See D.C. Masters, *The Winnipeg General Strike* (1950; Toronto, 1973), 124–6.

74 'Strike Leaders Leave for Winnipeg Today,' *Manitoba Free Press*, 15 July 1919.

75 LAC, RG 13, Access 87–88/103: box 36, file 9-A-1688, pocket #2, Meighen to Edward Anderson (letter), 18 July 1919.

76 See 'Ottawa's Position in the Charitonoff Case,' *Manitoba Free Press*, 18 January 1919, 13.

77 LAC, RG 13, Access 87–88/103: box 36, file 9-A-1688, pocket #2, Andrews to Meighen (letter), 18 July 1919. Another name had been added: J. Farnell, a returned soldier involved in the riots.

78 Ibid.

11 THEY ARE ALL DANGEROUS

1 *Western Labor News*, 1 August 1919.

2 'Secured consent Robert Myre Noble Police magistrate to act on Board we all approve his appointment please appoint immediately.' LAC, RG 13, Access 87–88/103: box 36, file 9-A-1688, pocket #2, Andrews to Meighen, 11 July 1919.

3 LAC, RG 13, Access 87–88/103: box 36, file 9-A-1688, pocket #2, Andrews to Meighen (letter), 2 July 1919.

4 LAC, Immigration Board Hearing, vol. 4, Samuel Blumenberg, 14 July 1919, 1.

5 *Manitoba Free Press*, 31 December 1937.

6 Roy St George Stubbs, *Prairie Portraits* (Toronto, 1954), 148–9.

7 In 1906, the new immigration act incorporated for the first time the principle of deporting persons who had become members of the undesirable classes after their entry to Canada: criminals, public charges, and the infirm. In 1910, sedition was added to the grounds for deportation. See 'An Act respecting Immigration,' chapter 27, *Statutes of Canada 1910*, 15. For the debate on the bill, see Canada, House of Commons, *Debates*, 19 January 1910: 2133f. Ostensibly introduced to provide a more effective administration of what Minister of the Interior Frank Oliver termed 'exclusion provisions,' the legislation was apparently prompted by fears of the growing influence of the IWW. See section 13 of the act, *Statutes of Canada 1910*, 211. Section 41 had never been applied by the Laurier government. The new sedition clause – tailored for the Citizens – had left the operation of the boards of hearing largely unchanged. Eric Lyle Dick, 'Deportation under the Immigration Act and the Canadian Criminal Code, 1919–1936,' MA thesis, University of Manitoba, 1978, 4.

8 LAC, RG 76, vol. 627, file 961162, Agitators, pt. 1. Thomas Gelley, Esq., Acting Commissioner of Immigration, Winnipeg, to W.D. Scott, Assistant Deputy Minister Immigration, 20 June 1919.

9 On 2 July 1919 Andrews told Meighen, 'There are two or three that

can be deported on account of improper entries, and I think where we find it difficult to get evidence under Section 41, these men should all be deported if we have any legal ground for deportation.' LAC, RG 13, Access 87–88/103: box 36, file 9-A-1688, pocket #2, Andrews to Meighen (letter), 2 July 1919.

10 The relevant portions were section 33, subsection 7. LAC, RG 76, vol. 627, file 961162, Agitators, pt. 1. William Scott, Assistant Deputy Minister Immigration to Thomas Gelley, Acting Commissioner of Immigration, Winnipeg, 17 June 1919. *Manitoba Free Press*, 23 August 1919.

11 Telephone interviews and email correspondence with Harvey Blumenberg, Minneapolis Minnesota; Eleanor Blumenberg (wife of Sam's son Charles Karl Blumenberg, originally named Karl Marx Blumenberg), Santa Monica, California, 14 December 2007.

12 Henry Trachtenberg, '"The Old Clo' Move": Anti-Semitism, Politics, and the Jews of Winnipeg, 1882–1921,' PhD diss., York University (Toronto), 1984, 2: 648.

13 *War, What For?* 'One of the most Radical plays ever produced on any stage,' Grand Theatre, *The Voice*, 11 June 1915, 3. On the second Battle of Ypres, see Desmond Morton and J.L. Granatstein, *Marching to Armageddon: Canadians and the Great War 1914–19* (Toronto, 1989), 62–3.

14 *Winnipeg Citizen*, 16 June 1919.

15 LAC, Immigration Board Hearing, vol. 4, Samuel Blumenberg, 14 July 1919, 2.

16 Ibid., 1.

17 Ibid., 2.

18 Ibid., 2–3.

19 Ibid., 4, 3.

20 Ibid., 4, 3–4.

21 Ibid., 4, 5.

22 Ibid., 4, 7.

23 Domicile had been defined in the amendments to the Immigration Act in 1910. During debate, Minister of the Interior Frank Oliver explained that '[we] give the privilege of Canadian citizenship to a man, who although not born in Canada has resided here for three years.' Even without becoming a British subject through naturalization, an immigrant to Canada could acquire rights of citizenship through domicile. Canada, House of Commons, *Debates*, 21 March 1910, 5802–3. In the act, domicile was defined as 'the place in which a person has his present home, or in which he resides, or to which he returns as his place of present permanent abode, and not for a mere special or temporary pur-

pose. Canadian domicile is acquired for the purposes of this Act by a person having his domicile for at least three years in Canada after having been landed therein within the meaning of this Act' (2(d)). Time in jail or a mental asylum for the insane didn't count. Canadian domicile would be lost if the person voluntarily resided outside Canada and intended to make his permanent home outside. *Statutes of Canada 1910*, 205–6. Section 3 of the Immigration Act protected those with domicile from summary deportation for being found among 'prohibited classes' of immigrants. A 1919 amendment to the Immigration Act increased to five years the required period of residence needed to gain domicile.

24 LAC, Immigration Board Hearing, vol. 4, Samuel Blumenberg, 14 July 1919, 6.

25 Ibid., 7.

26 *Revised Statutes of Canada, 1927*, vol. 1, 2079.

27 LAC, Immigration Board Hearing, vol. 4, Samuel Blumenberg, 14 July 1919, 8.

28 Ibid., 9–10.

29 LAC, RG 13, Access 87–88/103: box 36, file 9-A-1688, pocket #2, Andrews to Meighen (letter), 2 July 1919.

30 Donald Avery, 'Ethnic and Class Relations in Western Canada during the First World War: A Case Study of European Immigrants and Anglo-Saxon Nativism,' in David Mackenzie, ed., *Canada and the First World War: Essays in Honour of Robert Craig Brown* (Toronto, 2005), 286. Avery also notes that in early 1919 the federal government had considered a policy of mass expulsion of approximately 88,000 'enemy aliens.' The policy was rejected 'because of both its likely international repercussions and the demands it would make on the country's transportation facilities at a time when the troops were returning from Europe.' Avery, 'Ethnic and Class Relations in Western Canada During the First World War,' 281.

31 Steve Hewitt, *Riding to the Rescue: The Transformation of the RCMP in Alberta and Saskatchewan, 1914–1939* (Toronto, 2006), 93.

32 LAC, RG 13, Access 87–88/103: box 36, file 9-A-1688, pocket #2, Andrews to Meighen, 14 July 1919.

33 LAC, RG 13, Access 87–88/103: box 36, file 9-A-1688, pocket #2, Andrews to Meighen, 16 July 1919.

34 LAC, Immigration Board Hearing, vol. 4, Samuel Blumenberg, 14 July 1919, 13.

35 Ibid.

36 Ibid., 15.

37 LAC, RG 13, Access 87–88/103: box 36, file 9-A-1688, pocket #2, Meighen to Andrews, 18 June 1919.

38 LAC, Immigration Board Hearing, vol. 4, Samuel Blumenberg, 15 July 1919, 23.

39 Ibid., 24. LAC, RG 13, Access 87–88/103: box 36, file 9-A-1688, pocket #2, Andrews to Meighen, 16 July 1919.

40 LAC, Immigration Board Hearing, vol. 4, Samuel Blumenberg, 15 July 1919, 29–41.

41 Ibid., 9.

42 Ibid., 103.

43 Ibid., 4. Anticipating sedition trials, RNWMP Commissioner A.B. Perry in January 1919 instructed his constables: 'Where a treasonable or seditious speech is anticipated, it should be taken down by a short-hand writer and in a case of great importance, two shorthand writers should be employed acting independently.' See LAC, RG 18, Royal Canadian Mounted Police, vol. 599, file 1309–35, Circular memo 807, Re: Bolshevism, 6 January 1919, quoted in Hewitt, *Riding to the Rescue*, 77.

44 LAC, Immigration Board Hearing, vol. 4, Samuel Blumenberg, 15 July 1919, 15–16.

45 Ibid., 19–20.

46 Ibid., 4, 22.

47 Ibid., 26–7.

48 Ibid., 27–9.

49 Ibid., 32.

50 Ibid., 33–4.

51 Ibid., 36–8.

52 Ibid., 40.

53 LAC, Immigration Board Hearing, vol. 4, Samuel Blumenberg, 16 July 1919, 59–60.

54 Provincial Archives of Manitoba, J.C. Walker Collection, Interview with W.P. Fillmore, Tape C 2381, side 1. *Winnipeg Free Press*, 3 May 1978.

55 LAC, Immigration Board Hearing, vol. 4, Samuel Blumenberg, 16 July 1919, 57.

56 LAC, Immigration Board Hearing, vol. 4, Samuel Blumenberg, 15 July 1919, 57–8.

57 For the telegrams between Andrews and Meighen disclosing Andrews's failure to adhere to the terms of the Immigration Act in making these arrests, see LAC, RG 13, Access 87–88/103: box 36, file 9-A-1688, pocket #2, Meighen to Andrews, 17 June 1919 (telegram), #2400.

58 *Manitoba Free Press*, 28 June 1919.
59 LAC, Immigration Board Hearing, vol. 4, Samuel Blumenberg, 15 July 1919, 58–60.
60 LAC, Immigration Board Hearing, vol. 4, Samuel Blumenberg, 17 July 1919, 61–4.
61 No birth certificate has been located. Schoppelrei gave a variety of locations for his birth, including Quebec, Connecticut, San Francisco, and Ohio (where he spent some time in the Franklin Boys Home). LAC, RG 18, Royal Canadian Mounted Police, vol. 3314, H.V. – 1 (vol. 4), Winnipeg General Strike and Riot 1919, Winnipeg, Manitoba, Immigration Board Hearing, Oscar Schoppelrei, 16 July 1919, 3 p.m., 8–9. Quebec: LAC, Attestation Paper, No. 2380872, Canada Over-Seas Expeditionary Force. Connecticut and Ohio: Joy Rodriguez (granddaughter of Schoppelrei) to Tom Mitchell (email), 21 November 2007.
62 Province of Manitoba, Consumer and Corporate Affairs, Manitoba Finance, Vital Statistics, Deaths, Marriages search, 'Database searches,' 'Schoppelrei,' at http://vitalstats.gov.mb.ca/Query.php. The son was Oscar Mallinson Schoppelrei. Joy Rodriguez (granddaughter of Schoppelrei) to Tom Mitchell (email), 21 November 2007.
63 LAC, RG 13, Access 87–88/103: box 36, file 9-A-1688, pocket #2, 'Report on the Situation at Winnipeg: 14 June 1919.'
64 LAC, RG 150, Accession 1992–93/166, box 8700 – 43, See Discharge Certificate, Private Oscar Schoppelrei, in 'Schoppelrei, Oscar.' LAC, Immigration Board Hearing, Oscar Schoppelrei, 16 July 1919, 3 p.m., RG 18, vol. 3314, H.V. – 1 (vol. 4), Winnipeg General Strike and Riot 1919, Winnipeg, Manitoba, 8–9 (hereafter, LAC, Immigration Board Hearing, vol. 4, Oscar Schoppelrei).
65 The recruitment numbers turned out to be small. Nevertheless, formal US objections to the practice date from as early as the fall of 1915. Ronald G. Haycock, 'The American Legion in the Canadian Expeditionary Force, 1914–1917: A Study in Failure,' *Military Affairs* 43, no. 3 (9 October 1979), 116.
66 LAC, Immigration Board Hearing, vol. 4, Oscar Schoppelrei, 16 July 1919, 9.
67 Ibid., 6–8.
68 Ibid., 5–8.
69 See The Military Voters Act, 1917, part IV, sec. 2 (c), 314, *Statutes of Canada, 1917* (Ottawa, 1917). The authors would like to thank Lyle Dick for pointing out the relevance of the Military Voters Act.

70 LAC, Immigration Board Hearing, vol. 4, Oscar Schoppelrei, 16 July 1919, 18–19.

71 Ibid., 11–12.

72 Ibid., 14.

73 Ibid., 15.

74 LAC, Immigration Board Hearing, vol. 4, Oscar Schoppelrei, 17 July 1919, 20.

75 LAC, Immigration Board Hearing, vol. 4, Oscar Schoppelrei, 16 July 1919, 21.

76 LAC, Immigration Board Hearing, vol. 4, Oscar Schoppelrei, 17 July 1919, 20.

77 LAC, RG 13, Access 87–88/103: box 36, file 9-A-1688, pocket #2, Andrews to Meighen (letter), 18 July 1919.

78 LAC, Immigration Board Hearing, vol. 4, Oscar Schoppelrei, 18 July 1919, 26–7.

79 *Dos Yiddishe Vort*, 1 August 1919, quoted in Trachtenberg, '"The Old Clo' Move,"' 664–5.

80 LAC, Immigration Board Hearing, vol. 4, Oscar Schoppelrei, 18 July 1919, 27.

81 Ibid., 29.

82 Ibid., 42–4.

83 Ibid., 35.

84 Ibid., 37–42.

85 Ibid., 43, 46.

86 LAC, RG 18, Royal Canadian Mounted Police, vol. 3314, H.V. – 1 (vol. 4), Winnipeg General Strike and Riot 1919, Winnipeg, Manitoba, Immigration Board Hearing, Solomon Almazoff, 16 July 1919, NAC, 86 (hereafter, LAC, Immigration Board Hearing, vol. 4, Solomon Almazoff), 1–3.

87 LAC, Immigration Board Hearing, vol. 4, Solomon Almazoff, 16 July 1919, 5–6.

88 Ibid., 6–8. According to Henry Trachtenberg, the Jewish community held Almazoff in high regard, and worried deeply about his imprisonment. 'The Winnipeg Jewish Community and Politics: The Inter-War Years, 1919–1939,' *MHS Transactions* 3, no. 35 (1978–9), 7.

89 LAC, Immigration Board Hearing, vol. 4, Solomon Almazoff, 16 July 1919, 8. Henry Trachtenberg reports that Almazoff 'addressed a Jewish audience at the Liberty Temple in January 1918 on the Russian revolution, which he described as "the Greatest Happening of the Twentieth Century."' '"The Old Clo' Move,"' 867–8 n. 81.

90 LAC, Immigration Board Hearing, vol. 4, Solomon Almazoff, 18 July 1919, 18–19.

91 Ibid., 20.

92 See 'Bolsheviki in the United States,' *The Literary Digest*, 22 February 1919; 'Bolshevism's Heaven on Earth,' *The Literary Digest*, 22 March 1919; 'America Safe from Bolshevism,' *The Literary Digest*, 29 March 1919.

93 *Statutes of Canada, 1919*, Consolidated Orders Respecting Censorship, Order II, section 7 of PC 1241, 22 May 1918, lxix, stated: 'In any prosecution or proceeding brought, had or taken under this order by or on behalf or by the direction or under the authority of the Attorney General of Canada all matters alleged in the information, charge or indictment shall be without proof rebuttably [*sic*] presumed to be true.' In other words, if the Attorney General of Canada charged someone, that person was automatically guilty.

94 LAC, Immigration Board Hearing, vol. 4, Solomon Almazoff, 18 July 1919, 27–8.

95 Trachtenberg, '"The Old Clo' Move,"' 867–8 n. 81.

96 LAC, Immigration Board Hearing, vol. 4, Solomon Almazoff, 18 July 1919, 19–21.

97 Ibid., 29–32.

98 Throughout the transcript of the immigration hearing for Michael Charitonoff, also known as Max Charitonoff, his name appears incorrectly spelled as 'Charitinoff.' See, for example, Library and Archives Canada, RG 18, Royal Canadian Mounted Police, vol. 3314, H.V. – 1 (vol. 4), Winnipeg General Strike and Riot 1919, Winnipeg, Manitoba, Immigration Board Hearing, vol. 4, Michael Charitonoff, 16 July 1919, 1–3 (hereafter LAC, Immigration Board Hearing, vol. 4, Michael Charitonoff).

99 Trachtenberg, '"The Old Clo' Move,"' 668.

100 LAC, Immigration Board Hearing, vol. 4, Michael Charitonoff, 16 July 1919, 5–6.

101 LAC, Immigration Board Hearing, vol. 4, Michael Charitonoff, 17 July 1919, 4, 9.

102 Ibid., 10–11. On 23 September 1918, Charitonoff had been charged with possession of prohibited literature, a pamphlet entitled *Who Needs the War?* He was also charged with being a member of a prohibited organization and with sending money to the Russian Bolsheviks. Advised that he would probably be fined $100, Charitonoff pled guilty, but Hugh John Macdonald sentenced him to three years in a penitentiary and a fine of $1000. On his behalf, the Winnipeg Trades

and Labor Council mounted a campaign, declaring that the incriminating pamphlet belonged to his wife's Russian nurse, and that the money had been sent to Kerensky's Minister of Finance. The sentence was successfully appealed. Trachtenberg, "'The Old Clo' Move,'" 652–4.

103 LAC, Immigration Board Hearing, vol. 4, Michael Charitonoff, 17 July 1919, 11–13. On the Soviet Bureau and Martens, see Todd J. Pfannestiel, *Rethinking the Red Scare: The Lusk Committee and New York's Crusade against Radicalism, 1919–1923* (New York, 2003), 37–53.

104 LAC, Immigration Board Hearing, vol. 4, Michael Charitonoff, 16 July 1919, 5–6. *Western Labor News*, 13 December 1918.

105 LAC, Immigration Board Hearing, vol. 4, Michael Charitonoff, 17 July 1919, 14.

106 Ibid., 17–18.

107 Ibid., 22–4.

108 *Western Labor News*, 25 July 1919.

109 LAC, RG 13, Access 87–88/103: box 36, file 9-A-1688, pocket #2, Meighen to Andrews (telegram), 18 July 1919.

110 LAC, RG 13, Access 87–88/103: box 36, file 9-A-1688, pocket #2, Andrews to Meighen (letter), 18 July 1919.

111 Gregory S. Kealey supplies a partial list of secret agents from 1919–20: (1) F.E. Reithdorf, Secret Agent 50, a.k.a. Frederick Edwards; (2) Roth, Secret Agent 6; (3) Dourasoff, Secret Agent 14; (4) Jones, Secret Agent 58, Vancouver; (5) A.B. Smith, Secret Agent 61, Victoria; (6) F.H. Colam; (7) F.W. Zaneth; (8) George C. Evans; (9) R.M. Gosden; (10) Devitt, Vancouver; (11) W.P. Walker, Edmonton; (12) Eccles, Vancouver; (13) Spain, Vancouver; (14) Orton Hall, Vancouver; (15) Davies, Vancouver; (16) Willie, Vancouver; (17) Lawrence, Vancouver; (18) Kobus; (19) Kylick; (20) Harry Daskaluk, Secret Agent 21; (21) Gore Kaburagi or Goro Karbarugi; (22) John Leopold; (23) T.E. Ryan; (24) John Veloskie; (25) Julius Chmichlewski. See 'Appendix 1: RNWMP/RCMP Secret Agents, 1919–1920,' 205, in Gregory S. Kealey, 'The Surveillance State: The Origins of Domestic Intelligence and Counter-Subversion in Canada, 1914–1921,' *Intelligence and National Security* 7, no. 3 (1992), 184–91.

112 LAC, RG 13, Access 87–88/103: box 36, file 9-A-1688, pocket #2, Andrews to Meighen (letter), 18 July 1919.

113 Provincial Archives of Manitoba, J.S. Woodsworth Papers, P-5609, file 20, B. Zeglinski to D. Ireland, 13 November 1919, quoted in 'Winnipeg Defence Committee Newsletter,' 17 December 1919.

12 THEY STARTED THE FIRE

1 LAC, RG 18, Royal Canadian Mounted Police, Detective Sergeant Albert E. Reames to The Commissioner, RNWMP, 30 July 1919.

2 University of Manitoba Archives and Special Collections, MSS 48, PC 58, Pitblado Family Fonds, Series 3, Isaac Pitblado, box 6, folder 32, Isaac Pitblado, '60 Years at the Bar – the Pitblado Story,' 31 January 1950.

3 For an illuminating account of how narrative and the courtroom are implicated in the making of legal meaning, see Martha Merrill Umphrey, 'Dialogics of Legal Meaning: Spectacular Trials, the Unwritten Law, and Narratives of Criminal Responsibility,' *Law & Society Review* 33, no. 2 (1999), 393–423.

4 Bryce M. Stewart, *Canadian Labor Laws and the Treaty* (New York, 1968), 135.

5 Under the Industrial Disputes Investigation Act. See Judy Fudge and Eric Tucker, *Labour Before the Law: The Regulation of Workers' Collective Action in Canada, 1900–1948* (Don Mills, 2001), 54–8.

6 See, for example, PAM, Preliminary Hearing, J.R. Ong, Transportation Engineer, Winnipeg Electric Railway Company, 1448–51; William M. Gordon, Superintendent of the Western Division of the Dominion Express Company, 609–11; Charles H. McNaughton, Managing Director of the Artic Ice Company, 616–18.

7 *Statutes of Canada, 1892*, 64.

8 Ibid. On the history of sedition legislation in Canada, see William E. Conklin, 'The Origin of the Law of Sedition,' *The Criminal Law Quarterly* 15 (1973), 277–300.

9 In 1892 the text of the proposed Criminal Code definition of sedition was discussed and amended but not quoted in full during the debates in the House of Commons. See Canada, House of Commons, *Debates*, 19 May 1892, col. 2829–37. Only in 1919 was the proposed 1892 definition quoted in the *Debates* when Solicitor General Hugh Guthrie reviewed proposed changes to the Criminal Code dealing with sedition. See Canada, House of Commons, *Debates*, 10 June 1919, 3285–90, esp. 3289. For the creation of the Canadian Criminal Code, see Desmond H. Brown, 'Parliamentary Magic: Sir John Thompson and the Enactment of the Criminal Code,' *Journal of Canadian Studies* 27, no. 4 (1993), 30–1.

10 Canada, House of Commons, *Debates*, 19 May 1892, col. 2837.

11 Conklin, 'Origin of the Law of Sedition,' 284.

12 *Revised Statutes of Canada, 1906*, vol. 3 (Ottawa, 1906), 36.

13 Brown, 'Parliamentary Magic,' 38.

14 Provincial Archives of Manitoba, GR 950, Attorney-General's
    Records, Central Registry, Bill of Indictment, King vs. Russell (1919).
    See also the indexed copy of the indictment in PAM, MG 14, C 64,
    box 4, Pitblado 'Scrapbook – Winnipeg General Strike Trials,' 1–19.
15 Conklin, 'Origin of the Law of Sedition,' 279 n. 2.
16 *R. v. Manshrick* (1916), 27 C.C.C. 17 at 24, 32 D.L.R. 584, 27 Man. R.
    94, quoted in Conklin, 'Origin of the Law of Sedition,' 283.
17 PAM, Robert Graham fonds, 121–2.
18 PAM, Preliminary Hearing, Magistrate Noble, 1299.
19 PAM, Preliminary Hearing, RNWMP Detective Hugh Campbell, 1300.
20 PAM, Preliminary Hearing, Magistrate Noble, 588.
21 Ibid., 1296.
22 *Toronto Daily Star*, 22 March 1920.
23 See, for example, the testimony of William Campbell Muir, superin-
    tendent of the Canadian Northern Express Company. PAM, Prelimi-
    nary Hearing, William Campbell Muir, 878–85.
24 PAM, Preliminary Hearing, 1–3.
25 For a complete list of everyone whom the Citizens considered impli-
    cated, see PAM, 'Particulars,' 20th day of January, A.D. 1920, Alfred
    Joseph Andrews, Counsel for the Crown, 2–3, 9.
26 PAM, Preliminary Hearing, F.B. Perry, 8–12.
27 PAM, Preliminary Hearing, Sgt. Francis Langdale, 15–22. See also
    Manitoba Free Press, 22 July 1919.
28 PAM, Preliminary Hearing, Sgt. Francis Langdale, 32, 39.
29 Ibid., 41–2.
30 LAC, RG 13, Access 87–88/103: box 36, file 9-A-1688, pocket #2,
    Meighen to Andrews (telegram), 21 July 1919.
31 P.D. Mignault, 'The Right Honourable Charles J. Doherty,' *The Cana-
    dian Bar Review* 9, no. 9 (November 1931), 629, 631.
32 The St James Club, the Club Lafontaine, and the University Club in
    Montreal; the Rideau Club in Ottawa. Henry James Morgan, *The
    Canadian Men and Women of the Time*, 1st ed. (Toronto, 1898),
    275–6; 2nd ed. (Toronto, 1912), 333. W. Stewart Wallace, *The Macmil-
    lan Dictionary of Canadian Biography* (Toronto, 1976), 216. Robert
    Craig Brown and Ramsay Cook, *A Nation Transformed: Canada
    1896–1921* (Toronto, 1974), 191.
33 Canada, House of Commons, *Debates*, 19 August 1914, 20.
34 Ibid., 25 September 1919, 586.
35 'The Late C.J. Doherty, P.C., K.C., D.C.L.,' *The Canadian Bar Review*
    9, no. 8 (October 1931), 539.
36 LAC, Borden Papers, reel C-4334, Robert Borden to C.H. Cahan, 19
    May 1918: 5642; ibid., Robert Borden to Charles Doherty, 21 May

1918: 56643. Historians have generally ignored the role of the state in manufacturing a basis for the repressive measures of 1918. For an account of the developments arising out of these early discussions, see Gregory S. Kealey, 'The Surveillance State: The Origins of Domestic Intelligence and Counter-Subversion in Canada, 1914–1921,' *Intelligence and National Security* 7, no. 3 (1992), 179–210; Gregory Kealey, 'The Early Years of State Surveillance of Labour and the Left in Canada: The Institutional Framework of the Royal Canadian Mounted Police Security and Intelligence Apparatus, 1918–26,' *Intelligence and National Security* 8, no. 3 (July 1993), 129–48; A. Ross McCormack, *Reformers, Rebels, and Revolutionaries: The Western Canadian Radical Movement 1899–1919* (Toronto, 1977), 149–53; and Steve Hewitt, *Riding to the Rescue: The Transformation of the RCMP in Alberta and Saskatchewan, 1914–1939* (Toronto, 2006), 75–9.

37 LAC, Borden Papers, reel C-4334, C.H. Cahan to Honorable Charles Doherty, Minister of Justice, 20 July 1918: 56656–61.

38 Joan M. Jensen, *The Price of Vigilance* (Chicago, 1968), 22.

39 Ibid., 87.

40 Ibid., 234. On Lt. Col. Charles Vincent Massey and the war, see Claude Bissell, *The Young Vincent Massey* (Toronto, 1981), 100–2.

41 LAC, Borden Paper, C4334, Robert Borden to C.H. Cahan, 19 May 1918: 56642. On Cahan, see Gregory S. Kealey and Andrew Parnaby, 'The Insider: Charles Hazlitt Cahan,' *Beaver* 81, no. 4 (August–September 2001), 14.

42 LAC, Borden Papers, reel C-4334, Robert Borden to C.H. Cahan, K.C., 19 May 1918: 56642.

43 LAC, Borden Papers, reel C-4334, A.S. Sherwood, Chief Commissioner of Police, to the Honorable Minister of Justice, Re I.W.W., and kindred organizations, 16 June 1918: 56651–3.

44 LAC, Borden Papers, C-4334, C.H. Cahan to Doherty, 20 July 1918: 56656–61.

45 On Newcombe, see Philip Girard, 'E.L. Newcombe,' *Dictionary of Canadian Biography*, forthcoming.

46 LAC, Borden Papers, reel C-4334, C.H. Cahan to Doherty, 14 September 1918: 56665–83.

47 *Statutes of Canada, 1918*, vols I–II, PC 2381, 25 September 1918, lxxi–lxxii, & PC 2384, 25 September 1918, lxxvii–lxxx. For the reference to US statutes, see the similarity of the Canadian OICs and American immigration legislation, penalizing 'any association, organization, society or corporation, one of whose purposes or professed purposes is to bring about any governmental, political, social, industrial, or economic change within Canada by the use of force, violence or physical

injury to person or property.' Barbara Roberts, *Whence They Came: Deportation from Canada, 1900–1935* (Ottawa, 1988), 82.

48 LAC, Borden Papers, reel C-4334, C.H. Cahan to Doherty, 26 September 1918: 56692–6.

49 Kenneth McNaught and David J. Bercuson, *The Winnipeg General Strike: 1919* (Don Mills, 1974), 81.

50 LAC, Borden Papers, reel C-4334, C.H. Cahan to Doherty, 26 September 1918: 56692–6. LAC, RG 13, Justice, Series A-2, vol. 2159\File: 1919-166, Access code: 32\Establishment of Public Safety Branch–Abolition of Public Safety Branch, National Archives of Canada, Order in Council, 2 October 1918. Cahan lasted until January and then quit, alleging lack of support for his work. See LAC, Borden Papers, reel C-4341, C.H. Cahan to Right Honorable Sir Robert Borden, 28 May 1919: 61631–2. By Order-in-Council, Cabinet ended the brief life of the Public Safety Branch on 16 January 1919. See LAC, RG 13, PC 104, 16 January 1919.

51 Charles Doherty speech, *The Empire Club of Canada Speeches 1921* (Toronto; The Empire Club of Canada, 1923), 5 http://www.empireclubfoundation.com/results.asp?Index=British+Empire.

52 LAC, Borden Papers, Milner to Borden, 23 July 1919, quoted in Aloysius Balawyder, *Canadian-Soviet Relations between the World Wars* (Toronto 1972), 30. No information is available about whether this report was accurate or not.

53 Robert Craig Brown, *Robert Laird Borden*, 2 vols. (Toronto, 1975–80), 2: 179.

54 Henry Borden, ed., *Robert Laird Borden: His Memoirs*, vol. 2 (Toronto, 1969), 1008.

55 Mignault, 'The Right Honourable Charles J. Doherty,' 629, 631.

56 LAC, RG 13, Access 87–88/103: box 36, file 9-A-1688, pocket #2, Meighen to A.L. Crossin, 21 July 1919.

57 *Statutes of Canada, 1919*, Consolidated Orders Respecting Censorship, Order II, section 7 of PC 1241, 22 May 1918, lxix. For the wording, see note 1247.

58 See telegram, Doherty to Colonel E.J. Chambers, 19 July 1919, NAC, Access, 'Winnipeg' Justice (pocket #1). For permission to proceed, see Doherty to Andrews, 26 July 1919 (letter), NAC, Access, 'Winnipeg' Justice (pocket #2). Following Russell's conviction in December 1919, Andrews and his colleagues also undertook the opposition to Russell's appeal before the Manitoba Appeal Court and the Judicial Committee of the Privy Council. The arrangements made for Andrews and his associates to appear for the Crown at the Russell appeal suggest how the Province handled the federal entry into Manitoba's legal jurisdic-

tion. Andrews coached Doherty to wire the attorney general of Manitoba that the federal Department of Justice wished to oppose Russell's application to appeal and, if unsuccessful, to fight the appeal itself. Doherty was directed to ask the attorney general to authorize Andrews and 'such counsel as [Andrews] … may appoint to appear on his behalf without expense to the provincial attorney general.' The attorney general stipulated that the request come directly from Doherty rather than from Andrews. NAC, Justice, Access, RG 13, pocket #1, Andrews to Doherty, 29 March 1920. Evidently, Doherty agreed, since Andrews, Pitblado, Coyne, and Sweatman appeared when Russell's case came before the Manitoba Court of Appeal on 8 January 1920. The Crown's arguments were sustained on 19 January 1920. Given the unanimous rejection of his appeal, Russell could not appeal to the Supreme Court. However, he could and did seek a hearing before the Judicial Committee of the Privy Council. See NAC, Justice, Access, RG 13, pocket #1, Andrews to Doherty (telegram) [n.d.].

59 LAC, RG 13, Access 87–88/103: box 36, file 9-A-1688, pocket #2, Doherty to Andrews, 26 July 1919 (letter); ibid., Andrews to Meighen (telegram), 18 July 1919. See also *Statutes of Canada, 1919*, Consolidated Orders Respecting Censorship, Order II, section 7 of PC 1241, 22 May 1918, lxix.

60 LAC, Immigration Board Hearing, Vol. 4, Solomon Almazoff, 18 July 1919, 29–32.

61 LAC, RG 13, Access 87–88/103: box 36, file 9-A-1688, pocket #2, Andrews to Doherty, 6 August 1919 (telegram) and Doherty to Andrews, 8 August 1919. The technicality upon which they prosecuted Miller was that *Die Volk Stimme* didn't forward the necessary copies to the censor. Henry Trachtenberg, 'The Winnipeg Jewish Community and Politics: The Inter-War Years, 1919–1939,' *MHS Transactions* 3, no. 35 (1978–9), at http://www.mhs.mb.ca/docs/transactions/3/jewishpolitics.shtml, 25 April 2009.

62 *Manitoba Free Press*, 23 July 1919.

63 *Manitoba Free Press*, Wednesday, 30 July 1919. LAC, RG 18, Royal Canadian Mounted Police, Detective Sergeant Albert E. Reames to the Commissioner, RNWMP, 30 July 1919.

64 Roy St George Stubbs, 'Life Story of A.J. Andrews,' *Winnipeg Free Press Magazine*, 15 June 1940, 5.

65 PAM, Preliminary Hearing, RNWMP Sergeant Albert Reames, 77–82. The reference is to Friedrich Engels, *Socialism, Utopian and Scientific* (London, 1892).

66 *Manitoba Free Press*, Saturday, 6 August 1919. LAC, Preliminary Hearing, J.B. Coyne, 951–7.

67 PAM, Preliminary Hearing, RNWMP Sergeant Albert Reames, 101–5.
68 *Manitoba Free Press*, Saturday, 6 August 1919.
69 Ibid.
70 See PAM, Preliminary Hearing, E.J. McMurray, 937.
71 *Manitoba Free Press*, Saturday, 6 August 1919.
72 *Manitoba Free Press*, Saturday, 2 August 1919. PAM, Preliminary Hearing, W.E. Davis, 893–5.
73 PAM, Preliminary Hearing, W.E. Davis, 905.
74 Ibid., 902.
75 PAM, Preliminary Hearing, RNWMP Sergeant Albert Reames, 108.
76 Ibid., 111.
77 Ibid., 141.
78 *Manitoba Free Press*, Thursday, 23 July 1919. For Reames's verbatim testimony on these meetings, see PAM, Preliminary Hearing, RNWMP Sergeant Albert Reames, 83–92.
79 PAM, Preliminary Hearing, RNWMP Sergeant Albert Reames, 144–7.
80 Ibid., 166–9.
81 Battsford was born in Minneapolis in 1893. During the First World War, he served in France with the Canadian Expeditionary Force, and in October 1918 he rejoined the *Free Press* as an editorial cartoonist and reporter. By 1939, he was living in Garden City, New York, and working on the comic strip 'Mortimer and Charlie.' The authors would like to thank Michael Dupuis for this biographical note.
82 PAM, Preliminary Hearing, B.T. Battsford, 1155, 1157–8.
83 Ibid., 1158–9.
84 Ibid., 1162–3.
85 Ibid., 1165.
86 Ibid., 1185–9.
87 Ibid., 1182.
88 Ibid., 1181–2.
89 Ibid., 1184.
90 LAC, RG 13, Access 87–88/103: box 36, file 9-A-1688, pocket #2, Andrews to Meighen (letter), 18 July 1919.
91 PAM, Preliminary Hearing, Harry Daskaluk, 1328–30.
92 Ibid., 1332. On Cassidy, see David Bercuson, *Fools and Wise Men: The Rise and Fall of the One Big Union* (Toronto, 1978); and Todd McCallum, 'The Strange Tale of Tom Cassidy and Catherine Rose, or Free Love, Heterosexuality, and the One Big Union,' *Journal of the Canadian Historical Society*, new series 9 (1998), 125–54.
93 PAM, Preliminary Hearing, Harry Daskaluk, 1345.
94 Ibid., 1341–3, 1347.

95 LAC, RG 13, Access 87–88/103: box 36, file 9-A-1688, pocket #2, Andrews to Meighen (letter), 18 July 1919.

96 PAM, Preliminary Hearing, Harry Daskaluk,1356.

97 Ibid., 1335–6.

98 C.W. Parker, ed., *Who's Who and Why – A Biographical Dictionary of Men and Women of Western Canada* (Vancouver, 1913), 447. Linda McDowell, 'Some Women Candidates for the Manitoba Legislature,' *MHS Transactions* 3, no. 32 (1975–6), 8.

99 See 'Alderman Queen's Bolshevism,' *Winnipeg Telegram*, 18 January 1919.

100 PAM, Preliminary Hearing, Genevieve Lipsett Skinner, 261, 271. See also *Manitoba Free Press*, Friday, 25 July 1919.

101 PAM, Preliminary Hearing, Mrs Niblett, 1261.

102 PAM, Preliminary Hearing, Genevieve Lipsett Skinner, 266.

103 PAM, Preliminary Hearing, Mrs Niblett, 1271–5.

104 PAM, Preliminary Hearing, W.S. Thompson, 367–8.

105 Ibid., 377–80.

106 PAM, Preliminary Hearing, Mayor Charles Gray, 434.

107 Ibid., 440.

108 Ibid., 442–3. Later, W.J. Price, a civic employee, testified that he had been ordered on strike by the president of the Civic Employees' Federation with 'the threat that if he did not quit work he would never be allowed to work with any civic employee again.' See PAM, Preliminary Hearing, W.J. Price, 605–9.

109 PAM, Preliminary Hearing, Mayor Charles Gray, 521.

110 Ibid., 445.

111 Ibid., 475.

112 Ibid., 474.

113 Ibid., 445–6.

114 Ibid., 447.

115 Ibid., 448.

116 Ibid., 450.

117 PAM, Preliminary Hearing, Howard Rosling, 669–80.

118 PAM, Preliminary Hearing, Mayor Charles Gray, 459.

119 *Manitoba Free Press*, Wednesday, 6 August 1919.

120 PAM, Preliminary Hearing, Mayor Charles Gray, 451. For a fuller account of this incident, see chapter 1.

121 Ibid., 471.

122 Ibid., 488.

123 Ibid., 528.

124 Ibid., 529.

125 Ibid., 535.

126 Ibid., 537.
127 Ibid., 549–50.
128 Ibid., 553.
129 Ibid., 556–7.
130 Ibid., 569.
131 Ibid., 564–5.
132 Ibid., 559.
133 Ibid., 559–60.
134 PAM, Preliminary Hearing, William Gordon, 616, 627.
135 PAM, Preliminary Hearing, Mike Stodnick, 823–4.
136 PAM, Preliminary Hearing, Robert Snook, 763–7. At some unspeci-
     fied time, Snook got into an argument with Andrews about legal fees.
     Unable to get satisfaction, Snook slipped his dump cart into a Win-
     nipeg parade from a side-street. On the cart was written, 'All lawyers
     are crooks. A.J. Andrews is the biggest one.' Police escorted Snook
     out of the parade, but a few blocks later, he re-entered it. After the
     process was repeated a few times, police assigned a man to keep
     Snook out of the parade. Roy St George Stubbs, 'Life Story of A.J.
     Andrews,' *Winnipeg Free Press Magazine*, 15 June 1940, 5. See also
     Gordon Goldsborough, 'Albert Robert "Ginger" Snook (1835–1926),'
     Manitoba Biographies, Manitoba Historical Society, at http://www
     .mhs.mb.ca/docs/people/snook_ar.shtml#1, accessed 8 June
     2009.
137 PAM, Preliminary Hearing, Alexander Fraser, 639–40.
138 Ibid., 641.
139 PAM, Preliminary Hearing, John Sparling, 729.
140 Ibid., 698, 707. The agreement had been negotiated prior to the begin-
     ning of the Strike, but wasn't signed until 27 May.
141 PAM, Preliminary Hearing, John Sparling, 725.
142 PAM, Preliminary Hearing, Robert Graham, 1076–7.
143 PAM, Preliminary Hearing, J.K. Sparling, 713–14.
144 Ibid., 739.
145 *Manitoba Free Press*, Thursday, 31 July 1919. Only part of this
     appears in the transcript of the preliminary hearing, presumably
     because the court recorder felt that it wasn't intended to be part of the
     public record. PAM, Preliminary Hearing, 743–4.
146 PAM, Preliminary Hearing, Edward Parnell, 1041–2, 1054. Except
     for Botterell, these are names that appear on the Citizens' post-Strike
     congratulatory telegram to Prime Minister Borden. See chapter 2.
147 PAM, Preliminary Hearing, Edward Parnell, 1054–7.
148 Ibid., 1058–9, 1063.
149 Ibid., 1059–62.

150 Ibid., 1060.

151 Ibid., 1061.

152 PAM, Preliminary Hearing, B.T. Battsford, 1166–7.

153 PAM, Preliminary Hearing, Edward Parnell, 1066–8.

154 Ibid., 1068.

155 Ramsay Cook, ed., *The Dafoe-Sifton Correspondence 1919–1917* (Altona, 1966), 39.

156 PAM, Preliminary Hearing, Edward Parnell, 1072.

157 PAM, Preliminary Hearing, John Botterell, 1081. Canada Bread Company manager W.P. Riley denied being a member of the Citizens, even though his name appeared on the congratulatory telegram that the Citizens sent to Borden. PAM, Preliminary Hearing, W.P. Riley, 1114. Botterell's name didn't appear on the telegram. Executive Citizens Committee of One Thousand to Robert Borden, 18 June 1919, NAC, Access, 'Winnipeg' Justice, pocket #2. Riley's reticence is in keeping with that of many Citizens, particularly since he (unlike Botterell) ran a retail business that would be susceptible to boycotts.

158 PAM, Preliminary Hearing, J.E. Botterell, 1093–5.

159 PAM, Preliminary Hearing, J.E. Botterell, 1099.

160 Ibid., 1099–100.

161 Ibid., 1089.

162 PAM, Preliminary Hearing, Robert Graham, 1077–8.

163 PAM, Preliminary Hearing, E.J. McMurray, 1478.

164 PAM, Preliminary Hearing, Magistrate Noble, 1477.

13 POOR HARRY DASKALUK

1 LAC, RG 18, Royal Canadian Mounted Police, vol. 3314, H.V.-1 (vol. 5), Winnipeg General Strike and Riot 1919, Winnipeg, Manitoba (hereafter LAC, Immigration Board Hearing, vol. 5, Samuel Blumenberg), 1 August 1919, 109.

2 Ibid., 111.

3 Ibid., 5, 114.

4 Ibid., 116.

5 LAC, RG 18, Royal Canadian Mounted Police, vol. 3314, H.V.-1 (vol. 5), Winnipeg General Strike and Riot 1919, Winnipeg, Manitoba (hereafter LAC, Immigration Board Hearing, vol. 5, LAC, Immigration Board Hearing, vol. 5, Solomon Almazoff), 8 August 1919, 3.

6 Ibid., 2.

7 PAM, Preliminary Hearing, Harry Daskaluk, 1329.

8 *Manitoba Free Press*, 14 August 1919.

9 LAC, Immigration Board Hearing, vol. 5, Solomon Almazoff, 14 August 1919, 66–8.

10 'General Strike Must Paralyze Industries to Be Effective,' *Manitoba Free Press*, 20 December 1919, 19.

11 PAM, J.S. Woodsworth Papers, P-5609, file 20, 'Winnipeg Defence Committee Newsletter,' 17 December 1919.

12 PAM, J.S. Woodsworth Papers, P-5609, file 20, B. Zeglinski to D. Ireland, 13 November 1919, quoted in 'Winnipeg Defence Committee Newsletter,' 17 December 1919.

13 PAM, J.S. Woodsworth Papers, P-5609, file 20, Harry Daskaluk to My Dearest friend, undated, quoted in 'Winnipeg Defence Committee Newsletter,' 17 December 1919.

14 LAC, RG 13, Access 87–88/103: A-1688, pocket #2, Andrews to Meighen (letter), 18 July 1919.

15 LAC, Immigration Board Hearing, vol. 5, Solomon Almazoff, 14 August 1919, 94.

16 Ibid., 112.

17 Ibid., 102, 123–4.

18 LAC, Immigration Board Hearing, vol. 5, Solomon Almazoff, 15 August 1919, 117.

19 Ibid., 15 August 1919, 116–17.

20 Ibid., 123–4.

21 Ibid., 118.

22 Ibid., 146.

23 Ibid., 128.

24 *Dos Yiddishe Vort*, quoted in Henry Manuel Trachtenberg, '"The Old Clo' Move": Anti-Semitism, Politics, and the Jews of Winnipeg, 1882-1921,' 879, note 146.

25 LAC, Immigration Board Hearing, vol. 5, Solomon Almazoff, 15 August 1919, 139. This was probably true. In November 1918, with the tacit support of the British and other allied governments, Admiral Aleksandr Vasiliyevich Kolchak emerged as the 'supreme ruler and supreme military commander' in Western Siberia. Kolchak's regime was characterized by 'an unholy mixture of Great Russian chauvinism, xenophobia, and anti-semitism.' Pogromists' activities went unpunished and largely unrestrained under Kolchak. In July 1919, 2000 Jews died during the Ekaterinburg pogrom that took place in the wake of 'one of the most humiliating White defeats at the hands of the Red army of the Jew Bronstein, better known as Trotsky.' N.G.O. Pereira, *White Siberia: The Politics of Civil War* (Montreal and Kingston 1996), 138–9.

26 LAC, Immigration Board Hearing, vol. 5, Solomon Almazoff, 15
    August 1919, 139.
27 *Winnipeg Telegram*, 18 August 1919. A reporter quoted Almazoff,
    'Why should I desire here what I escaped from there?' but the sentence
    never appears as such in the transcript of the hearing.
28 LAC, Immigration Board Hearing, vol. 5, Solomon Almazoff, 15
    August 1919, 142.
29 Ibid., 148–9.
30 Ibid., 156.
31 Ibid., 152.
32 LAC, RG 13, Access 87–88/103: A-1688, pocket #2, Andrews to
    Doherty, 16 August 1919. Within a couple of years, Almazoff showed
    up in New York as an 'active member of the Workers (Communist)
    Party,' as secretary of ICOR (Organization for Jewish Colonization in
    Russia), and as a writer for the Yiddish-language newspaper *The
    Morning Freiheit*. In 1954, under the name of Sol Almazov Pearl, he
    was the subject of a denaturalization suit for failing to reveal his Com-
    munist connections before his naturalization. He wrote a number of
    Yiddish books and died in New York in 1979. See Roz Usiskin,
    'Moses Almazov and the Winnipeg General Strike, Part I & Part II,'
    Outlook 33, no. 3 (April/May 1995), 13–14, and 33, no. 4 (June 1995),
    10, 30–1. For his New York activities, see Melech Epstein, *The Jew
    and Communism: The Story of Early Communist Victories and Ulti-
    mate Defeats in the Jewish Community, U.S.A., 1919–1941* (New York,
    1959), 413 n. 44. See also S. Almazov, *Ten Years in Biro-Bijan
    1928–1938* (New York, 1938); Henry Srebrnik, 'Diaspora, Ethnicity
    and Dreams of Jewish Communists and the Birobidzhan Project,' in
    Gennady Estraikh and Mikhail Krutikov, eds, *Yiddish and the Left*
    (Oxford, 2001), 80–108; and Henry Srebrnik, 'Leadership and Control
    within an American Jewish Communist Front: The Case of the ICOR,'
    SHOFAR 16, no. 3 (Spring 1998), 103–17. See also 'Sued over Citi-
    zenship,' *New York Times*, 5 February 1954. For an obituary, see *New
    York Times*, 24 April 1979.
33 *Manitoba Free Press*, Wednesday, 13 August 1919.
34 Blumenberg and his family lived in Duluth, Minneapolis, and Los
    Angeles, where he set up a cleaning business. In February 1939 he was
    sentenced to a term of one to five years in San Quentin Prison for his
    part in a conspiracy described by the *Los Angeles Times* as 'plotting
    terrorism affecting price-cutting cleaners and dyers.' He died in 1946
    or thereabouts. *Los Angeles Times*, 16 February 1939. Telephone con-
    versations and email, Tom Mitchell with Harvey Blumenberg (Min-
    neapolis Minnesota) and Eleanor Blumenberg (Santa Monica, CA),

wife of Sam's son Charles Karl [Karl Marx] Blumenberg, 14 December 2007.

35 LAC, RG 13, A-2, vol. 240, no. 1992-1919, Department of Immigration, 'Oscar Schoppelrei,' Deputy Minister of Immigration and Colonization to E.L. Newcombe, Deputy Minister of Justice, 7 August 1919.

36 Ibid.,' Memorandum for Mr. Chisholm, no. 1992, Re Appeal of Oscar Schoppelrei, 14 August 1919, 2.

37 LAC, RG 13, A-2, vol. 240, no. 1992-1919, Department of Immigration, 'Oscar Schoppelrei,' W. Stuart Edwards, Acting D.M.J to the Deputy Minister, Department of the Interior, 16 August 1919.

38 LAC, RG 13, A-2, vol. 240, no. 1992-1919, Department of Immigration, 'Oscar Schoppelrei,' Memorandum for Mr. Chisholm, no. 1992, Re Appeal of Oscar Schoppelrei, 14 August 1919, 2.

39 Following Schoppelrei's deportation to the United States in 1919, he met and married Bessie Lillie on 2 July 1920, in Hennepin, Minnesota. They had three children together. Bessie and Oscar divorced on 1 December 1927 in Milwaukee, Wisconsin. Personal email to Tom Mitchell from Joy Rodriguez, Schoppelrei's granddaughter, 21 November 2007.

40 *Manitoba Free Press*, 15 August 1919, 10. LAC, RG 13, A-2, vol. 240, no. 1992-1919, Department of Immigration, 'Michael Charitonoff,' quoted in Eric Lyle Dick, 'Deportation under the Immigration Act and the Canadian Criminal Code, 1919–1936,' MA thesis, University of Manitoba, 1978, 63.

41 Dick, 'Deportation under the Immigration Act,' 63.

42 *Manitoba Free Press*, 15 August 1919.

43 LAC, RG 13, A-2, vol. 240, no. 1992-1919, Department of Immigration, vol. 5, 'Max Charitonoff,' quoted in Dick, 'Deportation under the Immigration Act,' 63.

44 *Manitoba Free Press*, 15 August 1919.

45 LAC, RG 13, Access 87–88/103: A-1688, pocket #2, Andrews to Doherty, 16 August 1919.

46 LAC, RG 13, Access 87–88/103: A-1688, pocket #2, Doherty to Andrews, 19 August 1919.

47 LAC, RG 13, Series A-2, vol. 241, file no. 2241, Memorandum prepared for E.L. Newcombe, Deputy Minister of Justice, 10 September 1919, quoted in Dick, 'Deportation under the Immigration Act,' 64.

48 Dick, 'Deportation under the Immigration Act,' 64. Unlike his fellow defendants, Charitonoff lived a comparatively uneventful life after 1919. While his political sympathies may have remained on the Left, he ended his wartime political and journalistic activism. From 1920 to

his death in 1960, Charitonoff was a sales manager for J. Werier & Co., a retail and wholesale furniture and hardware business established by his brother-in-law, Joseph Werier. Charitonoff's nephew through marriage, Val Werier, a noted columnist with the *Winnipeg Tribune* and *Winnipeg Free Press*, and author of at least one article on the Strike, knew his uncle well, but couldn't recall Charitonoff ever speaking about the events of 1919. Werier only discovered Charitonoff's role in the 1919 crisis via press clippings after Charitonoff's death. See Manitoba Vital Statistics, at http://vitalstats.gov.mb.ca. For Charitonoff's obituary, see *Winnipeg Free Press*, 22 February 1960. Joseph Werier's obituary appears in *Winnipeg Free Press*, 1 March 1956. Val Werier, 'Low Wages, Long Hours Led to Strike (Winnipeg General Strike, 1919),' *Winnipeg Free Press*, 18 June 1994, A6. Telephone conversations, Tom Mitchell with Val Werier, Friday, 13 and 17 June 2008.

49 LAC, RG 13, Access 87–88/103: box 36, file 9-A-1688, pocket #1, Andrews to Meighen (telegram), 17 June 1919.

50 LAC, RG 13, Access 87–88/103: box 36, file 9-A-1688, pocket #1, The Government of the Dominion of Canada in Account with Travers Sweatman, Winnipeg, 14 August 1919.

51 LAC, RG 13, Access 87–88/103: box 36, file 9-A-1688, pocket #1, The Government of the Dominion of Canada in Account with J.B. Coyne, K.C., Winnipeg, 14 August 1919.

52 LAC, RG 13, Access 87–88/103: box 36, file 9-A-1688, pocket #1, The Department of Justice in Account with Andrews, Andrews & Company, Winnipeg, 16 August 1919. The bill also included $1196 for work by Andrews's legal partners S.L. Goldstine, Herbert Andrews, and F.M. Burbidge.

53 At the end of August, F.M. Burbidge submitted additional accounts associated with the sedition cases. NAC, Justice, Access, RG 13, pocket #1, F.M. Burbidge to W. Stuart Edwards, 28 August 1919.

54 LAC, RG 13, Access 87–88/103: box 36, file 9-A-1688, pocket #1, Angus A. McLean, Comptroller, Royal North West Mounted Police, to The Deputy Minister, Department of Justice, 8 August 1919.

55 LAC, RG 13, Access 87–88/103: box 36, file 9-A-1688, pocket #1, W. Stuart Edwards to The Comptroller, Royal North West Mounted Police, 3 September 1919.

56 LAC, RG 13, Access 87–88/103: box 36, file 9-A-1688, pocket #1, W. Stuart Edwards to The Comptroller, Royal North West Mounted Police, 8 September 1919.

57 LAC, RG 13, Access 87–88/103: box 36, file 9-A-1688, pocket #1, Angus L. McLean, Comptroller, Royal North West Mounted Police, to

W. Stuart Edwards, Assistant Deputy Minister of Justice, 9 September 1919.

58 LAC, RG 13, Access 87–88/103: box 36, file 9-A-1688, pocket #1, Andrews to W. Stuart Edwards, 15 September 1919.

59 LAC, RG 13, Access 87–88/103: box 36, file 9-A-1688, pocket #1, W. Stuart Edwards to Andrews, 19 September 1919.

60 LAC, RG 13, Access 87–88/103: box 36, file 9-A-1688, pocket #1, Andrews to Doherty, 21 May 1920.

61 LAC, RG 13, Access 87–88/103: box 36, file 9-A-1688, pocket #1, W. Stuart Edwards to the Minister of Justice Re Winnipeg Strike, 19 September 1919.

62 LAC, RG 13, Access 87–88/103: box 36, file 9-A-1688, pocket #1, Andrews to Doherty, 6 October 1919.

63 Canada, House of Commons, *Debates*, 7 May 1919, 2173.

64 *Statutes of Canada, 1919* (Ottawa, 1919), 121.

65 Canada, House of Commons, *Debates*, 7 May 1919, 2172.

66 Canada, House of Commons, *Debates*, 8 May 1919, 2244.

67 Library and Archives Canada, RG 2, vol. 1233, PC 2106, 10 October 1919.

68 LAC, RG 13, Access 87–88/103: box 36, file 9-A-1688, pocket #1, E.D. Sutherland, Auditor General, to E.L. Newcombe, Deputy Minister of Justice, 3 February 1920 (letter).

69 By Order-in-Council, cabinet closed the Public Safety Branch on 16 January 1919. See LAC, RG 13, PC 104, 16 January 1919.

70 LAC, RG 13, Access 87–88/103: box 36, file 9-A-1688, pocket #1, E.L. Newcombe to E.D. Sutherland, Auditor General, 6 February 1920 (letter).

71 After 1977, the auditor general's role was expanded to include the broader mandate of how the government administered its business. The authority of the auditor general did not extend to these matters in 1919. See archival description of the Office of the Auditor General Fonds, R711-36-9-E (Series), National Archives of Canada.

72 Jonathan Swainger, *The Canadian Department of Justice and the Completion of Confederation, 1867–1878* (Vancouver, 2000), 131–2.

73 LAC, RG 13, Access 87–88/103: box 36, file 9-A-1688, pocket #1, Andrews to Doherty, 6 October 1919, and W. Stuart Edwards to Andrews, 16 October 1919 (telegrams).

74 LAC, RG 13, Access 87–88/103: box 36, file 9-A-1688, pocket #1, Andrews to Doherty, 6 October 1919, and W. Stuart Edwards to Andrews, 20 October 1919 (telegrams).

75 LAC, RG 2, vol. 1235, PC 2244, 6 November 1919.

76 LAC, RG 2, vol. 1235, PC 239, 31 January 1920.

77 In addition to the hefty lawyers' fees mentioned, the federal government had to send cheques to the attorney general of Manitoba for jurors' fees ($14,184), the cost of a court reporter ($4111), and the transportation and lodging of witnesses ($13,576). Dominion of Canada, *Sessional Papers*, 1920, vol. 4 (Ottawa 1921), part 3, *Sessional Paper No. 1*, Auditor General's Report, part ZZ, War Appropriation Act: Expenditures, Justice Department, ZZ13.

78 The cheques included S.L. Goldstein ($8376), T. Sweatman ($4162.50), Herbert Andrews ($1255.50), J.B. Coyne, K.C. ($7150), I. Pitblado, K.C. ($6615), and A.J. Andrews, K.C. ($3201.05). See LAC, RG 13, Access 87–88/103: box 36, file 9-A-1688, pocket #1, W.S. Edwards to Andrews, Andrews, Burbidge & Bastedo, 18 May 1920.

79 LAC, RG 13, Access 87–88/103: box 36, file 9-A-1688, pocket #1, Andrews to W. Stuart Edwards, 21 May 1920.

80 LAC, RG 13, Access 87–88/103: box 36, file 9-A-1688, pocket #1, Andrews to Doherty, 21 May 1920.

81 See handwritten summary of payments to Andrews et al. contained in Justice Department files, item 638 (3 pages). LAC, RG 13, Access 87–88/103: box 36, file 9-A-1688, pocket #1. The 1919–20 costs appear in W. Stuart Edwards to Andrews, Andrews, Burbidge & Bastedo, 3 July 1920, LAC, RG 13, Access 87–88/103: box 36, file 9-A-1688, pocket #1. Dominion of Canada, *Sessional Papers*, 1920, vol. 4 (Ottawa, 1921), part 3, *Sessional Paper No. 1*, Auditor General's Report, part ZZ, War Appropriation Act: Expenditures, Justice Department, ZZ13. The costs for the R.B. Russell appeal to the Privy Council appear in Dominion of Canada, *Sessional Papers*, 1922, vol. 1 (Ottawa, 1923), part 2, *Sessional Paper No. 1*, Auditor General's Report, War Appropriation Act: Expenditures, Justice Department, L46.

82 *Statutes of Canada, 1920*, 385.

83 The amounts were Andrews $5150, Pitblado $300, Coyne $2171, and Sweatman $1950. This doesn't include 'miscellaneous' fees and a bill from the McDonald Detective Agency. LAC, RG 13, Access 87–88/103: box 36, file 9-A-1688, pocket #1, Andrews to W. Stuart Edwards, 7 October 1920.

84 LAC, RG 13, Access 87–88/103: box 36, file 9-A-1688, pocket #2, W. Stuart Edwards to Deputy Minister of Justice, 20 October 1920.

85 *Manitoba Free Press*, Monday, 18 August 1919.

86 *Manitoba Free Press*, 20 August 1919.

87 *Manitoba Free Press*, 21 August 1919.

88 *Manitoba Free Press*, 21 August 1919.

89 *Manitoba Free Press*, 20 August 1919.

90 'Returned Men Demand Aliens Be Sent Home,' *Manitoba Free Press*, 4 February 1919, 6.
91 *Manitoba Free Press*, 21 August 1919.
92 The Citizens' League included the president, Isaac Pitblado; first vice-president, A.K. Godfrey; second vice-president, Dr W.F. Taylor; third vice-president, Major N.K. McIvor; honorary secretary, Fletcher Sparling; and honorary treasurer, W.H. McWilliams. Also on the executive were A.L. Crossin, D.J. Scott, Burton McLean, Thomas Boyd, F.E.H. Luke, George Guy, F.W. Adams, W.A.T. Sweatman, Capt. F.G. Thompson, Dr E.S. Moorhead, George W. Markle, Edward Parnell, A.L. Bond, J.E. Botterell, A.B. Stovel, C.C. Ferguson, Robert Jacob, R.A.C. Manning, Duncan Cameron, G.J. Baker, Louis Leipsic, George Munro, E.C. Ryan, C.J. Brittain, T.J. Langford, M.F. Christie, D.B. Mulligan, J.A. Woods, Horace Chevrier, J.C. Waugh, D.A. Clark, W.W. Richardson, H.M. Tucker, A.E. Rowland, G.W. Northwood, Thomas Sharpe, Dr Halpenny, R.H. Smith, J.G. Sullivan, C.W.O. Lane, A.J. Bonnett, C.A. Richardson, R.L. Smith, D.N. Finnie, Thomas L. Waldon, Norman Leach, H.D. Campbell, S.M. Campbell, and D. Drehmer. Although neither Botterell nor Thompson were listed in the Citizens' congratulatory telegram to Ottawa, both were clearly members.
93 *Manitoba Free Press*, 19 November 1919, 11.
94 *Manitoba Free Press*, 6 November 1919, 5.
95 *Manitoba Free Press*, 23 September 1919.
96 *Manitoba Free Press*, 8 August 1923.
97 Stovel attended the conference as a delegate of the Winnipeg branch of the Canadian Manufacturers' Association. *Manitoba Free Press*, 9 October 1919, 5.
98 Report of the Proceedings of the National Conference on Character Education in Relation to Canadian Citizenship (Winnipeg, 1919), 36.

14 DUTY TO GOD, COUNTRY, AND FAMILY

1 Provincial Archives of Manitoba, Robert Graham fonds, 112–13.
2 Provincial Archives of Manitoba, MG 19, A 14-2, no. 54, Crown Counsel's Address to the Jury (A.J. Andrews K.C.), 23 December 1919 (hereafter, PAM, Crown Counsel's Address), 1.
3 PAM, 'Particulars,' 20th day of January, A.D. 1920, Alfred Joseph Andrews, Counsel for the Crown, 5–6.
4 'A.J. Andrews Makes Sensational Statement,' *Winnipeg Tribune*, 15 August 1919. See also LAC, RG 13, Access 87–88/103: box 36, file 9-A-1688, pocket #2, Andrews to Meighen, 25 June 1919.
5 For a discussion of the granting of bail to the Strike leaders, see Leslie

Katz, 'Some Legal Consequences of the Winnipeg General Strike,' *Manitoba Law Journal* (1970), 39–52.

6 LAC, RG 13, Access 87–88/103: box 36, file 9-A-1688, pocket #1, Andrews to Honourable E.L. Newcombe, Deputy Minister of Justice, 18 September 1919.

7 Metcalfe, born in Portage la Prairie in 1870, was an effective campaigner for the Liberals. Jack Walker summarized Metcalfe's judicial reputation: 'On the bench Metcalfe displayed an ability to handle complex points of law. He was regarded as an able judge; he enjoyed lecturing at the law school. Though given to occasional fits of bad temper and biting sarcasm, he was generally well liked in the legal profession.' J.S. Walker, Q.C., unpublished manuscript, June 1991, 115–16.

8 E.P. Thompson, 'Subduing the Jury,' *London Review of Books* 8, no. 22 (18 December 1986), 12.

9 The complete questionnaire ran as follows: 'Give approximate age from appearance. Is he married? Is he a returned man: if so was he a volunteer or a conscript? How many children, if any? If sons, did they go to war? If they went to the war, did they go as volunteers or conscripts? Do they personally know any of the men being tried for Sedition or are they friends or friendly? What are his views as to the Union Government War Policy? Is he a Laurier Liberal, Conservative or Unionist? Is he a Socialist? Is he an O.B.U.? What is his present occupation? Has he a trade? Was he ever a member of a Union? What are his views on Bolshevism? Is he now a member of a Union? What does he think of Trades Unionist Leaders and their methods during the last twelve months? What does he think of the Winnipeg Strike? Does he think it was justified? What does he think of the Citizens' Committee of 1000 and their work? Does he blame the Government for taking methods to put down the strike? Does he blame the Government for the shooting which took place during the riot? Does he own his own home? Is he in your opinion liable to be sentimental in his judgment? Do you recommend him for the position?' Col. Starnes conveyed the RNWMP actions to Commissioner Perry, complete with a copy of the questionnaire. If the use of the RNWMP was a routine procedure in such investigations, Starnes wouldn't have needed to let Perry know. See LAC, Records of the Royal Canadian Mounted Police, RG 18, Royal Canadian Mounted Police, vol. 3314, file HV-1, vol. 6, 'Winnipeg General Strike and Riot,' Supt. C. Starnes to the Commissioner of the Royal North West Mounted Police, 5 November 1919. A bill from the McDonald Detective Agency submitted to the Justice Department by Andrews on 5 January 1920 indicates that the agency was

involved in this jury investigation. See NAC, Justice, RG13, Access, Pocket #1, Invoice, McDonald Detective Agency, 5 January 1920.

10 Access to the jury list by anyone other than the officers of the court responsible for summoning a jury panel was strictly prohibited. Under article 180 of the Criminal Code, anyone who influenced or attempted 'to influence, by threats or bribes or other corrupt means, any juryman in his conduct, whether such person has been sworn as a juryman or not' was subject to a sentence of two years' imprisonment. The Code also prohibited wilful 'attempts in any other way to obstruct, pervert or defeat the course of justice.' *The Revised Statutes of Canada, 1927*, vol. 1 (Ottawa, 1927), sec. 180 (b) (d), 720. The provincial Jury Act stipulated that 'neither the jury panel nor the name of any person on such panel, shall be communicated, either verbally or otherwise, to any person whomsoever, until such panel is returned into court by the sheriff.' This provision could be set aside only 'upon an order of the court or of a judge.' *Statutes of Manitoba, Consolidated Amendments* (Winnipeg, 1924), sec. 48, chap. 108, 798.

11 Jack Walker, *The Great Canadian Sedition Trials: The Courts and the Winnipeg General Strike 1919–1920* (Winnipeg, 2004), 6–7.

12 'Climax Reached on Monday in Great Fight over Trial Jury,' *Western Labor News*, 30 January 1920, 1.

13 Walker, *The Great Canadian Sedition Trials*, 176. For Deputy Sheriff Pyniger's testimony, see *Winnipeg Telegram*, 26 January 1920. For McMurray, see Masters, *Winnipeg General Strike*, 121.

14 Walker, *The Great Canadian Sedition Trials*, 176–7. 'Climax Reached on Monday.'

15 *Winnipeg Evening Telegram*, 27 November 1919. We are forced to rely often upon newspaper reports: only Andrews's summation to the jury and Metcalfe's charge to the jury remain extant.

16 On the power to reject jurors, see E.P. Thompson, 'Subduing the Jury.' *Winnipeg Evening Telegram*, 27 November 1919.

17 The amended Criminal Code had been assented to on 7 July 1919, and had been in effect since October.

18 *Winnipeg Evening Telegram*, 27 November 1919.

19 The jurors were farmers Edward Heney and Theo Nugets [Nugent] from Sanford, T.W. Smith from Emerson, William Hassett from St François Xavier, Roy Tolton from Otterburne, Albert A.[E.] Anderson from East Selkirk, Joseph Frechette from St Pierre, D.H. Pritchard from Carmen, and William Heale from Teulon; merchants William McClymont from Hazelridge and Harl Woodhead from Morris; and manager C.T. Fisher from Norwood. *Winnipeg Evening Tribune*, 24

December 1919. Andrews used the same jury selection technique for
the trials of the remaining Strike leaders beginning in January 1920.
He told Charles Doherty that there were 250 names on the jury list,
and that he was taking steps to obtain the list and to make arrangements to secure information about potential jurors. See LAC, RG 13,
Access 87–88/103: box 36, file 9-A-1688, pocket #1, Andrews to
Doherty, 25 December 1919. The private McDonald Detective Agency
was retained for this purpose. See LAC, RG 13, Access 87–88/103:
box 36, file 9-A-1688, pocket #2, Macdonald [*sic*] Detective Agency
bill for service, 5 January 1920. The jury was composed of D. Bruce,
Carman; G.C. Glenny, St Marks; A.H. Quick, Emerson; George Morrison, J.M. Henderson, and John Stephens, Hazelridge; James Jack and
James Kirkpatrick, Ridgeville; A. Davidson, Sperling; Herman Johnson, Lundar; Thos. Spence, Greenridge; and Alex Sinclair, Tyndall.
See *Manitoba Free Press*, 25 January 1920. In order to get the 12
jurors, Andrews had stood aside 31 others.

20 *Winnipeg Evening Tribune*, 29 November 1919.
21 *Winnipeg Evening Tribune*, 15 December 1919.
22 PAM, Crown Counsel's Address, 143.
23 *Winnipeg Evening Telegram*, 22 December 1919.
24 *Winnipeg Evening Tribune*, 22 December 1919. See also *Winnipeg
Evening Telegram*, 22 December 1919. In cases as unprecedented as
the prosecution of R.B. Russell and the Strike leaders, it is hard to
imagine what 'authority' Metcalfe had in mind. Perhaps the most obvious example of his bias was his collaboration with the Citizens to suppress the fact that the trials were instituted under the legal provisions
for a private prosecution.
25 When Dixon also asked, 'Is Hugh Phillips, K.C., representing His
majesty in the case of The King vs. F.J. Dixon, by virtue of being
retained or instructed by the Attorney-General of Manitoba?' the
answer was 'Yes.' Asking by what method Phillips had been
appointed, Dixon was told, 'The same as in all cases where the Department retains counsel, namely, by the Attorney-General without any
Order-in-Council.' For the exchange, see *Journals of the Legislative
Assembly of Manitoba* (Winnipeg, 1920), 69–70. The Manitoba Attorney General prosecuted Dixon for seditious libel, but he was acquitted.
On the Dixon case, see Harry Gutkin and Mildred Gutkin, *Profiles in
Dissent* (Edmonton, 1997), 36–43, and *Dixon's Address to the Jury and
Judge Galt's Charge to the Jury* in *Rex v. Dixon* (Winnipeg, 1920).
26 PAM, Crown Counsel's Address, 143–4. In May 1920, Justice Minister
Doherty in the House of Commons confirmed that 'the Dominion
Government [was] represented by counsel' at the sedition trials and

that the Dominion government had 'retained' counsel for the trial. While the Dominion government could *retain* counsel for any purpose it chose, it had no constitutional authority to prosecute criminal cases in Manitoba other than authority through the War Measures Act. For the full exchange with Ernest Lapointe, see Canada, House of Commons, *Debates*, 10 May 1920, 2181.

27 'General Strike Must Paralyze Industries to Be Effective,' *Manitoba Free Press*, 20 December 1919, 19.

28 PAM, Crown Counsel's Address, 6–7.

29 Ibid., 8.

30 *Evening Tribune*, 25 November 1919.

31 Ibid.

32 PAM, Crown Counsel's Address, 9–10. Andrews anticipated the defence claims that section 590 of the Criminal Code protected strikers from prosecution if they were engaged in acts taken for the 'purpose of furthering a trade combination.' This protection, Andrews noted, was qualified by the words 'unless such act is punishable by statute,' and all the acts included in the indictment were punishable by the Criminal Code, the Industrial Disputes Investigation Act, or provincial statutes prohibiting the breaking of contracts. PAM, Crown Counsel's Address, 10–11.

33 For a discussion of the law of sedition as it applied to the Russell case, see Desmond H. Brown, 'The Craftsmanship of Bias: Sedition and the Winnipeg General Strike,' *Manitoba Law Journal* 14 (1984), 1–33.

34 Crown Counsel's Address, 4. See *R. v. Manshrick* (1916), 27 C.C.C. 17 at 24, 32 D.L.R. 584, 27 Man. R. 94, quoted in William E. Conklin, 'The Origin of the Law of Sedition,' *Criminal Law Quarterly* 15 (1973), 283. 'Sedition Case Heard at Morden,' *Manitoba Free Press*, 2 November 1916, 6. 'Sedition Case to Be Heard Today,' *Manitoba Free Press*, 23 November 1916, 5. 'Manshrick Fined $700 for Sedition,' *Manitoba Free Press*, 27 November 1916.

35 PAM, Crown Counsel's Address, 4–5.

36 Ibid., 47.

37 Ibid., 5.

38 Ibid., 19.

39 Philip Viscount Snowden, *An Autobiography: vol. I, 1864–1919* (London, 1943), 473.

40 PAM, Crown Counsel's Address, 45.

41 Ibid., 46.

42 Ibid., 43.

43 The indictment was mainly the handiwork of Pitblado, who, Andrews recalled, 'prepared the cases for me so thoroughly that all I had to do

was to follow his instructions.' Roy St George Stubbs, 'A.J. Andrews: Nestor of the Manitoba Bar,' *Canadian Bar Review* 24, no. 3 (March 1946), 193. Pitblado kept a copy of the indictment in his personal papers. See the indexed copy of the indictment in PAM, MG 14, C 64, box 4, Pitblado 'Scrapbook – Winnipeg General Strike Trials,' 1–19.

44 PAM, Crown Counsel's Address, 20.

45 Ibid., 23.

46 St George Stubbs, 'A.J. Andrews: Nestor of the Manitoba Bar,' 185.

47 PAM, Western Legal Archives Biography File, Joseph Thorson interview, 'A.J. Andrews.'

48 Roy St George Stubbs, 'Life Story of A.J. Andrews,' *Winnipeg Free Press Magazine*, 15 June 1940, 5.

49 Telephone conversation, Tom Mitchell with Wallace Tolton (Swan River, MB), Roy Tolton's son, 24 November 2007.

50 Telephone conversation, Tom Mitchell with Lucien Fréchette, Joseph Fréchette's son, 20 November 2007.

51 *Rockwood Municipality – 100 Years of History* (Stonewall, 1982), 236–7.

52 Sanford–Ferndale History Committee, *Sanford–Ferndale 1871–1987* (Sanford, 1989), 423–4.

53 Neil Semple, *The Lord's Dominion: The History of Canadian Methodism* (Montreal and Kingston, 1996), 63.

54 PAM, Crown Counsel's Address, 39.

55 J.S. Walker, Q.C., unpublished manuscript, June 1991, 115–16.

56 PAM, Western Legal Archives Biography File, Joseph Thorson interview, 'A.J. Andrews,' Stubbs, n.p.

57 PAM, Legal Archives of Manitoba, A.J. Andrews, Biography File, Notes from the Records of the Benchers of the Law Society of Manitoba.

58 Walker, unpublished manuscript.

59 PAM, Western Legal Archives Biography File, Joseph Thorson interview, 'A.J. Andrews.'

60 On Rev. Alfred Andrews, Sr, see the report of his death in the *Manitoba Free Press*, 19 November 1919. On Ivens's removal from McDougall in June 1918, see *Manitoba Free Press*, 19 June 1918.

61 PAM, Crown Counsel's Address, 61.

62 Ibid.

63 Telephone conversation, Tom Mitchell with Mrs Hassett and her husband Frederick, William's son, 20 November 2007.

64 PAM, Crown Counsel's Address, 62.

65 Ibid., 24.

66 *Winnipeg Free Press*, 1 June 1933.

67 Douglas Owram, *The Government Generation: Canadian Intellectuals and the State 1900–1945* (Toronto, 1986), 80.

68 *Winnipeg Evening Tribune*, 18 December 1919.

69 PAM, Crown Counsel's Address, 24–5.

70 Email to Tom Mitchell from Jane Stevenson, volunteer with the Valley Regional Library and Morris Museum Archives, 25 November 2007. Telephone conversation, Tom Mitchell with Barbara Brown (Toronto), a relative of Maria Jane Haining (Woodhead's wife), 28 November 2007.

71 History Committee, Dugald Women's Institute, *Springfield – 1st Rural Municipality in Manitoba 1873–1973* (Dugald, 1974), 191.

72 For an astute analysis of the SPC in 1919, see Gerald Friesen, "'Yours in Revolt": Regionalism, Socialism and the Western Canadian Labour Movement,' *Labour/Le Travail* 1 (1976), 139–57.

73 Anna Tillenius, Learned Friends: Reminiscences – Pitblado & Hoskins, 1882–1974 (Winnipeg, 1974), 37.

74 PAM, Crown Counsel's Address, 39.

75 Ibid., 31.

76 Ibid., 27–8.

77 Ibid., 30.

78 Ibid., 29.

79 Ibid., 66. Effective 26 October 1917, after negotiating an armistice with the new Bolshevik regime, Germany 'transferred the best part of its eastern army to the Western Front, in preparation for what it hoped to be the war-winning offensives against the French and British.' John Keegan, *The First World War* (New York, 1998), 342. The next fall, the Canadian Expeditionary Force indeed suffered great losses at Cambrai (just south of Flanders), which, for rhetorical purposes, Andrews annexed to Flanders Plain. See 'Canadian [*sic*] Face 100,000 Germans North Cambrai,' *Manitoba Free Press,* 2 October 1918, and 'Canadians Win Battle of Cambrai,' *Manitoba Free Press,* 7 October 1918, 9. Under the heading 'Western Canadian Casualties,' the *Manitoba Free Press*, 14 October 1918, carried a report including hundreds of names of soldiers from the western provinces 'Killed,' 'Wounded,' 'Gassed,' 'Died of Wounds,' or in that dreaded category, 'Missing.'

80 PAM, Crown Counsel's Address, 26.

81 Ibid., 26.

82 Theodore Nugent – misspelled in press reports as 'Nugets' – farmed in the Sanford region southwest of Winnipeg. Sanford–Ferndale History Committee, *Sanford–Ferndale 1871–1987*, 423–4. For the Great War record see 210–11.

83 *Rockwood Municipality – 100 Years of History* (Stonewall, 1982), 236–7. On the service of Frank Heale in the Great War, see p. 151.

84 PAM, Crown Counsel's Address, 69.

85 'The Shoals of Pernicious Leadership,' *Winnipeg Citizen*, 22 May 1919.

86 PAM, Crown Counsel's Address, 69–70.

87 St Clements Historical Committee, *The East Side of the Red: A Centennial Project of the Rural Municipality of St. Clements 1884–1984* (East Selkirk, 1984), 440–2. Telephone conversation, Tom Mitchell with Allan Anderson, Albert's grandson, 30 November 2007.

88 PAM, Crown Counsel's Address, 72.

89 E.J. McMurray had charged the Citizens' Committee with committing 'sedition, as criminal as that which [Russell] was accused.' *Winnipeg Evening Tribune*, 10 December 1919.

90 PAM, Crown Counsel's Address, 144.

91 Ibid., 38.

92 Ibid., 50.

93 Ibid., 71.

94 Ibid., 72.

95 Ibid., 78.

96 Ibid., 76. The *Marxian Socialist* was the newspaper of the Socialist Party of North America. The SPNA was not on the list of banned organizations in the original PC 2384, but was added a month later. Founded in 1911 by former members of the Socialist Party of Canada who objected to the SPC's reformist tendencies, the SPNA remained a marginal political organization with about 100 members in locals situated in southern Ontario. See Ian Angus, *Canadian Bolsheviks: The Early Years of the Communist Party of Canada* (Montreal, 1981), 6. Angus has found no surviving set of the *Marxian Socialist*. A couple of individual issues survive, but do not name an editor. Email, Ian Angus to Tom Mitchell, 28 November 2007. See also Peter Weinrich, *Social Protest from the Left in Canada 1870–1970: A Bibliography* (Toronto, 1970), 399, no. 5212.

97 PAM, Crown Counsel's address, 77. Gerald Friesen says, 'From the context and content, I have concluded that the articles entitled "Revolution," "Industrial Ownership," "The Way Out," and "Reconstruction or Revolution" (*Machinists' Bulletin*, November and December 1918, March and April 1919) were written by Russell, Johns, or their associates.' Gerald Friesen, *River Road: Essays on Manitoba and Prairie History* (Winnipeg, 1996), 145 n. 14.

98 PAM, Crown Counsel's Address, 77.

99 See the events of 1 June in chapter 5.

100 PAM, Crown Counsel's Address, 110, 143–4.

101 *Manitoba Free Press*, 7 December 1899, 4. For an account of the 1899 election, see Larry Fisk, 'Controversy on the Prairies – Issues in the General Provincial Elections of Manitoba 1870–1969,' PhD thesis (University of Alberta, 1975), 170–83.

102 PAM, Crown Counsel's Address, 66–7.

103 Ibid., 96.

104 Ibid., 102.

105 Ibid., 104.

106 PAM, The King vs. R.B. Russell Seditious Conspiracy, 23 December 1919, Mr Justice Metcalfe's Charge to the Jury, 10–11.

107 Ibid., 61.

108 Ibid., 43–6.

109 PAM, Crown Counsel's Address, 143.

110 Provincial Archives of Manitoba, The King vs. R.B. Russell Seditious Conspiracy, 23 December 1919, Mr Justice Metcalfe's Charge to the Jury, 31. See Brown, 'The Craftsmanship of Bias,' 1–33. It is believed that the stress of this and the other Strike trials destroyed Metcalfe's health. He took a long vacation in the spring and summer of 1920, but when he returned he had no energy or capacity for sustained work. He was appointed to the Manitoba Court of Appeal, but was hospitalized in February 1922, and was dead by early April. For obituaries, see *Manitoba Free Press*, 4 April 1922; *Winnipeg Tribune*, 5 April 1922; and Provincial Archives of Manitoba, Western Canadian Legal History, Biographical File, T.L. Metcalfe.

EPILOGUE: ECHO

1 LAC, Records of the Royal Canadian Mounted Police, RG 18, RCMP, vol. 3314, file HV-1, vol. 6, 'Winnipeg General Strike and Riot,' RCMP Report, 7 April 1920.

2 Adam Smith, *An Inquiry into the Nature and Causes of the Wealth of Nations*, vol.1, ed. R.H. Campbell and A.S. Skinner (Indianapolis, 1981), I.viii.13, 84.

3 *Manitoba Free Press*, 20 April 1920.

4 Ed Parnell, Fletcher Sparling, A.K. Godfrey, W.P. Riley, H.M. Agnew, D.A. Clark, D.J. Dyson, and M.F. Christie were the Citizens. Ironmaster Thomas Deacon, general manager of the Winnipeg Electric Railway A.W. McLimont, and W.H. Carter had worked closely with the Citizens during the Strike. As well, a number of the board members seem to have been close relatives of former Citizens. 'Manitoba Employers' Association Annual,' *Manitoba Free Press*, 21 February 1921, 4.

5 On Roland and his possible involvement in the publication of the *Winnipeg Citizen*, see chapter 2, n. 195.

6 Museum of Manitoba, *The Payroll and Labor Legislation Review* 1, no. 1 (March 1922). The authors would like to thank Sharon Reilly, curator of social history at the Museum, for providing copies of *The Payroll* and *Special News Bulletins* and related materials on the Citizens' Committee of 100 and Citizens' Committee of 1000.

7 Glenbow Museum, Thomas Underwood fonds, M-1261-58, Employers' Association of Manitoba Newsletters, *Special News Bulletin* #321, 23 May 1923, 2.

8 Ibid., *Special News Bulletin* (confidential bulletin to members) #273, Employers' Association of Manitoba, 8 November 1922.

9 Ibid., *Special News Bulletin* #276, 15 November 1922. In 1931, Roland, on behalf of the Employers' Association, urged R.B. Bennett that the authority of the courts be enlarged for 'the purpose of investigating and keeping in touch with the revolutionary propaganda and the activities of the Communists in Canada.' C.F. Roland, managing secretary of the Employers' Association to R.B. Bennett, 21 April 1931, quoted in Aloysius Balawyder, *Canadian–Soviet Relations between the World Wars* (Toronto, 1972), 280–1.

10 Philip Taft, 'Violence in American Labor Disputes,' *Annals of the American Academy of Political and Social Science* 364 (March 1966), 138.

11 Thomas Underwood fonds, *Special News Bulletin* #275, 15 November 1922.

12 Ibid.

13 Museum of Manitoba, Chas. F. Roland, General – Secretary to the Honorable John Bracken, 14 December 1922, attached to *Special News Bulletin*, 20 November 1922. For an account of the schools that the *Bulletin* objected to, see D.I. Victor, 'Radical Jewish Education and Its Educational Institutions in Winnipeg (1914–1983),' in Daniel Stone, ed., *Jewish Life and Times*, vol. 3, *Jewish Radicalism in Winnipeg, 1905–1960* (Winnipeg, 2003), 77–82.

14 *The Canadian Forum* 1, no. 1 (October 1920), 30–4.

15 O.D. Skelton, 'Making Bolsheviks,' *Queen's Quarterly* (January–March 1920), 319–21. See also W.C. Clark, 'Oscar Douglas Skelton (1878–1941) obituary,' Foreign Affairs and International Trade Canada, 2 September 2008, from the *Proceedings of the Royal Society of Canada, 1941*, 141–7, http://www.international.gc.ca/odskelton/obit-necro_clark.aspx?lang=eng, 8 January 2009.

16 *Manitoba Free Press*, 8 April 1929.

17 *Manitoba Free Press*, 23 May 1929.

18 Roy St George Stubbs, 'Life Story of A.J. Andrews,' *Winnipeg Free
   Press Magazine*, 15 June 1940, 5.
19 Travers Sweatman's son Alan became a principal with Thompson
   Dorfman Sweatman LLP, which today has 69 lawyers. Its offices are
   on the 19th to the 23rd floors of 201 Portage Avenue. Thanks to Trevor
   Anderson and Roland Penner for explaining the historical permutations
   of Winnipeg law firms.
20 St George Stubbs, 'Life Story of A.J. Andrews.'

Index

and racism, 126–30, 132, 275–6;
replaced by Citizens' League,
292–5, 318; and returned soldiers, 107–12, 120, 123–4,
126–30, 134–5; and Robson
Commission, 196; and Special
Police, 136–43; volunteers, 36,
44, 67, 78, 99–100, 116, 120,
123, 125, 136–7, 176, 363n92;
Winnipeg Citizen, Committee
appears as, 16–17
Citizens' Industrial Alliance, 173
Citizens' League of Winnipeg,
292–5, 318, 413n92
Citizens Protective Association,
15–16
Clark, Douglas A., 64, 343–4n148,
345n161, 413n92, 421n4
Clarke, G.B., 282
class, 34–5; Dafoe on, 75; fluidity,
31–2; middle-class values, 33;
and status, 24, 30, 33–4, 65;
three-class model, 30, 333n120;
Weber on, 34; working-class
hierarchy, 34. *See also* Winnipeg, class and ethnicity
closed shop, 319, 321
Coetzee, J.M., 152
Coleman, D'Alton C., 144
Collins, Dr Herbert O., 12
commercial society, 5, 7, 9, 11, 79,
88–9, 325n9, 337n40
Committee of Forty Citizens, 50,
170
Committee of One Hundred (Winnipeg Patriotic Fund), 50
common law, 42, 56, 58, 74, 76,
80, 84, 86, 88–9, 102, 125, 137,
217, 219–20

communism, 252, 319–20; First
International, 19, 24, 326n4;
Second International, 19, 160
Communist Manifesto, The, 251–2,
314
Connor, Ralph. *See* Gordon,
Charles
conspiracy. *See* Bolshevism
constitution, 14, 27–8, 56–7,
70–92, 95–6, 99–100, 102–3,
106, 108, 118, 127, 134–7, 154,
157, 160, 168, 173–4, 201, 203,
211, 239–40, 242, 245, 256, 268,
276, 280, 293, 297, 299–302,
308, 314–16, 321, 348n11; 'constituted authority,' 27, 29, 42–4,
56–8, 78, 80, 116, 252, 256–7,
266, 268, 277, 375–6n19; and
contracts, 84; and criminal prosecutions, 100, 148–9, 175–6,
179, 185, 187, 190, 205, 213,
238, 249–50, 301, 416–17n26;
and general strikes, 85, 106; and
immigration hearings, 216–20,
230–1, 235, 250, 280; and individual rights, 76, 89; and postal
service, 78; and the press, 82–4;
and Special Police, 136–7,
152–3, 159; and Winnipeg
police 78, 106, 272. *See also*
permission signs
Coppins, Fred, 152, 155–8, 229,
283–4, 321, 372–3n35
Coyne, J.B., 7, 64, 101, 113, 145,
155, 204, 301–2, 382–3n24,
401–2n58; age, 355n135; background, 57, 63, 342n136, 381n7;
Committee of One Hundred, 51;
compensation from Ottawa,

4n148, 350–1n57; and Citizens'
Committee of One Hundred,
48–9; and Citizens' League, 294,
413n92; describes Citizens'
Committee of 1000, 51–2, 86,
274–7; and Employers' Association, 421n4; as mayor, 322; and
Winnipeg Citizens' Alliance,
47–9, 63, 175
Parry, David M., 173
*Payroll and Labor Legislation
Review, The*, 319
Penner, Jacob, 355n146
Penner, Roland, 4, 423n19
Permanent Court of International
Justice, 249
permission signs, 11–12, 24, 27,
29, 43, 72–3, 76–8, 96, 107–8,
116, 153, 268
Perry, F.B., 104, 130–1, 143–5,
149, 159, 179, 186, 191, 193,
197, 220, 243, 288, 362n58,
393n43, 414–15n9
Phillips, Hugh, 80–1, 164, 193,
195, 205–6, 210–11, 351n64,
416n25
Pigeon, E. Leslie, 294
Pitblado, Edward, 109, 310
Pitblado, Isaac, 7, 32, 60, 76, 78,
101–2, 109, 131, 133, 141, 145,
155, 216, 231, 274, 301, 310,
382–3n24; addresses Moose Jaw
delegation, 115–17; age,
355n135; arrest of Strike leaders, 166, 177–8, 184–5, 343–
4n148, 417–18n43; background
and career, 37–9, 41, 55, 63,
381n7; calls for martial law,
120; as Citizens' spokesperson,

24, 37, 42, 64, 128, 196, 205–6;
Committee of One Hundred, 51;
and common law, 85–6; compensation from Ottawa, 104,
287–8, 291, 412nn78, 83; and
Fort William delegation, 54, 57,
65, 341n114; life after Strike,
322; and police loyalty oath,
113; president of Citizens'
League, 294, 413n92; prosecution of Strike leaders, 238, 305;
Russell appeal, 401–2n58
Pitblado LLP, 322
Police Commission, 160, 273,
368n62; and Andrews, 114, 122;
and Citizens' Committee,
112–14, 121–2, 151; and complaints against police, 141; and
constitution, 136–7; demands
loyalty oath, 110, 112–14, 139,
140, 273; and Graham, 110–11;
police dismissed, 150; police
vote to join Strike, 110; and
Sparling, 111–14; and Special
Police, 138–40, 153, 161; and
street railway, 111
Postal and Railway Mail Service
Employees Bill, 322
preliminary hearing, 237–78
Pringle, Gustavus, 194, 385n3
Pritchard, Bill, 4, 93, 143, 196–7,
237, 243, 251–2, 305, 307–8,
317–18, 362n58, 375–6n19,
385n6
private property: Adam Smith on,
88, 337n40; Andrews and, 42,
73, 314–15; Blackstone on, 86;
and Citizens' discourse, 76, 98,
126, 297, 320; and communism,

THE CANADIAN SOCIAL HISTORY SERIES

Terry Copp,
The Anatomy of Poverty:
The Condition of the Working Class
in Montreal, 1897–1929, 1974.
ISBN 0-7710-2252-2

Alison Prentice,
The School Promoters:
Education and Social Class in
Mid-Nineteenth Century
Upper Canada, 1977.
ISBN 0-8020-8692-6

John Herd Thompson,
The Harvests of War:
The Prairie West, 1914–1918, 1978.
ISBN 0-7710-8560-5

Joy Parr, Editor,
Childhood and Family in Canadian
History, 1982.
ISBN 0-7710-6938-3

Alison Prentice and
Susan Mann Trofimenkoff, Editors,
The Neglected Majority:
Essays in Canadian Women's History,
Volume 2, 1985.
ISBN 0-7710-8583-4

Ruth Roach Pierson,
'They're Still Women After All':
The Second World War and
Canadian Womanhood, 1986.
ISBN 0-7710-6958-8

Bryan D. Palmer,
The Character of Class Struggle:
Essays in Canadian Working Class
History, 1850–1985, 1986.
ISBN 0-7710-6946-4

Alan Metcalfe,
Canada Learns to Play:
The Emergence of Organized Sport,
1807–1914, 1987.
ISBN 0-7710-5870-5

Marta Danylewycz,
Taking the Veil:
An Alternative to Marriage, Mother-
hood, and Spinsterhood in Quebec,
1840–1920, 1987.
ISBN 0-7710-2550-5

Craig Heron, *Working in Steel:*
The Early Years in Canada,
1883–1935, 1988.
ISBN 978-1-4426-0984-6

Wendy Mitchinson and
Janice Dickin McGinnis, Editors,
Essays in the History of Canadian
Medicine, 1988.
ISBN 0-7710-6063-7

Joan Sangster,
Dreams of Equality:
Women on the Canadian Left,
1920–1950, 1989.
ISBN 0-7710-7946-X

Angus McLaren,
Our Own Master Race:
Eugenics in Canada, 1885–1945, 1990.
ISBN 0-7710-5544-7

Bruno Ramirez, *On the Move:*
French-Canadian and Italian Migrants
in the North Atlantic Economy,
1860–1914, 1991.
ISBN 0-7710-7283-X

Mariana Valverde,
'The Age of Light, Soap and Water':
Moral Reform in English Canada,
1885–1925, 1991.
ISBN 978-0-8020-9595-4

Bettina Bradbury,
Working Families:
Age, Gender, and Daily Survival in
Industrializing Montreal, 1993.
ISBN 978-0-8020-8689-1

Andrée Lévesque,
Making and Breaking the Rules:
Women in Quebec, 1919–1939, 1994.
ISBN 978-1-4426-1138-2

Cecilia Danysk,
Hired Hands:
Labour and the Development of Prairie
Agriculture, 1880–1930, 1995.
ISBN 0-7710-2552-1

Kathryn McPherson,
Bedside Matters:
The Transformation of Canadian
Nursing, 1900–1990, 1996.
ISBN 978-0-8020-8679-2

Edith Burley,
Servants of the Honourable Company:
Work, Discipline, and Conflict
in the Hudson's Bay Company,
1770–1870, 1997.
ISBN 0-19-541296-6

Mercedes Steedman,
Angels of the Workplace:
Women and the Construction of Gender
Relations in the Canadian Clothing
Industry, 1890–1940, 1997.
ISBN 978-1-4426-0982-2

Angus McLaren and
Arlene Tigar McLaren,
The Bedroom and the State:
The Changing Practices and Politics
of Contraception and Abortion in
Canada, 1880–1997, 1997.
ISBN 0-19-541318-0

Kathryn McPherson, Cecilia
Morgan, and Nancy M. Forestell,
Editors,
Gendered Pasts:
Historical Essays in Femininity and
Masculinity in Canada, 1999.
ISBN 0-978-0-8020-8690-7

Gillian Creese,
Contracting Masculinity: Gender,
Class, and Race in a White-Collar
Union, 1944–1994, 1999.
ISBN 0-19-541454-3

Geoffrey Reaume,
Remembrance of Patients Past:
Patient Life at the Toronto Hospital
for the Insane, 1870–1940, 2000.
ISBN 978-1-4426-1075-0

Miriam Wright,
A Fishery for Modern Times:
The State and the Industrialization
of the Newfoundland Fishery.
1934–1968, 2001.
ISBN 0-19-541620-1

Judy Fudge and Eric Tucker,
Labour Before the Law:
The Regulation of Workers' Collective
Action in Canada, 1900–1948, 2001.
ISBN 978-0-8020-3793-0

Mark Moss,
Manliness and Militarism:
Educating Young Boys in Ontario for
War, 2001.
ISBN 0-19-541594-9

Joan Sangster,
Regulating Girls and Women:
Sexuality, Family, and the Law in
Ontario 1920–1960, 2001.
ISBN 0-19-541663-5

Reinhold Kramer and Tom Mitchell,
Walk Towards the Gallows:
The Tragedy of Hilda Blake, Hanged
1899, 2002.
ISBN 978-0-8020-9542-8

Mark Kristmanson,
Plateaus of Freedom: Nationality,
Culture, and State Security in Canada,
1940–1960, 2002.
ISBN 0-19-541866-2 (cloth)
ISBN 0-19-541803-4 (paper)

Robin Jarvis Brownlie,
A Fatherly Eye:
Indian Agents, Government Power,
and Aboriginal Resistance in Ontario,
1918–1939, 2003.
ISBN 0-19-541891-3 (cloth)
ISBN 0-19-541784-4 (paper)

Steve Hewitt,
Riding to the Rescue:
The Transformation of the RCMP
in Alberta and Saskatchewan,
1914–1939, 2006.
ISBN 978-0-8020-9021-8 (cloth)
ISBN 978-0-8020-4895-0 (paper)

Robert K. Kristofferson,
Craft Capitalism:
Craftworkers and Early Industrializa-
tion in Hamilton, Ontario, 1840–1871,
2007.
ISBN 978-0-8020-9127-7 (cloth)
ISBN 978-0-8020-9408-7 (paper)

Andrew Parnaby,
Citizen Docker:
Making a New Deal on the Vancouver
Waterfront, 1919–1939, 2008.
ISBN 978-0-8020-9056-0 (cloth)
ISBN 978-0-8020-9384-4 (paper)

J.I. Little,
Loyalties in Conflict:
A Canadian Borderland in War and
Rebellion, 1812–1840, 2008.
ISBN 978-0-8020-9773-6 (cloth)
ISBN 978-0-8020-9525-1 (paper)

Pauline Greenhill,
Make the Night Hideous:
Four English Canadian Charivaris,
1881–1940, 2010.
ISBN 978-1-4426-4077-1 (cloth)
ISBN 978-1-4426-1015-6 (paper)

Rhonda L. Hinther
and Jim Mochoruk,
New Directions in the History of
Ukrainians in Canada, 2010.
ISBN 978-1-4426-4134-1 (cloth)
ISBN 978-1-4426-1062-0 (paper)

Reinhold Kramer and Tom Mitchell,
When the State Trembled:
How A.J. Andrews and the Citizens'
Committee Broke the Winnipeg
General Strike, 2010.
ISBN 978-1-4426-4219-5 (cloth)
ISBN 978-1-4426-1116-0 (paper)